THE CLAIRMONT FAMILY LETTERS, 1839–1889

THE PICKERING MASTERS SERIES

THE CLAIRMONT FAMILY LETTERS, 1839–1889

Edited by
Sharon L. Joffe

Volume I

LONDON AND NEW YORK

First published 2017
by Routledge
2 Park Square, Milton Park, Abingdon, Oxon OX14 4RN

and by Routledge
711 Third Avenue, New York, NY 10017

Routledge is an imprint of the Taylor & Francis Group, an informa business

British Library Cataloguing in Publication Data
A catalogue record for this book is available from the British Library

Library of Congress Cataloging-in-Publication Data
Names: Clairmont, Claire, 1798–1879 author. | Joffe, Sharon Lynne, editor.
Title: The Clairmont family letters, 1839–1889 / [edited by Sharon L. Joffe].
Description: Milton Park, Abingdon, Oxon; New York, NY: Routledge, 2016. | Series: The Pickering masters series | Includes bibliographical references and index.
Identifiers: LCCN 2016003434 (print) | LCCN 2016015149 (ebook) | ISBN 9781138758070 (volume 1) | ISBN 9781315543901 ()
Subjects: LCSH: Clairmont, Claire, 1798–1879—Family. | Clairmont, Claire, 1798–1879—Correspondence. | Shelley, Mary Wollstonecraft, 1797–1851—Family.
Classification: LCC CT788.C475 A4 2016 (print) | LCC CT788.C475 (ebook) | DDC 929.20973—dc23
LC record available at https://lccn.loc.gov/2016003434

ISBN: 978-1-8489-3553-2 (Set)
eISBN: 978-1-315-54386-4 (Set)
ISBN: 978-1-1387-5807-0 (Volume I)
eISBN: 978-1-315-54390-1 (Volume I)

Typeset in Times New Roman
by Apex CoVantage, LLC

Publisher's Note

References within each chapter are as they appear in the original complete work

CONTENTS

ACKNOWLEDGMENTS

The Carl H. Pforzheimer Collection of Shelley and His Circle, The New York Public Library, Astor, Lenox and Tilden Foundations is the source of all the letters, photographs, and documents contained in this collection. Permission to publish in full the manuscripts from the later generations of the Clairmont family held in the Pforzheimer Collection was granted by the Carl H. Pforzheimer Collection and by Mr. Hans Jörg Bally, Dr. Claus Bally, and Mr. Peter Bally, Clairmont family heirs.

A collection of this scope would not have been possible without the assistance of the following people, to all of whom I owe a deep debt of gratitude:

Dr. Elizabeth Campbell Denlinger, the Curator of the Carl H. Pforzheimer Collection of Shelley and His Circle at the New York Public Library. Dr. Denlinger kindly gave me permission to work on the Clairmont letters and to make them available to scholars in book form.

Mr. Charles Cuykendall Carter, the Assistant Curator of the Carl H. Pforzheimer Collection of Shelley and His Circle at the New York Public Library

Mr. Hans Jörg Bally, husband of the late Mary Claire Bally-Clairmont, and Mr. Peter Bally and Dr. Claus Bally, his second cousins. Dr. Claus Bally shared information about the Clairmont family, and Mr. Peter Bally provided me with documents, photographs, and information pertaining to the Clairmont and Bally families. Mr. Hans Jörg Bally, Mr. Bally and Dr. Bally granted me permission to publish all documents, letters, and photographs from the later generations of the Clairmont family held in the Carl H. Pforzheimer Collection. Mr. Peter Bally also granted permission to publish the photograph of Mary Claire Bally-Clairmont in this collection. It has been an honor to be associated with extended members of the Clairmont family. Sadly, Mr. Hans Jörg Bally passed away on 26 December 2015, shortly before the publication of this collection.

Professor Antony Harrison, the Chair of the Department of English at North Carolina State University, and Professor Thomas Birkland, the Associate Dean for Research and Engagement in the College of Humanities and Social Sciences at North Carolina State University. Professor Harrison's financial support for this project is gratefully acknowledged, as is Professor Birkland's generosity in awarding a College of Humanities and Social Sciences Scholarship and Research Award for this project.

In addition, I would like to offer my thanks to following individuals for their invaluable assistance:

To Dr. Stephen Wagner, former Curator of the Carl H. Pforzheimer Collection of Shelley and His Circle, for providing me with access in 2004 to the then-uncataloged materials.

To Dr. Doucet Devin Fischer, the editor of *Shelley and his Circle.*

To Ms. Pernille Valentin, Ballyana Stiftung für Familien- und Industriegeschichte, Switzerland, for her assistance in putting me in contact with Mr. Peter Bally and Dr. Claus Bally.

To Mr. Herbert Fischer, who kindly forwarded archival information pertaining to the Clairmont family, who spent time researching the family on my behalf, and who generously provided additional photographs of the Clairmont family grave in the Evangelischer Friedhof Matzleinsdorf.

To Heraldic-Genealogical Society Adler, Vienna, tng.adler-wien.eu for permission to publish their photographs of the Clairmont tomb and Charles Clairmont's death announcement.

To Dr. Endre Domiczi, the Head of the Dean's Office, Faculty of Agricultural and Food Sciences, University of West Hungary, for granting me permission to publish the image relating to Wilhelm Clairmont while he was a student at Altenburg.

To Dr. László Varga, University of West Hungary, Sopron, Hungary, for facilitating my request for information about Wilhelm Clairmont's stay in Altenburg.

To Mr. Attila Németh, Secretary, University of West Hungary Alumni Association, for sending information and photographs from the university records pertaining to Wilhelm Clairmont and Rudolf von Hauer.

To Mr. Leopold Mikec Avberšek, Archival Adviser and Senior Librarian, Regional Archives Maribor, Slovenia, for providing information about Wilhelm Clairmont's farm, Nikolaihof.

To Ms. Margaret Woods, Armidale Family History Group, Armidale, New South Wales, Australia, for her invaluable assistance with the Australian section of the book. Her dedication to this project is gratefully noted.

To Mr. William Oates, University Archivist, University of New England, New South Wales, Australia, for graciously searching through documents pertaining to Wilhelm Clairmont's Australian sojourn and for granting access to the Dangar papers in the university's archive.

To Mr. John Dangar, for his generosity in sharing his family's copy of the mortgage agreement signed between William Dangar, Wilhelm Clairmont, and Julius Duboc for the acquisition of Kangaroo Hills.

I also wish to acknowledge the assistance of the following individuals:

Kimberley Smith, Editor, Routledge Historical Resources, Routledge Revivals and Routledge Library Editions; Robert Langham, Senior Editor, History, Routledge; Holly Smithson, Production Editor, Law and Major Works, Routledge; Lisa Williams, copyeditor; Mark Pollard, Publishing Director, Pickering & Chatto Publishers; Dr. Bruce Barker-Benfield, Senior Assistant Librarian, Bodleian Library, Oxford, United Kingdom; Anthony (Bill) Dangar; Dr. Ulrike Denk, Academic Staff,

Archiv der Universität Wien, Austria; Professor Dr. Ulrich Fellmeth, Archiv der Universität, Universität Hohenheim, Stuttgart, Germany; Vicki Parslow Stafford; David Suttor; Dr. Hermann Zeitlhofer, Bibliothek der Gesellschaft der Ärzte (Library of the Society of Physicians), Vienna, Austria; Haidee Jackson, Keeper of Collections, Newstead Abbey, Nottinghamshire; Shirley Bazley, Merimbula-Imlay Historical Society, Merimbula, New South Wales, Australia; Carol Churches, Bathurst Family History Group and Bathurst Historical Society, Bathurst, New South Wales, Australia; Dr. Ekaterina Obuchova, The Byron Society in Australia; David Rymill, Archivist, Hampshire Archives and Local Studies, Hampshire Record Office, Winchester, Hampshire, United Kingdom; Gina Hynard, Archives and Local Studies Assistant, Hampshire Archives and Local Studies, Winchester, Hampshire, United Kingdom; Rhian Dolby, Hampshire Archives and Local Studies, Hampshire Record Office, Winchester, Hampshire, United Kingdom; Sally Miller, Chair, Hampshire Gardens Trust Research Group, Hampshire, United Kingdom; Dr. Ruth Koblizek, Curator, Picture Archive. Medizinische Universität Wien, Austria; Dr. Steven Tötösy de Zepetnek, Purdue University; Martina Pelz, Bibliothek der Gesellschaft der Ärzte (Library of the Society of Physicians), Vienna, Austria; Claudia Köpf, Bank History Archives, Communications and Financial Literacy Division, Österreichische Nationalbank, Vienna, Austria; Christine Bryan, Archivist, Australian National University Archives Program, The Australian National University, Canberra, Australia; Pat Raymond, Research Officer, Bega Valley Genealogy Society, Pambula, New South Wales, Australia; Jim Hynd, Snowy River Shire Historical Society, Berridale, New South Wales, Australia; Kate Epstein; Ann C. Sherwin, American Translators Association-Certified Translator from German to English; Dr. Maria Pramaggiore, Maynooth University; Dr. Jeanne Moskal, University of North Carolina at Chapel Hill; Dr. Walt Wolfram and the Faculty Research and Professional Development Committee at North Carolina State University; Gary Wilson, Bibliographic Specialist, North Carolina State University Libraries; Dr. Agnes Bolonyai, Department of English, North Carolina State University; Stephanie McBroom, Department of English, North Carolina State University; and Dr. Catherine Mainland, Department of English, North Carolina State University.

This project would not have reached completion without the assistance provided by Arlo Pignotti, whose initial transcriptions of the letters were so expertly undertaken.

I thank Dr. Mohan Ramaswamy, Associate Head for Research and Graduate Services, North Carolina State University Libraries, for his invaluable assistance with formatting the bibliography for this book.

I am especially grateful to the following graduate and undergraduate students at North Carolina State University, whose excellent work contributed to this project's completion: Carlene Kucharczyk, Anja Reiner (who translated many of the individual German words and phrases into English), Grisha Mirzoev, and Beatrice Ferrari (Italian translations).

I would also like to acknowledge the generosity of Peter Lang Press for allowing me to republish sections from my book, *The Kinship Coterie and the Literary Endeavors of the Women in the Shelley Circle* (2007).

My family and friends were highly supportive of my endeavors. I am particularly thankful to my late father, Philip Joffe, and to my mother, Dr. Ada Joffe, for their encouragement and guidance. I also thank my brother, Dr. Ian Joffe, and my sister-in-law, Leila Joffe.

My deepest thanks go to my husband, Dr. Chris McKenna, for his constant support of the project, for his enthusiastic encouragement when obstacles presented themselves, and for his excellent editorial advice.

Finally, I dedicate this book to my daughters, Amanda and Ashley, and to my husband, Chris.

EDITORIAL STANDARDS AND PRACTICES

This collection contains all the extant English-language letters of Antonia, Pauline, Clara, Charley, and Ottilia (von Pichler) Clairmont housed in the Carl H. Pforzheimer Collection of Shelley and His Circle in the New York Public Library. It also contains all of the extant English-language letters of Wilhelm Gaulis Clairmont to his parents, to his aunt Claire, and to his brother and sisters, as well as a sample in the appendix of Wilhelm's English-language letters to his wife, Ottilia, some of which contain significant German-language sections.[1] Additionally, I have included all of Pauline Clairmont's correspondence to her brother, Wilhelm, and his correspondence to her, as well as the English-language correspondence of Ottilia's sister, Alma von Pichler, and two letters by Alexander Knox, Clara Knox's husband. These letters form part of the Pforzheimer Collection's holdings of Clairmont family papers and assist in telling the complete story of the Clairmont family.

All the letters in this collection are published here for the first time, apart from a very few that appeared in the footnotes to *The Clairmont Correspondence* as corroboration or elaboration, and I have re-transcribed these few. Although I have searched widely, I have been unable to locate at press time any surviving and unpublished letters by any of the correspondents represented here outside of the Pforzheimer Collection. It is possible that private collections hold such letters, although the Clairmont clan has had no living descendants since the death of Mary Claire Bally-Clairmont in 2009, and she was the donor, along with her brother Christoph Clairmont, of these letters to the Pforzheimer Collection.

Although some of the letters contain grammatical and syntactical errors and spelling errors, they are transcribed here exactly as they were written. A few contain words I could not read, and even if the context clarifies the meaning, I did not provide my guess. The letters are written in English, and all of the writers, except possibly for Antonia Clairmont, learned English in childhood. A good deal of the errors are Antonia's. Pauline and Wilhelm, who learned German from their mother and English from their father, make more occasional mistakes. Wilhelm's English-language mastery noticeably improves as he ages, no doubt as a result of his long sojourn in Australia.

I have followed the principles Betty Bennett and Marion Kingston Stocking set out in their respective editions of Mary Shelley's letters, *The Letters of Mary*

Wollstonecraft Shelley, and the Clairmont family's correspondence, *The Clairmont Correspondence*. My standards and practices are as follows:

1 I have arranged the letters chronologically, beginning with the first extant letter from 1839. I have also included in the chronological arrangement those letters that lacked either a year or a month, but from whose context I was easily able to determine the date.
2 Each letter has been assigned two numbers, one recorded at the top of the letter and one following each letter. I assigned the first number of each letter chronologically, from the earliest to the latest extant letters, thereby making it simple for readers to follow the linear order of the collection. The second number is the call number assigned by the Pforzheimer Collection and follows each letter. When the Pforzheimer Collection acquired the Clairmont family papers, the documents were assigned to "Clairmontana," a call number system that identified documents relating to Claire Clairmont. Every letter has been given a reference number that begins with the indicator CL'ANA. In this collection, the words "Unpublished. Text: M.S., Pf. Coll.," precede each CL'ANA number. With this identifier, each letter is designated as previously unpublished and a manuscript within the Carl H. Pforzheimer Collection of Shelley and His Circle, The New York Public Library, Astor, Lenox and Tilden Foundations.
3 The Pforzheimer Collection holds over 400 items pertaining to Wilhelm Clairmont. Of these, he wrote about 250 autograph letters to his wife, Ottilia. Wilhelm's letters to Ottilia are numbered CL'ANA 0118–0156 and CL'ANA 0421 (which contains a total of 211 letters under that call number). Although Ottilia was primarily the recipient of the contents of CL'ANA 0421 through letters written to her either by Wilhelm or by her children, a few letters from Antonia, Pauline, and Wilhelm to other recipients are interspersed. I include in this collection the English-language letters catalogued in CL'ANA 0421 and written by Antonia, Pauline, and Wilhelm to addressees other than Ottilia. Additionally, I provide some examples of the CL'ANA 0421 English-language letters from Wilhelm to Ottilia in the appendix to this collection.

  Most of the 211 letters in CL'ANA 0421 are German-language letters and some are dated beyond the date range of this edition. These 211 letters are identified by the general number CL'ANA 0421, with an additional Arabic numeral appended to each as a unique identifier. These 211 letters are divided between three boxes, each of which is numbered numerically. The boxes are further subdivided into a number of bundles, which have alphabetical designations. Each CL'ANA 0421 call number indicates the box, bundle, and letter numbers. Christoph Clairmont, Wilhelm and Ottilia's grandson, expressed his regard for the CL'ANA 0421 letters in a notebook he included in his gift to the Pforzheimer Collection: "Letters numbered 1–211 are inventoried with <u>very</u> brief contents in this booklet . . . Most letters are by Willy to Tilly – my grandfather and grandmother respectively. A few are in English. Some of my comments and red pencil marks refer to particularly interesting letters. C. Clairmont Feb 12, 1998".

4 The names of the writer and addressee appear at the top of each letter.

5 I have faithfully reproduced each letter's date and have retained any inconsistencies in the way that the writer chose to date his/her letter, such as incomplete dates or abbreviated names of months. When a date is absent but can be determined from the letter's content or from the postmark on the envelope or aerogramme, the presumed date appears in a square bracket at the top of the letter. Similarly, when a date has been written at the end of a letter, I have recopied the date in square brackets at the beginning of the letter. If I am not able to determine the date from the letter or from the postmark, I have indicated the possible date in square brackets with the abbreviation for circa (c.) placed next to it.

6 I have not corrected any spelling and have faithfully retained the letter writers' orthographic faults. I have provided an explanatory note if a word was written in a particularly egregious manner. I have indicated words missing in the manuscript due to tears in the paper or due to inkblots. Illegible words are represented by the word "illeg". in square brackets. Many of the letters were written on fine onion-skin paper and they proved somewhat difficult to read.[2]

7 I have not corrected any syntactical errors and have left punctuation flaws uncorrected. When the writers omitted to capitalize letters, particularly at the beginning of a sentence, I have followed the original manuscript exactly.

8 The writers frequently used dashes or multiple spaces instead of periods at the end of their sentences and I faithfully reproduce these forms. Writers of that era would often use dashes or multiple spaces as an informal way of ending a sentence. However, I have regularized the size of the dashes and spaces.

9 Most letters have accompanying notes, which are numbered separately for each individual letter.

10 I have indicated with a note the beginning of any cross-writing. This technique was used to save money and consisted of horizontal and vertical writing crossing together on the same page.

11 Any additions to a letter by the original writer (such as a word or sentence added above the text) have been silently incorporated into the letter.

12 I have retained abbreviations but have included a note to the unabbreviated word if further clarity is required.

13 I have followed the paragraph breaks employed by the letter writers but have regularized the size of each paragraph's indentation. I have standardized the alignment of all end addresses and final greetings.

14 I have included translations of any foreign-language phrases or sentences in the notes. For a complete German letter or for a German paragraph included within an English letter, I provide the German text followed by an English translation. The translator's name is noted after each complete German letter or paragraph of some length.

15 All legible deletions have been included but struck through. Illegible deletions are noted by the word "illeg". in square brackets, but struck through. Additional editorial symbols follow in this text.

16 The letter writers frequently signed their names using abbreviations or shortened forms. Wilhelm typically signed his letters WGC Esq (Wilhelm Gaulis Clairmont, Esquire), but his signature was often illegible. I have therefore standardized his signature to WGC when his signature was unable to be read. Antonia and Pauline often signed their names using their initials, which I have retained.

17 I used Google Maps to calculate all distances between towns and cities in the notes, but the dates of access vary. I include in the bibliography one citation to cover all Google Maps information: www.google.com/maps/. Information pertaining to the various Banat villages comes from the website "Banat: Donauschwaben Villages Helping Hands" (http://www.dvhh.org/banat/).

18 I reference Pauline Clairmont's unpublished Australian journal, currently held by the Pforzheimer Collection. Pauline paginated her journal, which bears the number CL'ANA 0176.

19 After each letter, I have included the following:

   a The address of the recipient transcribed from the envelope. If an envelope has been lost, the words "no envelope" appear after the letter. I have indicated each new line of the address with a slash mark (/). I have retained incorrect spellings and have underlined words that were underlined on the envelope.

   b Any legible postmarks on the envelope. If a postmark (or part of a postmark) is illegible, it is noted by "[illeg.]". I have indicated postmarks on the front of the envelope by "Front postmark" and on the back of the envelope by "Rear postmark". I omit the words "Front postmark" or "Rear postmark" if no postmarks were recorded on either the front or the back of the envelope or if they were entirely illegible. As some envelopes had two or more postmarks, I have separated them by a semicolon. I have used a slash (/) to indicate divisions within the postmark.

   c The CL'ANA number assigned by the Pforzheimer Collection.

20 I have provided a bibliography of sources consulted after the Introduction and after each of the two section headings. I have also included additional bibliographic information in the notes for sources not cited in these three bibliographies.

Notes

1 The Pforzheimer's holdings include some 250 letters from Wilhelm to Ottilia that do not appear here. Most of these letters were written in German (Kurrent, or old German script), with some English letters interspersed. As this collection centers around Claire Clairmont and the letters written primarily to her, Wilhelm and Ottilia's story is beyond the scope of these volumes. I hope that a future edition will publish Wilhelm and Ottilia's letters more completely. I have included a sample of Wilhelm's English language letters to Ottilia in the appendix to this collection.

2 See C. Golden, *Posting It: The Victorian Revolution in Letter Writing* (Gainesville: University of Florida Press, 2009).

LIST OF ABBREVIATIONS AND IDENTIFICATION MARKS

Abbreviations

CC	*The Clairmont Correspondence*
LMWS	*The Letters of Mary Wollstonecraft Shelley*
Novels	*The Collected Novels and Memoirs of William Godwin*

Identification

Following the precedent set by Marion Kingston Stocking in *The Clairmont Correspondence*, each letter in this collection is followed by the identifier: Unpublished. Text: M. S., Pf. Coll., CL'ANA number. Each letter is thereby designated as previously unpublished, and a manuscript within the Carl H. Pforzheimer Collection of Shelley and His Circle, The New York Public Library, Astor, Lenox and Tilden Foundations. The CL'ANA number follows the identifying information.

INTRODUCTION

The correspondence of Antonia Ghi(s)lain von Hembyze Clairmont (1800–1868) and her children, Pauline (1825–1891) and Wilhelm Charles Gaulis (1831–1895), to the children's aunt, Claire Clairmont (1798–1879), Antonia's sister-in-law, contains the reconstructed narratives that form the basis of this collection. These prolific letter writers represent part of a larger kinship circle that includes the more recognized and celebrated authors William Godwin (1756–1836), Mary Wollstonecraft (1759–1797), Percy Bysshe Shelley (1792–1822), and Mary Wollstonecraft Shelley (1797–1851). Until fairly recently, the letters contained in this volume of Antonia and four of her children, Pauline, Clara (1826–1855), Wilhelm, and Charles Gaulis (1835–1856), remained in the possession of Johann Christoph Clairmont (1924–2004) and Mary Claire Bally-Clairmont (1922–2009), Wilhelm's grandchildren. Christoph and Mary Claire bequeathed the letters, as well as journals and photographic prints belonging to their family, to the Carl H. Pforzheimer Collection of Shelley and His Circle at the New York Public Library. The English-language letters – an extraordinary set of documents – tell multiple narratives. On a standalone basis, each of the letters (some perhaps more eloquently written than others) represents a link in a contemporary social history of a nineteenth-century family living in Europe and Australia who confronted a host of confounding and age-specific anxieties, amongst them conflicts in Europe and in particular the Austro-Hungarian Empire, woes in the European financial markets, and the effects of Australian pioneer life on immigrants to that country. Furthermore, the letters inform our understanding of the Shelley–Godwin circle through the experiences and thoughts of their descendants. Chiefly, the letters provide researchers with additional resources for evaluating internal Clairmont family dynamics, for augmenting our understanding of the competing philosophical principles held by various Shelley-circle members, and for reclaiming the largely forgotten voices of many within that extended circle as part of a resurgence in Shelley-circle scholarship.

Critics have recognized the significance of Mary Shelley's relationship with Claire Clairmont, who was her stepsister. Following the publication of Betty T. Bennett's three-volume edition of Mary Shelley's letters (*The Letters of Mary Wollstonecraft Shelley*, 1980–1988) and Marion Kingston Stocking's editions of *The Journals of Claire Clairmont* (1968) and *The Clairmont Correspondence* (1995), scholars such as Daisy Hay (*Young Romantics*, 2010) and Janet Todd (*Death and the Maidens: Fanny Wollstonecraft and the Shelley Circle*, 2007) have examined the multiple connections between Claire and the Shelleys. Since Claire was herself a prolific writer, her correspondence with other participants within the Shelley circle continues to influence critical impressions of the principal members of the Shelley coterie. While *The Clairmont Correspondence* includes Claire's letters to Antonia, Pauline, and Wilhelm, the volume omits their responses, which provide useful background information regarding many of the incidents so exceptionally recounted in Claire's letters to them. This two-volume edition redresses that omission by providing readers with access to these forgotten manuscripts, providing additional insight into conflicts to which she was a party. For example, the letters in this current collection yield further insight into the rift between Claire and Mary Shelley over Clara Clairmont's marriage to Alexander Knox, making them valuable additions to the Shelley–Clairmont narrative. They also diminish and negate Shelley-circle claims that Claire's presence was an annoyance to some. For example, while Mary Shelley sometimes found Claire tiresome (she wrote to Percy Shelley on 18 October 1817, "Clare is forever wearying with her idle & childish complaints" [*LMWS* II: 57]), and Claire herself recorded in her journal entry of 4 July 1820, "Heigh-ho the Clare & the Ma/ Find something to fight about every day" (Stocking 1968: 153), Claire's generosity towards her Clairmont relatives, evidenced in this collection, rewrites the narrative. In spite of her own straitened circumstances, Claire provided financially and emotionally for her brother's children and his widow, serving as a unifying link for the Clairmonts and dispensing advice and money when they applied for it, which was often.

Moreover, if Claire's travels in Stocking's editions of her letters and journals read like a nineteenth-century European travelogue, Pauline's and Wilhelm's sojourns in places as far-flung as Australia and the Banat[1] offer readers a catalogue of relevant and historically significant place names and cultural experiences that are connected to historical events that occurred in the nineteenth-century British and Austro-Hungarian Empires. Sharing their father's British and their mother's Austrian national heritage, Pauline and Wilhelm moved from Austria to England and then on to Australia and back to Europe without any sense of cultural disruption, and their correspondence provides readers today with a glimpse of contemporary life in nineteenth-century Australia as well as in Vienna and in the Austrian Banat. Their epistolary record of a broad range of political, economic, and social matters in the nineteenth century provides modern readers a window onto the daily lives of people in Britain, in its Australian colony, and within the Austro-Hungarian Empire. Antonia's, Pauline's and Wilhelm's life-writing offers primary evidence as to what it may have meant to be a member of a family with impressive social and artistic connections (the Shelleys were members of the Baronetcy, and Wilhelm regularly associated with the sons of the Hungarian ruling class); however, the letters also demonstrate how more mundane or earthly concerns could temper such lives, including the chronic inability to earn a substantial living wage, unrequited love, and non-marital sexual experiences that contravened the social mores of the time.

Due to the efforts of Donald H. Reiman (editor of *Shelley and his Circle* from 1965 to 1992) and Christoph Clairmont, these documents became available to the public in the late 1990s. In August 1997, Christoph Clairmont, then a professor at Rutgers University in the Department of Classics, contacted Reiman, whom he had met at a conference organized by the Society for Textual Scholarship at City University of New York to offer the extant Clairmont papers in his and his sister's possession for the Carl H. Pforzheimer Collection of Shelley and His Circle, a collection housed at the New York Public Library. The Pforzheimer Collection thus received the papers in two installments between 1997 and 1998 (conversation with Elizabeth Denlinger). This two-volume collection marks the first time researchers and historians can peruse these letters outside of the library. It aims to restore these lost voices, bringing their perspicacious observations of nineteenth-century life on two continents to a broader audience.

While the letters alone provide a vivid and fascinating narrative, this introduction aims to contextualize them within the larger framework of the Godwin–Wollstonecraft–Shelley–Clairmont circle to enrich the reader's experience of them. Born outside of London on 27 April 1759, Mary Wollstonecraft would become the center of this circle. She was the first daughter and second child of Edward John Wollstonecraft and Elizabeth Dickson Wollstonecraft. Her upbringing, which featured an abusive and oft-drunken father who dominated her too-compliant mother, led Wollstonecraft to equate marriage with servitude and dominance. For years she avoided the institution, seeking emotional and intellectual refuge in multiple forms of self-education, in learning, in writing, and in her female friendships, initially with Jane Arden and later with Fanny Blood. These particularly close female bonds, her expressed distaste for marriage, and her notions regarding the importance of the maternal bond remained principal subjects of her writing. For example, both *Mary* and *Maria* explore the nature of maternal and sororal bonds, while Wollstonecraft's polemic tracts – like *A Vindication of the Rights of Woman* – address the issues of women's education and social status. Wollstonecraft's unconventional social preferences rankled many in London society who revered the notion of domesticity that had anointed the home as "a refuge from a hostile and competitive social world" (Kelly 1992: 12). Wollstonecraft's rejection of this ideal placed her outside of the social norms of her age; indeed, when Gary Kelly claimed that both "revolutionary threat" and "feminist protest" during the 1790s threatened the "domestic affections" of England, he could have been speaking of her, and he accurately described the marginalization of women such as Wollstonecraft because of their opinions (Kelly 1992: 12).

Wollstonecraft's espousal of the doctrines of the French Revolution, her subsequent move to France to live according to the Republican ideals of the Revolution, and her affair with the American adventurer Gilbert Imlay (possibly 1754–1828) marked her as a pariah. Although the relationship with Gilbert Imlay culminated in the birth of their daughter, Frances (Fanny), in May 1794 – and thereby provided

Wollstonecraft with "the combination of domesticity, professionalism and egalitarian erotic love" she had so actively sought (Kelly 1992: 149) – Imlay's subsequent infidelity and Wollstonecraft's corresponding bouts of depression heavily clouded the relationship. In 1795, Gilbert Imlay sent Wollstonecraft, Fanny, and Fanny's nurse Marguerite to Scandinavia, where Wollstonecraft's secret mission, undertaken on Gilbert Imlay's behalf, was to track down his missing treasure ship. Her poignant letters to Gilbert Imlay remain preserved in her book, *Letters Written during a Short Residence in Sweden, Norway and Denmark* (1796), and in them her deep love both for him and their daughter appears on every page. Their relationship dissolved in 1795, however.

While the philosopher William Godwin had despised Mary Wollstonecraft on their first meeting at the home of publisher Joseph Johnson in 1791, he thought differently of her after he read her *Letters from Norway* and when she attended a party he held in his "little deserted mansion" on 22 April 1796 for twelve people (*Novels* I: 51). The guests also included Elizabeth Inchbald, Samuel Parr, Thomas Holcroft, and James Mackintosh.[2] Perhaps Wollstonecraft was seeking a more satisfactory form of companionship than Imlay had provided. Godwin quickly recognized the affair they began thereafter as "friendship melting into love" (*Novels* I: 129). Godwin and Wollstonecraft's subsequent epistolary writings attest to the intense physical and emotional relationship that ensued as a result of their April rapprochement. Writing to Wollstonecraft on 13 July, Godwin passionately recorded his feelings:

> Shall I write a love letter? . . . No, when I make love, it shall be with the eloquent tones of my voice, with dying accents, with speaking glances . . . with all the witching of that irresistible, universal passion . . . Shall I send you an eulogium of your beauty, your talents & your virtues? Ah! That is an old subject; beside, if I were to begin, instead of a sheet of paper, I should want a ream.
>
> (Clemit 2011: 171)

In short order, they married in March 1797 but maintained separate residences while Wollstonecraft attended to her novel *Maria, or The Wrongs of Woman* as well as Fanny, who was three. On 30 August 1797, Wollstonecraft gave birth to their daughter, Mary, but she died of puerperal fever on 10 September. Her death thus ended Godwin's short period of domestic bliss and left the bereft widower with two small children to raise.

Wollstonecraft's reputation suffered a colossal blow in the years following her death, in part due to Godwin's own candid depiction of her life in his *Memoirs of the Author of a Vindication of the Rights of Woman* (1798), a work that refused to whitewash the incidents that had led to her notoriety. Published a mere four months after her death, the memoir eventually provided conflicting perspectives for her daughters, who would come to know both the maternal and the notorious aspects of their mother's personality through this work. Depicted by Godwin as a "worshipper of domestic life" whose light was prematurely "extinguished for ever" in death (*Novels* I: 132, 141), Wollstonecraft had provoked intense emotions within a husband who believed he had "never loved till now; or, at least, had never nourished a passion to the same growth, or met with an object so consummately worthy" (*Novels* I: 129). Yet at the same time, the *Memoirs* also furnished Fanny and Mary with unvarnished accounts of Wollstonecraft's failed relationships and her thwarted suicide attempts (she attempted suicide twice) that would eventually provoke antithetical responses in her children. Mary Shelley idealized her mother and revered her for the qualities Godwin had lauded, but Fanny Imlay would, tragically, follow in her footsteps, committing suicide in 1816.

Godwin's choice of Mary Jane Vial (1768–1841) as their stepmother would eventually factor into both Mary and Fanny's impressions of their mother. The mother of two small children of her own, namely Charles Gaulis Clairmont (1795–1850) and Clara Mary Jane (later Claire) Clairmont, the "widowed" Mary Jane married Godwin in 1801. This introduction will refer to Clara Mary Jane as Claire throughout, as she was Claire during the period this collection of letters covers. Scholars have questioned the legitimacy of Mrs. Clairmont's widowhood. It had long been supposed that there never had been, in fact, a Mr. Clairmont, and that Charles and Claire had different fathers, neither of whom their mother had ever married. As William St. Clair notes, if this were indeed the case Mrs. Clairmont would have had every reason to construct the fiction: "To be the unmarried mother of one could be passed off in the mid-1790's as a proper gesture of social defiance. To be the unmarried mother of two by different fathers was harder" (St. Clair 1989: 250). Indeed, St. Clair records that in 1830 their mother told Claire and Charles that Karl Gaulis of Switzerland, a man who had anglicized his name to Clairmont before dying of cholera while visiting Hamburg in 1798, had fathered them (1989: 249). Though St. Clair assumes Charles was "almost certainly" the son of Gaulis (1989: 250), he asserts that Claire's father was in all likelihood "a man – about whom nothing is yet known – with whom Mary Jane took up after Gaulis had gone abroad" (1989: 250). The matter stood there until 2010, when Vicki Parslow Stafford discovered the truth of Claire's paternity. Searching through documents deposited by Dodson and Pulman, Solicitors, in the Somerset Archive and Record Service Office (in Somerset, United Kingdom), researching her own family history, Stafford came upon a cache of letters that confirmed Claire's paternity. Roughly sixty extant documents from 1798 to 1814 reveal that John Lethbridge of Sandhill Park, an estate in Bishops Lydeard, Somerset, grudgingly accepted that Claire was his daughter and provided Mary Jane Vial (her birth name) with funds for the girl's support.[3]

While Godwin's wives may have had unconventional sexual histories, he had transformed himself from committed bachelorhood to a devoted family man in just a few years. Indeed, when Wollstonecraft's sisters offered to raise Fanny after Wollstonecraft's death, Godwin refused. He and his second wife produced William Godwin (Junior) in 1803. While the household suffered from a chronic absence of money, the children had intellectual stimulation, as they often had exposure to distinguished guests like Samuel Taylor Coleridge, Charles Lamb, and Aaron Burr. Moreover, Godwin and his wife took the children on educational trips as well as on outings to the seaside at Margate and Ramsgate. However, the second Mrs. Godwin was an unpleasant stepmother, and her pride in her own children and frequent disregard of her stepdaughters created difficulties for both Fanny and Mary. The former responded to Mrs. Godwin's acrimony by seeking approval and complying with her parents' rules. Mary Shelley, on the other hand, tended to oppose her stepmother.

The competing loyalties and affections that originated in the Godwin home may have prompted the anxieties about Mary Shelley and her son, Sir Percy Florence Shelley (1819–1889), evident in this collection. Betty Bennett and Charles Robinson observe that for Mary Shelley the shared family space provided "immediate lessons in complex politics: a half-sister, step-brother and step-sister, baby brother; a step-mother, with whom she did not get on; a beloved learned father committed to maintaining ideals and his family life; and above the mantle, the ever present portrait of Mary Wollstonecraft reminding her of her own special heritage" (1990: 6). John Williams records that Mrs. Godwin provided a "busy, but not an overly loving home" environment (2000: 20). Todd explains: "Fanny and Mary were not close but both suffered from their relationship with their stepmother: where Mary turned her desolation outwards, openly hating Mary Jane as 'odious' and 'filthy', Fanny turned her inwards, feeling the need, in her insecurity and reverence for Godwin, to mitigate the faults of the woman who was his wife" (Todd 2007: 65). Williams postulates that Mary Shelley "grew to loathe her stepmother" (2000: 21), but offers some sympathy for the critically much-maligned Mrs. Godwin by stating that Aaron Burr was probably the only person who spoke of her positively (2000: 24).[4] In her defense, parenting five children under the specter of Wollstonecraft, a figure against whom (as Williams notes) "she knew only too well . . . she would always be compared" (2000: 25) could not have been easy. Her husband had called her predecessor "the greatest ornament her sex ever had to boast" (*Novels* I: 131). Moreover, Mrs. Godwin encountered strong opposition from Godwin's friends, "none of whom were willing to read on after the exquisite chapter of Godwin and Wollstonecraft had been brought to its dramatic conclusion" (Williams 2000: 26).

Mary would find love instead with Percy Shelley, whom she met in 1812. Percy was already the father of two children, Eliza Ianthe (later Esdaile, 1813–1876) and Charles Bysshe (1814–1826), though he was estranged from their mother, the former Harriet Westbrook (1796–1816). An admirer of both her parents, Percy saw in Mary a combination of their most admirable qualities. Attractive, interesting, and appreciably alluring, Mary probably excited Percy in a variety of ways. On 28 July 1814, Percy and Mary, by then lovers, departed with Claire for the Continent. Percy and Mary's relationship would be both fruitful and tragic. Their elopement led to a joint literary production, a collection of letters and poetry titled *History of a Six Weeks' Tour* (1817). Emulating Wollstonecraft's *Letters from Norway*, a book of travel literature which the couple read on their journey through Europe, the volume included Percy Shelley's "Mont Blanc" and Mary Shelley's travel responses to European cities, mores, and people. Between 1815 and 1819, the Shelleys had four children – a daughter never named, William, Clara, and Percy Florence. They buried all but the last. In 1816 both Fanny Imlay and Harriet Westbrook committed suicide, Mary and Percy married in 1816, and Claire's daughter with Lord Byron, Clara Allegra (born 1817), died in 1822; she was Claire's sole offspring. Scandal, rumor, and allegations of incest marred these years as well. This series of losses reached its apogée when Percy Shelley and his friend Edward Williams drowned in Italy in 1822. Thereafter, Mary Shelley returned to England, where she lived until her death in 1851.

Claire regularly lived with the Shelleys over the years, an arrangement which frequently caused Mary Shelley some consternation. Claire entered into a relationship with Lord Byron in 1816, and gave birth to their child in 1817. Yet Byron soon grew disgruntled with Claire, and he permanently severed their relationship. He permitted Claire custody of Allegra for a single year, then sent for the child to live with him in 1818 despite the dissolute environment in which he lived.[5] According to St. Clair, for instance, Allegra was not only raised "among the stinking hounds, the gibbering monkeys, the polluting peacocks, and the scented whores who frequented Byron's palace at Venice," but Byron generally treated his daughter "like a toy" (1989: 463). He sent Allegra to live with Maria Gisborne, Mary Shelley's close friend, for a time, then placed her in a convent school at Bagnacavallo, in Ravenna. Claire pleaded with Byron to allow her access to Allegra, but he did not, and the girl succumbed to typhoid fever in 1822. Claire was perhaps seeking succor for her grief when she became a governess after Allegra's death, and took a motherly interest in her young female charges in particular. Later, when she took her niece Pauline and grandniece Georgina Hanghegyi (1864–1885) into her home in Florence in the 1870s, vowing to educate and support Georgina financially, she may have been acting on the same instinct. Charles Clairmont would provide Claire with seven nephews and nieces on which to shower her devotion, which Mary's son Percy Florence also received. Claire's half-brother married Antonia Ghi(s)lain von Hembyze, the daughter of Georg von Hembyze and Anna Schönbichler, in Austria in 1824. Together, Charles and Antonia raised seven children: Pauline, Clara, Wilhelm, Hermine (1832–1847, known as Mina), Emily (1833–1856), Charles Gaulis (Charley) and Sidonia (1836–1856, Sidi).

Charles was an exceptional English teacher who lived his adult life in Austria but retained British citizenship. Of Charles's significant linguistic accomplishments, Ernst Joseph Görlich notes that Charles was one of the first to provide English-language instruction in Vienna: "Einer der ersten, der in Österreich englische Sprache und englisches Wesen vertrat, war Charles Gaulis Clairmont, der dem Kreis um den großen englischen Lyriker Shelley angehörte" ("Charles Gaulis Clairmont, who belonged to the circle of the great English poet Shelley, was one of the first to represent the English language and English character in Austria" [Görlich 1970: 124, translation provided by Anja Reiner]). In fact,

Charles was a teacher of the Viennese nobility and counted the brothers of Kaiser Franz Joseph I (namely, Archdukes Ferdinand Max and Karl Ludwig) among his students. In 1838, Charles secured a prestigious position as an English teacher at the Theresianum Ritterakademie, a private institution for the children of the aristocracy (see CL'ANA 0319). He also gave private English lessons to members of the Austrian nobility, as the letters in this volume describe, and from 1839 onwards he served as a professor of English at the Universität Wien (University of Vienna). In addition to teaching, Charles also wrote books for English-language learning. His *Reine Grundlehre der englischen Sprache* ("Basics of English Language," first published in 1831) continued on through six editions, while his *Vollständige englische Sprachlehre* ("Complete English Grammar") was republished on twelve separate occasions. In 1845, he published his *First Poetical-Reading Book in the English Language*, which was dedicated to Mary Caroline, Archduchess of Austria, by her "humble servant and teacher". Signing himself "Your Imperial Highness' very devoted and attached Servant," Charles lauded the Archduchess and her "exquisite taste . . . evinced in our national poetry". The title page of this book identified Charles as "Professor Extraordinary of the English Language and Literature at the Impl. and Rl. University of Vienna and at the Impl. and R. Ter. Academy of Nobles".[6] Consequently, he represented an important Austrian cultural figure who was well respected by his students and their parents, as Herbert Huscher confirms. Antonia also gave English lessons and published a reading primer, *Erste Schritte zur Erlernung der englischen Sprache, für Kinder von sechs bis zehn Jahren* (1845, "First Steps to Learning the English Language, for Children Ages Six to Ten"). Unlike Mary Shelley and Charles, Claire herself wrote for publication only once, a short story entitled "The Pole," which appeared anonymously.[7] A remark to Jane Williams suggests she felt the burden of her literary family: "in our family if you cannot write an epic poem or novel that by its originality knocks all other novels on the head, you are a despicable creature not worth acknowledging" (*CC* I: 295). Yet she was a prolific correspondent and Mary Shelley and other family members admired her letters for their perspicacity and their poetic qualities.

Claire's devotion to her brother's children would disrupt her relationship with Mary Shelley, her principal correspondent, just two years before Mary's death. Claire's niece, Clara Clairmont, joined Claire in England in 1849. Claire did not join a visit Clara paid to Mary, Sir Percy Florence, and his wife Lady Jane Shelley soon after her arrival. Clara met Alexander Knox (1818–1891), a friend of Percy Florence's, at this time, and a whirlwind courtship ensued. The pair married some weeks later without Charles and Antonia's permission – and completely against Claire's wishes. She began an epistolary and social battle against the Knoxes that lasted for six years, until Clara died in 1855. Claire had been close to her stepsister's son, and his support of Knox was devastating to Claire. Charles and Antonia sought to repair the rift between Clara and Claire, but it, as well as the rift with the Shelleys, never healed, even though Knox financially supported his wife's surviving relatives. The letters in this collection provide insight into these ruptures, perhaps rendering Claire's behavior more explicable if not excusable. No such rift marred Claire's close relationship with Charles, his wife Antonia, or the rest of their children. And it is to members of this family that she wrote many of her letters and whose correspondence to her forms the basis of this collection. While six of Charles's seven children survived him – Mina died in 1847 of consumption[8] – Antonia and Claire buried four more, all of them the victims of illnesses, within six years of his death. Only Pauline and Wilhelm outlived Antonia.

Charles and his family lived through the revolution of 1848–9, and some of Antonia's letters in this collection reference her concerns for her family, the activities of the military, and her family's reaction to the political events. Claire evidently was worried for her family's safety, and Charles wrote to her on 10–11 November 1848 to placate her and to "put [her] out of all suspense about us" (*CC* II: 487). Mary Shelley was similarly concerned. Writing to Claire on 19 October 1848, she noted: "No further news in this Mornings Times from Vienna – I am very anxious for Charles" (*LMWS* III: 348). Although Charles sympathized with the revolutionaries, he stayed loyal to the imperial family. As Stocking asserts, many revolutionaries "remained attached" to the royal family, "hoping for a constitutional monarchy free from the repressions and censorship of the police state. Charles Clairmont was therefore not inconsistent in uniting his liberalism with a loyalty to the Habsburgs, on whom he was dependent" (*CC* II: 493). Görlich also shows Charles's advocacy for a unified Austria and Germany under Austrian leadership: "In bezug auf Deutschland wünscht er in einem Brief vom 7. Juni 1848 [wünscht er sich] ein stärkeres Eingreifen Österreichs in die deutschen Verhältnisse und selbstverständlich den österreichischen Kaiser als Oberhaupt eines erneuerten Deutschen Bundes" ("With regards to Germany, he advocated in a letter dated 7 June 1848 a stronger intervention by Austria in the German situation and, of course, the Austrian Emperor as head of a renewed German federation" [Görlich 1970: 124, translation provided by Anja Reiner]). Furthermore, Görlich confirms that Charles stayed loyal to Austria: "So bleibt er selbst in den größten Stürmen der Revolution 'habsburgisch' gesinnt, was wohl mit dem Kreis zusammenhängt, in dem er verkehrte" ("Thus, even in the greatest storms of revolution, he stays Habsburg-minded, which probably correlated with the set he socialized with" [Görlich 1970: 124, translation provided by Anja Reiner]). Unfortunately, Charles collapsed in 1850 while dining at the Archduke's residence and could not be revived (see CL'ANA 0042 and CL'ANA 0295). This produced a set of unexpected financial hardships only partially relieved through Claire's generosity. His widow not only buried four of her children in six years, but also discovered his adulterous relationship with Mrs. Kollonitz. Antonia's letters describe her devastation, as she became Claire's willing correspondent.

The portion of Claire's life her correspondence with Antonia covers, from 1850 until Antonia's death in 1868, has been heretofore largely known to scholars through Claire's correspondence in Stocking's collection. This collection of Antonia's letters therefore explains more fully Claire's life and her generosity towards her brother's family. Furthermore, these letters describe Claire's kindness to Pauline and her illegitimate daughter, Georgina Hanghegyi, after Georgina came to live in Florence with Claire in the 1870s. Reading these letters in conjunction with Claire's correspondence in Stocking's collection provides evidence of Claire's continued support of her brother's extended family. One measure Claire took to provide financially for Georgina was to attempt to sell a set of cherished Shelley papers that she yet possessed. She told Edward Trelawny, one of the participants in the Pisan Circle of 1821, that "the only thing that would tempt me to sell them would be if I could get a considerable sum for them. In that case I would sacrifice my feelings for the sake of making a small provision for a little Orphan girl that lives with me, and whom my niece kindly gives lessons to, to enable her by and by to earn her own livelihood" (*CC* II: 620). In a later letter to her executor Bartolomeo Cini, Claire further elaborated on her motive:

> I hope he will sell the letters, for I want if I can get it an addition to my Income; it is enough for me as it is – but I want so much to give a tolerable education to dear Georgina – and that I cannot do on my present resources. And you know that now it is absolutely necessary for a young girl who probably will have to do something towards earning her livelihood to be well educated. For my self I would not sell my letters – but to benefit Georgie I will.
>
> (*CC* II: 634)

The letters in this collection provide additional information about these papers and about the social history that formed the background to Henry James's story *The Aspern Papers*. In his novella, James based his characters and their attempts to sell the valuable Shelley papers on Claire's and Pauline's stories. Claire died in Florence on 19 March 1879 and was buried in the Camposanto della Misericordia di Santa Maria all'Antella. She composed her own epitaph, which was etched on her tombstone: "She passed her life in sufferings, expiating not only her faults but also her virtues" (*CC* II: 664). Unfortunately, the church underwent renovations in the early twentieth century, and Claire's bones were reinterred under the pavement. Today, a stone marker on the ground marks her final resting place. Her life history, expunged from the pages of Lady Jane Shelley's 1859 *Shelley Memorials*, remained relegated to the margins of the Shelley-circle story. This collection, like that of Stocking's, thus seeks to redress the wrong by providing a correction to the omission.

Pauline and Wilhelm's long lives and strong epistolary connections give them prominence in this collection. Indeed, their international travels are well documented in this set. Wilhelm lived with his aunt in England for a time after his graduation from the Gymnasium[9] in Austria, studying farming techniques at Queenwood College in Hampshire. He subsequently moved on to Hohenheim (Germany) and then Altenburg (Hungary), where he studied additional agricultural practices. Wilhelm's chosen vocation as a farmer took him to venues located across Europe and as far away as Australia. Pauline went with him in 1853, seeking their fortunes, both for their own support and that of their mother. Wilhelm worked on a variety of farms in Australia while Pauline served as a governess to the Suttor family before they returned to Europe. Wilhelm then relocated to the Banat region. The letters in this collection document their experiences in great detail and section introductions provide more information about the siblings' various activities on both continents.

Pauline's social behaviors frequently mirrored those of her aunt, Claire, and, although she would probably have been somewhat loath to admit it, Pauline's enjoyment of her sexual relationships and her many flirtations became echoes of Claire's former past. Like Claire, she was content to indulge in a host of sexual affairs, none of which culminated in marriage. Pauline's letters never mentioned her relationship with William Henry Suttor, Junior (1834–1905), but it dominated many of the unpublished journal entries she wrote between 1855 and 1857. He was a pastoralist, future politician, and the eldest brother of the children to whom she was governess in Australia. At the time of their affair, she was thirty and he was twenty-two, and he was the only man Pauline claimed to have loved. While the journal occasionally referenced other men who admired her, Pauline set down the full history of her love affair with Willie in a combination of French, German, and (primarily) English entries. While she masked his identity by referring to him variously as W., Guillaume, and Willy, it is unmistakable. Unfortunately for Pauline, Willie eventually redirected his passions towards one of Pauline's pupils, Adelaide Agnes Henrietta Bowler. Pauline, however, continued to voice in her private writings both an unabated interest in Willie and her stunned disappointment over what she considered to be his betrayal of her, not only because he forsook her, but also because of the wife he chose. In Pauline's opinion, Adelaide had little to offer Willie. As she observed, Adelaide was "a girl who [could] barely read & write who would never from year's end to year's end open a book who does not understand the poetry in our nature & whose conversation is utter commonplace" (CL'ANA 0176: 13–14).

Willie was himself a prolific writer in his later adulthood, and his 1877 collection of short stories entitled *Australian Stories Retold; and, Sketches of Country Life* appears to contain a number of veiled references to Pauline. He professed that the stories contained in the section "Sketches of Country Life" had been "derived almost wholly from my own experiences. The descriptions of men and scenery are exactly set down as they appeared to me" (Suttor 1887).[10] Certainly, many of the tales seem to be situated in Bathurst, where he lived, while the descriptions of the homestead they foregrounded clearly evoked his father's estate, Brucedale, given its many varieties of flowers plus the picturesque cottage, veranda, and vineyard frequented by "a sixteen year old called William" (Suttor 1887: 62–63, see also Norton and Norton 1993: 116, 176). Willie's story "A Cattle Muster on the Plains" features an unnamed female character whose personality traits appear to be drawn from Pauline: "[A] late arrival from England, but has lived much on the Continent, and being somewhat self-willed, would defy conventionalities and make one of the party" (Suttor 1887: 82). The story "The Van Dieman's Land Ghouls" records that "Tennyson must surely have seen Tasmania in a dream when he wrote the 'Lotus Eaters'" (Suttor 1887: 53), a comment suggesting Pauline's influence on the work, given that she probably shared her fascination with Tennyson's poetry with him during their romance.[11]

Wilhelm would stay in Australia until 1861, but Pauline would leave in 1857. Her letters to Wilhelm and to Claire recount an adventure-filled life. As a brilliant pianist (see CL'ANA 0405), an adventurous woman, and a trusted governess, Pauline seemed to ignore the mores of her time. According to this collection's letters, Pauline smoked, flirted with men, sought out and engaged in numerous relationships, and traveled by herself – behaviors nineteenth-century society considered shocking for a woman. Yet her independence was not unfettered. Not only do her letters and her journal testify to the difficult life she endured as a woman in the Australian bush and to the constraints of her lack of financial independence, but the arrival of her daughter, Johanna Maria Georgina Hanghegyi (b. 21 January 1864), was a life-altering event. Pauline concealed her maternal relationship in order to avoid being ostracized by an austere Austrian public, and she never divulged Georgina's father's name. "Hanghegyi" was her own coinage. Herbert Huscher has suggested that Hanghegyi represents an "attempt at a translation of the name Clairmont into Hungarian, *hang* being sound, especially clear or shrill sound (compare 'clarion'), and *hegy*, mountain" (1955: 47). Pauline sent the girl to live with Countess Károly, for whom she had formerly served as a governess, in Hungary, where she would visit her daughter a few times each year. Pauline lived with Antonia in Baden until her mother's death from cancer in 1868, and then, in the 1870s, Pauline resided in Florence with Claire. In 1871, she brought Georgina to live with her and Claire in Italy. Despite her bright and treasured sense of independence, however, sorrows would continue to haunt Pauline, who remained with Claire until the latter's death in 1879. Georgina died as a young adult in 1885, six years prior to Pauline's accidental death in 1891, when she fell to her death while walking in Öblarn, Steiermark (Styria), while on an excursion with her nephew, Paul Clairmont.[12] Her death was recorded in *Das Vaterland* of 15 July 1891, where she was listed as the sister of W. G. Clairmont of Reisnerstrasse 40, Vienna. She was buried in Öblarn.[13] Like Claire, Pauline was dedicated to her family. Walter Clairmont told Stocking in a letter dated 16 June 1949 that he was "a witness of her inalienable devotion to her brother and his offsprings" (Stocking 1978: 374).

Wilhelm would outlive his sister by four years. His surviving letters to Pauline and to Claire documenting his post-Australian years all appear in this collection. Wilhelm left Australia on 22 January 1861, sailing on the *Behar*, bound for Alexandria, Egypt. His unpublished "Sands and Kenny's Diary 1861" (CL'ANA 0177, unpublished manuscript, Pforzheimer Collection) records his departure from Sydney, from where his journey took him to Suez, then through Cairo and to Alexandria. From Alexandria, he continued towards Florence via Nubia, Malta, and Messina. Finally reaching his destination on 28 March, he surprised his aunt

Claire (see CL'ANA 0245) in a reunion he recounted in his diary: "Saw A Claire at Hotel Schneider She has become much older looking She has lost some teeth and lisps in consequence She was affectionate & vivacious She offered to lend me £500 for stocking a farm or £1500 for purchasing land in a warm climate". The following day, his diary confirms, he saw Claire yet again: "Dined with A Claire – rain all day took leave from her at 9 ½ pm".[14] Finally, Wilhelm returned home to Baden, Austria, on 4 April, and in his journal he documented his reunion with Antonia and Pauline. The reunion was joyous in spite of the failure of the Australian experiment. While the siblings' Australian sojourn was not a financial success, ironically it may have saved their lives; four of their siblings died of the various diseases that particularly plagued Europe in the mid-nineteenth century in their absence.

On his return from Australia in 1861, Wilhelm began farming as a tenant farmer in the Banat, in part of the Austro-Hungarian Empire which is Romania today. The journal Wilhelm kept between March and June 1861 of his travels across the Austro-Hungarian Empire searching for a suitable property resembles a nineteenth-century geographical primer/compendium of place names and locations throughout present-day Croatia, Slovenia, and the Czech Republic. His early association with the sons of the Hungarian magnate class at Altenburg provided him with connections he desperately needed to succeed in his uncertain search. While a substantial British expatriate community existed in various continental locations, Eastern Europe remained far less commonly traveled. Yet as a young Austrian of British descent, Wilhelm occupied the quite unusual position of being able to describe, in English, his subsequent experiences in the Banat. His letters to Claire illuminate for readers of English a part of a nineteenth-century continental and Eastern Europe which was embroiled in a set of social and political difficulties and anxieties whose lead combatants continue to populate history books today. Wilhelm's letters to Claire document and identify these issues and conflicts, as well as describing some of the magnates associated with nineteenth-century Austro-Hungarian politics such as Count Esterházy and Prince Schwarzenberg.

As in Australia, Wilhelm proved unsuccessful as a farmer in the Banat, almost certainly because he underestimated the difficulty of the terrain and the harshness of the weather. He worked as a tenant farmer on the estate of the brother of one of Wilhelm's Altenburg friends, Rudolf von Hauer, in Bobda, a village located today in Western Romania near to Timişoara. Conditions made it extremely difficult to eke out a decent living. Pauline joined him in 1863, and spent two years with him working on the farm, attending to his health, and keeping house for him. She left in 1865 and later returned to Baden to assist Antonia, who had been diagnosed with cancer. In 1866, Wilhelm married the daughter of a Viennese privy councilor, Ottilia von Pichler (1843–1913), whose correspondence to Claire features in this collection. Ottilia's sister, Emily, had previously married Rudolf von Hauer, and the two families lived in close proximity to one another for a while. While the marriage was happy, famine and drought afflicted the area and posed great difficulties. By 1870, he was forced to make a change. First he became a tenant farmer on a homestead he called Beleci, and then he and Claire purchased Nikolaihof, a farm property in today's Slovenia, some 650 kilometers west of Timişoara. Neither plan succeeded, and by 1874 the family finally returned to Vienna, where Wilhelm became a surveyor of Crown properties after proving incapable of sustaining his growing family through any of his several farming enterprises.

Wilhelm and Ottilia raised three children: Walter Claire (1868–1958), Alma Pauline (1869–1946), and Johann Paul (1877–1942). If the couple struggled together financially, their thirty-year marriage appears to have been a very happy one. Wilhelm's death notice recorded that he died on 26 December 1895 at 10:15 p.m. at the age of 65 years. He was buried in the family crypt in Matzleinsdorf on 27 December. The certificate listed his children and spouse as survivors.[15] Ottilia died in 1913. Of the three children, only Paul produced grandchildren. Paul's son, Christoph, was an archaeologist who, together with his wife, Victorine Clairmont-von Gonzenbach, published many volumes documenting his archaeological digs in Israel, Yugoslavia, and elsewhere. Christoph's sister, Mary Claire Bally-Clairmont, lived with her husband, Hans Jörg Bally, in Switzerland, where she died in 2009. Since neither Mary Claire nor Christoph had children of their own, with their deaths the Clairmont side of the Shelley circle ended.

This collection restores the voices of those extended Clairmont family members who were closest to Claire and, by extension, to Mary and Percy Florence Shelley. Both Pauline and Wilhelm came to know the Shelleys rather intimately during their respective stays in England, and Antonia met Mary Shelley during her sojourn in England with Charles in 1828. The Clairmont family's association with the major participants in the Shelley circle, together with their lifelong friendship with Claire, makes these forgotten voices particularly relevant to Shelley-circle studies. The collection serves too as a way to close the Shelley circle by bringing into its fold the marginalized voices of those in the Clairmont family.

Notes

1 This collection contains additional information about these locations in the introductions to the sections containing the letters written from them.

2 Among Godwin's intellectual circle, Inchbald was a celebrated actress and novelist, Parr was a scholar, Mackintosh was the author of *Vindiciae Gallicae* (1791), and Holcroft was a playwright, philosopher, and scholar.

3 See https://sites.google.com/site/maryjanesdaughter/home

4 Burr visited the Godwin home and apparently enjoyed Mrs. Godwin's company.

5 British law gave fathers full custody of their children (St. Clair 1989: 463), a situation confronted by Wollstonecraft, Mary Hays, and others. Anne Mellor asserts that writers such as Wollstonecraft, Ann Radcliffe, Hays, and Mary Shelley argued for "a radical reform of the social construction of gender" in their texts (Mellor 2000: 105). These women countered the traditional patriarchal social and legal systems existing in England by advocating egalitarian marriages and a redistribution of family roles in defiance of prevailing legal orders.

6 Impl. and Rl. are abbreviations for Imperial and Royal (k.k. in German, kaiserlich-königlich), while the R. Ter. Academy stands for the Ritterakademie Theresianum.
7 The story was published in 1832 in *The Court Magazine* and again in *The English Annual* of 1836. The writer was identified as "the Author of 'Frankenstein'".
8 See CL'ANA 0055 for Wilhelm's account of his sister's death.
9 Equivalent of secondary school.
10 Unnumbered prefatory pages.
11 See CL'ANA 0210 and also CL'ANA 0423, a copy of "The Charge of the Light Brigade," probably penned in Pauline's hand (unpublished manuscript, Pforzheimer Collection).
12 Wilhelm's son.
13 Austrian Newspapers Online, Austrian National Library, http://anno.onb.ac.at/cgi-content/anno?aid=vtl&datum=18910715&seite=5&zoom=33 (p. 5).
14 Wilhelm's diary was not paginated.
15 Photograph of the death notice provided by Heraldic-Genealogical Society Adler, Vienna.

Bibliography

Anonymous, *Picture of Vienna Containing a Historical Sketch of the Metropolis of Austria, a Complete Notice of all the Public Institutions, Buildings, Galleries, Collections, Gardens, Walks, and Other Objects of Interest Or Utility, and a Short Description of the most Picturesque Spots in the Vicinity, with a Map of the Town and Suburbs* (Vienna: Braumüller & Seidel, 1844).

Austrian Newspapers Online, Österreichische Nationalbibliothek (Austrian National Library), http://anno.onb.ac.at/

Bennett, B. T., *Mary Wollstonecraft Shelley: An Introduction* (Baltimore, MD: Johns Hopkins University Press, 1998).

Bennett, B. T. and C. Robinson (eds), *The Mary Shelley Reader: Containing Frankenstein, Mathilda, Tales and Stories, Essays and Reviews, and Letters* (New York: Oxford University Press, 1990).

Clairmont, A., *Erste Schritte zur Erlernung der englischen Sprache, für Kinder von sechs bis zehn jahren* (Vienna: Braumüller & Seidel, 1845).

Clairmont, C. G., *First Poetical Reading-Book: Being a Progressive Collection of the Most Interesting Pieces in Verse in the English Language; Beginning with the Simplest Poems – Poetisches Lesebuch für Anfänger* (Vienna: Braumüller & Seidel, 1845).

Clairmont, C. M. J., "The Pole," in C. E. Robinson (ed.), *Mary Shelley: Collected Tales and Stories* (Baltimore, MD: Johns Hopkins University Press, 1990), pp. 347–372.

Conger, C. M., F. S. Frank, and G. O'Dea (eds), *Iconoclastic Departures: Mary Shelley after Frankenstein* (Madison, NJ and London: Fairleigh Dickinson University Press, 1997).

Dabundo, L. (ed.), *Jane Austen and Mary Shelley, and Their Sisters* (Lanham, MD: University Press of America, 2000).

Davidoff, L. and C. Hall, *Family Fortunes* (London and New York: Routledge, 2002).

Dowden, E., R. Garnett, and W. Rossetti, *Letters about Shelley: Interchanged by Three Friends – Edward Dowden, Richard Garnett and Wm. Michael Rossetti* (London: Hodder and Stoughton, 1917).

Eberle-Sinatra, M. (ed.), *Mary Shelley's Fictions: From Frankenstein to Falkner* (Basingstoke and New York: Macmillan Press, 2000).

Favret, M.A., *Romantic Correspondence: Women, Politics, and the Fiction of Letters* (Cambridge and New York: Cambridge University Press, 1993).

Fisch, A.A., A.K. Mellor and E.H. Schor (eds), *The Other Mary Shelley: Beyond Frankenstein* (New York: Oxford University Press, 1993).

Garrett, M., *A Mary Shelley Chronology* (New York: Palgrave, 2002).

Godwin, W., *The Collected Novels and Memoirs of William Godwin*, ed. P. Clemit, M. Hindle, and M. Philp (London: Pickering and Chatto, 1992).

——, *The Letters of William Godwin*, ed. P. Clemit (Oxford: Oxford University Press, 2011).

Goerlich, E., "Charles Gaulis Clairmont," *Wiener Geschichtsblätter*, 25 (1970), pp. 124–125.

Google Maps, 2014–2015, Web, various dates, www.google.com/maps/.

Hay, D., *Young Romantics: The Shelleys, Byron and Other Tangled Lives* (London: Bloomsbury, 2010).

Hebron, S. and E. Denlinger, *Shelley's Ghost: Reshaping the Image of a Literary Family* (Oxford: Bodleian Library, 2010).

Hirst, T.A. and J. Tyndall, *Introductory Lecture to the Course on Natural Philosophy: At Queenwood College, Hampshire* (Romsey: C.L. Lordan, 1853).

Huscher, H., "Charles und Claire Clairmont," *Englische Studien*, 76 (1944), pp. 53–117.

——, "Claire Clairmont's Lost Russian Journal and Some Further Glimpses of Her Later Life," *Keats–Shelley Memorial Bulletin*, 6 (1955), pp. 35–47.

——, "Charles Gaulis Clairmont," *Keats–Shelley Memorial Bulletin*, 8 (1957), pp. 9–18.

——, "The Clairmont Enigma," *Keats–Shelley Memorial Bulletin*, 11 (1960), pp. 13–20.

James, H., *The Aspern Papers and Other Stories* (Oxford and New York: Oxford University Press, 1983).

Joffe, S., *The Kinship Coterie and the Literary Endeavors of the Women in the Shelley Circle* (New York: Peter Lang, 2007).

Jones, F. (ed.), *Maria Gisborne & Edward E. Williams, Shelley's Friends* (Norman, OK: University of Oklahoma Press, 1951).

Jones, F.L., "Mary Shelley and Claire Clairmont," *South Atlantic Quarterly*, 42 (1943), pp. 406–412.

——, "A Shelley and Mary Letter to Claire," *Modern Language Notes*, 65:2 (1950), pp. 121–123.

Jump, H.D., "'A Meritorious Wife': Or, Mrs. Godwin and the Donkey," *Charles Lamb Bulletin*, 90 (1995), pp. 73–84.

Kelly, G., *Revolutionary Feminism: The Mind and Career of Mary Wollstonecraft* (New York: St. Martin's Press, 1992).

Leslie, L., "The Fact That Is in Fiction: Autobiography in Claire Clairmont's 'The Pole'," *Keats–Shelley Review*, 20 (2006), pp. 69–88.

Levine, G. and U.C. Knoepflmacher (eds), *The Endurance of Frankenstein: Essays on Mary Shelley's Novel* (Berkeley: University of California Press, 1979).

Mathewson, G., "Claire Clairmont on Shelley's Circle," *Notes and Queries*, 20 (1973), pp. 48–49.

Mellor, A., *Mary Shelley: Her Life, Her Fiction, Her Monsters* (New York: Methuen, 1988).

——, *Mothers of the Nation: Women's Political Writing in England* (Bloomington: Indiana University Press, 2000).

Morrison, L., S. Stone and P. Feldman, *A Mary Shelley Encyclopedia* (Westport, CT: Greenwood Press, 2003).

National Center of Biography, *Australian Dictionary of Biography*, Web, http://adb.anu.edu.au/

National Library of Australia, Trove, Newspapers Online, http://trove.nla.gov.au/newspaper/

Neuer Nekrolog der Deutschen: 26 Jahrgang (Weimar: B. Fr. Voigt, 1850).

Norton, J. and H. Norton, *Dear William: The Suttors of Brucedale: Principally the Life and Times of William Henry Suttor Senior ("Dear William"), 1805–1877* (Sydney: Suttor Pub. Committee, 1993).

Owens, R., "In Defense of Mary Godwin," *Charles Lamb Bulletin*, 146 (2009), pp. 72–76.

Poovey, M., *The Proper Lady and the Woman Writer: Ideology as Style in the Works of Mary Wollstonecraft, Mary Shelley, and Jane Austen* (Chicago: University of Chicago Press, 1984).

Reiman, D.H., K. N. Cameron, D. D. Fischer, et al., *Shelley and his Circle, 1773–1822* (Cambridge, MA: Harvard University Press, 1961–).

St. Clair, W., *The Godwins and the Shelleys* (New York: Norton, 1989).

Seymour, M., *Mary Shelley* (New York: Grove Press, 2000).

Shelley, J., *Shelley Memorials: From Authentic Sources* (Boston: Ticknor and Fields, 1859).

Shelley, M.W., *The Letters of Mary Wollstonecraft Shelley*, ed. B.T. Bennett (Baltimore, MD: Johns Hopkins University Press, 1980).

——, *The Journals of Mary Shelley, 1814–1844*, eds. P.R. Feldman and D. Scott-Kilvert (Oxford and New York: Clarendon Press and Oxford University Press, 1987).

——, *The Novels and Selected Works of Mary Shelley*, eds. P. Clemit and N. Crook (Brookfield, VT: Pickering & Chatto, 1996).

——, *Maurice, Or, the Fisher's Cot: A Tale*, ed. C. Tomalin (Chicago: University of Chicago Press, 1998).

Snape, W.H., *Queenwood College, Near Stockbridge, Hampshire* (etching) (Wellcome Library, London, 1891).

Stafford, V.P., "Claire Clairmont, Mary Jane's Daughter," https://sites.google.com/site/maryjanesdaughter/home, 26 September 2015.

Stocking, M.K. (ed.), *The Journals of Claire Clairmont* (Cambridge, MA: Harvard University Press, 1968).

——, "Miss Tina and Miss Plin: The Papers behind the Aspern Papers," in D. Reiman (ed.), *The Evidence of the Imagination* (New York: New York University Press, 1978), pp. 372–384.

—— (ed.), *The Clairmont Correspondence: Letters of Claire Clairmont, Charles Clairmont, and Fanny Imlay Godwin* (Baltimore, MD: Johns Hopkins University Press, 1995).

Sunstein, E.W., *Mary Shelley: Romance and Reality* (Boston: Little, Brown, 1989).

Suttor, C., *Charlotte Augusta Anne Suttor Diaries, 1848–1853* (Bathurst, NSW: State Library New South Wales, 1848–1853).

Suttor, W.H., *Australian Stories Retold; and, Sketches of Country Life* (Bathurst, NSW: G. Whalan, 1887).

Todd, J. (ed.), *The Collected Letters of Mary Wollstonecraft* (New York: Columbia University Press, 2003).

——, *Death and the Maidens: Fanny Wollstonecraft and the Shelley Circle* (Berkeley, CA: Counterpoint, 2007).

Williams, J., *Mary Shelley: A Literary Life* (New York: St. Martin's Press, 2000).

Wollstonecraft, M., *The Works of Mary Wollstonecraft/Mary, a Fiction. The Wrongs of Woman: Or, Maria* (London: Pickering, 1989).

LIST OF ILLUSTRATIONS

Volume I

EDITORIAL SYMBOLS

~~word~~	Deleted legible word
[illeg.]	Illegible word
[~~illeg.~~]	An illegible word that has been deleted
c.	Editorial conjecture, typically used for a date
/	Line changes
{tear}	The manuscript is torn and is illegible
{ink}	An inkblot is visible, rendering the word(s) illegible
{section/line cut out of page}	Physical cut in the paper, made by an unknown person

INDEX OF LETTERS

Abbreviations for names of letter writers and recipients:

Claire Clairmont: ClC
Antonia Clairmont: AC
Charles Gaulis Clairmont: CGC
Pauline Clairmont: PC
Wilhelm Gaulis Clairmont: WC
Ottilia Clairmont: OC
Emily Clairmont: EC
Sidonia Clairmont: SC
Charles Gaulis Clairmont (Charley): ChC
Alma Clairmont: ACC
Clara Knox: CK
Alexander Knox: AK
Alma von Pichler: AP
Edward John Trelawny: EJT
Emma Taylor: ET

Volume I

	Date	CL'ANA Number	From	To	Page
1)	12 Dec 1839	CL'ANA 0405	AC	ClC	1
2)	8 July 1846	CL'ANA 0401	AC	ClC	5
3)	18 March 1847	CL'ANA 0404	AC	ClC	10
4)	20 August 1847	CL'ANA 0397	AC	ClC	14
5)	1 Dec 1848	CL'ANA 0402	AC	ClC	17
6)	18 Dec 1848	CL'ANA 0403	AC	ClC	20
7)	12 June 1849	CL'ANA 0041	WC	ClC	24
8)	18 June 1849	CL'ANA 0188	CK	ClC	26
9)	18 June 1849	CL'ANA 0201	AK	WC	27
10)	3 July 1849	CL'ANA 0058	WC	CGC & AC	28

11)	9 July 1849	CL’ANA 0189	CK	ClC	31
12)	24 July 1849	CL’ANA 0191	CK	WC	32
13)	1 August 1849	CL’ANA 0057	WC	CGC & AC	36
14)	16–17 August 1849	CL’ANA 0056	WC	CGC & AC	39
15)	11 September 1849	CL’ANA 0400	AC	ClC	43
16)	2 November 1849	CL’ANA 0055	WC	CGC & AC	49
17)	21 November 1849	CL’ANA 0054	WC	CGC & AC	55
18)	25 December 1849	CL’ANA 0059	WC	CGC & AC	58
19)	30 December 1849	CL’ANA 0060	WC	E, ChC,& S	66
20)	30 January 1850	CL’ANA 0042	WC	ClC	70
21)	12 February 1850	CL’ANA 0042	WC	ClC	72
22)	19–22 February 1850	CL’ANA 0212	PC & AC	ClC	74
23)	19 April 1850	CL’ANA 0043	WC	ClC	77
24)	25 April 1850	CL’ANA 0399	AC	ClC	80
25)	8 c. May 1850	CL’ANA 0396	AC	ClC	82
26)	17 c. May 1850	CL’ANA 0375	AC	ClC	85
27)	2 June c. 1850	CL’ANA 0395	AC	ClC	87
28)	21 July 1850	CL’ANA 0044	WC	ClC	89
29)	22 July 1850	CL’ANA 0319	AC	ClC	92
30)	11 August 1850	CL’ANA 0045	WC	ClC	95
31)	18 September 1850	CL’ANA 0398	AC	ClC	97
32)	3 December 1850	CL’ANA 0046	WC	ClC	100
33)	Undated, c. 1850	CL’ANA 0369	AC	ClC	105
34)	2 March 1851	CL’ANA 0047	WC	ClC	107
35)	27 June 1851	CL’ANA 0394	AC	ClC	110
36)	24 August 1851	CL’ANA 0421	AC	ClC	114
		Box 1, bundle a, numbers 8–10			
37)	19 October 1851	CL’ANA 0048	WC	ClC	116
38)	24 October 1851	CL’ANA 0370	AC	ClC	119
39)	6 December 1851	CL’ANA 0049	WC	ClC	121
40)	1 February 1852	CL’ANA 0371	AC	ClC	123
41)	17 February 1852	CL’ANA 0372	AC	ClC	125
42)	9 March 1852	CL’ANA 0050	WC	AC	127
43)	16 May 1852	CL’ANA 0052	WC	ClC	129
44)	6 June 1852	CL’ANA 0053	WC	ClC	131
45)	12 September 1852	CL’ANA 0206	PC	ClC	133
46)	24 December 1852	CL’ANA 0051	WC	ClC	134
47)	10 April 1853	CL’ANA 0373	AC	ClC	135
48)	8 July–31 July 1853	CL’ANA 0210	PC	ClC	153
49)	21 November 1853	CL’ANA 0374	AC	ClC	159
50)	22 November 1853	CL’ANA 0232	PC	AC	161
51)	4 January 1854	CL’ANA 0377	AC	ClC	164
52)	22–27 March 1854	CL’ANA 0209	PC	ClC	166
53)	30 May 1854	CL’ANA 0378	AC	ClC	171
54)	22 June 1854	CL’ANA 0244	ChC	ClC	173
55)	3 July 1854	CL’ANA 0185	ChC	ClC	174
56)	18 August 1854	CL’ANA 0065	WC	ClC	175
57)	21 December 1854	CL’ANA 0376	AC	ClC	177
58)	8 July 1855	CL’ANA 0233	PC	EC	178
59)	23 August 1855	CL’ANA 0066	WC	ClC	181
60)	7 February 1856	CL’ANA 0379	AC	ClC	184
61)	15 February 1856	CL’ANA 0067	WC	ClC	185

62)	5 April 1856	CL'ANA 0380	AC	ClC	187
63)	22 April 1856	CL'ANA 0392	AC	ClC	189
64)	26 April 1856	CL'ANA 0382	AC	ClC	191
65)	8 May 1856	CL'ANA 0381	AC	ClC	192
66)	24 May 1856	CL'ANA 0071	WC	ClC	193
67)	14 June 1856	CL'ANA 0387	AC	ClC	196
68)	16 June 1856	CL'ANA 0385	AC	ClC	197
69)	21 June 1856	CL'ANA 0383	AC	ClC	201
70)	29 June 1856	CL'ANA 0421	AC	ClC	203
		Box 1, bundle a, numbers 8–10			
71)	5 July 1856	CL'ANA 0384	AC	ClC	204
72)	14 July 1856	CL'ANA 0386	AC	ClC	206
73)	19 July 1856	CL'ANA 0388	AC	ClC	207
74)	7 August 1856	CL'ANA 0389	AC	ClC	209
75)	3 September 1856	CL'ANA 0073	WC	ClC	211
76)	27 September 1856	CL'ANA 0391	AC	ClC	213
77)	11 October 1856	CL'ANA 0393	AC	ClC	214
78)	18 October 1856	CL'ANA 0344	AC	ClC	216
79)	19 October 1856	CL'ANA 0390	AC	ClC	218
80)	25 October 1856	CL'ANA 0345	AC	ClC	221
81)	1 November 1856	CL'ANA 0346	AC	ClC	223
82)	8 November 1856	CL'ANA 0347	AC	ClC	225
83)	15 November 1856	CL'ANA 0348	AC	ClC	226
84)	28 November 1856	CL'ANA 0069	WC	ClC	227
85)	1 December 1856	CL'ANA 0068	WC	ClC	229
86)	21 December 1856	CL'ANA 0349	AC	ClC	231
87)	26 December 1856	CL'ANA 0350	AC	ClC	232
88)	29 March 1857	CL'ANA 0070	WC	ClC	234
89)	2 July 1857	CL'ANA 0072	WC	ClC	236
90)	12 October 1857	CL'ANA 0074	WC	ClC	239
91)	9 November 1857	CL'ANA 0075	WC	ClC	240
92)	3 December 1857	CL'ANA 0076	WC	ClC	242
93)	c. 2 January 1858	CL'ANA 0351	AC	ClC	244
94)	3 January 1858	CL'ANA 0352	AC	ClC	246
95)	18 January 1858	CL'ANA 0353	AC	ClC	247
96)	30 January 1858	CL'ANA 0354	AC	ClC	250
97)	12 February 1858	CL'ANA 0355	AC	ClC	252
98)	23 March 1858	CL'ANA 0356	AC	ClC	254
99)	27 March 1858	CL'ANA 0077	WC	ClC	255
100)	27 April 1858	CL'ANA 0078	WC	ClC	258
101)	1 May 1858	CL'ANA 0358	AC	ClC	260
102)	13 May 1858	CL'ANA 0357	AC	ClC	262
103)	17 May 1858	CL'ANA 0359	AC	ClC	264
104)	3 June 1858	CL'ANA 0079	WC	ClC	267
105)	25 June 1858	CL'ANA 0361	AC and ClC	ClC AC	269
106)	2 July 1858	CL'ANA 0362	AC	ClC	272
107)	4 July 1858	CL'ANA 0080	WC	ClC	274
108)	29 July 1858	CL'ANA 0363	AC	ClC	276
109)	4 August 1858	CL'ANA 0364	AC	ClC	278
110)	8 August 1858	CL'ANA 0365	AC	ClC	280
111)	10 August 1858	CL'ANA 0366	AC	ClC	282

112)	16 August 1858	CL'ANA 0368	AC	ClC	284
113)	28 August 1858	CL'ANA 0367	AC	ClC	285
114)	15 September 1858	CL'ANA 0339	AC	ClC	289
115)	5 October 1858	CL'ANA 0340	AC	ClC	291
116)	16 October 1858	CL'ANA 0341	AC	ClC	294
117)	31 October 1858	CL'ANA 0081	WC	ClC	296
118)	15 November 1858	CL'ANA 0342	AC	ClC	297
119)	28 November 1858	CL'ANA 0360	AC	ClC	299
120)	31 December 1858	CL'ANA 0343	AC	ClC	301
121)	15 February 1859	CL'ANA 0338	AC	ClC	304
122)	27 February 1859	CL'ANA 0337	AC	ClC	306
123)	1 March 1859	CL'ANA 0082	WC	ClC	309
124)	21 March 1859	CL'ANA 0336	AC	ClC	312
125)	3 April 1859	CL'ANA 0335	AC	ClC	315
126)	11 April 1859	CL'ANA 0207	PC	ClC	317
127)	15 May 1859	CL'ANA 0334	AC	ClC	319
128)	27 May 1859	CL'ANA 0333	AC	ClC	321
129)	22 June 1859	CL'ANA 0332	AC	ClC	323
130)	30 June 1859	CL'ANA 0331	AC	ClC	326
131)	4 July 1859	CL'ANA 0083	WC	ClC	327
132)	10 July 1859	CL'ANA 0330	AC	ClC	328
133)	25 July 1859	CL'ANA 0329	AC	ClC	329
134)	29 July 1859	CL'ANA 0084	WC	ClC	331
135)	1 August 1859	CL'ANA 0085	WC	ClC	333
136)	25 August 1859	CL'ANA 0328	AC	ClC	335
137)	29 August 1859	CL'ANA 0327	AC	ClC	337
138)	4 September 1859	CL'ANA 0326	AC	ClC	339
139)	7 October 1859	CL'ANA 0086	WC	ClC	342
140)	5 November 1859	CL'ANA 0087	WC	ClC	343
141)	8 January 1860	CL'ANA 0323	AC	ClC	344
142)	2 February 1860	CL'ANA 0322	AC	ClC	345
143)	23 February 1860	CL'ANA 0324	AC	ClC	347
144)	28 February 1860	CL'ANA 0088	WC	ClC	349
145)	7 April 1860	CL'ANA 0089	WC	ClC	350
146)	4 May 1860	CL'ANA 0090	WC	ClC	352
147)	25 May 1860	CL'ANA 0091	WC	ClC	354
148)	3 September 1860	CL'ANA 0092	WC	ClC	355
149)	5 September 1860	CL'ANA 0325	AC	ClC	357
150)	2 October 1860	CL'ANA 0093	WC	ClC	359
151)	30 October 1860	CL'ANA 0094	WC	ClC	360
152)	10 December 1860	CL'ANA 0095	WC	ClC	361

LETTERS FROM 12 DECEMBER 1839–10 APRIL 1853

1 • Antonia Clairmont to Claire Clairmont

267 Wallner Strasse Vienna[1]
12th Dec. 1839.[2]

My dearest Claire![3]

We are all erring mortals; in proof of which poor dear Toni, whom you supposed to be the only one not liable to be ill, is the only one who is ill at present;[4] I am sitting on the sofa with a very bad ruhmatism[5] in my thigh, wrapped up in flannels it would do Mamma good to see me so like a gouty old Lady I look.[6] Thank God I can move my hands, but I write very badly owing to a little trembling. The contents of yours gave us great joy, it has removed a load from our minds, to think that Mamma is provided for for a couple of years is a blessing indeed, if she would come now, she might almost live on that capital here, and all our sorrows were ended for ever, however we see already she has made up her mind not to do that; and so we must submit to her; on your account we are most sorry; because you might live cheerfully and happily with us, instead of suffering from uncertainty and care as you do in your present mode of life. Our business goes on as usual, I have a few little girls that come to me, and I might have more but for want of time; it is true that more and more English men are coming to settle as masters here; but Charle's reputation is such, that it has nothing to fear from such newcomers, perhaps those cheap masters might injure the classes, but till now we have not perceived any evil influenze, except the making Charles uneasy; the poor fellow's hard time begins now again; his lessons go on without interruption from 7 in the morning till 9 in the evening with a short half hour for dinner, and another for tea. –[7]

Since writing this I have been in bed four days with very bad pains and fair hopes of spending the winter more or less on the sofa; you may imagine what a trial this is for a [illeg.]ing economical housekeeper! though I took to my bed with the firm resolution to bear it out stoutly, and not to be cast down, but when I think of candles and butter more used, vegetables spoiled, potatoes thrown away, and meat that is not made go far enough, can you wonder when I confess myself entirely failed, and fretful and fidgetting as any cinic[8] would wish to see one. Today I could no longer bear it, and got up, and crept into the nursery, where

I found the Bonne d'Enfans,[9] changing her Bonnet, whilst the children were all unwashed, and the linen not put by since three days, nor last weeks stockings mended; the cook in full dress receiving visit and the housemaid was nowhere to be found; surely the servants are nowhere so bad than here; lazy, dirty, and good for nothing in every respect; but no more of them; let me rather try to be as amiable as possibly can be in this present dilemma.

Again I have been forced to leave off, and shall not say much more there are several points in your letter, that Charles wants to answer, I will only add about Mrs Wright, ~~that~~ I am the more inclined to take and love her boy, as I heard from Mr Richter that he is a very quiet boy, and besides she Mrs. W. is so kind to you that we are glad to show our grateful sense for it. You say nothing about Emily; how is she? soon to be married or no?[10] the wizest thing for you to do were to get your things in order, and bring young Emilie's yourself, instead of looking for a situation; I had half a mind to send over Pauline next summer, as a Lady of our acquaintance goes there in spring and returns in autumn; but partly I am afraid she would be a burthen to Mama, and partly I wish her to be a year older, on account of her studies not being finished, especially her music, in which she makes astonishing progress;[11] we have this winter taken a first rate master for her at 5.s. per lesson, she goes on improving rapidly, perceptible almost at every lesson and it would be a pity to break off, at such a time when she is too young to go one alone, so I suppose I must give up my project and wait for another year; Mrs Moreau is likewise satisfied with them, and they adore her; they are both good looking girls;[12] Pauline has more improved in this point[13] than Clary which was the first as I told you already; William gives me most trouble just now; some of his evil propensities may have been his fathers too, when a boy; but he, who wants to be faultless in my eyes, even to doubing his douts,[14] is too reserved as to converse with me on such subjects; therefore I can gather no lights, but my own wisdom to guide me on my difficult way. The others are all well and going on as they should. Mina and Emy[15] prefer french to English for the present but Charley[16] stoutly maintains he is an English boy. When I told them that a young English friend will come to stay with us, they were so glad, and look forward with the greatest impatience to see him.

Good bye dearest Claire I can say no more, but do not think I am ill, it is only a very ~~dangerous~~ tedious thing, but not a dangerous one. do write again very soon we wish also much to hear from Mama.

ever yours A.C.

No envelope

Unpublished. Text: M.S., Pf. Coll., CL'ANA 0405

1 *Picture of Vienna Containing a Historical Sketch of the Metropolis of Austria* (1844) describes certain aspects of Viennese life in this period. Street numbers, the unnamed author noted, ran "from

1 to 1214, indiscriminately through the town" (p. 10), making it difficult to locate addresses. The book's list of house numbers and the street on which they stood reveals that the Clairmont's house, number 267, was on Wallnerstrasse. Houses numbered 263, 265 through 273, and 276 were also located on Wallnerstrasse (Vienna: Braunmüller and Seidel, 1844) p. 111.

2 This letter, dated 1839, is the earliest extant letter of Antonia Ghi(s)lain von Hembyze (1800–1868), the daughter of Georg von Hembyze and Anna Schönbichler, who married Charles Gaulis Clairmont (1795–1850) in 1824. Parish birth records for Charles and Antonia's children identify Antonia as the daughter of Georg von Hembyze, a "Zollamts Oberbeamter" (customs office official). A document signed by Konstantin Bouhelier Beaulier of Belgium (Flanders), and dating back to the eighteenth century, shows the Hembyze family tree with its Belgium connections (see Pforzheimer Collection, unpublished manuscript, CL'ANA 0415). Charles was an English language teacher in Vienna. His children's birth records listed his profession as "englischer Sprachmeister" (German for "master of the English language").

Charles first moved to Vienna in 1819. Marion Stocking explains that the Austrian authorities deemed Charles and Claire (1798–1879), who was visiting him at the time, as "subversive[s]" in 1822, and ordered them to leave Vienna, acting on an anonymous letter Count Joseph Sidlnitzky, chief of the Police and Censorship Office, had received (see Charles's letter to Mary Shelley, *CC* I: 202–9). Bias against their step-father, William Godwin, and against Percy Bysshe Shelley probably prompted the authorities to single them out for expulsion. Walter Clairmont (Charles's grandson) confirmed the family connection in a document written in 1933 (CL'ANA 0428, unpublished manuscript, Pforzheimer Collection). Walter Clairmont observed: "Da die Stiefschwester Mary Godwin die Frau des berühmten englischen Dichters Shelley wurde, traten sie in enge Beziehungen zu den Familien Shelley und Byron. Die Freundschaft meines Großvaters mit Shelley ist aus jeder englischen Literaturgeschichte zu entnehmen". (Translation by Anja Reiner: "Since [their] step-sister Mary Godwin became the wife of the famous English poet Shelley, they [Charles and Claire] maintained a close relationship with the families of Shelley and Byron. My grandfather's friendship with Shelley appears in English literary history").

Charles secured the aid of many important Viennese families who petitioned on his behalf to allow him to stay. Signatories included Count Dietrichstien-Prosekau-Lestic, Princess Grassaltowitsch née Esterhazy, Baron Gump and Baron Eskeles (*CC* I: 206). As a result of these requests, the authorities granted Charles permission to remain in Vienna where he taught English for many years. Claire stayed until 1824, when she became a governess in Russia, an employment in which she would continue for some years. In July 1828, Charles and Antonia left for London with their two children, Pauline and Clara. They stayed for two years, then returned to Vienna. Writing to Mary Shelley from Tauplitz, Austria, Claire asked about her brother's children, inquiring if they were "pretty". She also asked Mary Shelley to share information about Antonia (*CC* I: 253). By 1839, Charles and Antonia had seven children. The parish register of the Church of St. Michael in Vienna (Michaelerkirche) provides their birth names: Pauline (Pauline Maria, 1825–91), Clara (Maria Johanna Klara Gaulis, 1826–1855), Wilhelm (Wilhelm Karl, 1831–95), Hermine (register information unavailable, 1832–47), Emily (register information unavailable, 1833–56), Charles Gaulis (Carolus Borromaeus, 1835–56), and Sidonia (1836–56). The register also records the birth of "Bertha," daughter of Charles and Antonia, in 1828. No further information about Bertha is known. The announcement of Emily Clairmont's death on 2 March 1856 in the 6 March 1856 edition of *Wiener Zeitung* lists her as Emma Clairmont (Austrian Newspapers Online, Österreichische Nationalbibliothek, http://www.anno.onb.ac.at/cgi-content/anno?apm=0&aid=wrz&datum=18560306&seite=11&zoom=1, p. 11). Of the seven Clairmont children, only Pauline and Wilhelm would survive their mother.

3 See Introduction for more detailed information about the family.

4 Antonia was known as Tonie to her family. She was 39 years old at the time this letter was written.

5 Antonia misspelled the German "Rheumatismus" and the English "rheumatism".

6 Antonia referred to Mary Jane Godwin (1768–1841), Claire's mother and wife of William Godwin (1756–1836). Marion Stocking records that Mary Jane Godwin had moved by 1837 to "a retired spot at the beginning of Kentish town" (*CC* II: 354). In 1838, Claire wrote to Mary Shelley to ask

whether she had seen Mrs. Godwin. Claire informed Mary Shelley that her mother corresponded very "seldom" with her (p. 354). Mrs. Godwin died in 1841 and was buried beside Godwin and Mary Wollstonecraft in old St. Pancras's Church. After Mary Shelley's death in 1851, her son, Sir Percy Florence Shelley, authorized the bodies of Godwin and Wollstonecraft to be exhumed and then reburied in St. Peter's Church, Bournemouth. See Introduction for information about Mary Jane Godwin.

7 In *Picture of Vienna*, the author documented the presence of private schools for language instruction in Vienna: "English gentlemen or ladies, intending to pass some months in Vienna, and wishing during their stay to acquire a knowledge of German, cannot do better than to apply to Prof. Clairmont, Wallnerstrasse, Nr. 267" (p. 88). Charles was highy acclaimed as an instructor (see Introduction to this collection for information from Ernst Joseph Görlich).

8 cynic.

9 French for "nurse maid".

10 In a letter to Mary Shelley from Paris, dated 2 June 1843, Claire stated that she had received a letter from "Emily" who informed her that Mrs. Wright had married Count de Witts and had "given up business," and that she considered the marriage not "prudent" (*CC* II: 377). Stocking identifies Emily as Emily Godwin, wife of William Godwin, Jr., (1803–32), named Mary Louisa Eldred but known as Emily. The son of William and Mary Jane Godwin, William Godwin, Jr. married Emily in 1830, and died without issue in 1832. Stocking was unable to identify Mrs. Wright, Count de Witts, or Mr. Richter.

11 Pauline was extremely musical and played the piano. Her letters from Australia reference the piano she played as a governess at Brucedale (see CL'ANA 0210 and CL'ANA 0232). Charles Clairmont told Mary Shelley that Pauline was "considered one of the best female dilettanti" in Vienna and that she could earn her living with her piano playing. He called her "Beethoven mad" (*CC* II: 462).

12 Writing to Mary Shelley from Moscow in 1824, Claire expressed her dissatisfaction at having to keep up with so many correspondents. She evidently wrote to "two Moreaus at Vienna," one of whom Stocking identified with some probability as Jeanne Hulot Moreau, widow of General Jean Victor Moreau (*CC* I: 214). In 1845, Claire told Mary Shelley that she was visited in Paris by two friends from Vienna whom Stocking identified as the Moreaus. In 1849, Charles and Antonia wrote to Claire about their daughter, Clara, noting that "poor old Mrs. Moreaux used to swear by her" (*CC* II: 504).

13 Pauline was considered extremely attractive, although she was plagued with bad teeth. In a letter to Wilhelm dated 9 June 1878, Pauline decried the loss of her teeth, saying it was far worse a condition than Wilhelm's grey hair (see CL'ANA 0421, Box 3, bundle g, number 207). She also complained of becoming "stout". Charles Clairmont told Mary Shelley that Pauline had "a very pretty face" (*CC* II: 462) but that Clara, although less "delicate" than Pauline, was in fact the prettier sister (p. 462). Pauline's Australian lover, Willie Suttor, described her in his *Memoirs*: "I was a boy of eighteen and she a woman of twenty-eight . . . She was a short dark woman with jet black silky hair, dark brown eyes and very pretty hands and arms and a certain spice of devilry in her that made her (undeciphered word) to a raw country lad with all his passions just ripening unto manhood strength. I think she left us in 1857 having just taught me what it was to feel what love of a woman was like" (quoted in Voignier-Marshall, p.29). In her own journal, written in 1855 while she was living in Australia, Pauline compared herself to the woman Willie Suttor would eventually marry, Adelaide Agnes Henrietta Bowler. According to Pauline, while Adelaide had beauty and youth on her side ("You have beauty I have the mind you have youth I have experience"), Adelaide's face was completely out of proportion: "& then her features are of that kind that will very soon look wizened – Nose and chin meeting – & though on the whole she is very handsome, yet I do not think I have in my face a feature so out of proportion as her nose is – But then I being plain one bad feature would not strike on so much" (CL'ANA 0176 pp. 10, 15; unpublished journal, Pforzheimer Collection).

14 Antonia meant to write "doubting his doubts".

15 Hermine was known as Mina, and Emily as Emmy or Emy.

16 Charles Gaulis Clairmont was known as Charley.

2 • Antonia Clairmont to Claire Clairmont

My direction – Madame Clairmont Nrs 57.58. Weidling 8th of July 1846
Weidling bei Klosterneuburg[1]

My dearest Claire.

Yesterday I was in town and Charles gave me your two last letters,[2] and I sit down immediately to relieve your fears on Charles' account and to thank you for your affectionate solicitude for his and our sakes; Charles is better in so far that he is going out, but there is still the same stiffness about the limbs; the arm is stiff and writing easily fatigues him, also ~~has~~ doctor Boehm has forbidden it.[3] the leg is rather stronger, but going up our high staircase must naturally weaken it, therefore Doctor B advises most strenuously to take another lodging, which however is not so easily done, good lodgings being scarce unless you pay a high price;[4] doctor B now seems to think the cause of the disease to be in the liver in that case a trip to Carlsbad[5] will be found necessary which I should greatly regret, not so much on account of the expense but because I am convinced Charles would feel so low and melancholy, separated from us all without occupation, always brooding on the future, that he would never reap the benefit from the waters that might accrue if taken with a mind free from cares: on the other hand if he were to spend the two months of the boys' holidays entirely at Weidling, enjoying the pure air, repose, and the cheerful society of his children it would do more for him, than either the waters of Gastein[6] or Carlsbad; his disease having been brought on by over exertion, repose and quiet both of mind and body will cure it; this I represented to Dr. B. and he fully agreed with me as to the moral view of it, but said he would be guided in his final judgment by the effect of the baths he is now taking; so very likely no journey [Badreise][7] will be necessary, but if it were my dearest Claire, pray do not distress yourself for the means we are fully able to meet the expense, if for such a purpose one must not regret a sacrifice. I am indeed deeply touched with your kindness and generous love; would to God I had other means of proving it to you but words; but never, never, kind and liberal sister, can we accept more from your kindness than the promised £80 pr annum; if Mrs. S.[8] will or can add something – as you seem to hint – £20 or 25 or whatever it may be, it will be a blessing to us; but you my dear Claire, neither I nor Charles could bear the idea, that after a life of storms and vicissitude you should deny yourself every comfort that your ill health or habits and an advancing age require, in order to support us; you do not seem to be aware of the immense benefit you are already conferring; for is it not the reliance on your promise that keeps up my courage now in this tying moment? without it I own, my heart would sink within me in bleak despair; but now secret tears of thanks to God mingled with those of pain when I first heard of his illness – for I was already at W: – you may well think, I was not unprepared for a catastrophy of that cost I saw him running on in his headlong career where he would not be stopped and have been expecting to see him sink these last six years; many is the hour I have sat in painful meditation, how shall I do when he fails? what can I undertake, – and now the dread moment seems to come God has put a guardian angel on my path, and that guardian angel are you my dear Claire, you are our benefactress, such unexpected such essential help, that I should blush to accept more; if Mrs. S. can add nothing no matter £80 is a great sum; and though our wants be many, let my own and my children's activity supply the rest, and with the help of God we shall succeed, besides Charles' state of health is not so bad but we may hope if he will only be reasonable, and not begin his lessons too early, so as to bring on a relapse; I am sorry you are again prevented from coming here this summer, for I relied on your influenze with him on that point. But ~~whether~~ let me now speak of the future. You speak of our retiring in the country, that I am afraid is impossible, though it would meet all our wishes as to taste, because we cannot afford to live without gaining something, and what should we do with the boys? they must have the advantage of studying; ever since Charles' great illness I had the wish of retiring from Vienna and settle in some smaller town where living was cheaper, and we should find some occupation which with the stipend you so generously fixed would carry us through, but Charles treated it as a ridiculous idea, to give up a prosperous business, numerous connexions, to go and teach English in a town where one does not even know whether anybody has a wish of learning it; there is certainly some truth in this, so the matter dropt, but last winter when he had the attack of deafness, which considerably frightened us, I again recurred to the old project; but he would not hear of it; "what would Claire say, if we were to sell Weidling ~~again~~, it would seem so vaccilating, as if we did not know our own minds; the town I fixed upon is Grätz;[9] there is a university, so the boys could receive their education at home, instead of the house at Weidling we should buy one at a suburb of Grätz, which then would be a real dwelling house for the family towards whose maintenance a garden and a couple of fields well managed would go a great way, I might also take a ~~some~~ a few young ladies as boarders, the Styrian[10] nobility is poor, but I have been assured that an establishment for education is wanted there and would have some chance; but yet it is a difficult thing to begin, both Pauline and Clara are afraid of the risk, and though I feel sure we should all be benefitted in the end I cannot impart that conviction, to the others, so all will remain as it is. Of Weidling I can only say that we need not regret the bargain at all, our little garden is very productive, I mean the newly created kitchen garden; the field the same: the crop of potatoes very promising till now no trace of illness; we shall have about {tear} bushels to sell besides our own stock for winter and seeds; we have peasant peas and beans without end and all sorts of cabbage and lettuce; a piece of ground I sowed with turnips and they succeed too; we have had endless raspberry currants tarts and gooseberry fool,[11] all our shrubs bearing already, the trees we planted have of course no crop to offer, but we hope for next year. the meadows we have let, as also the wine cellar, they bring in about £15 of which the taxes are to be deducted about £5; we are just now making the repairs and then it will be all in the completest order, and the most comfortable dwelling house one can imagine; If we could live here all the year

round, I would keep a cow, and a couple of ~~geese~~ pigs and poultry, which would all tell in the kitchen department; the more I am convinced of the utility a little farm well managed might be to the family, the more I am desirous of realising my project about Grätz where we might join it with giving lessons and the means of education for our boys. In Weidl:[12] though the farm would succeed but the two last advantages are wanting; and as we only spend part of the year here and 2 parts in town, we have no chance of making that profit of the former as if nursed all the year round; well for this year at all events I can do nothing, and as I do not wish to harrass Charles' mind I shall say no more of it for the present; in so far my dear Claire I must own I feel reluctant that the few friends to whom I imparted my scheme seemed rather to take Charles' view of it than mine; Clärchen is now at home we are all overjoyed to have her again, she is a sweet good child and the Rismondo's hardly knew how to part with her, they made her leave all her winter clothes behind hoping she would come again to Görz till the autumn,[13] but I cannot spare her for the moment, her presence will be a consolation to me, in case Charles should fall ill there is nobody to nurse him, Pauline being engaged in out of door lessons, and I in my school; If it had been the will of Providence to send a repetition of the stroke, and poor Charles became seriously ill, then I could not have done without her; but that we need not fear, if he will only allow himself the necessary repose, not only now but always, also in the winter;
Now I will give you a statement of our money affairs; some years ago I told you we had saved about £500, this sum I am sorry to say has not much increased since then, having now two boys at school which cost a great deal but still it ~~has~~ is not less; we have paid £500 on the house and have £100 besides the necessary provision for the summer; these 100 pounds ought to remain intact except in case of Charles' going to some Bathing place, but what harasses him so much is that in Sept: another installment on the house pr £50 will fall due, but even that is cared for; ever since Sidi's illness took that turn as to show she would ~~be~~ remain sickly and deformed it has been my wish to buy an ~~one~~ small annuity of 12 or 15 pounds for her poor little life after my death, for this purpose I had already saved 60 pds in the saving bank;[14] this money then shall go to pay the installment, and I hope God will spare my life a few years longer, so that I may be able to accomplish this task which I have much at heart; the others are all strong and healthy, but this poor child, it would be hard indeed to leave her entirely to depend on the kindness of her brothers and sisters, however strong and durable that tie may be. So you see kindest and best of sisters that there is no need of your great anxiety, pray then keep quiet lest you injure your health; about our retrenching, little can be done we did not indulge in any unnecessary expenses, besides we ought to take a lower and consequently dearer lodging,[15] and if Charles goes on with his lessons, he will want to hire a carriage at least for half the day, besides provisions rise every day, wood, since the introduction of the railroads[16] has doubled its price, where then is the road to retrench under such auspices? Now good bye my dearest Claire I hope this letter will bring some quiet to your mind by showing you Charles has a partner willing and able to fulfil her duties, and who is not scared at the idea it

is now her turn to work in order and to give him rest; you know woman is always superior in bearing domestic misfortunes. Now God help you my dear Claire if your health permits you answer me soon, do give my best thanks to Mrs S.[17] for her kind sympathy. ever yours most affectionately

A.C.

the children are all well and happy even Sidi in spite of her complaint grows quite [illeg.] and stout in this good air. the affair with [illeg.][18] is quite off, thank God – Pauline now has an offer of an elderly lover but has decided against it.[19]

Address: Aerogramme: à/ Mademoiselle/ Mademoiselle Claire Clairmont/ 24. Chester Square/ London
Postmark: WIEN/ 10. JUL.

Unpublished. Text: M.S., Pf. Coll., CL'ANA 0401

---

1 Charles and Antonia Clairmont owned a house in Weidling, about 10.5 kilometers north of the capital city, Vienna. Weidling is located in the municipality of Klosterneuburg, Austria. Antonia described the "pure air" and the "very productive garden" at Weidling and the "beautiful tranquility and delicious air of this place" (see CL'ANA 0400). She also confirmed that, by December 1848, the house was "paid out and well furnished" (see CL'ANA 0403 and CL'ANA 0212). In his letter to Claire of 10–11 November 1848, Charles wrote from Weidling about revolutionary activity in Vienna. He described how the windows of their Weidling home were made to "tremble and clatter" from the "bombardment" in Vienna (*CC* II: 487). In *Picture of Vienna*, the author identified "Klosterneuburgh" as a "town of 3000 inhabitants" which was located "about 8 English miles from Vienna". The author observed that the town's "chief interest" was the monastery of St. Augustin, which dated from the twelfth century and which had an enormous wine cellar (pp. 147–50). The German word "bei" means "near" or "close to".

2 These letters have not survived.

3 Known alternatively by these various spellings, Dr. Boehm, Dr. Bohm, or Dr. Böhm, he was evidently the Clairmont family's physician. In 1848, Charles wrote to Claire from Weidling, noting that his friend Mr. Böhm had fled from the town for fear of being "pressed into the service of the Nat. Gd" (*CC* II: 491). It is possible that Dr. Böhm was of Jewish origin given his absence from the city. In the revolutionary activity of 1848, the state denied Jews their rights as citizens and also forced many of them into military service. Charles recorded in his letter that another of his friends had fled as "Jews especially" found conditions unsafe (p. 492). See also Werner Mosse (ed), *Revolution and Evolution, 1848 in German-Jewish History* (Tübingen: Mohr, 1981), p. 9. After Charles's death in 1850, Dr. Böhm offered to become the guardian of Antonia's children (see CL'ANA 0212).

4 See note 15.

5 The town of Carlsbad is located today in the Czech Republic some 420 kilometers north-west of Vienna. Known as Karlovy Vary, the spa town is renowned for its hot springs. In 1830, Claire suggested that Mary Shelley spend her summer at Carlsbad to "set up" her health and to prepare her for the winter (*CC* I: 270); she told Jane Williams Hogg (1798–1884) in April 1830 that she was going to Carlsbad in May (*CC* I: 275). Jane's common-law husband, Edward Williams, drowned with Percy Shelley in 1822. Jane later entered into a relationship with Thomas Jefferson Hogg (1792–1862), Percy Shelley's Oxford University friend and author of *The Life of Shelley*.

6 Another spa town, located 396 kilometers south-west of Vienna, Bad Gastein was known for its thermal waters. It was a well-considered nineteenth-century spa town. Emperor Franz Joseph I and Empress Elisabeth of Austria are known to have visited the spa.

7 German for "spa travel".

8 Mary Wollstonecraft Shelley (1797–1851), step-sister of Charles and Claire Clairmont, and step-sister-in-law of Antonia.

9 Known today as Graz and located about 198 kilometers south of Vienna, the city is Austria's second largest. Graz boasts six universities today. Its oldest, the University of Graz (Karl-Franzens-Universität Graz) was established in 1585. In 1871, Wilhelm moved to Marburg (today, the city of Maribor in Slovenia), some 50 kilometers from Graz.

10 Located in the south-east of Austria, Styria is one of the nine Austrian federal states (Bundesländer). Graz is its capital city. Styria is known as Steiermark in German.

11 A fool is a dessert made of custard and stewed fruit.

12 Weidling.

13 Clara Clairmont was known as Clärchen or Cläri. Antonia's sister, Marie, had married Mr. Rismondo who was a lawyer. They lived in Görz, a city some 489 kilometers from Vienna and located in northeastern Italy. Known today as Gorizia, from 1848 onwards the town was – at various times – under Austrian, Italian, and Yugoslavian rule. While Gorizia is now part of Italy, the town of Nova Gorica was established in 1948 on the Slovenian side of the border with Italy to incorporate areas of Gorizia not included in the Italian city following the Second World War (The Editors of Encyclopaedia Britannica. "Gorizia". *Encyclopedia Britannica Online*. Encyclopedia Britannica Inc. n.d. Web. 9 May 2016. http://www.britannica.com/place/Gorizia).

In November 1845, Charles wrote to Claire of Clara's trip to Görz. He informed Claire that Clara was in "Gorica or Goertz – near Trieste in Illyria" with her aunt and uncle, who had asked to let her stay for another winter. Charles hoped that she would have the opportunity to learn Italian (*CC* II: 463). Trieste is a port in the north-east of Italy. During the nineteenth century, Trieste was part of the Austro-Hungarian Empire.

14 In November 1845, Charles wrote to Mary Shelley and described Sidi's illness. He explained that Sidi had been a healthy child until 1842. According to Charles, Sidi was "seized with a scrophulous complaint," where ulcers covered her body and her eyes became fixed rigidly in her face and incapable of movement. Charles explained that, since Sidi's illness, her body had ceased developing and had turned "dwarfish and deformed". Nevertheless, he did confirm that she was overall "lively and healthy" with a good appetite (*CC* II: 464). He praised her intelligence, her ability to play cribbage, her sense of humour, and her love of order.

15 Antonia referred to the stair case in her lodging (a "lower" lodging). A lodging on a lower floor would be more expensive as it would involve fewer stairs.

16 Robert Kann records that Austria "pioneered" the railroad in Europe. The first railroad was opened between 1825 and 1827 and the line ran from Budweis (Budějovice today, in the Czech Republic) to Linz, Austria, and covered a distance of about 77 kilometers. While horse-drawn cars were employed on this railroad, steam locomotives began running from Floridsdorf (one of Vienna's districts) to Deutsch-Wagram (a distance of some 14 kilometers) in 1836 (*A History of the Habsburg Empire: 1526–1918* [Berkeley: Univ. of California Press, 1974], p. 286). Eric Brose explains that, by the late 1830s, plans were made to link Vienna with Galicia, Budapest, and Trieste. In 1841, there were almost 500 kilometers of railroad track in the Austrian empire. By 1847, the railroad covered some 1,350 kilometers (*German History 1789–1871* [New York and Oxford: Berghahn Books, 2013], p. 189).

17 Mary Shelley.

18 Illegible initial. Possibly S or J.

19 Antonia wrote this final paragraph on the side of the fourth page. Pauline's love affair with Willie Suttor was well-documented in her Australian journal, as were her flirations with other men (see Introduction to this collection and the introduction to Pauline's Australian sojourn). See also CL'ANA 0208. For Pauline's "solo" trip to Venice, see CL'ANA 0088.

3 • Antonia Clairmont to Claire Clairmont

Vienna 18th March[1] [1847]

My dearest Claire.

Yesterday the 17th a person called and delivered into my hands the sum of 786 fC.M.[2]paid by ordre of Miss Clairmont – Charles having been from home he could not sign the receipt and so that post day was lost and you will stay three days longer before you receive Charles signature. How can we ever thank you enough for your generous help! we were afraid circumstances might prevent you to send it, as we heard very discouraging accounts about the opera house, the more rejoiced and happy are we now.[3] I must again and again repeat you do not know how great a benefit you are conferring; I cannot believe you can spare so large a sum without some inconvenience to yourself; comforts denied, pleasures renounced, not lost, but made over to others who will ever feel grateful to you. Charles' not writing is a good sign, it shows him to be occupied; his health is not quite recovered, but we thank God it has not suffered during the fatigue of winter; the intense cold we had affected him, the stiffness in his limbs could not be expected to go off during the winter, we must hope this from the warmer season; his going again to Gastein has already been fixed by Dr Böhen,[4] and we can now look forward to it with a tranquil mind;[5] your egg system he has not yet adopted, not having fully digested it, but it could not have come more seasonably than just now when fresh eggs are so temptingly coming in; besides on the very day when your letter arrived but before we read it, he had complained of pain in the side and said whether it might not result from the liver and he had not better try Carlsbad instead of G.[6] all of which coincided with your view of the case, he intends writing to you whenever he finds a moment, probably the Easter holidays. The children are all well, of the boys we have excellent account, Charley got the first prize in the half yearly examination, and William is the 2d in his class;[7] Charley's 12th birthday is on the 22d his sisters are now busy making up some little gifts for him, to arrive just on the right day, they girls[8] were all clamorous for the permission, to let them come down to spend the Easter holidays with us, but I was obliged to refuse on account of the expense; there has been a great deal of illness in Vienna, we too have lost a valued friend, poor Mrs. Moreau, fell ill in nursing a friend at whose house she had been staying for that purpose it was with difficulty she was transported home, and never left her bed –[9] poor Mrs Herz[10] is to be pitied, having never been for a moment separated from her mother she must feel her loss intensely; she is now surrounded by her husband's family a {tear} of purseproud jews, and even the comfort of a daughter is denied her; having o{tear} 2 boys of her own, and one by the fir{tear} the little girl she had died some years ago Paul has made a most disgraceful marriage with a French milliner, which however has never been recognized by the family, and may have embittered the last years of his mothers life.

Of Weidling I cannot say much, the frost has just been broken, so we have hardly been thinking of sowing and planting; we are quite at a loss whether or no to plant potatoes, the price of seed is so high, and as we are not there, and must trust everything to menials, we are liable to be cheated. In the Easterweek I shall go out to look round a little to see what is to be done; there is no doubt it might be made very profitable, if one could reside there, but four months in the year is not enough. When I am once out there I will write you a long circumstantial account of all, in answer to something you mentioned about W. in one of your former letters. The good people of this town are all mad with Jenny Lind[11] there was never such enthusiasm! for your sake I wish~~ed~~ she might be kept to fulfill her original engagement at the Opera house, as yet we don't know how it will turn out; she never appears without having wreaths and garlands showered upon her by the admiring adoring public.

Charles[12] bids me add that it is considered as quite sure Miss Lind's engagement with Lumnley is to be fulfilled. he sends best love. ever

yours affectionately Antonia C.

Address: Aerogramme: à/Mademoiselle/Mademoiselle Claire Clairmont./ Chester Square. 24./ London.
Postmark: WIEN/ 19. MAR:; AUTR. [illeg.]/ 25/MAR[illeg.]/ 47

Unpublished. Text: M.S., Pf. Coll., CL'ANA 0404

---

1 This letter dates from 1847, as the aerogramme postmark confirms. Antonia stated in the letter that Charley was turning 12 years of age. He was born in 1835.

2 In *Picture of Vienna*, under the section entitled "Value of money," the author described the two different types of currency used in Vienna: "*Schein* or paper money; the other *Conventions-Münze* or good money" (p. 39). The author recorded that only C. M. (Conventions-Münze) was used for large transactions, while Schein was offered for smaller purchases. Another term for "Schein" was "Wiener-Währung" (abbreviated as W.W. and translated as Viennese Currency) while "Silber" (Silver) was the term used for C. M. According to the author, one Florin in C. M. was equal to two and a half Schein. C. M. was not frequently used and was often not in circulation. In *Beyond Nationalism*, István Deák explains that the Austrian currency was the Gulden and that it was written as "fl" (Florins). There were 60 Kreuzer (kr.) in a Gulden. Fl. C. M. was worth 2 fl. 50 kr. W. W. In 1858, the Österreichische Währung became the new form of currency. The Gulden was then divided into 100 Kreuzer (New York: Oxford University Press, 1990), p. 115.

3 Claire considered herself relatively well-off by the mid-1840s. After the death in 1844 of Sir Timothy Shelley, Percy Bysshe Shelley's father, Claire received £12,000, the result of a bequest from Percy Shelley's will. In his will, Percy Shelley left the bulk of his estate to Mary Shelley. As well as to Claire, Percy Shelley left bequests to his children, to his first wife, Harriet Shelley (who would commit suicide in 1816), and to his friends, Thomas Jefferson Hogg, Lord Byron, and Thomas Love Peacock. In the draft copy of his will, dated 24 June 1816, Percy Shelley stated: "To Mary Jane Clairmont (the sister in law of Miss Godwin) ~~12 6~~ 12,000, one half to be laid out in an annuity for her own life, & that of any other person she may ~~ch~~ name if she pleases to name any other, the other half to be at her own disposal" (Kenneth Neill Cameron [ed.], *Shelley and his Circle 1773–1822* [Cambridge, MA: Harvard University Press, 1970], vol. iv, p. 703). Cameron explains that Percy Shelley based his will of 24 September 1816 on this draft copy and that he left $6,000 to Claire and an additional $6,000 to his trustees "to invest in the purchase of an annuity 'for the life of the said Mary Jane Clairmont and the life of such other person as the said Mary Jane Clairmont

should name (if she should be pleased to name one) . . .' These bequests were repeated in his next will, on February 18, 1817" (p. 712). Cameron further records that Mary Shelley told Leigh Hunt that the bequest was in fact twice what Percy Shelley had intended. In spite of Mary Shelley's assertion, Claire received the full $12,000 after Sir Timothy's death.

Mary Shelley had advised Claire to invest the money wisely so that it did not lose interest (*LMWS* III: 125, 127, 132, 134, 140–2). Initially, Mary Shelley had proposed sharing with Claire the cost of an opera box which they hoped to rent to others. But as Mary Shelley decided to invest elsewhere, Claire invested £4,000 of her income and purchased Box 23 at Her Majesty's Theatre in London in 1845. Her letters to Mary Shelley from 1845 discussed the purchase in great detail. She was hopeful that the purchase would yield a good interest income, positing that the purchase of a whole box would solve her "present difficulties" (*CC* II: 434). Indeed, Claire considered herself to be financially comfortable and she was relatively generous in her support of her brother's family. Unfortunately, the purchase of the opera box proved a financial disaster for her.

4 Antonia wrote either "Böhen" or "Böhm". It is unclear in the manuscript.

5 See CL'ANA 0401.

6 Gastein.

7 Wilhelm and Charley were both considered good students. The Pforzheimer Collection includes prospectuses written in Latin from the Gymnasiums they attended: Gymnasii Ad Scotos (Charley) and the Gymnasii Mellicensis (Wilhelm). Charley studied religion, Latin, Geography, and Arithmetic while Wilhelm studied Greek, Geography and History, Mathematics, Religion, Culture, and Interpretation of Style. See CL'ANA 0060. Charley's school was known as the Schottengymnasium and it was run by the Benedictine Order. The Irish monks who founded the monastery in the twelfth century were known as "Schotten" whose name reflects the Latin name for Ireland, "Scotia Maior" (Dr. U. Denk, Universität Wien, personal communication: 2 March 2015).

8 The word "girls" is inserted above the line.

9 See CL'ANA 0405.

10 Unidentified. Antonia's anti-Semitism reflected attitudes common to Austrians at the time. Anti-Semitism flourished even though Jews held important positions in industries such as banking and commerce. Before 1848, Jews were not permitted to reside in Vienna. Marsha Rozenblit notes that, by 1840, about 2,000 Jews lived in Vienna, the vast majority of them tolerated by the authorities who only allowed wealthy merchants to settle in the city. By 1848, the number had risen to 4,000. Rozenblit suggests that, after the Revolution and the easing of the rules which prevented Jews from living in Vienna, the number of Jews residing in Vienna rose dramatically. By 1869, there were 40,000 Jews in Vienna and over 73,000 by 1880 (in Jonathan Frankel, ed., *Assimilation and Community: The Jews in Nineteenth-Century Europe* [Cambridge: Cambridge UP, 1992, p. 226]). Rozenblit explains too that, in spite of Emperor Joseph II's Edict of Toleration of 1782, which removed or relaxed many of the discriminatory laws against Jews ("Toleranzpatent"), Jews in Vienna "endured endless restrictions, oppressive taxes and a profoundly precarious legal status" (p. 227). This marginalization was a continuation of pervasive historical anti-Semitism in Austria. See also CL'ANA 0326, CL'ANA 0324 and CL'ANA 0421, Box 3, bundle g, number 185.

11 Johanna Maria Lind (Jenny Lind, 1820–1887) was also known as the "Swedish Nightingale". Born in Sweden, Lind was a soprano who performed to great acclaim in Europe and America. She first appeared in London in 1847 at Her Majesty's Theatre where Claire owned her box. She performed as Alice in Giacomo Meyerbeer's opera, *Robert le Diable*, causing Queen Victoria to write in her diary, "The great event of the evening was Jenny Lind's appearance and her complete triumph" (quoted in Isabelle Emerson, *Five Centuries of Women Singers* [Westport, CT: Greenwood Publishing, 2005], p. 155). Lind's agent was Benjamin Lumley. Lumley began managing the theater in 1842 but he ran into tremendous difficulties by 1847 when a rival company installed itself in Covent Garden. Many of Lumley's singers and musicians defected to the rival company. Lumley was thus forced to go to extraordinary means to bring singers to the stage and he believed that Jenny Lind would be his company's saving grace (*LMWS* III: 295, 329). After much anxiety,

(Henry Scott Holland includes in his *Memoir of Madame Jenny Lind-Goldschmidt* a letter to Lumley from singer Luigi Lablache urging him to encourage Lind to perform in London [Cambridge: Cambridge UP: 1891], p. 58), Lind finally appeared on stage. She was an overwhelming success. The reviews following her performance were complimentary and Lumley, who was in the midst of a fray with his rivals at Covent Garden, considered the opera saved. See also CL'ANA 0373.

12 Antonia wrote this final section on the cover of the aerogramme.

4 • Antonia Clairmont to Claire Clairmont

Weidling the 20th August 1847.

My dearest Claire.

Your kind letter reached me yesterday and I sit down immediately to answer it; – your goodness almost overpowers me – is it possible you would make such a sacrifice for the dear boy's sake as to go and live in a village, out of the reach of your friends? of society and the stir and resources of a great town which you are so accustomed to? how will you spend your long winterevenings in the country? or what if you should want physical advice? have you considered all that?[1] As for Willy, I should prefer it of all things – to receive his proffesional education as an agriculturist in England is beyond what I ever dared to wish[2] – I consider it also of more advantage to his intellectual developement, to spend the next two or three years in which his estimation of things and manners are formed in an enlightened country, and to have him removed from the narrow bounds of an Austrian university education and the society of the flat youths he would have had to associate with whose mental faculties are mostly drowned in the most frivolous love of trifling amusements, but not such as are fit for young people – they neither of them know how to throw a ball or any gymnastical ~~amusements~~ diverson – dancingparties concerts and lovemaking to little girls in trousers are the order of the day. – children are regularly taken to balls at ten and twelve years of age – they are more like little men and women – One remark I have however to make – will it not be necessary for him to study Physiks,[3] Chemistry and Mechanics before he begins the practical course of instruction? it seems to me that, that will be absolutely necessary, he might perhaps devote next winter to it, and go to England in the Spring – but you have certainly considered all that and will tell me the result; Charles seems more to lean towards a mercantile life, but I can't help giving a sigh to think his tall thin figure bent down on the writing desk day after day, instead of strengthening his fine limbs by some active occupation and movement in God's free air! He is now full six feet English – but wanting nerve and grace, that will come in time, his character is like most tall men's, gentle and placid, kind and affectionate – there is nothing brilliant in him, but a fund of good and promising qualities, a slow but clear understanding open to conviction, simple in his tastes and habits, punctual and true with a strong sense of his duties and the best temper in the world such is the boy from whom to part even now cost me tears, but cheerfully will I submit to it – for his own good; he is not so active now as he ~~go~~ used to be, that is owing to his growing so very fast – with regard to your remark about the children's diet I am so fully of your opinion that it has been repeatedly an object of dissent between Charles and myself; he being always furious against suppers insisting it being fully enough for any man to eat substantial food once a day – every year in the holidays I made a fresh trial and always was defeated – this year I again found it necessary – and so the first evening of the boys return, without saying anything, I had only 3 cups brought in for Papa Pauline and Clara – ~~and~~ besides a ham and some vegetables declaring ~~we should~~ all the rest should take supper in future; poor Charles made a face like a thundercloud so that the whole assembly was awestruck – but I was afterwards obliged to tell him of Emmy's illness to convince him what the too early use of tea brings to, and how natural it was to give nourishment not stimulants to growing children – Emmy has had no fit since I last wrote for which I am truly grateful. I did not think of giving the children beer, it is a practice not known here – and Weidl. being a wine district, we have none – but on our removal to town I will make the trial, Emmy likes it, perhaps it is a sort of instinct that her nature requires it. Charles is not gone to Gastein – he had such a distaste for that journey, and was so irritable and nervous so miserable and cross all the time the scheme was in agitation that I was afraid of a bit of illness from mere vexation, and lost all courage to urge him any further, nobody else having the right of doing so, he {tear} it entirely, and came out here last Sunday, when he ought to have been already far on his road – in radiant good humour which did all our hearts good, and not a word of Gastein was mentioned any more, his health improves with his spirits, he has begun to drink Creutzbrunnen wasser[4] which he says agrees very well – and we must hope for the best.[5] We have an excellent fruit year; such abundance of apples pears and plums as never was seen; potatoes are likewise very promising, no traces of illness as yet; every day we go to the field and bring in a basket of vegetables of some kind or other; this morning we went out before breakfast to get beans and peas for winter crop – and it is always remarked {tear} Charley and Willy are sooner fatigued exhausted and com {tear} of heat and hunger than Sidi and Emmy, which shows that im Grossen wie im Kleinen[6]– men are less able to bear and conquer small difficulties than women. I have not told you that Charley brought the first prize and Willy the second – the joy of our meeting was however greatly diminished by poor Minna's loss; the poor boys hardly had an idea that she was seriously ill[7] and do not think the children have forgotten their aunt; it is rather a fault of omission on my side than want of affection in them; just now little Sidi flitted by and enjoined me not to forget their best love to Aunt Claire, they are all good and affectionate, the elder ones know your goodness to us; they thank you for having thought of them in chusing your letter paper.[8]

accept once more my dearest Claire my warmest thanks for your ready assistance and the kind sympathy you take in our children's welfare; I am also much pleased with your agreeing so entirely ~~with~~ in my views, and fully approve of your remark on the effects of constant occupation on the mind and temper – I know that on this consideration every compliance from my side on domestic arrangements or the minor concerns of life is Charles' due but I cannot deny that I find it more difficult in things which must affect the comfort of his old age and almost impossible if the question is of the future welfare of the children. Let us hope that Providence will not put me to the proof so far; but will send relief by your means and in your shape. Good bye my dearest Claire I embrace you most warmly – I don't think the culprit will be in a hurry to write to you, he will be at a loss to explain for his not going to Gastein.

ever yours most affection.

A.C.

You don't mention Mrs. Shelley's health? how did the sea air agree with her?[9]

Address: Aerogramme:
Mademoiselle/ Mademoiselle Claire Clairmont/26 Osnaburgh Street/
Regent's Park. London./ England.

Postmark: WIEN/ 22. AUG:/ OES[illeg.]REICH/24 [illeg.]

Unpublished. Text: M.S., Pf. Coll., CL'ANA 0397

---

1 Claire had proposed that Wilhelm study in England and she offered to sponsor her nephew.

2 The letters that follow provide an account of Wilhelm's relocation to Queenwood College.

3 Antonia added the English plural ending to the German word, "Physik".

4 Antonia's spelling for Kreutzbrunnen water. This is a type of mineral water from Marienbad. Marienbad today is part of the Czech Republic. See A. Granville, *The Spas of Germany* (London: Henry Colburn, 1837), pp. 128–9.

5 Antonia left a space in the document.

6 German for "[events] large and small". The phrase means "overall" or "in general".

7 Hermine died of consumption in 1847. Stocking includes in her collection a letter from Charles to Claire which Herbert Huscher originally published in "Charles und Claire Clairmont". In this letter, Charles described his daughter in the most positive of terms. He refused to allow a priest to attend Hermine's deathbed, stating that she was "a spotless being" (*CC* II: 482). He referenced her domestic abilities, her kindness to others, her love of books, and her consoling ways.

8 The back page of this aerogramme has the address and these final lines of the letter.

9 Mary Shelley had gone to Brighton. In June 1847, she told Claire that Brighton was too noisy (*LMWS* III: 316), and on 1 August she declared that she was "bored" in Brighton (p. 325) and that the noise and heat were considerable (p. 325). By August 31, she was back in London.

5 • Antonia Clairmont to Claire Clairmont

Vienna 1st of Dec. 1848.

My dearest Claire.

Yours containing the post bank Bill arrived yesterday, and a thousand thanks and blessings on you for it; Charles had already set off for Ollmütz[1] the day before, but he left me directions what to do; I went to Mr Biedermann[2] and got it cashed, he paid me 220 fl C.M.[3] and once more of my best thanks for your generous assistance – I shall now be able to clear all the claims, that will fall due between now and the new year, and still be able to spare the expense for Willy's journey should you decide upon calling him near you – I am then alone with the three youngest children, and can live with the strictest economy – I shall let two rooms that will bring in something; besides less fuel and light is required, if before we had 4 stoves to heat now we heat but one, instead of 3 large lamps, one small one serves us now, and thus I hope to make up for decrease of income, and make things go as far as possible; in so far I have also dismissed one servant
I am glad of Charles' absence, retrenchments of this sort are very painful to him, whilest to me they are a consolation, I feel I am doing something towards my object; but also in other respects it is better for him, these horrid staircases he need not mount and descend the whole day, not having so many lessons, he will have time to take his meals properly and rest a little after them, and ~~rest a little~~ if he do indulge in a little comfort, it needn't be shared by 7 persons, which is the case at home, for he will never suffer me to put an extra dish on the table for him, and it was really painful to me, to see him dine on the simple fare, ~~I~~ my larder lately afforded – this moment I got a letter from him; he has been extremely well received and the two Archdukes[4] have already begun to take their lessons, some of the court people too, they live so near together if not at the same house, so next door, Pauline has two lessons promised, so you see it will go well, lodgings are not very plentiful at Ollmütz they have nothing found as yet, and complain of horrid bad inns. Things will go better when has all his little comforts around him, his own good bed, teapot and breakfast cup et et. Pauline is with him to nurse or amuse if need should be. I have advertised for my school, what success is uncertain, till now I have hopes of 6 scholars, if their number increase to 15 I shall be very happy indeed; to day Charley's school or rather the Humanitäts Classen[5] were opened, and the first salutary effects of our young and much abused liberty are shown in a new and most judicious distribution of school hours, and the entire omission of church service; the latter is most wise measure, for churchgoing was carried to such a degree, it made the young people both indifferent and careless of religion to spend so much time there ~~at church~~[6] – of the university and Polytechnic[7] we know nothing as yet. the two little girls were extremely sorry to leave Weidling, and come to town, they have all a great inclination for the country Willy among them; soldiery he detests, being of a retired turn, simple wants and habits, shall I tell you; that he will be most happy to come to England, or will you consider it as indelicately pressing the matter upon you? Clary has got your letter

and answered it too she is quite happy at having got into correspondence with you – We hope the family of Lichtenstein[8] will go to spend the winter at Ollmütz, then Clara would have the pleasure of her father's and sisters company – Countess Wimpfen[9] was not in town – she had her share of the troubles at an earlier stage of the business, at Venice when she was detained hostage by the insurgents – excuse this very bad scramble, but since in town we have been immensely busy to restore order and cleanliness, for our town lodging as well as the country home served as an asylum to some friends, but now every thing is bright and shining, curtains and window cushions washed and got up, pictures cleaned and arranged every thing done to satisfaction – I missed Pauline very much; Clary not she is no great hand in things of this sort; Emmy and Sidi were a great help; the former is now 15 – and the latter makes in up in[10] understanding what she is wanting in strength.
Now good bye my dearest Claire Charles will write to you as soon as he is a little settled – the children send their best love, of the cannonading Emmy was most afraid, having been in town with us on the memorable 6th of oct. when the Arsenal was stormed, and we felt as if our house was hit every time so near was the report.[11]

yours affectionately
A.C.

Friday 1st Dec.

Address: Aerogramme: To/ Miss. Clara Clairmont./ Field Place, Horsham/ Sussex/ England.
Postmark: WIEN/ 5. DEC/; HORSHAM/DE 8/ 1848/A

Unpublished. Text: M.S., Pf. Coll., CL'ANA 0402

1 The town of Olomouc (known as Olmütz in German) is located in the Czech Republic today, some 297 kilometers north of Vienna. In December 1848, Emperor Franz Joseph I (1830–1916) was crowned Emperor of Austria and Apostolic King of Hungary in Olmütz. By 1867, Austria and Hungary were designated equal partners in the Dual Monarchy which would last until the end of the First World War in 1918. Franz Joseph would rule the empire until his death in 1916. The kingdom was alternatively known as the Austro-Hungarian Empire, Austria-Hungary, and the Austro-Hungarian Monarchy. Vienna served as its capital city.

In his letter to Claire of 10–11 November 1848 (*CC* II: 487–92), Charles informed his sister that the Archduchess Sophie had asked him to come to Olmütz to teach English to the young Archdukes and the children of other aristocratic families. Charles proposed to take Pauline with him and to leave Antonia and the rest of the family at Weidling. He expressed concern too about the interruption to his sons' education, as he anticipated that schools in Vienna would remain closed for the year. He hoped to find someone to teach Wilhelm in Olmütz. Charles also recorded that he had written to the Archduchess to request an extension on his decision to move to Olmütz, hoping first to see if his services at the Theresianum (Theresianische Akademie Wien) were still needed.

Archduchess Sophie was the wife of Archduke Franz Karl. Her son, Franz Joseph, would be crowned Emperor in December 1848. Her second son, Ferdinand Maximilian (1832–1867), became Emperor of Mexico in 1864. Maximilian was executed in 1867 (see also CL'ANA 0295).

2 Charles wrote to Claire in November 1848 to ask her for financial assistance. He told her that, if Mr. "Biedermann" were in town, he would be able to obtain what he needed with his own signature as proof. Biedermann, he noted, had fled town, because as a Jew he did not feel it was safe (see CL'ANA 0404).

3 See CL'ANA 0401 and CL'ANA 0404.

4 Charles was the tutor of Maximillian and his younger brother, Karl Ludwig (1833–1896). See Herbert Huscher, "Charles und Claire Clairmont" (pp. 65–6). Huscher quotes from R. Glynn Grylls, who confirmed that Charles saw the young Archdukes daily.

5 German for "Humanities Department".

6 In *Europe in 1848: Revolution and Reform*, Heinz-Elmar Tenorth observes that after the Revolution of 1848–9 in Austria, "there were no lack of plans for reform and restructuring, nor of demands for a liberal educational system . . . an independent ministry of Education was created for the first time, the dominance of Catholic clergy in secondary schools and universities was temporarily reduced, and laws were passed concerning duration and subject matter of secondary school education" (p. 737). While in 1849, churches were restored to their "old rights . . . [and] from this time on, an alternative form of public education existed, which was then introduced in wide-ranging reform after 1866/67" (Dieter Dowe, [ed.], [New York: Berghahn Books, 2001], p. 737).

7 In his November letter to Claire, Charles mentioned his concern that both the University and the Polytechnical School in Vienna would remain closed for a year (*CC* II: 487). Known today as the Technische Universität Wien, the Polytechnical School was founded in 1815 as the k.k. Polytechnisches Institut (Imperial and Royal Polytechnical Institute). In 1872, it became known as the Technische Hochschule and in 1972 as the Technische Universität Wien. See www.tuwien.ac.at. The University of Vienna (Universität Wien) was founded in 1365 and is the oldest university in Austria.

8 Clara had given lessons to the children of the Prince and Princess of Liechtenstein. In July 1849, after Clara's elopement with Alexander Knox, Charles told Claire that he had reminded Clara that she would have "lost all character" with people such as the "princess L – " had he and Antonia not protected her character (*CC* II: 504). In *Picture of Vienna*, the author provided a list of the palaces in Vienna and included the palace of Prince Liechtenstein, located on Herrngasse and the "entailed family mansion of prince Liechtenstein, in the great Schenkenstrasse. One of the finest buildings in the whole city, by Dominic Martinelli" (p. 46).

9 The wife of Franz von Wimpffen (1797–1870), an Austrian General who was also head of the Austro-Hungarian Navy between 1851 and 1854. Von Wimpffen fought during military campaigns in Bologna, Trieste and Vicenza.

10 As written in the letter.

11 On 6 October 1848, fighting broke out in Vienna when some Austrian soldiers refused to follow orders to march against the Hungarian Magyars. Students and other disenfranchised soldiers and workers took the part of the dissenting soldiers in an ensuing bloody conflict. By 26 October 1848, Vienna was bombarded and subdued by the anti-revolutionary forces of Alfred, Fürst zu Windischgrätz (Prince of Windischgrätz, 1787–1862). Those responsible for the uprising on 6 October were punished. Emperor Ferdinand I (1793–1875) fled to Olmütz as a result of the incident and his nephew, Franz Joseph I, succeeded him in December (*CC* II: 492–3; Tóth, I. G., *A Concise History of Hungary*).

Charles mentioned the "bombardment" to Claire in his letter of 10–11 November 1848. He explained that their windows were made to "tremble and clatter" (*CC* II: 487). On 23 October, cannon fire was apparently heard at Weidling. Charles described in some detail the devastation wreaked on Vienna as a result of continuous cannon fire. On 7 October, the Zeughaus (Armoury) was stormed and destroyed. Between 1849 and 1856, the Zeughaus was rebuilt on a different site.

6 • Antonia Clairmont to Claire Clairmont

Vienna 18th dec. [1848]

My dearest Claire.

This morning at 5 o'clock Willy set off with the railroad, you may therefore expect him about the 26th or so. your desire to let him go by Ostende[1] met our intentions, for Charles had already fixed that route for him before going away to Ollmütz – but I was greatly relieved by your directing him to Brighton at once without passing through London, which would have been rather difficult for so inexperienced a traveller – but now everything is smooth and easy; Capt. Andoe[2] gave so much good and useful advice and notes and directions about places of stoppage, inns, porters custom house, and so forth, that I think he will get on well; he does not come to you as an Austrian, but a Brittish subject – on Capt. A's advice, I went with him to the English Embassy and asked a passport for him ~~as~~ he being the son of an Englishman and entitled to it by right of law et. et.[3] – and after a little consideration they gave it; so you have no bother with the Austrian Embassy nor have we here with the Police for leave of absence,[4] and so; I think Charles will be very happy to hear it – to day he reaches Ollmütz and will spend a day with his father and sisters, for we hope Clara will come to see him[5] – I gave him your last letter that they might all read, and find consolation in thought how much love and kindness expect him there for the parting is painful however happy we may find ourselves in his going – your assurances touched me to tears, you will find him meriting all – he is so pure and innocent, so good never he hurt his parents by a disrespectful look or word obedient, sensible, open to advice, steady beyond his years, never a lie sullied his lips, simple in his wants, you will find all this to be true, not merely a fond mothers praises. another sourse of consolation I found in your saying you address a daily prayer for our welfare to the Almighty; Oh could I ever hear Charles utter such words! I may then hope that also in this most important point you will act a mother's part to the dear boy – he is not quite what I wish him to be - living so long in a monastery, where he saw the insidious ways of the clergy on ~~the~~ one hand – on the other was wearied with too much religious exercises, he lost all respect and grew indifferent the more so as at home he soon found out thought the same – but I hope in time he will perceive it was the form and not the matter, is in fault;[6] I put a book of devotion in his trunk calculated to carry conviction to the most refined understanding and made him promise to read at least one chapter every week it is not a catholic prayer book, but by the most powerful protestant writer <u>Zchokke</u> a swiss clergyman, I dare say the work is translated into English – but you know German well enough to read it; it is one vol: out of 6.[7] I [8]was really pained to find you will send him money to Ostende; he would have been quite well with what I gave him – such is the state of his finances – from here to Dresden[9] he goes with Austrian money 30fl C M. from Dr: to Ostende is Prussian money for which purpose I exchanged him 32 Dollars – then I paid in 34 fl 30 x[10] good money at Mr Biederman's for which he received a Bill for Ostende for three pounds – so he is well furnished – if he saves the three pd or any part of it, I told him to keep it for any little wants he may have – he will have to buy a hat the calabrese[11] he wore here, several of our English friends here were of opinion, he could not appear with in England, so he took a cap for the journey, which is moreover preferable [~~illeg.~~] in every thing else he is provided for a long time; his wardrobe and linen is just as it was, I could not make any additions the time was so short [exeipt[12] a black satin waistcoat Capt: A telling us he could not wear a white one][13] and as he is still growing it would be a waste to give him more clothes. I gave him 6 pair of gloves, because I think this a dear article in England and two pair of new strong boots, he must find his own clothes, I shall always find means to [illeg.] with him a small bill of 5 or 6 pounds every 6 months, without troubling Charles for it, it shall be furnished of my own little economies – since my marriage I have always been saving – when we returned from England we were poor indeed, Charles had to borrow money to furnish our lodging; that is now 18 years ago where we began anew housekeeping – first we paid off our debts, then the yearly increase of family the education of the two elder ones, my savings all went to suffice the wants of the increasing household, later I bought silver spoons, linen, beddings – or I put the money in the stocks, always wishing to make a small provision for Sidi,[14] sometimes I sold out again ~~but~~ I have now £120 in the stocks, but they are so low I should get but 60, if obliged to sell now – besides it brings me £6 interest which is just half of the sum I mean to allow Willy – but you will ask in what my savings consist? Charles was in money affairs unlike most other husbands, he never gave any fixed sum, but I had the key of his desk and took out what I wanted, certainly I never abused his confidence, but was the more careful, but I began early to give a lessons even when the children were quite young, or when he composed a new book, I copied all and corrected the press, ~~then~~ for which he always made me a present with some share of the Honorar;[15] then I myself composed a small book for young children which brought me in £20 at once,[16] but when my school began, I became rich indeed, first I paid the clothing for myself and family at least the girls – then the rest I divided in half, one I put to the kitchen expenses the other into my own private cashbox, and in this manner I was enabled to go on satisfactorily; since Charles' ill health, I haven't of course put by any thing but many a grateful prayer I sighed out to Him if enabled to meet any larger expense without troubling Charles such as perhaps Willy's black suit, of which I wrote you last spring – or the bill for wood et et. If it were not for the troubles of the moment brought on by the disastrous turn of things, as by Charles' ill health, I think we might look back with satisfaction upon the result of our exertions of these eighteen years; we have a comfortable and gentil lodging well furnished always considered upon a moderate footing; the house at Weidling is now paid out and well furnished, besides we have done for our children rather more than our circumstances warranted and shall reap our reward in their success in life the consciousness of this keeps me always quiet and cheerful even in the calamities of the moment, the clouds will blow over and we shall have a clear sky the only thing that really vexes and troubles me is Charles' imprudence and obstinacy with regard to his health – money embarrassments may change but, a ruined health not – he is well I hear, about his income I know nothing as yet, but trust it must be pretty well, and that we shall be enabled to make up the sum for Gastein, without accepting your generous assistance beyond Willy's – how I thank God the dear boy is in safety, for we do not know what they will at again by next spring – good bye dearest Claire thousand and thousand thanks and blessings, you say you are laconic, but your words go straight to the heart, now it is 8 o'clock evening, the dear ones are all assembled now at Ollmütz reading your letter and blessing you and so do we – the children send their love – Emmy and Sidi some cuffs[17] of their own work and Charley some letter covers, ever yours gratefully and affectionately.

A.C.

Address: Aerogramme: à/ Mademoiselle/ Mad[lle] Claire Clairmont/ at Colonel Pringle's.[18] 5. Brunswick Square/ Brighton/Sussex/ England
Postmark: [illeg.]/DEC 25/1848

Unpublished. Text: M.S., Pf. Coll., CL'ANA 0403

---

1 Ostend is a port-city in Belgium on the North Sea. In 1846, a ferry service began from Ostend to Dover. Mail was frequently routed through Ostend for England, as many of the postmarks on the Clairmont letters indicate. Some of the Clairmont letters include handwritten directions, "Via Ostend". Ostende is the German for Ostend (Oostende in Dutch and Ostende in French).

2 Captain Andoe was a friend of both the Clairmonts and Mary Shelley. An Austrian, he spent time in England and provided much needed assistance to Antonia and her family. Clara Knox also mentioned meeting Andoe in her letter to Claire (see CL'ANA 0188 and CL'ANA 0189).

3 Charles Clairmont and his children retained their British citizenship, as a document from 1880 shows. Sir Henry George Elliot, "Her Britannic Majesty's Ambassador Extraordinary," granted Wilhelm a document in Vienna which gave "Mr. William Gaulis Clairmont, British subject, travelling on the Continent, accompanied by his wife and his three children" the right to "pass freely without let or hindrance and to afford him every assistance and protection of which he may stand in need". The document is now amongst the Clairmont papers (CL'ANA 0408, unpublished manuscript, Pforzheimer Collection).

4 In *Picture of Vienna*, the author noted that any visitor to Vienna's environs would need, upon arrival, to leave his passport with the police and then, within twenty-four hours, to appear at the police station to receive his "Aufenthalts-Karte" (German for "residence card," and spelled "Aufenthaltskarte"), granting him permission to stay for six weeks (p. 39).

5 See CL'ANA 0402 for information about Clara Clairmont's whereabouts. Pauline was with Charles in Olmütz.

6 Antonia was Catholic while Charles was Protestant. Wilhelm attended the Gymnasium of Melk Abbey in Lower Austria. See note 7, CL'ANA 0404, and CL'ANA 0060.

7 Johannes Heinrich Zschokke (1771–1848), a German-born, Swiss writer who wrote both literary and philosophical works. Antonia probably alluded to his *Stunden der Andacht* which was published in 1806 and translates as "Hours of Devotion" (Bäbler, J.J., "Zschokke, Johannes Heinrich Daniel" in: *General German Biography* 45 (1900), pp 449-465 [Online version]; URL: http://www.deutsche-biographie.de/pnd118637266.html?anchor=adb).

8 Antonia left a large space in the letter before starting this sentence.

9 Vienna is located about 479 kilometers south-east of Dresden. Dresden is 860 kilometers east of Ostend. There are 166 kilometers from Ostend to Dover. Dr: is the abbreviation for Dresden.

10 Antonia wrote the letter x, which was the abbreviation for Kreuzer (kreutzer, in English). See CL'ANA 0404 for more information about Austrian currency.

11 Calabria is a region in the south of Italy. A calabrese hat would have been conical-shaped and possibly had a ribbon tucked into its headband or attached to the cone.

12 Misspelling for "except".

13 Antonia placed these words in square brackets.

14 See CL'ANA 0401.

15 German for "professional fee".

16 In 1845, Antonia wrote a book entitled *Erste Schritte zur Erlernung der englischen Sprache, für Kinder von sechs bis zehn Jahren* ("First Steps to Learning the English Language, for Children ages six to ten"). The book juxtaposes lines of English with lines of German, with the German text inserted above the English lines. The title pages lists the author as "Antonia Clairmont, geb. Ghylain v. Hembyze" ("born Ghylain von Hembyze"). In the German-language foreword, Antonia opined that few books had been writen about English language learning for younger children, and in particular books which provided broad grammatical knowledge. She expressed her belief that mastery of a foreign language occurred more quickly and with greater ease in younger students and her hope that her book would help support early language learning. She expressed her desire that young mothers, in addition to teachers, would use her book to educate their children.

The text is structured as follows: The content pages list stories in both German and English. Examples of the German stories include "Der Schneefall," "Samuel und Heinrich," and "Der Franzose" (Antonia translates them as "The Fall of Snow," "Sam and Harry," and "The Frenchman"), while the English selections include chapters about animals and their behaviors, such as "The Ant," "The Rattlesnake," and "The Stork," and stories like "The Purple Jar" and "The Cherry Orchard" (in which Antonia depicts a character named William). The nursery rhyme section includes selections such as "King Arthur's Pudding," "The three Children," "Jack and Jill," and "Oranges and Lemons". The book begins with an explanation in German of the English alphabet and provides phonetic pronunciations of each letter. In each of the earlier lessons, Antonia includes German translations beside the English sentences. Many of Antonia's characters have Clairmont or Shelley family names. In one of the lessons, Antonia gives her young protagonist one of Claire's names (Jane). In another lesson, which Antonia titles "Charles and Jane," students learn that Charles is a "good boy . . . we all love him, and he loves us . . . Jane! she is a sweet child" (p. 15). Another story revolves around a character named Fanny, possibly named for Mary Wollstonecraft's daughter Fanny Imlay who died in 1816. "The Fall of Snow" tells the story of a boy named Willy, while "The Dormouse" introduces readers to a character named Mary. In the later lessons, Antonia writes only in English. She provides a list of English "common phrases" with the accompanying German translation for each one. There are sentences to describe various activities and events. Section headings include: "Weather, Health, Clothing, Needlework, Breakfast and Tea (where Antonia provides a sentence about Charley, "Let Charley have some tea for his breakfast" p. 112), Dinner, Time, Dwelling-house, Furniture, Relationships and Domestic Connexions, Animals, Birds and Poultry, Fishes and Insects, Parts of the Body, Fruit and Flowers, Plants and Trees, Religion and religious Ceremonies". The book also introduces a few English nursery rhymes which, Antonia notes in the foreword, she believes are particularly effective in helping students with memorization and retention. She also provides an appendix in which she conjugates some verbs in both German and English (Vienna: Braumüller & Seidel, 1845).

17 A band to finish the bottom of a sleeve.

18 Colonel and Mrs. Pringle were Claire's friends. Antonia referred to them on numerous occasions in her correspondence. Claire told Mary Shelley that Colonel Pringle's regiment was located at Winchester and that the Pringles had "lovely children" who would perform difficult deeds for a show of "kindness" (*CC* II: 444). See also CL'ANA 0191.

7 • Wilhelm Gaulis Clairmont to Claire Clairmont

Malling[1] 12th June 1849.

Dearest aunt.

I hardly know what to say to your letter, but that the difference of opinion concerning the marriage existing between you and my sister grieves me very much.[2] I do not know what you have to say against it, nor do I know what she has to say for it, so it naturally is impossible for me to speak at all upon the subject; but on the whole I cant help thinking the affair by far not so entirely settled as you seem to do, for considering that they know eachother only so short a time it always is possible that yet some disagreement may happen. I had a letter from lady Shelley[3] the other day, in which she speaks in highly favourable terms of Mr Knox; so you see from ~~the~~ one side I hear all good from the other all bad, so that I dont know what to make of it – I shall be very glad to see you dearest aunt, and hear from your own mouth what you think. –

I thank you many times for the money succours you sent me, it was very welcome to me for I should have had not what to pay my bill with, next Thursday; the 5 £ note arrived quite save[4] and sound and is now in my possession. I aad[5] here a little account – to tell you what I spent – the other ten pound on –

My health is perfectly well. I only whish[6] you had as little to complain of, as I have but I trust that a little London change will do you good; I understand Miss Hammond[7] is arrived. I hope that the society and conversation of so intimate a friend as she seems to be to you will also help to restore your health a little.

Now, dearest aunt, I must conclude for I am in a hurry I am your ever attached nephew

William.

Mr & Mrs Black's best compliments[8]

Address: No envelope

Unpublished. Text: M.S., Pf. Coll., CL'ANA 0041

---

1 Malling is located in Kent, England. West and East Malling are towns in the county of Kent, some 56 kilometers from London.

2 In late April 1849, Clara Clairmont traveled from Vienna to London to join Wilhelm, who was staying with Claire. From January through April 1849, Mary Shelley urged Claire and Wilhelm to visit her at Field Place in Sussex (*LMWS* III: 355, 356, 358, 359, 360, 363, 366, 367), and she extended her invitation to Clara: "By this time Cleary I hope is with you . . . Pray come with her as soon as you like" (*LMWS* III: 367). Claire responded that Wilhelm's health was precarious, that she would remain with him in Kent, and that she would not be able to meet Clara at Field Place (*CC* II: 501). Claire asked Mary Shelley to receive her niece alone: "So seeing every thing in this uncertainty, I think it best to propose that Cleary should come alone – with the proviso that if I can come I will" (*CC* II: 501). Clara therefore arrived unaccompanied in England and went to stay with the Shelleys at Field Place. There, she met Alexander Andrew Knox (1818–1891), a Trinity College friend of Sir Percy Florence Shelley (1819–1889) who had traveled

to Italy and Germany in 1842–3 with Percy Florence and his mother. Within a week of their meeting and without her parents' consent, Clara and Knox were engaged. They married on 16 June 1849. Mary Shelley's apparent support of the marriage angered her stepsister enormously. Claire accused Mary Shelley of poor chaperoning and of encouraging her niece (at least in Claire's opinion) "to outrage every law of natural tenderness, every filial duty, every family tie" (*CC* II: 533). The incident caused a rift that never repaired. After Mary Shelley's death on 1 February 1851, Claire wrote to Percy Florence of the "contemptuous way" she was treated in his house and of her anger at the ball the Shelleys had held to celebrate Clara's marriage to Knox (*CC* II: 536 and *LMWS* III: 391–2). Percy's wife, Lady Jane Shelley (1820–1899, and whom he had married in 1848), held a different view of Mary Shelley's involvement in Knox and Clara's courtship. In a conversation with Maud Rollston many years later, Lady Jane Shelley denied Mary Shelley's approval of the match: "When I told Mary she was much troubled, and said, 'Don't allow it, dear, don't allow it; they don't love each other, and the Clairmont blood always brings misery'" (quoted in *CC* II: 508).

Both Charles and Antonia Clairmont took more a moderate stance in response to their daughter's marriage. While Charles was initially stunned by the news (*CC* II: 503), he looked forward to a reconciliation between Claire and her niece. He characterized Clara's behavior as "foolish," but assured Claire that he did not suspect his daughter of "dissimulation" (*CC* II: 505). To Charles's letter, Antonia added: "we have had a terrible time of it, and shall thank God if Knox is not quite as bad as you at first seemed to think; but at the Shelley's we are both highly incensed, we see from Cläry's letter that they all urged her to consent to this hasty marriage before she left Field place; I begged and entreated her to withdraw her confidence from one who could make so unworthy a use of it; but it will be impossible for her to avoid seeing them, if her husband wishes it" (*CC* II: 507). Antonia forgave her daughter for the marriage (*CC* II: 507), which Clara Knox's few surviving letters suggest was happy until her death in 1855 (see *CC* II: 509, CL'ANA 0188, CL'ANA 0189 and CL'ANA 0191). Knox continued to support both Wilhelm and Charley Clairmont after their sister's death. Wilhelm told Claire that he refused to intervene in her dispute with the Shelleys because Knox had promised Antonia £20 a year for as long as Charley remained a student (see CL'ANA 0052).

3 Lady Jane Shelley, wife of Sir Percy Florence Shelley and daughter-in-law of Mary Shelley. Lady Shelley was a great favorite of Mary Shelley for whom she cared until Mary's death in 1851. In Lady Shelley's *Shelley Memorials*, published in 1859 and for which she served as editor, she expunged all negative aspects of the Shelleys' lives and instead provided a sanitized version of events. Percy and Jane had no children of their own, but adopted Bessie Florence Gibson, Lady Shelley's niece from her first marriage. Bessie married Lieutenant Colonel Leopold James Yorke Campbell Scarlett.

4 Wilhelm misspelled "safe".

5 He meant "add".

6 Wilhelm's spelling for "wish".

7 Marianna Hammond was a governess and friend of both Mary Shelley and Claire. In 1840, Claire wrote to Mary Shelley about Hammy (as she was known), calling her a "darling" with "so tender and affectionate a disposition" (*CC* II: 355). Emily Sunstein records that Mary Shelley spent time in Paris in 1840 with Claire and Marianna (p. 351), and that she saw Marianna at Kissengen in Bavaria in 1842 when Mary Shelley, Percy Florence, and Knox traveled to the spa town (p. 357). Sunstein notes too that Marianna and Mary Shelley attended the opera and theater together in 1844. See *Mary Shelley: Romance and Reality* (Baltimore, MD: Johns Hopkins University Press, 1989), p. 365. Betty Bennett speculates that Claire met Marianna through the Mason family (*LMWS* III: 28). Lady Margaret Mount Cashell (Claire Tomalin spells the name as Mountcashell) was one of Claire's closest friends in Italy. As the former wife of Lord Mount Cashell, Margaret styled herself as Mrs. Mason and was the mother of two daughters, Lauretta and Nerina, by George William Tighe. Nerina Tighe would marry Bartolomeo Cini, Claire's close friend whom she hoped would be the executor of her will (he died, however, some years before Claire). Claire was still corresponding with Hammy as late as 1875 when she told Cini that she had received a letter from Hammy (*CC* II: 624). See also CL'ANA 0394 for more information about Lady Mount Cashell and Cini.

8 Unidentified. Wilhelm could not be referring to John Black, the editor of the *Morning Chronicle*, as he was unmarried. See CL'ANA 0058.

8 • Clara Knox to Claire Clairmont

June 18 1849.

Dear aunt

I beg your pardon for not having sent a written answer to your kind note and thanks for the pretty cap – but I was afraid of making the boy wait too long and thought you could do without my note better than without your box. So I made haste and unpacked that –

I hope you are well We are both well and very happy; we have been to Rishmond[1] were we spent a delightful day, and we mean to go on a train as long as we can for it is very pleasant –

Pray give my compliments to Mrs Bird[2] and tell her I was very sorry not to have had an opportunity of wishing her goodbye before I left her house so abruptly, but I shall make a point of calling ere long. My boy[3] joins me in all kind things to you –

Ever yours
Clari Knox.

If Captain Andoe should remain in town untill next week I think it would be more suitable that I should defer seeing him untill then. If however he is leaving town at once I would not omit seeing him on any account. Pray drop me a line about this.[4]

Address: No envelope

Unpublished. Text: M.S., Pf. Coll., CL'ANA 0188

1 Richmond, about 9 kilometers from London.

2 According to Huscher, the Post Office directory listed George Bird (a surgeon) as "occupier" of the home in which Claire resided ("The Clairmont Enigma," p. 20).

3 Her husband, Alexander Knox. See CL'ANA 0201.

4 On 15 August 1849, Antonia and Charles wrote to Claire asking her to instruct Wilhelm to write to Andoe for information about Clara and Knox (*CC* II: 518).

9 • Alexander Knox to Wilhelm Clairmont

[18 June 1849]

My dear W. Clairmont – I need not say how much pleasure it will give me, I will not say, to make your acquaintance, but to gain your friendship, as well as that of all those who are so closely connected with my dear dear[1] wife – Believe me none of you have any cause of anxiety about her future fate whilst it is in my keeping – if I can help it she never shall know an anxiety or a care, or have cause for one.

I was so very sorry that we were compelled to be so precipitate in our measures, for as a mark of respect to her family I would have preferred waiting the return of a letter from your father; but, (although I cannot explain all until we meet,) we felt that our only means of avoiding great trouble and annoyance was to keep our own counsel and act for ourselves – I am sure no one who was interested in my dear little Clari's happiness, would have interposed the obstacle of a moment to our marriage, but I was not so sure, that the absolute and plain truth about us would have been told – under these circumstances we thought it best to act for ourselves; and let the blame fall upon me alone if anything has been done amiss – but no one who sees how happy we are will blame us at all –

Whenever you think that it will suit your convenience to come to London, you will always find a home and a most hearty welcome here – and your sister the same as ever, only I hope somewhat happier. Meanwhile until we meet – Believe me to be

always most sincerely yours
A. Alex. Knox.

77. Warwick Square. Pimlico.
June $^{18}/_{49}$.

Address: No envelope

Unpublished. Text: M.S., Pf. Coll., CL'ANA 0201

1 Double repetition of "dear" in the letter.

10 • Wilhelm Clairmont to Charles and Antonia Clairmont

Malling 3rd July 1849.

Dearest parents.

It may seem impudent on my part, that I should endeavour to say anything about so serious an affair. as just occupies our minds; on the other hand however I think it a hard thing for poor Clara that she should be condemmed in that way without having anybody to plead her cause. ~~for her~~. – You will now say; how is it that you did not say all you have to say with A.C.'s[1] letter? In answer to this question, which it is [~~illeg.~~] probable, you will put to yourselves, let me deviate in only a few words from the chief and original tenour of this letter. – When A.C. first came from London (29th June) down to Malling – she darted quite unexpectedly, without my knowing of her being here, into my room and made me a terrible scene; she worked herself into a terrible state of fury and at last said: that if I would not side with her. throughout this affaire, she would give me money and I was to go home instantly!; I was not prepared for such a decided step but however assented at last for a variety of reasons; first because I thought Clara more in the wrong than A.C. than because I ~~thought~~ did not consider myself entitled to take without your consent such steps as would have caused my being sent back to Vienna, and lastly because I thought it safest in a dilemma to choose from two ways the one that you have in your power to go back again if necessary. (I allege all these motives that you may see that I had at least good intentions if I perhaps did wrong.) I accordingly kept my lip~~p~~s sealed hermetically during the three first days; but now A.C. seems to forget the affair at least she is very kind and cheerful again with me; however I hope this will be sufficient reason why I could not write yesterday, so as I should have liked exactly; for she would have misinterpreted the slightest word and then we should have had a new row. besides I think Aunt Claire is likely to forget the whole affair much sooner if she is allowed to give uninterrupted vent to her feelings, than if by constant arguing and proveing her guilt /: for this would be the consequence of my defending Clara:/ all the different disagreable recollections were kept fresh in her memory. I trust you will after these explanations understand the tone of my postscription to A.C.'s long letter from the 2nd July; which you ought to have received the day before this. A.C. desires Papa to send a very severe and reprimanding letter to Clara and I totally agree with her in the opinion that it will have an excellent effect. Her husband being a man of the world must see himself how she committed herself in leaving her aunt and putting herself in that way into the hands of strangers.[2] It will accordingly not only make him respect [~~illeg.~~] our family so much the more but it will also show him at once, that he is sure to have constant advocats of the right, the true and the just in his new parents of law, a feeling which certainly will exercise influence over him; as for Clara the good effects of sound reason and serious reprimandings are quite evident. Now you will say: how very altklug[3] of that boy to talk in such a way; and so it would be, I dare say, wasn't it that I brought up this way of reasoning not perhaps ~~to~~ with the erroneous intention of improving anybody's opinions on the subject or anything of that kind, but merely in order to found the following argument upon it viz. –: that if the letter is to have the desired, above mentioned good effects it also must have certain qualities; that is I mean to say: that if this letter is to convince her of her guilt and make her really acknowledge her faults, it must not go one jota[4] beyond the truth; for it's known how difficult it is for human nature to find fault with itself, even with the best intention of seeing the truth; thus I think she will on finding one reproach that she knows herself unguilty of, think the whole the work of her aunt~~s~~'s disinclination or perhaps even revenge; where as I am most firmly convinced that she will and must come to rights again if her dearly beloved parents point out to her ~~these~~ as most grieving and hurtful offenses these very wrongs, that I am sure her own conscience is mortifying her about already now. – I think I am now arrived at the point of my arguments. viz. that the letter to Cl. ought to convince her of her [~~illeg.~~] guilt and in order to obtain that object ought to strictly true. I accordingly proceed to say, that I do not think that A.C.'s accusations are all strictly true. I naturally can not judge Clara's behaviour or pass a regular opinion over her [~~illeg.~~] howl[5] conduct because this requires experience, sound settled principles, knowledge of the world etz. still I can see wether single accusations are quite sound. So for instance she accuses her for having been quite reckless for you, and us all; this I positively know and can prove ~~to be~~ not to be the case; for although the accusation might perhaps be merited with regard to her not waiting for your approval, still it is unmerited in all the other senses in which it easily might be understood. – It can not be denied that A.C. is of an extremely imperious and despotic disposition, this frequently gives arise to little disputes the worst of which is that A.C. sees every where some secret plot[~~illeg.~~] or intention; and if you give your real cause she only says that she has been very much in the world, knows human nature thoroughly, has an eye as sharp as an eagle and that you are much to young to deceive her. I dont mean to say that she does so always, but she treated me in this way several times and so I naturally suspect that with Clara in whom she has so much less confidence this was the case still oftener. besides she sneaked before the Shelley's and other things which I dont believe to be ~~through~~. true. I hope dearest parents you wont misunderstand me; I dont think of excusing Cl's real guilt but I only wanted to mitigate A.C.'s accusations, where it is possible, to a little degree. As for the marriage itself all has been as legal and regular as possible. – I dont think, I confess, A.C. has behaved very well on one point and that is that she makes the busiest job of informing about among all her acquaintance, even those that have been quite laid by and tells them the whole affair in the least favourable light; even to quite common people as the old woman whom I lived with –, she talks with an indelicacy about it, as I should not have expected. Yesterday she [~~illeg.~~] went in a ~~a~~carriage down to Black;[6] and bid me come down an our[7] afterwards on foot. I immediately suspected the reason (for this she had never done before) and really heard her talking about it when I arrived; for you know the groundfl~~o~~or parlours with the large windows entering into the garden. – She says she was so very ill in L.[8] but now I find out by and by from her own narrations that she successively invited all her friends to [~~illeg.~~] tea

in order to communicate to them the great news. What I said about her health in yesterdays letter was a modyfied extract of what she bid me to tell you; my private opinion does not even go so far.
I wish you would keep this letter a secret to A.C. because she would be most suspicious and angry at my not showing her what I wrote; also to Clara I think it would be better a secret. – I hope you are all quite well, and in good health; I am glad that there is nothing illegal in the marriage itself. Knox is an exceedingly clever man and may make her very happy.[9] No[10] goodbye dearest parents. many kisses to Paulin and all the others. your obedient son.

Willy.

Address: Aerogramme: via Ostend./Charles Clairmont Esqr./
Vordere Schenkenstrasse N° 35–1st. Stock/ Vienna./ Austria.[11]
Postmark: Dover/ JY 4/ 1849

Unpublished. Text: M.S., Pf. Coll., CL'ANA 0058

1 Wilhelm and Pauline often referred to Claire as A.C., A.Cl. or A^t in their letters. In a letter from 2 July that has been lost, Claire evidently wrote to Antonia and Charles about the marriage. Their letter to Claire of 14 July referenced the 2 July letter which they claimed was a "thunder stroke" to them (*CC* II: 503).

2 Claire blamed the Shelleys for Clara's marriage to Knox, because Clara had been visiting them unaccompanied when the two met and became engaged without her parents' consent.

3 German for "precocious".

4 German for "iota".

5 whole.

6 Probably John Black, editor of the *Morning Chronicle*. Both Antonia and Charles remained skeptical that Knox worked for the *London Times* and they wanted Claire to ask Black to confirm this fact (*CC* II: 517–18).

7 An hour.

8 London.

9 Both Antonia and Charles were eager to find out more about Knox. In her note to Claire (appended to Charles's letter of 14 July 1849), Antonia expressed the hope that Knox was "not quite so bad" as Claire had intimated (*CC* II: 507). On 15 July, Charles informed Claire of the letter he received from Knox in which Knox described his family. According to this letter, Knox was the second son of George and Letitia Knox. His father was a merchant in Jamaica while his mother had died during childbirth. At the time of his marriage to Clara, Knox was thirty-one years of age. He had attended Trinity College, Cambridge, and was a lawyer by profession. He apparently wrote for the *Times*, for which he received £720 a year in addition to the pay he received for his work as a lawyer and a writer (*CC* II: 514).

10 Wilhelm probably meant to say "now".

11 "Stock" refers to the floor or story.

11 • Clara Knox to Claire Clairmont

July 9th 1849[1]

My dear aunt

I am at a loss how to apologize for my remissness in not writing before this – however you will I hope make some alowance for circumstances under which I am sure, few young women would willingly be very busy with their pens – Besides we have been jaunting about a great deal –

So much so that I have not even seen Captain Andoe – although he was kind enough to call three times, never finding us at home – On our going to his lodgings we met with [illeg.] [illeg.] [illeg.], so I was actually compelled to enter into correspondence with him or I should never have had a chance of seeing him – He will come and take tea with us and so I shall at length enjoy a Vienna gossip revelry – I have had a most kind and affectionate letter from my parents today – which adds greatly to my high spirits and if possible to my happiness.[2]

I hope dear aunt you are better in health and spirits now than you have been for some time back – and that the air and food of Malling will soon quite restore you. Many thanks for the trouble you took in packing and sending my box and excuses for having occasioned it.

I am now going to write to Willy – who has become an intolerably bad correspondent – and whom I have serious thoughts of cutting dead if he does not retourner sur ses pas[3] – He is not a bride, I fancy – and has no right de se faire précieux.[4]

Goodbye dear aunt. Hoping ~~to~~ soon to hear that you are well and in good spirits.

always yours
Clari Knox

Address: No envelope.

Unpublished. Text: M.S., Pf. Coll., CL'ANA 0189

---

1 Clearly, on 9 July, Clara had no idea of Claire's outrage at her marriage and continued to write in an affectionate manner to her aunt.

2 While Charles and Antonia were disappointed by Clara's hasty marriage, they sought reconciliation with her nonetheless. On 15 July, Charles told Claire that he was going to give Clara £50, noting that it was "hardly reputable" for him to allow his daughter to marry without "some little fitting out" (*CC* II: 512). In this same letter, Charles voiced his hope for a reconciliation between Claire and the rest of the family, expressing a desire that Claire not regret having assisted his family all the years (*CC* II: 514). See also CL'ANA 0041.

3 French for "retrace his steps".

4 French for "to be affected".

12 • Clara Knox to Wilhelm Clairmont

July 24th 1849.
77. Warwick Sqre

My dear Willy,

I received both your letters – the first I confess made me very sad – I did not expect you would write to me in that way – I do not however wish to say anything about it as I feel sure you did not mean to be unkind to me and will ever be my dear old Willy boy – As to the inquiry you seem so very anxious to make me answer, my aunt must be very well aware that I never told her Lady Shelley[1] had spoken ill of her – because it is not true.

I am happy to hear you are taking the sea baths – pray write soon dearest boy and give me a full account of your health – ~~it~~ you said nothing about it in your last three or four letters and I am very anxious to know all about it – how is your poor long back? and do you often catch colds and coughs! do you still use that iodine Salbe[2] and the inhalations, and are the glands on the whole grown bigger or smaller?[3] do you take a good deal of exercise and do you swim? – I put all these questions for fear you should try to [illeg.] me with a bündig[4] statement, as: I am well – or very well or pretty well – which would be very unsatisfactory. Please, answer me scrupulously.

Andoe took tea with us one evening last week – I felt very funny hearing myself called „Madam" by him. he told me you had written to him from Brighton[5] and gave me hopes of going to pay you a visit – which I should be very glad of for I am sure it would give you great pleasure to see and talk to a Vienna friend – and besides since there seems to be no chance at all of your coming to London I should be very happy at least to get the directest news possible from you – through a person that had just seen you – that would be better than lots of letters – besides I dislike letters more and more – they are almost always too warm or too cold and they are unfri[illeg.] things often – for like mysterious talismans they still retain a dark and fearful power to inflict pain when the Spirit that has [illeg.] the [illeg.] is passed and gone – and letters are often dictated by a mischievous but passing Spirit of anger or excitement or sorrow – but pray, do not dear boy make all this stuff an excuse for not writing to me very soon – after all letters from those we love are a great comfort and bless the man that invented posts and post offices.

Alexi and I are now beginning to lead a very settled life. We have gone through a regular cours of visiting and I have become initiated to my household duties and now everything goes on so smoothly and quietly as if we were Philemon and Baucis.[6]

We read a good deal of German together – Alexi is very fond of it and will soon be as good a German scholar as I can make him – he has such an astonishing talent for languages. – The quickness with which he seizes and puts to right in his mind our puzzling round-about German constructions is quite wonderful and his pronunciation promises to be pure Saxon, which he is very proud of – he very [illeg.] schätzingly[7] calls me a little Vienesse for saying schprechen schtehen[8] etz

and insists upon pronouncing his st and sp in the hanoverian way[9] – We go to the country as often as we can; the environs of London are so delightful; the parks too are beautiful and have been of great resource to us, but now they are burnt up by the sun and look as yellow as the Vienna Glacis.[10]
We have been twice to Gravesend;[11] and once we enjoyed ourselves very much cruising about in the yacht of a friend of Alexi's, a very amiable and good natured young man whom Alexi is particularly fond of and who will I think become an habitué[12] at our house –

I forgot to thank you for sending the little coffee pot – it is of invaluable use to me; I use it every [~~illeg.~~] afternoon for Alexi's black coffee, which I make myself whilst he reads his odious news papers – a necessary evil for men. During that time, the practical occupation of [illeg.] is a great relief to me. – Andoe seemed rather piqué[13] rather at my father's not answering his letter – I forgot to mention that when I last wrote to Vienna – but I hope papa will not delay writing to him much longer – in fact I don't understand why he did, till now.
Poor mama, you see is dragging on in town – why I cannot think – for I am sure Pauline would be very glad to live with Papa and Charley boy – yet for the sake of poor Paulines health I am very happy to know her in the country. I wish her health were seriously looked to – or that she would at least give up that unfortunate smoking or that any one at home had [~~illeg.~~] influence with her. It is such a very sad thing. – I must now wish you goodbye my dearest Willy. – Give my kindest remembrances to my aunt; I hope she is well – and how are the Pringles?[14] do you see much of them; pray give my compliments to Mrs Pringle and Miss Ramsbottom[15] if you do –
– Now goodbye, be a good boy and write soon.

Address: No envelope.

Unpublished. Text: M.S., Pf. Coll., CL'ANA 0191

---

1 Lady Jane Shelley. After Mary Shelley's death in 1851, Claire wrote to Sir Percy and chastised him for having given a ball in honor of Clara's marriage to Knox. Claire believed that the Shelleys endorsed the marriage which occurred against Claire's wishes (*CC* II: 536). See also CL'ANA 0374 for an account of Claire's disagreement with Lady Jane Shelley.

2 German for "ointment".

3 Wilhelm's health was always a source of concern for his family and Claire was intent on his bathing at the sea, which was considered a curative for many types of disorders. Alastair Durie explains the enormous influence of Sir John Floyer's *History of cold bathing* (1702) in bringing the concept of sea-bathing to the attention of the public. Sea-bathing became an alternative to "taking the waters" at a spa ("Medicine, health and economic development: promoting spa and seaside Resorts in Scotland" in *Medical History*, 2003, 47: 195–216). Louise Miskell records that sea bathing was considered a "health and leisure activity among the fashionable elite" of the early nineteenth century (Peter Borsay and John Walton, eds., *Resorts and Ports: European Seaside Towns since 1700* [Bristol: Channel View Publications, 2011], p. 113).

In a joint letter from Charles and Antonia to Claire of 12–15 August 1849, Antonia referred to Wilhelm's thick neck, which her physician, Dr. Boehm, attributed to a swollen thyroid gland.

According to Boehm, patients who were susceptible to "weakness in the Bronchia, or to scrophulous complaints" developed swollen thyroid glands as a "protection" against other diseases. The swelling, Boehm assured Antonia, was benign. Boehm also advised that Wilhelm should live in a milder climate and that he exercise in the outdoors (*CC* II: 516). On 29 August 1849, Charles expressed his delight on hearing that Wilhelm's "Gland" was "doing well" (*CC* II: 524).

Iodine inhalation was used to treat disorders of the respiratory system. In 1834, Charles Scudamore described how a patient experienced "good effects" and "great relief" of his "bronchial symptoms" after being prescribed a "plan of inhalation, using the iodine mixture with conium" (*On the Inhalation of Iodine and Conium in Tubercular Phthisis*, London: Longman, 1834, p. 109). In an article published the *London Journal of Medicine* (1851), Dr. John Snow explained that inhalation was frequently a preferred method to digestion as inhalation did not exacerbate stomach disorders and that unpleasant tasting medicines were rendered more palatable when inhaled. He cited the "irritating effects on the stomach" of iodine in endorsing inhalation of the medication (Snow, J., "On the Mode of Communcation of Cholera". 1855. Web. 9 March 2015. http://johnsnow.matrix.msu.edu/work.php?id=15–78–2F).

4 German for "succinct".

5 Christopher Chalkin records that bathing started at Brighton in the 1730s and that Brighton, Margate, and Ramsgate were the largest of all the English resorts by 1801 (*The Rise of the English Town, 1650–1850* [Cambridge: Cambridge University Press, 2001], p. 14). In *British Spas from 1815 to the Present*, Phyllis Hembry explains that one of the major reasons for Brighton's "period of success . . . as a coastal spa was its easy access from London. The opening of the Brighton Road and introduction of mail coaches brought to it fashionable people . . . And the beginning of Brighton's decline as a spa coincided with the coming of the railway, which brought the trippers who came in their thousands to enjoy the seaside attractions of the beach, promenade and Chain Pier, and changed the nature of the resort" ([New Jersey: Fairleigh Dickinson Univ. Press, 1997], p. 114).

6 From Ovid's *Metamorphosis*, Philemon and Baucis were an elderly couple who gave food and shelter to Zeus and Hermes. The gods rewarded them by ensuring neither would have to live without the other, and that they would die at the same time.

7 Clara combined the German word "Schatz" (in this case, a pet name meaning "treasure") with the English ending "ingly" to create an adjective that means "treasuringly".

8 Clara wrote "schprechen" by which she meant to say "sprechen" (German for "talk" or "speak"). She wrote "schtehen" instead of "stehen" (German for "stand").

9 Hannover (German for Hanover) is the capital city of the German state of Lower Saxony. See Charles Russ, *The Dialects of Modern Germany: A Linguistic Study* (Stanford, CA: Stanford University Press, 1989), for a study of German dialects.

10 A glacis is a type of defensive fortification, typically constructed of stone or earth. Until the early part of the nineteenth century, Vienna was ringed by a wall and an earth glacis. In *Harper's Hand-Book for Travellers in Europe and the East*, W. Pembroke Fetridge notes that "Vienna is of a nearly circular form, being twelve miles in circumference. The old city, or city proper, is, however, scarcely three miles round; it was formerly inclosed by fortifications: there, however, have been converted into a public promenade; known as the *Bastei*. Immediately outside of this is a wide esplanade, called the *Glacis*, which is laid out in delightful walks and gardens" ([London: Harper and Brothers, 1864], p. 236). In 1857, plans were made to destroy the glacis and fortifying wall and to construct the Ringstrasse which was completed by 1880. The Ringstrasse is a circular boulevard which surrounds the center of Vienna.

11 Gravesend is located in northwestern Kent, about 44 kilometers from London. It is located on the Thames River just before the river enters the Thames Estuary. It is a well-known area for sailing.

12 French for "frequenter".

13 French for "piqued".

14 Colonel and Mrs. Pringle were friends of Claire and of Mary Shelley. On 26 June 1845, Claire told Mary Shelley that the Pringles were "quite unworldly minded people" who admired "genius"

and were "free from prejudices of all kinds" (*CC* II: 444). Mary Shelley told Claire that Colonel Pringle seemed a "most good humoured agreable man" (*LMWS* III: 192) and Mary Shelley's letters confirm that she took an interest in the Pringle family and in sustaining the friendship. In August 1848, she expressed a desire to entertain them and in October 1848 she exclaimed that "with the Pringles, Sanfords & ourselves you [Claire] will have a little society" (*LMWS* III: 348). Writing to Claire, Mary Shelley asked to be remembered to the Pringles whom she wished "every happiness" (*LMWS* III: 354), and she also recorded her feeling of "love" for them" for the comfort" they provided Claire (351). On 10 March 1850, Claire told Wilhelm that she could "never sufficiently repay" the Pringles for their kindness to her (*CC* II: 530). She compared their warmth to Mary Shelley's "cold sharp manners" and told Wilhelm that a woman would never fall in love in a short period of time in the Pringle's home, alluding of course to Clara's romance with Knox which occurred while Clara was residing with the Shelleys (*CC* II: 530).

15 The Ramsbottom family features fairly significantly in the Clairmont family's letters. Ada Ramsbottom and her sister, Emily Ramsbottom Wilbraham, were Claire's friends. Their parents were James and Emma Ramsbottom. On 7 May 1845, Claire sent Mary Shelley a letter of introduction to Ada whom she called a "charming girl," and very "domestic" (*CC* II: 429–30). On 23 June 1845, Mary Shelley responded to Claire, informing her that she had invited both sisters to a party to celebrate the Regatta in Putney. Claire wrote back, confirming that Ada greatly admired Mary Shelley. On 28 June 1845, Mary Shelley recorded in a letter that Ada and her sister had attended her party and she noted her satisfaction with Mrs. Wilbraham's looks. Mrs. Wilbraham apparently wore "rouge" (*LMWS* III: 189). Mary Shelley did not, however, mention Ada, an omission on which Claire remarked in her letter of 4 July 1845. Mary Shelley responded on 7–10 July 1845, praising Mrs. Wilbraham's complexion and noting that she had not said much to Ada, but that she had found Ada to be a pleasant young woman (*LMWS* III: 194). By October 1845, Mary Shelley was writing to Claire about prospective wives for Percy Florence and she mentioned Ada Ramsbottom (*LMWS* III: 243).

13 • Wilhelm Gaulis Clairmont to Charles Gaulis Clairmont and Antonia Clairmont

Brighton August 1st
1849.

Dearest parents.

It is but with very a different feeling from hitherto that I take up my pen to write to you, for indeed this unfriendly feeling between A.C. and Clara as well as the false position I am put into by it,[1] grieve me very much; and still on the other hand I understand that you must ~~have~~ be very anxious to hear from us and Clara; and so I think it despite my disinclination a necessity to write. – I will first acquaint you with what has happened since I last wrote, before I can make you understand our relative positions. – Clara having intimated to A.C. that lady Sh.[2] had spoken ill of her, A.C. desired me to write to my sister in order to learn the particulars; in return to which ~~answers~~ question Clara answered the following words.: "As for the question you seem so particular to have answered [~~illeg.~~] my aunt must be very well aware that I never said so, because it is not true". I abstain making any remarks on these words, for it is sufficient, that she by them accuses AC. in a very violent way of a lie. I am sorry to say that the mental agitations and sufferings following thereby, had a very sad effect on A.C.'s state of health; for with her all these attacks seem to go to the chest and at the same time impeed the digestion. I need not say how unhappy it makes me to think that AC. has really has behaved so very kindly towards us all, should reap such fruits for her sacrifices and that from Clara, who I hoped would be the likliest to recompence in some measure A.C.'s kindness, which I feel I myself shall not be able to do. However, ich muß zur Sache[3]; for my time is very short. A.C. accordingly resolved that she could not go on any longer in this way with any one who had attacked her honour in that way; moreover she thought it impossible that she could go on guiding and protecting me as long as I had intercourse with any such individual as this must do away with all the power of moral influence.[4] She accordingly announced to me that if I wished to enjoy any longer [~~illeg.~~] her protection I must firmly and resolutely make up my mind to renounce every intercourse with Clara. The chief object of this letter is to lay before your judgement my decision, and to tell you that I thought myself not only justified, but even bound to obey to this demand of A.C.'s in the strictest sense of the word. My reasons for doing so are the following: 1st because it is evident to me that through out the whole affaire A.C. was the injured party to whom apology and reparation is due, in which your last letter confirms me 2~~nd~~ly because I consider that Clara ought to learn by a very stern and decided conduct on our side that her <u>real</u> friends dont approve of her late ways of going on 3<u>rd</u>ly because I think that she perhaps by this obstinacy of conduct (if this be not to[5] violent a word) may at last make up her mind to yield and having so time to think over the whole affair perhaps freeer from strange influence may come to acknowledge her fault. This is all I feel or think upon the subject and I hope you will give your approbation; I need not say that I am still very fond of dear Clara but at the same time I cant help

thinking that she comitted a great fault in her late conduct, but by fare[6]a ~~still~~ greater one in denying her error, from false shame, moreover as she by this act, which taking a moral view of it does not even deserve the name of a good but only a right action, would restore peace and happiness to her whole family.
A.C. wishes me to have an other month's seabathing[7] during which time I am to frequent one of the neighbouring farms; then she had an idea of sending me to an agricultural college in Hampshire where I should have the advantage of seeing the management of a farm of + 800 acrs.[8] and besides to learn bookkeeping and all the scientific p{tear} of agricultural business; which would give me extreme pleasure, for you know that I think I am rather a little behind in these parts. at all events I can promiss that there shall be no want of application on my part. – This extremely tedious thing my gland, is growing very much smaller now with seabathing so that in comparison with what it was it scarcely is comprehensible. – England being such a very manufactural country all the people here from a feeling of patriotism ware flanell[9] or gore[10] or something or other in order to raise the manufactures; you may imagine that I shant be one of the exceptions so I must begin now to ware flanell too.[11] I delight very much in the seabathing; the first time I swam in ruff[12] sea the waves were even 10 feet high and I got rather severely handled, however now I know better how to manage it; in the calm sea it's quite delicious for expanding my <u>four</u> legs I can float on the surface of the water without the slightest movement and this is a very agreable feeling because ~~it is~~ you nowhere feel the fulcrum upon which your body rests, which you must even on the very best sopha. How is Charley getting on ? I hope he is very diligent in Geometrie[13] and Algebra for especially the latter and Mathematics are the sole foundation for the study of any other science.[14] I hope dear Mama is recovered from her attack of D.[15] A.C. thinks it highly important to take ice water now. Now goodbye dearest parents do write as soon as possible to your affectionate

son William.

address changed to:

47 Norfolk Square Brighton.

This time just now, was a time of the greatest pleasure for me for many years. A.C. I hope will write soon; just now she is not able to do so, but I trust she soon will. - Goodbye - A.C. sends her kindest love to you all; - you had better address: <u>postoff [illeg.]</u>[16] <u>[illeg.]righton</u>, because we may change this lodg[17] [illeg.]dbye.[18]

Address: Aerogramme: via Ostend./ C. G Clairmont Esqr./
Vordere Schenkerstrasse N° 35 1[t] Stock/ Vienna./ Austria
Front postmark: Aus ENGLAND/3/8/Per AACHEN[19]
Rear postmark: BRIGHTON/AU 2/ 1849/D

Unpublished. Text: M.S., Pf. Coll., CL'ANA 0057

---

1 Claire was furious with Clara over the marriage and made it clear that Wilhelm's success in England was contingent on his breaking off contact with his sister.

2 Lady Jane Shelley. See CL'ANA 0191 for Clara's response to this allegation.
3 Wilhelm meant to say "I must get down to business," but he omitted the word "kommen" which means "get".
4 Charles Clairmont told Claire on 12 August 1849 that he approved of Wilhelm's decision not to visit Knox and Clara, but that he was not opposed to Wilhelm corresponding with his sister (*CC* II: 518). In this same letter, Antonia forbad Wilhelm from visiting the Shelleys ("their society can do him no good and may do him harm" [*CC* II: 517]), and reiterated Charles's wish that Wilhelm only visit Clara once the estrangement between Claire and Clara was over. Expressing her optimism, she asked Claire whether Clara had already contacted her.
5 too.
6 far.
7 See CL'ANA 0191.
8 From 1849 until 1850, Wilhelm attended Queenwood College near Stockbridge in Hampshire. Stockbridge is a town in west Hampshire, located about 112 kilometers south-west of London. Marion Stocking incorrectly identifies the college as "Greenwood College" (*CC* II: 524). The Hampshire Gardens Trust provides the following information: The Rolle family owned the original property until the early nineteenth century. In 1839, the reformer Robert Owen leased the site. He constructed Harmony Hall on it in 1842, aiming to conduct an experiment in communal living. Harmony Hall was designed with 80 rooms and was intended to house some 700 people. By 1845, Owen was bankrupt and he rented the building to the Society of Friends (the Quakers). The buildings became known as Queenwood College and a school was established to teach science, physics, and agriculture. George Edmondson served as principal until 1863. A 1902 fire destroyed the school, and the buildings were torn down in 1904. The grounds were then employed for agricultural endeavours. Only the original school teachers' cottages survive today, as well as parts of the retaining walls and entrance gate pillars (Hampstead Garden Trust, "Queenwood College". Web. 6 May 2016. http://research.hgt.org.uk/). See the 1849 engraving in this collection by J. Harwood depicting Queenwood College which was included in the "Synopsis of the Course of Education at Queenwood College" in 1849.
9 Wilhelm's spelling for "wear" and "flannel".
10 Unidentified.
11 "Flanell," with a capital f, is the German spelling for "flannel"; however, Wilhelm omitted to capitalize the word.
12 Wilhelm's spelling for "rough".
13 German spelling for "geometry".
14 On 12 August 1849, Antonia told Claire that Charley was going to enroll in the "Polytechnic" and continue studying Latin with a private tutor (*CC* II: 516). On 29 August 1849, Charles wrote to Wilhelm, confirming that they had employed a tutor to teach Charley geometry (*CC* II: 523).
15 Probably dysentery. Rehydration was often prescribed as a cure.
16 A red wax seal partially covers the words "postoffice Brighton".
17 A red wax seal covers these words.
18 Wilhelm wrote this last paragraph on the front of the aerogramme.
19 "Aus" is German for "from" and "Per" is German for "going via". Aachen is a German town situated on the border between Germany, Belgium, and the Netherlands.

14 • Wilhelm Gaulis Clairmont to Charles Gaulis Clairmont and Antonia Clairmont

Brighton 16th August
finished 17th 1849.

Dearest parents.

I am now writing for A.C. who bids me say that she has been wishing to write to you every day for three weeks, but she has been to indisposed that she has not been able; and she now is so unwell that she can not write otherwise than through me. She was very well at Malling, but these insolences of the Shel.s[1] and Knoxe~~e~~'s have so upset that she never has had a days health since Clara's marriage. About Pauline she wishes me to say thus: that she certainly thinks it would be a good thing for her to be married and she thinks that by her being with the Kn.[2] has a chance of getting a good husband, and for this she conseled the step of her coming to England; but of course she never ment to insist upon it if it is against your judgement. She thought it was well, that you should know the carte du pays[3] and therefor she informed you of what probabilities there were of her getting a husband; but she leaves it entirely to you to judge wether you will accept the probabilities or no.[4] My aunt will always be ready to be an aunt to Paula if she comes; if she does she thinks no time is to be lost, and she thinks in the present uncertain state of affairs[5] in Vienna as many of you as can should certainly get out of it. Mama asks in her letter whether my aunt told to me and Clara of her opinion of the Shell. A.C. answers that she told us every thing because she never would think of having secrets with her own relations, so Clara knew perfectly well what she put her foot into, but she was so infatuated that she would not believe one word my aunt said to her. and Mr K. of course is furious against my aunt for speaking so openly all she knew about him; now A.C. says she is determined to make the Shel.[6] pay the piper for it. A.C. says you ask why she never complained of the S. before; and she said that she never mentioned particulars about them, but always complained bitterly of them to you at Paris; and told you there that Mr Trelawny[7] had told her many years before that Mrs S. was the bitterest enemy she ever had. – With regard to myself steps have been taken for placing me at Queenwood colledge in Hampshire. The principal is Mr Edmondson a quaker; the whole institution seems to be a very good one there is a farm of 800 acr.[8] and besides I shall have all the advantages of a Scientific education; lectures upon chymistry, geology ~~etz~~. bookkeeping etz an other great advantage will be my having there the opportunity of studying all the first books that have been written in English upon Agriculture and it's different branches[9] This I ~~can~~ think can only be done effectually under the guidance of some one well acquainted and able to pass an opinion upon this part of the English literature; besides they have a library there;[10] for the dearness of books would be an other impediment to reading them all; but if I have studied and compared them all successively I always will be able to have a few as constant companions. As far as I can see from the prospectus they also seem to

take a very sound view of sciences; in so far as it appears to me, they take them for what they really are viz the foundation rules upon which every single, little process in nature takes place and to which we consequently must [~~illeg.~~] [~~illeg.~~] refer as the only councellors not interfearing with the processes of nature; for the art of Agriculture is in fact nothing else but that. –
My aunt applied to my sister through me to assist in paying part of the expenses and my sister[11] has offered to pay about £ 40 or 50 but the thing is not yet quite settled.[12] My aunt told you that she would find out who Mr K. is; she had heard that he had a rich father living and she was in hopes it was so as it might have proved a benefit, but she has now found out Mr. K's godfather who tells her that his father really is dead, that the family are very poor so all hope is cut off from that quarter. – I can not go to Queenwood just now, because Clara delays answering and Lumley does not pay A.C.[13] and so she has not the £ 25 which it is necessary to pay down on my first entrance at Q. colledge.[14]

I am very glad to tell you that with the seabathing my gland has almost entirely disappeared; I also feel on the whole very much stronger and healthier. I had now for a month a little brush up for my German with Miss Beste[15] the governess of Mrs. Pring{tear}[16] children; she is Hanoverian[17] and a very amiable agreable young woman; ~~and~~ I had many amusing German [illeg.] with her, but now they are all gone off to London, which I am very sorry for. I hope that you are [~~illeg.~~] both quite well dearest parents, and [~~illeg.~~] Pauline and the others; are you at Weidling or in town and is it tolerably peacible ? the Hungarian accounts sound rather dismal for Austria, today the Times say that she is going to take recourse to a pacification; how I do wish it soon be over!

A.C. desires me to tell you that ~~Lady~~ Mrs Sh. never has sent your letter, which you ~~desired~~ wished her to forward to A.C., to her; this is I think a great piece of insolence.

[written on aerogramme envelope]
I hope you will write immediately for I am most anxious to hear from you; perhaps I shall be already in Queenwood on the return of your letter.
address: postoffice Brighton. – Pray tell me how Charley is getting on and what you hear of Prof. Schrötter, for you said in your last: "he is disappeared" but [~~illeg.~~] although I think he is a Liberal still I cant conceive what reason he should have to fly;[18] and do not forget that Braumuller owes me still the last Heft[19] of Schrotters Chymistry[20] which I wish very much for as it is all about the organic Chymistry and because I cant have the whole bound before I receive the last. Now good bye dearest parents do write soon to your affectionate son.

William

Ich hätte gern deutsch geschrieben aber der [illeg.] wollte mich nicht lassen: wie Ihr wohl sehet ist das seine Dictation mit Ausnahme der letzten Zeilen und der bezüglich der Anstalt in Queenwood.[21]

English Translation (German transcription and English translation provided by Ann Sherwin):

I would have liked to write in German, but the [illeg.] wouldn't let me; as you can probably see, this is his dictation, with the exception of the last few lines and the one regarding the academy in Queenwood.

Address: Aerogramme: via Ostend./C. G. Clairmont Esqr./ Vordere Schenkenstrasse № 35. 1st Stock./ Vienna./ Austria./ paid. franco.
Postmarks: BRIGHTON/AU 17/ 1849; Aus England/ per Aachen franco;

Unpublished. Text: M.S., Pf. Coll., CL'ANA 0056

---

1 Wilhelm referred to the Shelleys in the following terms in this letter: Shel, Mrs. S., Mrs. Sh., Shell, the S., Shel.s.

2 Wilhelm used K. or Mr. K. to refer to Knox. The term "Knoxes" refers to Clara and Alexander.

3 French. Literally, the "map of the country". In other words, "how the land lies".

4 Wilhelm incorrectly spelled a number of words in these earlier letters. His orthography improved as his facility with the English language became more apparent.

5 After the 1848 Revolution with its ongoing political crises, political instability plagued Austria and Hungary. In April 1849, the Hungarian government declared itself free from Hapsburg rule but Hungary was under Austrian rule by August.

6 Shelleys.

7 Edward John Trelawny (1792–1881) was a friend of Claire, and of Percy and Mary Shelley. The Shelleys, Claire, Lord Byron, Trelawny, Leigh Hunt, and Edward and Jane Williams formed part of the Pisan circle of 1821 (see CL'ANA 0432). In 1858, Trelawny published *Recollections of the Last Days of Shelley and Byron* in which he chronicled the lives of Byron and Shelley. In 1878, he published a revised version of the text as *Records of Byron, Shelley, and the Author*. In his letter of 19 September 1858 to Captain Daniel Roberts (builder of the *Don Juan* which Shelley was sailing when he drowned in 1822), Trelawny stated that his "book is brief and to the point and has elevated Shelley and shown Byron as he was. My wish was to tell nothing but the truth, tho' I could not tell the whole truth" (H. Buxton Forman, ed., *Letters of Edward John Trelawny*, [London: Oxford University Press, 1910], p. 216). Writing to Claire in 1870, Trelawny recorded that Mary Shelley's "jealousy must have surely vexed Shelley – indeed she was not a suitable companion for the poet . . . Mary was the most conventional slave I ever met – she even affected the pious dodge, such was her yearning for society – she was devoid of imagination and Poetry – she felt compunction when she had lost him – she did not understand or appreciate him" (p. 229). Trelawny was buried next to Shelley in the Cimitero Acattolico (non-Catholic cemetery) in Rome. See also CL'ANA 0319, CL'ANA 0431, CL'ANA 0432, CL'ANA 0433, and CL'ANA 0434.

8 The *Illustrated London News* of 13 January 1849 notes that Queenwood College "in addition to the usual course of classical and commercial study, provides on a farm of 800 acres, for such young men as wish to turn their attention to agriculture, an opportunity to make themselves acquainted with it, both practically and scientifically" ("Notices of the Public Press". Hampshire Record Office: 47M66/12/1).

9 The prospectus from Queenwood College described the "Course of Instruction" offered at Queenwood. For each student, the school aimed to "strengthen his body by muscular, and his mind by intellectual exercise . . . By Chemistry, for example, his powers of observation are sharpened, and by Mathematics he is trained to accurate deduction . . . though we store the mind with words and rules, our ultimate aim is to make the Memory serve as a kind of quarry to the Understanding, whence the latter extracts the blocks by which her edifices are raised". The school consisted of two "departments entirely distinct – that of the School, and that of the Farm; – the former devoted to the general Education of Youth, the latter to the Education of Practical Agriculturists". Students received instruction in "Mathematics, Natural Philosophy, Chemistry, Classics, Modern

Languages, History, Geography, Grammar, Geodesy, Mechanical and Landscape Drawing, Painting, and Music". The prospectus notes that lectures were given in "a fine room capable of accommodating upwards of one hundred persons" and that "a large and healthful Play-ground is attached to the College, in one angle of which an extensive Gymnastic Apparatus is erected, where the pupils exercise under proper supervision . . . Thursday afternoon is a fixed holiday, but additional holidays for games of cricket, &c. are not refused, if earnest work during class-time gives the boys a claim to the indulgence" ("Queenwood College, Near Stockbridge, Hants," Hampshire Record Office: 47M66/12/1).

10 The terms of the school included the payment of "Fifty Guineas per Annum" for "Board and Education, the use of the School Library and Philosophical Apparatus" ("Terms, &c. of Queenwood College, Near Stockbridge, Hants". Hampshire Record Office: 47M66/12/1). A guinea was equivalent to about £1.05 or 21 shillings.

11 Clara.

12 Annual costs, in addition to the fifty guineas, included four guineas for "Laundress and Sempstress". The condition of terms notes that "Medical Attendance, Lessons in Music, Musical or Mathematical Instruments, Chemistry Tests, Pocket-money, and Books which a Pupil may require for his exclusive use, or which he may take out of the establishment with him, are extras" ("Terms, &c. of Queenwood College, Near Stockbridge, Hants". Hampshire Record Office: 47M66/12/1).

13 Lumley did not pay Claire her rental income from the opera box.

14 The Queenwood prospectus states that payments are to be made "half-yearly, *in advance*" to Mr. Edmonson.

15 Julia Beste was the German governess of the Pringle children. See also CL'ANA 0043 and CL'ANA 0056.

16 Although the page is torn and unable to be read, it is clear that Wilhelm wrote Mrs. Pringle's name.

17 See CL'ANA 0191.

18 While Stocking states that Schrötter was unable to be identified, he was in fact a renowned Austrian chemist. Priesner records that Anton Konrad Friedrich von Schrötter (1802–75) worked at the University of Vienna and was a professor of Chemistry at the Technische Universität Wien from 1843 onwards. He discovered red phosphorus in 1845, a non-toxic form of phosphorus used in the production of matches. Red phosphorus or "Schrötterscher Phosphor" (Schrötter's Phosphorous) was named for him (Claus Priesner, "Schrötter, Anton". Web. 27 September 2015, http://www.deutsche-biographie.de/sfz14722.html). According to the *Biographical Encyclopedia of Scientists*, (John Daintith, ed., [Philadelphia: Institute of Physics, 1994]), Schrötter lectured in Birmingham in 1849 on his discovery, which Arthur Albright, producer of phosphorus, then incorporated into the various products Albright produced at his factory in Birmingham (p. 801). Schrötter evidently returned to Austria as he later became chair of Chemistry at the university. Writing to Wilhelm on 29 August 1849, Charles stated that Schrötter had gone to England but that he was still receiving his salary. Although the reason for Schrötter's flight was unclear to Charles, he informed his son that Schrötter had been "accused of making and furnishing Gunpowder in the Octr. days". Charles also indicated that he would not "neglect" Schrötter's work when it "appears" (*CC* II: 523). The political climate in Vienna at the time made it difficult for liberal-thinking academics to flourish.

19 German for "book".

20 Schrötter was the author of *Die Chemie nach ihrem gegenwärtigen Zustand* (1847–9), a two-volume book. The title translates as "Chemistry According to its Current State".

21 Wilhelm wrote these German words on the back of the folded aerogramme.

15 • Antonia Clairmont to Claire Clairmont

[11 September 1849]
Weidling 11th

My dearest Claire.

I am now come out ~~here~~ to spend a month here, and to day Charles sent me Willy's last dated the 5th; I have not seen him, but it seems you have not received his last to you where he spoke about Willy's going to Hohenheim[1] – I feel such a desire to write to you, that I must sit down and do so without waiting for Charles' coming out, and hearing what he has done, if he too has written you must excuse the double postage; I am so grieved that you who have been all kindness to us, should have such ill return from one of our family; I can't conceive it from Clara, she, so affectionate and generous a character – I can only think that Knox sees all her letters, and therefore she must style them so stiffly – but yet, I think ~~I~~ fully with Charles we have no right to come upon the Knoxes for Willy's education, nor should I like to be under obligation to them; however I dare say Charles has discussed this chapter fully to you, nor will I speak of Pauline's going there till I have seen Charles, but I will only say, what I wish to say to you; my heart bleeds to think that on our account you are in money difficulties and embarrassments,[2] from which we cannot contribute anything to free you; and to know your health failing without friends or relations near you to take care of you; not that the loss of the S's is much to be regretted, having ever been as you call them your bitterest enemies – but it is the load on your mind, the affection of your spirits, I should wish to remove; to effect this, the best thing would be for you to come and pay us a visit; for you it is not a great affair having no furniture or household goods, as I understand you always live in furnished lodgings – the journey does not cost much; and you might have Andoe for a companion; let Willy go to Hohenheim, and you come to Vienna, and if you like it and you feel well and comfortable, air, climate and our manners agreeing with you, our endeavours to prove our gratitude succeeding, I think that quiet of mind which all these unfortunate occurrences have nearly destroyed might be restored to you; in a pecuniary view it would be most advantageous; about £80 per annum would pay your board and lodging, [except you desire a separate servant][3] in the spring you might come with Sidi and Emmy to Weidling, to enjoy the beautiful tranquility and delicious air of this place; society you can have plenty and I am sure the best houses in the town will be open to receive you; I don't care for it, and never go out nor ever did, my children always sufficing me, but that is no rule for you, besides you will have Charles, who I am sure loves you best upon earth; and do not my dearest Claire let the fear of our climate deci~~e~~de you against it, if my scheme should find favour in your eyes – now if you can make up your mind to it, so it should be done; you must let me know immediately, that I can make arrangements about ~~the~~ a room for you; then you should send off Willy for Hohenheim, that he may not miss the time for he must be there on <u>the 1st of Oct.</u>, then you arrange your affairs and set off with Andoe for Vienna where your arrival will be hailed with pleasure, if Lumley does not pay you, I would take bills from him, if once here, there would be no such pressing necessity for money, life being so much cheaper for you in a family, than now; but for your present difficulties let us enact the fable of the lion and the mouse; you know, I have £100 in the stocks, it is the savings of 15 years and I consider it as Sidi's property; but I will sell out 50 pounds and send you the money if you are in want of it; to be sure the Exchange is still high, and the stocks are not quite up, so that you would lose a good deal upon it, but if you wish it, it shall be done instantly; besides it would be settled again in your receiving money from England, the Exchange would be in your favour again – the other 50 pd. shall be devoted to Willy at Hohenheim if necessary; it will be sufficient for the 1st term and farther on God will help. I hope I am doing right, at least it is my constant endeavour to do for the best; If only you will consent to your coming here, you will then find that you can benefit us without stinting and embarrassing yourself, and I shall find that I can in some measure prove my sense of your great goodness to us all, in trying to make you comfortable and happy; we have now a very nice lodging in the very best part of the town, in a first floor, and if you say, you will come I shall try to get another room added to it, for our apartment would not allow of ading you one, but there is another lodging empty next door to ours and perhaps we can arrange it as I said: but write as soon as possible. Now good bye my ever dear sister and may God lead you to be propitious to my wishes and to decide accordingly; you would also be enabled to observe and judge of Charles' health; and then we should alltogether consult about our future proceedings after Willis' studies are finished, which by letter is almost impossible. Sidi Emmy and Charley send their best love to their kind aunt and beg her to come without fail. Ever yours affecty

A.C.

Liebster Willy.[4] Weidling, 11te Sept: 1849.

Jezt werdet ihr wohl [illeg.]s Brief mit dem Vorschlag daß du nach Hohenheim gehen sollst schon erhalten haben; ich weiß nicht ob du die Briefe an T.C. liesest aber hören wirst du wohl alles was die unsrigen enthalten; ich wünsche sehr daß du nach H. gehst, und habe eben denn T.C. den Vorschlag daß sie zu uns nach Wien kommen sollte, sie würde sich gewiß bei uns gefallen wenn sie nur erst hier wäre. Das Leben würde ihr weit weniger kosten und die Ruhe und Ordnung ihr wohl thun; wünschte sie Gesellschaft zu sehen so könnte sie genug haben; suche ihr nur das alles recht deutlich zu machen, und sie dafür zu stimmen, sollte es ihre trotz unserer Bemühungen ihr den Aufenthalt hier angenehm zu machen nicht zu sagen, so würde sie in einem jährlichen Hiersein gewiß so viel erspart haben als die Reise hin und her kostet; so daß sie also doch keinen Verlust hätte; es würde sie zerstreuen und erhohlen und ihre Gesundheit wiederherstellen; wegen Pauline's Kommen kann ich nichts sagen weil ich den Papa nicht gesehen; wenn ich wüßte daß sie bei K's wohnen kann und Leckzionen geben, so würde ich es recht gerne sehen, weil es natürlich für Cläry sehr angenehm wäre und sie wünscht es auch; aber bis wir nicht wissen wie es mit K's Einkünften steht wird sich Papa schwerlich entschliessen sie gehen zu lassen. Du warst krank armes Kind, und ich war nicht bei dir, schreibe mir nur gleich und adressire Weidling weil ich noch wenigstens 14 Tage hier bleibe; die drei Kleinen haben jezt alle gefleckt d. h. they had the measles; ich glaube du hattest sie nicht nimm dich also in Acht – Emmy machte heuer die Bekanntschaft mit der Spieß Sophie von St. Pölten, sie ist mit Zimmers verwandt und war auf Besuch hier; sie sprachen sehr viel von dir; Poßl läßt dich grüßen in Briefen, gesehen habe ich ihn nicht; Emmerich Zimmer ist jetzt Pionier Kadett in Tulln – Onkel E. war gefangen in ~~Petr~~ Großwardein, jezt ist er ~~aber~~ zwar frei aber noch nicht zurück sondern von Pest aus hat er uns geschrieben. H. M. L. Blagoer ich pensionirt – sein Bruder geht wieder nach Siebenbürgen, die Frau mit den Kindern bleibt wieder wie vorher hier – Raffy ist zu klein zum Militär, ist folglich berechtigt zu haus zu bleiben und sich seinen Hang zur dramatischen Kunst zu überlassen – der Faullenzen – Gestern waren wir auf dem Harschberg – es ist ganz unbewohnt, das Gebäude verfällt ganz; man sagt der Besitzer ein [illeg.]tetiks sei in Ungarn gefallen. Die Besitzung wird wahrscheinlich heuer und aufs Frühjahr in die Auction kommen und verkauft, ich höre daß es ohne der Mühle auf 9000 fl geschätzt ist. Wenn es 2 Jahre später wäre, könnten wir daran denken, so nahe bei Wien und so viel Grund, es ließe sich schon [illeg.] Versuch machen; ich mache jezt verschiedene Veränderungen im Haus; im Kutscherzimmer einen Rauchfang damit es die Türkinn bewohnen kann Dann werden die Salon[illeg.] in die Stadt geführt und das Billiard hinüber gestellt, damit künftigen Sommer die oberen Wohnung vermiethet werden kann leztlich habe ich dem Hauer aufgesagt, und seine Wohnung wird hergerichtet und dann wird sie der Chirurg Ofner beziehen, so wird dann das Haus ein Erbringung von 380 f jährlh abwerfen und wir doch die große Wohnung mit 10 Zimmer für uns behalten. Ich plaudere aber in den Tag hinein und hätte viel wichtigere Dinge zu sagen; nämlich über deine vorgeschlagene Reise nach H. wenn ~~wir~~ch nicht so viel Vertrauen hätte~~n~~ in dich so würde ich diesen Schritt nicht vorgeschlagen haben ich hoffe aber mein lieber Sohn wird meine Erwartungen nicht täuschen und obwohl du dort ganz dir selbst ~~vor Augen~~ überlassen immer Gott und deine Pflichten vor Augen haben – wenn ich dir sage liebster Willy daß ich wenn nöthig für deinen Studien die 500 f von den gewißen 5 pro ctigen nehme die ich für keinen andern Zweck in der Welt angegriffen hätte, so hast du dadurch den besten Beweis wie sehr mir deine Zukunft am Herzen liegt, auch bin ich so überzeugt daß du das sauer erworbene nicht vergeuden wirst, daß du so sparsam bist wie ich selbst; und hoffe auch mit deiner Hülfe, wenn wir einmal recht thätig sind zusammen, die jezt nett [illeg.] Summe wieder zu erstatten; und daß jedenfalls die Sidi an dir einen Bruder hat von Vater- und Mutterstelle vertreten; da ich Papas lezten Brief nicht gesehen habe so weiß ich nicht was er geschrieben hat. nun schreibe augenblicklich was geschieht – ob die Tante sich entschließt zu kommen und ich die 500 fl.~~wegen~~ die ich ihr angetragen schicken soll, oder ob ~~du mei~~ sie es vorzieht zu bleiben und du nach Hohenheim gehst; wenn die Tante dir in diesem Falle nur das Reisegeld geben kann, dasandere wirst du vermittelst Wechsel in

Stuttgart finden, dein Einpacken und Reisebedürffnisse bleibt dir selbst überlassen, aber da ist es nicht aus mit dir, wie man hier sagt – jezt lebe wohl liebstes Kind, viele Küsse und Grüße. Charley und Emmy sind enorm gewachsen; leztere ist ein hübsches schlankes Mädchen auf den H[illeg.] Schlag. sie ist so groß wie ich. Gustl Nell ist bei Görgen, aber ich glaube es ist eine [illeg.] um vom Militär frei zu werden. Papa lezter Brief wo er wegen G. schrieb ging am 27ten v. m. ab, ihr hättet ihn am 5t schon haben sollen

Deine Dich innigst liebende Mutter

A.C.

I hope to God my dear Claire you will come to Vienna so that nobody may take Willy's going to H. as a sign of disagreement between us.[5]

English Translation (German transciption and English translation provided by Ann Sherwin):

Dearest Willy,

By now you will probably have received [illeg.]'s letter with the suggestion that you should go to Hohenheim; I don't know if you read the letters to T. C.[6] but you will probably hear everything that ours contain; I very much wish for you to go to H.[7] and have just suggested to T. C. that she should come to us in Vienna, she would surely like it here with us, once she gets here. It would cost her much less to live, and the tranquility and order would be good for her; if she wished company, she could have enough. Just try to make all this clear to her and get her to agree to it. If she does not approve, despite our efforts to make her stay here pleasant, then in an annual stay she would certainly have saved as much as the cost of the round trip, so that she at least wouldn't lose anything; it would divert and refresh her and restore her health; as for Pauline's coming, I can't say anything because I have not seen Papa; if I knew that she could stay at K's and give lessons, then I would be very much in favor, because it would naturally be very nice for Cläry, and she also desires it; but as long as we don't know what K's income situation is, Papa will hardly decide to let her go.

You were sick, poor child, and I was not with you. Just write to me right away and address it to Weidling, because I will be staying here at least another 14 days; the three little ones are all spotted now, i.e. they had the measles; I don't think you have had it, so be careful. – This year Emmy became acquainted with Sophie Spiess from St. Pölten;[8] she is related to Zimmers and was here for a visit; they spoke of you a great deal; Possl sends you greetings in letters; I didn't see him; Emmerich Zimmer is now a pioneer cadet in Tulln, Uncle E. was taken prisoner in ~~Petr~~ Großwardein;[9] ~~but~~ he is free now but not back yet; he wrote to us from Pest. H. M. L. Blagoer is retired – his brother is returning to Siebenbürgen,[10] the wife and children are staying here as before. Raffy is too small for the military and is therefore entitled to stay home and yield to his penchant for the dramatic art – of loafing. – Yesterday we were at the Harschberg – it is totally unoccupied; the building is completely in ruins; they say the owner, a [illeg.], was killed in action in Hungary. The estate will probably come up for auction and be sold this year and in the spring. I hear that it is appraised at 9000 gulden without the mill. If it were 2 years later, we could think about it, so close to Vienna and so much land, It would be worth a try. I am now making several changes in the house; in the coachman's room a chimney, so that the Turkish woman can live there. Then the parlor [illeg.] are being taken into the city and the billiard table moved over, so that in future summers the upstairs apartment can be rented out; finally, I gave Hauer his notice, and his apartment will be renovated, and then the surgeon Ofner will move into it.[11] So then the house will yield an income of 380 gulden annually, and we will still keep the large apartment with 10 rooms for ourselves. But here I am rambling away, and I have much more important things to say – namely, about your proposed trip to H. If I didn't have so much confidence in you, I would not have suggested this move. But I hope my dear son will not prove my expectations wrong; and although you will be left entirely on your own there, that you will always keep your eyes on God and your duties. – When I tell you, dearest Willy, that if necessary I am taking the 500 gulden for your studies out of the certain 5%, which I would not have touched for any other purpose in the world, then you have the best proof of how very much I care about your future; I am also confident that you will not waste my hard-won funds, that you are just as thrifty as I am; and I also hope that with your help, when we are actually working together some day, that to repay the net [illeg.] sum; and that in any case Sidi will have in you a brother in father's and mother's place; since I have not seen Papa's last letter, I don't know what he wrote. Now write immediately what will happen – whether Aunt decides to come and whether I should send her the 500 gulden ~~for~~ that I offered her, or whether ~~you thi~~ she prefers to stay and you are going to Hohenheim; if Aunt can just give you money for the fare in the latter case, you will find the rest in Stuttgart through currency exchange; packing and travel needs are left up to you, but it isn't all over for you, as they say here. – Now, farewell, dearest child. Many kisses and greetings. Charley and Emmy have grown immensely. The latter is a pretty, slender girl at the [illeg.] Schlag.[12] She is as tall as I am. Gustl Nell is at Görgen's,[13] but I believe it is a[illeg.] to get out of military service. Papa's last letter, in which he wrote about G., went out on the 27th of last month. You should already have received it on the 5th

Your loving mother
A. C.

Address: Aerogramme: Miss Claire Clairmont./ Post office./
Brighton./England.
Postmark: WIEN/ 13 SEP:/

Unpublished. Text: M.S., Pf. Coll., CL'ANA 0400

1 In his letter to Claire of 12 November 1849, Charles proposed that Wilhelm attend the Land- und Forstwirtschaftliche Academie Hohenheim in Hohenheim, Germany. Charles expected Wilhelm to begin in March 1850. The former agricultural academy is part of the Universität Hohenheim today. The university is located in Stuttgart, Germany, and enrolls over 9,000 students. According to information provided by the University, in 1847 the academy enrolled about 100 students who studied subjects connected to agricultural concerns under seven professors and nine assistants: forestry, bee-keeping, veterinary science, pomiculture and vegetable gardening. Classes were also offered in accounting, law, and agricultural civil engineering. Additionally, students received instruction in the natural sciences, mathematics, and physics ("University of Hohenheim". Web. 11 March 2015. https://www.uni-hohenheim.de/60695?&L=1#jfmulticontent_c148405–3). Charles noted that Württemberg (the state in which Hohenheim was located; today the region is part of the state of Baden-Württemberg) was politically peaceful in 1849 and that he saw no danger in Wilhelm's attending college in the area (*CC* II: 525). In the same letter, Antonia referenced Wilhelm's remark about Claire's inability to support him in the future. Not wishing for Wilhelm to be a burden to Claire, Antonia noted that they had "no choice" but to have him relocate to Hohenheim (p. 528).

2 Claire was continually in financial difficulty. Her situation would improve, however, in 1844, after the death of Sir Timothy Shelley when she would come into her legacy (see CL'ANA 0404).

3 Antonia enclosed these words in square brackets.

4 Antonia included this letter to Wilhelm together with her letter to Claire.

5 Antonia wrote the final sentence on the folded section of the aerogramme, above the address.

6 German for "Tante Claire" (Aunt Claire).

7 Hohenheim.

8 Spies, Zimmer, Uncle E., H. M. L. Blagoer, and Raffy are all unidentified. St. Pölten (Sankt Pölten) is about 66 kilometers west of Vienna.

9 Tulln an der Donau is a town in Austria, about 44 kilometers north-west of Vienna. Großwardein is the German name for Oradea, a city in Romania today.

10 German for Transylvania, in Romania.

11 Hauer and Ofner were Antonia's tenants.

12 The context does not allow for an adequate translation.

13 Unidentified.

16 • Wilhelm Gaulis Clairmont to Charles Gaulis Clairmont and Antonia Clairmont

73. St. John's Wood Terrace, Avenue Road, London. November 2nd 1849.

Dearest parents. – We had at last (28th Oct) your long expected letter, deciding about what I was to do for this winter, but I am very much astonished to find, that you make no mention whatever of A.C.'s letters, in which I think she answered to you her intention of resigning every responsibility with regard to myself. You then say that both your minds were made up with regard to the pursuit of my career that you wished me to spend this winter if possible in London to perfect myself in the language and in those sciences, that are likely to be of use to me in afterlife, and that I am to go to Hohenh[1]. by next spring. I will then speak about my stay in London, ~~being~~ this being the point first to be settled, and leave the Agriculture and H. plan for the latter part of my letter.

After the explanations that have passed between A.C. and you and me and with regard to ~~A~~ the bad state of A.C.'s finances and other affairs sufficiently discussed, I hardly think it necessary to enter upon a new declaration, for you will I suppose be able to understand the whole state of things without it. but let me at once tell you, that Mr. Knox has offered me to come and live with them in their house, under the condition that the plan should meet with your approbation and I therefor now write to obtain it from you. It is difficult for me to say anything on that point, because your judgment alone can decide, but if the circumstance of my being here, having seen him and spoken with him entitle me to speak about it, I certainly should beg you to give your consent to the plan.[2] Circumstances have altered, or a different knowledge of circumstances has reached us since you last wrote; We know that K. is a man of resourses, for Clara tells me that she regularly every first of the month takes charge of his 60£; that he is employed on the Times there is no doubt from a great variety of circumstances; he does come forward from his own accord, and make the offer in the most friendly and delicate way, and as for the evil sources from which he draws his ~~resources~~ money this is only a supposition and not sufficiently ascertained to be an obstacle. I did not entertain for a moment the idea, that you should apply to him for assistance, but I do not on the other hand see any reason, why you should object to my accepting anything from him since he by marrying Clara has not only made himself a member of our family but has also thereby contributed to put me into the disagreable position I am in at present. So if you have no objection to the execution of this plan, I shall move there as soon as we obtain your consent, which I hope you will transmit as quickly as possible that I may get the sooner into a settled state.

I now come to an other point of your letter viz. my final destination. I hardly know how to thank you dearest papa, for the kind, generous and sacrifizing tone, in which you speak about it in your last letter. and indeed I think you are too generous in thinking of making debts on the Weidling house for only one single member of our family, a sacrifice which I am sure, I should feel very uncomfortable in accepting with no consolation but the hope of its perhaps at one time turning to the benefit and profit of you all. You say if I think a countrylife and agriculture would suit my taste, and I see my way in it, these are two important points gained, and if I give you positive assurance of it, you will immediately take the necessary steps. I think I need not hesitate in saying that an agricultural life in the country would suit my taste, for although A.C. thinks that after the refined state of England, I shall not be pleased with the raw and uneducated society of an Hungarian or Austrian village, where you intend to place me, still I think that my ideas of happiness in the country are such, as not to suffer from this obstacle, ~~and~~ but in the contrary do consider it as certain, as a thing under such circumstances can be, for I think no one can at the time he chooses a profession for himself be quite positively assured that it will be agreable to him all his lifetime but he must choose what seems most in accord both with his inclinations and faculties at the time he makes his choice. As for the seeing my way I cannot be quite so decided, as in the first. for I fear it requires great capital to begin with, and besides it depends so much on the country in which I am to settle. Mr Coulson,[3] whom you will perhaps still remember said the other day that agriculture, was in all countries especially in Europe a profession the least remunerative of all; certainly there are many things to be said in reply to that;: that one has not so many wants, expenses, etz. but still it would be a very pitiable thing if we afterwards found unforeseen obstacles start up, and were obliged to live on in a kind of struggling existence. But put this aside, the great question before we can answer the above is: in what country are we all to settle? In Austria I think it would be very dangerous, at all events there are two great reasons which ought to make us consider the thing well, before we decide upon it. 1st all the physicians here seem to think that I possibly may escape the effects of the rigorous climate, because as they say no one can tell before hand the resources of nature in the individual constitution; but all seem to agree that it is very probable or at least possible that I should suffer from it; and that at all events every body with such a delicacy in throat or chest and such a tendency to inflammation or any other disorder usually if circumstances at all enable him to do so, seak a moderate climate. 2ndly It is here the general and public opinion, that it would be down right folly to settle in Austria, in a country where such strong and sudden changes must bring on reactions for many years yet to come, where intestine wars have been raging in so fearful a way, and the violence and passion of parties is yet hardly checked by the rigidity of Martial law; a country which for the last 30 years of peace has been sinking always more and more into debt, and which - from its late extraordinary war expenses and the terrible confusion of its finances will by a very heavy and severe taxation, which has partly begun already, have to bear for many years the consequences of this disastrous state of things; a country as yet one might say with out constitution or laws, just stirred up to a state of fermentation and brought to a crisis, of which we have no guarantee whatever, ~~of~~ how it will end, which Party will finally triumph or the time and manner in which it is likely to return to a settled and secure state not to speak of all the laws concerning landed property the right of possession etz. wich we do not know as yet, but which naturally would affect us in a direct way. – At all events I think it would be difficult to say anything certain before ~~and~~ the state of siege is done away with, and we see how the new diet will act, and then even that will be but a very weak guarantee for the future. – Considering all that, it seems to me so very much more desirable that I should settle in one of the English colonies, rising countries, where land is bountiful, competition not so strong, and a man with thorough knowledge of his business, activity perseverance and honesty besides, almost sure to make his fortune. In Austria migrations certainly are not so frequent, and therefor the idea is apt to appear startling or visionary for the beginning, but here where there are annually as many as 60–70 000 souls emigrating one knows perfectly well that it is a very good plan, and frequently of the highest profit to the people engaged. A.C. Knox and Mr. Coulson have personal acquaintances who went out with only £300 and made a splendid fortune. A Mr Charles Robinson[4] friend of Mrs Shelley's spent up to his thirtieth year the whole of his little fortune in London without being able to succeed; he went out with no more than £5 in his pocket, and returned after 8 years stay a wealthy man. He ~~was~~ now spent two years here to perfect himself in farming and ~~is going~~ went out again this October. A.C. dined with him at the S.'s shortly before I came over. he told her that the climate was so beautiful, that he slept almost all the nights in the open air under a tree and many other nice things. One more case let me state. A Mr Beary, a common Yorkshire farmer who married Miss[5] a cousin of Mrs Shelley's also emigrated and I understand without a farthing to help him self with.[6] He has now so far ammeliorated his condition that he possesses an income of no less than £10.000 a year and maintains by pensions several of his poor relations whom he had left in England when compared to himself rich. He has now retired to Sydney but farmes all his estates by stewards and bailiffs; and if I do go out I naturally should have an introduction to him and all others to ~~that~~ whom good A.C. could by her numerous friends and connections get me one. for Mr. Coulson also told me of a young lawyer and Mr Jones[7] of a young surgeon whom they had (according to English customs) to educate in their profession and both although decided blockheads and without the least success in England made quite a handsome career there. At all events [~~illeg.~~] there is as much hope or chance of my succeeding there as in Austria (I think in private more) not taking into consideration the climate, which is as people assure me, fast adapted for and sought by people with complaints like mine. Mr Taylor a cousin of Col Pringle's[8] a gentleman of the very highest connections here is going out this winter because he suffers from Bronchiatis and Col. Pringle thinks of perhaps [~~illeg.~~] following him there with his family this would then be a most excellent thing because I should have someone where to go to. How ever I will not overload you in that way, but let us come to a conclusion at last. I am fully aware that you can not immediately give your approval to so important a plan as this and I think you will grant that also the Austrian plan has its difficulties; so on the whole it's rather a difficult thing to settle, but let us consider it as fixed for the present that I am to pursue the agricultural career and that I am to go to Ho~~n~~henheim by next April, for the rest we can, I trust, settle during the two years of my apprenticeship. What the doctor thinks about the Wurtemberg winters you will see, and wether this be an impediment I leave to you to decide. – With regard to A.C.'s assistance she repeats, that she always will continue in her friendly feeling towards us all, ~~but~~ and will do every thing she can to assist and help you, but at the same time she not only disapproves of the Austr. and even the Wurtemberg plan, but also the unsettled and uncertain state of her moneymatters absolutely keeps her from making any precise promise, without incurring the danger of being obliged to cause afterwards some distressing disappointment which would be exceedingly painful to her.

Now then for this most tedious subject, my health. A very clever physician here, who has now been watching me for a week gives upon my asking him to give me an idea, of what I am to tell you the following written communication, which I would send you if it was not for the postage: "My dear Sir. Stated briefly this is your case. The larynx is the seat of a chronic inflammation Although there is now very little ~~danger~~ inconvenience, yet it is necessary that you should be careful for a long time to come. The frequent occurrence of this condition is sometimes the prerunner of disease of the lungs especially when any disposition exists. You ask me wether I think the climate of Wurtemberg would suit you. As a general remark the warmer and more genial the climate, the better for you; and I certainly should fear in your case the rigour of the Wurtemberg winters.[9] You have now no lung disease, but bear well in mind how rapidly you have been growing lately, that a sister died of consumption,[10] and that your larynx seems prone to become affected. It is very important that you should be favourably circumstanced for the coming 3 or 4 years at least, as regards climate. ~~at least~~ I dont think there is much cause for apprehension from the neck – tumour, although it needs watching. As the state of your health must influence your arrangements for the future, I have then frankly and briefly given you my opinion". this is exactly the same opinion that Lawrence at Brighton,[11] (nephew of the famous Lawrence[12] that you knew) and Turley[13] gave who is a firstrate London practitioner, which he was obliged on account of his health, and we thus find 2 very clever men coincide in one view of my case. I naturally can not say anything of my own, but must content myself with what they tell me; all I know is, that since I have been in England this constant expectoration that I used to have, has to a great degree left me as likewise the occasional dryness and [~~illeg.~~] irritation in the throat and want of breath returning only at times, and never so violently as in Vienna on the other hand I think that my voice has grown worse for I recollect that shortly before I left (September in Trudau) I could and did sing and call for 3 hours without feeling any consequences, whereas now I get hoarse from reading for half an hour aloude. I dont know what to say after this about Hohenheim will you, or will you not approve of it; at all events it would be of no use spending the summer there, if my studies are to be interrupted again for the winter; otherwise I think the plan would be very good. I should like it very well and it only depends upon wether you would like to risk it or not. I dont see any means of managing my agricultural education in England. –

What you said dearest papa about employing my time now in London shall not be forgot, if possible I shall frequent the lectures upon Chymistry and Geology and others that might be of use to me; in the same way I shall read as much as possible; Davy's Chymistry on Agriculture[14] is very dear it costs even second hand 15 s. I am now daily copying and did so all the summer; and A.C. tells me to my greatest pleasure that I have improved in Ortheography. With regard to Schrotter's Chymistry[15] I should very much like to have that Heft,[16] but I cannot tell you this time wether it is the right one - because my books are
packed at the bottom of my trunk and I have no time to unpack now – Goodbye then dearest parents. do at all events write soon about K. the rest may be settled afterwards. your affectionate son WGC

I have arranged this letter abominably I am in such a hurry I cant alter it

Address: Aerogramme: Via Ostend./Clairmont Esqr./
Freyung N° 238. 1 Stock 2t Stiege/ Stadt./Vienna/Austria.
Postmark: WIEN

Unpublished. Text: M.S., Pf. Coll., CL'ANA 0055

---

1 Charles told Claire that Antonia had sent Wilhelm a prospectus for the school in Hohenheim and that the school "bears a high character" (*CC* II: 521). He calculated too that the school would prove less expensive than an English college and that it would provide Wilhelm with an introduction to the "systematic cultivation of extensive forest lands," a branch of education not taught in England and one with which a young Austrian man would surely need to be familiar, in Charles's opinion, in order to farm in his native country. According to the institution's prospectus, education at Hohenheim cost £30 for the first year of studies and £20 for the second year. Board and lodging cost £16 a year with an additional £2 for laundry, use of the library, and fees for servants. Charles estimated the cost to be around £70 a year and about £20 less than the fees at Queenwood (p. 521).

2 On 29 August 1849, Charles expressed concern for Claire's ongoing discord with Clara. Regarding Wilhelm, Charles told Claire that Wilhelm was "very much attached" to Clara and that he did not want to prohibit Wilhelm from communicating with his sister (*CC* II: 520–2). On 12 November 1849, Charles informed Claire that he had received a letter from Wilhelm, requesting consent to stay with the Knoxes until his departure for Germany. Charles indicated to Claire that he had given Wilhelm his consent, particularly as Claire did not raise any objection to such a stay (*CC* II: 525) but he reiterated that Wilhelm needed to depart around 20 March 1850 for Hohenheim.

3 Walter Coulson (1795–1860) was a barrister as well as editor for *The Traveller*, an evening newspaper which later became known as *The Globe and Traveller*. During his tenure as editor, the paper became more radical than it had been. He was also a parliamentary reporter for the *Morning Chronicle* and provided a home for John Black (see CL'ANA 0058) on Black's retirement from the paper in 1843. On 19 March 1849, Mary Shelley promoted the idea of a relationship between Claire and Coulson, noting that Coulson would make a "good husband" and stating that she wished "with my whole heart he were yours" (*LMWS* III: 308). On 11 April 1849, Claire told Mary Shelley that "dear" Coulson came to visit her and that she was pleased to see him (*CC* II: 496). Mary Shelley responded by saying, "I am very glad that you had this pleasure & that a lump of sugar tumbled into your cup – I hope the relish of the sweetness still continues – & that another lump will come soon" (*LMWS* III: 365). The relationship did not, however, prosper.

4 Charles Robinson was the youngest brother of Isabel Robinson, Mary Shelley's friend. In 1839, Charles left for Australia to make his fortune. Betty Bennett records that Robinson lived in New Zealand, where he was a police magistrate and a farmer until 1858 when he returned permanently to Europe (*LMWS* III: 4).

5 There is a space in the letter with no name included.

6 Elizabeth Wollstonecraft Berry was Mary Shelley's cousin. She was the daughter of Edward Wollstonecraft, the brother of Mary Wollstonecraft. She married Alexander Berry and they immigrated to Australia in 1819. Betty Bennett records that, by the time of his death in 1873, Alexander Berry owned an estate in Australia of 65,000 acres (*LMWS* II: 321). On 3 August 1839, Mary Shelley wrote to Elizabeth Berry to tell her that Charles Robinson would be contacting her on his arrival in Australia and that he had a letter of recommendation from their aunt, Everina Wollstonecraft (1765–1843). See *LMWS* II: 321.

7 Unidentified. Possibly Colonel Jones, a friend of Mrs. Godwin's and Claire's. Writing from Florence on 2 June 1835, Claire told Mary Shelley that Colonel Jones had not received "the order". Stocking records that Mrs. Godwin had been informed in March by Colonel Jones that he would not be able to send anything to Italy at that time but that he would be happy, at another time, to take something to Claire (*CC* II: 323, 325).

8 See CL'ANA 0191.

9 See Antonia's summary of Dr. Böhm's opinion in CL'ANA 0191.

10 Hermine Clairmont died in 1847.

11 In *A Peep Into the Past: Brighton in the Olden Times*, John Bishop records: "Out of the 76 'physicians,' &c., practicing in Brighton in 1850, – not of few of whom were eminently skilful in their profession, as the Messrs. Lawrence (father and son) . . ." (Brighton: J.G. Bishop, 1892), p. 373.

12 The London Medical Directory for 1845 lists William Lawrence, a surgeon who practiced at St. Bartholomew's Hospital and the London Fever Hospital. He also worked at the London Ophthalmic Hospital (C. Mitchell, London, 1845, The Hathi Trust Digital Library). Mary Shelley was a friend of Lawrence and Marilyn Butler speculates that Lawrence's scientific theories influenced Mary Shelley's *Frankenstein* ("*Frankenstein* and Radical Science" in *Frankenstein: The 1818 Text* ed. J. Paul Hunter [Norton: New York, 1996]). Miranda Seymour identifies Lawrence as the doctor Godwin consulted in 1812 about Mary Shelley's health: ". . . he sought a second opinion on his daughter from a brilliant young doctor called William Lawrence, then at the start of his medical career" (*Mary Shelley*, p. 71).

13 Edward Astbury Turley was a London surgeon who published *First Lines of Education: a Course of Four Lectures delivered to the Members of the Literary and Scientific Institution, Worcester* in 1839. John Forbes records that Turley was a phrenologist (*The British and Foreign Medical Review*, [John Churchill: London, 1840], pp. 243–4).

14 Sir Humphrey Davy's *Elements of Agricultural Chemistry in a Course of Lectures* was published in 1813.

15 See CL'ANA 0056.

16 German for "book".

17 • Wilhelm Gaulis Clairmont to Charles Gaulis Clairmont and Antonia Clairmont

London 21st Novemb. 1849.

Excuse the quantity of little scraps, but I was afraid of exceeding the quarter of an ounce and thereby causing you double paying.

Address WGC to the care of Mrs Knox.

9. Hyde Park, Gate South
Kensington London

My dearest parents.

I ~~have~~ received yours of the 7th Nov. about a week ago, but delayed answering, till I might have something decisive and certain to say. I will then at once tell you, that, as Clara and K. are going to move to Kensington[1] where they will enter their new house probably about the end of this week, I have not yet joined them, as their first house was not sufficiently furnished; but if every thing goes as we expect, I shall join them next week. A.C. also said she would move over to Kensington so that I might the oftener have the pleasure of seeing her; and I hope everything is quite right with regard to that affair. I next come to speak about ~~my~~ the employment of the ~~my my~~ time I have yet to spend in England; and I hope that the plans and arrangements we have made in that respect will meet with your full approbation. I shall read and translate into English as much as I possibly can, and have no doubt, that with such advisors I have, they choice of my lecture, will be such as will satisfy you, both with regard to the style and the subject. Besides this I intend reading Euclide[2] as far as I can get in it, and going through once more two German works I have brought with me one scientific "[illeg.] Mathematik, the other what they call [illeg.] lectures on "Physik"[3] in English I think natural Philosophy –

All these studies I naturally might carry on without any additional expence for masters etz. but the chief delight of my plans for the present would be the frequen~~tation~~ing of a german colle~~d~~ge for Chemistry in Oxfordstreet, where analytical chemistry is taught practically. My greatest wish is to frequent this institution for 3 months 3 times a week ~~wh~~ and if I attended regularly and with diligence and fervour I might be a ready [~~illeg.~~] enough [~~illeg.~~] chemist for [~~illeg.~~] common analysis. This once obtained would not only advance me one great (and in fact the first) step towards my final destination but it also would give me such manual dexterity, and practical, experimental knowledge in Chemistry,[4] as would enable me to pursue this study alone with the greatest advantage or at any public laboratory like Hohenheim at all events with definitely greater advantage, than without it; for in such laboratories where every [~~illeg.~~] experiment is carried on in common or public, the professor will always prefer to avail him self of the help of those who show the most scientific and practical ability and then this preference ~~in itself~~ and through it ~~your~~ one's previous knowledge becomes a new source of learning in the same way as interests laid to the capital bring again interests – However I think that, besides learning something by this course, which I perhaps other wise will not learn at all, at [illeg.], and learning with so much more advantage what I should learn ~~advantage~~ mediocriter – but middlingly without it, it would also enable me to preserve so much of my time for either other theoretical studies or practical observations, for without ~~without~~ a good preparation this science both from its high importance and its enormous (Umfang scope)[5] would claim the most of my time I do not think that there can be any doubt of the excellent services this course would be of to me nay I think these to be so highly beneficial as to form an easy balance against the comparatively well surmountable obstacles, which [~~illeg.~~] as you may imagine consist in the expenses; the fee is £7 add to this £2–10 for an apparatus and 10s. for the purchase of a book necessary and an other fee for "the keys" (I suspect nothing but a kind of Trinkgeld[6]) and the whole ammounts to £10 about. This to be sure appears an extravagant sum for Vienna and even for England it is very much, but then it must be recollected what enormous advantages I should reap from it, and that a huge box of apparatus and the book would be mine and espe~~e~~cially the first necessary friends for my life. – When I told Clara of the affair she said to me that she had 400fl. in Vienna and that she had written to you already several times about it, thinking that [~~illeg.~~] it would be of very great use to me, in doing the best for my education, till I went to Hohenh. Clara said she never knew of any so very strict demarcation of the little savings between us brothers and sisters, and that she and Paulin had always assisted each other, when the one had money and the other wa{tear} need, and that she would have been very glad under any circumstances to do something for me, but that now that she was married and settled, she would feel the greatest pleasure in aiding me in some way, especially as the advantage I could reap from the money was so much greater than it would be to her for she does not want it at all, and as she would be quite ready to accept the obligation from me if we were in the contrary circumstances. I might say I dont think there is any objection to an offer of that kind from a sister and hope you will agree with me on that point; the only question is wether you are not in need of the money yourself, or perhaps counted on it for Hoh. as this will be such a tremendous expense. In that case it is selfevident that the whole falls to the ground; but if that be not the case, and you approve both of the Chemistry plan and the acceptation of the offer Clara told me beg you to transmit £ 15. as something must be allowed for the loss of exchange and the selling out for Clara tells me that it was in Metallics[7] which are in <u>London</u> by today's paper 87½ so they are perhaps 90 in Vienna. but this of course could only be thought of under the above mentioned condition. The transmission might be managed by Reuter, he lives 4 Moorgate Chambers City,[8] where I could easily fetch the money from, for I have been there once already.

I have been twice at the laboratory to see it and learn the particulars of it. The head director is Dr. Hofmann a Professor from a German University and a German.[9] That of course would be of great consequence for me not only for the sake of explanation and the translation of the scientific language, technical terms, names of all the acides etz – but also do I think that he would take more interest in me; I have not yet seen him however. the circumstance of his being a German induced me to ask the assistant who showed me the whole, wether[10] they had not had a visit from [illeg.]. Schrötter this summer.[11] Upon my mentioning his name he doubled his politeness, showed and explained me everything, and told me that Schrötter had been [~~illeg.~~]3 months here and was a friend of Hofmann's and had made several most interesting experiments of his own discovery in their laboratory – Now pray let me beg you ~~to~~ if you intend to send the money, to send it as soon as possible, because the sooner it comes, the more I can profit with not more expence – Many, many thanks dearest parents for all ~~the~~ your kindness and patience in all the troubles I cause you, but I hope that it will come to a good end. your most affectionate & grateful son

WGC

Address: Aerogramme: via Ostend./C.G. Clarimont, Esqr./Stadt Freyung № 238/2te Stiege 1^{t} Stock./ Vienna./Austria
Front postmark: [illeg.]/21NO21/1849
Rear postmark: WIEN

Unpublished. Text: M.S., Pf. Coll., CL'ANA 0054

1 Kensington is about three kilometers south-east of the center of London.

2 Euclid was a Greek mathematician who wrote the *Elements*, a thirteen-volume work about geometry and other mathematical branches. Euclid lived in Alexandria, Egypt, around 300 BCE.

3 German for "Physics".

4 In March 1850, Claire expressed delight at Wilhelm's progress in chemistry, the most "useful" subject besides engineering, in her opinion (*CC* II: 530).

5 The word "scope" is written above the German word, "Umfang," which is a direct translation of "scope".

6 German for "tip".

7 Carl-Ludwig Holtfrerich records that, in the earliest years of the nineteenth century, Austria found itself in a position to be unable to repay its debts as a result of its ongoing war with France. In 1802 or 1803, Austria converted its unpaid bonds into new ones called Bethmann bonds. However, once Austria began paying its interest in paper money, investors had little desire for the bonds: "An attempt at a solution was the issue of what were called 'Métalliques' in 1816. These were bonds on which the interest was paid in coins" (*Frankfurt as a Financial Center*. [Munich: Beck, 1999], pp. 109–11)

8 The word is unclear – it could either be Reuter or Benter. The *London Standard* of 30 April 1863 noted the receipt of a telegram by "Mr. Benter's office" and the *London Daily News* of 27 February 1865 recorded the receipt of a telegram by "Reuter's Telegram Company". Charles told Claire on 10–11 August 1848 that "Reuter was no longer in London" (*CC* II: 492). Stocking was unable to identify Reuter but believed he might have been a banker, given the context of Claire's letter.

9 Imperial College London provides the following information: The Royal College of Chemistry was founded in 1845 by John Lloyd Bullock and John Gardner. August Wilhelm von Hofmann was appointed the college's first professor. The college was located in Oxford Street. After its merger with the Royal School of Mines in 1853, the college moved in 1872 to South Kensington ("Imperial College London". Web. 12 March 2015. http://www.imperial.ac.uk/centenary/timeline/1845.shtml). Von Hofmann's primary area of research was on aniline, an organic base used in the production of explosives. He also discovered formaldehyde (The Editors of Encyclopaedia Britannica. "August Wilhelm von Hofmann. *Encyclopedia Britannica Online*. Encyclopedia Britannica Inc. n.d. Web. 9 May 2016. http://www.britannica.com/biography/August-Wilhelm-von-Hofmann).

10 Wilhelm added the letter "h" above the letter "w".

11 The initial is illegible. See CL'ANA 0056.

18 • Wilhelm Gaulis Clairmont to Charles Gaulis Clairmont and Antonia Clairmont

Queenwood, Stockbridge, Hants.[1] _____ Queenwood, 25th Decemb. 1849.____

My dearest parents.[2] By the time this letter reaches you, all your anxiety and doubts with regard to the money affair will no doubt be perfectly removed through Clara's letter, which also will explain my continued silence, for the Queenwood plan not being settled till the 1~~9~~5th inst., I waited till then in order to kill the two birds with one stone, but my departure for the college being fixed for the 19th inst; the whole of my time, I mean of these four intervening days, was taken up by making a few necessary preparations for the winter, and on my taking leave from the Knoxes 19th, we settled, in order to save you postage, that Clara should write immediately, and I wait another week or fortnight, in order to be able then to give you a more satisfactory account of my new position. Urged by a second letter from you which the K.s sent me the 23rd I now sit down to write a very long letter, but before I begin about Queenwood I will first settle the businesspart. The money I received at Reuter's[3] office all save £42. taking at the same time a trip to that part of London lying on the eastside of the bank, seeing the docks, all the low sailor streets with plenty of drunken men, and groups of Germans standing about and talking, seeing the tunnel, making a purchase of two tin medails under the waters of the Thames for 8d returning through a number of filthy coalwarfs [~~illeg.~~] by Bermondsey on the Surryside.[4] – The money I gave to Clara, and she said to me, that she intended ~~to~~ or rather did actually give it me all. On seeing the letter to Hofmann I was of course quite charmed and thanked you many times in my heart, for the kindness with which you thought of every thing, and ~~papa's~~ the trouble it must have given dear papa to walk out as far as the Winden[5] and all that, and I proposed to Knox that I would arrange the laboratory affair immediately; he however proposed the plan, that the 42£ should be kept for Hohenheim, and that I should spend the remaining 3 months on some farm or agricultural college at their expence, which would differ but slightly from the costs of my maintenance in London. After some looking about we found this place, and as I was convinced that you could have no possible objection and ~~that~~ I thought it would be more beneficial to me than the Chemistry course, and besides I should have had to pay the £10 out of the 42£ whereas now I have no expense of the kind, so I accepted it at once, and off I bolted for this place. – A.C. says K. is a most consumate rascal, he could not bear the idea of anyone being in the house to watch his movements, and he accordingly contrived to get me out; this of course may be true for what I know, because I cant read the thoughts of his soule, but I think that in our actions we cant regard such vague suspicions untill they come to have a more material foundation, for without casting the slightest doubt upon A.C.'s imputation, I think I may yet say as a general rule that interpretations of this kind might be made to even the very best of actions. One thing I must say, that the few days I spent in K's house there was a man there who the told me was a sailor out of service and whom they had taken in from charity till he should find a place; wether true or not, I know not; but I did not tell that to A.C. However I will return to my [illeg.]. You see thus, that by this arrangement these ten £ have been saved, which will come in very well for Hohenheim but I will first tell you what my ideas are. From the original £ 42–£ 34 are but left. £8 having been spent by me; this I know will appear an enormous sum to you, but I can assure you that I was as economical as possible. 22 f cm. I paid to the dentist one of the first of London,[6] and that is the only money I gave away with all my heart for I hope he did me very much good; he pulled out one enormous root, which that rascal Weiger[7] bro~~e~~ke and mutilated to such a degree that he was obliged to dig it out of the gum, before it could be pulled out, an operation so severe that he said to me after it was over, he did not know what we should have done, if it has not been for the Chloroform[8] because the ~~operation~~ pain was so acute and the operation so long that no man could stand it. The first time I went there the Chloroform could not be got to act although he gave me 3 [illeg.] and I enhaled for 13 minutes. I was very intoxicated and felt the stupifying effects for a quarter of an hour afterwards but never senseless. He said it was with the exception of one the only case he had ever met with. The second time however I fasted and fatigued myself with walking and so it did act, and the operation went off well enough. To my greatest dismay he then informed me that I had 4 teeth decaying fast, all of which ~~shoul~~ would have been lost had it not been for his help in time. He stopped three of them with pure gold ramming in as much of it as would go into the hollow. the fourth he stopped with paste. He said he could promise that the gold ones would last me all my life and the paste one a very long time unless some disorder of the stomach destroy them, and as he is very well off, and known to be one of the first dentists in Europe I am very much inclined to believe him.[9] I shall go, and let him look into my mouth before I leave England; how I wish that all the poor younger ones might be taken to him, for he says I should have had the same fate as Pauline and Clara, whose teeth were also beginning to go;[10] the stopping he managed so cleverly that although it was very nervous making and disagreable still without the slightest actual pain. – The remainder of the £8 was spent in my journey between here and London, because I had to come down previously in order to settle the affair; than in the purchase of several little things such as comb and brushes (which alone cost me 7 shillings). paper thick leather working gloves for the winter etz. and ~~one~~ £1. is still in my purse, but I consider it as spent because it will barely suffice to pay my journey back to London and different little expenses here such as postage etz. The remaining £ 34 are in Clara's hands, and the question is: how much do you think shall I have yet to spend and how much shall I be able to save for Hohenheim. My wish is that 30£ should be put by but than I do not know wether it will be fisible, and of course it would be a very akward thing if you were to count upon 30£ as a certainty and I were then obliged to rep of £1 or so as a matter of bare necessity for completing my journey; but it just strikes me that, ~~as~~ £30 will do and you need not send anything at all to Stuttgart because one only pays fulljährig[11] in advance. 150f for instruction etz + 80f for board + 10f. for servants and the museum will leave me yet 60f which will provide amply for washing, light, books, paper and other expenses, (even if I were obliged to take of 10 – or 15 florins as an addition for my journey. Of course I shall do every thing in my power to preserve the £ 30 intact, for this would then perhaps enable me to proceed to Vienna next September without causing you any expense till next October My journey from here to Hohenh. will amount I should guess to £6. The expenses necessarily attending the preparations of a journey will be not less than £ 2 or 3 including perhaps some expence for my wardrob; now A.C. promised me that she would help me on in this most ~~expensive~~ costly branch of expenditure and if she and the K's each give me an odd pound or so, (my 30£ being converted already here in Würtemberg paper money) I hope it will be practicable. At all events you will be free for the present and should anything go wrong, the amount I shall want, will not be high and it always will be time to send it; but if I rush in to a banker's the first day I reach London and convert the £ 30 into W. money K. and A.C. will be obliged to supply my journey. You would oblige me very much by troubling capt Andoe for a rough estimate of the traveling expenses. the nearest way is I think via Cologne and up the Rhein.[12] Also should I like to know wether they have at Würtemberg the Bavarian coin, or their own – he speaks of florins in his prospectus; now I know that there are two sorts of florins, one kind of which 24f. constitute in Mark Silbers,[13] and one of which only 20f go to the Mark. At any rate it is possible that their [~~illeg.~~] florin is of a greater value than the Austrian fCM.[14] and that of course would make a difference in our calculation; also should I wish to know what subdivision there is, wether also be [illeg.] or what kind of smaller coin; for this would give a clearer insight. I think I have said all that is necessary concerning that affair, and ~~shall be~~ am most anxious to have all good advice you can give me, for I dont know how far my judgement and my good will and intentions will go. One thing more; you will say: how foolish to have the expence of the remittance of the money to England, if it was destined for Hohenh. the funds might have risen, there would have been four months more interest etz. why ~~hav~~ not send it to Stuttgart at the proper time i.e. 3 months hence? In answer to that I can not tell you what the Knoxes previous plans were, but for myself I knew nothing of the Queenwood plan before the money arrived in England, and then of course it was too late.

28th Decemb. My time is now no more so free as it used to be, which obliges me, when I want to write a long letter, to write it in different Abschriften.[15] I will now tell you all about Queenwood, I know as yet, but as I think this will just afford a suitable opportunity to write to the little sisters & Charley without ~~wasting~~ sending more wa~~i~~stepaper, I will leave such details, as might amuse them and give you some insight into my new position at the same time for a separate sheet. You must not however expect any clear account because the vacations are just now, lasting till the 17 Jan. during which period of course all the masters are absent, so that my profit chiefly consists in what I read, having the library at my disposition, and in what practical knowledge I can gain on the farm working about the fields and the farmyard, for even the manager who at the same time teaches practical agriculture is absent;[16] so that my sources of learning are rather limited for the present. The library contains a very nice collection of books scientific, instructive and amusing the branch I particularly cultivate is the practice of agriculture treated as such in a scientific way without entering into the special sciences on which the whole is based. I think this is the English forte, and I certainly do wish to take some of the best books with me in spite of the awfully high prices. I am reading a practical treatise on maures[17] and a very large and voluminous work on farming in general; this latter is sectioned the first in the English literature, and contains many engravings, plans plates and woodcuts, its price is alas! – £2, 14 and owing to [illeg.] [illeg.] its recent publication is not yet to be had second hand; I will however try to scrape up as much as I can from the pocket money A.C. gives me, for the book would be an invaluable treasure and councellor for my life. There are besides this a few or special branches of farming such as measuring, breeding & rearing of cattle etz. which I also very much wish to have. [~~illeg.~~] – The principal, as they call him, is a quaker, and has been a good deal in Russia;[18] besides him there is a Swiss[19] to teach German and French and an Englishman. who has been abroad for seven years, three of which he spent at the famous Hofwyl in Switzerland (Fellenberg's institution of which I think F. Po[illeg.]at used to talk) he is of course a very good German scholar and a very liberal and enlightened man in every respect although one of my schoolfellows (a Highlander and awful tory) calls him a low freetrader and chartist.[20] The rest of the mastery I do not yet now. Mr Edmondson, the Quaker and head[illeg.] has only returned today having left the day after I came, so that I know little of him too. He seems however exceedingly Jesuistical, and has a very contracted uncomfortable making look about him; both he and the Hofwyl man have already set about proving [illeg.] that Hohenheim was not so good as Queenwood for one reason and an other, but as I do not know either as yet I cannot say anything. Knox paid £16 s.15 for these months ending about the 18. or 19th March. I thank you very very much dear mama for your kindness in saying that you would yet consent to a change if I wished it; I think since I have gone so far I had better pursue the course; although I must confess that I do not see my way quite so clear as one might in an other profession still I hope that in some way or other it will succeed; better we may emigrate, or we may have a brewery connected with the farm, or if a farm on our own account do not succeed, I may perhaps unite with it a place on some Herrschaft,[21] or we may take farm students as many farmers do here; and so I hope that by some means or other all will go ~~write~~ right – My wardrob, which you ask me to detail in your last, is good enough for the present. My farming dress consists of the famous old green brown great coat, I think 5 years of age, the celebrated red and black woolen [illeg.] shawl, my students trousers and very stout heavy boots; not to mention a waistcoat of some kind for I always wear my coat buttoned up to the chin. My black dress coat looks well enough yet it only is growing slightly too small over the chest the two wings or flaps scarcely meeting, which is put down to "foreign fashion". I wear it out as much as I can, and I have a good opportunity too because they have here the terrible habit of dressing for dinner in the middle of the day. My brown Quäker[22] is [illeg.] fast; my heavy brown coat has little service because it is not cold enough; in its stead for going to church etz I always wear a light great coat more adapted for this climate, A.C. gave it me. my black pantaloons are rather getting a little shiny; I wear them on Sundays and for half toilet, but good A.C. provided me with a very fine new pair, which I have as yet scarcely worn. My shirts are in a wretched state, none of the Vienna ones wearable in a decent place, all the fronts torn and patched up the [~~illeg.~~] laundresses tear them so;[23] some I have actually been obliged to throw away (I am speaking of the 6 or 8 day shirts) the nightshirts are not so bad; I have 4 new day sh. of linnen with fronts of fine linnen, I couldnot do without those.[24]

The little note to A.C. I forwarded the day I received it; she has written to me since but did not mention it at all. Pray answer me in your next all the questions I made concerning Würtemberg and also wether I am to take my passport as an Englishman or as an Austrian. Now dearest parents goodbye, I think I have said every thing but remembered the new year which I hope you will spend very happily and cheerfully together thinking very often of your obedient and [~~illeg.~~] affectionate son

W.G.C.

My address I have given you at the top of the letter; Stockbridge is the county town and nearest place of importance, although in itself a very old, but small town, Hants is the usual abbreviation for Hampshire.[25]

[Insert:]

As for my illness you need not be uneasy in the least; to be sure I was three weeks in the Dr's hands, but then I was not a day in bed but walking about just as if nothing was the matter; it is rather awkward to tell but since it might make you uneasy if I did not tell you, I will; my urin was in disorder ~~it~~ forming always deposits and cristals;[26] he said I wanted Alkalies and that it came from "high living" eating to much animal food (I suppose because it AC was so afraid of the Cholera,[27] she would give me only so few vegetables and no fruit) the Dr also said something about the liver and kidneys but I think it is all well now, although these cristals make their appearance sometimes yet[28]

By the delay of this letter I have an opportunity of wishing you all a very happy new year and everything to go prosperously and well with the beginning of this new half century. I thought many times of you and wished very much to be with you and share your domestic circle. I went to Salisbury with two of my fellow colleagues. it is by railway only a quarter of an hour; I thought it a nice little town the cathedral is splendid[29] I think as large as the Stefanskirche,[30] and because there are no pews it appears even larger than it is; they sang a beautiful "anthem" a psalm gesetzt[31] by Mozart. We sat in the Chorstüle[32] still remained of ancient Catholic times and it reminded me very much of the [illeg.]

you[33] will write very soon and give me news of [illeg.], O. Georg Mr [illeg.] Mr [illeg.], Battaglia, cpt. Andoe[34] and all other friends and please write very explicitly about Hohenh. Clara is very well

Address: No envelope

Unpublished. Text: M.S., Pf. Coll., CL'ANA 0059

---

1 Hants is the abbreviation for Hampshire.

2 Wilhelm left a relatively large gap between the opening salutation and the start of the letter.

3 The original either reads "Benter's" or "Reuter's". See CL'ANA 0054.

4 Wilhelm misspelled the names of the wharves he saw along the river. The south bank of the Thames is known as the Surrey side. Bermondsey is part of the Borough of Southwark and is located on the south side of the Thames. In *Oliver Twist*, Charles Dickens negatively depicted Jacob's Island in Bermondsey: "In such a neighborhood, beyond Dockhead in the Borough of Southwark, stands Jacob's Island . . . In Jacob's Island, the warehouses are roofless and empty; the walls are crumbling down; the windows are windows no more; the doors are falling into the streets; the chimneys are blackened, but they yield no smoke. Thirty or forty years ago, before losses and chancery suits came upon it, it was a thriving place; but now it is a desolate island indeed. The houses have no owners; they are broken open, and entered upon by those who have the courage; and there they live, and there they die. They must have powerful motives for a secret residence, or be reduced to a destitute condition indeed, who seek a refuge in Jacob's Island" (*Oliver Twist*, [New York: Oxford University Press, 1994], p. 382). Dickens's description evokes the squalor that Wilhelm encountered on his visit. Today, a historic marker pays tribute to Dickens's famous description: "In the early nineteenth century this area was a notorious rookery or slum. Dickens used it in his novel 'Oliver Twist'. He set Fagin's den in one of the warehouses and the evil Bill Sykes met his grisly end in the ooze bed of Folly Ditch" ("Jacobs Island Residents Association". Web. 23 April 2015. http://www.jira.org.uk).

5 Unidentified.

6 S. Gelbier records in "125 years of developments in dentistry" (*British Dental Journal* 199, Nov 2005, p. 685–9. Web. 10 May 2015. http://www.nature.com/bdj/journal/v199/n10/full/4813002a.html) that until 1858, dentists in England had "no proper training or qualifications". The Dental Hospital of London and the Metropolitan School of Dental Science opened in 1858 and provided training to 43 "practitioners" who received their degrees in 1860. Gelbier also explains that dental care improved significantly during the Victorian era as a result of industrialization. While some dentists received proper training, many were untrained and the profession became an extra source of income for "surgeons, blacksmiths, jewellers, wig-makers" (pp. 746–50).

7 See note 8 below.

8 The use of chloroform as an anesthetic began during the nineteenth century. Surgeons used it routinely during the Crimean War (1853–56). In 1861, Charles Jackson wrote in *The Boston Medical and Surgical Journal*: "In Austria, by orders of the Government, one ninth of the bulk of chloroform is added to ether, and this is employed in the Austrian hospitals and armies. Its introduction was effected by Dr. Weiger, of Vienna, and it is stated that no fatal accidents have thus far arisen from its use" ("Action of Chloroform on the Blood," [David Clapp, Publisher: Boston, 1861], vol. 64, p. 179). See also CL'ANA 0268.

9 Gelbier (see note 6) explains that, before 1870, excavators, chisels and burs (rotary cutting tools) were used to cut into enamel. Before 1880, when amalgam was used as a material for filling cavities, dentists would use "tin or cohesive gold" to fill cavities: "Layers of gold foil were inserted into cavities and welded together by pressure from hand and later mechanical springloaded pluggers" (*British Dental Journal* 199, pp. 536–9).

10 See CL'ANA 0421, Box 3, bundle g, number 207.

11 Wilhelm added the English word "full" to the German word "-jährig". From this word, it appears that Wilhelm attempted to communicate that fees were only paid once a year and in advance.

12 German for the Rhine River.

13 The Mark was the German unit of currency. "Silber" is the German for silver. Charles Conant explains that silver was the "principal metallic stock" of Germany until 1873 when gold became the standard (*A History of the Modern Banks of Issue* [New York: Putnam's Sons, 1909], p. 196).

14 See CL'ANA 0404.

15 German for "manuscripts".

16 Richard Davis was the "farm superintendant" for Queenwood College. The following were all instructors at the college: Dr. John Tyndall (Natural Philosophy and Mathematics), Dr. Heinrich Debus (Chemistry), Mr. John Prout (Classics and History), Mr. J. Haas (Modern Languages and Foreign Literature), Mr. Richard Wright (Geodesy), Mr. R. P. Wright (Painting and Drawing), and Mr. William Cornwall (Music). The "farm department" at Queenwood enabled students to spend a part of each day in "assisting in carrying out practically the most approved methods of Agriculture". The prospectus also confirmed that the farm at Queenwood provided "ample arena for Field Practice" in the field of Geodesy. See "Prospectus for Queenwood College". Hampshire Record Office: 47M72/4.

17 French for "moors".

18 The *Illustrated London News* of 13 January 1849 reported that George Edmondson "is not merely an agriculturalist, but an experienced teacher, who is imbued with a deep consciousness of the importance of school, as an introduction to life". The newspaper noted too that Edmondson worked in Russia, and that he helped reclaim the land around St. Petersburgh on behalf of Emperor Alexander (Hampshire Record Office: 47M66/12/1).

19 Mr. J. Haas, instructor of Modern Languages and Foreign Literature, came from "M. de Fellenberg's Institution in Hofwyl, Switzerland" ("Queenwood College, Near Stockbridge, Hants," p. 4. Hampshire Record Office: 47M66/12/1). Philipp von Fellenberg established a school in 1799 in Hofwyl, Switzerland, that taught academic subjects and provided agricultural training (The Editors of the Encyclopaedia Britannica. "Philipp Emanuel von Fellenberg". *Encyclopaedia Britannica Online*. Encyclopaedia Britannica Inc. n.d. Web. 13 March 2015. http://www.britannica.com/EBchecked/topic/203997/Philipp-Emanuel-von-Fellenberg). According to the *Illustrated London News* of 13 January 1849, Queenwood followed the principles of the Hofwyl School: "The celebrated establishment of M. de Fellenberg, at Hofwyl, is the model, to a great extent, of Queenwood College, as far as the principles upon which it is conducted are concerned" (Hampshire Record Office: 47M66/12/1). The newspaper compared Edmondson's educational philosophy to that of Fellenberg's, noting that both men aimed to develop their students' minds in addition to giving them appropriate vocational training. The name F. Po[illeg.]at is unidentified.

20 Chartism was a movement that demanded parliamentary reform in Britain between the years 1838 and 1848. In particular, the Chartists called for universal male suffrage and yearly elections. The movement declined after 1848.

21 German for an estate possibly belonging to a baron or to a member of the landed gentry.

22 Wilhelm probably meant "Quäkerhut," which is German for a type of hat that Quakers would wear.

23 Pupils paid four guineas per year for laundry service.

24 Each student was expected to purchase the following required items recorded on the "List of Clothes, &c., Required at Queenwood College". Pupils were to have "not less than": "3 Suits. 6 Shirts. 3 Night-Shirts. 3 Night-Caps. 6 Pairs worsted or 6 Pairs Cotton Stockings. 6 Pocket-handkerchiefs. 3 Neck-kerchiefs. 12 Collars. 6 Towels. 3 Pairs Shoes. Umbrella. Slippers. Small-tooth Comb and Brush. Clothes Brush. Hair do [Brush]. Tooth do [Brush]. Bible. Silver Spoon. Do [Silver] Fork" (Hampshire Record Office: 47M72/5). "Do" is the abbreviation for ditto.

25 In "Queenwood College, Near Stockbridge, Hants," the author recorded that Queenwood was located between Salisbury and Winchester and was about three hours' journey from the Waterloo terminus of the London and South-Western Railway. Dunbridge was the closest railway station.

26 Crystals in urine (crystalluria) are often associated with kidney stones or with stones in the bladder or ureter. Red meat and cheese are highly acidic food products which can contribute to kidney stones. A diet rich in greens such as spinach can reduce the risk of stones.

27 Outbreaks of cholera occurred in much of Europe in the nineteenth century. Significant outbreaks occurred in London in 1831–2, 1848–9, 1853–4, and 1866. In 1848–9, 14,137 people died in London while 10,738 people died in the outbreak of 1853–4 ("Cholera and The Thames". Web. 13 March 2015. http://www.choleraandthethames.co.uk/).

28 Wilhelm wrote the following paragraph on the back of the insert.

29 Construction on Salisbury Cathedral, located in Salisbury, Wiltshire, began in 1220. Originally a Roman Catholic cathedral, it has been a Church of England cathedral since the reign of Henry VIII. The cathedral's official name is The Cathedral Church of the Blessed Virgin Mary ("Salisbury Cathedral". Web. 29 April 2015. http://www.salisburycathedral.org.uk/).

30 St. Stephan's Cathedral in Vienna. The original church was built in the twelfth century. The Roman Catholic cathedral is Vienna's largest cathedral ("Domkirche St. Stephan zu Wien". Web. 29 April 2015. http://www.stephanskirche.at).

31 German for "scored".

32 German for "choir chairs". Wilhelm's spelling was incorrect ("Chorstühle" is the correct form of the word).

33 This final sentence was written on another small insert.

34 Uncle Georg was Antonia's brother (O. is the abbreviation for the German word, "Onkel"), Georg von Hembyze. See CL'ANA 0398 for information about Battaglia.

19 • Wilhelm Gaulis Clairmont to Emily, Charley, and Sidonia Clairmont

Queenwood, 30 Decemb. 1849.

My dear Emmy, Charley and Sidi.

For our mutual benefit I will write to you in English, but since this is the the first time I do so, and I know that you would most likely prefer a German letter instead, it may be perhaps very [illeg.] to reconcile you in the beginning by a most humble apology to the nature of this odious epistle. Charley I thank very much for his nice letter, but only I thought it very nasty of him (and I consider that he ought to be stupf ed[1] for it by you two) that professing at first to greet in all your name, he afterwards did not give me a little bit of news of the sisters, but I hope that you will make up for all that some day. As I have nothing better to amuse you with, I will tell you something concerning myself. I am now as you know at Queenwood an agricultural college in the middle part of the South of England; the building with the farmyard stands quite solitary in some kind of a Kessel[2] formed by slight elevations on all sides but one narrow valley like outlet which descends below the level of the building; this consists of 2 parallel running buildings fronting the East and connected by one other stretching in the middle between the two from East to West and thus fronting north and South;[3] there is ample room, fine lecture halls, dining rooms etz. the kitchen is as usually in England on the cellar floor and the same the dining room only in the opposite building; as it would thus be very inconvenient to carry the dinner for 80 persons, upstairs, accross a court and downstairs on the other side the have a kind of tunnel railway[4] from the dining room under the court to the kitchen; it is about 4 feet square and there is a little wooden machine with wheels placed on the rails ~~on~~ which is laden with the dishes etz. and then halled over by a rope. The farm contains 750 acres. there are 20 horses, 12 cows more than 100 pigs 500 sheep so that you see it is a very large concern. As for the school it is divided into two parts the juniors and seniors. the first are kept just in the same way as we were at Melk.[5] the latter to whom I belong have their private rooms,[6] and have permission to walk out etz only they must be at home at all the meals and in the evening when it grows dark. I get up every morning at 5. by six I go down to the farm where I begin working either chopping turnips called "Sweeds"[7] for the cows or cleaning a stable or combing the horses or something of that kind, at 8 we breakfast and ~~at~~ then I go in the fields working till dinner at 1. after dinner I either go out again or I read and study at home. As soon as the session commences I will begin analytic chemistry and also shall we have a lecture or rather conversation on practical agriculture every evening; there the events of the day on the farm are talked over, models of agricultural machines explained and examined, books upon similar subjects read and discussed. – I hope that Charley is getting on very emsig ly[8] with his mathematics only recollect dear Charley that whatever branch of practical business you choose it always will constitute the basis of the knowledge by which you are to learn your livelyhood, if you want to be an engineer you want mathematics, an architect, a farmer, a förster, a Maschinist,[9] they all acknowledge Mathematics to be the basis of their profession so never mind the "[illeg.]! [illeg.]! but [~~illeg.~~] very diligently.[10] Now goodbye to you all, many kisses to the sisters and I hope that they are both very good cooks and stocking menders, so that we always may have plenty to eat and to cloth with.

Goodbye.

Liebe Paulin. Heute ist der 2t Jänner 1850 es ist also schon eine ganze Woche verfloßen, seit ich diesen Brief begonnen, und heute erst sende ich ihn ab. Nun ich hatte immer so viel zu thun, daß es mir unmöglich war. Diese Tage lebte ich immer in einer fieberhaften Gährung die entsprechend nur durch den bezeichnenden Ausdruck "Aufregung" angedeutet werden kann denn da gewispelt wurde daß den Sylvesterabend eine "party" seyn sollte, so war meine Neugierde aufs heißste verspannt wie sich dies nach Quäkerprincipien modificirte, gesellschaftliche Unterhaltung, als wirkliche Unterhaltung ~~modificieren~~ beweisen würde.
Um 7 Uhr nahm man thee und kaffeh und "Sundry" biscuits und Kuchen, um 8 Uhr machte sich die ganze Masse nach dem Gebeth in ein Sitzzimmer in welchem die Knaben unter der Anleitung ihres deutschen Sprachmeisters einen Christbaum aufgestellt hatten, welche Sitte hier nicht existiert. Der Quaker nahm dann seine Sitz in einem Presidenten stuhl von wo aus er Sundry Gedichte auf die Gelegenheit vor las die alle sehr [illeg.] waren, man brachte dann einen Haufen schöner Kupferstiche die angesehen wurden, aß wieder Kuchen, Pomeranzen, Apfel etc. Da meine Befürchtung nähmlich die Abwesenheit von kaltem Fleisch und Punch oder Wein sich bestättigte so war ich in einem großen Mops. Die 7 geladenen Damen (Herren waren keine, ich vermuthe weil sie meinen Ansicht theilten) nahmen dann mit den 3 kleinen Mädchen Abschied (11 Uhr) und wir (die Familie Edm. Lehrer und Schule) blieben noch bis 1 Uhr auf um welche Zeit wir nachdem jedes eine [illeg.] Chocolat und vier Stück Kletzenbrot gegessen, zu Bette gingen. Jetzt ade liebe Paulin, mir ist leid, daß mein Papier zu Ende ist, ich mochte dir noch vieles sagen.

Its pretty cold with us; I have had one days skating, but there is no proper piece of water here about[11]

English Translation (German transcription and English translation provided by Ann Sherwin):

Dear Paulin. Today is the January 2, 1850, so a whole week has gone by since I started this letter, and I am only now sending it off. I always had so much to do that I just couldn't get to it. These days I've been living in a feverish ferment that can only be appropriately referred to with the descriptive term "excitement". Since it was whispered about that there was to be a party on New Year's Eve, I had become extremely curious as to how this social event, modified according to Quaker principles, would actually prove to be entertaining. At 7 o'clock we had

tea and coffee and sundry biscuits and cakes; at 8 o'clock, after the prayer, the entire party moved into a sitting room in which the boys, under the supervision of their German language teacher, had set up a Christmas tree – a custom that doesn't exist here. The Quaker then took his seat in a presidential chair, from whence he read aloud sundry poems for the occasion, all of which were very [illeg.], then a horde of beautiful copper engravings were brought in and viewed, and more cakes, Seville oranges, apples, etc. were consumed. Since my fear – namely the absence of cold meat and punch or wine – was confirmed, I was in a big sulk. The 7 invited ladies (there were no gentlemen, because they shared my view, I suspect) and the three little girls said farewell (11 o'clock), and we (the Edm.[12] family teachers and school) stayed on until 1 o'clock, at which time, after each of us had eaten a [illeg.] of chocolate and four slices of Kletzenbrot,[13] we went to bed.
Now, goodbye, dear Paulin. I'm sorry that my paper is full. I wanted to say much more to you.

Address: Aerogramme: Via Ostend/ C.G. Clairmont, Esqr./ Stadt, Freyung, N° 238, 2[t] Stiege 1.[t] Stock/ Vienna. Austria.
Postmark: STOCKBRIDGE/ JA 2/ 1850

Unpublished. Text: M.S., Pf. Coll., CL'ANA 0060

---

1 Wilhelm added the English past participle (-ed) to the German word "stupfen" which means "to nudge" or "to prod".

2 German for "basin".

3 Wilhelm accurately described the external appearance of Queenwood. A picture of Queenwood College published on 13 January 1849 in the *Illustrated London News* shows the two buildings with the connection, as Wilhelm explained in his letter. In another picture (included in this collection), the surrounding grounds appear impeccably laid out and one can see well-tended and extensive lawns in the background.

4 Wilhelm wrote the number 2 above the word "tunnel," and the number 1 above the word "railway".

5 Wilhelm attended the Gymnasium of Melk Abbey in Melk, Austria, 87 kilometers west of Vienna. The Pforzheimer Collection has Wilhelm's school report (recorded in Latin) for the year 1846–7 at the "Gymnasii Mellicensis". Wilhelm earned the comment of "primam eminenter"(first class) for each of his subjects, which included Greek, Geography and History, Mathematics, Religion, Culture, and Interpretation of Style. Wilhelm (his name was recorded in Latin as "Guilielmus Clairmont") was one of fourteen students in his class. The school is still in existence today. Alma Crüwell-Clairmont, Wilhelm's daughter, stated in her Herkunft der Familie Clairmont, testimony written in the 1930s about her family's origins, that Wilhelm was baptized and educated in Catholic establishments at Melk and possibly the Schottengymnasium, in accordance with the religion of his mother, but that he converted to his father's Anglican religion before his marriage in 1866 (CL'ANA 0419, unpublished manuscript, Pforzheimer Collection). See also note 7, CL'ANA 0404.

6 The school's policy on "domestic arrangements" stated that Edmondson was responsible for ensuring "the physical comfort and health of the whole establishment" and *Chambers's Edinburgh Journal* of March 1849 declared: "We have heard much of Queenwood, as agreeably uniting the character of a home with that of a public academy for boys," corroborating the school's general statement that "the objects aimed at in Queenwood College, are, to maintain for Pupils a *home*, in the true sense of the word; and, to surround that home by educational appliances, the best the times will afford" ("Queenwood College". Hampshire Record Office: 47M66/12/1).

7 Wilhelm misspelled the word “swede,” a type of turnip.
8 Wilhelm fused English and German. He combined the German word “emsig” with the adverbial ending to create a word that meant “diligently”.
9 The German word “Förster” means a “forester” and the German word “Maschinist” refers to an “operator, machinist, or engineer”.
10 Wilhelm repeated an unidentified word.
11 These final words appeared on the back of the aerogramme.
12 Edmondson.
13 A traditional Austrian fruit bread made with dried pears, raisins, dates, and nuts.

20 • Wilhelm Gaulis Clairmont to Claire Clairmont

Queenwood, January 30th
1850.

My dearest aunt.

According to your desire, I send off this answer immediately by which means I am certain you must have it by to morrow the 31st. Their address in Vienna is as follows:
Freyung, No 238, 2te Stiege, 1t Stock.[1]

Vienna.

With regard to keeping you au courant of my future destination, I shall of course always be but too happy to do so as long as you will be kind enough to take an interest in it, which I am sure, you always will. but the truth is, that ever since I have left London, nothing decisive or at least <u>more</u> decisive has been said or done for you recollect, that already at that time papa wrote to say that he considered it a settled thing that I was to go to Hohenheim. A letter I had a few days ago from Mama speaks in a similar style and says that I was to have a letter shortly from Papa in which all the minutiae concerning travelling arrangements, money-matters etz. would be detailed. She also writes that a~~n~~ Vienese Merchant of the name of Mr Genersich,[2] who visits occasionally at our house is going to come to London on business for a few days and that if possible I shall have some letters by him, but when, and wether he is in reality coming I do not yet know.
What you say of Miss Beste[3] is very true and the more I think of it the sadder it makes me that you are deprived of so agreable and so amiable a companion, who would have proved such a very great support to you in every respect. – I was greatly astonished to hear of her having had an attachment to some one I knew. I remember your telling me of something of the kind in Germany, but that you can not be alluding to now; as you doe not tell me his name I suppose both~~e~~ common sense and etiquette will forbid me to ask it, but I do confess that all my study and labour to find it out was in vain for the only young man I ever saw her with was captain Ramsbottom,[4] and him you certainly can not mean!? – So I do not know what to make of it.
As I ~~will~~ shall be most likely answering Capt. Andoe's note, I write to ask you wether I may return your compts to him, and what report I may give him of your health and state of mind, after which he most particularly inquired.
I am now in a great hurry and cant say anymore, but beg that you will excuse me on account of the spead with which I despatch this should it turn out very incomplete. With my best thanks for all your cares for me, believe me ever to be

your most dutyful nephew
W.G.C.[5]

M[rs] M[illeg.] wife of a medical man
Lewisham.[6]

M[rs] Hyde

Ware Valley[7]
D[r] [illeg.]

Address: No envelope

Unpublished. Text: M.S., Pf. Coll., CL'ANA 0042[8]

---

1 Charles and Antonia's address in Vienna: Freyung, No. 238, 2nd Staircase, 1st Floor. Freyung is located in the first district of Vienna. According to a *Picture of Vienna*, Vienna had twenty-three squares at the time and "Freiung" was one of them (p. 42). The palace of Count Harrach with its books about agriculture as well as a notable collection of prints was located in Freiung (p. 71), as was the Schottenhof, the "monastery of the Scotch Benedictines" (p. 47).

2 Unidentified.

3 On 21 January 1851, Claire wrote to Wilhelm stating that she had received a letter from "dear" Julia V. Beste announcing her forthcoming marriage to a German man who was Julia's brother's friend. Julia also intended to settle in Bordeaux (*CC* II: 535) and she sent her best wishes to Wilhelm. Claire described Julia as "gentle" and "considerate," saying that she would make a good wife to her new husband. Claire also expressed regret to think that Julia would no longer be living in England. See also CL'ANA 0043 and CL'ANA 0056.

4 *Burke's Peerage* of 1890 notes that Edward Bootle-Wilbraham married Emily Ramsbottom, daughter of James Ramsbottom (Edmund Lodge, London: Hurst and Blackett, 1890), p. 369. Their daughter's name was Ada Constance, possibly named for her aunt, Ada Ramsbottom. Captain Ramsbottom was likely a brother of Ada Ramsbottom.

5 Wilhelm wrote the notes that follow on the back of the final page of the letter.

6 Lewisham is a borough of London and is situated about 11 kilometers south-east of the city.

7 Wilhelm could have referred either to the Wear Valley which was a district in County Durham or the city of Ware. He probably meant the Wear Valley which was incorporated into the Durham County Council in 2009. Mrs. Hyde is unidentified.

8 This letter and the next are both numbered CL'ANA 0042.

21 • Wilhelm Gaulis Clairmont to Claire Clairmont

Queenwood 12th February
1850.

My dearest aunt.

With my eyes still full of tears and my mind scattered and broken I take the pen to inform you of the dreadful news Mr Edmondson[1] communicated to me this morning. I can't tell you anything nearer, because I have not had a letter yet; but probably you will find all in the enclosed letter, that our dear, dear, beloved father is no more. I am so grieved that I can hardly yet believe it, ~~in~~ I am incapable of comprehending as yet the whole amount of the misfortune and seem to my self in a deep dream of sorrow and disbelieve; I can not collect my thoughts, but I thought it was my duty to write to you immediately so I did it. Paulin wrote to Knox about it, and he to Mr Edmondson who told it me, in an excessively kind and considerate way preparing me first – There was also a very kind letter of Knox for me in which he invites me to come to London, if I wish; I have however refused it – I would not do it on any account. I am here, with if not exactly so deeply sumpathizing[2] yet with very kind people and left to my own thoughts I will bear the blow much better than in town which in itself makes me always melancholy and where I should always be remembered of bygone circumstances and events, which I feel convinced deeply grieved my poor father shortly before his death. so I (also with Mr Edmondson's counsel) refused the offer at once.
Pauline writes that he was dinning at the Arshduk'es and accordingly not expected home that day (2nd February) when between 8 and 9 in the evening. a stranger was announced at Mama's bearing the onepage that Papa had dropped down senseless in the room during a visit. Mama immediately set out with Pauline but it was too late. They had taken him to the hospital and bled him ~~but~~ he expired in half an hour; and was no more when Mama arrived.[3]
Dr Böhnn had seen him the same day, and perceived not he had symptoms of apoplexy.[4] The funeral was on the 5th February.
What my feelings are I can not describe to you; the more I think over it, the ~~more~~ heavier the blow seems to me; I conclude now dearest aunt for I can not write more for the present I know you always will be my kind and affectionate aunt.

your obedient nephew
William.

Address: No envelope.

Unpublished. Text: M.S., Pf. Coll., CL'ANA 0042

1 The principal of Queenwood, George Edmondson.

2 Sympathizing.

3 Herbert Huscher wrote that Charles "am 2. Februar 1850 in Wien auf der Straße einem Schlaganfall erlag" ("on February 2, 1850, [Charles] died of a stroke in the streets of Vienna") ("Charles

und Claire Clairmont," p. 65). The *Neuer Nekrolog der Deutschen*, (entry 373 in "New Necrology of Germans") provides details about Charles's life. According to the entry, K. Gaulis Clairmont was a teacher of language and literature at the University of Vienna and the Theresianum. He was known for his publications, specifically *Reine Grundlehren der englischen Sprache mit einem ersten Lesebuche*, *Zweites Lesebuch der englischen Sprache*, *Vollständige englische Sprachlehre*, *Handbuch englische Sprache* and *Poetisches Lesebuch für Anfänger* (Translation: Basics of the English Language with a First Reading Book, Second Reading Book in English, Complete English Studies, Pocket Guide to the English Language, Poetric Reading Book for Beginners). His age was listed as 55 years (Ilmenau: B. F. Voigt, 1854), p. 978. Charles was buried in the cemetery in Währing in the eighteenth district of Vienna. The cemetery was closed in 1888 and is a city park today (Schubert Park). Charles's gravestone was moved to the Matzleinsdorf Evangelical Cemetery (see the photograph of the Clairmont family tomb in this collection). According to the testimony of Alma Crüwell-Clairmont (c. 1930s): "Sein Grabstein liegt nach Auflassung des Währinger Friedhofs auf unserer Gruft am Matzleinsdorfer evangelischen Friedhof" (CL'ANA 0419, p. 1, unpublished manuscript, Pforzheimer Collection). Translation: "After the closing of the Währing Cemetery, his gravestone is now located in the (family) tomb in the Matzleinsdorf Evangelical Cemetery". Mary Claire Bally-Clairmont included a note about the Clairmont family tomb on the back of a photograph of the site: "at the churchyard of Matzleinsdorf in Vienna: tomb (in german gruft) Nr. 3 bought by the Clairmont family in 1850; first burial for Charles Gaulis Clairmont; then his daughters Sidonia and Emily; no idea where his wife Antonie is buried. Next William Gaulis = Willhelm, a.s.q". (no CL'ANA number, Unpublished document, Pforzheimer Collection).

4 Internal bleeding, caused by a hemorrhage.

22 • Antonia Clairmont and Pauline Clairmont to Claire Clairmont

Feb. 19th [1850][1]

My dearest best aunt, I can not express to you, how much I was touched by your dear letter, and indeed I long to be with you & try by my affection & my cares to make up to you for all the sufferings of this life. Besides this sad mis fortune which has cast us all down, you have many griefs, you are alone, your health is not very strong, I am sure I could do something to make your life more agreeable. Mama will write to you all the details about money matters & all that, & her plans for the future, so I need not say anything about it, indeed Mama has so many cares now, so much to do & to think of she is occupied day & night. I too, have begun my lessons again, I have a good many, for I have several of poor Papa's; so that our life is pretty much the same as it was before, except of an evening, but then I feel sad & lonely At that time dear Papa used to come home & as he always went to bed very early, I generally went to him, & then we had a little chat together, that was my happiest hour of the day for me;[2] he showed so much interest for every thing that I had done, he was so kind so affectionate I think that none of my family feels this loss as much as I do – my heart is so full on this subject, I cannot find the right words to express all my sorrow; this event has thrown such a dark shade over my whole life, it seems to me as if I never could become as gay & lighthearted as I was before. It was the ideal of my whole life to be with Papa to take care of his old age, perhaps once to come over to England with him, how happy he would have been; and oh, now all is past, all is lost, & I am quite alone. – At the same time I cannot help thanking & admiring Providence that has turned aside from us the still more terrible feeling at seeing our dear father suffer for years & years; if the stroke had come on with less violence, if but his tongue or his eyes had been palsied, if he had been confined speechless or motionless to his sick chamber, he whose mind was so active, whose feelings were yet so fresh & lively! What would have been our feelings if we could not have given him all the comforts without which life is really a plague All this we have been spared, & it is a selfish though very pardonable feeling of pain, if we mourn at his having been taken from us so suddenly. Now, dear aunt you may imagine that being the eldest it is my most ardent wish to be able to do something for my family for as you will see by mamma's letter we are not in brilliant circumstances. Though I am pretty well off here, yet I think that I might do more if I was in England, for a small sum for instance 10£, very easily saved in England would be of great assistance to persons living in Germany.[3] I therefore wish to ask your advice on this subject. But first I wish you to be persuaded that I will not be a charge to any of my relations in England; I do not go with the intention of accepting alms from any one, I think I can get on very well with what my dear father has given me; a good education. If therefore I come to England to give music or German lessons, or look for ~~find~~ some place in a family I shall only beg you dear aunt to introduce me to some families, & to tell me whether you think that I might without injuring my reputation live in a boarding house where I pay for all that want, & have my day free for giving lessons. In Vienna any young person might do so, but I do not how one might judge me in England. This is all I have to say, I hope that your answer will be favourable, for I should be very glad to go to England. Pray dearest aunt write us very soon, & be so kind as to answer me these important questions.

Your most affcte. niece
Paula.

22[4] [22 February 1850]

My dearest Claire.

~~We have~~ I received your last to me after poor Charles's death; the stroke was so sudden and ~~for~~ unlooked for – I have not yet recovered it, and yet never was presence of mind more necessary than in my case – what heavy duties devolve on me, and how slender the means to fulfil them – Charles died intestate[5] – not a word of a will nor any provision whatever to protect me from the law, which is in Austria particularly hard to the widow – what you say about the English birthright of my children was my first thought, but at the Embassy they were very cool about it – would Mrs Clairmont like to pay the probate duty[6] in England which is a very heavy one, they asked – and Capt. Andoe whom I had asked to act as guardian flatly refused – he said, the responsibilities of an Engl guardian were heavy indeed, and he could not undertake them – I thought of calling home William and have him declared of age, and named as guardian, but without money one can't do any thing – all I found in Charles's desk was about £40–20 more came in for lessons outstanding, half of this sum was swallowed up in funeral expenses mourning for all the family, et et. then there are some bills to be paid trifling indeed but when the stack of cash is so small every shilling is felt – there are also two bookseller's accounts which were due at the new year – they are about £15 – and then last of ~~of~~ all the rent with £28 due on St. George 24th April – so what could I do? I felt grateful, relieved and soothed when our friend Böhen[7] and Dr Budinsky[8] ~~of~~ whom I have mentioned to you in former letters – came and voluntarily offered – the former to be guardian~~s~~ to my poor orphans, the latter to take my affairs in hand without a farthing of fee, to advise and help me in all things – God bless them both, it was He sent them to help me on my weary path; the only property left, is the Weidling house and Charles books with the sale of the latter I hope to cover the cover[9] the above deficit, for the £60 would go far enough, besides I have still a stone to provide for poor Charles – the house will be valued (we bought at £600) and then sold – half of it belongs to me and half ~~of~~ to the deceased – and that half is taken hold of by the authorities and put by till the children are of age – we live now by the produce of my lessons and Pauline contributes, but she is putting by money for journey to England - you seem to think we ought all to come over ~~all~~, but how should we live there? what could I do to earn something? I'm sure I should not know; and who are the relations to protect me? You, all generous and kind as you are, had not even the means to do something for dear Willy, whom your own free offers to provide for him had drawn from his fathers house; and besides it would be madness to think you should provide for a family of 5 persons – for only Pauline could earn something in England – and you would not have me depend on Mrs Shelley?[10] No here I must remain, I have connexions, I have means of earning something with my lessons, education for Charley is much cheaper, he is only 14 years old; God will give [illeg.] health and strength, to go through with it I ~~was~~ am greatly relieved to know your religious feeling if Charles had had any spark of it, all would be better, Pauline is like Cläry – but my fault it is not – thank God Willy is better – I am taking a 100 steps to ameliorate my condition, if I succeed in any of them I shall let you know – after what I told you of Andoe you will hardly want to know his direction – Pray write soon ever yours

A.C. the children send their love.

Address: No envelope

Unpublished. Text: M.S., Pf. Coll., CL'ANA 0212

---

1 This letter from Pauline, and the following one from Antonia, were written together on the same paper.

2 See introductory material to The Australian Sojourn in which Pauline described sitting around the family table.

3 By 1850, Pauline was in England living with Claire. She left for London on 26 April 1850 (see CL'ANA 0399).

4 This letter's year is undated, but it dates to 22 February 1850, given the context. The letter "t" next to the date probably indicates that Antonia intended to write the letters "ter". In German, the date would read "zweiundzwanzigster".

5 Without a will.

6 Probate refers to the legal steps that have to be executed after an individual's death. Probate includes appraising the deceased's property, attesting to the validity of the will, paying any debts owed by the deceased, and distributing the estate amongst the deceased's heirs. George Horsey explains that the Probate and Administration Act of 1857 gave English executors the ability to assess the deceased's property in order to determine whether or not probate duty would need to be paid on the estate (*The Probate and Administration Act, 1857, with the Rules and Orders of the Court of Probate* [London: Shaw and Sons, 1858], p. 143). The executor had the right to decide the value of the deceased's property "in order that the proper and full stamp duty may be paid on such probate or administration" (p. 143).

7 See CL'ANA 0401.

8 The *Hof-und Staats-Handbuch des österreichischen Kaiserthumes* of 1844 listed August Budinsky ([Wien: Hof- und Staatsdruckerei, 1844] p. 644) as a practicing justice and court advocate (Hofs- und Gerichtsadvokaten) in Vienna. In the 1859 edition, he was listed as "Wilhelm August Budinsky, Hof-u. Ger. Adv. in Wien" (Wien: Hof- und Staatsdruckerei), p. 87.

9 Correctly transcribed from the original letter.

10 Mary Shelley. After Clara's marriage, the relationship between the Clairmonts and the Shelleys suffered irreparable harm.

23 • Wilhelm Clairmont to Claire Clairmont

Hohenheim April 19th
1850.

My dearest aunt.

As you must have had the letter I posted in Belgium after my passage, I thought it would be better for me to wait a few day longer, in order to be enabled to say a little more concerning my new position. – I need not mention that the whole of my journey passed off without an accident; I went by Ostend and Cologne, up the Rhine to Mayence, from there via Frankfort, Heidelberg and Heilbron to Stuttgardt.[1] – Hohenheim lies about 5 miles from Stuttgardt, and arriving here early in the morning of the 5th inst. I may say I accomplished the whole in 6 days. – The Rhine charmed me excessively, I never imagined it so beautiful. – Heidelberg where I had to stop for about 10 hours also pleased me very much; I filled up my time there very agreably by taking a walk in the neighbouring mountains where I saw the old residence of the former Granddukes of Baden;[2] nevertheless I strongly noticed that uncleanliness that you so frequently used to complain of in other nations when compared with the English.–

Hohenheim has a very beautiful situation; it lies on a kind of plateau, which rises in a steep acclivity from the very walls of Stuttgardt and continues all over the southern part of Würtemberg down to the valley of the Danube and the Alps of Switzerland;[3] the air is thus very good and pure and as for health I think there is every thing that might be desired. The food is also good; there is a table d'hôte for dinner in which I joined breakfast and supper every one provides for himself privately; I always keep a large loaf of bread in my room. for breakfast I ~~always~~ get a glass of milk from our cowstable; this is by far the best mode of breakfast not only cheaper and more wholesome but in this case also better than tea or coffee made by those negligent servants. For dinner we ~~always~~ have soup, beef and either a roast or a pudding; it is of course by far[~~illeg.~~] not so substantial as the English dinner but yet pretty tolerable. Supper I usually get at the traiteur[4] who has his establishment in the building; I take either beef or veal and a glass of beer. As I breakfast at 7 in the morning and dine at the Arcadian[5] hour of noon I am always quite over ready for supper at 7 in the evening – at a quarter to ten I go to bed.

The masters are all seemingly very clever men the farm is also very large and I have no doubt that my time will be profitably employed

I think I have now told you the greatest part of what might prove interesting of my affairs and shall now enjoy an agreable chat with you the second part of which I hope to have very soon. – First – about your health; I hope this is quite well now; the mild spring air cannot fail to in fluence it beneficially; and how are you off with regard to lodging; ~~and~~ will you leave [~~illeg.~~] Regent's Park and go somewhere in the neighbourhood of Kensington Gardens or Hyde Park? or will you perhaps go down to Malling again?[6] that was after all I think the finest place we ever went to. From Mama I now expect a letter very soon, for I have not heard from her [~~illeg.~~] ever since I left Queenwood, where her last one reached me.

By the by in looking over a newspaper yesterday I accidentally cast my eye on a correspondence from Hanover, and read ~~the~~ as follows~~ing~~: “Our new laws for the press have just come out and will be brought to operate now. The first case will take place on the 2nd May; it is an action against Mr Gerding Dr juris and lawyer in Celle[7] brought against him in consequence of an article published in the Hanoverian gazette in which he warns the people from a confederation of the monarchs, saying that things must not be unconditionally trusted to, since they had failed in their promises too. I suspect you recollect this to be Miss Beste’s brother in law; he does however not seem to think much of it, for I constantly see his name in the debates of the Hanoverian house, where it appears he plays a very prominent part as leader of the “Linken” the liberal party. –[8]

My room is very badly furnished, and I have been obliged to hire a few things in order to be enabled to store away all the various objects in my possession. I got a bookshelf. on which I keep my invaluable treasure of books, at the very reasonable sum of 6 d in the same way I hired a chest of drawers and a lamp the first for 3 sh. the letter for 1 s. and all that for the whole of the 5 months. You may imagine how glad I shall be to go back to Vienna and see Mama but yet we shall never be so happy again as formerly. there will always be something wanting. it will never be the same again. I dare say I shall leave here about the last week of August.

Now goodbye dearest, best aunt, pray continue for ever so kindly towards me as you have began, and believe me always to be

your obedient nephew.
W.G.C.

My address is
45 Hohenheim, Stuttgardt.
Würtemberg.

The general religion here is the Lutheran or protestant; this I am very glad of because of all events they dont starve one on Fridays[9]

Address: No envelope

Unpublished. Text: M.S., Pf. Coll., CL’ANA 0043

---

1 Ostend is in Belgium. Mayence is the French for Mainz or Mentz as it was known in English. Heilbronn is located in Germany, some 53 kilometers north of Stuttgart.

2 Heidelberg, Germany, is located in the state of Baden-Württemberg. Schloss Heidelberg (Heidelberg Palace) was the seat of the Palatine electors (http://www.schloss-heidelberg.de/).

3 Hohenheim is located in Germany near to the city of Stuttgart. Today, the area is part of the German state of Baden-Württemberg and Stuttgart is its capital city. When Wilhelm was a student at Hohenheim, Wilhelm I was the ruler of the independent kingdom of Württemberg with its capital city of Stuttgart. Wilhelm I ruled from October 1816 until June 1864 when his son Karl I

succeeded him (The Editors of Encyclopaedia Britannica".Württemberg". *Encyclopaedia Britannica Online*. Encyclopaedia Britannica Inc. n.d. Web. 8 May 2016).

Wilhelm attended the Königlich Württembergische Land- und Forstwirtschaftliche Academie Hohenheim (the Royal Württemberg Agricultural and Forestry Institute, Hohenheim) from 5 April 1850 until 20 August 1850. According to information provided by the University, the institute was founded by Wilhelm I in November 1818 and became an academy in 1847 with "seven professors: two for Agriculture, one of whom was also the director, two for Forestry, one each for Technology, Natural Sciences, Mathematics and Physics". Together with their teachers and nine assistants, students studied "Veterinary Science, Pomiculture and Vegetable Gardening, Bee-keeping, Accounting, Law and agricultural Civil Engineering". By 1848, there were over 100 students enrolled in the college. Authorities continued to add different faculties through the nineteenth century and into the twentieth century. After the Second World War, the college reorganized by adding new departments and faculties. By 1967, the school was renamed the Universität Hohenheim ("Universität Hohenheim". Web. 16 May 2015 and 13 September 2014. https://www.uni-hohenheim.de).

Records of the college register provide information for Wilhelm's stay while at Hohenheim. The register states that Wilhelm was born in London on 20 May 1831 and that his student number while at Hohenheim was 1262. His designated course of study was agriculture ("Landwirthschaft"). The record shows that he took the following subjects: agricultural economics, agronomy, fruit tree breeding, cattle, horse breeding, agricultural technology, geometry, mechanics, and botany. The registry also provides "testimonies" for each student and Wilhelm is rated as "very good" for "diligence". For "knowledge," no remarks are recorded as Wilhelm apparently did not have the opportunity to take part in testing. Another directory records Wilhelm's later profession as an "estate tenant" in the Banat (Dr. Ulrich Fellmeth, Universität Hohenheim, Stuttgart, Germany, personal communication: 15 September 2014).

4 French for "caterer" or German for "head of canteen".

5 A reference to the idealization of Arcadia, the home of the Greek god, Pan, and to Virgil's *Eclogues*.

6 Claire's multiple address changes provided evidence of her peripatetic nature. In 1849, she wrote from West Malling, near Maidstone, Kent. In July 1849, Charles addressed his letters to her at Brighton. By November 1849, Claire was writing from 73 St. John's Wood Terrace, London. In August 1850, she had moved to 2 Acacia Terrace, St. John's Wood. By 1851, her address had changed once again. She was then living at 42 Gloucester Place, Hyde Park.

7 The city of Celle is located in the district of Celle in Lower Saxony, Germany. *Hubbell's Legal Dictionary for Lawyers and Businessmen* listed Dr. Gerding as a lawyer licensed to practice in Celle, Germany (J. H. Hubbell, [Cambridge: Houghton and Company, 1882], p. 874).

8 The German word, "Linke," meaning "the left" (politically). The suffix "en" refers to a plural form. Gerding is identified in a work by twentieth-century artist, Vollrad Kutscher (born 1945). Kutscher created "12 Shining Examples from Celle" ("twelve miniature portraits painted on glass lenses over halogen light"), a photograph of which appears in the catalogue of *The First 24-Hour Museum of Art* (Art Foundation Celle, 1998), pp. 44–5. It identifies Gerding as "Dr. Carl Friedrich Adolf Gerding (1807–1854) Lawyer, leader of the bourgeois revolution in Celle, founder of the People's Association [Gründer des Volksvereins]" (p. 81).

9 Catholics abstained from eating meat on Fridays. They also fasted on Good Friday, and on the Fridays during Lent.

24 • Antonia Clairmont to Claire Clairmont

25th[1] [April 1850]

My dearest Claire.

I write a few lines only to tell you that Pauline sets off to morrow evening 26th and will arrive on the 1st or 2d of May, ~~if~~ no unforeseen delay ~~should~~ occur on the road; she has the highest recommendations one can have, both with regard to her musical attainments and to the general respectability of herself and family, and some pleasant introductions of most distinguished kind, one to the dutchess of Kent[2] by good kind Count Menzdorf,[3] and another to Lady Flora Macdonald[4] by Miss H. the governess of Archduchess Mary Caroline[5] so that she comes into the immediate neighbourhood of Her Majesty the Queen[6] and can hardly fail of success if her endeavours are equal to her good luck; your last letter which I quite innocently asked to see, shows what the contents of hers was to you; thanks to you my dear Claire for being just to me; I am also glad to see Willy is so – as to my violence of temper, you might inquire of all my children whether they ever knew me quarrelling or disputing with any body, or whether discord or enmity and disagreements with friends or acquaintances were ever heard of in our family? and whether I did not often, when warning them of the dangers of gossiping or scandal a common fault with many women – showed them how happily we lived in that respect; and indeed I must say that I have never had to suffer from the ill-will of others, the few friends I have are such indeed, and there was only <u>one</u> that hurt and wounded and illtreated me and besides him my two eldest daughters they gave me pain and grief; but Clary had of late years improved, and I wondered she should have spoken so to you, but it is clear that you fully understood my motives; Emmy and Sidi are more of my character, so as also Willy, of Charley I am not yet sure, but being so like his father in person, I am afraid he will turn like him in character; [illeg.] I am more desirous to keep him with me, that I may do my best – though I sometimes think education is very little indeed, for Pauline and Clara are just the contrary of what I wished them to be; with regard to my going to settle in England, you see now what my personal objections are, pray excuse me but I think the English are more selfish than less enlightened nations and I could not be happy there; I do not expect to find much happiness any where; Good by my dear Claire I think we two should visit each other {tear}all your being English.

Willy has written once; he gave me a full account of the £10 he received from you he is thank God punctual and orderly in his habits. no answer from Court and my affairs are always in the hands of the <u>Magistrat.</u>[7] the books I have sold pretty well, so that I have my rent which I have to pay today £28 – alas – and besides £40 ready money to help out when my lessons ease – I shall also sell some of the furniture, when I move autumn. Now God bless you. I hope you will get on well with Pauline; but I am glad you told her about the social position of females in England – I am never believed – I am yours most gratefully

A.C.

freiung.238. 2de Stiege. 1st Stock.

Aerogramme: Address: Miss Claire Clairmont/ 2. [illg.]side Terrace Ordnance Road/ St John's Wood./ London/ England.
Postmark: [illeg.]/ $^{25}/_{4}$ /5.E; [illeg.]AP[illeg.]/1850; WIEN/25. APR/

Unpublished. Text: M.S., Pf. Coll., CL'ANA 0399

---

1 While the letter itself is undated, the postmark confirms the date of 25 April 1850.

2 Victoria Mary Louisa, Duchess of Kent (1786–1861) was the mother of Queen Victoria (1819–1901). She also had two children by her first marriage, to Ernich Charles, Prince of Leiningen. Her marriage to Queen Victoria's father, Edward, Duke of Kent, who died in 1820, began in 1818 (Elizabeth Longford, "Victoria, Princess, duchess of Kent (1786–1861)", *Oxford Dictionary of National Biography*, Oxford University Press, 2004 [http://www.oxforddnb.com, accessed 8 May 2016]).

3 Count Alexander von Mensdorff-Pouilly (1813–1871) was a well-connected general and diplomat. Alan Palmer explains that von Mensdorff's mother was Princess Sophie of Saxe-Coburg and Gotha, making him a first cousin of Queen Victoria (p. 139). Palmer states that von Mensdorff was "so courteous a gentleman" who "understood the nature of the Monarchy better than most of his successors" (*Twilight of the Habsburgs*, [New York: Atlantic Monthly Press], 1994).

4 Flora Clementine Isabella Macdonald was a lady-in-waiting to Queen Victoria from 1847–1874. The Museum of London has in its collection a figurine of Flora Macdonald made in 1951 as part of an exhibit about the 1851 Great Exhibition.

5 Princess Maria Anna of Bavaria (1805–1877) was the twin sister of Archduchess Sophie (1805–1872) whose husband was Archduke Franz Karl of Austria (1802–1878).

6 Queen Victoria. Victoria succeeded to the throne in 1837.

7 Municipal authorities.

25 • Antonia Clairmont to Claire Clairmont

Freiung 238. 8th [c. May 1850]

My dearest Claire.[1]

Pauline has been gone this week or more she set off on the 26th and yesterday I received a letter dated Berlin. she is staying with Baroness Prokesh[2] the wife of our ambassador at the Prussian Court; I hope she has written to let you know the reason of this long delay; B. Prokesh very fond of her and introduced her to several people who will be useful to her in her carreer in London; but perhaps you have heard from her; with regard to Charley, what you say quite coincides with some informations Andoe received from a friend of his to whom he wrote at my request, and I had before written to Knox to tell of the difficulty I had in deciding upon such a step but for a definite letter I wanted to wait till I heard from them on Pauline's arrival, as I had charged her to tell them verbally all my reasons for disliking the sea for Charley, if I could place him with an engineer; I should be glad to have him spend the next 3 or 4 years in England, not only for the sake of his general education but also because our Polytechnical[3] school is the seat of radicalism, and that I fear his understanding and judgment will be clouded and I beg you to accept of Charles' spectacles, he wore them always[4] prejudiced before his reason is formed, but a friend of ours tells me the praemium[5] to a good engineer is at least £300, and that is far above what I could afford, on the other hand, what you say about the Shelleys makes me alltogether disinclined to send him; for he would be entirely under their influence, and how far desirable would that be? he is very young and flexible – Andoe will come very early this year, he intends being in England by the middle of June, you can speak it over with him and he can also tell you the present state of politics what new cause of dissatisfaction the people of Austria have had lately, and how that made me wish anew to send Charley away; because little good is boding to our poor country; in letters it is so difficult to give a full statement – ~~what~~ he is also informed of poor Charley's bad ways, I told it him in order to make him repress any report that should happen to spread at the Verein[6] of which he is a member, and he also did so; your sympathy my dear Claire is soothing; but you have had to suffer yourself therefore you know what it is; do not say much about it to Pauline, it will only make her irritable; yesterday I went with the children to the churchyard to see the tombstone,[7] it is ready and Pauline has made a slight sketch of it; it is pretty but simple; I thank you much for the 10 pds, it is a great sum here – I am not in want of money till now, because I have odd little things to sell, and my lessons are going on till the end of May or so; I have paid my rent for summer, and am looking out for a smaller lodging, but they are horrid and comparatively much dearer; if the house at W.[8] were only sold all would be well then, I should have a little interest, at present I have nothing at all – Charley is not at all disinclined to embrace his brothers proffession but for the next two years it would make no difference at the Polytechnick[9] – I thank God my dear all has come so as it did – if Charles had lived to know his secret discovered to me, how miserable would he have been, and could I have preserved even outward peace, or could I have remained quiet knowing these shameful transactions – or would he ever have broken off his old ways ?[10] we must bow our heads and thank Him, for he did all for the best; if this catastrophe had taken place five years ago, how much more difficult would it have been to me to complete the children's education and five years later might have brought more misery; well I understand now a hundred things I could not unriddle before; I hope to God she has no bond or writing of some sort or other, to come and claim the little inheritance – I shall be in anxiety about that till the 28th of May – that being the termin[11] set by authorities before the close of the Abhandlung[12]; I can not measure the depth of the grief I should have to suffer if he had been a loving husband and a companion but that he never was. – you see however how things are. - there would have been no need of your assistance then nor now if the money had not gone in that way, we might have lived comfortably and have now retired upon a modest independence, which he might have enjoyed 20 years longer, if he had lived regularly – I always think his irregularities began whilst he was separated from me, going to Vienna before me, and then he was too weak to resist and break off – – – so heartless, and careless of my feelings, and fate in my old age only a hardened libertine could have shown himself – and he must needs come to you for money, and my earnings all went into the household without his ever thanking me for it; now I understand the system of concealing he generally practiced with me, everything was concealed from me, the smallest trifle, even if he bought something, it was to be concealed – do excuse me dearest Claire this subject must give you pain, I'll no more enter upon it – pray write soon again, and tell me how Pauline behaves; what you say about Cläry grieves me deeply; the children miss aunt Claire and beg her to come and see them, and indeed it would not be bad; I have now a fine room to offer. yours most affecty

A.C.

Address: No envelope

Unpublished. Text: M.S., Pf. Coll., CL'ANA 0396

---

1 Although this letter is undated, it was evidently written in 1850, shortly after Pauline's 26 April departure.

2 Baron Anton von Prokesch-Osten (1795–1876) was Austria's ambassador to Berlin from 1849–1852. *The International Monthly Magazine of Literature, Science, and Art* (New York: Stinger & Townsend, December to March 1850–1) recorded the following: "A History of the Greek Revolution is soon to be given to the public by Baron Prokesh Osten, who for many years was the Austrian ambassador at Athens, and who now fills the same office in Berlin. Of course his book will be published at Vienna" (p. 188). Baroness Prokesch-Osten was born Irene Kiesewetter von Wiesenbrunn (1811–1872). She was a celebrated pianist who was known as "one of the foremost pianists in Vienna" and who accompanied the composer, Franz Schubert (Peter Clive, *Schubert and His World* [New York: Oxford University Press, 1997], p. 94). Schubert composed *Kantate für Irene Kiesewetter* in her honor.

3 The Technische Universität Wien was founded in 1815 as the k.k. Polytechnisches Institut (Imperial and Royal Polytechnical Institute). The letters "k.k". stand for "kaiserlich und königlich" which translate as "Imperial and Royal". Today, it is Austria's largest scientific and technical research institution ("Technische Universität Wien". Web. 5 April 2015. https://www.tuwien.ac.at). See also CL'ANA 0402.

4 Antonia wrote the words ("I beg you to accept of Charles' spectacles, he wore them always") upside down at the bottom of the page.

5 Antonia meant "premium," but she confused the German "Prämie" with the English "premium".

6 German for "club" or "union". On 12 November 1849, Antonia assured Claire that all three of her younger children were "good and dear children" (*CC* II: 529).

7 Charles was buried in the cemetery in Währing. See CL'ANA 0042.

8 Weidling.

9 William Johnston explains that the Austrian educational system was reformed in the 1850s and that students were educated to "engage in research". The educational focus shifted from religion and "obedience to the state" to a research-based system. According to Johnston, students were required to spend eight instead of six years in Gymnasium. Instructors were hired to teach in their particular areas of specialization instead of serving as generalists. Ritterakademien ("Knight's Academies") were academies for the children of nobles and they adhered more closely to the existing regulations (*The Austrian Mind* [Los Angeles: University of California Press, 1983], p. 67). Antonia misspelled the German word, "Polytechnik".

10 Charles had conducted an extra-marital affair with Mrs. Kollonitz. See CL'ANA 0395.

11 German for "meeting" or "appointment". The word is a German noun and should be capitalized.

12 German for "treatise" or "written representation of a situation".

26 • Antonia Clairmont to Claire Clairmont

17th[1] [c. May 1850]

My dearest Claire.

My last letter explanative of Paula's stop at Berlin must have been lost and my supposition of her silence proves quite correct; I had a letter from her dated Berlin 4th of May, saying that she stopped with Baroness Prokesh the wife of our ambassador at the Prussian court; we know the family very well and Lady P. always was a particular friend of Pauline's; she also said that she was so well received, and saw a ~~grea~~ great many people who would give her letters for England; Lord Westmoreland,[2] and others, and that she would ~~go~~ continue her journey with a friend of Baroness P's. and would write again when in England. I, knowing her extreme giddiness in matters of business wrote to you directly to explain, but it appears the letter missed, and to day I also received one from Clary; she too is in the most cruel anxiety about her so she has not written to her either: I find her stay at Berlin very improper on account of all the letter of recommendations she has got from high quarters, which I told you off, it seems so neglectful and disrespectful; and impolitic besides, for the season will be over, the people dispersed, and she will have missed the right moment for presenting herself – But that is the way with her any transitory pleasure carries away every thing, and prudence is put aside; I wonder her chest is not arrived I gave your direction, it must soon come, will you have the kindness and pay the carriage out of the £10 she is to receive from you? Captain Andoe intends leaving Vienna by beginning of June he is not here at present having taken a trip to Pesth, but I shall see him before he goes and give him your message. Good bye now dearest Claire, I am in a great hurry being unwilling not to lose to day's post, to put you out of anxiety I wrote also a few times to Clary to quiet her fears – my affairs are not formanded a bit, but the contrary it will be lucky if I have ended ~~in~~ 6 or 8 months hence His majesty did not grant my petition but sent it to the Ministerium,[3] to make it go the usual way, so after 3 months waiting, I ~~am told~~ received notice to put in my regular petition at the Theresianum[4] which means nothing more then, he does not intend doing any thing more for me than the common course of things will allow – the regular petition I can't present till the Abhandlung[5] – transactions of the civil authorities, are finished, so another 4 weeks at least must elapse before I can stir in the matter, and then every body will be gone to the country – I am much vexed at all this unnecessary but yet unavoidable delay – Good bye now I hope you are well, have you heard from Willy? do pray make your letters a little longer

ever yours affectionate
A.C

Captain A.[6] knows all – he and Böhm – the children send their best love, they are all well and well behaving, I have no trouble with them God bless them –

Freiung 238.2te Stiege. 1ter Stock.[7]

Address: No Envelope

Unpublished. Text: M.S., Pf. Coll., CL'ANA 0375

---

1 This letter has no year, but the context dates it to 1850 and probably sometime in May after Pauline's stay in Berlin.

2 John Fane, 11th Earl of Westmoreland (1784–1859), was the British Plenipotentiary to Prussia.

3 German for "Ministry".

4 See CL'ANA 0319.

5 German for "written representation".

6 Andoe. See note 2, CL'ANA 0403.

7 "Stock" refers to the floor/story while "Stiege" is German word for "the stairway".

27 • Antonia Clairmont to Claire Clairmont

2t June [c. 1850]

My dearest Claire.

I can not let Capt Andoe go without some lines to you, though you are in my debt for two letters, which is however not meant as a reproach, but an excuse rather for my writing again. I tremble with anxiety to hear from you how you are satisfied with Paula, having made such painful experiences in Clara's case, ~~which~~ who was always so much prepossessed in your favour, and went over with the certainty to love you so well, ~~as~~ being her father's only sister! and to find you all she wished me to be; – I have written to Knox to thank him for his kindness to Willy, and I let him into the secret of poor Charles' errors[1] – in that I had several reasons, and I think you will agree with me; first I wanted to ask him several questions about his will and life insurance, then to show why Charles did not write and to let him see what misery is caused by such proceedings, and also in case you should chance to drop a word, that it might not be turned towards you; and so I hope I have done right; I charged him to keep it secret; and with regard to his wife[2] tell her or not as he thought fit;
you will hear from Paula's letter the hopes I have of keeping Willy here near me instead of sending him again to Würtemberg – however every thing is so vague and uncertain that I cannot say; I mean so or so, but must take patience – I add here a sort of prospectus of the colonies [3]about to be established in Hungary under the special protection of government. perhaps I shall find my self there some day or other – if only my affairs were once in order, the house sold, my petition answered, so that I might leave Vienna for that place is hateful to me; there has just been Mrs Walter's[4] maid to ask for Pauline's direction; I gave it but let her understand to frank her letters for it would not do to overcharge Paula with postages, for Mrs Walter's interest; I also plainly told her P. could not see Mrs Palsky[5] so she knows it at once, it is by far the best way Pauline will explain all this if you do not understand it; Pray my dear Claire you mentioned once about some reports you heard in disfavour of P. and C.[6] what would that have been and who were the persons, for I have no idea, can you tell me?

The abhandlung[7] is now at a close, and thank God, till now I have not heard of my claims having come forward; but other things I continually hear, which show what a complete dupe I was and have been these twenty years. yet it is not known generally; several inferiors know of it; Good bye now dearest Claire, my money affairs go on so, so, I am still selling off one thing or other, and hope I shall have help sent when needed – your own words "God will reward you" are often present to my mind putting assist instead of remand – I trust in him! the children send their best love, I embrace you and remain ever your affectiona{tear}

A.C.

To Miss Claire Clairmont.[8]

Address: No envelope

Unpublished. Text: M.S., Pf. Coll., CL'ANA 0395

---

1 In her letter to Antonia of 1 August 1850, Claire chastised her sister-in-law for writing letters to both Mary Shelley and to Knox. Claire expressed her "great pain" over the knowledge that Antonia had told Knox "of my Brother's errors". She was also upset that Antonia had written to Mary Shelley (*CC* II: 532). Claire feared that Knox would divulge all to the Shelleys, thereby "putting a weapon into her hands to injure our family" (p. 533). Claire drew an analogy between Mary Shelley's friendship with Knox (she had long suspected an affair between Mary Shelley and Knox and she indicated as much in her letter) and Charles Clairmont's relationship with Mrs. Kollonitz, and she urged Antonia to consider how she would feel if Claire were to write to Mrs. Kollonitz "after the injuries she has inflicted upon our family". Claire concluded by suggesting that Mary Shelley was "an enemy" and Antonia a "traitor" (p. 533).

2 Clara Clairmont.

3 This "prospectus" is missing.

4 Unidentified.

5 In "Claire Clairmont's Lost Russian Journal," Herbert Huscher records that Wilhelm told his family that Miss Miller, who resided with Claire in Florence, was "with Mrs. And Mr. Pulsky" (p. 42). Huscher misspells Miss Müller's name. Evidently, the Pulskys employed Miss Müller and perhaps Pauline. See CL'ANA 0289 and CL'ANA 0320. Antonia spelled the name as either "Pulsky" or "Palsky".

6 Pauline and Clara.

7 Antonia wrote the word without a capital letter.

8 Antonia wrote these words on the back page of the letter.

28 • Wilhelm Clairmont to Claire Clairmont

Hohenheim, July 21st
1850.

My dearest aunt.

I am quite astonished to see by the almanac that very nearly a month has passed since I had your last letter, indeed I am quite ashamed of so [~~illeg.~~] longe a silence, but time does pass so very rapidly that one is not at all aware of it, besides I am always very busy. I need not say how glad I was to have again some news from you, but above all things I was glad to think that your health is at least in pretty good condition. I am sure that this summer will contribute very much towards its restoration, the winter of course was not very favourable for that but now I feel convinced you will be improving from day to day and be stronger and healthier than ever, especially since the sickly matter has been removed from your system by this decisive crisis.

I thank you very much dearest aunt for the kind manner in which you always think of me and the trouble you take about my health;[1] your letters are a constant proof of it; yet I am very sorry to say that it is out of my power to employ this remedy you mention in your last about the ice water, for ~~there is~~ neither ice nor ices are to be had either in our establishment or anywhere else 6 miles around so I shall have to put this off until I come to Vienna. –[2] The Brighton plan is of course unfeasible under the present circumstances, and I must console myself as well as I can for the lost hope of seeing all of you; perhaps it will be some other time.

I dare say you have heard of the gigantic step the Austrian cabinet has taken in removing Haynau.[3] It all depends whether this measure was resorted to from a serious conviction of what is most urgent necessity to the country, or whether it was merely hurt pride in the young emperor a feeling one could well enough imagine for it appears the General neglected his commands in the most arbitrary manner. The people here all seem imbibed with the idea of a general war; indeed the English farmer when walking through his quiet fields grumbling may be about the "damned freetraders" is nevertheless an enviable being when compared with these [illeg.] wretched creatures. I have been in several villages that have lost more than two thirds of their population by emigration and Würtemburg is one of the few German countries that favours the English colonies in Australia in preference to America.[4] they all write with great pomp that they have now become subjects of the Queen of England; but it seems on the whole they get on very well, for their relatives always receive urging letters to follow them and indeed they[5] state of things here is entirely calculated to make one inclined for similar propositions – Nevertheless I cant help thinking that the worst is over now in Austria. for this measure will answer many purposes; by dismissing it so unceremoniously they wish to assume an appearance as if they disapproved his former line of conduct, and by thus making him appear the author of a great deal of mischief the[6] hope to turn all the blame of the past year on his shoulders whilst they themselves seem guiltless. If this little stratagem succeeds and all the wrath and ire of the people be concentrated on that unfortunate man, and the court party seem purified in the eyes of the people at large I have no doubt it will work in a very conciliatory manner.[7]

I am very much obliged to you for your offer of sending me something; you know the ~~his~~ only things I want are books and cloths. of the latter I hope to have enough. to get through the winter and the former I know not whether you and capt. Andoe will approve of it. My great desire is to have "The Farmers library, Animal Economy published by Knight 2 large Qarto vols. with a great number of prints and engravings. (second hand.) it is an excellent work the greater part of it by Youatt.[8] M[r] James Hall, <u>Medical Bookseller, St. Aldersgate street City</u> offered it me for 14 sh. which is comparatively very cheap; the others asked for 16 or 18 sh.; of course he might send it to your house; but the work is rather voluminous and it would first be necessary to ask capt. Andoe whether he could take it, it is the usual Quarto size each volume rather above an inch thick; but [~~illeg.~~] it is to be seen in any of the larger bookshops in Oxford Street

Address: No envelope

Unpublished. Text: M.S., Pf. Coll., CL'ANA 0044

---

1 In her letter to Wilhelm of 10 March 1850, Claire inquired about her nephew's health. She asked if he drank beer and if he felt weak. She also questioned Wilhelm about the nature of his breathing (*CC* II: 530).

2 Hydrotherapy was used as a cure for a variety of ailments in the nineteenth century. Vincent Priessnitz promoted the cure at a spa in Gräfenberg, Austria in the 1830s. He would induce sweats in his patients, which he would then follow with "cold baths". Patients were also exposed to the "cold douche," a procedure during which they were showered with icy water. According to Roy Porter, "Priessnitz's establishment became immensely popular; in 1839 it played host to one monarch, one duke, one duchess, 22 princes and 149 counts and countesses. Bored with Bath, the British upper classes arrived in the 1840s" (*The Greatest Benefit to Mankind: A Medical History of Humanity*, [New York: Norton, 1997], p. 392).

3 Julius Jacob Freiherr von Haynau (1786–1853) was a general in the Austrian army known for his brutal behavior during military action. In 1848–9, he was responsible for the execution of twelve men in the Italian city of Brescia and thus became known as the "hyena of Brescia". In 1849, he became commander of the Hungarian army and conducted vicious campaigns during military conflicts (I. Rév, *Retroactive Justice*, [Stanford: Stanford University Press, 2005]. p. 77). He was attacked while in London in 1850 and a plaque to commemorate this incident was erected on Park Street. The plaque reads as follows: "An International Incident Occurred Here – 1850. General Haynau 'The Austrian Butcher' was recognized and attacked by Barclay & Perkins Draymen". The visual engraving shows Haynau being whipped by two draymen ("Open Plaques". Web. 6 April 2015. http://openplaques.org/plaques/11882). The word "Freiherr" means a Baron.

4 See CL'ANA 0071 and CL'ANA 0075 for information about German immigration to Australia.

5 Wilhelm wrote "they" for "the".

6 they.

7 Theodore Martin, in *The Life of His Royal Highness the Prince Consort*, describes the attack on Haynau. Martin recorded that an "evil reputation preceded him. His several measures of repression at Brescia and other places in Italy, and subsequently in Hungary – still more, charges of having

flogged women among the Hungarian insurgents, and encouraged reprisals happily little known in modern warfare, had made his name a byword as a monster of cruelty". According to Martin, Haynau was attacked with a "truss of straw" and he was "pelted with a shower of missiles". He was even "dragged along the road by his moustache" ([London: Smith, Elder, and Company, 1876], p. 324).

8 Wilhelm referred to *The Farmer's Library, Animal Economy*. Charles Knight published it in London in 1847–1848. The authors were William Youatt and W.C.L. Martin. The two-volume work explained animal breeds, management of the breeds, and diseases affecting the various animals. Chapter headings in Volume I included "The Ox" and "The Horse" while Volume II was devoted to a study of "The Sheep," "The Dog," "The Hog," "Poultry," and "Bees".

29 • Antonia Clairmont to Claire Clairmont

22nd-7-1850.

My dearest Claire.

I put off writing to you so long, always hoping I should be able to tell you something conclusive of my affairs, but alas, by the new law arrangements that are taking place through out the whole monarchy, every thing is put out of order, and slow and heavy as legal proceedings always are, it is much worse now – the worst thing is that I have not even put in my petition to the Theresianum.[1] I may not till I have not done with the civil authorities – and there has been appointed a new director there – that is a disadvantage too; this newcomer ~~did~~ has not known Charles nor his active exertions for the institution; our laws for guardianship are only calculated for large fortunes, in a case as mine they become harassing and disturbing; tho [~~illeg.~~] I am named guardian of the children and the care of maintaining and educating them is left solely to me, yet with the money I am not to be trusted – the wife has no right whatever to any of the property of her deceased husband, if not legalized, by some writing or agreement, a line of his hand is sufficient, but if nothing of the sort is found, the law has the right to sell everything and put the money by for the children; now Charles' personal property has been valued at £35 – for in consideration of my paying taxes to the state in my own right as school mistress they allowed half of the town furniture to belong to me – this sum I must lay down at the Majistracy[2] – raised by 1/3 – in order to have the free use of the effects – if I do not, they seize upon them and sell them by auction, to secure the money for the wards – and what did I do with the things? the watch I keep for Willy, the linen and clothes Charley now wears, some other valuables I put by for them and divided them amongst the others in short what I sold was about 5 pounds worth. Yet I am required to pay such a sum as the above out of my own means, in order to secure those dear relics from being sold to strangers – the half of the house has been valued at £280, and by a mistake of the appraisers the whole of the Weid:[3] furniture has been put in the valuation though half of it belongs to me, so I am short of 15 or 20 pds. to rectify which would have caused so much rewriting, stamps, and loss of time, that I said for God's sake let it pass besides I had nearly £20 of small fees to pay in the course of the affairs, which is a great sum for me – and I have not yet done of course thank God the books were not all put in the valuation, I don't know what I should have done – well when all the formalities are gone through, I am either required to pay down the whole, or have it secured upon the house; the first is preferable because it will leave me a free agent with regard to selling, as in the second I shall be dogged and fettered and every step I wish to take, I shall want the concurrence of the Chancery, so I shall prefer the first, but not having the capital myself, I shall be obliged to borrow it, till the house is sold – and so my little property ~~capital~~ will dwindle away into nothing – well, as God Almighty directs; you said He will reward me – if he will only assist me so far as to finish my boys' education and gives Willy health – as to reward, how could there be compensation for my sufferings – about Willy's going to spend his holydays at Brighton I have to say, that I shall have no obligation to his going if he comes here to Altenburg,[4] but in case of his continuing at H.[5] I should much regret not seeing him at all this autumn for my heart yearns after him, but even then if it is for his health I must not mention my own feelings, but I should like soon to know what is going to be done – as for Pauline I think it could not be so difficult to find a place for her, to be sure it would be a good thing to have her settled; your judgment of her is very true and just, if she were married, to a good man, capable of guiding her she will turn out well – it was partly her giving lessons, which gave her that feeling of independence and habits of free movements so pernicious in a young female – therefore Emily shall never give lessons, rather gain her livelyhood with needlework, and remain under my own eye – she is a good child and a dutiful one – Mrs. Shelley's letter I have answered already, in a simple and polite way, having considered her note as a matter of etiquette, I answered it as such;[6] what you say about dividing the children is true, but if fate wills it so I cannot counteract, think only of my poor miserable finances, I shall be happy and think myself rich with 80 pds per an. pension and all – how could I go to England? I grieve to think that so many fine spots are on this globe, and yet I forced to remain here where detested recollections assail me on all sides; let me see Willy first, ascertain the state of his health and hear what our physicians say of it, and in the course of this winter my affairs must be concluded, then I shall be able to decide upon some ~~thing~~ step to be taken – Charley remains at his studies as <u>Technicker</u>[7] he is growing so immensely now, a head taller than I. Good by now my dearest Claire, with my best thanks for all your kindness for Pauline I remain yours most affecty. A–C. the children send their best love.

Address: No envelope

Unpublished. Text: M.S., Pf. Coll., CL'ANA 0319

---

1 According to the archives of the Universität Wien, Charles was a substitute teacher of English Language and Literature at the Theresianische Ritterakademie (the Theresianum), a school for young noblemen founded by the Empress Maria Theresia in 1746 (see CL'ANA 0396). On 7 January 1840, the Government of Lower Austria (Niederösterreich in German) granted Charles permission to give English language and literature lectures at the university level (Dr. Ulrike Denk, Universität Wien, personal communication: 20 February 2015). Lower Austria is one of the nine Austrian Federal States. *Picture of Vienna* (1844) records that the "imperial Theresian Academy" was located on "Favoritten Strasse" and that it was established in 1745 for "young catholic noblemen". The unnamed author describes the school as an "enormous palace" with a "park, botanical garden, swimming school, riding school and extensive library (p. 85). The book describes the curriculum: "After completing the regular course of studies, consisting of humanity, philosophy, law and European languages every pupil has claims to a place in some office of the legislature, with a small salary" (p. 85). On 10–11 November 1848, Charles told Claire that he was continuing in his position although he was concerned about the school's future. The school, he noted, was one of the "principal schools" and therefore was part of the great movement towards reform that resulted

from the Revolution. He explained that, during a previous attempt at reform, certain classes were marked to be "excluded" from the school's curriculum. English language instruction was not considered a "necessity" and Charles feared losing his position. He questioned whether Count Taaffe, the Curator of the Theresianum, would retain him and recognized that his retention would be based on whether Taaffe considered English a necessary subject for students to study (*CC* II: 488). On 12 November 1849, Charles told Claire that he continued to work at the Theresianum but that he chose not to receive his salary, as he preferred to wait until April when his half year's rent would come due (p. 526). As Charles died in February 1850, Antonia retrieved his money from the Theresianum.

Years later, in her letter of 30 May 1875, Claire wrote to Edward Trelawny that Charles had been denied a position as an English professor in Vienna because Mary Shelley had made negative comments against Austria in her book, *Rambles in German and Italy* (1844). This assertion was false, as the fact that Charles was employed at the Theresianum by 1840 reflects.

Today, the Theresianum is still located on Favoritenstrasse in Vienna. The school's website explains that the institution is "one of Austria's oldest schools and can look back on a long tradition of providing top-class education . . . [O]ur pupils . . . should be able to fully develop their potential and thus become open-minded European citizens, ready and willing to take on positions of responsibility in society, as the school's founder Maria Theresia intended" ("Stiftung Theresianische Akademie Wien". Web. 6 April 2015. http://www.theresianum.ac.at/en/home/).

2 Wilhelm meant to write "magistracy".

3 Weidling.

4 In late 1850, Wilhelm began studying at k.k. höheren landwirthschaftlichen Lehranstalt in Ungarisch-Altenburg (Altenburg, Hungary). Altenburg is located in northwestern Hungary about 87 kilometers south-east of Vienna and is known as Mosonmagyaróvár in Hungarian. Today, the academy forms part of the University of West Hungary. While the University of West Hungary is in Sopron (about 90 kilometers south-west of Mosonmagyaróvár), the Faculty of Agricultural and Food Sciences continues to be located in Mosonmagyaróvár. The educational mission of k.k. höheren landwirthschaftlichen Lehranstalt survives in the instruction provided by the Faculty of Agricultural and Food Sciences ("University of West Hungary". Web. 2 October 2014 and 16 May 2015. http://www.uniwest.hu).

5 Hohenheim.

6 In her letter to Antonia of 1 August 1850, Claire expressed her anger over Antonia's correspondence with Mary Shelley. See CL'ANA 0395.

7 German for "technician" or "engineer". The correct spelling is Techniker.

30 • Wilhelm Clairmont to Claire Clairmont

Hohenheim Aug. 11
1850.

My dearest aunt.

This morning I had your kind letter; and as I was just about setting off for Stuttgardt I first sit down to write a few lines and post the letter immediately myself. Many thanks dearest aunt for your never ceasing cares; and your affectionate feeling for me. I need not say that I accept the proposition you make with all my heart; I have just been to s~~ay~~ee our Director:[1] by the 18th August I am ready to star.t and so I think I may indulge in the hope of seeing my dear kind aunt and Paula before many days will have ellapsed.

My journey from London to Hohenheim ~~here~~ cost me £ 6 and that from Vienna to London £ 10. In the first case going from Stuttgardt to ~~Vienna~~ London £ 5 will suffice for the £6 were owing to an overweight of luggage. from London to Vienna I hope that from £ 8–9 will do for my first journey was in winter which always is more expensive. as for sending the money the speediest method would be to include a five pound note in a letter, but then the[~~illeg.~~]re is the risk of its being lost and I know not whether it can be assured; indeed I hardly think it can. otherwise I know no method of doing it, then by sending ~~my~~ the sum with my name to Benedict brothers in Stuttgardt[2] in which case you might pay it to any City merchant for instance to your own bankers Paul; that is at least who I understood Mr Benedict's direction when I asked him. I almost think sending it in a letter would be the best. for the other way will take so very long. and it is of importance that I should profit of the last days of August – In case you are in Brighton already and I know your directions I might go the shortest and cheapest way via Strassburg, Paris and Dieppe to Brighton, for in London I could in no way stop very long because time is flying away. – It will not be necessary for me to ask Mama's permission, but of course I will let her know. Now good bye dearest aunt if all goes well I hope to be with you very soon. The S.'s[3] I will not see of course

ever your affectionate nephew W.G.C.

I think I have thus said every thing that is necessary: I shall be ready to start by the 18th. Please give me also your exact address; if London shall I join you in the old lodging in Acacia terrace?[4] I think you do best by sending the money in the letter but not paying the letter.

once more Good bye.[5]

My dear Pauline! please tell Clara of what has been decided, and excuse me for not writing to her about it in case I should have no time the last moment.

Address: No envelope

Unpublished. Text: M.S., Pf. Coll., CL'ANA 0045

1 Dr. Heinrich Wilhelm von Pabst served as director of the academy in Hohenheim. In October 1850, he left Hohenheim to assume directorship of the Agricultural Academy in Altenburg. See CL'ANA 0319 and CL'ANA 0046. Wilhelm thus enjoyed von Pabst's leadership at both of the agricultural institutions he attended in Europe.

2 Benedict Brothers was a banking house in Stuttgart. Members of Stuttgart's Jewish community who served as bankers, merchants, and court agents, owned it. In the nineteenth century, Moses Benedict (1772–1852) founded a private bank together with his brother Seligmann (1770–1842). The bank was known as Benedict Brothers (Yad Vashem. "Stuttgart". Web. 6 April 2015. http://www.jewishgen.org/yizkor/Pinkas_germany/ger2_00141.html). Moses's son, Adolf Benedict (1801–1876) also worked at Benedict Brothers (Hofmann, Rolf. "Family Sheet Baruch Benedict of Kriegshaber & Stuttgart". Web. 6 April 2015. http://www.alemannia-judaica.de/images/Images%20190/FS-BENEDICT-BARUCH.pdf).

3 Shelleys.

4 Claire provided her address as 2 Acacia Terrace, Ordnance Road, St. John's Wood in her letter to Antonia of 1 August 1850 (*CC* II: 532).

5 The preceding paragraph was written on the top of the second page of the letter. The following paragraph was written at the bottom of the second page of the letter.

31 • Antonia Clairmont to Claire Clairmont

[18 September 1850]
18th Weidling

My dear Claire.

Yours reached me duly and I should have answered directly but for my being constantly engaged with the workpeople at the unfortunate Wasserleitung,[1] which is undergoing a great repair, and cost me a great deal of money, it is however of too much consequence to the house, to risk the loss of the water, so I must go through with it though I can but ill afford it. I am extremely sorry my dear Claire you should be hurt or grieved by any step of mine, the two notes[2] that passed were mere matter of convenience, or ettiquete an thing that was proper to be done, and nothing more – I detest family quarrels, and will not contribute to carry them on; Clara is married, and all we could say and do, will not change it, it will only make her uncomfortable;[3] I have just had a letter of her telling me of the letter you made Pauline write to Mrs S.[4] in consequence of which the two sisters are in discord; might they not reproach you with setting niece against aunt and sister against sister? and what good is the result of it?[5] I find it even highly improper for a young girl to step forward to take up a cause her own father choose to let at rest; she ought to have been guided by her father's behaviour, and not openly disapprove it by her actions;[6] and if ~~Pau~~ Mrs S. chose she might do Pauline serious injury in public opinion, just when she must try to find a footing and make or establish her character in the world – [7] and yet Clara remains married, nor is her husband's connexion with the S[8] at all changed – so what is your object? would it not be better to leave them alone and let the two sister enjoy a quiet intercourse, which may not perhaps last very long – Clara says and assures us of her happiness in her husband – let her enjoy it; the delusion will break too soon; oh my dear Claire; if I think of all that may lie in wait for her! blessing on her blindness – she is now in the sunshine of life, how soon will clouds arise, poor girl; just now I received Willy's letter, he tells me of your kindness to him, he seems in such good spirits, I am happy and grateful to you, and fully and entirely forgive you the nasty insinuations in your last about my paying regard to riches[9] – you cannot mean it, you were irritated, in ill health when you said so – I will forget it, but you must recall it. I am not mercenary, and do not care for riches nor do I like to play the poor relation or sycophant rather eat dry bread – ~~and~~ work hard, and trust in God; if only 2 years were passed and dear Willy's education finished, then I hope to have some support in him! what he tells me of his health is astonishing; I begin now and then ~~of the po~~ to consider the possibilities of emigrating to some warmer climate on his account – but the journey is so expensive I shudder when I think if it; when he is once here we shall talk it over, and consider all the chances; at all events his education must be finished first; – [10]

I am under great uneasiness of how my school and lessons will turn out this winter for now when every thing depends on their success, it is of more consequence than formerly; I wish to God I could spend a couple of months in England, it would do my English a great deal of good; a Mr de Lambert[11] who was formerly at Pesth[12] giving lessons has come here and received the Place at the Theresianum; as for a Pension nothing is decided as yet; it is even supposed it will depend entirely on account of, or under plea of our possessing that poor Weidling house; that is the favour of the Great; unfortunately people think we have saved a great deal of money; he had such a good income, is the general cry, I cannot explain where the money went to; when I had delivered my petition to his Majesty, sometime after Countess Schönborn[13] sent to me a gentleman Mr Battaglia[14] to know what I received from England, the Ctss S. knew Mr Clair:[15] to have received money from England regularly, whether it was possible that support was now withdrawn entirely, which I could best prove by showing your letter,[16] and was greatly commented upon the next time I saw the Ctss herself, and yet nothing is done for me. If I can only sell the remaining books – Good bye now my dear Claire, I hope you will write soon, and direct to town, for I shall go there by the 1[17] to receive dear Willy; it would have been a good opportunity for you to come to Vienna; but I have let half my Lodging, so no room to receive you. the children send their best love, and all beg you to come with Willy, they say it would be so nice to have Aunt Claire here. Ever yours

affect. A. C.

Address: Mademoiselle/Mad[lle] Claire Clairmont/Poste restante[18]/ Boulogne sur mer/France.
Front postmark: Wien/ 24 SEP
Rear postmark: Calais/ 26/ SEPT./ [illeg.]; [illeg.]/ SEPT./50

Unpublished. Text: M.S., Pf. Coll., CL'ANA 0398

1 German for "water pipe".

2 Antonia's letters to Mary Shelley and to Knox. See CL'ANA 0310 and CL'ANA 0395.

3 See CL'ANA 0041 for information about Clara's marriage to Knox.

4 Mary Shelley.

5 Pauline arrived in England in May 1850, expecting to secure a position as a governess or as a teacher of German and music (see CL'ANA 0399 and CL'ANA 0212). Claire told Antonia in her letter of 1 August 1850 that she had shown Pauline letters from Mary Shelley confirming, in Claire's opinion, the relationship between Knox and Mary Shelley (*CC* II: 533). Pauline therefore wrote a letter to Mary Shelley, addressing this issue, which led to a disagreement with Clara Knox. Just as Claire had encouraged Pauline to write to Mary Shelley, Claire later urged Wilhelm to write to Sir Percy Florence Shelley about the family dispute (see CL'ANA 0052). Claire also attempted to persuade Wilhelm to tell Sir Percy that his wife, Lady Jane Shelley, had been involved in Clara's marriage plans, but Wilhelm declined to write such a letter as he feared that Knox would discontinue his support of Charley's education (see CL'ANA 0052).

6 Charles Clairmont evidently hoped to reconcile with his daughter as he encouraged Wilhelm to correspond with Clara after her marriage (*CC* II: 518), and he communicated to Claire his plan to send money to Clara: "I was going to say it is hardly reputable for me to let Clary marry without some little fitting out; my intention is therefore to give her £50 (*CC* II: 512). On 29 August 1849,

he expressed concern over the "State of affairs" between Claire and the Knoxes: "You seem to wish I should forbid all correspondence; I do not think this politick, for W: although he considers (her) Clara quite in the wrong, is very much attached to her, and I fear such a prohibition from me might only lead to murmurs and perhaps dissimulation, which I would of all things avoid" (*CC* II: 520–1).

7 Claire's letter of 1 August 1850 in which she expressed concern that Mary Shelley and Knox shared information may have prompted Antonia's fear that Mary Shelley would injure Pauline in "public opinion". However, in her letter of 6 September 1853, Claire absolved Mary Shelley of criticizing her to Clara and instead blamed Lady Jane Shelley for speaking "ill of me" (*CC* II: 545).

8 Shelleys.

9 In her letter of 1 August 1850, Claire accused Antonia of pandering to the Shelleys because of their wealth: "Be assured the Shelleys have been the very first to despise you for your letter and are highly pleased to think they have found in you a person who will swallow from them because they are rich, any insult they like to offer" (*CC* II: 533).

10 In previous letters, Claire had expressed concern for Wilhelm's health. On 11 April 1849, she noted that Wilhelm's "glands are very bad again lately" (*CC* II: 496). Charles thanked Claire for organizing "sea bathing" for Wilhelm, which Charles hoped would "restore the sort of equilibrium that is disordered in his system" (*CC* II: 512). Claire also encouraged Wilhelm to drink a pint of beer a day, offering to pay for it (*CC* II: 535).

By 1849, Charles had made all the arrangements for Wilhelm's future educational training and he asked Claire to assist him financially (*CC* II: 521–2). Claire declined, perhaps because she was still angry about Clara's marriage (see CL'ANA 0394), and Knox provided the needed funds instead.

11 Eduard Labbat de Lambert. Huscher identified de Lambert as "Dr. der Philos., Lehrer der englischen Sprache und Literatur an de K.K. Universität und Professor derselben an der Theresianischen und orientalischen Akademie, beeidigter Dolmetsch des K.K. Landesgerichts" (English translation: "Doctor of Philosophy, Teacher of the English language and literature at the K. K. University and a professor of English language and literature at the Theresianium and Oriental Academy, and a sworn interpreter at the K. K. regional court"). See "Charles und Claire Clairmont," p. 74. Huscher also notes that de Lambert succeeded Charles after Charles died in 1850.

12 The two formerly two separate cities, Buda and Pest, were united in 1873 to create the modern city of Budapest.

13 Countess Ernestine von Schönborn was a friend of Archduke Francis and Archduchess Sophie. Charles taught English to von Schönborn's children and to the royal children. It appears that Charles had told von Schönborn about his fiscal woes and that she provided Antonia with access to financial advice after Charles's death. Antonia hoped to receive a pension from the Crown.

14 See CL'ANA 0059.

15 Clairmont.

16 Probably a reference to Antonia's letter of 12 November 1849 in which she alluded to Wilhelm's request to live with Clara and Knox because of Claire's refusal to provide Wilhelm with further financial support (*CC* II: 529). See also CL'ANA 0055.

17 first.

18 French for "general delivery". Typically, the words "poste restante" were written on the envelope of a letter to indicate that the mail should be held at the post office until collected by the recipient.

32 • Wilhelm Gaulis Clairmont to Claire Clairmont

3rd Decemb. U. Altenburg.[1]
1850.

My dearest aunt.

I write by return of post in order to acknowledge the receit of your letter of the 27th [illeg.] and to thank you for the five pound note you included; it comes very à propos for my finances are not very brilliant; besides I have no doubt I shall at least make £1 on it so as to get £6 in Austrian money for it, because the value of silver and consequently foreign money is so very high;[2] Two days ago it was 52 per cent. now Silver is still 32 per cent above par. It is not yet decided whether I am going to have the place or not, and as for my future prospects in Austria I can not as yet see clearly enough what awaits me. I have not seen the Countess Schönborn[3] because she was out of town during my sojourn there, I do not think that I shall find much success in taking a situation; it is more likely that I may try to get a situation at one of the Agricultural colleges which are going to be established all over Austria; I think I may say that I am farther advanced in sciences than the greater part of my schoolfellows here, besides ordinary breeding and but somewhat of a gentleman is a thing not at all in common currency here; so that even that would give me some advantage over my competitors; if not over all, yet over many. Dir Pabst[4] who is now a great man in Austria and into whose hands all those things are put, seems to ~~be very fond~~ have taken a liking to me; at least he treats me with great kindness. You must however recollect that this is only a vague kind of project which I have not even told of to Mama. and who knows perhaps my throat if it continues in that state of weakness, may prove an obstacle, preventing me from talking which I should be obliged to do; Therefor I beg you that you will tell no one of it because it is t~~a~~edious to ~~talk~~ have such uncertain plans talked of. – As for Hungary there is no doubt, that a great deal might be done; but there is one great barrier there is no one to your work, because the people are not enough or too lazy. Thus you see vast tracts of land, excellent soil but not cultivated; On my way to Vienna I have to cross a heath through which we drove for more than 2 hours a good trot without ever seeing a house or a tree. Land is now comparatively dear, because as I have told you before, the value of paper currency has sunk so very much and the people are inclined to be afraid of a national bankruptcy; I dont think there is the slightest idea of any such thing; yet we are made to feel all the doleful consequences as if it actually existed. no one sells land or anything like real property unless he is obliged. In general land is cheapest the farther south and eastward you go, close to the Austrian ~~p~~borders it is dearest; average price of land here is from £6 to 8 per Austrian acre which is equal to 1 2/5 English acre.[5] One of the young men here bought an farm which he is going to manage for himself next year, and he paid £10 per acre. This was a small farm of 100 and some odd acres; but all people assure me that you get larger ones of 800 and 1000 acres, which are above the reach of the smaller capitalists, at 25 and 30 per cent cheaper, The usual rent of land is 6 1/2 or 5 per cent; the taxes imposed something like 4 per cent. but all agree that the latter will be raised to very nearly the double. Here in this neighbourhood there are no small farms whatever to be sold; but farther inland there are ~~and~~ sometimes at ama~~n~~zingly cheap prices; great caution and circumspection is requisite in bargains of that kind so as not to be deceived by the apparently low price; the distance of any market town may be enormous, the fields may be in such a state as not to yield anything for the next 5 or 6 years. it may be indispensibly necessary to lay out great sums in repairing the buildings or roads through the estate, and last of all you may not be able to get workmen at any price for the Hungarians are a singular people and no one can understand them except who has seen it himself. Of estates with a title I have not heard anything in this neighbourhood. I shall however inquire.

I am sorry to hear dear aunt that you have had such turmoil with this wretched Operabox; if you could but manage to get rid of it in a decent way; this year however I have no doubt it will do well for the season will be a splendid one. The engraving of the Chrystall palace pleased me very much;[6] pray send me another print concerning the exhibition if there exists one; for that interests me very much – I now am reading W. Irving's Sketchbook[7] which interests me exceedingly; what capital descriptions he sometimes ~~of~~ gives of English scenes and character. almost as well as Dickens. – This reminds me of a question that I have to put to you, it is a line of W. Scott[8] which I can not understand: Canto I. chapt. 13. Onward amid the copse ' gan peep – A narrow inlet etz – (Lady of the lake –) I can not understand this phrase at all; what is 'gan ? – then there is the word stalwart. A stalwart stag, a stalwart arm.[9] Pray dear aunt be so kind as to give me an explanation of this in your next letter.

Miss Beste has I trust by this time got over all the fatigues and endurances of a winter's ~~travel~~; journey and is now save[10] and sound in London; do not forget to give her my best remembrances. the Pringles will be glade[11] enough for having her again; but Miss Ada ?[12] I envy her for being in England; it is a different thing from what it is here; the people are all so idiotic; only think the postmaster here wanted me to pay 55 [illeg.] for your last letter which was paid, because the fool took the number of my house 55 for the postmark. If it depended on myself you need not doubt I would most willingly go to England or to the Colonies; but I can not leave Mama just as I am growing up and getting fit to do something towards support{tear} her. her affairs are not at all in a good {tear} and it is to be questioned whether she will {tear} able to go on very long; perhaps in 4 years I shall at any rate be enabled to offer her at least a lodging somewhere on a farm house or in the country; this would be something at any rate.

Now Goodbye dearest aunt, thank you once more for your kindness and do write as soon as you can, particularly how your health is; I have had a slight attack of fever which went off of itself; I consulted however the Doctor (who at the same time is my Professor and a very clever man)[13] whether there was any danger of the Hungarian fever.[14] he said however this was not the season, nor did I appear to have a constitution liable to suffer much from it; but he said what you must particularly guard against is simply the taking cold; he forbid me wine which is drunk so much here, but he allows me beer which I take almost daily. I also had that hacking cough returning, he drove it away by a simple medicine consisting of oil of amands, gum arabic, gimamre[15] and some ingredients like that; it has not returned since. My throat continues well both in and out side. I wonder what the S.'s[16] are doing in Hants.[17] once moor[18] goodbye. your dutiful nephew

W.G.C.

Address: Aerogramme: Miss Clairmont/ Carlo Cottage, Waverly Place/ St. John's wood/ England. London
Postmark: Ung. Altenburg/ $^{6}/_{12}$

Unpublished. Text: M.S., Pf. Coll., CL'ANA 0046

---

1 Wilhelm began his studies at the academy in 1850. Records from the university's register provide information about the courses he studied (such as anatomy and meteorology), the fact that no disciplinary actions were taken against him, and his personal information. The register documents that Wilhelm was born in Vienna on 28 May 1831 and that he was a Catholic. He completed his studies in 1852. In 1865, Professor Hugo Hippolyt Hitschmann, a former student at the school and later a professor, collected information on some 2,000 former students, including Wilhelm. He published this information in *Verzeichniss der Lehrer und Studirenden der erzherzoglichen landwirthschaftlichen Bildungsanstalt und der k. k. höheren landwirthschaftlichen Lehranstalt zu Ungarisch-Altenburg 1818–1848 und 1858–1864* (Ung. Altenberg: Alexander Czéh, 1865 [translation: "Register of Teachers and Students of the Archducal Agricultural Academy and the k. k. Higher Agricultural Academy of Altenburg-Hungary 1818–1845 and 1850–1864]). See note 4, CL'ANA 0319. *Verzeichniss* records Wilhelm's name as "Wilhelm v Gartlis Clairmont" instead of Gaulis. Hitschmann provides Wilhelm's semester of entry to the college ("1850–51"), his birthdate, place of birth, and his profession (pp. 10–11). Under the column headed "Gegenwärtig" (German for "currently"), Wilhelm is listed as a "Gutspächter bei Temesvár in Ungarn" ("an estate tenant near Temesvar in Hungary"). Professor Hitschmann also collected photographs of the students and the university archive has photographs in its files of of Wilhelm and his friend, Rudolf Hauer (Mr. Attila Németh, Secretary of the Alumni Association, University of West Hungary, personal communication: 1 October 2014). See the photograph of Wilhelm from the university records in this collection.

2 Charles Conant notes that paper money was the main form of currency used in the Austrian empire from 1800. However, he argues that the reliance on paper money posed a "serious detriment" to commercial activities in the empire in that war and the "over-passed" limit on the amount of money in circulation contributed to this "downward course". Conant explains that in 1806 paper money "circulated for only half its value in silver, which was then the metallic standard . . . The need for funds was so urgent that decrees were issued ordering the transmission to the Treasury of silver vessels, jewelry . . . which were paid for in paper money at three times their specie value" (pp. 219, 222). At the beginning of the Revolution of 1848, the government created laws to prevent gold and silver from leaving the country and then replaced small coins – six kreutzer and ten kreutzer – with bank and Treasury bills (p. 226). Charles Kindleberger notes that after the financial crisis of 1873, "high agio [exchange rate] on silver built up until 1879," after which it decreased following the declining price of silver. By 1892, gold replaced silver as the standard of value and bank notes were linked to the gold standard (*A Financial History of Western Europe*, [London: George Allen, 1985], p. 130).

3 See CL'ANA 0398.

4 Professor Hitschmann includes a brief biography in his *Verzeichniss* of Professor Heinrich Wilhelm von Pabst. Hitschmann records that Pabst was born in 1798 in Maar in the Grand Duchy of

Hesse and that he held the degree of Doctor of Philosophy. From October 1850 until March 1861, Pabst served as director of the agricultural institute in Altenburg. In 1864, by the time Hitschmann published the *Verzeichniss*, Pabst was serving as an assistant head of a government department and chair of the department of Rural Management (land improvement) in the k. k. Ministry for Trade and National Economy in Vienna. He was an honorary member of many national and international educational associations (p. 4, Prefatory material). Ulrich Fellmeth notes that Pabst implemented "a new university constitution" while at Hohenheim but that he left the academy due to a dispute with the Württemberg ministry. He published prolifically and made enormous contributions to the field of agricultural sciences. He died in 1868 (Fellmeth, Ulrich. "Pabst, Heinrich Wilhelm von". *New German Biography* 19 (1999), p 738 f [Online version]. Web. 16 May 2015. http://www.deutsche-biographie.de/ppn116013990.html).

5 The *Farmer's Magazine* of January – June 1873 notes that one Bavarian acre is "equal to about five-sixths of an English acre" (London: Rogerson and Tuxford, 1873) p. 289.

6 Designed by the architect Joseph Paxton (1803–1865), the Crystal Palace was built in Hyde Park, London, to house the Great Exhibition of 1851. The Crystal Palace's website provides the following information: Over six million people visited the glass structure during the six month-long exhibition. In 1852, the building was re-erected on Sydenham Hill. A fire destroyed it in 1936. Today, the Crystal Palace Museum in London retells the story of the original palace's construction and its subsequent move to Sydenham Hill. The museum is housed in a building constructed by the Crystal Palace Company, which built the original palace ("Crystal Palace Museum". Web. 6 April 2015. http://www.crystalpalacemuseum.org.uk/).

7 Washington Irving (1783–1859) was an American writer who wrote *The Sketch-Book of Geoffrey Crayon, Gent.* in 1819. The book consists of 34 essays and includes the short stories, "The Legend of Sleepy Hollow" and "Rip Van Winkle". Mary Shelley considered him a friend and she told Louisa Holcroft in 1825, "Remember me to him & tell him I claim his promised Visit when he does come" (*LMWS* I: 464). Sunstein references Mary's friendly interest in Irving, recording that Mary Shelley confessed it to their mutual friend, John Howard Payne. Sunstein explains that Payne showed Irving Mary Shelley's letter in which she asked Payne to give her love to Irving, thereby "exposing her to humiliation . . . and probably chilling whatever interest Irving may have had in her" (pp. 267–8).

8 Sir Walter Scott (1771–1832) wrote his six-canto-long narrative poem, *The Lady of the Lake; A Poem*, which was published in 1810. The correct line is "Onward, amid the copse 'gan peep/ A narrow inlet, still and deep,/ Affording scarce such breadth of brim/ As served the wild duck's brood to swim" (*Project Gutenberg* I, xiii).

9 Canto I, verse XXVIII: "'I never knew by one,' he said/ 'Whose stalwart arm might brook to wield/ A blade like this in battle-field.'" Canto I, verse XXIX: "This morning with Lord Moray's train/ He chased a stalwart stag in vain,/ Outstripped his comrades, missed the deer,/ Lost his good steed, and wandered here.'"

10 safe.

11 glad.

12 Ada Ramsbottom (see CL'ANA 0191, CL'ANA 0042, CL'ANA 0351 and CL'ANA 0231).

13 Probably Dr. Anton Masch. Hitschmann's list of people associated with the school k.k. höheren landwirthschaftlichen Lehranstalt identified him as a "med. Dr.,"; and a professor at the academy from October 1850 until 1863 (*Verzeichniss*, prefatory material, no page number).

14 Charles Creighton describes Hungarian fever as "notorious," noting that the fever "had become the dreaded name for war-typhus of a peculiar malignity and diffusive power. It had been so often engendered since the 16th century in campaigns upon Hungarian soil as to have become known everywhere under the name of that country" (*A History of Epidemics in Britain* [Cambridge: Cambridge University Press, 1894], p. 32). Typhus is a highly infectious disease that is often transmitted by lice, ticks and fleas to humans living in close quarters. The onset of the disease is marked by headaches and fever.

15 Wilhelm probably meant "amandes," the French word for almonds. "Gin amer" probably refers to "bitter gin," a mixture of gin and tonic used to treat malaria. Gum arabic was used as a medicinal

agent to assist with a variety of ailments, particularly those associated with painful stomachs and throats.

16 Shelleys.

17 Abbreviation for Hampshire.

18 more.

33 • Antonia Clairmont to Claire Clairmont

[undated, c. 1850]

My dear Claire.[1]

I received yours of the 24th with the half note included, and sit down directly to answer and thank you once more for your kindness, I have also lying before me a letter to Willy to tell him of it so he will shortly write to thank you himself and also tell you what his hopes and views for the future are; but at all events he can't get a place before his studies are over, which will not be till autumn; whether it will then maintain him, the first year is still the question things do not go swimmingly in the Imperial service,[2] especially now where we are in full retro grade to the old state of things, when seniority was everything and merit nothing – letters are most insufficient things but if you will read mine through again, you will find, I have already written to the Knoxes, about my money affairs, to tell them for the next two or three years till the boy's education is finished I shall want some assistance, and as for selling the house, I am always trying to do so, but cannot find a purchaser; I only said, I cannot borrow upon it, without laying my embarrassments bare to all the world, which would be highly detrimental to the children; you ask, how it came the half of the house belonged to me, I'll tell you; when we bought it Charles and Mr Turk the former proprietor were settling the points of the contract, which a notary was taking down, when Turk said, how now Mr. Clairmont don't you present your wife with the country house? Charles hesitated, but on the notary's saying, oh surely half of it? he bowed assent, and so thanks to the interference of these two strangers, I became half proprieter, otherwise, every farthing would would[3] have been wrenched out of my hands by the authorities; was I not obliged to buy off from the magistrate the watch and gold pencil which Ch.[4] wore, and which I wanted to give to Willy and Charley? I had to pay 6 guinees[5] in the masse;[6] on my expostulation that I wanted to give it to ~~the children~~ my sons they said, it was joint property of all the children, and they not being of age they couldnot claim it now. His not making a will proceeded merely from a coward fear of looking forward to death and eternity; he may have draped hints of dying ~~it~~ in his letters to you in order to interest you for the children; he always seemed or pretended to seem greatly to rely on you with regard to them; the children are provided for he would say, to any expostulation of mine on the score of expenses – perhaps he tried to persuade himself of it to silence the occasional warnings of conscience which he must have experienced but enough of this most painful and harrassing subject; whatever is laid to my share, I shall bear with patience and fortitude, if only my boys are got through to do us credit and honour; once it has been in my power to change my childrens fortune for I had an offer of marriage, and a good match it would have been, but I could not make up my mind, after all the sufferings I had gone through and I don't think my duty to my children could have imposed such a sacrifice ~~to~~ on me; even at my age, a mercenary match seems to me an indignity, and in every other point of view it would have been distasteful absurd and ridiculous, a widow near 50 with 6 children to marry again?[7] surely my children could not but agree with me, if they knew of it, but I did not tell them – Good bye now my dear Claire, I hope and wish you will get through all your difficulties; this year is also for you, as for me, a bad one. I have sent over a book to be published in London – Knox has undertaken it, if he succeeded it will be a good thing. E. and S.[8] send their love. ever yours most gratefully A. C.

Address: No envelope

Unpublished. Text: M.S., Pf. Coll., CL'ANA 0369

1 This letter is undated, but the context dates it to sometime in 1850.

2 A position in the Imperial service meant that Wilhelm would have been a public servant, working for a governmental organization.

3 Antonia wrote the word "would" twice.

4 Charles.

5 Antonia combined English ("guinea") and German ("Guinee").

6 Antonia again confused the English ("in the mass", meaning "on the whole") and the German ("Masse," meaning "the bulk").

7 Antonia was born in 1800.

8 Emily and Sidonia.

34 • Wilhelm Gaulis Clairmont to Claire Clairmont

Altenburg, March 2. 1851.

My dearest aunt.

I thank you very much for the half £5 note which you enclosed in your last letter, and which I received duly on the 26 of last month. Your supply comes very much à propos just now for I am going to Vienna in a fortnight, to spend there most likely my last holy days I am to enjoy as a free man; I mean to say an individual not yet chained and checked by worldly business matters. You will certainly agree with me that riding is a most essential thing for a farmer not only for its locomotive facility, but also in valuing and judging of horses. There are riding schools in Vienna where they give the lessons at 2 sh.[1] so that about 25 lessons would make £2.10. Now since it is very likely that a long time may elapse without any such opportunity for me to learn riding, I should not wish it to pass without my profiting of it. I must however see how the state of Mama's finances is, for if she is very badly off, the realization of my scheme for which you have now given me some hope will be impossible, as the £5 you sent me will have to go towards the defray of other immediate expenses.

The news of Mrs. Shelley's[2] death I had first from the papers and afterwards learnt it from Mama but I do not know any of the particulars nor what was the cause of her sudden death; but in fact it does not interest me very much. What you say about Percy's[3] proceeding after her death is really horrifying – I should not have believed it unless it was you that told it me. I wonder whether they did that according to Mrs. Shelley's will or whether it was their own idea? do you know? If there be no other circumstances with which I am not acquainted, and which possibly might soften the case, it is indeed an outrage at which barbarians in the time of paganism would have shuddered; it is a sacrilege – a violation of the most sacred laws – I can not conceive how for the sake of their own name they could dare to do such a thing for it is so atrocious a deed that it can not escape the notice of the public. I wonder what they would say in their defence. Did you make any reply after having received the news by your lawyer?[4] I should never have believed that the daring imprudence of these people should go so far. Pray do tell me in your next, what has happened since, and whether you intend to undertake anything against them and whether I could do anything although I do not see what from this distance – writing a letter would be as good as nothing. He would either return it by Post or not notice it. – At any rate Mrs S's death must be considered as a favourable omen by those who take any interest in Clara for it can not but tend to loosen the connection between K. and the S's.[5]– I even hailed it as the sign and indeed the beginning of a new and better turn of things where I saw all my sanguine hopes destroyed by your last letters.

What you tell me about Miss Beste pleases me very much. I really pity her for her for her fate. I don't think she can be very happy with the Pringle's, pray when you next see her, will you give her my best complts. And tell her I hope she has not yet forgotten me.

I thank you very much too for your information concerning Walter Scott. I like him best of the few poets (English and German) I am capable of enjoying. I have now begun the Lay of the Last Minstrel,[6] but I hardly know whether it equals the Lady of the Lake.

Our examinations are to begin the day after tomorrow and are to last till 15 inst. I hope all will go well enough; somewhere about the 16th I shall go to Vienna to stay there 3 weeks or so. So pray direct your answer Freyung No. 238 Vienna.[7] I suppose you know that I had robbers in my room between 2 and 4 o'clock in the afternoon whilst I was in school; they must have been frightened away for they only took my great brown pilot-coat and a new pair of large farming boots which I got for the snow, leaving a silver spoon of mine and several small articles on the table; happily the whole winter was excessively mild, so that I could do with the nice coat we bought in Bondstreet.[8] I need not say what excellent service the corduroy unmentionables[9] and the stockings did me which you sent me to Queenwood. Now goodbye dearest aunt. Pray give me news of Pauline in your next it is so long since I heard of her. I am very sorry that England is no longer to profit by L. Palmerston's[10] talents you may imagine the triumph of the papers here. If Austria had such a man they would stick tighter to him. And Lord John R.[11] too. I daily pray to God that Lord Stanley[12] may not succeed; indeed I think that if Lord John falls, yet his party can not fall for the Whigs[13] are strongest now - pray tell me your opinion on that point.

Your affect nephew
W. G. Clairmont.

Address: No envelope

Unpublished. Text: M.S., Pf. Coll., CL'ANA 0047

---

1 shillings.

2 Mary Shelley died on 1 February 1851. Her death certificate states that she died of "Disease of the Brain Supposed Tumour in left hemisphere, of long standing, Certified" (Death Certificate, General Register Office, London. *LMWS* III: 389). Betty Bennett cites Dr. Abraham Lieberman who suggests that Mary Shelley may have died of meningioma, a tumor that spreads from "the covering of the brain" to the brain itself (*LMWS* III: 389). Bennett notes that Mary Shelley asked to be buried beside her parents, Wollstonecraft and Godwin. A letter to Alexander Berry dated 7 March 1851 reveals that Lady Jane Shelley knew of this wish. Wollstonecraft and Godwin were interred in St. Pancras's Church, and Lady Shelley stated that it would have "broken my heart to let her loveliness wither in such a dreadful place – we have therefore removed them to a vault in the churchyard at Bournemouth . . . there she rests with her father on one side of her & her mother on the other" (*LMWS* III: 395).

3 Sir Percy Florence Shelley. He authorized the exhumation of the bodies of his grandparents, Wollstonecraft and Godwin, who had been buried in St. Pancras's Church in London (where they had married in 1797) and had them reinterred with Mary Shelley's body in St. Peter's Church in Bournemouth. The body of the second Mrs. Godwin remained in St. Pancras's churchyard. Today, the original stone markers remain on the church ground, which also contains the mausoleum of Sir John Soane and the Thomas Hardy tree, with its collection of gravestones removed in the 1860s to

allow for the construction of the Midland railway line. Hardy, at that time an architect's apprentice, was responsible for overseeing the exhumation of the bodies and the removal of the graves in the way of the proposed railway line. Stones from the exhumed graves were placed at the foot of an ash tree, known as Hardy's Tree, and remain today (S. Joffe, *The Kinship Coterie and the Literary Endeavors of the Women in the Shelley Circle*, [New York: Peter Lang, 2007], p. xiv).

4 On 2–5 February 1851, Claire wrote to Percy Shelley and reprimanded him for not having told her of his mother's death. She asked for the particulars of Mary Shelley's demise and praised her nephew as a good son to her stepsister. She also chastised Percy for his role in Knox and Clara's marriage and the celebratory ball given in its honor. She concluded the letter by stating that she had loved Percy as if he were her own child but that his lack of feeling towards her and Charles was a "deadly blow" (*CC* II: 536–7).

5 Knox and the Shelleys.

6 Sir Walter Scott wrote this six canto narrative poem in 1805.

7 *Picture of Vienna* listed the location of number 238 as "Freiung" (p. 111). The correct spelling is Freyung.

8 A street in London, known for its expensive and high-fashion shops. Horatio Nelson lived on Bond Street.

9 undergarments.

10 Lord Palmerston. Henry John Temple, 3rd Viscount Palmerston (1784–1865), served as Prime Minister for two terms (1855–1858 and 1859–1865). Palmerston was originally a Tory, but joined with the Whigs around 1830. As foreign secretary in Lord Russell's government, Palmerston's support of causes that appealed to the Radicals angered his fellow ministers. His support of Napoléon III led to Palmerston's dismissal in 1851 (Southgate, Donald. "Henry John Temple". *Encyclopaedia Britannica Online*. Encyclopaedia Britannica Inc., n.d. Web. 8 April 2015. http://www.britannica.com/EBchecked/topic/440205/Henry-John-Temple-3rd-Viscount-Palmerston).

11 Lord John Russell. First Earl Russell (1792–1878) served as Whig Prime Minister for two terms (1846–1852 and 1865–1866). He was at odds with Palmerston, whom he forced to resign in 1851. Palmerston had supported Napoléon III's coup of December 1851, greatly embarrassing Lord Russell. The following year, Lord Russell's government was forced to resign ("Past Prime Ministers". Web. 8 April 2015. https://www.gov.uk/government/history/past-prime-ministers).

12 Edward Smith Stanley, 14th Earl of Derby (1799–1869), served as Prime Minister for three terms (1852, 1858–1859, and 1866–1868). Originally a Whig supporter, he joined the Tory Party in 1837 ("Past Prime Ministers". Web 8 April 2015. https://www.gov.uk/government/history/past-prime-ministers).

13 Whigs were members of the English political party that supported political and social reform and limited monarchy. The Tory (Conservative) Party favored the monarchy and was seen as the more conservative political party.

35 • Antonia Clairmont to Claire Clairmont

Wieden 790. Bärenmühle.[1] Vienna. 27th June 1851.

My dear Claire.

I received yours containing the half tenp. note and some days later the second half in a letter of Willy's; accept my best and warmest thanks for your assistance; but why did you add that unkind and reproachful letter? Willy tells me you are so kind and amiable to him, why are you not so to me? what have I done to deserve that cutting language? you ask me to break with Cläry and side with you, at least you do so distinctly in this letter,[2] your allusions in former ones I did not clearly understand; in answer to this I must ask, had there been any fresh provocation given on the part of the Knoxes when you wrote that letter before Christmass? recollect how matters stood at Charles' demise – Cläry had been married above half a year, and Charles had had written several letters to her, he had not written to Mr K. but we know why, and more than that, he had accepted pecuniary obligations from him, which I highly disapproved of at the time: when you withdrew your hand from dear Willy and the letters that ought to have informed us of it were as you said lost, for we never got them, Knox came forward and paid Willy's schooling at Gueen'swood,[3] Charles having suffered him to do so was under obligations to him,[4] and might therefore be said to have sanctioned the marriage the term at Gueen'swood was not yet over when poor Willy was without a father, and then again Mr K came forward and furnished the means for his going to Hohenheim so it is to his assistance the dear boy owed 9 months useful instruction, and shamefully callous and selfish we both must be if we could ever forget that, and break with him now – even if Cläry were not my daughter I should feel grateful and obliged to Mr K. for his assistance, given in the second instance at least, in the moment of darkness around me, when I saw others withdrawing whom I might have thought my friends, or my childrens. what pretence then should I take now to break as you call it. And why continually rake up the old ashes again, is it Christian like to do so? isn't peace and harmony better than siding and disputeing – about Sir Percy's[5] behaviour you cannot doubt my having felt for you, but what good would Willy's interference have done?[6] a student, a mere stripling, not of age – he could not force him nor expostulate – if you had not any moral influence with Sir P what else should? if he had any of the gratitude for past benefits which you seem to object to in my case towards K.[7] he could not have acted so, he must have recollected that Mrs G[8] had been ~~was~~ the protectress of his mother's[9] youth; and himself, how often was the pudding ready for him or the desert kept, and playthings prepared against his visits to his grandfather, I recollect well several instances, when the little Hudsons[10] were invited to meet him – no doubt, if Sir P. had been a Roman, he would have been subject to heavy punishment, but in the present day ingratitude is no longer a crime; I should surely have written to you, but having done so, shortly before I waited for an answer from you, I hear from Willy you never received that letter, the more ~~so~~ I must thank you for your assistance; the ten pounds will just do to pay for Charley's outfit, for he is to leave me for Moravia,[11] on the 1st of August, where he is to pass two years in order to get practical information in farming and it was a matter of great anxiety where to get him the necessary stock of clothes and linen, and pay half a years stipend in advance, consisting in £ 30 pr. as. and some more extras which will come to £8 ~~pr~~ more, this with his clothes, books, boots et et and a little pocket money he will cost me £ 50 p.a. I shall now be able to meet these demands by the further help you promised; as Charles, that man without principles and conscience left me and his children nearly beggars, spending his income in his vile selfishness upon his vicious tastes and pleasures,[12] how am I to provide for the education of two sons without assistance of some sort or other, the little pittance I have, will with my own earnings barely suffice for myself and the two girls, my other resources are now exhausted; I have some good books left, but can find no purchaser for them that's all that's left; so for the next four years, I shall be obliged to look to you for some assistance for your brother's sons; and do not think it is the least of my hardships to sue for and accept bounty when unwillingly granted – since Charley's destiny to Moravia has been fixed, I have also written to Cläry for the same purpose, Pauline too must contribute something, but I know she will gladly do so; it is only the innate consciousness that I have by no action of mine deserved my hard lot, enables me to bear up against it, agravated as it is by the pain of separation of all I hold dear – When Willy went away the affair of Charley had only been in contemplation, but since a visit of Dr Pabst's[13] God bless him – enabled me to tell him, and by his kind interference he procured that place and I closed immediately – having been recommended by him is a great advantage to Charley I cannot write to Willy not knowing where he is, perhaps you can let him know of the receipt of his, and of his brother's destiny; I hope Willy's return will be early enough for the brothers to meet – Sidi and Charley send their best thanks for their intended present, Emmy having gone to the country, with the Family of Countess Pergen[14] to perfect the children's English I have written to, about it; your concluding remarks are both bitter and unjust; I am neither calculating nor siding with any one, if I have lost your affections I must bear it as I do my other misfortunes undeserved I shall sincerely regret it – my whole crime was my having answered a few lines to Mrs S's insignificant note,[15] from that time forward you were quite changed towards me, and your letters that used to be a source of consolation, gave pain and vexation, however as I learnt to love you for your attachment to your brother, I shall do so now for your kindness to his children and remain yours gratefully.[16]

A.C.

Address: Via Ostende/ To Miss Clairmont/ 75. Gloucester Place/ Hyde Park Gardens/ London/ England.
Front postmark: WIEN/ 30 JUN.
Rear postmark: 1 A[N] 1/ JY 4/ 1851

Unpublished. Text: M.S., Pf. Coll., CL'ANA 0394

---

1 Wieden is the fourth district of Vienna and the location of the Theresianum. *Picture of Vienna* called it a "suburb" of Vienna and stated that 894 houses had been constructed in "Old and new Wieden" by 1844 (p. 41). The book included the Freihaus in Wieden under the general heading "Remarkable buildings and gardens in the suburbs". According to the book's author, the Freihaus was "the largest private building within the lines of fortification. It has 6 courts, 31 staircases, 300 lodgings; contains above 1000 inhabitants" (p. 49). The Freihaus belonged to the Starhemberg family. Bärenmühle was the name of the building in which Antonia resided.

2 The letter to which Antonia referred has been lost. However, on 21 January 1851, Claire wrote a kind and accommodating letter to Wilhelm. She purchased six pairs of stockings for Wilhelm and arranged for them to be sent to Queenwood. She also told Wilhelm to ask Mr. Edmondson to provide him with a pint of beer a day, particularly as three doctors had recommended that Wilhelm drink a portion of beer a day. She promised to pay for the expense and asked Wilhelm to confirm the arrangement. She told Wilhelm that she did not want him to alter his diet which clearly agreed with his constitution (*CC* II: 535).

3 Antonia's spelling for Queenwood. The second letter is unclear and is either the letter "n"or the letter "u". Stocking refers to Queenwood as Greenwood (*CC* II: 524).

4 Antonia placed the letter X above the word "him" and on the left side of the page, she added these words: "and might therefore be said to have sanctioned the marriage".

5 Sir Percy Florence Shelley. Percy Shelley drowned in 1822 and his first-born son, Charles Shelley (born in 1814), died in 1826. Thus Percy Florence was the sole surviving male heir when his grandfather, Sir Timothy Shelley, died in 1844, leaving Percy Florence the baronet. His half-sister, Ianthe (1813–1876) married Edward Jeffries Esdaile in 1837 and they had seven children. Charles and Ianthe were the children of Percy's first wife, Harriet Westbrook (1796–1816). Harriet committed suicide by drowning herself in the Serpentine River in Hyde Park. She was pregnant at the time, but not with Shelley's child.

For further particulars of the letter Claire wrote to Percy Florence on 2–5 February 1851, see CL'ANA 0047. She recorded in that letter her dissatisfaction with his treatment of her.

6 Evidently, Claire had asked Wilhelm to write to Percy Florence Shelley but he declined to do so. On 16 May 1852, Wilhelm again referred to his aunt's request. See CL'ANA 0052 and CL'ANA 0053.

7 Knox was assisting both Wilhelm and Charley by paying their educational expenses, a fact both Claire and Antonia knew.

8 Mrs. Godwin. In 1801, William Godwin married Mary Jane Vial. See Introduction and CL'ANA 0405.

9 Mary Shelley.

10 John Corrie Hudson (1796–1879) was the executor of Godwin's will. Mary Shelley wrote to Hudson on 8 April 1836 to ask him to accompany her to see Mrs. Godwin following Godwin's death, noting that her stepmother would prefer him to anyone else (*LMWS* II: 269).

11 Moravia was part of the Austro-Hungarian Empire from 1867 until 1918. It is located in the Czech Republic today. Olmütz (Olomouc) is one of Moravia's principal cities. In 1848, Charles Clairmont traveled some 297 kilometers north of Vienna to Olmütz to teach English to the young Archdukes. See CL'ANA 0402. In his unpublished journal of 1861, Wilhelm recorded visiting Moravia and sensing the presence of his deceased brother Charley in various locations. On 19 April 1861, he documented in his journal that "everybody speaks of poor Charley with great kindness – the

locality and everything else reminds me painfully of him" (CL'ANA 0177, unpublished manuscript, Pforzheimer Collection). On 20 April 1861, he met with Sophie Gratichy: "I took more than usual interest in her presence [as] she was very much attached to Charlie; she & her parents spoke very much of him as did all the people there and at Hostitz" (CL'ANA 0177).

12 Clearly Antonia referred to Charles's affair with Mrs. Kollonitz.

13 Wilhelm's school director at both Hohenheim and Altenburg. See CL'ANA 0046.

14 Count Johann Anton von Pergen (1804–1873) married Philippina Batthyány-Strattmann. They had two children ("Johann Anton von Pergen". Web. 24 April 2015. http://de.rodovid.org/wk/Person:855793).

15 See CL'ANA 0395.

16 On 12 July 1851, Claire told Bartolomeo Cini (1809–1877) that family commitments had her "chained" to England. She explained that she was responsible financially for assisting Charles's children and that she had to spend a year and a half with Wilhelm in the country while he studied agriculture. She noted too that Pauline had come to live with her after Charles's death: "life took me over, without leaving me the least possibility of doing what my heart desired to do" (*CC* II: 539).

Cini was the husband of Catherine Elizabeth Raniera Tighe (1815–1874). Janet Todd, Claire Tomalin, Sunstein and Stocking tell the history of Catherine Elizabeth, who was known as Nerina. Her mother, Margaret King (1773–1835), had been the pupil of Mary Wollstonecraft in 1786. Margaret's marriage to Stephen Moore, Earl of Mount Cashell (1770–1822), made her Countess Mount Cashell but she fell in love with her husband's friend, George William Tighe (1776–1837, known as "Tatty"). She left her family (she had eight children with her husband) and she moved to Pisa with Tighe. They had two daughters, Nerina and Anna Laura Georgina (Laurette). Margaret began to go by the name of Mrs. Mason, in honor of Wollstonecraft's 1788 fictional governess in *Original Stories from Real Life*. Writing about the choice of name, Tomalin states: "According to what she later told Claire Clairmont, this was at the insistance of Tighe; and since he did not want her to take his name either, she chose to be called 'Mrs. Mason', the name of the good governess in the children's stories by her own well-remembered governess, Mary Wollstonecraft" (p. 30). The couple married in 1826. Mary Shelley was a friend of the family and wrote her story, *Maurice, or the Fisher's Cot*, for Nerina's sister Laurette. Cristina Dazzi, wife of Nerina's great-great grandson, found the lost manuscript in 1997, which bears the following inscription: "For Laurette from her friend M[rs] Shelley" (Mary Shelley, *Maurice, or the Fisher's Cot*, ed. C. Tomalin [Chicago: University of Chicago Press, 1998], i).

Claire enjoyed a friendship of many years with the Cini family. Tomalin states that the Cinis "were an old landowning family, able and respected" (p. 53) and she quotes from Claire's letter of 22 February 1835 in which Claire told Cini after the death of Margaret Mason that his family and her nephew were the "beings most dear to me in the whole word" (p. 65). In 1875, Claire wrote to Cini asking him to be the executor of her will and thanking him for his "kind friendship" (*CC* II: 624). Her will itself, dated 2 December 1876, instructed Cini to be the executer, for which she left him Percy Shelley's inkstand. Pauline exchanged the inkstand for a portrait of Lady Mount Cashell (see *CC* II: 662 for a description of the allocation of Claire's belongings). Claire's will also entrusted Cini with the sale of the Shelley letters. She left instructions asking him to invest the proceeds in stocks, the interest of which was to be paid to Pauline and then, after Pauline's death, to her daughter Georgina Hanghegyi. Claire also left to "my dear and beloved Cini" her funeral expectations. As Cini died in 1877, Claire added a clause on 21 July 1877 which named Cini's son, John Cini (Giovanni), as executor.

36 • Antonia Clairmont to Claire Clairmont

Vienna 24th Aug: 1851.

My dear Claire.

This morning dear Willy set off with the steamboat for Altenburg, he stopt with us but three days, and these were taken up in arranging his things et But the first free moment shall be devoted to pouring forth my thanks to you for your generous help in the moment of need; If I have been able now to provide for Charles' wants, and pay his first quarter, if I see Willy furnished with all he wants, returning cheerfully to his studies, instead of having his young mind cramped, his spirits weighed down with cares and anxiety, and can look forward with less anxiety to the dreary unproductive season till my lessons begin again, it is to you I owe it, and I shall ever bless you in my heart for it; if once you see your nephews grown up, good and upright men, able to take their place in society as gentlemen and be a credit and an honour to their family, you will feel rewarded for all you do towards attaining that desired end; Willy is already on the best way; let us hope that Charley will follow his example, and that his present flightiness will ~~steady~~ sober down into a more steady character – In my last I mentioned Dr Pabst's kindness in interesting himself for Ch:[1] and he proved as true as his word; on the 1st of August Charley begins his new career, in Moravia under the direction of a very able man, a Mr Kraus, where he is instructed in practical farming – for board and lodging Washing attendance I have to pay £ 25 pr an: and twelve pounds more for instruction; so altogether £37 besides his clothes books and pocketmoney – after two years spent there he will repair to Altenburg for two years, and then he will be ready with his studies; no fear of further success, if he goes on well for ~~it~~ agriculture is an open field for merit and Knowledge in Austria; what I foresaw long ago comes now to pass; at last the eyes of the nations open and intelligence wonders how the richest sources of national wealth could so long have been neglected or shamefully illused by a perverted system of management.

Charley and Sidi send their best love and thanks for their present, we exchanged the money, and Sidi intends buying a dress for the autumn for it, for now it has been put into her saving box; Charley will get a portfolio or writing book; which he wished very much to have but I could not afford one; for the ten pound note I got 123fl the exchange was higher than now, for 402 pre paid – now I received 350f; once more my best and warmest thanks, my dear Clara for this most timely assistance – I did not show William your last letter; ~~whether~~ he had[2] time to tell you about my new edition of the dialoge book?[3] it is now ready and looks very nice, I should have liked to send you a copy, but was not yet completed – now I must wait the result, of my endeavours; I hope it will have a good sale; I reduced it a little, ~~and~~ in size, which enabled me to reduce the prize too; the dear expense of the edition pr. 1500 copies is £ 60, which money I got [~~illeg.~~] by the interference of a friend, from the saving bank; 40 pound. I must give commission; ~~will~~ my gain will come to about £ 60, ~~p~~ but can only hope in two or three years, first I must cover the debt; – if this edition sells well, as there is every chance it will

I shall the better sell the copyright, it is something to look to for the future. Good bye now my dear Claire, write to me soon if after the 5th Aug direct Weidling bei Klosterneuburg[4] as we shall go there directly after Charley's departure.

ever yours affect:
Antonia Cl.

Weiden. Bärenmühle[5]
790.

Address: No envelope.

Unpublished. Text: M.S., Pf. Coll., CL'ANA 0421, Box 1, bundle a, numbers 8 – 10.[6]

---

1 Charley.

2 Antonia inserted the number "2" above the word "he" and the number "1" above the word "had". Clearly, she intended this sentence to read as a question: "had he time to tell you about my new edition of the dialog book?"

3 See CL'ANA 0403.

4 See CL'ANA 0401.

5 See CL'ANA 0394.

6 Christoph Clairmont enclosed letters 8–10 (CL'ANA 0421) in an envelope on which he wrote the following: "Dates: 29.8.51/29.6.56/26.12.63/ Letters of/ Antonia Cl. – d'Hembyze/(1800–1868)/to Claire Cl. In Florence./ she is wife of Charles/Gaulis Cl./1795–1850/ (and is my great great grandmother)". In actuality, Antonia was Christoph's great-grandmother.

37 • Wilhelm Gaulis Clairmont to Claire Clairmont

Ung.[1] Altenburg. 19th Octob. 1851–

My dearest aunt.

I was absent from Altenburg now for more than six weeks having spent my autumn holydays on a geological tour in the Austrian part of the Alps for which I had been engaged and my travelling expenses paid by the Geological Society in Vienna. On my return to this place I found your letter,[2] which judging from its date must have arrived soon after my departure and consequently have been waiting a very long time; this accounts for my not answering immediately as you desired it. however I hope I shall be just in time for you say you are going to stay at your present lodgings till the end of Octob; and today being the 19th it may reach you yet.

The letter you mention as having been lost, is sure to be mine. at any rate I dispatched one somewhere about the end of July or beginning of August immediately on my return from England, for I dare say you recollect, you requested me particularly to give you immediate news of my safe arrival.

There is hardly any thing interesting I could tell you with regard to ourselves. Mama fretts on in her usual way; she will be moving to town tomorrow; now she has at any rate a few lessons to look forward to and £20 Knox promised to send in the course of the winter; she got through the summer with the aid of your £40 which you sent by me, but if it had not been for that, she should be in debt already; for there were several extraordinary expenses this year; such as a repair of the roof of the Weidling house an other heavy expense brought upon us by this unfortunate house is the indemnification[3] paid to the former Lord of the manour. This gentleman having had the right to buy certain taxes from our house which were abolished by the reforms of 1848, it was fixed by government that the third part of the capital, where of the taxes due should be considered as interest at 4 percent shall be paid to the Lord of the manour by the proprietor.

We do not however gain the slightest advantage by paying of that capital, for the rates and taxes we now pay to Government alone are so much increased that they exceed by 50 percent what we formerly had to pay both to Government and, to the Lord of the manour.

Mama has found out that going expressly to town for the sake of giving lessons, there is but very slight profit to repay her exertions; ~~the~~ moving, the very high rents of town lodgings, the carriages she occasionally wants and living in town all is so excessively expensive that her lessons hardly pay the outlay; on the other hand the Weidlinghouse owing to her continued absence is quite neglected, every thing gets stolen and thieved; the house itself is a completely dead capital, because there is no one there to let the lodgings so Mama has serious thoughts of going to Weidling next spring and never returning to town any more; she calculated that having no rent to pay the expense of the town rent and the moving alone would pay her and the children's living the summer through; she hoped that with some slight alterations in the house she could get two tolerably decent and one peasants lodging which if let, and there is very reasonable hope of her succeeding in that, would do something towards her maintenance in winter. Charley will be on her hands for the next four years and so long there is no hope for pecuniary independence, as for myself I hope to earn my own bread by this time next year or at any rate the succeeding spring for it is very customary to make young men serve the first year without any "salary;" my schooling has lasted a very long time it is true and a great deal of money has been spent for my education by all my relations; but at any rate I have the good conscience of having made the best of my time and having learnt as much as I could and so I do not think any one will find it sanguine in me to hope to get through the future as least as well as the ordinary run of people.

My Geological tour was highly instructive and amusing to me. we wandered full six weeks through the mountains pioneering our way without road or path through valleys and forests and across rivers and brooks by the mere aid of maps and the magnetic needle; we passed through beautiful scenery, but we had a deal to endure especially in bad weather; I was however very cautious, and made a point of changing stockings and putting on my slippers the first thing on reaching my quarters for the night whenever I had wet feet which was very frequently the case; and it was a consolation to me to find that despite the deal of roughing I went through I never felt the slightest indisposition nor even as much as an irritation of the throat.

As for my "cash in hand" it is not very brilliant yet I am not in immediate want; having lived for six weeks at the expense of the Geol. Society and some days with Mama I was enabled to save part of the £5 you gave me in England, besides there is ~~my~~ a quarter of my stipen[4] coming due but this is but £3–10s. However if you could manage to send me £5 I should be very glad for I shall have to buy a wintercoat the English one from ~~Bichie~~ Bondstreet being too light for these winters.[5] – besides my rent must be paid and it has been raised too in consequence of our number having augmented from 40 to 100 students whom it is very {tear} difficult to accommodate in such a little place. But pray my dear, dear aunt do not stint yourself, for you know I am a young fellow and can bear such little privations much better than you, a little cold wont kill me; and you are in serious crisis now – you must not give in – it is just such a position as Mama is in now; the calls must be paid, for if they be not, you loose the point you have been struggling for and aiming at for the last three years. I am so much obliged to you dear aunt for the kindness you have for Pauline and the care and trouble you take to bring about some fortunate change of her position Mama had a letter from her some time ago. it was from Brighton; she did not seem in very good spirits. – Charley is getting on pretty well in his practical career; he is in Moravia; Mama has had two very satisfactory letters from his principal. Now goodbye dearest aunt pray let me hear soon of you and give my best kisses to Pauline from me your dutiful nephew

W.G. Clairmont

My direction: Ung. Altenburg – Austria.

Pray give my best remembrances to Miss Beste and tell her how sorry I was to leave England so suddenly without taking leave of her: but it was impossible otherwise.

We had our vintage at Weidling just before I came away – I munched enormous quantities of grapes; they are excellent. the vines are all of the very best quality; Papa had received them from different horticultural societies; there are some French ones too.

they were all set the first and second year he had the house and turned out very well indeed; if Mama was there she might manage to sell part of them, but so it will be lost and stolen.[6]

Goodbye once more.

Mamas direction in town
949 Rauhensteingasse Wien.[7]
she said she was going to write to you.

Address: Aerogramme: Miss Clairmont/ 6. Waverley
Place/ St. John's Wood./ London/ England.
Postmark: Aus Oesterreich; UNG ALTENBURG/[illeg.]/10

Unpublished. Text: M.S., Pf. Coll., CL'ANA 0048

1 "Ung" is the abbreviation for "Ungarisch" (Hungarian).
2 The letter has been lost.
3 Compensation for damages or expenses incurred.
4 stipend.
5 See CL'ANA 0047.
6 Wilhelm wrote this final paragraph on the cover of the aerogramme.
7 Mozart's last residence was 8 Rauhensteingasse, which intersects with Himmelpfortgasse. A *Picture of Vienna* lists number 949 as being on Himmelpfortgasse. The two roads are 850 meters from one another.

38 • Antonia Clairmont to Claire Clairmont

Rauhensteingasse. 949. 24th Oct 1851.

My dearest Claire.

I received your last at Weidling, and put off answering because I did not well know my new direction, which I wished to give you, so I waited till the moving was over; we are settled, but what a sad change from the cheerful sunny Weidling to this dark dungeonlike place, never a glimpse of sun not even light we have, it is now two o'clock and I have hardly light enough to write this, I pity the poor girls; and yet bad as it is it comes to £25 with taxes and all, lodgings are so immensely risen in Vienna; I have advertised for my classes and must expect the result but this is the last winter I shall spend in town, if I cannot sell W. I shall move there and thus at least rentfree and make the most of my little farm and house; for now I am cheated out of every thing, and then Willy can advise me; for as Charley is no more here for my lessons it is not worth while to pay such high rent, pay washing and wood, and neglect my little property in the country; I should have done it this year already, but for another trial I wished to make of ~~making~~ selling the Copy-right of the Grammar,[1] which I did not succeed in last year. With Charley I have every reason to be satisfied also as to the arrangements made for him; Mr Kraus is a very sensible active and kind man, whose letters show the mental attention he pays to his pupils welfare; Mrs Kraus is an amiable woman and very kind to Charley and attentive to his wants; they live in plenty, which is a great thing for a growing lad; as he spends most of his time in the open air, he brings a sharpened appetite home 4 times a day; I praise God he is no more to sit down to a sickly evening meal of tea or coffee, as he had had to do at home; but what can one do, every thing is so dear in town, one can not afford to buy meat. Poverty is a sad thing, I never coveted riches and always was moderate in my desires, but when the most needful things are wanting, and you do not know to provide for the next day that is a bitter thing; I am trying now to sell the remnant of Charles' library; at the value of about a thrid[2] it would have been about £30, yet I have but 9 offered and shall be obliged to accept of that pittance; and to think that the father of those poor children who are even now objects of charity went on buying those dear books year after year, knowing what sums he spent decides on his own individual pleasures, without thinking either of me nor of them! such heartless selfishness is unequalled; I cannot help poring over the past and wondering what were my sins to deserve so hard a lot; my greatest fault was blindness in too much confidence; God forgive him I shall try to do so.[3] I have just had a letter from Willy where he tells me he found one of yours on his return to Altenburg telling of unfavourable things about your shares[4] yet you promised him some help for a winter great coat, a thousand thanks my dear Claire, I was very anxious on that point; the few days he spent with us we were very happy and I feel more and more convinced he will be the support of his family in time; we had a very fine crop of grapes this year, and wished we could send you some of them; you will have heard from Paula that poor Emmy returned home ill, she arrived the very day I had your letter; she is now quite well, but I am afraid of making another trial of placing her again and yet necessity is imperious; I don't wish to have the nature of her complaint known, it might injure her she is a very pretty girl, just 18, the dear children are very cheerful, more than I could have expected in this dismal hole a lodging where never a ray of sunshine appears; good bye my dearest Claire ever

your grateful and affect.
A.C.

Address: No envelope

Unpublished. Text: M.S., Pf. Coll., CL'ANA 0370

---

1 See CL'ANA 0403.

2 Antonia's spelling for "third".

3 Again, Antonia referenced Charles's relationship with Mrs. Kollonitz.

4 On 12 July 1851, Claire wrote to Bartolomeo Cini (see CL'ANA 0394). She thanked Cini for providing her with information about the Orleans stocks. She felt "reassured" by his information and stated that she also had an interest in the "railroad". She observed that, if she lost money on one investment, she would gain on the other (*CC* II: 539). On 16 March 1852, she again discussed her stock purchases, telling Pauline that she was undecided about selling her "french rail-ways. Some wise and experienced men say, if I were you, I would sell at the greatest loss every thing" (*CC* II: 540).

39 • Wilhelm Clairmont to Claire Clairmont

December 6th 1851 Altenburg.

My dear aunt.

We have now been snowed up for more than a fortnight; and every communication with Vienna or any other place even by rail interrupted – but now the highest road is passable again and so I seize the first opportunity to write to you in order to acknowledge the receit of the second half five pound note and to thank you for your kindness – I got a white shaggy winter great coat in which they tell me my figure from a distance looks like a polar icebear – however it is a capital thing for keeping one warm in our cold climate. – I hope to run up to Vienna for a few days at Christmas; mostlikely Charley will be there too and so I trust we shall spend a few pleasant days together; Mama is shifting on in her old way, in her last letter she told me there was some faint hope of selling the house, it is not however likely that the ~~sale~~ purchase should be contracted before spring, because the buyer thereby gains the interest on his capital the winter through; whereas the house brings him no percentage during winter because the lodgings will only let in the summer season. –
I was told by a gentleman coming from England that all the country was raving mad for Kossuth[1] so that even the Times paper which had taken a more conservative turn was burnt by the ~~publ~~ people in public and was now utterly deserted. of course I do not believe it to be true, yet it proves {tear} that there a striking interest is shown in behalf of the Hungarians by a great part of English nation and this is what displeases the people very much. –
I am rather afraid this letter will be too late to find you at [Sud][2] brook Park but no doubt they will send it[3]{tear} you, it must be a very dull place for you, living with so many sick and ailing people[4] – it is apt to make one melancholy hearing constant complaints about one, so much more when one finds them just and people's claims to pity and commiseration are just. Now goodbye dearest aunt. I cannot write more for the moment for the end of the year drawing near, I am very busy just now, besides its hard up to the post hour already – Many kisses to Pauline and believe me ever to be your

dutyful nephew
W.G. Clairmont

Address: Aerogramme: Miss Clairmont/ Sud Brook Park/
Petersham, Surry/ England.
Postmark: UNG: ALTENBURG/ $^{6}/_{12}$

Unpublished. Text: M.S., Pf. Coll., CL'ANA 0049

1 Lajos Kossuth (1802–1894) led Hungary in its fight for independence from Austria. In 1847, Kossuth was elected to represent Pest in the Diet (Parliament) and he became leader of the opposition. In 1848, Kossuth called for a change in the prevailing political order and for the implementation

of social and political changes. His embrace of Hungarian nationalist policies made him extremely popular in the country. He was Finance Minister of Hungary in Count Lajos Batthyány's government. By September 1848, after Batthyány's resignation, Kossuth became leader of the National Defense Committee. By January 1849, Kossuth concluded that peace between Austria and Hungary was unattainable and, on 14 April 1849, he proposed that Hungary declare its independence from Austria. However, by August 1849, after a series of political setbacks, he resigned and went into exile. He never returned to politics and lived in exile the rest of his life. See István Tóth, *A Concise History of Hungary* [Budapest: Corvina Books, 2005].

In 1851, Kossuth went to England. In her article, "The Invention of a Hero: Lajos Kossuth in England (1851)," *European History Quarterly*, 43 (1), 2013, pp. 5–26, Zsuzsanna Lada documents that the British press had little interest in Hungarian affairs prior to the Revolution of 1848. She observes that Britain received its news directly from Viennese or German newspapers and that British reports therefore reflected an anti-Hungarian bias in spite of the attempts by Ferenc Pulszky, Kossuth's representative in England, to alter the views of the British press: "Conservative papers such as the *Morning Chronicle*, the *Morning Post* and *The Times* were not amenable: in the wake of the Russian intervention they unequivocally channelled anti-Hungarian views and were in favor of Austria" (p. 11). According to Lada, Pulszky prepared the British public for Kossuth's arrival as he "stage-managed" Kossuth's image (p. 7). He was entirely successful in that many newspapers, the *Daily News* in particular, supported the Hungarian cause. Lada records that when Kossuth arrived at Southampton on 23 October 1851, "he was given a true hero's welcome . . . The multitude that turned out was several thousand strong" (p. 9). Lada concludes that Kossuth's popularity in England in 1851 can be linked to "the importance attached to English national identity, with which the Kossuth cult was deeply intertwined in the eyes of all those Englishmen that celebrated him" (p. 21).

2 The page is torn, so the word "Sud" is unclear. Wilhelm probably meant to write "Sud Brook" (see address).

3 The page is torn here. The missing word appears to be "after".

4 Sudbrook Park was a well-respected water-cure institution in the nineteenth century. Dr. James Ellis succeeded Dr. Joseph Weiss in 1845 and a notice in *The Athenaeum* of 25 July 1846 recommended Dr. Ellis to the public. Dr. Weiss wrote: "I beg respectfully to recommend Dr. James Ellis as a Physician in whose knowledge and skill of the Hydropathic treatment I entertain in the fullest confidence" (*The Athenaeum for the Year 1846* [London: James Holmes, 1846], p. 746). An advertisement from *The Athenaeum* of 14 August 1858 described Sudbrook Park as a "hydropathic establishment" offering treatment that was "agreeable . . . Thousands of sufferers have been cured when all other curative means had failed". James Ellis, M. D. was listed as the doctor for the clinic ([London: J. Francis, 1858], v 2, p. 187). Today, Sudbrook House and Park form part of the Richmond Golf Club.

40 • Antonia Clairmont to Claire Clairmont

[1 February 1852]
Rauhensteingasse949.
Vienna ½ 1852

My dear Claire.

You will excuse my long delay in answering your letter, I had hoped to tell you something decisive about the sale of the house, but alas my hopes were disappointed, and I am as far as ever from gaining my point; I have now determined upon going to settle at Weidling entirely; at least, I shall have no rent to pay, and may be sell it easier when there myself; the more so is my lessons fall off, I had only 2 this winter! I am now trying to sell the last remnants of the books to pay Charley's next quarter – Willy poor boy is near crying to see those dear and good books go and at such prices, but what can I do – it was madness to lay out so much money on books for a man in his situation, and with other certain claims on his income. to day is the anniversary of the most dreadful day in my life two years have passed, and as yet let me own to you, I am far from having attained to accord forgiveness as a Christian, much less as an injured wife and mother; I cannot yet forgive; I have suffered too much – and even now – can I speak to my children of their father in exhorting them to their duties or directing their views on high? admonish them to follow the path trod by him ?– an unnatural silence must close my lips, to go farther would be playing a part – I approve in so far of Willy's knowing the truth; at least, I shall not be misjudged by him though for his sake I would have wished to have it witheld. Christmas passed well enough thanks to Pauline's gift, which enabled me to pay the journey and a new coat for Charley <u>which</u> he stood much in need of; I was happy in the sight of my dear boys – Willy my pride and hope, Charley the sunshine of the family; there was laughter, joke and merryness, to do one's heart good; Willy took Charley into examen ~~but~~ and was very well satisfied with the result; also Mr Kraus gives most satisfactory account of him, he is fond of his business and enters most zealously into it. Mrs Kraus is a kind motherly woman attentive to his comforts and health in cleanliness and good living which is attested by his growth and healthy fresh face; you say you shall not be able to send me anything this year, it will be very hard for me, for the expenses for the two boys are imperious and cannot be avoided; let us hope you will be able to help me a little; for my means are all exhausted now; Emmy and Sidi send their best love, they bought each a dark dress of the half sov.[1] you sent them, Sidi continues at her school, and Emmy is a sort of a daily governess at Cts Pergen's;[2] she goes there at 12 and returns at 7 – her health does not allow her taking a regular place; they continue their piano. By the bye, I never mentioned Mr. Falcon[3] whom you sent to me; he is a nice young man, but I don't understand why he was forced to leave France; we see now little of him; since Charley is gone, I don't encourage his coming nor any other of our acquaintance; for at our state of finances a cup of tea to our friends is a sacrifice, besides, I keep no servant now, Sidi and I take care of the concerns of our little menage and God knows I am above being ashamed of poverty, but I can do little good to my friends now nor make them comfortable. Good bye my dear Claire your

Affectionat[illeg.] A. C.

I continue in this lodging till the end of April then in Weidling. Do write me very soon.
How is Pauline why doesn't she write to me?[4]

Address: No envelope

Unpublished. Text: M.S., Pf. Coll., CL'ANA 0371

---

1 Sovereign. British coin, worth about £1.

2 See CL'ANA 0394.

3 The ink has smudged on this name, but Antonia meant to write Mr. Falcon. In her letter to Antonia of 19 July 1856, Claire asked whether "young Falcon" was still in Vienna. Stocking identifies him as "probably the son of Sophie Kazloffsky and Charles Falcon" (*CC* II: 570). Bennett identifies Sophie Kazloffsky as Claire's friend (*LMWS* III: 154). In January–February 1844, Claire informed Mary Shelley that, while Madame Kazloffsky married her husband (a prince) in a church, "Emperor Nicolas" (probably Nicholas I of Russia, 1796–1855) did not sanction the marriage (*CC* II: 384). In 1844, Claire wrote to Mary Shelley to inform her that Sophie Kazloffsky would marry Charles Falcon, the son of a banker who lived in Naples (*CC* II: 410). Mary Shelley replied, "I am so glad of your pretty Sophie's match – she was a Lady which her Mother was not – & certainly she could only diserve her in consequence" (*LMSW* III: 154). On 12 May 1845, Claire wrote from Clichy, France, to ask Mary Shelley to purchase "five papers of pens" for Sophie Falcon and to send them to M. Ivanoff in Paris (*CC* II: 430). Mary Shelley responded on 17 May that she would (*LMWS* III: 180). In August 1856, Claire begged Antonia not to allow a certain Miss Falcon to stay in her home because she feared that Wilhelm and Miss Falcon might enter into some kind of a relationship (*CC* II: 576). Miss Falcon was possibly the sister-in-law of Sophie Falcon. Claire confirmed that she "well knew" Sophie Falcon before her marriage to Charles Falcon, but that she had lost contact with her. She described Antonia's prospective lodger as a penniless young woman who was in ill health. In a line that confirms Miss Falcon was Sophie Falcon's sister-in-law, she said she was convinced Miss Falcon's brother – juxtaposition reveals him as Charles Falcon – had told Miss Falcon about Antonia and her children and their kindness towards others.

4 This final sentence was written upside down on the bottom of the third page.

41 • Antonia Clairmont to Claire Clairmont

17th Feb: 1852.

My dear Claire.

This moment I receive yours with the half note included, and sit down directly to answer and thank you most warmly for this new proof of your kindness and care for dear Willy; you have taken a load off my mind, for I expected every day to hear from him, knowing he must be in want of money, and yet my utter inability to furnish it, and the misery of cramping the poor boy's spirits by the dreadful feeling of poverty and indigence hovering over his young head; this you have for the time averted, and once more accept my best and warmest thanks for it; my position is indeed a most trying and difficult one; you advise me to make debts on the house; if you know all the details of my position, you will see the obstacles to my doing so any further; you shall also see what the Knoxes have done for me, and if I did not speak more fully on these subjects before, it was not from a wish to have secrets; silence on my part was but natural after your declaration, soon after your brother's death – of your utter inability of assisting me and mine – to enlarge on my difficulties, or the assistance received from others I should have deemed indelicate and painful to both of us; but you knew of Knox having paid Willy's expenses at Hohenheim for full 6 months at Hohenheim which I would never have done, and which together with his stay at Greenwood College[1] laid the ground – to his present and future success – what he has since done you shall hear directly; when a man dies in Austria, without leaving a will or marriage contract, whatever the position of the family may be, all he leaves is considered as the children's property, taken hold of by the authorities, valued, sold by auction and the money, after deduction of costs et et fees dues and taxes put by against their coming of age; whilst the care of the education and maintenance of the family is left entirely to the widow; well, Charles, not even doing me the poor justice of saving me by one line, of a last disposition from all this, I came within the pale of the law; every thing was reduced, and but for the half of the house being secured to me, I should have found myself bereft of every thing; the house we had bought at £700, it was reduced now at under 600, I succeeded also in saving most of the books from the valuation and a good deal of the furniture; Pauline could tell you all that verbally – after all the proceedings were concluded, taxes et et paid, a sum of £ 240 was pronounced as the children's property, viz. £40 each, and the choice was left me either to deposit that sum at the Chancery, or have it ~~averaged~~ mortgaged on the house; Dr Budinsky my advocate whom God may bless – advised me to do the former, ~~an~~ as leaving me free mistress of selling the house without having to fear the Court of Chancery's interference – he, knowing me, even procured me the necessary money; Pauline being already of age, and knowing the circumstances did not claim her share – I only wanted therefore £200; since then Clary has become of age, but W. sent me a power of attorney, the money to be made over to me; this was but natural, but yet I am thankful for it, he might have claimed it; lawyers do sometimes add things you know; I repaid those £ 40, and so my debt is reduced to 160 – but last summer repairs had to be done I had a bill presented this new year of £30, and of course not having the means of paying it, a friend procured me the money from the savingsbank, so you see, the house though nominally unencumbered, is in fact indebted to a third and if I wished to take money upon it these two parties would come forward, to be inscribed first; there would be difficulty of finding money upon a third mortgage or Satz[2] as we call it in German, then it would be talked about and known, and have humiliating for Charley and Willy, have impeding to every endeavour to rise and get a footing in society such a report would be; however poor, a person may still enjoy respectability but one involved in debt loses even that, and ~~that~~ surely I should be as soon as I made the attempt to take money on the W.[3] house; you will now understand how impossible it is for me to follow your advice; and that instead of clearing present difficulties it would only augment them; I repeat once more that I want no help for myself and the two girls, we shall live as thousands do, suffering for the sins of others, you shall not hear me either repine or complain of any privation; you know that K offered to take Charley over to England which I did not accept, but I had the less scruple of telling them of my difficulties in providing for the education when I also wrote to you on the same point so this winter I received £10 from Clary and I am to have 10 pds more between now and spring; dear generous Pauline contributes her share most joyfully, blessings on all, that are kind to my boys.

In spite of all my cares and troubles I can fully enter your difficulties; and it must be a painful thought, to have failed in both your speculations, with the box as well as the shares, for so it appears; you might have such a fine income instead of uncertainty and calls for payment; but surely the opera cannot remain shut during the season, that would be unheard of. Let us hope for the best. I shall not write to Willy till after the receipt of your next. Sidi and Emmy send their best love, ever you grateful

A.C.

Address: No envelope

Unpublished. Text: M.S., Pf. Coll., CL'ANA 0372

1 Antonia's spelling for Queenwood College.

2 German for "rate".

3 Weidling.

42 • Wilhelm Gaulis Clairmont to Claire Clairmont

[9 March 1852]

My dearest aunt.

Mama tells me in her last letter from Vienna that you enclosed a £5 note for me; never did such a supply come to any person so à propos as this for I was in a very bad need for money from several reasons. Spring will be setting in now and I want summer clothes as I have non[1] [~~illeg.~~] left from last summer; this is one care off my mind; formerly I should not have much troubled my self about such a trifle as dress but I must confess that I have now come round from what you used to term my philosophical turn of mind. I have had many proofs now, that if I wish to maintain that superior position in society to which my education entitles me, this must necessarily be aided by a favourable outward appearance not only with regard to manners but also with regard to dress. I have seen that not only fools but also wise men are apt to judge of a man by his coat or at least to treat him accordingly and it has often occurred to me ~~what~~ all you used to say to me on this point, [~~illeg.~~] the truth of which I am now only capable of apreciating. You must not then think that its vanity or vulgar dandyism ~~whe~~ that makes me wish to appear well dressed, it is the mere conviction that it is necessary for being well received in the world and pushing on ones way – I shall have finished the regular college course at the end of July next and then shall take a situation immediately; for the beginning it will not be very brilliant I shall think myself lucky if I can manage to ~~appear~~ [~~illeg.~~] live and make a decent appearance on my [illeg.] salary, but in 4 or 5 years I hope I shall be working my way towards an agreable independence; for I am the first out of a hundred students here,[2] besides I know many people employed in [~~pra~~] business already ~~which~~ whom I may safely consider inferior to me, so I do not see why I should not succeed in pushing my way too.

It is very long dear aunt you have not written to me, indeed you owe me a letter still, for I have not had an answer to my last, unless ~~indeed~~ it should have been lost. I had for some time the intention of writing to you but always being so very busy I delayed it until Mama's news came when I at once resolved to thank you for your kindness. But it now strikes me that I do not even know your direction and so this letter shall have to wait till I come to Vienna, which will be in another week. – It is a long time I have heard nothing from Pauline, the last news I had from her was that she was going to return to ~~Mr~~ Lady ~~something~~ Barrington's in Berks.[3] I wish she was some thing of a farmer, for close to the place she is living at, is the farm of Mr Pusey's the famous agriculturalist[4] (not Dr –) [5] and then she might give me some description of it or anything interesting that is going on there.

You must not think dear aunt that I am still labouring under my old mania for books; it is true I am very fond of them still, but for the moment I have enough of them. I must tell you though, that irrespective of the information I got out of them the capital is nearly paid back in specie[6] for I turned them to excellent use in translating different things and although they pay one miserably yet I have made a few pounds by it. Now goodbye dearest aunt many thanks for your kindness,

I see you have not forgotten me even if you do not write, but I know it costs you an effort to sit down and write a long letter to go by foreign post so just write me a few lines to tell me you are well, ~~an~~ how you will spend the summer and whether you intend going to Brighton again. I hope the Pringles are well and little Violet![7] My best compliments to Miss Beste. Your affectionate nephew

William G.C.

Altenburg 9 March 1852.

Address: Aerogramme: Miss Clairmont/ 42. Gloucester Place/ Hyde Park/ London/England.
Postmark: WIEN/[illeg.]

Unpublished. Text: M.S., Pf. Coll., CL'ANA 0050

---

1 none.

2 Wilhelm's report cards, housed in the Pforzheimer Collection, document his academic successes. See photographs in this collection of his various school certificates.

3 Berkshire, some 96 kilometers west of London. Pauline worked as a governess in England.

4 Philip Pusey (1799–1855) was a Tory Member of Parliament and an agriculturalist. He helped establish the Royal Agricultural Society of England in 1840 and he wrote forty-seven articles for the *Journal of the Royal Agricultural Society*. In the *Dictionary of National Biography* (London: Smith, Elder & Co., 1896), Ernest Clarke records that Pusey's estate in Pusey, Berkshire, consisted of about 5,000 acres and that Pusey "showed himself a very practical agriculturist. . . . He tried innumerable agricultural experiments, and frequently arranged for trials of implements on the estate" (p. 63). In 1851, Pusey was named chairman of the "agricultural implement department of the Great Exhibition, and, as a royal commissioner, came much into contact with Prince Albert" (p. 63).

5 Edward Bouverie Pusey (1800–1882), younger brother of Philip Pusey. Edward was a theologian who was educated at Eton and Oxford. He was Regius Professor of Hebrew at Oxford University from 1828–1882 ("Edward Bouverie Pusey". Project Canterbury. 1933. Web. 17 May 2015. http://anglicanhistory.org/bios/ebpusey.html).

6 Specie refers to coins instead of paper currency.

7 On 26 June 1845, Claire told Mary Shelley that the Pringle children were "pretty . . . lovely . . . so full of character" (*CC* II: 444). On 10 March 1850, Claire wrote to Wilhelm about Lion and Ada Pringle and, on 21 January 1851, she mentioned two of the Pringle children, Zifi and Elly. Violet is probably Elly, whose full name was Emily Georgiana Violet Pringle. Born in 1839, she married Lieutenant-Colonel John Peyton but died in 1866 in India where she was buried ("The Peerage". Web. 10 April 2015. http://www.thepeerage.com/p64637.htm#i646368).

43 • Wilhelm Gaulis Clairmont to Claire Clairmont

[16 May 1852]

My dearest aunt.

I received your last letter about a fortnight ago, but it was totally impossible for me to answer immediately, as you requested me to do, for I was so overrun with business that I could not find a free hour, and as I did not like to write quite a short note I deferred it till now. Matters stand very ill with us now; Mama is unwell for a considerable time, she is in bed it seems with a low fever, and the worst is that she is in great money anxiety for her income has ceased now, since she is in the country Charley wants his quarterly fee paid, constant repairs are going on in the house and there is no hope of either selling it or letting the lodgings for this season which is now already very far advanced. – her money will be gone soon, and if once she gets into debt every hope is lost. – As for myself I am precisely in the same or even a still more melancholy position; my funds are reduced to £ 3 and that is to last me till September for Mama cant send me anything and there are but £ 5 which I am to get ~~from~~ for translations. so that £ 8 is all I have for the next 4 months – I shall have to make debts, but I dont know whether any one will lend me any money, although until now I have been very punctual in paying all my bills. – I am working night and day in translating and writing for an agricultural paper, but they pay very badly, besides the work goes on very slowly so that I earn but little by it. If you could send me the five pounds you promised in your last letter I should be very glad for it would do a deal towards helping me out of my difficulties.

I thank you very much for the trouble you took in pointing out to me some of the faults I made; it is of great service to me since I have no other authorities, whom to improve my English by except the dictionary.

You request me to write to Percey and remonstrate with him on the pain he ~~caused~~ allowed his wife to inflict upon you and us all – it is a difficult task ~~for~~ to remonstrate on a thing the truth of which it is so difficult to prove, though we may be convinced of it –; for he would simply say that neither he nor his wife had anything whatever to do with Clara's marriage; ~~but~~ or the more likely thing is that he would not take the slightest notice of my letter; and so our purpose ~~s~~would not be gained.[1] – The chief difficulty however is that K. promised to send Mama £ 20 every year as long as Charl.'s education lasts and I am afraid he would seize upon this as an opportunity of shaking off his obligations towards us.[2] I am afraid I can not in the present critical moment risk to deprive Mama of any pecuniary support, without the certainty of some great end being gained. – If they are determined to go on in ~~a~~ their hostile way my letters will not put a stop to it. Pray consider of that dear aunt and tell me what you think. My best compts to the Pringles and Miss Beste. the French papers[3] I think are rising now –

Yours affectionate nephew
WGC

Alten[illeg.].16 May 1852
My direction in full is:
W G. Clairmont
U Altenburg. Austria. (the U before Altenburg means "Ungarisch)

Address: Aerogramme: Miss Clairmont/ 16. Westbourn Street/ Hyde Park/ England. London
Front postmark: UNG: ALTENBURG/ $^{17}/_{5}$
Rear postmark: AACHEN/ $^{21}/_{5}$/ BAHNHOF

Unpublished. Text: M.S., Pf. Coll., CL'ANA 0052

---

1 See CL'ANA 0394 and CL'ANA 0047.

2 See CL'ANA 0373, CL'ANA 0390 and CL'ANA 0394.

3 Probably a reference to stocks or bonds.

44 • Wilhelm Clairmont to Claire Clairmont

[6 June 1852]

My dearest aunt.

I received your last letter today and write according to your request by return of post; I thank you very much for the £ 5 note half of which you enclosed, it will be of very great service to me for I was in very sad need for money –[1] Mama too was very ill so much so that the doctor apprehended real danger; so that on the whole I spent a very dismal time – she now writes me that she is better but I dont know how far I may believe her letters, for she will never tell us when she is unwell or something ailing her. – There was another thing which made me rather lowspirited, an affair which in fact is not yet settled. I had a tolerable situation promised me by the end of the summer when I shall have finished my studies here; [~~illeg.~~] it is quite a wild desert in the southern borders of Hungary a place abounding with wild beasts and robbers and ~~in~~ every thing except civilized people; yet I should have liked to accept it because I should have had a tolerable pay and a comparatively influential position, but it now seems that I shall not get that place for want of sufficient knowledge of the Hungarian language; so I am once more at a loss what to do with myself.
What you tell me about Pauline is very astonishing; I never heard anything of this Mr Jarrant, who and what is he ? She would not think of marrying an adventurer going to some out of the way place in the colonies ! and besides I can not conceive her not writing to her mother herself on so important a subject. –[2]
As regards my letter to Sir Percey I do not think you quite understood what I intended to have said viz. that [~~illeg.~~], I doubted whether a fat, phlegmatic fellow like himself would much care about any letter disturbing his indolent quietude – as for servility no one would think of making a reproach of the kind either to you or to me.[3]
Now Goodbye dearest aunt. I shall of course hear soon of you again;

your affectionate nephew
W. G. Clairmont

6th June 1852.
U. Altenburg. Austria.

Address: Miss Clairmont/12. Horbury Terrace/Notting hill gate/London.
Front postmark: UNG: ALTENBURG/ $^{7}/_{6}$
Rear postmark: PRESSBURG/$^{3}/_{6}{}^{4}$; Coeln./[illeg.]/Verviers.[5]

Unpublished. Text: M.S., Pf. Coll., CL'ANA 0053

1 In her letter to Pauline of 16 March 1852, Claire mentioned having sent £5 to Wilhelm (see *CC* II: 539).

2 On 12 July 1851, Claire wrote to Cini, stating that her niece wanted to marry and that she would need to provide assistance (*CC* II: 539). She did not mention her niece's name, so there is no way to determine if she meant Emily or Pauline. Emily became engaged in 1855. Pauline would leave for Australia in 1853, disproving thereby Wilhelm's assertion that she would not think of "going to some out of the way place in the colonies".

3 Claire still felt anger towards Sir Percy Florence Shelley and she continued to suggest that Wilhelm contact him. Wilhelm had already refused to write to Sir Percy, but evidently Claire persisted in making the request.

4 Pressburg is known today as Bratislava and is the capital city of Slovakia.

5 Verviers is in Belgium.

45 • Pauline Clairmont to Claire Clairmont

Septb 12. [1852]
Holme Hall.

Dearest Aunt

How extremely kind of you to think of the dear children & also of Willy – indeed I cannot find words to express how deeply sensible I am to every thing you do for them – I am however sadly afraid that you are putting yourself to much inconvenience on our account – if it is in the least degree unpleasant for you to send me the £10 pray do not think of it any more – I will be extremely economical with the £5 that I have already received & for which I beg to accept my warmest thanks. – Yesterday I had a letter from Willy – he did not mention having heard from you so probably your letter has not reached him yet – He is as I thought with Mama at Weidling she is very busy getting his things ready – but she says as you that Charley must not go till his health is quite strong & he has left off growing. – Willy says he will ~~be~~ leave Vienna on the tenth of Octb. at least he believes so but cannot decide anything before having heard from the Knoxes
Clari has not written to me so I suppose they have not yet landed anywhere.
I hope you will write as soon as you are at leisure & tell me if you are quite well & will stay at Hoarbury[1] Terr. till I come to London.
Once more many many thanks for your kindness & believe me your most

aff[t]
Paul[illeg.].

Address: Miss Clairmont/12. Hourbury Terr./ Notting Hill/London.[2]
Rear postmark: HOLME; UNG/13SP13/1852; YORK/SP 12/ 1852

Unpublished. Text: M.S., Pf. Coll., CL'ANA 0206

1 Pauline misspelled Horbury Terrace.
2 She meant to write Horbury Terrace, Notting Hill Gate.

46 • Wilhelm Gaulis Clairmont to Claire Clairmont

[24 December 1852]

My dear aunt[1]

I am very sorry at the idea of no more seeing you I never thought the Dutch man would think of sailing on Christmas day and in that case I should have spent tomorrow with you. However they are quite positive they will not wait a moment longer than till tomorrow morn. – I have just come all the way from Shadwell[2] where the ship is at present lying. I should ~~come~~ go to see you now
I have still got to move my things from the Chambers to here because I shall sleep here this last night. Many thanks dearest aunt for all your kindness and regards for me I hope I shall see you very soon again and in good health and spirits
Give my best remembrances to all the [illeg.] and believe me always to be your most

affectionate nephew
WG Clairmont

24 Decemb. 1852
12 St. James Place.
I enclose you Charley's direction which I forgot to give you the other day. and a little note for Pauline.[3]

Address: Miss Clairmont/ 42. Gloucester Place/ Hyde Park. London
Rear postmark: FARRINGTON/MR16/1852/B; [illeg.]/852

Unpublished. Text: M.S., Pf. Coll., CL'ANA 0051

---

1 Wilhelm concluded his studies at Altenburg by the end of 1852. He was 21 years old at the time and he and Pauline would leave Europe for Australia in January 1853. Pauline was 27 years old.

2 On the north bank of the Thames River and entrance to the London docks.

3 These enclosures have been lost.

47 • Antonia Clairmont to Claire Clairmont

[10 April 1853]

Weidling $^{10}/_{4}$ 1853.

My dear Claire.

I received both your letters, the reason of my not answering your first directly was simply the fear of increasing your uneasiness instead of allaying it; you know my affairs, and they can't change for the better, at least not till Charley's studies are over; my house brings me in about £30, my own rent and fuel included – my pension is 10, so with these ~~thirty~~ forty pds I and Sidi must continue to subsist, and I should be able to manage it, no matter how, but for Charley's wants; his salary is £15 per ann. – we must thank God to have it – but yet I can't let the poor boy starve his board and washing comes to double the sum. then there are his clothes and boots – besides other things; when he entered his present place at Lichtensteins,[1] it was stipulated, that he must make two examinations in the course of the first year, one at Easter, and the other at Michelmass;[2] but he dear boy partly from ambition partly to please me and and save a second journey, made both at once and got first rate certificates – but the expenses the fees for the examinations were 4 guineas then the journey up to town and down again. his journeys backward and forward from here new clothing he wanted – it came altogether just to ten pds. I knew that expense was coming, but the whole winter, I looked quietly forward, trusting your promised amount in April would make matters even, but when that hope was destroyed, I had great sorrow how to provide the money, without making the dear fellow feel it too much – Clairy sent something but it was not enough, besides she begged half of it might be for his birthday present, for he was 18 on the 22th March – and the first birthday I had none to give – I had a bitter time of it; by the sale of some furniture and one or two old trinkets, I have now paid all but his tailor's bill with 32 fl that is about 3 pounds and if Heaven helps me to let part of my lodging for summer, that'll be cleared too; so you see, it was better not to write to you, till I was partly relieved of my cares, than to make partake of them; I wish rather I could have shared my happiness and joy with you during the last night of Charley's stay; he had just been absent 6 months, but that time had made a wonderful change and improvement in him, a gay thoughtless lad he went, and returned a man, in earnest attention to his duty, and zeal to take Willy's place or rather follow his footsteps; full of affection and gratitude to me; all tenderness to his sisters; Oh my dear Claire if you could see him you would dote on him, I do not speak of his looks, though he is one of the handsomest lads one could set eyes on about an inch ~~wanting of~~ within Willy's size, and so well made, slender yet strong, and agile untainted as yet by vice of any kind; Oh surely I may not complain of hardship or privation, as long as I have the blessing of seeing my children pursue the right road to virtue and duty – we spent some happy days, Emmy too came to see us, they are all three so fond of each other – all cares were forgot – we thought of our dear absent ones – and of the time when we again see them. I hurts me to the soul, to hear you always reflect upon Pauline and Clara – I know their faults too well, but some of them of which you accuse them are not of the number; Gossip and scandal mongers are every where busy, and you seem too apt to lend an open ear to bad tongues, even when you must know them to speak false, how else could you listen to the absurd report about the Shellies making me an allowance, you know that Mrs. S. never did the least thing for her brother not even then when she came to her fortune; who should think of it now – besides they are perfect strangers to me – and do you think I would be a pensioner upon anybody? I had rather live upon bread and potatoes than be dependant upon the bounty of others; if I accept assistance from yourself or Knox for the education of my sons, that is quite a different thing, it is a noble end, a sacred duty, a capital laid out on high usury, and will bring credit to the whole family, that aim gained, I shall sit down quietly to my little pittance, happy to think, that poor as it is, it will, in case of my death, secure bread to poor Sidi; if only God preserve my life for the next three years, when Charley is 21, then I hope all will be well; Now my paper is quite full and I have not said a word on your affairs – it is indeed a sad thing that you have to invest at such an unfavorable moment, but it is the smaller evil and therefore not so heavy if you consider how lately you trembled for the capital – I cannot yet reconcile myself to the idea that the Opera house should remain shut because the manager is bankrupt[3] – is the whole nation to remain without opera? we have a dreadful winter, just now it begins to snow as if we were in January. the children send their best love; I did as you desired – for in fact I have no secret now for them, Sidi is 17, Charley 18 – Emmy 19

Goodbye ever yours A.C.

Address: No envelope

Unpublished. Text: M.S., Pf. Coll., CL'ANA 0373

1 Unidentified.

2 She meant Michaelmas, the 29 September and the day of St. Michael and All Angels, observed by the Catholic Church and the Church of England. In England, it is one of the four quarter terms of the year.

3 See CL'ANA 0404. Middleton notes that by 1856, Lumley was unable to pay his debts as Jenny Lind's retirement from the stage in 1849 had contributed to his financial troubles. From 1853 until 1855, Her Majesty's Theatre was closed and Lumley, who had sought refuge in Europe, remained on the continent. In March 1856, Covent Garden burned down and he therefore returned to London to reopen Her Majesty's Theatre hoping to improve his financial prospects. By 1858, he was forced to give up the theater due to an inability to pay back his loans (L. M. Middleton, "Lumley, Benjamin (1811/12–1875)", rev. John Rosselli, *Oxford Dictionary of National Biography*, Oxford University Press, 2004; [http://www.oxforddnb.com.prox.lib.ncsu.edu/view/article/17174, accessed 8 May 2016].

Image 1 Portrait of Claire Clairmont by Amelia Curran (NA 271)

Source: Newstead Abbey

Credit Line: Courtesy of Nottingham City Museums and Galleries (Newstead Abbey)

№ 51.

Paulis Clairmont Carol. Austr. Vienn. Ex a did.

primae Grammaticae classi egregiam publ. operam dedit, atque in tentamine publico prioris cursus semestris anni 1845.

a morum cultura	classi	primae eminenter
e doctrina religionis		primae eminenter
e studio linguae latinae		primae eminenter
— — geographiae et historiae		primae eminenter
— — arithmeticae		primae eminenter

adscriptus est.

Viennae in Gymnasio C. R. ad Scotos
die 3. mensis Martii anni 1845.

Vidi
Conradus Luttinger m.p.
Praefectus Gymnasii.

Maurus Schinnagl m.p.
Professor publicus.

Image 2 Report card of Charles Clairmont, Jr., 3 March 1845.

Source: Clairmont family papers. Mar. 3, 1845. recto Manuscript.

Credit Line: The Carl H. Pforzheimer Collection of Shelley and His Circle, The New York Public Library, Astor, Lenox and Tilden Foundations.

Image 3 Image of Queenwood College, included in the "Synopsis of the Course of Education at Queenwood College", 1849, belonging to the collection of the Aylward family of Lockerley and deposited at the Hampshire Record Office in 1966. J. Harwood (artist or possibly engraver).

Source: Hampshire Record Office: 47M66/12/1

Credit Line: Hampshire Record Office, Winchester, Hampshire, United Kingdom.

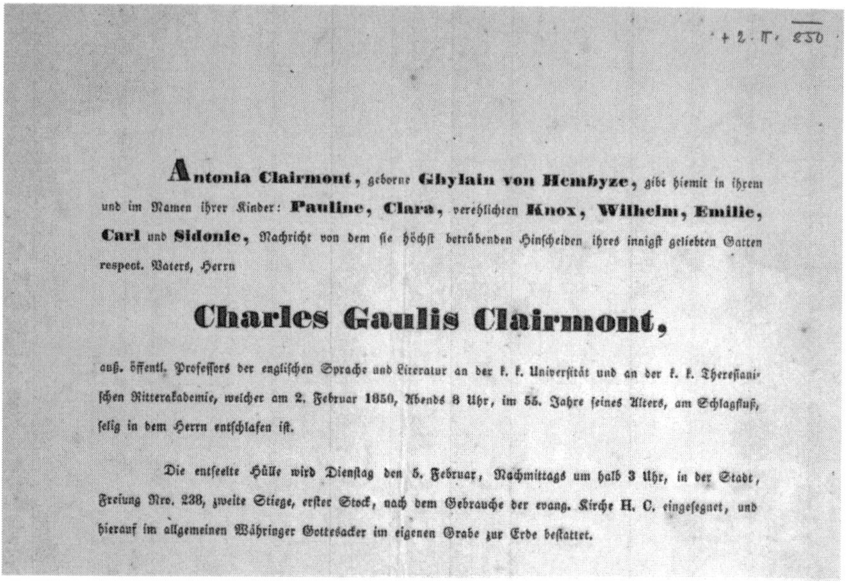

Antonia Clairmont, geborne **Ghylain von Hembyze**, gibt hiemit in ihrem und im Namen ihrer Kinder: **Pauline**, **Clara**, verehlichten **Knox**, **Wilhelm**, **Emilie**, **Carl** und **Sidonie**, Nachricht von dem sie höchst betrübenden Hinscheiden ihres innigst geliebten Gatten respect. Vaters, Herrn

Charles Gaulis Clairmont,

auß. öffentl. Professors der englischen Sprache und Literatur an der k. k. Universität und an der k. k. Theresianischen Ritterakademie, welcher am 2. Februar 1850, Abends 8 Uhr, im 55. Jahre seines Alters, am Schlagfluß, selig in dem Herrn entschlafen ist.

Die entseelte Hülle wird Dienstag den 5. Februar, Nachmittags um halb 3 Uhr, in der Stadt, Freiung Nro. 238, zweite Stiege, erster Stock, nach dem Gebrauche der evang. Kirche H. C. eingesegnet, und hierauf im allgemeinen Währinger Gottesacker im eigenen Grabe zur Erde bestattet.

Image 4 Death Notice (Die Parte) of Charles Gaulis Clairmont.

Source: Heraldic-Genealogical Society Adler, Vienna, tng.adler-wien.eu

Credit Line: Heraldic-Genealogical Society Adler, Vienna, tng.adler-wien.eu

Antonia Clairmont née **Ghylain von Hembyze,** on her own behalf and that of her children: **Pauline, Clara** (married name **Knox**), **Wilhelm, Emilie, Carl,** and **Sidonie,** hereby gives notice of the passing of their dearly beloved husband and father,

Charles Gaulis Clairmont,

Professor Extraordinary of English Language and Literature at the Imperial Royal University and the Imperial Royal Theresian Knight Academy, who died blest in the Lord on February 2, 1850, at 8 o'clock in the evening, in his 55th year of life, of a stroke.

The lifeless remains will be consecrated on Tuesday, February 5, at half past two in the afternoon in the city, Freiung no. 238, second staircase, one floor up, according to the custom of the Evangelical Church of the Helvetic Confession, then laid to rest in a private grave at the General Währing Cemetery.

(English translation provided by Ann Sherwin).

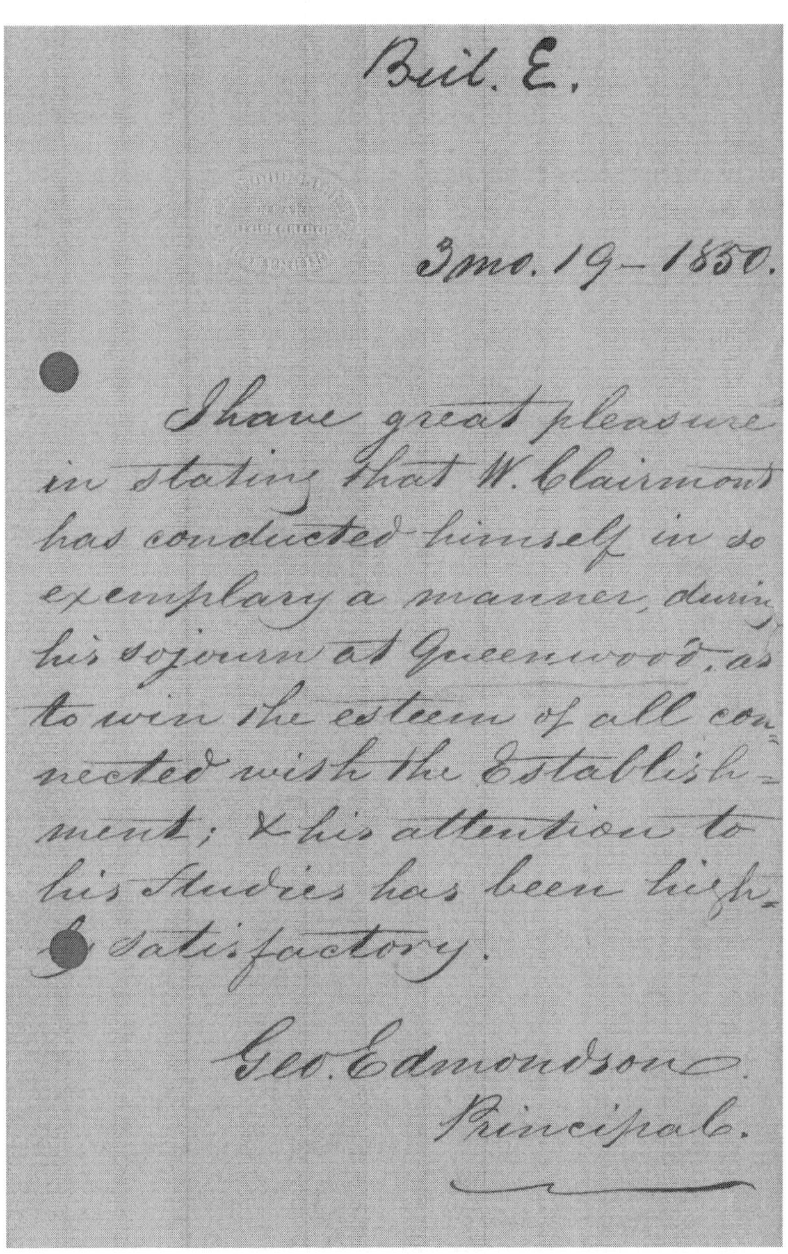

Beil. E.

3mo. 19 – 1850.

I have great pleasure in stating that W. Clairmont has conducted himself in so exemplary a manner, during his sojourn at Queenwood, as to win the esteem of all connected with the Establishment; & his attention to his Studies has been highly satisfactory.

Geo. Edmondson.
Principal.

Image 5 Autograph letter from George Edmondson, principal at Queenwood College, regarding Wilhelm Clairmont, 19 March 1850.

Source: Clairmont family papers. Mar. 19, 1850. p. 1 Manuscript.

Credit Line: The Carl H. Pforzheimer Collection of Shelley and His Circle, The New York Public Library, Astor, Lenox and Tilden Foundations.

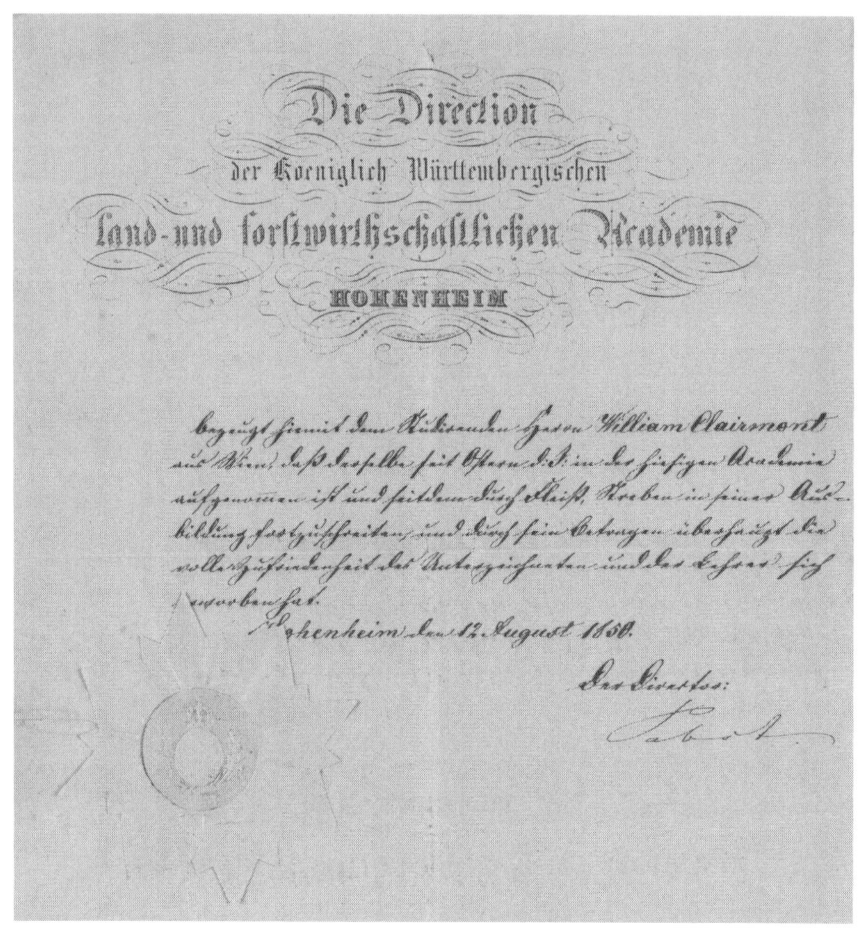

Die Direction
der Koeniglich Württembergischen
Land- und forstwirthschaftlichen Academie
HOHENHEIM

Image 6 Document from the Royal Württemberg Land and Forestry Academy, Hohenheim, regarding Wilhelm Clairmont, 12 August 1850. The German text reads as follows: Die Direction der Koeniglich Württembergischen Land- und forstwirtschaftlichen Academie HOHENHEIM bezeugt hiemit dem Studirenden Herrn William Clairmont aus Wien, daß derselbe seit Osterd:d: in der hiesegen Academie aufgenommen ist und seitdem durch Fleiß, Streben in seiner Ausbildung fortzuschreiten und durch sein Betragen überhaupt die volle Zufriedenheit des Unterzeichneten und der Lehrer sich erworben hat. Hohenheim den 12 August 1850.Der Director: [sig.] Pabst

Translation: The Administration of the Koeniglich Württembergischen Land- und forstwirtschaftlichen Academie HOHENHEIM hereby certifies that the student Mr. William Clairmont of Vienna was accepted in this academy at Easter of this year and since then, through diligence and striving to advance his training and through his conduct in general, has performed to the full satisfaction of the undersigned and the instructors. Hohenheim, August 12, 1850. The Director: [sig.] Pabst (German transcription and English translation provided by Ann Sherwin)

Source: Clairmont family papers. Aug. 12, 1850. p. 1 Manuscript.

Credit Line: The Carl H. Pforzheimer Collection of Shelley and His Circle, The New York Public Library, Astor, Lenox and Tilden Foundations.

Image 7 Photograph of Wilhelm Gaulis Clairmont, from the records of k. k. höheren landwirtschaftlichen Lehranstalt zu Ungarisch-Altenburg (Imperial and Royal Higher Agricultural Academy of Altenburg-Hungary).

Source: University of West Hungary, Faculty of Agricultural and Food Sciences

Credit Line: Németh Attila, Óvári Gazdászok Szövetsége, Alumni Association, Nyugat-magyarországi Egyetem, University of West Hungary, Mezőgazdaság- és Élelmiszertudományi Kar, Faculty of Agricultural and Food Sciences, Mosonmagyaróvár, Hungary.

Image 8 Photographic portrait of Charles Clairmont, Jr.

Source: Visual materials from the Carl H. Pforzheimer Collection. c. 1855.

Credit Line: The Carl H. Pforzheimer Collection of Shelley and His Circle, The New York Public Library, Astor, Lenox and Tilden Foundations.

THE AUSTRALIAN SOJOURN

Historians have rarely mentioned Wilhelm from the time he moved to Australia in 1853. Owen Wright's book *Wongwibinda*, for example, acknowledges Wilhelm as a co-purchaser with Julius Duboc of the sheep run of the title (then named Kangaroo Hills), but states that "the history and character of Clairmont remains unknown" (1985: 62). He reproduces parts of the purchasing contract between Duboc and Wilhelm and the seller, William Dangar, but otherwise leaves Wilhelm a mystery and provides no information as to the level of Wilhelm's involvement in these matters. In *Our Grandchildren Won't Believe It*, Wright contributes a chapter on Kangaroo Hills in which he concludes that "William Clairmont" was "probably French" (McInherny and Schaeffer 2004: 72). Similarly, Jacqueline Voignier-Marshall records Wilhelm's arrival in Australia, but admits she knows nothing of him thereafter (1983: 25).

Wilhelm's letters home and local Australian newspaper articles attest that his eight-year stay in Australia involved a certain amount of excitement. He held a number of managerial positions on sheep runs, owed a farm that failed, and suffered an attempt on his life that left him injured. Pauline's four-year stay was equally eventful. On her arrival, she took a position as a governess, later fell in love with the son of her employers, and left Australia when her young admirer turned his attention to another woman. Wilhelm and Pauline set sail on the Dutch *Zeepaard* on 17 January 1853 with the expectation of achieving financial security in the fledgling colony. Wilhelm's letter of 2 November 1849 (CL'ANA 0055) referenced several people he knew who had done so, including Charles Robinson, Mary Shelley's friend, who returned "a wealthy man" (see CL'ANA 0055). He even mentioned a cousin of Mary Shelley named Alexander Berry, who earned a colonial fortune large enough to support his family back in England, and "personal acquaintances" of Walter Coulson (the editor of *The Traveller*) and Alexander Knox who "made a splendid fortune" (see CL'ANA 0055). With great optimism, then, the siblings arrived in Sydney on 6 May 1853, and *The Sydney Morning Herald* of 7 May 1853 (National Library of Australia, http://nla.gov.au/nla.news-page1507368) noted the presence of passengers including "Mr. and Mrs. Culvert, Mr. and Miss Clairmont" (p. 2).

Pauline's letters record that she found Sydney to be "a very bad place," and life there offered her only "a wretched existence" (CL'ANA 0210). However, shortly after her arrival, she went to work as a governess for the Suttor family on Brucedale, their estate near Bathurst – a town situated some 200 kilometers west–northwest of Sydney in New South Wales – a position the local newspapers and her journals reference, as well as her letters (see note 7, CL'ANA 0232 and note 6, CL'ANA 0210).[1] Pauline found the Suttors to be "kind generous and agreeable people" (CL'ANA 0232); however, she viewed Australian men as "worse tyrants here than in Europe," and to her the colonists seemed generally "narrowminded" (CL'ANA 0209).

Pauline's letters in this volume describe her employment as governess to Caroline Suttor (born 1841, and known to the family as Carry), the daughter of William Henry Suttor (1805–1877) and his wife, Charlotte Francis Suttor (1817–1879), and her cousin, Ruth Amelia Simpson (born 1838, and known within the family as Minna). Ruth was the daughter of George and Ruth Francis Simpson, Charlotte's sister.[2] While Charlotte Suttor's diary entry from October 1853 noted one of the new arrival's most charming qualities – "We engaged a lady as governess for Caroline she had just arrived in Sydney . . . her name is Clairmont she is an excellent musician" (quoted in Norton and Norton 1993: 139) – the new governess' letters contained in this volume indicate that even as Pauline enjoyed teaching the children and playing the piano which the family provided for them, she often sought moments of solitude available in the quiet Australian bush (see CL'ANA 0209). William and Charlotte Suttor would name Caroline's new sister born in November 1853 Sarah Pauline Suttor, suggesting their regard for their accomplished and impressive governess.

According to Ruth Teale, William Henry Suttor, the son of the family patriarch and original immigrant to the continent, George Suttor, had served as "overseer of his father's grant at Brucedale" since 1834. He managed both his father's 10,020 acres as well as his own allotment of 3,344 acres. By 1865, William held more than "600,000 acres on the lower Lachlan, Darling, Macquarie and Bogan rivers".[3] Members of the Suttor family still own land in this area, and even as this book goes to press, David Suttor, George Suttor's great-great-grandson, continues to raise sheep at Brucedale.

Pauline perhaps desired to play a role in the Suttor family lineage, as in the course of her affair with employer's son Willie Suttor she wished to marry him. She details her love affair with him and her sense of disappointment over the dissolution of her romance in her unpublished Australian journal, in a story that very much resembles Claire's failed romance with Byron (CL'ANA 0176, unpublished manuscript, Pforzheimer Collection). Willie, it seems, was initially smitten by Pauline, "the first woman of marked intellect and high attainments whom it had been my fortune to meet . . . She opened my eyes to the beauties of English literature, authors of whom I had scarcely heard before. And now couldn't help – thrown together so much as we were – feeling a stronger feeling than mere friendship for her" (in Voignier-Marshall 1983: 29). After Willie transferred his affections to Adelaide Bowler, Pauline recorded the age difference between herself and Willie, noting its role in the decline of the relationship. Indeed, Willie's overtly diminished affection towards Pauline was the deciding factor in her departure from Australia. Pauline so wished to keep Willie's affection and stay in Australia – eventually as his wife – and her journal reflects her despair over the events. Finally, an entry in her journal on 8 November 1856 suggests she had resigned herself to the impossibility of the situation: "I feel certain that AB[4] will make him an excellent wife five hundred times better I could have done. Would that I were gone although I wish to stay for Mrs. Suttor's sake . . . that my love for him sinks deeper & deeper into my heart – not even to his mother can I speak of it much less to any one else" (CL'ANA 0176: 166–167). She underscored her growing sense of dejection and abandonment by copying into her journal Robert Burns's poem "Wandering Willie". The once hopeful plea expressed in the poem ("Welcome now Simmer, and welcome my Willie,/The Simmer to nature, my Willie to me!"[5]) gives way to a hauntingly sad foreshadowing of an unfaithful suitor. Pauline's musings on her relations with Willie became even more frequent as her departure drew nigh. On 26 November 1856, she commented wistfully on his physical appearance: "Caught in an awful thunderstorm coming from Alloway Bank – Mrs. Sr[6] cannot believe that I am going – What beautiful eyes that boy has – I shall never forget my Australian lad – his eyes have an expression of deep & unuttered – something –" (CL'ANA 0176: 168). For his part, Willie alternated between flirtatious behavior towards Pauline and sheer indifference towards her whenever Adelaide or other family members were around, thus further intensifying Pauline's desire to leave. "I am impatient to be gone," she reported after one of Adelaide's visits, after which Willy finally "makes an effort" to treat his former lover with a modicum of affection (CL'ANA 0176: 176). In time, Pauline extended her sense of despondency even towards Brucedale, which she now found overcrowded and oppressive ("There are always so many people staying at Brucedale that one cannot enjoy one's life at all" [CL'ANA 0176: 182]). Her Australian journal recorded her pain over her unrequited love: "'Love lies bleeding'[7] those words that I heard & heeded not, sound now like a dirge – Oh Willie farewel you love me not – or you could not be so silent. The wind is howling loud & the clouds are sweeping over the cold sky – on such a night I stood on the Verandah at Wallawa & deeply did I long for you to love me & protect me though life. But you came not" (CL'ANA 0176: 183). As a result of her failed romance, Pauline decided to leave Australia and to return to Europe, thereby ending her association with Willie and the Suttor family. She left behind a position she had enjoyed and a country that she had considered her home.

Pauline's journal conflates the loss of Willie's affection with the loss of her father, Charles Gaulis Clairmont, underscoring the close Clairmont family connections:

> This day is always of sad recollection to me this day 10 years ago the Countess K. came into my room before breakfast & fatal & yet happy was the result – yes happy because I came here where I met the only man I have ever truly loved the one I shall ever love On this day far back in the recess of my childhood we used all to assemble round my fathers

> table – there were the mysterious presents for all, the children to the parents what their small means afforded & the parents to the children what was pleasing & useful – there we used to find long & secret wishes realized through the devining power of love there tears of gratitude & pleasure would fill our youthful eyes, & Father and mother stood by in silent pleasure watching the happiness of their children – Then came the family breakfast – the only one throughout the whole year & the harmony & peace was exquisite –. And now – where are they all gone? Around the small table shall sit but three where once were 9. their hearts are filled with sorrow – & mine is doubly so – & my eyes are full of tears when I think of Willie whom I am going to leave never to see again.
>
> (CL'ANA 0176: 184–185)

Willie's response to the affair with Pauline appears slightly more measured. In his Memoirs, while he described Pauline as "highly educated and accomplished," he noted that she had a "certain spice of devilry in her" that attracted a "raw country lad with all his passions just ripening into manhood strength" (quoted in Voignier-Marshall 1983: 29). Perhaps to justify the dissolution of their relationship, he subsequently identified Pauline's "little flirtation" with an older male cousin, noting that "she was never the same to me after that" (1983: 30); however, Pauline provided a different reason for the termination of the friendship with Willie.

As Pauline's impending departure for Europe allowed her to turn her thoughts once more to what she termed in her journal "the charms of Old Europe" and to recognize her permanent separation from Willie, she committed herself to a new cause – "the satisfaction of doing what I consider to be my duty" (CL'ANA 0176: 190) towards Antonia. As she wrote, "My mother my only friend there to you will I return you are the only attraction" (CL'ANA 0176: 195). That her mother welcomed the reunion seems evident in that she voiced regret in 1856 that she had not prevented her children's emigration (see CL'ANA 0384), although in 1860 (CL'ANA 0324) she would express the hope that Australia promised a healthy climate. Once Pauline finally left Australia on 19 April 1857 "with a whole cargo of strangers" (CL'ANA 0176: 220), she recorded in her journal her flirtations with others on board ship. Just as her aunt Claire had, she sought out the company of men whose attentions she enjoyed. On 7 August 1857, directly upon her arrival in England she traveled to join Claire. Pauline never again saw Willie Suttor.

Wilhelm would stay in Australia four years past his sister, although he had also found the Australian enterprise to be a challenge. As the letters will show, after his arrival in Sydney in 1853, he began working for Augustus Morris on the Tala (also known as Kieta) Station, located roughly 950 kilometers west of Sydney. Wilhelm's interest in farming led to the acquisition of Kangaroo Hills in 1855, a sheep station located 98 kilometers northwest of Armidale in New South Wales. Wilhelm and his partner, Julius Duboc, apparently purchased some 26,000 acres of land from pastoralist William Dangar (Wright 1985: 12). After owning it for a mere two years, Wilhelm and Duboc were forced to return ownership to Dangar, as per the mortgage agreement, as they were unable to make payments on the property.[8] The sale proved abortive, and Duboc and Wilhelm suffered tremendous financial losses, to the extent that an advertisement in *The Maitland Mercury and Hunter River General Advertiser* recorded Wilhelm's attempts to rid himself of his sheep stock. On Saturday, 24 November 1855, and again on Wednesday, 28 November 1855, Clairmont, Duboc and Company of Kangaroo Hills, Armidale, advertised "3000 store sheep for sale".[9] According to Wright, Duboc variously blamed their Kangaroo Hills failure on the climate, lack of high quality shepherds, and the poor wool market (McInherny and Schaeffer 2004: 73). Wilhelm's letters to Claire and Antonia largely focus on a climate unsuited to sheep farming. Yet Kangaroo Hills later appeared to become a thriving concern. An advertisement for its sale in *The Sydney Morning Herald* of 16 February 1859 offered "a first-class station, well grassed and watered, and in full working order . . . The Kangaroo Hills Run is so well known to all New England squatters as to need very little embellishment . . . parties desirous of entering upon pastoral pursuits would do well to contrast the small quantity of stock sold with the run with its large grazing capabilities, and to avail themselves of this opportunity of securing a large and valuable station, with good improvements and in good working order".[10] The newspaper termed the station "very extensive and valuable".

In 1856, Antonia informed Claire that she had asked Alexander Knox to forward Wilhelm funds for return passage to Europe, but he refused, deeming it "madness" to give up on the colonies so quickly (see CL'ANA 0385). After the failure of Kangaroo Hills, Wilhelm went to work for the Twofold Bay Pastoral Association, an enterprise controlling 400,000 acres consisting of seven businessmen: two sets of brothers – John Edye, James, and William Montagu Manning, and Robert and Edwin Tooth – and Thomas Sutcliffe Mort and John Croft. James Manning had been educated in Hohenheim some years before Wilhelm attended the school, and it is evident from Wilhelm's letters that he had developed a close and continuing association with his fellow alumnus. Between 1857 and 1861, Wilhelm spent some time working on Cuba, a pastoral run that the Association owned, which is situated near today's Darlington Point, or some 631 kilometers southwest of Sydney.[11] Local newspapers recorded the presence of Wilhelm in the area at least as early as the tail end of 1857, when the Sydney newspaper *The Empire* noted on 10 December 1857 that bank orders drawn by W G. Clairmont, Esq., Cuba Murrumbidgee, in favor of three men, had been stopped. The newspaper reported that the orders were "fraudulently obtained from Mr. Clairmont" the previous August.[12] Just over a month later, on 16 January 1858, *The Goulburn Herald and County of Argyle Advertiser* offered a reward of thirty pounds for the "apprehension and conviction of the three men . . . now at large, who committed a violent and murderous assault upon Mr. W.G. Clairmont, in the woolshed at Cuba Station on the Murrumbidgee River, on the 1st September last, and who did then and there forcibly extort certain orders from him under peril of his life".[13] In keeping with the tenor of their relationship, Wilhelm did not report this assault to either his mother or his aunt.

While Wilhelm's association with the Twofold Bay Pastoral Association marked a turn in his fortunes, it also heralded the end of the Australian period in his life. Beginning in 1858, as told in both his letters home and references in local newspapers, Wilhelm spent some years living with the Mannings and working on the Kameruka station,[14] an estate of 192,260 acres the company had acquired in 1852.[15] The dissolution of the Twofold Bay Pastoral Association in 1860 led to Wilhelm's departure from Australia in 1861.[16]

Notes

1 The family patriarch, George Suttor (1774–1859), emigrated from England in 1800. Together with his wife Sarah (1775–1844), he obtained a land grant to a farm located on the Bathurst Plains from Governor Sir Thomas Brisbane. According to historian Geoff Smith, Brisbane originally granted Suttor permission to choose his own land in Bathurst, but by the time Suttor actually arrived in 1822 to stake his claim, settlers with prior claims had overrun it. Thus the Suttors turned their attention instead to the land north of Bathurst, which resulted in their selection of Brucedale in the village of Peel. Smith opines that, in their choice of Brucedale, "no doubt, the history of Peel began on that day" (1998: 2). The Brucedale property, which initially consisted of some 300 acres, continued to expand as additional grants were awarded over the years.

2 See "Francis Descendants," Web, 20 October 2014, http://www.asletts.com/node/6.

3 Teale, R., "Suttor, William Henry (1805–1877)," *Australian Dictionary of Biography*, National Centre of Biography, Australian National University, 1976, Web, 1 November 2014, http://adb.anu.edu.au/biography/suttor-william-henry-1269/text7733.

4 Adelaide Bowler.

5 *The Complete Poetical Works of Robert Burns*, ed W. Henley and T. Henderson (Boston: Houghton Mifflin, 1900), p. 283.

6 Suttor.

7 William Wordsworth's poem, "Love Lies Bleeding" (1845).

8 Wright indicates that there is no official record of Duboc and Wilhelm's stay at Kangaroo Hills, since the license for the run was never officially transferred to them, which appears to be an error because historian William Gardner (1802–1860) had recorded in his *Alphabetical List of Settlers in the New England and Macleay Districts* the sale to Wilhelm and Duboc before placing the word "left" in the record.

9 National Library of Australia, http://nla.gov.au/nla.news-page129370 (p. 3); and National Library of Australia, http://nla.gov.au/nla.news-article709175 (p. 1).

10 National Library of Australia, http://nla.gov.au/nla.news-page1492577 (p. 7).

11 The *Australian Dictionary of Biography* records that John Peter became licensee of Cuba, and that by 1848 Peter was "licensee of Cuba, Gumly Gumly, Ugoble and Sandy Creek" ("Peter, John (1812–1878)," *Australian Dictionary of Biography*, National Centre of Biography, Australian National University, 1974, Web, 31 October 2015, http://adb.anu.edu.au/biography/peter-john-4392/text7157.

12 National Library of Australia, http://nla.gov.au/nla.news-page5720756 (p. 5).

13 National Library of Australia, http://nla.gov.au/nla.news-article118248598 (p. 2).

14 Situated in the Bega Valley on the South Coast of New South Wales, about 500 kilometers south of Sydney, Kameruka was originally started by the brothers George, Alexander, and Peter Imlay, but after a series of financial difficulties the property passed into the hands of the brothers James and William Walker. They later sold it to the Twofold Bay Pastoral Association. See Vicky Small, *Kameruka* (Canberra: Pirie Printers, 1989).

15 On 1 February 1860, *The Goulburn Herald NSW* offered rams for sale: "Some of the late Twofold Bay Pastoral Company's celebrated stock". W. G. Clairmont of Kameruka, Merimbula, was listed as the company's agent. See National Library of Australia, http://nla.gov.au/nla.news-article103400826 (p. 3).

16 Although Small provides two different accounts of the subsequent ownership of Kameruka in the wake of the partnership's dissolution, it appears likely that James Manning purchased Kameruka outright in 1861. Small suggests that Manning left Kameruka by 1864 (1989: 18), while Suzanne Edgar claims that he had been forced to sell it in 1862 to Robert Tooth (Edgar, S. "'Manning, James Alexander Louis (1814–1887)," *Australian Dictionary of Biography*, National Center of Biography, Australian National University, 1974, Web, 17 November 2014, http://adb.anu.edu.au/biography/manning-james-alexander-louis-4149/text6654). Kameruka still exists today as an estate of some 3,000 acres which, according to Bruce Ryan, represents "the largest individually owned holding in the Bega Valley" (1964: 103). In terms of its legacy, Ryan claims that of the many attempts by "men of imagination" at "recreating an English agrarian social system" in Australia, "today only Kameruka enshrines what might have been" (1964: 121).

Bibliography

Barker, T., *A History of Bathurst* (Bathurst, NSW: Crawford House Press, 1992).

Bartley, N., *Opals and Agates, Or, Scenes Under the Southern Cross and the Magellans: Being Memories of Fifty Years of Australia and Polynesia* (Brisbane: Gordon and Gotch, 1892).

Bayley, W.A., *Behind Broulee: History of Eurobodalla Shire, Central South Coast, New South Wales* (Moruya, NSW: Eurobodalla Shire Council, 1973).

Burrowes, G. (dir.), *Return to Snowy River* (Video DVD, Walt Disney Home Video, 2003).

Clarke, P., *A Colonial Woman: The Life and Times of Mary Braidwood Mowle, 1827–1857* (Sydney and Boston: Allen & Unwin, 1986).

Farwell, G., *Squatters' Castle: The Saga of a Pastoral Dynasty* (London and Sydney: Angus & Robertson, 1983).

Ferry, J., *Colonial Armidale* (St. Lucia: University of Queensland Press, 1999).

Fitzgerald, J., *Big White Lie: Chinese Australians in White Australia* (Sydney: University of New South Wales Press, 2007).

Frost, L., *No Place for a Nervous Lady: Voices from the Australian Bush* (Melbourne: McPhee Gribble/Penguin, 1984).

Google Maps, 2014–2015, Web, various dates, www.google.com/maps/

Jones, J., L. Smith, and G. Briscoe, "They used to Call it Sandy Blight: Aboriginal Health and Censorship in Australia," *Australian Aboriginal Studies*, 2 (2006), pp. 62–67.

McInherny, F. and T. Schaeffer, *Our Grandchildren Won't Believe It: A Local History of the Wongwibinda, Aberfoyle and Ward's Mistake Areas* (Armidale, NSW: Historical Group, 2004).

Mackaness, G., *Fourteen Journeys over the Blue Mountains of New South Wales, 1813–1841* (Sydney and Melbourne: Horwitz-Grahame, 1965).

Miller, G. (dir.), *The Man from Snowy River* (Video DVD, Fox Video, 2002).

National Center of Biography, *Australian Dictionary of Biography*, Web, http://adb.anu.edu.au/.

National Library of Australia, Trove, Newspapers Online, http://trove.nla.gov.au/newspaper/

Norton, J. and H. Norton, *Dear William: The Suttors of Brucedale: Principally the Life and Times of William Henry Suttor Senior ("Dear William"), 1805–1877* (Sydney: Suttor Pub. Committee, 1993).

Pearson, M., *Pastoral Australia: Fortunes, Failures and Hard Yakka: A Historical Overview 1788–1967*, Australia, Department of the Environment, Water, Heritage, and the Arts, Australian Heritage Council and J. Lennon (eds), (Collingwood, Vic.: CSIRO Publishing in association with the Dept. of the Environment, Water, Heritage and the Arts and the Australian Heritage Council, 2010).

Ryan, B., "Kameruka Estate, New South Wales, 1864–1964," *New Zealand Geographer*, 20:2 (1964), pp. 103–121.

Small, V., *Kameruka* (Bega, NSW: Kameruka Estates, 1989).

Smith, G., *100 Years Peel and District* (Bathurst, NSW: Geoffrey A. Smith, 1998).

Suttor, C., *Charlotte Augusta Anne Suttor Diaries, 1848–1*853 (Bathurst, NSW: State Library New South Wales, 1848–1853).

Suttor, W. H., *Australian Stories Retold; and, Sketches of Country Life* (Bathurst, NSW: G. Whalan, 1887).

Taylor, J. G., *The Social World of Batavia: European and Eurasian in Dutch Asia* (Madison: University of Wisconsin Press, 1983).

Voignier-Marshall, J., "Looking for Pauline Clairmont in N.S.W.," *The Byron Society in Australia Newsletter*, 7 (1983), pp. 25–31.

Walker, R. B., *Old New England, A History of the Northern Tablelands of New South Wales, 1818–1900* (Sydney: Sydney University Press, 1966).

Walsh, G., *Pioneering Days: People and Innovations in Australia's Rural Past* (St. Leonards, NSW: Allen & Unwin, 1993).

Wilson, G., *Murray of Yarralumla* (Melbourne and New York: Oxford University Press, 1968).

Woodland, J., *Money Pits British Mining Companies in the Californian and Australian Gold Rushes of the 1850s* (Farnham, Surrey, and Burlington, VT: Ashgate, 2014).

Wright, O., *Wongwibinda* (Armidale, NSW: University of New England, 1985).

LETTERS FROM 8 JULY 1853–10 DECEMBER 1860

48 • Pauline Clairmont to Claire Clairmont

Sydney[1] July 8th 1853.

My dearest Aunt,

It seems very long to me since the arrival of your last letter which was about 6 weeks ago[2] – Perhaps you think that my letters were not satisfactory but really one lives in the center of constant whirl, motion, excitement troubles & pleasures that it takes an amazing amount of collection to settle all one's thoughts & write a rational letter. You will be happy to hear that we both are doing well & likely to be flourishing in a very short time – Willy is gone 600 miles down the country on the Murumbidgee[3] on a sheep station of Mr Morris[4] I had one letter from him on the road – by this time he must have at the place of his destination but the letters take 8 days coming through the mail goes day & night. I myself am going away in a few days to Bathurst[5] to a very nice agreable family as far as I know them[6] – I prefered taking a permanent situation as Sydney ~~is a~~ that is giving lessons & living all the year round in ~~it~~ it is a wretched existence – Besides there are numbers of daily governesses as many ~~p~~ married ladies find it necessary to add something to their husband's income owing to the dearness of the most necessary articles of life – They take pupils at 2 & 3 guineas for 3 month – but well educated governesses there are <u>none</u> – when I found that my accomplishments were at such a premium I made my conditions accordingly – & think I shall be very comfortable & happy with my 3 pupils two girls & a boy[7] – We shall be in the country nearly in the bush – but the house they tell me is very comfortable, a horse will be at my disposal & a piano[8] in my own room. Does not all this seem very promising? – But now I will tell you how I spent my time – The plan in Sydney to procure as much comfort as possible for those that have no homes of their own, is of finding nice lodging houses – Quite an american fashion – the good lodging houses are expensive but besides being respectable enable one to make many agreeable acquaintances which otherwise would be very difficult – Thus I met a young man here who after a fortnight seemed desperately smitten & popped the question! He was so earnest about it that I was going to say yes – but Willy & several of my other friends advised me so strongly against it that at last I was~~t~~ persuaded to say no It was altogether a fruit of unripe & too quick growth – besides he was too unsettled in life rather careless & a great flir~~s~~t though he had arrived at the age of 30. On the whole I think that being in the colony does all the young men a great deal of good – they brush off a great part of their cockney prejudices & are more natural a agreeable in their manners than they are at home. I never was so much courted as here they are really all as you said "cap in hand" – Elegant women are at a [~~illeg.~~] Premium here, so Mr Blair[9] a very handsome young man, says who lives in this lodging house where I am but alas he is poor & proud – So we settled that it was no use thinking of marriage but we would contribute to our mutual amusement as long as we were both in Sydney – So there I see his beautiful bright eyes & his dark curls of hair daily – he reads Tennyson's poems[10] to me, & when we come to hear about love in a cottage[11] we shut up the book & sigh! – Is not that a pleasant little passe tems ![12] There are many balls & parties, I find myself remarkably well received every where so much so that I often wonder in secret what induces those rich people to be so very civil to a poor Miss Nobody like myself & a Governess too! Now I am all right though I had a good many troubles. Sydney it seems to me is a very bad place – a great many fashionable young men the governor's son's[13] at their head as wild as march hares both very handsome, a great many rich diggers still richer trades people for they are making money hand over fist – I think I never saw so many public houses & drunken people about as here all day long but the nights are comparatively quiet – Yesterday was the Major's fancy Ball[14] but I unfortunately could not go as all my things had been sent away to Bathurst with the drags.[15] The best place here for people with a little capital would be to set up a lodging house – You would have your board for nothing only the rent to pay – always lots of people if you choose to make the house agreeable comfortable & decent. They charge 2 or 3 guineas a week for a single small bedroom & common meals & drawing room. There are very few places of public amusement, & those that there are are[16] low places more calculated to attract diggers[17] & their class. I have not once been to the theatre Willy says it is too horrid for ladies to go to, one concert I heard & that is all So if people have an agreeable family to visit it is far preferable. It would be the thing for you who combine good house keeping with good manners & pleasant conversation.

Bathurst July 31st[18]

You will be pleased to hear dear Aunt that I have preferred settling in the country with a family to the uncertainty of lessons in such a low place as Sydney.[19] I have come to Bathurst with a very agreeable family; they are all kind to me as the day is long, I have 3 children to teach it is true, but every comfort & luxury. They keep a very nice carriage & what is more I can very often have a horse to ride. Travelling in this country is very defective nearly always on horseback the roads are in awful state so much so that the last mail was stuck in the mud & it was too[20] or 3 days before they could get men to dig it out. We are here within

20 miles of the diggings[21] & Mrs Suttor has promised to take me there when the days get longer. – In short I am as comfortable & happy as one can be – & only wish Willy would not keep me in such a state of suspense – I have not heard of him for the last month. Your last letter to him arrived the last day I was in Sydney, & I posted it the same day to his place. Till now I do not repent the state I have taken, & only wish more people would be induced to come out. There is an abundance of occupation particularly for the labouring class – Only think that common working men receive 10 s. p. week & are found in <u>everything</u> except clothes! A cottage rentfree 10 lb of meat 10 lb. of flower[22] 2 lb of sugar ½ of tea milk & vegetables for 1 individual! The servants are intolerably independent though they receive 12 s. p. week. In the lodging house where I was staying we had a china man[23] as servant, & when Mrs Armstrong[24] ordered him to do one thing or another he would say "You go & do it, you do nothing all day long" – at other times, he would lie in bed till 8 o'clock smoking opium, & at last he walked off without saying a word. Such are most of them here, & one has to beg & pray and be very[25]

Address: No envelope.

Unpublished. Text: M.S., Pf. Coll., CL'ANA 0210

---

1 *The Sydney Morning Herald* of 7 May 1853 records the 6 May arrival of the Dutch barque, *Zeepaard*, with passengers Mr. and Miss Clairmont aboard (National Library of Australia, http://nla.gov.au/nla.news-page1507368, p.2). The ship's captain was T. Giltjes, and Gilchrist, Alexander and Company served as agents. The *Zeepaard* departed from the Downs, in England, on 17 January 1853 and arrived in Port Jackson, New South Wales, on 6 May 1853. In addition to 28 crew members, there were four passengers on board.

2 This letter has not survived.

3 Knox financed Wilhelm and Pauline's Australian project. Wilhelm and Pauline were unassisted immigrants, meaning that unlike many others they did not have an Australian employee seeking inexpensive labor paying their passages. Upon arrival in the colony, Wilhelm began working on a farm in New South Wales, while Pauline became governess to the family of William and Charlotte Suttor at Brucedale near Bathurst in New South Wales (see CL'ANA 0209).

The Murrumbidgee River has its source in the Snowy Mountains in southeastern New South Wales, near the former gold mining town of Kiandra. The word itself means "big water" in the Wiradjuri language. The Murrumbidgee flows through the Australian Capital Territory. The river then continues through New South Wales and past the city of Wagga Wagga to join with the Murray River. See "Murrumbidgee River". The Editors of Encyclopaedia Britannica. *Encyclopedia Britannica Online*. Encyclopedia Britannica Inc., n.d. Web. 6 May 2016. http://www.britannica.com/place/Murrumbidgee-River

4 Augustus Morris (c. 1820–1895) was the Australian-born son of a former convict who had been transported to the colony. He was a pastoralist who managed and later purchased sheep stations and runs. Prior to 1853, Morris managed Tala, Yangar, Nap Nap, and Paika stations on behalf of William Wentworth. In 1853, together with pastoralists T. S. Mort, Thomas Holt, and T. W. Smart, Morris purchased stations from Wentworth in the Murrumbidgee area. He later "bought out" his partners to become sole owner (Barnard, Alan. "Morris, Augustus (1820–1895)", *Australian Dictionary of Biography*. National Centre of Biography, Australian National University. 1974. Web. 15 November 2014. http://adb.anu.edu.au/biography/morris-augustus-4250/text6867). Wilhelm evidently worked on the Tala station, which was also known as Kieta (CL'ANA 0065).

5 See CL'ANA 0209 for the history of Bathurst. See also the introduction to the Australian section for a history of the Suttor family.

6 In her journal entry of October 1853, Charlotte Suttor recorded her intial satisfaction with Pauline: "she is highly educated and brought out letters of introduction to some of the first people here. She is of German birth, her name is Clairmont she is an excellent musician and I hope, and think I shall find her what I wish, she is a most agreeable companion we pay her a high salary" (*Dear William*, p. 139 and Charlotte Suttor's journal, pp. 228–9). See Introduction to The Australian Sojourn for more information about Bathurst and the Suttor family. In November 1853, Sarah Pauline was born to Charlotte and William, named possibly for Pauline Clairmont. Jessie Augusta Francis (1842–1917), daughter of Henry Francis and Mary Ann Griffin, and niece of Charlotte Suttor, referred to her cousin Sarah Pauline Suttor as Pauline in her diary (*Dear William*, pp. 163–223).

7 Pauline taught Caroline Suttor (1841–1921), daughter of William and Charlotte Suttor, and Ruth Amelia Simpson (known as Minna, 1838–1880), daughter of Ruth Francis and George Simpson. Ruth Francis Simpson and Charlotte Augusta Francis Suttor were sisters. Marion Stocking incorrectly identifies Minna as William and Charlotte Suttor's daughter rather than as their niece via Charlotte's sister (*CC* II: 568, note 2). Caroline Suttor (Carry) married John Edye Manning (1831–1909), son of Edye and Fanny Manning, while Minna Simpson married Silas Fowler, a ship's officer ("Francis Descendants". Web. 2 November 2014. http://www.asletts.com/node/6). The "boy" Pauline mentioned was probably George Roxburgh Suttor (1844–1928), fifth child of William and Charlotte. Pauline was governess to her students at Brucedale, located some 12 kilometers north-east of the town of Bathurst (see CL'ANA 0209).

8 Jacqueline Voignier-Marshall notes that John H. Suttor, great grand-nephew of Willie Suttor, Jr. and then-owner of Brucedale when Voignier-Marshall visited the estate in 1982, recalled that Brucedale once had a piano ("Pauline Clairmont in New South Wales" p. 30).

9 While the identity of Mr. Blair is not conclusively proven, it seems likely he is the same Mr. Blair who, according to *The Sydney Morning Herald* of 9 July 1853, attended the Mayor of Sydney's fancy dress ball (National Library of Australia, http://nla.gov.au/nla.news-page1507710, p. 5). The newspaper article recorded that while most of the men were dressed in "warlike" costumes, the "presence of Peace" prevailed. It appears that there was also a rather large police contingent at the ball to monitor the attendees. The reporter contrasted the ball with disorderly conduct often seen on the streets of Sydney, noting, "good humour seemed to preside". Mr. Blair did not wear fancy dress, unlike many of the other attendees whose costumes the reporter identified.

10 Pauline Clairmont evidently enjoyed the poetry of Alfred, Lord Tennyson. The Pforzheimer Collection has in its archive a hand-written copy of Tennyson's "The Charge of the Light Brigade," possibly in Pauline's handwriting (CL'ANA 0432, Unpublished manuscript, Pforzheimer Collection).

11 An allusion most likely to Tennyson's "The Lord of Burleigh" with its line "Love will make our cottage pleasant".

12 Pauline's spelling for "passe-temps," French for "hobby, diversion or pastime".

13 Sir Charles Augustus FitzRoy (1796–1858) was the Governor of New South Wales from 1846 until 1855. In 1851, he became the governor-general of the Australian colonies. He had two sons, Captain Augustus Charles Lennox and George FitzRoy. George served as his father's private secretary.

14 See note 9.

15 A four-horse coach.

16 Pauline repeated the word "are".

17 Gold was found in Australia in great abundance in the 1850s, changing thereby the nature of the colonial enterprise. Many people rushed to the diggings hoping to make their fortunes. Charlotte Suttor recorded the discovery of gold in the Bathurst area in 1851, and she detailed the great sense of excitement over the discovery. "Everyone seems mad to go and dig," she wrote on 14 May 1851. Her excitement over the discovery seemed to wane somewhat when she expressed concern over the consequences of the gold rush: "I hope it will not lead to misery but I am much afraid it will" (*Dear William*, p. 129). In his personal narrative, George Preshaw explained the nature of

the gold digger, recording that the "true digger . . . is a brave, high-spirited working man, ready with his purse as a friend, or with his fist as a foe . . . I know no more hospitable individual, in the full sense of the word, than this honest, jolly, free-hearted spendthrift" (*Banking Under Difficulties* [New York: Arno Press, 1974], p. 59).

18 Jacqueline Voignier-Marshall documented her own impressions of Brucedale when she visited in March 1982: "I shall never forget arriving on that cool sunny morning in autumn. The gates, so typically Australian, were there in front of us with the name BRUCEDALE. Very excited, we opened them and drove on. The 'dust-road' was long and winding and cattle could be seen grazing in the surrounding landscape. Further on to the right we ascended a hill dotted with beautiful trees which altogether presented a breathtaking spectacle, indeed. A delightful old house appeared, with a spacious veranda around it and a galvinised iron roof which sloped gently down. In evidence also were the original pavement, front door, steps and windows with their wooden shutters" ("Pauline Clairmont in New South Wales," p. 27).

19 Charlotte Suttor recorded that Pauline began teaching Carry and Minna on July 25 1853 and that she found Pauline to be a "most agreeable companion" for whom she felt a "warm attachment". Charlotte Suttor further detailed the "trust" she placed in Pauline in terms of the education of Carry and Minna (*Dear William* p. 139 and Charlotte Suttor's journal, pp. 229–30). It is doubtful that Charlotte would have suspected the subsequent affair between Pauline and her eldest son, William Suttor, Jr.

20 Pauline's spelling for "two".

21 The gold rush in the area began officially with the discovery of gold in April 1851 at Ophir, 42 kilometers from Bathurst, although it was not the first such find. While some gold had been found prior to 1851, the gold rush began officially with this 1851 discovery. A May 1851 discovery of gold 45 kilometers from Bathurst at the town of Sofala fueled the frenzy. Charlotte Suttor would probably have taken Pauline to these diggings. *The Courier* of 21 June 1851 included a 4 June 1851 article from *The Bathurst Free Press* which described the discovery of seven pounds of gold at the Ophir diggings. The writer observed that, while writing his review, he saw "some twenty loaded teams and carts, and not less than a hundred people, all strangers, bound for the diggings". The same article concluded with an explanation of the number of diggers in the area: "We are credibly informed that no fewer than 1000 persons crossed the Ferry at Penrith, on their way to the diggings, on the 6th June" (National Library of Australia, http://nla.gov.au/nla.news-article2960714, p. 2). In June 1851, an Indigenous Australian worker found gold on the run of William John Kerr, brother-in-law of William H. Suttor and husband of William's sister, Elizabeth Mary Suttor. *The Bathurst Free Press and Mining Journal* of 19 July 1851 titled its discovery article, "A Hundred Weight of Gold" and boldly declared, "Bathurst is mad again. The delirium of golden fever has returned with increased intensity" (National Library of Australia, http://nla.gov.au/nla.news-page6172011, p. 2). The press reported that the gold weighed roughly 106 pounds, "all disembowelled from the earth at one time," and that the discovery "set the town and district in a whirl of excitement". *The Maitland Mercury and Hunter River General Advertiser* of 23 July 1851 compared the Californian gold rush to the Australian gold rush and, as a result of the discovery of gold near the Meroo Creek area where Kerr's run was located, the newspaper published the following: "whether the Californian gold fields exceed ours in general richness or not, no such quantity of gold as this has yet been found there in one mass. This finding of a hundred weight of gold, as it has been aptly termed, has produced considerable excitement in the colony . . . Increased immigration from neighbouring countries may be looked for as an immediate consequence, and the news will reach home just in time to swell the stream of immigration hither which the first intelligence of our gold discovery will have induced" (National Library of Australia, http://nla.gov.au/nla.news-page127012, p. 2). On 14 July 1851, Charlotte Suttor termed the Kerr find "the wonderful heap" and recorded that it was kept in the dining room cupboard until it could be placed in the bank (*Dear William*, p. 131).

The gold rush caused anxieties for many in the colony. Penelope Selby, who moved to Australia in 1840, recorded the discovery of gold in 1851 near Melbourne and expressed fears over the diggers' behaviors: "Indeed there is no telling where the discoveries will end. Meanwhile, labour has risen enormously, and it is said this crop of wheat will rot in the ground for want of men to reap. Woe to the country if such prove the case, for it will take all their gold next year to get bread" (in Frost, p. 147). Writing to England in 1876, governess Ellen Ollard observed that "people here are very different to what they are in England. Gold is their God" (Frost, p. 163).

William and Elizabeth Suttor Kerr built a house which still stands today ("Peel House") in Peel Village and which *The Bathurst Free Press* in October 1856 termed "a suitable mansion . . . erected by W. J. Kerr, Esq on a picturesque little hill overlooking the swamp" (*One Hundred Years of Peel and District*, p. 37). Elizabeth Suttor Kerr began a Church of England Sunday School (p. 154, 171) and *The Bathurst Free Press* recorded the opening of the school in November 1859 with forty children and four teachers at the Kerr's house (p. 59). Peel Church has a stained glass window dedicated to the memory of Dr. and Mrs. Kerr. Smith notes that Elizabeth Suttor Kerr donated £10 in 1857 to the Church of St. John the Evangelist building fund (p. 126).

22 Spelling for flour. Gerald Walsh records that shepherds made very little money (in the 1840s, shepherds earned £20 pounds per year – the figure increased to £30–40 per year by the 1870s) and that they were given weekly rations which consisted of ten pounds of meat, ten pounds of flour, two pounds of sugar and a quarter pound of tea (pp. 2–3).

23 In *Big White Lie: Chinese Australians in White Australia*, John Fitzgerald estimates that some 100,000 people entered Australia from China from the 1840s until 1901 and that they "moved and worked constantly between China and Australia . . . promoting international trade, bilateral diplomacy and cultural exchange between China and Australia" (p. 13). By the time the Australian Federation was established in 1901, Fitzgerald records a Chinese Australian population of 29,627 people. He also shows that Chinese Australians experienced extreme discrimination, buoyed by negative stereotyping and the "comic figure of John Chinaman that was frequently portrayed in the popular press of the day" (p. 19). He affirms that "the persistent deafness of white Australia was a necessary condition for the persistent exclusion of Chinese from Australia and from their claim to being counted as Australians" (p. 23). Pauline's remarks showed evidence of such stereotyping.

24 While the identity of Mrs. Armstrong is not conclusively known, it is probable that she owned or managed the boarding house in which Pauline resided while waiting to find employment after her arrival in Sydney. An advertisement that appeared in the supplement to *The Sydney Morning Herald* of 27 July 1853 advertising the sale of a five-ton wood boat provides some evidence as to her identity. Interested buyers were urged to apply at "Armstrong's Boarding House, next door to the Patent Slip Inn, King-street West" (National Library of Australia, http://nla.gov.au/nla.news-page1507810, p. 2S). Later, in 1867, the City of Sydney published its *Almanac and General Calendar for 1867* and listed "Mrs. A. Armstrong" as a boarding house owner who lived at 188 Princes Street (Sydney: John Sands, 1867, p. 404. Web. 4 July 2015. http://cdn.cityofsydney.nsw.gov.au/learn/history/archives/sands/1858-1869/1867-part4.pdf, p. 404.).

25 The letter is incomplete and ends here.

49 • Antonia Clairmont to Claire Clairmont

Weidling 21st Nov. 1853.

My dear Claire!

I have received both your letters; the reason I did not answer the first of the 25th august was simply this; I was much affected with it, you reproach me, you abuse my children and hurt me in many ways, I would not answer directly, but on reading it again in a fortnight or so, I saw you speak of departing for Bologne[1] not knowing any direction there I could not write, and was obliged to wait for further communication from you;[2] I too had a letter from Pauline quite as stinted and insufficient as yours, she only tells me that she has £50 ready for me, but I begged her not to send it,[3] for now as Charley is off my hands, I had much rather be satisfied with dry bread, than to accept obligations even from my own Children; her offer however made me quite happy; she is a good and generous character, and I hope to God will be happily settled some time or other – though what you say of her imprudence is but too true – of Willy I have hear nothing since the first letters from 31st May. Charley has now set off for England, and must be arrived by this time, but we have no news as yet[4] – I intend never more to mention Clari and Knox[5] in my letters to you, and I wish you would do the same; you hate and dislike them, and I think these feelings are kept up in you by persons about you whose interest it is, you should be on bad terms with your relations; otherwise it is impossible with your clear understanding and penetrating judgment, you should continue in such erroneous opinion; the faults you accuse Clary of, are not at all in her nature, and comparing Knoxe's actions with the caracter you gave him, it don't agree in the least, and thank God, it does not; I had much rather, you had been in error, than finding it true; you ask whether I had ever tried to make peace – I did so on both sides – but with little hope of success – as you will know from your own side – about my will – I have made none – for several reasons – in the first place I have so little fortune it is hardly worth while – but yet, I intended the little I have to secure to poor Sidi during her life, and name William as her guardian – his going away prevented my doing so, of Knox I did not think at all, on account of the distance; the most I am worth is ~~one~~ £1000 ~~pds.~~ if the house sells well; for such a trifleing affair, one cannot name a guardian so far off; so I ~~left~~ have only a letter in my desk directed to my children intimating my wishes with regard to Sidi; but Knox and Clari both promised me she should never want a home, and indeed wanted to have her immediately with them, if I could have spared her and made my mind easy on that account; for I am often low spirited and fearful what should become of the poor children, should I be called from them before we have joined dear Willy upon whom I look as their support in life – it is my best consolation and I cannot be thankful enough for it, that my children are all so united in love, and will help and support each other through life –

Why should you think me indifferent to your health and affairs? Oh do leave off that unkind tone I am at peace with the whole world, and wish to be so with you; the separation from dear Charley was most painful, we feel solitude doubly so since he is gone; Emmy continues with the family in town,[6] and comes now and then to see us; both she and Sidi send their best love; I am not well, far from it, pray write soon and tell me of your health and affairs; are you at Ramsgate for your health?[7] believe me yours

very sincerely A. C.

Address: No envelope

Unpublished. Text: M.S., Pf. Coll., CL'ANA 0374

---

1 A city in Italy (Bologna), about 111 kilomteres north-east of Florence.

2 Only one of the two letters Antonia mentioned has survived. On 6 September 1853, Claire wrote to her sister-in-law, bitterly chastising her for Clara's behaviour (see *CC* II: 543–7). She accused Antonia of "partiality" (p. 543) to Clara and attacked Clara for her attachment to Knox. In Claire's opinion, Clara practiced "insolence . . . impertinence and contempt" towards Claire (pp. 543–4). Moreover, Claire told Antonia that Clara's keeping Knox beside her "all day long" after a mere seven day's courtship displayed a lack of "deference for the common decencies of life" (p. 544). The letter also vented Claire's fury at the Shelleys for their reaction to Clara's marriage. Claire had particular anger for Lady Jane Shelley, and she recalled Clara saying that Lady Shelley had spoken negatively of her, although Clara later denied it. Claire also blamed Clara's behavior towards herself on the Shelleys' influence; she charged that Clara possessed "evilmindedness" and harbored a "stubborn determination to insult and to crush" her (p. 545). She had asked Pauline for information about Mary Shelley's health, and Clara's refusal to pass information along to Pauline likewise upset Claire. Claire believed that Clara found joy in hurting her and that the pain had been physical and mental. She blamed Clara for her own physical illness and depression. She also expressed concern that her conflict with Clara had divided her from Wilhelm (*CC* II: 543–7). See also CL'ANA 0191.

3 On 16 March 1852, Claire told Pauline that Knox should assist Antonia with £50 as part of his duty towards Clara's family. Antonia had considered borrowing money by using her Weidling property as collateral, but she decided against it (*CC* II: 540).

4 See CL'ANA 0244 and CL'ANA 0185. Charley arrived in England in 1854 where he was to study agriculture.

5 Claire was equally negative about Knox in her letter of 6 September 1853. She reminded Antonia that Knox had written a letter "full of vituperation of me" (*CC* II: 544) to Charles Clairmont and that Knox was party to a series of "wanton unfeeling insults" towards her (p. 546). Although Charles told Claire on 29 August 1849 that Knox had spoken in a negative way about her (p. 520), he appeared to retract his words in his letter of 12 November 1849. In that letter, he merely said that that Knox was "irritated" by Claire's attitude towards his marriage but that Charles did not detect anything "abusive" about Claire in Knox's letter (p. 527).

6 See CL'ANA 0377.

7 A town in east Kent, Ramsgate was one of the famous seaside resorts of the nineteenth century. Christopher Chalkin writes about the growing number of seaside resorts between 1750 and 1850 and explains that Brighton was "the largest resort in 1802, along with Margate and Ramsgate" (*The Rise of the English Town, 1650–1850* [Cambridge: Cambridge University Press, 2001], p. 14). Alan Armstrong records that "Visitors from London frequented the healthy resorts of Margate, Whitstable and Ramsgate and 'washing off the smoke at Margate' was said to be a fashionable diversion" (*The Economy of Kent, 1640–1914* [Suffolk: Boydell Press, 1995], p. 28).

50 • Pauline Clairmont to Antonia Clairmont

Bathurst Nov. 22.[1] [1853]

My dear mother

It seems a very long time since I heard of you last direct except the little note which you inclosed for me in one of Clary's letters – but I hope that the year which has nearly past since we left England has proved to you a little less burdened with care & anxiety than the preceding ones.[2] If I wanted to tell you all – our gettings on in this country I should scarcely know where to begin – From Willy I think you have heard lately though the poor fellow is very desponding – the fact is that it is much harder work for him to get on than we all expected, so much so that he seriously thinks of going back to Europe – but I think he has not given this country a fair trial & show a little more perseverance & endurance; the life he leads seems something quite barbarous[3] & in every letter he says that he would not for the world condemn you & his sisters to live in such a wretched place. But I dare say you have heard all the details from him, & I conclude that he will not wish Charley to come out, unless things were much altered. He is 600 miles from where I am a journey of 3 weeks there being no other mode of travelling than horseback – & whether I shall if he remains in the colony see him within the next 3 or 4 years is very doubtful.[4]

But it will be more satisfactory to hear that I am getting on very well comparatively speaking I mean that I am making more money than any person in my circumstances though it is a miserable pittance compared to what any fool of a man can earn. But I will not grumble as I have been really uncommonly fortunate, am enjoying all the comforts of a well furnished house live with most kind generous & agreeable people & receive a salary of £140. which will continue at least I hope for some years till Willy is able to offer you something better. Picture to yourself a charming part of the country something like the valley of Weidling only that the trees & the grass are brown instead of green. about an hours drive from the town of Bathurst[5] – & here we live quite secluded in the country quietly from one day to the other without excitement, or other pleasures than books & a good Piano[6] – You would scarcely know me as I sit nearly all day in my schoolroom with my cap on surrounded by the children – quiet silent as much as possible & pleased to go to bed early. It is not fashion in the country for Ladies to leave their house for a walk & for day together. I do not stir of ~~of~~ the little enclosure in front of our house except to go to church.[7] But nevermind – I am more submissive than I used to be & take all things as they come. My principal object is to make money not that I think of saving that part of your admonition I am afraid will enter my constitution but that I may at least have the satisfaction of knowing you my dear mother & my poor brother & Sister out of positive want – I had a letter from Claire a short while ago saying that her affairs were really in such a state that she could not possibly manage to send you any remittance nor even do any thing for Charley – Upon which I answered that I was afraid that either she or her advisers had managed her fortune very badly putting it all very civilly of course & that if it was any assistance to her, I would allow her twenty £ p. an. so as to save from utter ruin, & I would really not mind doing it as she has been kind to us in former days – at the end I could not help adding that I had got a little more knowing in the world, & might not say much on a subject but that I was not so easily duped as when she first knew me. Her hypocrisy is more than I can bear. But speaking of money dear Mamma I here inclose a Bill of Exchange for £50[8] & will as ~~if~~ I have before said send it every year so long as remain here which will I think be 3 years. If you wish it I will make it 80 next year but this year I want to send Ch.[9] £30 & besides Willy may want a little cash in case he should want to go home. For the present I can see no prospect of your coming out & even for Ch. I do not know what to advise. Living in town is so much above anything that all our forces put together could afford & as for the country life if you cannot build a place of your own – you must live in tents, – both alternatives out of the question. In case this bill should be lost I shall in another fortnight send another letter with a duplicate of it – & trust it will arrive safe in your hands in the shortest time possible which may perhaps be in the end of Feb or beginning of March. Pray give my love to my Darling Ch. & dear little Sidi & Emy I cannot fancy them grown up but still see them as I left them. Tell Sidi that I have still the dear little colar she worked for me – Believe me dearest mother with best hopes for your health & welfare your dutiful & affectionate

daughter
Pauline.

Address: No envelope.

Unpublished. Text: M.S. Pf. Coll., CL'ANA 0232

---

1 Pauline and Wilhelm left England on 17 January 1853. This letter dates to the end of 1853.

2 In *No Place for a Nervous Lady*, Lucy Frost notes the length of time it took for the mail to reach the Australian bush. Frost suggests that letters could take up to a year from Europe (p. 6).

3 See CL'ANA 0065.

4 Wilhelm was working on the Kieta run on the Lower Murrumbidgee. See CL'ANA 0065 and CL'ANA 0210.

5 Brucedale is 12 kilometers (7.5 miles) north of Bathurst. Pauline was correct in stating that the drive in a carriage took about an hour. The Long Riders Guild Academic Foundation estimates that horses can travel some eight to ten miles per house at a trot (Craft, Susan. "An Equestrian Writer's Guide". The Long Riders Guild Academic Foundation. 2014. Web. 29 October 2014. www.lrgaf.org).

6 See CL'ANA 0210.

7 The foundation for the Church of St. John The Evangelist in Peel was laid in 1860 and the church was consecrated by 1867. Pauline contributed £1 to the Church Building Fund (*100 Years of Peel and District*, p. 126) and £3 towards a fund to construct a National School House at Peel (p. 27). *The Bathurst Free Press and Mining Journal* of 17 February 1855 recorded her school contribution, together with a £25 contribution each from George Suttor and W. H. Suttor (National Library of Australia, http://nla.gov.au/nla.news-page6173100, p. 3). Theo Barker notes that, prior to 1880, education was undertaken by church schools, as no system for compulsory education existed at

that time in the colony. In 1848, the government instituted a National Education system providing subsidies for school buildings and teachers' salaries. Pauline's contribution went to fund the government-supported school building at Peel (*A History of Bathurst*, pp. 160–66). At the time of publication of this edition, the school building at Peel is still used as a meeting place for public functions (Carol Churches, Bathurst Family History Group and Bathurst Historical Society, personal communication: 2 October 2014, 7 December 2014, and 23 April 2016).

8 See CL'ANA 0374.

9 Charley.

51 • Antonia Clairmont to Claire Clairmont

[4 January 1854]

My dear Claire.

If I remember right I said in my last, Charley set off yesterday for England,[1] for I think it was directly after his departure I wrote; if I did not say more, it was from delicacy to you; you did not care so much about him when he was starving in Moravia[2] upon £15 pr. annum; your promise of 6 pds four times given, for dec: then Jan: then March – then for April where you had a dividend coming in, being at last revoked, would create some doubts in me whether you would like to see him; I have now however sent him your direction and the Knoxes is, East Sheen Surrey[3] – Perhaps Charley has been to see you already;[4] he is for the moment to complete his farming education in England I have had a letter from Willy but 6 months old; he had arrived at the sheep run where he is to spend the first year,[5] the hardships of the journey, and the state of his present way of living is such that I tremble to think of all that he is exposed to; the hut he lives in is without flooring and ceiling, only a roof of rushes, nor are there any windows, the light comes in ~~from~~ by the chinks in the boards that constitute the walls, of all the millions of objects of enjoyment in a civilized life to the poorest member of society, he has none – and if he should fall ill! Oh God Allmighty send him home safe, I shall not be happy nor quiet till I see him again. his letter is dated 13th of July and I had it 30th of December, so it has been nearly 6 months on the road; I have not yet answered him, because I should first like to go to town and make some inquiries about Hungary ere I write; and we have such a severe winter, I cannot brave the cold, having a bad cough; since the 6th of December we have had continual frost of 15 degrees Reaum:[6] our windows are frozen, the snow lies several feet deep, covering the hills around us, it is a beautiful sight from our window, but we have an hour's walk to the place where the coaches start from for town, and that is too much for me, nor can I afford a coach; I must therefore wait till the wheather gets milder; since residing in Wiedling[7] I am forgetting my English. I have not the command of the language to enter into answering some points of your letter, if German would you understand it? you are wrong in congratulating me and in bewailing – we have all our trials, and I hope with the help of God we shall bear ours, and conquer as far as possible for poor mortals. –

Emmy continues still with Mrs Löhner;[8] Sidi is pretty well in health, at present she acts as sick nurse to a poor little boy of 3 years old who has had a bad fall whose mother a neighbour of ours, is almost out of her senses, with the fear of losing him though she has 8 children besides; the little fellow will suffer only Sidi or his mother; Sidi is the best nurse I know, it is a pleasure to be ill to be nursed by her. I hope your eyes are quite well, and you are quite pleased with Ramsgate;[9] let me know when you have seen Charley and believe me ever yours

sincerely A. C.

Weidling $^{4}/_{1}$ 1854
you always the date.

Address: Miss Clairmont,/11 Acklow Square North/East Cliff/
Ramsgate/Kent, England.
Front postmark: KLOSTERNEUBURG/ 2 EXP. 6 JAN.; DOVER/[illeg.]/1854/A
Rear postmark: WIEN $^{6}/_{1}$ /[illeg.]

Unpublished. Text: M.S., Pf. Coll., CL'ANA 0377

---

1 Charley left Austria for England in 1854 in order to further his education in Scotland. Knox provided financial support. However, by the winter of 1855, Charley returned to Austria, sick with lung disease. He would die on 7 May 1856, a few months after his sisters, Sidi and Emily, who also died that same year. On 12 May 1856, Claire implored Antonia not to tell Pauline and Wilhelm of their brother's death until Antonia was certain that the siblings had come to terms with the earlier losses of Sidi and Emily. Saying that she disliked "deception," Claire nonetheless felt that Pauline and Wilhelm were "young and very sensitive" and in need of such protection (*CC* II: 549).

2 See CL'ANA 0373.

3 Clara and Alexander Knox lived at East Sheen, Mortlake parish, in Surrey County.

4 See CL'ANA 0244 and CL'ANA 0185.

5 Wilhelm began working at Kieta (see CL'ANA 0210 and CL'ANA 0065).

6 Réaumur scale. René-Antoine de Réaumur devised the scale, a commonly used temperature scale: "its zero set at the freezing point of water and its 80 degree mark at the boiling point of water at normal atmospheric pressure" (The Editors of the Encyclopaedia Britannica. "Réaumur Temperature Scale". *Encyclopaedia Britannica Online*. Encyclopaedia Britannica Inc., n.d. 24 October 2015. http://www.britannica.com/topic/Reaumur-temperature-scale). Other forms of measurement replaced the scale in the late nineteenth century.

7 Antonia misspelled Weidling.

8 Emily was a governess. See CL'ANA 0374.

9 Claire moved to the seaside town of Ramsgate, Kent, in 1852. Located some 125 kilometers southeast of London, the town includes as part of its geographic setting two chalk cliffs, East and West Cliff. Claire's home was located at 11 Arklow Square, East Cliff, but Antonia misspelled the address. However, by 1855, Claire had moved back to London.

52 • Pauline Clairmont to Claire Clairmont

Brucedale Bathurst New South Wales.[1]
March 22d 1854 & 27th

My dearest Aunt

Your kind letter from Dec 14 of last year reached me last night[2] – & I am very sorry to hear that you had not yet received the last letter which I wrote a long time ago immediately after your last but one arrived – as it must appear to you like very unfeeling neglect which I am very far from feeling towards you, as you have always been kind to me – but you have a stronger and better claim than that to my affection – you are my father's sister, & I should find it impossible to treat any one with neglect that he had loved. But by this time you must have received that letter I just mentioned & seen what I said about poor Willy – The poor fellow is in such low spirits that he scarcely ever writes even to me, as for European correspondents he has given them quite up I believe having no table nor paper to write on, no time to write, all his minutes being taken up in washing & mending his clothes cooking his dinner, seeing that he has the bread baking, & meat killing to do all by himself – I would willingly go & keep hut[3] for him if I could afford to give my situation. He means to stay at the that[4] wretched place till his engagement is over which will be in July next, & then come across the country to Bathurst – This is my plan – for he was going to leave Austr. without having according to my ideas given the place a fair trial. So I insisted on his coming here first & consult the friends I have made here, the only ones we have in this part of the world - & see if he could find some better employment before taking such an important step as returning to Europe. Pray dear Aunt excuse his not having written to you I feel sure that it is not neglect but low spirits & the want of writing material. We heard from the Knoxes a few ~~months~~ weeks ago since their return from Germany – they seem much delighted with their trip the same as my mother though I have not heard from her direct – I know very little about Charles' plans – he is in England but where I do not know at some school I expect – if Willy finally settles here he will have his brother with him – but as for Mama's coming I consider it an utter impossibility for an elderly lady to begin such a hard new life, & for a young girl to banish herself willingly in the scrub & become a squatter's[5] or scrubber's[6] wife & servant – Willy wrote to me a short time ago – Take care my dear sister you don't marry a squatter for it would be neither more or less than hiring yourself out for life time as maid of all work. I told him there was no fear of that, as I did not intend marrying at all – let not that vex you dear Aunt, – but men are worse tyrants here than in Europe – Regular turks (except the plurality of wi~~f~~ves) & if I hoped for more liberty I got out of the pan into the fire – for here I am literally imprisoned night & day in a house & garden a hundred yards square & as for going to any place beyond a mile it is such an unheard of piece of independance in the eyes of these narrowminded colonists, that the first & only time I attempted a little stroll by myself[7] – terror seized all the inmates of the house when they became aware of my absence horses were saddled, bellmen were sent out the native cooy[8] was sounded & at last they discovered me sitting under a tree at about 5 minutes walk from the house. Then there were questions asked, signs of terror & surprise given, what could have induced me to wander away in the bush, had I lost my way (I had only been absent half an hour) did I hear the bellman & the cooy why did I not answer the latter? Till I at last said – be quiet with all your nonsense, I only took a little walk to refresh my wearied spirit in the cool bath of solitude & commune with myself on the different duties I had undertaken – all of which was gibberish to them I dare say – for though all the people here are very kind & generous, they have no sort of refinement no early education no training of any kind no command over their thoughts & feelings no regards for each other, which they most likely do not feel the want of but which grates rather sharply on the strings of my soul, which I own are sometimes morbidly overstrung the same as yours – & then we clutch hold of some imaginary grief, hug it, weep over it, till we can weep no more, & then (I at least) get up & say what a fool I was! as if any thing in this life was worth crying for. – I'll make the best of it, & it is fortunate I have so many thoughts in my own head there's a precipice in my mind to the bottom of which I have never got – but really the solitude I live in would be appalling to many – not solitude – that blessing I never enjoy – but seclusion is the right word – my only pleasures are books & my piano & it is a good job I don't want to marry for I have not seen one man worth having. – it would be cruel to put a young girl who has seen nothing of life yet – like Emillie into such a place as this, profitable though it may be. I have told mama that she had much better remain quietly at Weidling where she is now & live comfortably on what K.[9] & I can contribute to her small income than come & knock about in this go-ahead boisterous unsettled country As to the climate we were quite mislead when we fancied it warm. It is a fine climate but warm only at noon clear blue sky, sun shine, & dusty & dry; in midsummer the mornings are very fresh & now in autumn very cold – the winter is as bitter as any continental winter can be, much severer than in England. I wish I could go to Java next winter, if Mrs S.[10] as she intends goes to England next year, I will go to Batavia.[11]

You wish to know whether I think that any of your friends would make mischief? Miss Hammond[12] would not I believe – I have for her the greatest respect, as well for her natural kindness, as for her worldly prudence. The Hunts[13] could not, you know them too well – Mrs Lynch[14] might I dare say be induced, if it answered her purpose – about the Pringles I don't know – I saw very little of them (in accordance with your wishes) You may remember perhaps that when I was in England I intruded very little upon your friends from a feeling of delicacy that you should not even seem to have a shadow of obligation for any thing they might do for me – I wished to owe everything to my own exertions – therefore I can not take upon myself to say what they would or would not do –

I sincerely hope my dear Aunt that your Operabox & all your other pecuniary concerns are going on swimmingly – could you not wind up all this tangled heap of botheration into an easy going reel of a settled annuity? Would not that be more comfortable?

I have made the acquaintance of M^rs^. R. Ramsbottom's family here they are a queer set – I wish you would tell me the name of the Lady to whom Mrs Smith[15] gave me a letter, but perhaps you have reasons of your own for wishing me not to know her – However that may be I trust you are in good health and satisfied with this long gossiping letter from your aff

Paula.

Address: No envelope.

Unpublished. Text: M.S., Pf. Coll., CL'ANA 0209

---

1 In the first volume of his book, *A History of Bathurst*, Barker provides an account of the history and settlement of Bathurst from the arrival of the colonists in New South Wales in the early eighteenth century until the decade of gold discovery in 1851–1862. Bathurst is located in New South Wales, some 160 kilometers west-northwest of Sydney. Barker explains that a 1784 Act of Parliament in Britain paved the way for Australia to become a penal colony and the first fleet of convicts arrived in Australia in 1788. As additional colonists arrived in the colony over a thirty year period, they began to migrate deeper into New South Wales. Many went in search of new grazing lands and spaces on which to farm cattle and sheep. Pastoralists, soldiers, free immigrants to the country and Australian-born descendants of the first waves of colonists began to dominate. In the early years of the nineteenth century, waves of colonists explored the region around Bathurst and created a road to traverse the Bathurst plains whose land had been deemed arable. William Cox, Lieutenant and Paymaster of N.S.W. Corps, recorded in his journal that the road "across the Blue Mountains" was first commenced in 1814 and that 100 miles had been completed by 1815 (*Fourteen Journeys Over the Blue Mountains*, pp. 34–62). The original inhabitants of the area, the Wiradjuris, came into contact with these colonists when the town of Bathurst was officially founded in 1815. Governor Lachlan Macquarie noted in his diary that the area of the Bathurst plains "is truly grand, beautiful and interesting forming one of the finest landscapes I ever saw in any country" (*A History of Bathurst*, p. 25) and J.T. Campbell, secretary to Governor Macquarie, recorded that, within ten miles of Bathurst there were at least "fifty thousand acres of land clear of timber," of which "fully one half of that may be considered excellent soil, well calculated for cultivation" (*Fourteen Journeys Over the Blue Mountains*, p. 71). On 7 May 1815, the future town of Bathurst was proclaimed and named for Lord Bathurst, Principal Secretary of State for the Colonies (p. 25). The Suttors began farming at Brucedale in 1822 when George Suttor (1774–1859) and his wife, Sarah Dobinson, obtained a grant from Governor Sir Thomas Brisbane to farm at Bathurst. Their descendants still own 2,800 acres of the original property about 12 kilometers north of Bathurst at the time of the writing of this text (Suttor, David and Suzie. "Brucedale Cottage". Web. 7 July 2015. http://www.brucedale.com.au/index.php). The Australian Heritage Database lists the property on its Register of the National Estate and describes it as being located 1.5 kilometers west of Peel. According to the register, Brucedale dates from 1837 and "the earlier timber and pise house built when the grant was first occupied by the Suttors still stands on the property" ("Brucedale Homestead". Australian Government, Department of the Environment. Web. 29 October 2014. http://www.environment.gov.au/cgi-bin/ahdb/search.pl?mode=place_detail;place_id=914).

2 This letter has not survived.

3 Pauline either referred to the shepherd's watch box, a small, moveable hut which served to protect the shepherd from the cold winters of New England, or – more likely – to the very basic hut in which a shepherd would have resided. R.B. Walker provides a photograph of a shepherd's watch box in *Old New England* (p. 86). In *Pioneering Days*, Gerald Walsh describes the shepherd's living conditions as "primitive. Accommodation was invariably a small hut of slabs, roofed with bark with an earthen floor and large fireplace. The hut was neither wind nor

rainproof. The only concession made for convenience was that it was usually located near a waterhole or creek" (p. 2).

4 Correctly transcribed from the letter.

5 Michael Pearson and Jane Lennon explain that Australia's history is closely tied to its legacy of pastoralism which, they argue, led to the territorial expansion of the continent, the creation of a unique Australian "identity", and the development of an economic system that continues to "shape" Australia today. Pastoralism, they opine, "is a pervasive creative force that has permeated almost everything that has happened in Australia since 1788 . . . Pastoralism is the foundation of some of the great legends of Australian life" (*Pastoral Australia*, pp. 1, 177). Pastoralists were land-holders who farmed and grazed sheep and cattle on large tracts of land, typically acquired by agreements with the Crown. The term "squatter" originally referred to men who farmed on unoccupied land, usually without official Crown permission. Walsh explains how Australian squatters pushed beyond the legal, recognized boundaries of the original Nineteen Counties to find new grazing pastures for their flocks. These squatters occupied land illegally, posing great challenges in the early years of settlement. By the 1830s, however, the Crown government implemented regulations and squatters were allowed to settle on Crown land with appropriate leases provided (see Walsh, *Pioneering Days* and CL'ANA 0066). By the 1860s, the pejorative connotations of the term "squatter" no longer endured. Walsh notes that "while in the 1830s and 1840s the squatter's life might well have been 'a sordid, filthy, existence' . . . from the 1860s, when an ever increasing number of properties were fenced and subdivided and often possessed a substantial homestead, the pastoralist had more time to devote himself to other interests including the arts, science and technology" (p. 229). George Farwell terms the squatter a "special kind of man . . . He was dedicated, inventive and hard-working, even if this dedication corresponded with self-interest and the hard work produced fortunes no others could amass . . . He was often ruthless, arrogant, disdainful of lesser orders; but he could also be liberal in his attitudes, extravagantly generous and devoted to the land that bred him" (*Squatter's Castle*, p. 9). Pauline's negative depiction of the squatter probably stemmed from pervasive stereotypes of the earlier squatting classes – men (sometimes former felons) who secured land for themselves without government consent.

6 A pejorative term for an inhabitant of the bush.

7 Charlotte Suttor wrote in her journal on 15 October 1853 that she and Pauline "took a very pleasant walk the murmur of the bees amongst the blossoms was really like Spring" (*Dear William*, p. 139 and Charlotte Suttor Diaries, p. 232).

8 *Collins English Dictionary* defines the word "cooee" as "a call used to attract attention, esp (originally) a long loud high-pitched call on two notes used in the Australian bush" ("cooee". *Collins English Dictionary – Complete & Unabridged 10th Edition*. HarperCollins Publishers. Web. 26 Jun. 2015. Dictionary.com http://dictionary.reference.com/browse/cooee). The *Oxford English Dictionary* cites the 1827 use of the word by P. Cunningham in *Two Years New South Wales* (ed. 2) II.i.23: "The calling to each other at a distance . . . [has] become of general use throughout the colony; and a new comer, in desiring an individual to call another back, soon learns to say '*Coo-ee* to him,' instead of '*Hollo* to him.' ("cooee | cooey, n. (and int.)". *OED Online*. Oxford University Press. September 2014. Web. 31 October 2014).

9 Knox.

10 Mrs. Suttor.

11 Batavia (today's Jakarta, the capital of Indonesia) was under Dutch occupation during the nineteenth century. Jean Gelman Taylor explains that qualified governesses were scarce in Batavia and that colonial newspapers were the source of advertisements for governesses. These governesses, Taylor records, did not need to have teaching credentials, as "conversational powers and accomplishments" were more highly valued (*The Social World of Batavia: European and Eurasian in Dutch Asia*, p. 139). Given the possibility that Charlotte Suttor would return to England, Pauline seemed to have considered Batavia as her next possible place of employment.

12 See CL'ANA 0041.

13 James Henry "Leigh" Hunt (1784–1859) and his wife, Marianne (1788–1857) were friends of both Mary Shelley and Claire. Hunt was an essayist, a critic, and editor of the *Examiner*. The Hunts had eight known children. Lucy Morrison and Staci Stone suggest that Mary Shelley and Marianne Hunt sympathized with one another because they had suffered an unwanted sister in their marriages (Claire cohabited with Percy and Mary Shelley while Marianne's sister "seemed to be in love with Leigh" (*A Mary Shelley Encyclopedia*, pp. 208–9). After Percy Shelley's death, the Hunts were a tremendous source of comfort to Mary Shelley. Leigh and Marianne's son, Henry, married Dina Williams, daughter of Jane and Edward Williams.

14 Unidentified.

15 Possibly Eliza Smith, daughter of the poet Horace Smith (1779–1849) who was a friend of Leigh Hunt and Percy Shelley. In 1817, Shelley and Smith wrote competing sonnets after visiting the British Museum. Smith wrote "On a Stupendous Leg of Granite" and Shelley "Ozymandius". In 2014, Nora Crook discovered thirteen unpublished letters written between 1831 and 1849 from Mary Shelley to Horace Smith and Eliza Smith.

53 • Antonia Clairmont to Claire Clairmont

[30 May 1854]

Dear Claire.

Though I am very unwell, as you will see by my handwriting, yet I will answer your letter directly, and shall endeavour to make my meaning as clear as my Knowledge of your language enables me to do; to enter at once, upon your two points; to supply the proofs of the truth of what I accused you of, I should have to copy out all your letters ~~of~~ from the time since Clara's marriage; you must recollect their contents;[1] Clari was called – cringing, flattering, sordid, coquettish bald reckless et et[2] – of Knox it runs – a young man that will plunge into every vice in order to get money – or – that vilest sort, a man kept[3] – or, Sir Percy said – it is Knox, made so many debts my mother must sell – in order to pay them[4] – with regard to his marriage you said, he would not have married her, but for the scenes I made – and later – he will bring his vicious friends around her, and divorce her when he is tired of her et what you said of his position in the Shelly family you will recollect, and many more things, I cannot get into so small a compass as this paper, but if you still think me to have been unjust, and require further proof, I might send your letters to Knox and leave it to him to satisfy your demand. he does not know till now, the character you gave him, for my desire of keeping the peace in the family made me withold all these painful things; but it is perhaps right he should know; how he has been represented; and how well his own actions during these five years have cleared away every shadow of doubt against him;[5] as to my meaning of traducing and calumniating – it is quite plain; calumniation is falsehood, untruth, fiction, therefore invented, and of course spread, else why invented? when you speak of Paul: and Clara's sordidness, a fault which all my my[6] children are free from, I can only take it as a wrong done to them, and not as a blame they ~~may have~~ deserved; every human action ought to be judged by its motive; I do not know yours in being so unkind to me and my children, nor can I guess to reason – have I in any way offended or hurt you? Let us conclude this tedious disagreeable affair; do not write to me any thing about your friends; rich people have friends. and a spinster lady's are sometimes more pliable than others, but that is your affair; I only wish for peace; the troubles and sufferings which providence sent me, I shall bear with christian fortitude, but those inflicted by the ill will of our fellow creatures are more difficult to bear.[7]

Sidi sends her best love,
and believe me yours sincerely

A.C.

Weidling 30th May
1854.

Address: Miss Clairmont/ 6 Waverley Place, St John's Wood/ London,/ England
Front postmark: KLOSTERNEUBURG/ 1EXP. 31 MAI.
Rear postmark: Wien $^{31}/_{5}$/ 11F.; BA/ 5 JU 5/ 1854

Unpublished. Text: M.S., Pf. Coll., CL'ANA 0378

---

1 Claire's vitriolic letter to Antonia of 6 September 1853 appears to have been one of the letters that engendered this response. See CL'ANA 0374.

2 Claire went so far as to call Clara a "fiend" in her letter of 6 September 1853.

3 Claire had previously alleged that Mary Shelley and Knox had been lovers. Knox had assisted Mary Shelley with legal matters pertaining to her problems with Ferdinando Gatteschi, who, in 1845, was blackmailing her by threatening to publish letters she had written to him. Emily Sunstein explains that Gatteschi had letters from Mary Shelley that proposed marriage and that Mary Shelley sought Knox's assistance to protect her own reputation and by extension her son's (pp 370–2). Knox arranged for the letters to be retrieved, and Percy Florence never knew of the situation. Claire, however, was aware of the situation and kept all of Mary Shelley's letters to her about the incident, in spite of Mary Shelley's request that Claire burn the letters about the affair (*LMWS* III: 212). On 16–24 September 1845, Mary Shelley wrote to Knox, calling him "my dear Friend," and noting his kindness: "How kind – how much more than kind you are". She also called on "Heaven" to "bless" him (pp. 206–7). On 13–14 October 1845, she told Claire that Knox was a "darling . . . how clever – how more than clever he is" (p. 233). By December, she gave Knox money "to settle his affairs," remarking to Claire, "I have given Knox a cheque for $100 – even that I have not – but the bankers will advance it – my poor poor Percy w^{d} he had no Mother to rob him in this wicked manner" (p. 267). Claire later misconstrued these communications to suggest that Knox and Mary Shelley were lovers, hence Antonia's use of the word "kept" in this letter.

4 Percy Florence was unaware of the Gatteschi affair that had caused Knox's financial debts and incorrectly attributed Knox's debts to profligacy.

5 Knox's generosity towards Clara's family, his support of Wilhelm's and Charley's education, and his kindness to Sidi led Antonia to view him more favorably than she had originally.

6 The word appears twice in the manuscript.

7 Even after Clara's death in 1855, Claire continued to wage war against the Knoxes. On 23 August 1856, she told Antonia that she had never intended to sever connections with "Knox and his Wife," but that she did so because "the more forbearance I showed the ruder they became" (*CC* II: 582). She accused Clara of calling her a "liar" and Knox of avoiding her (p. 582). See CL'ANA 0191.

54 • Charles Gaulis Clairmont (Charley) to Claire Clairmont

[22 June 1854]

Dear Aunt;

I am very sorry not to be able to accept your kind invitation as soon as Monday next, but I do not think I am strong enough for so long an excursion, as I have not yet been further than the garden since my arrival from Scotland.[1] If Monday week would suit you as well, I shall by that time be able to come, if I go on improving in strength, but my illness has been a very severe one.

Will you be kind enough to let me know whether I may come on the day I mentioned, or which day afterwards would be most convenient to you.

Pray believe me dear aunt yours most sincerely

C. Clairmont.

East Sheen. June 22. 1854.[2]

Address: Miss Clairmont/ 6. Waverley place/ St. Johnswood./ London
Front postmark: [illeg.]/JU 22;73
Rear postmark: East Sheen

Unpublished. Text: M.S., Pf. Coll., CL'ANA 0244

---

1 In January 1854, Charley went to Scotland to study agricultural practices. Knox provided the financial support for the endeavor. See Antonia's letter to Claire of 4 January 1854 (CL'ANA 0377) in which she noted that Claire had "revoked" her promise to give Charley financial assistance while he was at school in Moravia. By winter of 1855, Charley would return to Vienna where he would die in 1856 from tuberculosis. Antonia's letters chronicled her attempts to improve her son's health while Claire's letters were full of rancor, as she blamed Knox for Charley's illness (*CC* II: 578).

2 Antonia told Claire that Charley was living with the Knoxes in East Sheen, Surrey (CL'ANA 0377). Clara lived at East Sheen, Mortlake Parish, in the county of Surrey.

55 • Charles Gaulis Clairmont (Charley) to Claire Clairmont

[3 July 1854]

My dear Aunt[1]

I am glad to say that I am sufficiently recovered, to undertake a journey to town, and shall therefore be with you Monday next at 2.o'clock, if the weather permits. We have had no news from Willy lately. Hoping to find you in perfect good health I remain

Your affectionate nephew
Charley

Address: Miss Clairmont/ 6. Waverley St / St. Johnswood/ London
Front postmark: [illeg.] JU 3/ 54

Unpublished. Text: M.S., Pf. Coll., CL'ANA 0185

---

1 This letter dates to 1854.

56 • Wilhelm Gaulis Clairmont to Claire Clairmont

[18 August 1854]

My dear aunt,

The last letter I got from you was through Pauline and dated the 17th March from Ramsgate.[1] I am sorry to hear such bad accounts both of your health and your finances but every thing seems misery and every thing seems to go wrong in this world. As for myself I can report you little news; in fact I only write to let you know that I am still alive and still remembering you with a greatful heart. With the exception of a trifling complaint, I think it is a sort of inflamation of the eyes[2] to which the glaring sun and the extreme drought of the atmosphere makes almost all new comers subject I am all right and well – but I can not say I like Australia much and the resolution ~~of~~ to return~~ing~~ [~~illeg.~~] to Europe grows stronger in me every day. What I chiefly object to and will not under any terms consent to is being separated for good from my mother. I know it makes her unhappy and I will not do it on that account. You must not be frightened if you should suddenly some time next spring find a big tall man walk into your [~~illeg.~~] room with an uncouth sunburnt face and a beard that has not been shaved for years. I still continue at the same place to which I first came. I have now got a little more accustomed to the extreme roughness of bushlife[3] besides going about looking for a new situation would have caused me loss of time which I wanted to avoid; and perhaps I might have got from the frying pan into the fire. – I wish dear aunt I could know how you are now and whether you are enjoying yourself a little more than before I hope you do, that solitary, monotonous life in itself is enough to make you ill and low. Now Goodbye dearest aunt dont think because I write short letters I think the less of you, but long letters I can never find time to finish But now Goodbye from your affectionate nephew

W.G.C.
Kieta[4] August 18th 1854.

Address: No envelope.

Unpublished. Text: M.S., Pf. Coll., CL'ANA 0065

---

1 See CL'ANA 0377.

2 See CL'ANA 0067. Wilhelm's spelling of "inflammation". Gerald Walsh describes "sandy blight (trachoma) and rheumatism" as "occupational hazards" of farming in Australia (*Pioneering Days*, p. 4). Trachoma is a bacterial infection of the eye that can lead to blindness. Jones, Smith, and Briscoe explain that the disease is associated today with poverty and that it is highly contagious. In the early years of Australian colonization, poor living and hygiene conditions led to the spread of the disease. Jones et al. note that the increased rate of trachoma in some Indigenous Australian communities today is a result of "dry, dusty environments" (Jones, Jilpia, Smith, Leila, and Briscoe, Gordon. "*They used to call it Sandy Blight*: Aboriginal health and censorship in Australia".

Australian Aboriginal Studies. Vol 2, 2006. Aboriginal Studies Press. Web. 16 November 2014. http://lryb.aiatsis.gov.au/PDFs/aasj06.2_jones.pdf).

3 Australia presented many challenges for newly arrived immigrants in the nineteenth century. While the colony was originally envisioned as a penal colony, with the first convict ships arriving in 1788, immigrants in search of opportunities flooded its shores during this period. Two major industries heralded the growth of the Australian economy: farming and mining. The squatter in search of grazing lands and pastures, Farwell suggests, "provided the one dynamic force for an ingrown, unproductive colony of petty officials, idling soldiery and transported felons . . . These men transformed the once opprobrious term squatter – meaning those who squatted illegally on crown lands – to one of value and respect . . . it has authentic Australian overtones" (p. 10). The discovery of gold in the 1850s brought many immigrants with dreams of financial success.

Wilhelm was not affected by the gold rush and continued to pursue his vocation as an agriculturalist. While he later became a land owner himself and then a manager for the Twofold Bay Pastoral Association, his letters describe difficult early days in the colony. See note 3, CL'ANA 0073 for the account of a violent attack he suffered in the wool shed in this period.

4 Wilhelm wrote to Claire from Kieta, which was in New South Wales. Kieta was known as Tala or Kieta Nass Nass, and was originally owned by William Wentworth and his son-in-law, John Reeve. A series of advertisements from the beginning of 1853 showed Wentworth and Reeve seeking a buyer for the stations Tala, or Kieta Nass Nass, and Paika. An advertisement from *The Argus* of 31 March 1853 recorded that the stations, located on the Lower Murrumbidgee, consisted of some 90 miles and included creeks and lakes, about one million acres of pasture, and about 45,290 sheep and 4,000 cattle. The stations were located about 260 miles from Melbourne (National Library of Australia, http://nla.gov.au/nla.news-page508642, p. 8). Augustus Morris (see CL'ANA 0210) managed Tala/Kieta Nass Nass on behalf of William Wentworth until 1853 when he purchased it together with T. S. Mort, Thomas Holt, and T. W. Smart. Shortly after purchasing the stations from Wentworth, Morris became sole owner of the stations when he "bought out" his partners. In his Memoir *Opals and Agates*, Nehemiah Bartley described how he visited Wentworth's "great stations" of Tala, Yangar, and Paika in 1851 when drays would regularly travel the road either to Sydney or Melbourne, delivering supplies to the stations and taking wool back to the ports for transportation to wool markets. However, as a result of the discovery of gold, Paika remained unvisited and unsupported for two years as it was not profitable for suppliers to make the long trip to the wool stations. Suppliers recognized that they could make greater profits by making shorter trips to the gold diggings. Hence, Bartley observed that, by 1853, two years' supply of wool was stored at Paika, supplies were old and rancid, and conditions had deteriorated (pp. 65–6).

57 • Antonia Clairmont to Claire Clairmont

[21 December 1854]

My dear Claire.

Yesterday I had a letter from Willy, telling me that he intends leaving Kieta on the 1st of Jan. 855[1] and after visiting Paula hopes to take sail for Europe about 15th of Feb: so that about May we may hope to see and have him once more here no more to see him part; I was so affected with the happy news that I was taken with a violent fever, yet I wished to let you know, for however unkind you have been to me since sometime, yet I think you love the dear boy, and will be glad to hear of his return.[2] Sidi sends her best love, the dear child is always ailing this winter I hope you are in good health. yours most sincerely

A. Clairmont

Weidling 21/12 1854.

Address: No envelope

Unpublished. Text: M.S., Pf. Coll., CL'ANA 0376

---

1 Antonia inserted a line above 855.

2 As the letters will show, Wilhelm did not return from Australia until 1861. When he next wrote to Claire, he would be the owner of a station called Kangaroo Hills (see CL'ANA 0066). Pauline would return to Europe in 1857.

58 • Pauline Clairmont to Emilie Clairmont

Brucedale
Bathurst
New South Wales
July 8. 1855.

My dearest Emy

I have had your letter five days & not been able to answer it – whenever I tried to write my eyes came full of tears & I began to think of all that our dear Dohl[1] had ever said & done, & I could not write. Even now it seems impossible to tell you all I feel for such a loss is too great to admit of any consolation. I read her last letter again & remember how she made me promise to tell her if I was unhappy here in Australia & how pleased she was to go to Weidling the summer before,[2] & how full of love her kind heart was to her family & to Knox & how she would have anytime made any sacrifice in her power for those she loved – & to think that we must loose her, that I shall never hear that sweet little voice again oh Emy that make me so unhappy that I wish I too was in the grave & at rest –.
Es scheint mir alles wie ein Traum u manchmal geht es mir ganz aus dem Sinn u ich Denk mir bei tausend Kleinigkeiten die des Tages vorfallen, "das will ich der Clari schreiben u das will ich ihr schicken, das wird sie freuen, u dann fällts mir auf ein mal ein dß ich sie nie wieder sehen kann dß ich nichts mehr von ihr hören werd dß sie auf ewig fort ist – Meine liebe gute Emi jetzt da wir unsere schöne Dohl verloren haben, schmerzt es mich noch mehr dß ich oft gegen dich so unfreundlich war sie hat oft gesagt die arme kleine Emi thu ihr nichts – Ja liebe Emi die Trennung u Entfernung haben mich in vieler Beziehung verändert, ich glaub ein bischen weicher u besser gemacht aber ich werde doch immer ein derbes hartes gefühlloses Ding bleiben, aber die wenigen die von unserer familie zurückbleiben werd ich doch immer lieb haben – so sehr es so einem wilden bißigen Hund wie ich bin möglich ist – es ist an mir dich zu bitten die Vergangenheit zu vergeßen u wir wollen einander treue Schwestern sein – Ich wollte nur es stünde in meiner Macht Euch allen zu beweisen wie lieb ich Euch hab. – Im letzten Brief den Knox mit Claris Einverständniß schrieb sagten sie mir beide wie sehr Charley wünschte nach Australien zu kommen u jetzt da Willi sich entschloßen hat hier zu bleiben hoffen wir beide dß er so bald als möglich sich auf den Weg machen wird denn erstens wird es so viel angenehmer u leichter sein für zwei zusammen zu arbeiten, zweitens thut er so jeztl. nichts in Ost. u drittens u hauptsächlich glaub ich es wird seiner Gesundheit sehr vortheilhaft sein – wenn ihn uns der liebe Gott laßen will – es schwebt mir aber wie eine finstere ~~Ahlung~~ Ahnung vor dß er nicht davon kommt – das Klima hier ist warm u trocken u sonnig welches hoff ich ihm gut thun wird wenn ihn die Seereise nicht zu sehr schwächt. Ich hoffe die Mama wird nichts dagegen haben, u dß sich alles so fügen wird dß wir alle bei sammen sein können. – Über deine Verlobung liebe Emi hab ich mich sehr gefreut denn ich hör viel Gutes über dem jungen Mann u wünsche nur dß er dich glücklich

mache – u merk dir liebe Emi good temper ist eine Hauptbedingung zu einer glücklichen Ehe – Schreib mir etwas mehr Ausführliches über das "Wann u wo" – ich hoffe dß wenn die Zeit heran kommt werd ich dir einen Beitrag zur Aussteuer schicken können aber es muß nicht zu bald sein denn die letzten 50 f hab ich der Mama geschickt u die nächsten 100 hab ich versprochen dem Willi zu leihen wenn er nach Neuseeland geht – wo man durchaus Kapitel haben muß um anzufangen. Nun meine beste Emi leb wol, ich wünsch von Herzen dß es dir wol gehe wo du jetzt bist – so gut wie mir denn was äußerliche Umstände betrifft bin ich sehr zufrieden – ein ander mal mehr ich kuß dich tausend mal u bleib deine treue Schwester Pauline

English Translation (German transcription and English translation provided by Ann Sherwin):

Everything seems like a dream to me, and sometimes it slips my mind completely, and umpteen times a day when little things happen I think to myself, "I want to write that to Clari" or "I want to send her that, she'll enjoy that, and then suddenly it occurs to me that I can never see her again, that I will hear nothing more from her, that she is gone forever – my dear, good Emi, now that we have lost our beautiful Dohl, it pains me even more that I was often so unkind to you. Poor little Emi, she would often say, don't hurt her. – Yes, dear Emi, separation and distance have changed me in many respects, made me a little more gentle and better, I think. Even though I remain a rude, harsh, unfeeling thing, nevertheless I will always love few members of our family that remain – insofar as possible for a savage, vicious dog like me. It is up to me to ask you to forget the past; let us be true sisters to each other. If only it were within my power to demonstrate to all of you how much I love you. – In the last letter that Knox wrote, with Clari's permission, they both told me how eager Charley was to come to Australia, and now that Willi has decided to stay here, we both hope that he will start on his way as soon as possible. First, it will be so much easier and more pleasant for two to work together; second, he is not doing much of anything now in Ost;[3] third and most importantly, I think it will be very beneficial to his health – if it is the good Lord's will to leave him to us – but I have a dark foreboding that he won't get away. The climate here is warm and dry and sunny, which I hope will do him good, if the sea voyage doesn't sap his energy too much. I hope Mama won't have any objections and that everyone will give in, so that we can all be together. – I was very pleased about your engagement, dear Emi, for I am hearing so many good things about the young man and only hope that he makes you happy – and take note, dear Emi: "good temper" is a primary requirement for a happy marriage.[4] Write me more details about the "when and where" – I hope that when the time approaches I can send a contribution for your trousseau, but it must not be too soon, for I sent Mama the last 50 gulden, and the next 100 I've promised to lend Willi when he goes to New Zealand[5] – where capital is absolutely essential to make a start. Now, my dearest Emi, farewell. From my heart I wish you well where you are now, as well as I am; for as to external circumstances I am very content. More another time. I kiss you a thousand times and remain your faithful sister, Pauline

Address: No envelope.

Unpublished. Text: M.S. Pf. Coll., CL'ANA 0233

---

1 Clara's untimely death from consumption in 1855 was the first of a string of losses to the Clairmont family as three of her siblings followed in 1856 (Stocking cites "pulmonary consumption" as the cause of Clara's death. See CC: II 548). In both the English and German parts of this letter, Pauline referred to Clara as "Dohl". As this is neither a German nor an English word, it is entirely possible that it is a coined term of affection and that it means "doll". Pauline also wrote Clara's name as "Dohl" in her journal entry of 8 July 1855. Clara's loss prompted Pauline to write: "Dohl if you could have thought of the void your death would leave you would have cried tears as burning as mine, to think that your poor sister should be so unhappy – to think that her courage should be so broken down, hope energy & mirth gone, to think that she was so sad, that she only wished to be in the cold grave & at rest. Oh I hope dohl you never knew anything of this & this & much more would I bear if you could be saved even a moment's pain" (CL'ANA 0176, unpublished manuscript, Pforzheimer Collection).

2 See CL'ANA 0364.

3 German for Austria.

4 Emily was engaged to Frederic Drathshmid. See CL'ANA 0350.

5 See CL'ANA 0205.

59 • Wilhelm Gaulis Clairmont to Claire Clairmont

[23 August 1855]

My dear aunt.

I am very glad to be able at last to tell you something certain about my plans. I have fallen in with a young German[1] owning a few hundred pounds to which I added my savings and with this aided by Mr Morris[2] my former employer we bought a sheepstation in New England.[3] My share will amount to one third of all the profits in return for which I undertake the management of the affair without a salary. the station numbers 14.000 sheep and the price we gave for it will amount to about £10.000 – of this we pay £3000 the first year and the remainder in 4 more years in four equal instalments paying interest at the rate of 7%.[4] Our being void of capital and consequently having to take the thing on credit and pay heavy interest makes it rather uncertain for if we should have unfavorable seasons or low prices for the first few years we should in all probability fail; but as the money I embark is (with the exceptions of £40 which Pauline will contribute) entirely my own and as there is a very fair chance of success I think I am perfectly justified in running that risk; for unless I chance something I shall never get on. On the other hand that is to say if we succeed I shall at the end of 7 or 8 years be proprietor of 5000 sheep and having once a start of that description I have no doubt I shall soon get on, for the main difficulty is to make a beginning entirely without capital as I was – –

I hope Charley is on his way out; there will be no room for him on our station; that is to say the profits of it will be too small especially while the heavy debts are on it to pay him besides us three, but if he will take a situation as I did for the first few years he is sure to succeed hereafter as I will be able to assist him in a hundred different ways always of course provided our present project succeeds; that he must chance as I do myself.

I am sorry to see from your papers that Her Majesty's opera is getting on so ill it must be a source of great annoyance to you. I hope dear aunt your health is better than it was. Pauline & I spent a very sad time since we heard of poor Clara's sudden death, for we both liked {tear} but poor Knox must suffer even {tear} than we do. P. & I went to Sydney to {tear} where we spent a fortnight, we had a great number of invitations to the élite of Sydney society but I could not enjoy anything as I had to hurry & bustle about night & day in order to remove all sorts of difficulties in effecting this {tear} desired bargain. the colony has this great advantage over London that you require neither title nor money but simply the bearing of a gentleman to procure yourself admittance to very best society; and I must say one can hardly say enough of the hospitality and affability of rich wealthy colonists.[5] Now Goodbye dearest aunt, write very soon and direct as below; give me all particulars about your health and believe me always

your affectionate nephew
W.G. Clairmont

August. 23rd 1855.
Kangaroo Hills, Armidale[6]
via Sydney N.S.W.

Address: Aerogramme: Miss Clairmont,/ 6 Waverley place/
St. John's Wood/ London.
Postmark: 2 A^N 2/DE 29/[illeg.]

Unpublished. Text: M.S. Pf. Coll., CL'ANA 0066

---

1 Wilhelm purchased a share in Kangaroo Hills together with Julius Duboc (1829–1903), a German immigrant who arrived in Australia in 1853. In *Wongwibinda*, Owen Wright provides information on Duboc's life, stating that Duboc became a writer who worked at the University of Dresden after his return to Germany in 1857. The Duboc family papers are housed today in the State Library of New South Wales. Kangaroo Hills, now known as Wongwibinda, is some 60 kilometers from Armidale in New South Wales. In 1855, Duboc and Wilhelm purchased Kangaroo Hills from William Dangar (see introductory material to The Australian Sojourn). The agreement named Duboc, Wilhelm (whose last name was misspelled as "Claremont"), and Dangar in the purchase of Kangaroo Hills on "this tenth day of August 1855" together with "the sheep depasturing there, estimated 13,8000 of mixed sexes and ages" (University of New England Heritage Center, A0344 – Dangar papers. Armidale, New South Wales, Australia). In his list of property purchases of the New England and Macleay Districts, William Gardner recorded that Duboc and Wilhelm purchased the property, which was situated on the Sugar Loaf River in the area with the "native name" of "Ourconnan," in 1855, but Gardner added the word "left" next to the entry of their names, confirming that they had given up the property. Gardner, a historian who kept copious notebooks in which he recorded statistical information about the early years of the colony's history, detailed the purchase. While Gardner's record had a column for the station owner's occupation, he left this column blank in both Duboc and Wilhelm's case (University of New England Heritage Center, A0344 – Dangar papers. Armidale, New South Wales, Australia. *Resources of Northern Districts*, Vol. 1. A175. p. 130). The purchase agreement referred to Duboc and Wilhelm as "German Immigrants" and was signed by Augustus Morris who agreed to "accept the Bills referred to in the above Agreement (University of New England Heritage Center, A0344 – Dangar papers. Armidale, New South Wales, Australia). By November 1855, Wilhelm and Duboc tried to sell off some of their sheep: An advertisement in *The Maitland Mercury and Hunter River General Advertiser* from 24 November 1855 offered "3000 Store Sheep For Sale". Prospective buyers were encouraged to contact Clairmont, Duboc, and Company (National Library of Australia, http://trove.nla.gov.au/newspaper/page/129370, p. 3). Unfortunately, Duboc and Wilhelm were forced to relinquish ownership back to William Dangar as they were unable to make the payments. An advertisement in the *Armidale Express* of 7 March 1857 read as follows: "Kangaroo Hills Station. The above station is FOR SALE by private contract without stock. For particulars, apply to the undersigned on the station, or to Messrs Mather and Gilchrist, Armidale. R. Lakin" (Copy of the advertisement provided by John Dangar, Australia). In 1858, Dangar sold Kangaroo Hills to John and Christopher Allingham.

2 See CL'ANA 0210.

3 The New England region of Australia is located in the state of New South Wales. New England stretches for about 59,344 square kilometers from the Queensland border in the north to Walcha in the south. The area includes the towns of Armidale, Walcha, Uralla, and Tamworth ("Profile

of the Electoral Division of New England [NSW]". Australian Electoral Commission. Web. 23 October 2014. http://www.aec.gov.au/profiles/nsw/new-england.htm).

4 Wilhelm's purchase of Kangaroo Hills was closely tied to the history of land ownership in nineteenth-century Australia. The first grants of land given to settlers were in the Sydney area. However, as the population swelled, Governor Darling set a "bounds of settlement" in 1826 and again in 1829 which permitted colonists to apply for land grants in nineteen counties in New South Wales. Known as the "Limits of Location," the land extended some 200 kilometers from Sydney (in McInherny, p. 1). However, due to demands for land, enterprising pastoralists and squatters moved beyond the perimeter of the nineteen colonies and sought land further into New South Wales. Various land acts assisted in protecting Crown lands and in imposing license fees on pastoralists in the counties and beyond. Initially, in 1836, the Crown assessed run license fees of ten pounds annually. The Crown also assessed a fee on those pastoralists operating outside the "Limits of Location" for each animal owned. In 1847, the Order in Council, which was signed by Queen Victoria, authorized the grant of each license to be given for a period of fourteen years, thereby giving a measure of security to the pastoralists. Official run boundaries were also defined and William Dangar became the first owner of Kangaroo Hills. Wright suggests that Dangar leased Kangaroo Hills around 1842 but that his lease was only recorded in 1847/8 (in McInherny, p. 71). According to Wright, the District Commissioner, George James Macdonald, reported that there were "660 cattle, 6 horses and 5,600 sheep" on the run in 1844 (p. 71). As recorded in the contract, the number of sheep had grown to 13,800 by the time Duboc and Wilhelm purchased it.

Wright describes the Kangaroo Hills area as "undulating to hilly" with an altitude that varies considerably "so that the climate is seldom uncomfortably hot, but it can certainly be cold by Australian standards" (*Wongwibinda*, p. 1). Inclement weather, with some snow, frost, and high rainfall levels make it perpetually difficult to farm Merino sheep. In 1885, Albert Wright noted the presence of dingoes on the property (p. 77) which made fencing to protect the sheep an imperative.

5 See Pauline's letter of 8 July 1853 (CL'ANA 0210) in which she recorded how the colonists received her upon her arrival in Sydney. Her enthusiastic endorsement of the reception given in Sydney towards "a poor Miss Nobody like myself & a Governess too," reflected the almost-democratic nature of the colonial spirit.

6 Armidale today is an important town in New England and is situated about halfway between Brisbane and Sydney. Originally the home of the Anaiwan people, it was settled in the 1830s. Henry Dangar, father of William Dangar, was one of the earliest settlers who colonized the area in 1833. Various texts document the harsh treatment of the Indigenous Australians in the area. Furthermore, the importation of sheep into the area, starting in the 1840s, competed with the traditional macropod diet of the Anaiwan people and led to starvation and population decimation (Diprose, Philip. "Aboriginal Land Use in the Armidale NSW Area". Web. 23 April 2016. http://ochrearchives.blogspot.com/2006/08/aboriginal-land-use-in-armidale-nsw.html). Today, Armidale is home to the University of New England which was started in 1938 as New England University College (NEUC) and as a college of the University of Sydney. In 1954, NEUC became the independent University of New England ("University of New England". Web. 23 April 2016. http://www.une.edu.au/about-une/a-world-of-learning/origins). Armidale is some 90 kilometers from Wongwibinda, the current name for Kangaroo Hills.

60 • Antonia Clairmont to Claire Clairmont

[7 February 1856]

Landstrasse Rennweg.[1]
671. Vienna 7.2.56.

My dear Claire.

What misfortunes have come over me since you last heard from me; with the beginning of winter Charley's illness returned in full force and he has been in bed since then – Emmy has had a bad typhus fever – but when she had almost conquered, the danger declared to be over, our dear Sidi was taken ill and in short 12 hours, her angel soul passed on to that better world, when we shall once join her, but are now left to struggle and suffer –[2] Emmy has had a relapse and is more dangerous than before – if with God's assistance her life is saved, she will long be ailing, and an expensive journey to a bathing place in Moravia will be the only means to recover health to both Charley and Emmy – if you can do something for your brother's children to assist me to carry ~~out my~~ through the sufferings and troubles – so do so he who always looked upon as the support and prop of his children will see and bless you for it – I have many kind friends here who do their best to support me in the dreadful trials awarded to me, oh that you too might be of their number – if you can assist me with something send it by the English house John Henry Schröder & Co: London[3], to the Viennese house Stametz and Cop:[4] it will reach me safely – I cannot say any more

ever yours sincerely
Antonia Clairmont

Address: Miss Clairmont/ 6. Waverley Place/ St Johnswood/ <u>London</u>
Front postmark: Wien/ $^{7}/_{2}$/ 6 A
Rear postmark: FJ/ FE/ 1856

Unpublished. Text: M.S., Pf. Coll., CL'ANA 0379

1 Landstrasse is the third district of Vienna today. Rennweg refers to a road in the district.

2 Sidi died on 29 January 1856. By 1855, Charley had returned from Scotland, but he was gravely ill.

3 The firm of J. Henry Schröder was formed in 1818 in London. In 1804, Johann Heinrich Schröder joined the firm J.F. Schröder & Company, which was started by his brother Johann Friedrich Schröder in 1800. Today, Schroders is a major investment asset management company ("Schroders". Web. 12 April 2015. http://www.schroders.com/global/home).

4 The firm of J.H. Stametz and Company was located in Vienna and was one of the approved banking houses in the "List of Foreign Bankers" in *The Merchant's and Banker's Almanac* of 1855 ([New York: J. Smith Homans, 1855], p. 46). *Gaze's Tourist Gazette* ([London: Henry Gaze and Sons, 1895], p. 16) recommended J.H. Stametz and Co. as its Viennese banker.

61 • Wilhelm Gaulis Clairmont to Claire Clairmont

Kangaroo Hills
February. 15th
1856.

My dear aunt

I recd yours of the 27th Sept. only a few days back & was doubly rejoiced for it was the first letter I had from any of my European correspondents since I announced my intention of not returning at least immediately to Europe. I was grieved dear aunt to find that you suffered so much on my account thinking me exposed to the dangers of a voyage while I was in perfect safety on shore; I have for this very reason, and also because it must make me appear so very fickle minded and unsettled often wished I could avoid altogether mentioning any thing of my plans for the future to you or Mama but you would think this a very illplaced reserve whereas in reality it would not arise from any such feeling [~~illeg.~~] at all but simply from a desire not always to be leading you astray as to my whereabouts ~~by~~ through each successive letter ~~always~~ contradicting the contents of its predecessor. – The enterprise ~~of~~ which I wrote you in my last I had embarked in has since taken a ~~rather~~ decidedly unfavorable turn; wool is low, price of stock has fallen considerably & nobody inclined to transact business owing to the scarcity of money.[1] I fully expect that we shall be insolvent before the end of the year.[2] Of course it is a very heavy blow to me as it will put me in a worse position than I was when I first landed here, leaving me £100 in debt ~~but~~ and all the fruits of so much privation and many a day's hard labour thrown away but I try to be as philosophical as I can & to convince myself that I have no right to grumble as I entered on the enterprise with a full consciousness of its hazards and even on cool reflection thought myself justified to risk the small sum I had hitherto earned for even the chance of making at once such a great stride towards the accomplishment of my aim; I am spared ~~the~~ perhaps the worst part viz. that extreme bitterness of disappointment, as I knew from the first commencement what I was about; but still it is a dreary prospect to have to toil after this crisis is over for another twelve month at least to pay off any debt~~s~~ and then only be penyless – If I had not ~~that~~ a sort of almost conceited reliance in my own capabilities, if in fact I did not consider it more as a point d'honeur than a question of material gain I should feel very much inclined to give in, but as it is, my obstinacy gets excited and a desire manifests itself to defy the persecutions of fate & fight it out to the last.

About my health I can give you very good reports the climate of New England[3] where I now am is infinitely better than that of the hot low country of the Interior where I was before, it is cool and bracing and as there is enough rain here to enable you to grow vegetables we add to ~~the~~ beef & damper[4] the inestimable luxuries of lots of cabbages, salads & potatoes. I feel the benefit of this improved diet very forcibly for I have not been troubled here by any of the cutaneous complaints which persecuted me on the Murumbidgee in some of their most disgusting shapes.[5] My throat does not trouble me at all. – I am very uneasy about Mama;

post after post arrives and no letter from her since Octob. 8th 1854 perhaps she is angry with me for not returning this would make me truly miserable, I only did it for the best of all if I consulted my own inclinations I should not stop long among a set of semibarbarous shepherds & stockmen[6] in preference to returning to my relations & friends and the numberless agreements of a civilised life in Europe. Write soon and believe me dear aunt yours truly

WG Clairmont

Pray give my sincerest regards to the Pringles and direct Brucedale Bathurst.[7]

Address: No envelope.

Unpublished. Text: M.S. Pf. Coll., CL'ANA 0067

---

1 Owen Wright records that the price of Australian wool had plummeted by 1840 to one shilling and four pence a pound from two shillings and sixpence a pound in 1836. By 1849, the price was twelve pence a pound (in McInherny, p. 2).

2 Duboc himself wrote, of Kangaroo Hills: "Chance and miscalculation have played tricks on us. The wheat crop and wool clip have gone badly, a depressed market, higher wages than we had reckoned with and a very wet climate, which is bad for the sheep" (*Wongwibinda*, p. 62).

3 See CL'ANA 0066.

4 The Oxford English Dictionary defines "damper" as "a simple kind of unleavened cake or bread made, for the occasion, of flour and water and baked in hot ashes". The OED notes G.C. Mundy's use in 1852 of the term in *Our Antipodes* I.ix. 305: "The Australian bush-bread, a baked unleavened dough" ("damper, n". *OED Online*. Oxford University Press, September 2015. Web. 3 November 2015.http://www.oed.com/view/Entry/47092?redirectedFrom=damper#eid).

5 *The Sydney Morning Herald* of 29 October 1856 (p. 8) presented a report on conditions on the Lower Murrumbidgee. The prevalence of ophthalmia, an eye disease, was recorded amongst the settlers. According to the correspondent, the disease frequently reoccurred as a cure proved elusive. Remedies included applying silver nitrate or zinc sulphate to the eyes or lancing the eyelids. *The Sydney Morning Herald* of 15 December 1857 referenced a possible outbreak of smallpox on the Lower Murrumbidgee and reminded readers of a disease, probably smallpox, that had afflicted people some fifteen years earlier and which had disfigured many of the Indigenous Australians. The correspondent noted that the disfiguring skin disorder was known as the "devil-devil" (p. 8). (National Library of Australia, http://nla.gov.au/nla.news-page1498815 and http://nla.gov.au/nla.news-article13003992). See also CL'ANA 0065.

6 Wright records that Australian shepherds were originally convicts who performed the duties of shepherds as part of their sentences. Later, when convicts were no longer transported to Australia, squatters' agents in Europe encouraged immigration to Australia and many men found themselves working on remote stations, living in primitive huts, and shepherding flocks of some 1,000 sheep.

7 Wilhelm cross-wrote this final sentence. It is interesting to note that Wilhelm asked Claire to address letters to him to Bathurst. Although some 602 kilometers separate Bathurst from Kangaroo Hills, Wilhelm's recognition that his farming enterprise was doomed to fail caused him to ask his family members to write to him care of Pauline. He expected to be insolvent by the end of 1856, and he had no idea where he would be living by 1857. His request to have his mail sent to Pauline's address was probably a move to ensure delivery, since letters from Europe took many months to reach Australia.

62 • Antonia Clairmont to Claire Clairmont

Vienna 5th April 1856.

Landstrasse Rennweg
671.

My dear Claire.

I received both your letters with the inclosed ten pounds, and I thank you heartily and warmly for your assistance and the kind and feeling sympathy you express – I am also glad you have overcome your illness; we were both Ch. and I very uneasy on your account, having received notice from a Mrs or Miss Atherstane, that you could not be shown any letters – it was very kind of her to write, and I beg you will give her my best thanks; I hope you had a good nurse, and rejoice to hear you had kind friends around you to support and cheer you, in all you had to go through, and believe me truly grateful for writing two such long letters for dear Charley's sake, when you have hardly recovered from such a severe attack – you say you don't know the exact nature of the poor boy's illness – an inflammation of the lungs, badly treated at [illeg.] and not quite cured – was the beginning – he came home and I consulted the best physicians, and did what I could, they said he ought to spend the winter at Venice – but I could not do it, I had two other children to maintain and my house was not sold then, I could only make the two ends meet, and not even that since Charley and Emmy were at home the household expenses so much increased – we came to town after the house was sold,[1] to increase my income in some way either by giving lessons, or otherwise; when the cold set in poor Charley became worse, Emmy at the same time, she got the typhus, ~~and~~ but Charley soon rallied, was out of bed, grew quite strong again, and promised very fair, but two such lapses to fear, without bad consequences was not to be hoped; since Emmy's death,[2] he is getting weaker and weaker every day, he does not cough, nor are the other symptoms very bad, ~~but~~ he sleeps well and quietly the whole night, he shows no tendency to perspire, he has good appetite, not too much, but every day enjoys his meals, so far all is right, but for a low fever and want of strength, however we hope every thing of the fine weather and advance of season – his pulse is about a hundred, the last few days formerly it was more – 120 – his diet has been upon white meat or light game for months, and eggs and aspick[3] or a bit of fish for change; I would not let him want, I should rather have sold my last silver spoon; wine or beer he may not take – I have on[4] of the best physicians to attend him, and he calls every day – if he gets strength enough to travel we shall go a place in Moravia where an institution is for pulmonary patients, there we shall pass the summer months, and there ~~the~~ return, to go to Venice for the winter – you see that coincides entirely with your view of the matter, that he should go to Italy for the cold season – to Venice the journey is less expensive than to Pisa or Genoa – and then, I could never leave him or he separate from me, we can not therefore accept your kind offer of sending him to either of those places besides he could not travel alone – I shall thank God if we get him to Moravia, which is only seven hours distance from here by railroad – and then 6 german miles farther in the Carpathian mountains. He gets up every day for 4 or 5 hours but lies down on the sofa again, he is too weak to sit up – the first use we made of your present[5] was to take a girl to help in nursing him, for he worried himself continually on my account, and really I was near sinking under fatigue care and anxiety, so we are both relieved, and he begged me especially to thank you in his name – my sister Mary[6] I have not seen for years – and my brother but seldom, travelling is expensive though the distance is but small – since we are in town, George[7] comes to see us whenever he comes to town; but I have kind and affectionate friends here, that supported me through my heavy trials by kindness and sympathy. I am glad of the turn in the affairs with your box, and wish it may go well – oh my poor dear children far away – what will be their feelings when they hear of our misfortunes, poor Willy in his desert – who will help him to support himself, and poor Pauline – if I can only give them good accounts of Charley it will be a consolation at least – I have already written a second time – Goodbye once more my best thanks and love from Charley and self

yours most sincerely A. C.

Address: Miss Clairmont/ 17 Edwards / Portman Sq/ Lon{tear}
Rear postmark: AP [illeg.]/ 1856

Unpublished. Text: M.S., Pf. Coll., CL'ANA 0380

---

1 In her letter of 8 May 1856, Antonia noted that she received £700 for her Weidling house (see CL'ANA 0381).

2 Emily died on 2 March 1856 after suffering a relapse. Her death notice in the *Oesterreichisch kaiserliche Wiener Zeitung*, No 55 (Austrian Newspapers Online, Austrian National Library), on Thursday, 6 March 1856, stated her name as Emma Clairmont, "Tochter der Frau Antonia Clairmont, k.k. Professors-Witwe, alt 22 J., Landstrasse Nr. 671". Antonia's was listed as a "professor's widow" and Emily's age was recorded as "22 J" (22 years). See http://www.anno.onb.ac.at/cgi-content/anno?apm=0&aid=wrz&datum=18560306&seite=11&zoom=1, p. 11.

3 Aspic, a jelly mould made with meat and vegetables.

4 one.

5 It is evident that Claire continued supporting her brother's children financially.

6 See CL'ANA 0401.

7 Georg Ghilain von Hembyze, Antonia's brother. He lived in Wiener Neustadt, about 63 kilometers south of Vienna.

63 • Antonia Clairmont to Claire Clairmont

[22 April 1856]

My dear Claire.

A thousand thanks and blessings for your kindness and assistance – you do not; cannot know what relief you gave, what load of care taken off my mind; and Charley is so happy to see me so – now I can indeed do every thing that is necessary for the poor boy, I have already taken a summerlodging, to go there till it is time for Roznau[1] – I would have answered you directly, to pour out my thanks to you, but had to go to town first, to get the direction you desired me to send, and I here inclose the note I received at Stamez's[2]. I read part of your letter to Dr Hitchfeld, our physician – for he understands English, and is also physician at the English Embassy – no English doctor being here – he said he would write a few lines in French, so that Sir James C.[3] might fully understand the case beer and wine he cannot allow, but nourishing diet, he does – when your letter arrived I was just occupied in chopping the very things you recommend to make strong soup for him, as I do every day, and I always choose the meat myself, or some of my friends do it for me, that it may be prime and choice, nor does he want in little dainties to stimulate his appetite – we also long for the moment to get him to the country, but April is a raw windy month[4] and we may not yet venture in the open air with him, we are however in a tolerable good situation here, just opposite the Belvedere, and Schwarzenberg gardens,[5] and the great botanical gardens,[6] so that we have hardly any houses opposite – Dr H. is no Homeopath, but of the old school – he hates the Homeopathic system – but you do not seem to know, that I did change physicians – he was treated at first by our old doctor, but no success being visible, I reasoned just as you do – and went to the opposite method and we found considerable improvements of our present doctor – I am afraid you can hardly read this scrawl – my hands tremble and even words fail me – at every moment in the day I miss the dear lost ones – and yet I must appear cheerful to poor Charley – what you say about chicken panado seasoned with cherry[7] and beef tea with port will not be lost upon me[8] – even if Charley is not allowed to drink wine – he can take some in that shape, and I will give him a little every day – once more my best thanks, and I will write again in a week. Charley sends his best love and thanks. I hope you are quite recovered? my health changes with my prospects of my poor boy's recovery. ever yours gratefully
A.C.

Landstrasse. 671.
22- 4 - 56.

Address: No envelope

Unpublished. Text: M.S., Pf. Coll., CL'ANA 0392

---

1 Antonia probably meant Rosenau, a town some 144 kilometers west of Vienna.

2 See CL'ANA 0379.

3 Sir James Chambers was Claire's physician in England.

4 Claire blamed Knox for Charley's illness. In her letter of 16 August 1856, she questioned whether Knox had sent Charley to be examined by a physician before sending him to Scotland. Knox, she declared, did not take any "precaution" with regard to Charley's health (*CC* II: 578).

5 The official website for the Belvedere provides the following information: The Belvedere consists of two palaces (the Upper and Lower Belvedere) which were built for Prince Eugene of Savoy (1663–1736). The Palace Gardens were designed by Dominique Girard. Schwarzenberg Park was built by Count Franz Moritz Lacy in 1697. The estate was bought in 1715 by the Schwarzenberg family for whom it was renamed ("Belvedere". Web. 19 May 2015. http://www.belvedere.at/en and "Schwarzenbergpark". Web. 19 May 2015. https://www.wien.gv.at/umwelt/wald/erholung/schwarzenbergpark.html).

6 The Botanischer Garten (Botanical Garden of the University of Vienna) was founded by Empress Maria Theresia in 1754 and is located next to the Belvedere Gardens. It forms part of the Universität Wien.

7 She likely meant "sherry". See CL'ANA 0382.

8 Chicken Panado was a dish made for drinking and was recommended "for the sick". A recipe from 1812 advises the cook to proceed as follows: "Boil the breast of a chicken in a quart of water; take off the skin, cut the meat when cold, and put it into a marble mortar; pound it to a paste with a little of the water it was boiled in . . . boil it gently for a few minutes to the consistency you like; it should be such as you can drink it, though tolerably thick" (Elizabeth Alcock, *The Frugal Housekeeper's Companion* [Liverpool: James Smith, 1812], p. 212).

64 • Antonia Clairmont to Claire Clairmont

[26 April 1856]

My dear Claire.

Today being Saturday, I write a line as you desired me to do; on reading your last three or four times over, I took your advice, and got a bottle good old Tokay wine,[1] and gave the poor boy first half a wine glass full with a biscuit, and since then I increased the potion to a whole today is the fourth day, and we both think he feels the benefit of it already he feels stronger, and the pulse is not increased after the wine; I am quite happy and thank you a thousand times so does he. I have hopes to get a bottle of cherry from the Imperial cellar by particular protection; he will like it, and it will do him good. today he sat up in bed to take his dinner which he could not do this week past; his cough is not worse, he sleeps well, only the first day he took the wine his sleep was broken and uneasy but since then all is well. I must now conclude – good bye dear Claire perhaps I can give you better accounts next week, Charley sends his best love – ever yours gratefully

A. C.

Vienna 26-4-56.
Landstrasse, Rennweg 671.

Address: Miss Clairmont/ 17. Edward Street/ Portman Square/ London/ England.
Front postmark: Wien/ $^{26}/_{4}$/ 6A.
Rear postmark: FZ / 30 AP 30/ 1856

Unpublished. Text: M.S., Pf. Coll., CL'ANA 0382

---

1 Wine from the Tokaj wine producing region of Hungary or Slovakia. István Tóth notes that viticulture was extremely important in many Hungarian regions and that the Tokaj wine region had achieved world recognition by the seventeenth century for its sweet sack wine, aszú (*A Concise History of Hungary*, [ed.], István Tóth [Budapest: Corvina Books, 2005], p. 255). The drink is known as Tokay in English.

65 • Antonia Clairmont to Claire Clairmont

8th May 1856.

My dear Claire.

Yesterday 7th May at ½ past 2 in the afternoon my dear poor Charley departed this life for a better world where there are no cares no sorrows, he is an angel as pure and free from sin as dear little Sidi[1] – a thousand thanks for all your kind intentions towards them – I knew for some time his danger but it was doubtful, the doctor said it may go well, but it may take a bad turn and then it will be sudden, and I could never tell you because he read all my letters to and from you, and as he bore up so well after taking the wine, I was full of hope but God willed it other wise His will be done – I must now speak of other cares, the 50 pounds you had intended for the poor boys, benefit pray lend them to me, and I will pay them off by and by say next year half, and the second year the rest I have now the doctor's and apotheckary's bills to pay the rent for the summer lodging and the poor boys funeral which [illeg.] together will just be that sum and my finances are quite exhausted[2] – 6 months illness, and all the expenses of the two poor girls – no wonder – the 700 pds I got for the house,[3] I have invested with good security at 8 pr ct, so I can't get at any part of them nor should I like to do so, for it is the income I have to live upon, but I shall have few wants now, and can pay of the 50 pds if you can help me now in two years as I said before; [~~illeg.~~] I am sure the dear children in heaven will see, and thank for it; good bye dear Claire once more my best thanks ever yours affect.

A.C.

Address: Miss Clairmont/ 17 Edwards Street, Portman
Square/ London/ England.
Front postmark: Wien/ $^{8}/_{5}$/1M
Rear postmark: 12MY12/ 1856

Unpublished. Text: M.S., Pf. Coll., CL'ANA 0381

1 Claire echoed Antonia's expression in her letter of 12 May 1856 when she called Charley "a blessed Angel". She also referenced Antonia's "delicate" children whom she believed now lived in "a blissful abode" (*CC* II: 548).

2 Claire was adamant that Antonia keep the £50 and asked Antonia to consider it a gift. She offered to send Antonia more money if she required additional funds and she expressed happiness in the knowledge that the gift would relieve Antonia's mind of financial concerns (*CC* II: 548).

3 See CL'ANA 0380.

66 • Wilhelm Gaulis Clairmont to Claire Clairmont

[24 May 1856]

My dearest aunt.

I rec$^{\underline{d}}$ your letter of the 4$^{\underline{th}}$ Janry[1] already last month but I was immersed in such a press of business that I was obliged to lay it aside at the time and only now find an opportunity of answering it. I thank you most sincerely for your kind congratulations on my new undertaking[2] here, for although events since have proved them as erroneous they serve me as a proof all the same that you still continue with the same interest as formerly to watch my progress & wellfare; the conciousness of having at least left a few friends who in our misfortune still care for us and have sympathy with us is to me a great consolation in a position like the present, where everything around seems to threaten with an inevitable ruin of my prospects for a long time at least. I see from my journal that I wrote to you last, on the 14$^{\underline{th}}$ Febry.[3] I have no recollection at all of what I then wrote to you, although it is highly probably that already that letter must have contained some hints that our business here did not prosper as well as might be desired. Suffice it to say that since that time our prospects owing to a variety of reasons (among which are foremost a wet season, low prices of wool and great mortality among the sheep in this cold mountain country)[4] have been continually on the decline and that now we are on the verge of an insolvency; ~~afraid~~ it is only by dint of a most desperate arrangement which we are on the point of entering into now that we hope to avert this latter catastrophe; & even then we can only hope to save ourselves the nuissance of the publicity of [~~illeg.~~] legal proceedings against us, the pecuniary loss will be all the same amounting to all that we possess and in my case even worse leaving me £100 in debt, which are a matter not connected with the business & which I must strive to pay hereafter out of my future earnings. You must not think dear aunt that I am utterly prostrate at this sad state of my prospects, I felt it very bitterly at first, when the first bitter disappointments destroyed the hopes I rested on the success of the enterprise, but since that time the dreaded disaster has been growing so steadily and over clouding our horizon so gradually that I have had ample time to impress myself with a conviction of our inevitable destiny; the anticipation was worse than the calamity itself; now that it is actually about to come I can look on comparatively speaking at least quite coolly. Therefore my dear aunt dont give yourself any concern on my account; always preserve me your affection and rejoice at my successes but do not grieve at my reverses. After all my losses are not so very great; certainly they comprise the savings of 3 years hard work, but what are [~~illeg.~~] [~~illeg.~~] a few hundred pounds in comparison with the resources still left me in a sound brain and active body; there I have lost [~~illeg.~~] nothing indeed I rather gained for my health has ~~been~~ decidedly bettered itself during my residence in this cool, bracing mountain climate after the enervating heat of the inland level country and as for my mind, I am sure I have experience more than I wish to get again, and likely to impress itself the deeper on my mind the dearer it was purchased – I suppose it will be my destiny like that of most people not belonging to the privileged class of those "born lucky" to pass my life in strife in which the hight of success that one can aspire to is a fluctuating and periodical conquest over the surrounding difficulties so I have a right to consider a defeat at the outset though it be an entire route, as a steppingstone to future victories over the malice of fate. But I am very selfish dear aunt I am ~~not~~ saying ~~anything~~ all about myself and nothing about you; I hope the case about the opera is decided by this time & decided in your favour; why do you not have done at once with this humbuging opera and buy an annuity? at any rate you must get rid of the box as soon as a favorable turn in the lawsuit gives you half a chance of disposing of it.[5] and how is your health? where are you living? have you given up all thoughts of going to Italy ~~?~~ for a winter? Pray write to me soon & fully about yourself and believe me your affectionate nephew

W.G. Clairmont

May 24th 1856.[6]

Direct as formerly Kangaroo Hills Armidale
Sidney N.S.W.[7]

Address: No envelope.

Unpublished. Text: M.S. Pf. Coll., CL'ANA 0071

---

1 This letter has not survived.

2 The purchase of Kangaroo Hills.

3 The letter was dated 15 February 1856, and not February 14, as Wilhelm claimed.

4 See note 2, CL'ANA 0067, which provides information from Duboc's letter about the wet weather and the market conditions. Duboc also cited the impossibility of finding qualified shepherds as a contributing factor to the station's failure (in *Wongwibinda*, p. 62). John Ferry notes that migration to the area included a group of German immigrants William Kirchner had encouraged to live in the area. Kirchner worked with Henry Dangar, who preferred employing German-born shepherds on his runs (p. 47). In *Squatter's Castle*, Farwell quotes from Edward David Ogilvie's 1852 letter to Kirchner in which he confirmed Kirchner's intention to "import shepherds from Germany under indentures" and in which he stated his desire to hire six shepherds. Ogilvie apparently also informed Kirchner that many of the so-called shepherds from Germany were untrained in the profession (p. 194). Jürgen Tampke explains that Kirchner arranged the passages of some 4,000 migrant workers to Australia over a ten-year period that started in 1839 ("Germans". *Dictionary of Sydney*. 2008. Web. 8 November 2014. http://www.dictionaryofsydney.org/entry/germans). Tampke also notes that Kirchner was instrumental in creating a "German community" near Grafton, New South Wales, as a result of the soap and candle factory he set up in 1855 (*The Germans in Australia* [Melbourne: Cambridge University Press, 2006], p. 76).

5 In her letter of 13 September 1856, Claire recorded going to London to try and let her opera box for two years. Her agent, Mr. Mitchell, who assisted her in the endeavor, only offered her £220 for one year. She deemed this offer unsatisfactory and declined it. Claire therefore believed herself to be in financial difficulty. Given this failure, she considered asking Knox to support Wilhelm's passage home (*CC* II: 589–90).

6 Claire referenced Wilhelm's letter of 24 May 1856 when she wrote to Antonia on 13 September 1856. Stocking erroneously states that this letter did not survive (*CC* II: 591, note 1). Claire's

letter to Antonia stated that Wilhelm wrote to her from Kangaroo Hills, quoted directly from it ("Suffice it to say . . . possess"), and referenced Wilhelm's apparent ignorance of his sisters' deaths, from which she surmised that he had not yet received letters with this information. She also expressed concern that Wilhelm had not indicated whether or not Kangaroo Hills was to be relinquished. She offered to forgo certain necessities in order to pay for Wilhelm's and Pauline's passages home. She also suggested that Antonia ask Knox for £50 to pay for Wilhelm's passage home, arguing that Knox should "bear his share" (*CC* II: 587–590).

7 Wilhelm cross-wrote his address. Mail service in the colony was a weekly event for many years. Judith Norton documents that postal deliveries began in Sydney in 1809 and that weekly service to Bathurst began in 1823. Theo Barker explains that, while the first post office was opened in Bathurst in 1828, there was no permanent post office building until 1855, and the Mounted Police delivered the mail. Mail would leave Sydney by coach at 8am on Mondays and would then be transferred to a horse and rider at Penrith, some 145 kilometers from Bathurst. It arrived at Bathurst by noon on Wednesdays.

Claire suggested in her letter of 13 September 1856 that they not pay postage on Wilhelm's letters as it would have been more likely that he would have received them if postage was expected on delivery. She also informed Antonia that Wilhelm asked her to write to him at Kangaroo Hills, Armidale, Sydney, NSW.

67 • Antonia Clairmont to Claire Clairmont

Baden
Weikersdorf, 15
14 of June 1856.

My dearest Claire.

I write a line as you desired me to do – I should wish so much to see you, we could consider and discuss everything so well, which to treat by letter, I am quite incapable, don't you think the journey would do you good,? and the air here is so very pure and healthy; the expenses of the journey excepted you would live here very cheaply, if you would share my room you should be most welcome; or I could find another in the neighbourhood. now what do you think of my proposal? I am sure you should not have to regret, you would find yourself more strengthened by this trip and change of air – and then we would consider about the dear children what do you think? Kiss dear Paula to her I have not written – do prepare her, but then the letter announcing the fatal truth ought to follow immediately so as to shorten the pain of suspense – to Willy I have written – but will write again next post, then I should say something about their return, and yet it requires consideration ~~I~~ I cannot say all I wished to say, my head is so weak, perhaps you will soon write, to tell me what you think best; many thanks for your kind offer of assistance – my little income will fully serve all my wants – I shall always endeavour to thank God for all the blessings he has left me; and to bear in resignation what He thought fit to impose – yours ever most gratefully

A. Clairmont

Address: Miss Clairmont/ ~~17 Edwards Street, Portman Square~~/
Gate House [illeg.]/ Highgate/ ~~London.~~ / ~~England~~.
Front postmark: Baden; 12/JU 17/ 56; Red Stamp with
BADEN and 72 stamped over it.
Rear postmark: Duke S^t; FO/ 17 JU 17/ 1856

Unpublished. Text: M.S., Pf. Coll., CL'ANA 0387

68 • Antonia Clairmont to Claire Clairmont

Weikersdorf bei Baden[1]
nächst Wein.
16^{t} Juny[2] 1856.

My dearest Claire!

I received yours with dear Willy's inclosed;[3] not a wink of sleep closed my eye the whole night, poor boy what he has to suffer! but your letter contains such weighty matters I must try to answer all as clearly as I can – I agree with you, his disappointment will be the means of bringing him back[4] – however painful it is to him now we shall in the end rejoice in it – but he must return with a fair conscience and an umblemished reputation, the character he bears for rectitude and uprightness ~~moist~~ must not be soiled, therefore the 100 pds must be paid, and all must be done soon,[5] for time is our object, we cannot wait till he is actually in want of the money, ~~he~~ it must be sent directly – and I shall tell you how I mean to arrange the matter – Mr Maier[6] the banker whose direction I gave you for sending me the money, has always been extremely kind to me; I shall try to get a letter of credit for a hundred pds. on a Sydney house payable at sight to W.G.C. Mr Maier – God bless him, he has ever been kind to the widow and orphans, and he is particularly fond of Willy – will not require me, to pay the money in till it is actually drawen so there is no difficulty nor sacrifice to be made, and dear Willy gets the money in hand at the same time with our letters it will raise his spirits, and give him power to act; if he does not want ~~it~~ he will not draw it; and then it is all well – but perhaps he will want it for the voyage – dear Pauline sent me so much money she too, may be short, so it is every way a benefit – then you need not write to Suttor's [7]– even if W. does draw the money it won't be payable here before 7 or 8 months hence – if you can assist me a little in paying it off, you will do so I feel sure but if not a break in my capital must be made – and willingly, if my children are returned to me – I hope my dear Claire you are satisfied with this plan; but pray, send me, <u>the exact direction</u> I must put on the letter for the month of July so that I don't send it to a wrong place and lose a month – pray don't forget, I ought to send it off on the 1st July – Mr Maier is not in town now I hope to God he will return in time I have already written to Sophie Drathshm.[8] to make inquiries and send me word as soon as he arrives; I shall certainly write to Knox to tell him how affairs stand, and that I mean to call Willy back, but as to his sending any money for a scheme he does not approve of, seems to me out of the question, he offered to pay my passage out, but he won't ~~pay~~ help for Willy's coming home, for in every letter he says, it wont do to call him back, it would be madness, you won't think of et et,[9] I have just had a letter of him, and shall tell him all in my answer – but I know he will be furious; and therefore I won't ask him; also for Willy's sake, it would put him on such a dependent footing oh how much we should have to talk together if we could meet – you ask me to come over, if you repeat the invitation I shall with pleasure accept it, it is too tempting, but then my hopes of your coming here, this summer? what becomes of them? in one respect, it would have been better for you to come here, not only for your health's sake, which certainly would have been benefitted, but to see how things are here and to be enabled to judge as to the advantage of our settling in England or here – our choice must be guided by prudence – as to liking, where my children are, I shall be happy – so that is soon settled; but to take a farm is not done so easily, as you seem to think; Charley told me that Mr Wrigtt in Sottland[10] – on a farm of 500 acres had a capital of £12000 in it, and his father stocked the farm for him,[11] so, on 250 acres we should want half the capital; our fortune being so very small, it would hardly suffice for stocking the house, so most of the necessary capital must come from you, and should we be justified in accepting such generosity? would Willy think himself entitled to it after having just failed in a~~nd~~ similar undertaking? in going to England we become quite dependent on you, because we are strangers – here we have friends and connexions – when I shall tell you, I have got the letter of credit – you will have proof these are not empty words; money ~~is~~ goes farther than with you every thing being cheaper – you see my dear Claire how much there is to consider ere we can come to a resolution – the first thing is now, you to write me the exact direction for the precious letter to Willy, and to give me your approval of the arrangement – then to consider whether you could not come here instead of going to Cheltenham[12] – I have already begun to drink the waters, it is abominable stuff – and I am deeply touched with the thought, that owing to your great generosity to me, I enjoy this benefit, whilst you must miss it;[13] May Paula and Willy by love and affection repay you once, for I am not able to do anything to prove my gratitude. I can't think what the directing of W's letters to Bathhurst means[14] – should he have thought of leaving the place already in Feb: ? the dear poor things what sufferings await them – now they will have the first letter.[15]– they little know what is still in store for them. – a thousand thanks for copying W's letter – indeed yours are my only consolation – the inscrip:[16] is in the mason's hand and will be done by the first of July. ever yours most gratefully

A. C.

Address: Miss Clairmont/ ~~17 Edwards Street, Portman Square~~/
Garbrand Hall/ Ewell/ ~~London.~~/ Surrey/ ~~England.~~
Front postmark: Baden / $^{16}/_{6}$/ 5.E.; Epsom [illeg.]
Red One Penny stamp on the front of the envelope
Rear postmark: St M. S. / [illeg.]/ 21 JU 21/ 1856

Unpublished. Text: M.S., Pf. Coll., CL'ANA 0385

---

1 Literally, Weikersdorf next to Baden. "Nächst Wien" refers to this juxtaposition. Antonia was in Baden, a spa town, taking the waters. Baden (also known as Baden bei Wien) is located about 26 kilometers south of Vienna. Weikersdorf is a municipality some 60 kilometers south of Baden. On 6 September 1856, Claire told Antonia that she was glad to hear that Antonia would reside in Baden rather than in Weikersdorf or Vienna. Weikersdorf, she declared, was "too inanimate – too countrified for winter" (*CC* II: 583). Evidently Claire provided financial support for this endeavor.

2 Misspelling for "Juni" which is German for June.

3 Antonia's letter responded directly to Claire's letter of 12 June 1856. In that letter, Claire acknowledged receiving a letter from Wilhelm which she copied for Antonia. Her 16 June 1856 letter to Antonia also summarized Wilhelm's.

4 Claire was convinced that Wilhelm's financial problems would send him back to Europe and Antonia evidently agreed (*CC* II: 552).

5 In her letter, Claire told Antonia that she hoped Wilhelm would not pay his debts to rich people, but only honor those to impoverished people, believing that in this way he could retain his one hundred pounds (*CC* II: 553). She advised he should tell his rich creditors that he had no money in the hope that they would forgive his debts to them. If they refused, she argued, he should "go thro' the Court" to be freed of his debts and of any labor associated with a lack of payment. Antonia disagreed, stating that Wilhelm should pay his debts to protect his good name.

6 Possibly a relative of Salomon Mayer Rothschild (1774–1855), son of Mayer Amschel Rothschild, who founded the house of Rothschild (M.A. von Rothschild & Söhne) in Frankfurt. Mayer Rothschild's sons continued his legacy: Amschel in Frankfurt, Salomon in Vienna, Nathan in London, Carl in Naples, and James in Paris ("The Rothschild Archive". Web. 3 November 2015. https://www.rothschildarchive.org/archive/about_us/).

7 Claire offered to assume responsibility for the money if the Suttors would lend some to Pauline.

8 See CL'ANA 0350 and CL'ANA 0233. The Clairmonts were friends with the Drathshmid family and Emily was engaged to Frederic Drathshmid.

9 Claire suggested to Antonia that she should write to Knox and ask him to encourage Wilhelm to return to Europe. She also expressed the hope that Knox would assist with Wilhelm's passage home (*CC* II: 553).

10 The German for Scotland is "Schottland".

11 In her letter to Antonia of 23 June 1856, Claire termed the type of farm owned by Mr. Wright and the kind of farming he practiced "high farming". She explained that only people of significant means could undertake it, and that they were possessors of "small fortunes" (*CC* II: 561). She offered to assist Wilhelm financially with a farming enterprise.

12 A spa town in England, about 152 kilometers west of London. In her letter, Claire had expressed a desire to go to Tunbridge or Cheltenham to drink the waters (*CC* II: 553) but she explained that she did not have any money to pay for such a trip. She apparently hoped to get some money from renting her opera box by August and she planned to visit a spa town when her finances permitted such a venture.

13 Claire begged Antonia to partake of the waters in Baden as the best salutary remedy for the terrible suffering her sister-in-law had endured (*CC* II: 553).

14 Instead of directing them to Kangaroo Hills. Claire noted that Wilhelm had requested she write to him at Bathurst. She believed this meant Wilhelm might be leaving Kangaroo Hills to join Pauline.

15 The letter telling Wilhelm and Pauline of Sidi's and Emily's deaths.

16 Inscription. See the photograph of the Clairmont family memorial stone in this collection. The German inscriptions on the family memorial read as follows: "Familie/ Clairmont/ Wilhelm Gaulis/ Clairmont/ Geboren 28 Mai 1831,/ Gestorben 26 Dezember 1895/Ottilia Clairmont/ Geb: Von Pichler/ Geboren 22 Jänner 1843,/ Gestorben 20 Jänner 1913/ Gottlieb August Crüwell/ 1866–1931/ Alma Crüwell Geb. Clairmont/ 1869–1946/ Frida Clairmont geb Zucker/ 1875–1957/ Dr. Walter Gaulis Clairmont/ 1868–1958/ O Ewigkeit, du schöne,/ An dich mein Herz gewöhne". Gottlieb Crüwell was the husband of Alma Clairmont while Frida Clairmont was Walter Clairmont's wife. The words "geboren" and "gestorben" mean "born" and "died". The verse on the tombstone was written by the German Protestant preacher, Gerhard Tersteegen (1697–1769), and comes from the hymn "Nun sich der Tag geendet" ("Now ended the day"). The lines on the family gravestone translate as "O Eternity,you beauty, my heart has to grow accustomed to you". The left side of the stone devoted to Charles identifies him as "Professor der englischen Sprache/geb. zu Bristol in England am 4. Juni 1795/ gest. allhier am 2. Februar 1850". (Translation: Professor of the English Language/ born in Bristol, England, on 4 June 1795/ died here [Vienna] on 2 February 1850).

On 12 June 1856, Claire asked Antonia whether she had received her letter with the inscription she had written for Charley's tomb (*CC* II: 553). On 23 August 1856, she sent an inscription for the grave of her brother as well as for the graves of Sidi and Emily (*CC* II: 580–3). In that letter, she told Antonia that she found writing Charles's inscription very difficult. She acknowledged that Antonia had not loved Charles, and therefore she felt obliged to justify why she praised him more thoroughly. She reminded her sister-in-law that Charles had been a hardworking man who provided his family with financial support and who therefore deserved some praise. One "failing," she proclaimed, referring to his infidelity, did not outweigh all his other virtues (p. 581).

69 • Antonia Clairmont to Claire Clairmont

Baden 21^{t} June 1856.
15. Weikersdorf bei

My dearest Claire.

Do I not write too often? today being Saturday I write again though our letters have twice crossed – I received yours of the 16$^{\underline{th}}$[1] and you will by this time have got mine to tell of the safe arrival of yours with the copy of Willy's. thanks for all you said to the dear children, I most heartily agree in every word you say; on the second equally important subject of our future settlement, I shall not enter today, till I hear your answer to the suggestions I made on that point – yesterday I was in town, and got the bill, from Mr Maier whom God ~~shall~~ may bless for his great kindness to me; it is for a hundred pds[2] and I signed a letter of promise to pay it when drawn; I am now going to write immediately to the dear children and send it off ~~on~~ about the end of the month, and the duplicate a month later, and so I hope the chief difficulties to be smoothed – Mr M. has extensive estates in Hungary, and would have taken Willy on most liberal conditions,[3] and it was allmost ~~all~~ settled when Knox's letter came, and Willy preferred Australia;[4] since then M^{r} M had always said, he would take Charley as soon as his studies were completed; this hope was like a star to the poor boy, when his long cessation from studies began to pray upon his spirits – dear angels in heaven as they all are now – so I am sure for Willy to find a place ready and not only a lucrative one, but also a [~~illeg.~~] sphere of [illeg.] suiting to Willy's powers and knowledge for the estates are enormous and capital plenty – oh my dear Claire could we only talk together, I think a month's time we should have plenty of subject; is there a possibility of your coming over? you would be so much better able to judge; would see the difference in price – then the produce of interest upon capital is so much more than with you – I have full 8 pct upon mine whilst you have but 3; if I contrived to live respectably and bring up my children with so little as I have, what could one not do with such capital as yours? you say it is good to have two strings to one's bow; for Willy I have four or five good tough strings [5]– it is only 6 months back, that a gentleman called on me to ask when Willy would return, he was sent by Mr Zimmermann, the director of the Hungarian estates of Archduke Albrecht;[6] you may think that he (director) is a great man – he had been keeping a place open for him (for W.) and only after I had told him, that Willy had no thoughts of returning just now, he gave it away to another person; I may therefore say that as soon as Willy returns there will be an end of all care for him – another proof of the esteem our family enjoy, I have just had in an application from Count Menzdorf[7] to have poor Emmy as a governess to his children – this is not only one of the richest and highest, but most worthy and religious families, such as you seldom find in the high nobility; they live always on their estates in Moravia so he was a stranger to my misfortunes; as I should greatly wish to oblige him in complying with his request to find somebody – I thought of writing to you; but first asked his Lordship to state in a few lines some dates – these I will send to you, if you will kindly undertake the commission, the big point is that she must be a catholick, and know music – the late ~~Old~~ Count Menzdorf was always very kind to poor Charles and this is the eldest son, and besides first cousin to your queen;[8] I am going to write to Knox today – we shall see whether my opinion of him is correct but my dear Claire you have really wonderful talents for medical science, your supositions are quite true; my health is improving – the air here agrees better with me than at Weidling – I am much stronger, can walk better – and have not that extreme weakness in the spine that I used to have for so long a time generally in the summer as that I had to lie down 3 or 4 hours every day in order to keep up the rest of it.[9] Mrs Schauer and Jda[10] were much pleased with your kind mentioning they beg to be kindly remembered, and wish you should come here they know a little English. Now good bye my dear Claire, and best thanks for your sweet words of consolation – God bless you and believe me every yours most affectionately

A. Clairmont

Address: No envelope

Unpublished. Text: M.S., Pf. Coll., CL'ANA 0383

---

1 Claire had not put a stamp on her letter of 12 June and feared it had been lost. She wrote again to Antonia on 16 June to reiterate some of the points she had made in her earlier letter (*CC* II: 554).

2 See CL'ANA 0385.

3 On 23 June 1856, Claire responded to Antonia's comment of 21 June about Mr. Maier, and stated that Wilhelm should take a "good Intendentship with a good income" in Hungary (*CC* II: 560). On 28 June 1856, she again referred to "Mr. Myers" and the position Wilhelm would have found with him and expressed disappointment over the fact that Wilhelm had spent time in Australia (*CC* II: 561).

4 Claire had long blamed Knox for Wilhelm's Australian adventure. In her letter to Antonia of 16 June 1856, she argued that Wilhelm and Pauline should return from Australia to take care of their mother and to do their "duty" towards her. She also said she was confident that Wilhelm and Pauline would undertake such a duty "because there are no Shelleys or Knox's with them, to pervert their minds with a hundred dangerous sophistries" (*CC* II: 555). Claire had an elaborate plan for Wilhelm's future: he was to return to England and obtain a government position while she and his mother would live on a farm some twenty miles out of London that they would manage according to Wilhelm's dictates. Wilhelm, she explained, would return at night from London "to farm or to amuse himself". If the farm were profitable, Wilhelm would then give up his London position to farm full-time on another, larger farm (pp. 555–6).

5 Claire described her proposal that Wilhelm work in London while she and Antonia farmed as providing Antonia with "two strings to your Bow" (*CC* II: 556).

6 Archduke Albrecht, Duke of Teschen (1817–1895).

7 Antonia misspelled Count Mensdorff's name. See CL'ANA 0399.

8 Queen Victoria.

9 Claire advised Antonia to take some "clearing medicine" while at Baden and to drink "Marien Bad Waters". Marienbad is a spa town, located today in the Czech Republic. She also recommended some "opening medecine" (her spelling) to clear her mind from agitation (*CC* II: 556).

10 Mrs. Schauer was one of Antonia's friends. Her daughter's name was Ida, but Antonia misspelled it.

70 • Antonia Clairmont to Claire Clairmont

29th June 1856.
15 Weikersdorf bei Baden.

My dear Claire.

I cannot write much to day, for fear of making the letter too heavy; I here send you Count Mensdorff's letter, though your answer does not reach mine where I spoke to you about it, yet I hope you will kindly try to find somebody to suit them – you will see by his letter how amiable and perfect a nobleman he is, the Countess is a pattern of a woman, and they have four children a boy and 3 girls from 8 to 13 – oh my poor Emmy; what a house that would have been for her, to remain till her marriage! I think dear Paula was once in a catholic family; there you would perhaps first succeed, but you will best know the ways and means - it would be a new source of gratitude if you help me to oblige Count Mensdorff it was his father, gave Pauline the letter to the dutchess of Kent[1] – I felt almost inclined to go there myself till they find somebody, Willy's bill would soon be paid but I must not interrupt my baths, and as I bathe only every other day, I shall not have done for a good while, between I take the water, and in the afternoon I walk about in the fir woods that cover the hills round baden, extending for hours with wellmade roads and occasional places of rest – I thank God and you that I could come here; what a pity you cannot come, the more so as I am afraid there will be great obstacles to my coming in lateness of the season, for I could not leave here before beginning of Nov: I'll explain it another time – thank you dear Claire for both your letters, I had mine sent off the 28th so as to be in town for the post the next day, the very day when yours arrived, but I wish Willie's debts to be paid. and happy I shall be if this bill suffices; - the next time I will answer your last more fully – I wished to have your ideas to my last – and waited a day, for it is sunday today – but won't defer any longer – I hope soon to hear your health is improving – God bless you my dear Claire ever yours affect:

A.C.

Address: No envelope.

Unpublished. Text: M.S., Pf. Coll., CL'ANA 0421, Box 1, bundle a, numbers 8–10.

---

1 See CL'ANA 0389. The Duchess of Kent, mother of Queen Victoria. Count Mensdorff was a first cousin of Queen Victoria. His mother, Sophie von Mensdorff-Pouilly, and the Duchess of Kent were sisters.

71 • Antonia Clairmont to Claire Clairmont

5th of July 1856
15.Weikersdorf bei Baden

My dearest Claire.

I have just received yours of the 28th June.[1] Your news of the short passage, is a great blessing, the more so as it can be relied on; 53 days is a mere trifle, to what it was before; if they are ready by January to set off, we might see them by ~~g~~ beginning of March or so![2] May Good God, lend his help to bring them safely home! I think your view of Hungary is too severe, these reports are not to be trusted; things look differently at a distance, Capt. Andoe often used to say, it was wonderful what false notions the English had about Hungary;[3] to tell you the t~~h~~ruth, I within myself look with distrust upon England sometimes I think, if dear Cläry and Char: had remained here they would be well and happy; but we are all under the control of Him who guides us, and to whose power we must submit; so I am resigned to whatever may be the will of Heaven, thanking Him most fervently, that my children find such an affectionate friend and relation in you. You ask me why Willy went to Australia[4] when he had such good prospects here; I think I wrote you a long letter about it at the time he went: my children to be English subjects instead of Austrians seemed desirable to all parties, and I would not prevent Willy of trying to realise that wish, when an opportunity offered; but had I known Knox as I do now, I should have paused and thought twice upon any plan proposed by him; as for me, what a sacrifice to part with such a son! it is my only consolation in all my misfortune, that I never acted selfishly, but only what I thought for the good of my children; Of the cholera we know nothing except from your letter – not even the papers mention any appearance of it[5] – my health improves very much, though somewhat affected by the baths and the waters I can take long walks without much fatigue;[6] the air agrees well with me, woods and trees are the fittest society for my state of mind – I feel myself a burthen on my best friends; it seems selfish to intrude my sadness on them and disturb their cheerfulness. Have you got the letter of Count Mensdorff? and do you think you can do anything for him? I have not answered him till hearing from you what hopes there are; excuse the trouble I give you; but I told you my reasons. Mrs Schauer and Ida[7] beg to be most kindly remembered; I always read parts of your letters to them; they both admire you greatly; and wish to know you – perhaps this wish will be gratified, if the dear children arrive towards the spring, what would be more easy and natural than your accompanying them to Austria; if your affairs are settled, so that you can leave England by that time; the sale of the box will give you a great deal to do; how do you get on with it? Pray do write soon again your letters are my best consolation, thanks for your attention to my health but wine or beer is not at all for me, it heats me too much, I must take cooling things.[8] I shall be happy to think you out of London[9] – generous Claire, take my best thanks, ever yours sincerely A. C.

Address: No envelope.

Unpublished. Text: M.S., Pf. Coll., CL'ANA 0384

---

1 See *CC* II: 561–563.

2 In her letter of 28 June, Claire copied an excerpt from *The Times* in which it stated that a new Australian mail service had been awarded to the European and Australian Steam Company and would be fully operational from Liverpool to Sydney or to Melbourne by January 1857. The newspaper estimated that the journey from Sydney to Liverpool would take 53 days (*CC* II: 563). Claire was delighted to find that the journey would no longer require traveling via Cape Horn and that the new line would ensure that ships avoid the two Capes (Cape Horn and Cape of Good Hope), which would make for calmer, shorter journeys. Lucy Frost states, however, that from the early 1860s many ships from England to Melbourne still took over one hundred days to complete the passage (*No Place for a Nervous Lady*, p. 6).

3 Claire expressed disappointment that Wilhelm had gone to Australia and claimed that she and Antonia would have experienced less grief if he had settled in Hungary instead of in Australia. Yet she believed that Hungary was dangerous, with the poor roads, a lack of culture, adverse winters, a marsh-like environment, and prevalent disease in the absence of effective physicians. She likewise noted that the Revolution of 1848–1849 had made it a difficult place to farm. She based these concerns on books she had read and accounts by Englishmen who managed estates in Hungary. Therefore, Wilhelm could only consider Hungary if he found a job near a large town with appropriate amenities; Antonia should not support Wilhelm taking a position on a remote farm. Claire stated too that she planned to have an English physician examine Wilhelm's lungs once he returned to England and that she would discourage him from taking a position in Hungary if the physician found her nephew to be in poor health (*CC* II: 562). See also CL'ANA 0388.

4 In her letter, Claire stated that it was a "pity" that Wilhelm went to Australia, although she did acknowledge the positive experience of learning how to manage sheep. Claire also questioned Wilhelm's decision to go to Australia, noting that Knox probably encouraged Wilhelm to believe that he would make a great deal of money in Australia. She cautioned Antonia against depending on Knox's judgment, claiming that he had too many ideas in his own head and could not attend cautiously to the ideas of others (*CC* II: 562).

5 Claire warned Antonia to avoid Vienna due to the prevalence of cholera (*CC* II: 563). See also CL'ANA 0059.

6 Claire exhorted Antonia to watch daily the effect the waters had on her and advised her to avoid fruit and vegetables and to eat only meat and bread (*CC* II: 563).

7 Claire had sent good wishes to Mrs. Schauer and her daughter in her letter. On 31 May 1856, Claire told Antonia that she was pleased that Antonia was with Madame Schauer, drinking the Baden waters (*CC* II: 550).

8 Claire also advised a glass of wine or ale at dinner (*CC* II: 563).

9 Claire stated that she would soon be leaving London (*CC* II: 563).

72 • Antonia Clairmont to Claire Clairmont

15 Weikersdorf bei Baden.
14th July 1856.

My dear Claire.

I received yours of the 5th in due time to answer it by saturday,[1] but having written directly to Count Menzdorff, I waited, in case he should answer, but I will not delay longer, he may not think it necessary to do so directly, for I told him that you are just gone to the country,[2] but there is no doubt he will pay the journey, especially upon such high and trustworthy recommendation as you will procure; it is indeed an excellent idea, and I only regret it will give you so much trouble: I am very happy to think you in the country, enjoying air and quiet to strengthen your health after the fatigue of the winter; I am going on well; I have 25 baths, with 30 I will pause for a month and then begin again – thanks for your words of consolation; I do try to be resigned and patient, but it is difficult under such trials as mine – let me not enter this chapter – rather try to hope for P.s and W.s safe return – 32 years have I hoped and trusted and toiled cheerfully and what am I now? Good bye dearest Claire, I will never be a burthen upon my friends with my complaints so I conclude write soon ever yours affectly

A. C.

Address: Miss Clairmont/ Mrs. Innerarity's, South Street/
Epsom,/ Surry. /England.
Front postmark: Baden/ $^{14}/_{7}$ / 5.E.
Rear postmark: FP/ 18 JY 18/ 1856

Unpublished. Text: M.S., Pf. Coll., CL'ANA 0386

---

1 On 16 June 1856, Claire asked Antonia to write to her every Saturday (*CC* II: 556).

2 On 5 July 1856, Claire asked Antonia to write to Count Mensdorff and to inform him that she was ill and out of London for two months but that she would look for a governess for his family on her return (*CC* II: 564).

The Pforzheimer Collection has in its archive an undated document which appears to be from Antonia to Claire and was possibly originally included in this letter. The text of the note reads: "This was just sealed to go away, when a letter from Count M. came, he begs me to procure the exact direction of the Convent of the sacred Heart so that he can write or have written directly, so will you be so good and give me the direction; and do tell me how one addresses these nuns – in German we say Rev: Sister – Ehrwürdige, or Hochwürdige Frau the Lady Abbess is always called the Würdige Frau – how does one say in English?" The English translation for "Ehrwürdige, or Hochwürdige Frau" is "Reverend Lady" (CL'ANA 0421, Box 2, bundle c, number 75).

73 • Antonia Clairmont to Claire Clairmont

19 July 1856.
15 Weikersdorf bei baden.

My dearest Claire.

Your letters are so refreshing to me I am grateful for the love you bear the dear children, you will see all will go well, Pauline will stay with me, she will plenty of lessons here during the season, then Willy will find a good place, for I assure you once more he will have his choice, then we shall go and settle with him, and you will then come and spend at least the summers with us, and will then see, how erronous your ideas of Hungary are;[1] the Hungarian peasant is the most submissive and respectful to his betters you can imagine, it was Kossuth[2] made the revolution, the common people had nothing to do with it, but you will see – the Tyrol[3] is no country for the farmer, high mountains won't do to grow wheat and corn he must seek the ~~ground~~ plains and good roads, fertile soil and navigable streams all this he finds not only in Hungary but Moravia, Galicia and Croatien[4] is equally advantageous if he means to take a farm, but my advice will be a good situation. I had written to Knox when you desired me to do so, and have no answer as yet, the best proof how little he agrees with our view of the matter, and what we should have had to expect, had I sought his assistance in [~~illeg.~~] any way whatever – if once we met we shall have much to talk over – the reason why my coming this year will be difficult is this[5] – the term is for moving nominally at Michaelmass the 29th of Sept. but 14 days of grace are added, so that it is 13th of Oct: then I shall be at least a fortnight arranging my things; I have let my lodging on the Landstrasse[6] furnished; but linen cloths, books et I packed up and gave ~~it~~ to several friends to keep for me; these things I must gather sell part of them, bring them out here, for I intend staying here; I have a nice airy lodging and very cheap, but can't enter before the 13th of Oct, so that I shall not be in order before the beginning of Nov: and if winter sets in early we may be deep in snow by that time – so I think it better to give up the thought of it now, than hope for and be disappointed at last. I am glad the prospects of selling your box are so promising, it will be much better to have your capital placed so as to give a sure income; if you had confidence to place it in Austria you might have clear 5% of it, and I and the children ~~have~~ enjoy 3 more and your capital in no way endangered, think of this my dear Claire you could benefit us greatly without hurting yourself; the capital would not remain in our hands, but ~~would~~ be placed in the bank, and you should have the highest security for it – so tell me what you think about it? I would never advise your buying land in Hungary or anywhere – small estates are always proportionally dear, and large ones require large capital to work them, so I feel convinced to buy landed or other property would be ruin – but stocks and funds are the order of the day. No answer as yet from Count M.[7] what you say about poor Clary's living on tea is too true,[8] what have I tried to convince them of the badness of this system, but it was Charle's fault, he always encouraged them when I was for giving them substantial suppers instead of tea,[9] he spoke in the same strain about coarseness et et hereby destroying the children's confidence in my advice and opinion and strengthening all their perverse ways – always excepted Willy, he was ever sensible poor Charley was too young – but in spite of my earnest entreaties his father made him even breakfast on tea, from being his favorite he wanted the boy breakfast with him, whilst the other children got coffee and milk! with Emmy I had the greatest trouble in the world to make her eat a little meat, years after her father's death – for he had told them, that in England many people lived on vegetables, himself having done so for two years and more – so it all came; poor dear children! shall I ever see those that are still left; or will they too be called away! I hope my dear Claire your health is going on well and improving, we have a very fine summer, one thing I miss greatly, books none to be got, that is, nothing but stiff translations from the French which I cannot bear – English books I never see now; good bye believe me ever yours affecly

A.C.

Mrs Schauer's kindest regards, both wish very much to see you, and were pleased with your thinking of coming here.

Address: M$^{\underline{rs}}$ Innerarily's[10]/ South Street, Epsom/Surrey – England.
Front postmark: Baden/ $^{21}/_{7}$ / 1.E.
Rear postmark: FU/ 24 JY 24/ 1856

Unpublished. Text: M.S., Pf. Coll., CL'ANA 0388

1 On 28 June 1856, Claire expressed her misgivings about Hungary. See CL'ANA 0384.

2 See CL'ANA 0049.

3 A state in the western part of Austria with its capital at Innsbruck. It is located in the Alps.

4 Antonia combined the English word ("Croatia") and the German word ("Kroatien") when referencing Croatia.

5 On 22 June 1856, Claire informed Antonia that she was confined to her bed and unable to travel. She expected Antonia to spend the winter with her in England (*CC* II: 559).

6 On 16 August 1856, Claire asked Antonia to let her know when she had given up her lodging in the Landstrasse (*CC* II: 580).

7 Count Mensdorff.

8 On 12 July 1856, Claire expressed her belief that more young people died of consumption from drinking hot tea and coffee than from the weather. Children who drank cold milk were less likely to contract consumption, she affirmed, as hot liquids "destroy the strength and activity of the digestion". Clara, she confirmed, survived by drinking tea and eating bread and butter as her primary food sources (*CC* II: 567).

9 A light supper.

10 Antonia misspelled Mrs. Innerarity's name.

74 • Antonia Clairmont to Claire Clairmont

[7 August 1856]
15 Weikersdorf bei Baden.
7-8-56.

My dear Claire!

I have just received yours of the 2nd, and sit down directly to answer it, because I have reason to think my last of the 2nd has been lost, the servant maid whom I parted with since, dropped something to that effect and yet would not own it when asked – be sure my dear Claire that I will write to Willy about the things you mention, the more so as I am quite of your opinion as to the efficacy of the measures you propose, but on the other hand, I know too well, how superfluous young people deem such care, but be assured that I will enforce it as ever I can – my letter to the Lady Abbess is already off.[1] C.M.[2] begged me not to mention his name – I think it is because the dutchess of K.[3] ~~is~~ being also engaged in looking out for a governess for them, he does not wish to have it known that he also employs other~~s~~ means; so do not fret anymore about that and enjoy the repose so necessary for your health; you have done enough already, and if we are now successful with the Lady Abbess, and the young Countesses are presented three years hence to the Queen of England speaking English like natives – it will be all owing to your endeavours and suggestions. You speak of going abroad. you can hardly get to Italy without passing Austria, then I shall see you – and yet but lately you spoke of your not being strong enough to travel, and then there is the great difficulty of ~~of~~ returning in winter; that is the worst of it, as you suffer by the cold; the idea of seeing the dear children makes me bear up. I have a nice lodging – – that is, with drawbacks – you enter through the kitchen, and on one side there is a room and a cabinet – so you call, small rooms with only one window and no stove to them – on the other side there is also a room, with a separate entry, so that I can let it, or if any dear ~~guests~~ guests come there is a room ready to receive them; I should wish Pauline to come directly with Willy, so we have them here; she can remain with me at Baden, and there will be plenty of lessons here during the summer months, perhaps she might get appointed English teacher to the young archduchesses, the daughters of Arch: Albrecht and Hildegarde[4] – who ~~have a~~ reside here always in the summer – at all events, I am quite sure all will go well, if they are once here; how shall I thank you my dear Claire for the consoling words your letters contain; I read very often in the family lectures;[5] the sermons are beautiful, and show the weakness of human nature, but I am reading them to strengthen and improve my mind, I am alas, sinning against my own religion, because I ought not to read protestant books – what would those pious fathers themselves say if they knew it? I left my father confessor because he possitvely forbade my reading them, the present one permits it; we are poor miserable creatures! perhaps I ought to thank God he has called away the poor dears,[6] but I can not yet! the great heat is over with us, but we have most beautiful wheather my health is going on well, but the complaint I had is not going away, though I have now completed 30 baths. – The grave stone of poor dear Charley cost 75 fl; that is about 7 pds 10 s. but I am afraid my dear Claire you hurt yourself by this generosity; and pray send me the inscription for the two poor dears[7] for I should like to have that ready too by the 1st Nov: that is all souls day; when friends and relations visit the graves. Don't you find it rude, Knox never answered my letter? what do you say to such behaviour? he cannot be ill; but I forgive him – God bless you my dear Claire, and tell me more clearly about your going abroad and whether I may hope to have a glimpse of you; we should have so much to talk –

ever yours most gratefully
A.C.

Address: Via Ostende/ Miss Clairmont/ South Street, Epsom, / Surrey:/ England.
Front postmark: K.K. FAHRENDES/POSTAMP N[8]; EPSOM/ AU/ 1856/A
Rear postmark: FJ/ 11 AU 11/ 1856

Unpublished. Text: M.S., Pf. Coll., CL'ANA 0389

1 On 5 July 1856, Claire told Antonia that she did not know of any Catholic governesses in England but that she would obtain an introduction to the Abbess of the Convent of the Sacred Heart. She planned to ask the Abbess to recommend a decent young lady for the position of governess as "imposters," she opined, were so numerous in London (*CC* II: 564). On 26 July 1856, Claire informed Antonia that she had written to a friend to ask for the address of the convent. Her plan was to send the address to Antonia. Claire suggested that Antonia encourage Count Mensdorff to write directly to the "Lady Abbess," the head of the convent (*CC* II: 570). On 30 July 1856, Claire confirmed receiving addresses of two convents, the convent at Hammersmith (the Convent of the Good Shepherd) and the Convent of the Sacred Heart at Roehampton. She recommended the convent at Roehampton as being superior and she encouraged Antonia to tell Count Mensdorff to write directly to the Mother Superior, Madame Merilhon (*CC* II: 572).

2 Count Mensdorff.

3 See CL'ANA 0421, Box 1, bundle a, numbers 8–10 and CL'ANA 0399.

4 Archduke Albrecht, Duke of Teschen (1817–1895), and his wife, Princess Hildegard of Bavaria (1825–1864). They had two daughters, Maria Theresia and Mathilda (Royal Collection Trust, https://www.royalcollection.org.uk/collection/2907719/archduke-albrecht-of-austria-duke-of-teschen-with-his-family. 6 May 2016).

5 *Family Lectures: or, A Copious Collection of Sermons, Selected from the most Celebrated Divines, on Faith and Practice*. The text was published in London in 1795 and was printed for T. Longman, et.al.

6 Her children.

7 Sidi and Emily. See CL'ANA 0385. Claire sent the inscription on 23 August 1856.

8 The postmark is at the edge of the envelope and therefore the number of the post office has been left off. The German translates as "Travelling post office branch, number".

75 • Wilhelm Gaulis Clairmont to Claire Clairmont

[3 September 1856]

My dearest aunt.

Although I wrote to you only lately (August 14th) a long letter I commence another now to answer your last of the 20th May I have not time to write much but I will take your advice to write little rather than not at all. A thousand thanks dearest aunt for your kind letter and all the tokens of solicitous care it contains which you still continue to entertain for me – as regards my health you can make yourself perfectly easy I know fullwell that it is the only thing left to me worth taking care of – but you have touched on another subject viz the return of Pauline or myself to Europe; it is a very important one to us I have therefore considered over it with great care and will tell you what I think. I for my part should certainly like to return but I do not see how I could live in England. I am too old now to ~~return~~ live with you as formerly – to accept a clerkship and have to look forward to £100 a year as the highest attainable climax in this world is a career which would not only fail to satisfy my very excusable desire for a worldly position and an at least mediocre income but would even disagree with my physical requirements for I feel confident that 8 hours compulsory work at a desk would break me down – Glorious therefore as would be to me the idea of exchanging the miseries of bushlife for the agreements of civilized society not to mention the innumerable comforts of the old country I do not see how I can realize that idea for I can find no field in England for the particular sphere of action for which I have been trained.[1] if I saw a way of avoiding this difficulty, if I thought there was a chance of my obtaining employment in the country on a large farm or so nothing would please me better than the idea of living together with you & Mama.

With Pauline however it is altogether a different case. She can easily earn £50 or so to cover the greater part of her expenses which living together with you would be not nearly as great as mine; besides she would prove to you a much more acceptable companion than I. – I also fully recognise the propriety that one of us at least should return to Europe so that Mama may have somebody near her in case poor Charley should meet his doom.[2] I have written about all this to Pauline with a view of persuading her to accept your invitation to return to Europe & live with you and I hope it will soon be in my power to follow her – I cannot give you any more information about our business aspects because nothing as yet is decided. affairs linger on; I think we shall manage to sell off of course with a loss after we have taken off the ensuing clip which will be in January next.[3]

Now Goodbye dearest aunt pray continue to write often a letter with the European postmark on it always appears to me like a messenger from some higher region. poor Mama writes very rarely of late, I fear she is in very low spirits; I have often made myself serious reproaches for having left her [~~illeg.~~] or for not having returned sooner but I am now so tied by engagements that

I cannot for the moment return without actually bolting. Give my best regards to Col & Mrs Pringle and to Violet & believe me my dearest aunt your affectionate nephew WGC.

Kang. Hills
Septbr. 3rd 1856.

Address: Miss Clairmont/ care of Messrs Haggard & Hale/ 2 Angel court Throgmorton street./ City London.
Front postmark: PAID/FB/31 DE 31/1856[4]
Rear postmark: SYDNEY/[illeg.]

Unpublished. Text: M.S. Pf. Coll., CL'ANA 0073

---

1 The "miseries" of bushlife are well recorded in accounts from the time.

2 Charley died on 7 May 1856. The news had evidently not reached Wilhelm by September 1856.

3 By 1857, Wilhelm was writing to Claire from Cuba, a run located today near Darlington Point, New South Wales. Newspaper articles from the time recorded his presence in the area. In September 1857, Wilhelm was attacked in the woolshed at Cuba Station and a thirty pound reward was offered for the "apprehension and conviction of the three men . . . now at large" (*The Goulburn Herald and County of Argyle Advertiser* 16 January 1858, National Library of Australia, http://nla.gov.au/nla.news-article118248598, p. 2). The men "committed a violent and murderous assault upon Mr. W. G. Clairmont" (p. 2). Between the January 1857 clipping season and the September 1857 attack, Wilhelm and Duboc evidently sold Kangaroo Hills back to William Dangar. See CL'ANA 0066.

Walsh records that the world's first patent for a sheep shearing machine was granted to Australian J.A.B. Higham in March 1868 (p. 79) and that the first commercial sheep shearing machines were used in the 1870s. In previous years, farmers would hand clip their sheep. With flocks numbering in the thousands, hand shearing must have been particularly arduous for farmers like Wilhelm.

4 Wilhelm dated his letter 3 September 1856. The postmark on the accompanying envelope reads 31 December 1856. It is likely that the envelope and the letter are incorrectly matched.

76 • Antonia Clairmont to Claire Clairmont

[27 September 1856]

[illeg.] 27th. 1856
15 Weikersdorf bei[1]

My dearest Claire.

What can have prevented you from writing last Saturday? I hope it is not illness! to have you fall ill, and no friend no relation near you, would be truly afflicting; but let me hope your not writing has some other cause, perhaps you were removing to town. though it would be a pity, so soon; the autumn is so fine – we have beautiful wheather. Mrs Schauer left Baden today it will be a great loss for me, but I have had too severe a lesson, not to bear it patiently; my greatest pleasure in her society was in speaking of the past – and that, I felt, I ought not in justice to her indulge in, for she being an invalid, and a sufferer, ought to have had life presented to her ~~from~~ as a cheerful picture, and not such as I could show it her. therefore I think her a gainer by our separation and that thought consoles me; good bye my dear Claire, I hope to hear soon from you and that you are well – every yours affecty

A. C.

Address: Miss Clairmont/ South Street, Epsom/ Surry, England.
Front postmark: Baden/ $^{28}/_{9}$ / 4. E.; EPSOM/[illeg.]
Rear postmark: FB/ OC/ 1856

Unpublished. Text: M.S., Pf. Coll., CL'ANA 0391

---

1 The postmark confirms the letter's date of 27 September 1856.

77 • Antonia Claimont to Claire Clairmont

Baden 241. 11th Oct. 1856.
the new direction

My dearest Claire.

Owing to the bustle of moving into the town of Baden, and having to go to town to arrange with the Lady on the landstrasse, whose confinement, being happily over in good time, enabled me to bring out my furniture in fair wheather all this prevented my writing to you last Saturday, and have now in fact 3 of your letters to answer, for yours of the 22nd of Sept. arrived after I had sent of mine, but I will do it now; and begin with my news; Knox is going to send £50 to W. that is, 25 with the Nov. mail and the rest later; to Pauline – so there is one great care off our minds;[1] I have had a letter dated 6th June from dear P. an answer about poor Sidi; she mourns her so bitterly; and there are inclosed letters to Emmy and Charley[2] I have not had the courage to read them yet; Oh my dear Claire, do not fret and sorrow about the money – you say you would borrow from Mitche[3] do not grieve – you have done all you could do, in helping me this winter, not only, have you enabled me to do all for Charley to cheer his last days, to make him rejoice in your kindness, to ~~make~~ help me clear all obligations I had, and so the better enable me to pay the bill I sent; the consciousness of having done all this, should make me quiet and happy; so do not sorrow any more; we are poor mortals, and can only do our best, the rest we must leave to God! I am so sorry for your health – and charmed with your young friend; God bless her – and believe me I trust all to him – I have got acquainted with two old ladies – a widow and her sister in law – they are two wise old ladies – living together now 35 years – the husband and resp.[4] brother, having been dead these 20 years – they have a little ~~g~~ cottage and a garden which they work themselves and are so cheerful and happy – if we could live so together, how agreeable that would be; how I would nurse you and take care of you, or you of me, and neither of us be alone nor dependent upon a menial. about Fritz [illeg.].[5] you are quite in error, but another time more of this – I have told you already I <u>must pay</u> all my Australian letters otherwise your plan is good. but if Willy should arrive by Trieste should not you come here to see him directly – dear Pauline seems inclined to return, if they have only money for both – Mrs S.[6] sent me word, that she would do all she could to help poor P. to bear her grief – thank God she is with such kind friends – I must now conclude I am in great disorder, and shall be so till I enter my own lodging on 1st of Nov: you are right; occupation is the only consolation – I try to be always busy – rubbing furniture[7] washing horsehair[8] – curtains et et and taking long walks, so with the help of Him, I hope to get through the span of life, still awarded to me.

God bless you ever and ever

yours affectionately
A.C.

Address: Miss Clairmont,/ South Street, Epsom,/ Surrey, England.
Front postmark: Baden/ $^{11}/_{10}$ / 4.E; EPSOM/[illeg.]
Rear postmark: FM/14 O 14 /1856

Unpublished. Text: M.S., Pf. Coll., CL'ANA 0393

---

1 On 13 September 1856, Claire expressed that Knox should "bear his share" with regards to assisting the family financially, telling Antonia to write to Knox to ask him to send fifty pounds for Wilhelm's return passage (*CC* II: 590).

2 Clearly, by 6 June, Pauline had not yet received any letters with news of Emily's and Charley's deaths.

3 Mr. Mitchell, who assisted Claire with her opera box. On 5 June 1856, Claire told Antonia that she would not be receiving any money from Mitchell until August (*CC* II: 552). On 12 June, she told Antonia that she would go to Cheltenham or Tunbridge if she received money from Mitchell (p. 553). In her letter of 21 June, she reiterated her hope that Mitchell would send her money by August (p. 557). On 9 August 1856, she optimistically wrote that Mitchell would send her all that he owed her by the twentieth of August and that she intended to pay her lawyer's bill and keep the remainder for Wilhelm. She blamed her lack of money on the short opera season (p. 577). Finally, on 23 August, she told Antonia that she had written to Mitchell to ask for her money but that he had not responded. As a result, she expected not to hear from him for another week or two (p. 581), a delay that "vexed" her immensely (p. 583). On 13 September 1856, she informed Antonia that she had been to London to see Mitchell as she had hoped to let her box for two years. He apparently offered her only £220 for the year, attributing the low price to the opening of another opera company in Drury Lane. Claire was bitterly disappointed as she expected to get a minimum of £300 and therefore declined the offer (p. 590).

The Athenaeum of 1846 advertised that tickets for a performance by the Sacred Harmonic Society at Exeter Hall were available from "Mr. Mitchell, 39, Charing-cross" who was described as a "principal Music-seller" ([London: James Holmes, 1846], p. 611). *The Saturday Review* of 3 February 1866 noted that tickets for *Tobias* by Charles Gounod were available at "all the Libraries and Music-sellers': Mr. Mitchell's, Old Bond Street" ([London: Spottiswoode and Co., 1866], p. 149).

4 respective.

5 Fritz's surname is indicated by a single illegible upper-case letter.

6 Mrs. Suttor, Pauline's employer and Willie Suttor's mother.

7 Applying oil to furniture.

8 Horsehair was used in furniture production in the nineteenth century, specifically as a stuffing for chairs or as a fabric to cover furniture.

78 • Antonia Clairmont to Claire Clairmont

Baden 241. 18th Oct 1856.

My dearest Claire!

How sorry I am to hear you are always unwell, and cannot keep a servant to nurse you, and then to think, it is all owing to your kindness and generosity to me and the poor dear angels above; though I regret we are not together to assist and support each other yet I am glad I did not accept your invitation to come over; what a burden I should have been to you; I cannot but feel very lonely, the more for~~at~~ being kept at home by a bad cold and cough with a little fever; I shall try to find a few lessons; occupation would be the best cure for me. having been accustomed to constant activity and useful labour, think what a void my life must be – if it were not for the hope of the dear children, I would take children to board and lodge, or set up a school or take a small farm or anything but the complete idleness in which I live now – society disgusts me, only the two old ladies of which I wrote last I like to see, but they live very far off, a good half hours walk, so we can never spend the evening together, I mostly give them a call in the afternoon when I take my walk, as long as the wheather[1] will permit~~s~~ me to do it; I see by the newspaper that both the Operahouses will open for a few nights; isn't that quite uncommon, and will you not derive any profit from it?[2] I have now read the letters dear Pauline wrote to poor Char.[3] and E. would to God, I knew whether they have received all the news; I tremble for her life, she is so affected by the loss of poor dear Sidi and her anxiety and foreboding on Charleys account so great I wrote to her directly, and told her how kind you were to me, and how your assistance not only helped to cheer the last days of Ch: but also enabled me to bear the burthen of my sufferings more easily; how kind my other friends were; I think it will be some consolation in their depth of grief, to know I was not left alone, but supported by love and kindness: you once mentioned my sister and Gorice–[4] the least has been done by her – one single letter is all I saw from her hand – no sympathy there – I must conclude now – I live in the most dreadful disorder – all my things in trunks and packages about me, and cannot enter my lodging before the first Nov: then it wants cleaning – awfully long – good bye my dearest Claire believe me ever yours affectionately

A.C.

Count Mensdorf has found a governess, and sends his best thanks to you.[5] in the moment of sealing this a letter of dear Willy's arrived, but brings nothing new; it is 15th June, he mourns poor Sidis loss – my letter announcing it has been nearly 4 months on the road – so we may hope that they know all by this time, and also that the letter with the bill is now in Paula's hands; and I hope he will come directly as soon as he has the means in his hands – he says – "you may trust to my doing my utmost to return directly as soon as I have got rid of my affairs here,[6] but as yet nothing has been decided we had hoped to sell ~~it~~ underhand; but he says, if all is over I must first take a place to earn my passage money – he says nothing of debts so perhaps, all will go better than we think – I shall not now write, but with the next mail; Oh blessed thought that the means to return are already in his hands and I shall do my utmost to find lessons, to have a little ready money against his return ~~and~~ or to pay the bill when he has drawn it – he says his health is good, but in going uphill he has short breath – his letter is dated Armidale – but I shall direct Brucedale – for by the time ~~this~~ our present letters arrive~~s~~ he must have left Armid: most probably the affair~~s~~ will be ~~con~~ dissolved when the year is up[7] – Good bye dearest Claire – we now know him inclined to return, and may hope all will go well. his letter is German otherwise I would have copied out all he says of the concern, but it is in fact not more than I said already. Good bye.

Address: Miss Clairmont/ South Street,/ Epsom/Surry, England.
Front postmark: BADEN/ [illeg.]/$_{10}$/ 4.E.
Rear postmark: FT/ 22 OC 22/ 1856

Unpublished. Text: M.S. Pf. Coll., CL'ANA 0344

1 Antonia's spelling for "weather".

2 On 21 June 1856, Claire told Antonia that she was unable to join her at Weikersdorf, as she hoped to sell her opera box and that she was consulting various people about the matter (*CC* II: 557).

3 Charley.

4 Antonia's sister, Marie Rismondo, lived in Görz which is the German name for Gorizia. See CL'ANA 0401.

5 Antonia wrote the concluding paragraph on a separate insert.

6 Kangaroo Hills.

7 In August 1856, Claire wrote to Antonia and expressed the hope that Wilhelm was at Brucedale with Pauline. She stated that Brucedale was "well inhabited," with many wealthy families residing in the area, and she believed that Wilhelm would get assistance from these families (*CC* II: 576).

Wright reports the resale of Kangaroo Hills to William Dangar in 1857 or 1858. The Allinghams then purchased the run from Dangar in 1858. Wilhelm's letters from 1857 confirmed that he was working by that point at the Cuba run.

79 • Antonia Clairmont to Claire Clairmont

15 Baden 19th Oct 856[1]

My dear Claire.

Your eloquence is irresistible, so much so, that the letter to Knox is now actually written and sealed and shall go~~n~~ off this very afternoon. it is true that he was the instigator of the whole plan, Willy might be here well settled, and out of all difficulty if it had not been for this journey;[2] you say I praised Knox, and so I did; he intended to take care of poor Charley's education when he took him over to England, and I have no doubt would have done all, he promised, if the poor boy's health had allowed him to stay there, but he never sent any money to ~~Austria~~ me, never; I cannot enter, into an explanation of all that happened after Charleys return, but certain it is, that Knox's interference with both W. and Ch. has turned out most unfortunate as you say harum scarum[3] – let me turn my thoughts to dear W's affairs. Knox, in his letter of the 24th Aug. says, he has had a letter of P. and as she does not seem to know of all W's circumstances, I have tried to tell him, how affairs stand, and begged him if he would and could send W. £50 for his return, I would then most thankfully repay him, if only now he could come forward to assist us; I said also, that I wished to write to W. by the second of Oct, and begged him to answer me directly, whether I could inform W. that he – Knox – would send off the money on the 5th with the mail to Pauline, and that he W. could take his steps accordingly. I have just written to Willy, and as I told you in my last, I would do directed to Pauline, and in it I begged her, if Willy should be prevented of returning for want of money, to ask Mr S.[4] to advance £50, and I should then return it as soon as possible, in good bills on a Sydney house; by means of Mr Maier[5] so now my dear Claire I think all is done, that was in my power; and I shall not now write to W. till I hear from K. if he refuses, I shall not mention it at all to W., only repeat to him what I have now been telling him for the last 3 months continually that he should return instantly, if possible I shall speak the more decidedly, as I see the dear Boy has a decided preference for Europe, and feel convinced he will be happier here than there – for he has good prospects here; kind and powerful friends, and love and friendship will receive and greet him: his letters to you and me agree quite, in the first I had from March he tells me direct to Brucedale,[6] and in the one from May, to Kangaroo Hills, so I can only conclude that the catastrophe,[7] has been for some time postponed by the desperate arangement he mentiones, he also says, he cannot tell me anything for it does not depend upon him – I cannot send my letters without paying – we must pay for Australian letters: I wish my dear Claire I could do ~~any~~ something to lighten the load of care you have on your mind; but I think we may be quiet now; the bill ~~with~~ of £100 is on the road, that will be a great consolation to poor W. perhaps it will suffice for his journey; dear P. will perhaps like better to stay a year longer, than to quit the family so abruptly, she has been with so long; we can then also receive her better, when Willy is once settled; and do not fear the dear boy will want assistance if here – I will save and economise the whole winter against his return; I don't know about telling him about dear T.[8] I wanted to let it all alone; but I am not going to write just now; till I have K's[9] answer; so can ponder over it; last autumn, when we expected him home,[10] I wrote once that I had already tooked[11] out a little wife for him, but if he did not come soon I would give her to Charley; the letter I lately received was an answer to this; and he says, he would willingly take from my hand and on my recommendation a companion for life; it would give his loghut a more cheerful look et et I was touched to the heart, though he was but joking; he is the most gentle and affectionate creature on earth; but the more care we must take, the more careful of how we use the influence his kindness of heart allows us: to see him happily married is or rather will be my chief wish, for now I think only of his coming. Good bye my dear Claire, I hope you will tell me that you are in better health and your strength increasing, and I greatly regret you cannot go to Italy – of your last letter I have one question to answer, which in honesty I must – it is what you say about Tetty's health; she is well, but she has lost a brother a charming highly talented young man of Charley's age, his friend; he died of a pulmonary complaint; we all thought he must have injured his health on a tour he made in the autumn and never recovered – Poor dear. Tetty is 18, about my size rather smaller, and particularly well made and far from romantic; her mother a woman of good sense, good housekeeper and not at all a fine lady, ~~but~~ and she loved all my children as her own.

ever yours affect: A.C.

Address: Miss Clairmont/South Street/ Epsom./ Surrey, England.
Front postmark: EPSOM/ SP2[illeg.]/185[illeg.]; BADEN/ $^{21}/_{9}$/4.E.
Rear postmark: [illeg.]/24SP24/ 1856

Unpublished. Text: M.S. Pf. Coll., CL'ANA 0390

1 Antonia wrote October for the date. However, the postmarks on the envelope indicated September. It is possible that the envelope has been incorrectly matched with the letter.

2 On 6 September 1856, Claire encouraged Antonia to write to Knox to ask him to support Wilhelm's return to Europe. Claire proposed that Antonia tell Knox that she could no longer live without Wilhelm but that neither she nor Claire had sufficient money to pay for Wilhelm's return passage. Claire further exhorted Antonia to tell Knox that Wilhelm's continued absence and exposure to hardship would result in Antonia's demise (*CC* II: 585). Claire noted too that she would not be able to write directly to Knox herself, as such an appeal could be problematic (p. 585).

3 On 16 August 1856, Claire told Antonia that Knox's recklessness had caused all their problems and she described him as "harum-scarum himself and despising Prudence" (*CC* II: 578).

4 Mr. Suttor.

5 See CL'ANA 0350, CL'ANA 0383 and CL'ANA 0385.

6 Wilhelm clearly recognized that he would have to leave Kangaroo Hills and he asked his aunt to write to him care of Pauline at Brucedale, Bathurst (CL'ANA 0067). However, his 24 May 1856 request that Claire address her letters to Kangaroo Hills suggested he hoped that the enterprise might not fail after all (CL'ANA 0071). But by 1857 he was working on the Cuba run and by 1858 he was working on Kameruka station for the Twofold Bay Pastoral Association.

7 The loss of Kangaroo Hills.

8 Tetty Strimasko, a young lady whom Antonia hoped Wilhelm would eventually marry. She featured fairly regularly in Antonia's letters. On 23 August 1856, Claire announced that she wanted Wilhelm to marry an attractive, rich and decent woman, and that she had someone in mind for him (see *CC* II: 582). Antonia preferred Tetty for her daughter-in-law. But neither would prevail.

9 Knox.

10 Antonia wrote this letter on two sets of pages. There is an X before the word "home" to indicate the beginning of the second set of 2 pages.

11 Spelled as such.

80 • Antonia Clairmont to Claire Clairmont

241. Baden 25-10-56.

My dearest Claire

Your last gives me great uneasiness; if a complaint begins in the autumn it is so difficult to get rid of it; cold and damp are your great enemies, and that is just the season for them – I am so glad you have got such a kind affectionate friend, and cannot but grieve, I am not near you, to nurse and cheer you, with the hope of seeing our dear children – for it is that sustains me; and indeed my dear Claire you ought not give way – you have so much strength of mind, and religion, and besides all has been done on our side – so now we will rest on Him from whom success must come – I do not what to say about your sending £50 with the nov. mail – Willy does not say anything about debts in his last – perhaps affairs have turned out more favourable than he expected;[1] so he can take the bill, which must have arrived by this time for the journey; I shall tell him so and in fact have said so in several letters; and if Knox sends fifty, I think it will do – and so do not worry think rather of the time when they are here – and believe me if all goes well, and Willy is married – we shall not be happy if you are not with us; you must come and be with us, then we shall be happy – when I see my new friends, the two old ladies I mentioned, I always think how comfortable we might live together – and I am sure our air and climate would do you good – I am not yet settled and in order but one thing can tell you: our water has a little tinge of sulphur, and that has a most wholesome influenze on the bowels the baths I have now left off, on account of a bad cough which I caught in my present unsettled state – and which I am nursing most carefully to get rid off[2] before the cold sets in; I have hopes of letting my room but none with regard to lessons there being two English mistresses established here; and I, being old and sad and serious there is hope for me – now good bye my dear Claire, I most fervently hope to hear from your next that you are regaining strength and health and believe me ever yours affect:

A.C.

I am always afraid Pauline cannot leave the Suttors[3] so soon as to come with Willy and if he is once gone, she will come no more.

Envelope: Miss Clairmont/ South Street, Epsom/ Surrey, England
Front postmark: BADEN/ $^{26}/_{10}$/ 4. E.
Rear postmark: F[illeg.]/ 29OC29/ 1856

Unpublished. Text: M.S. Pf. Coll., CL'ANA 0345

---

1 Wilhelm confirmed the financial loss he suffered as a result of the Kangaroo Hills experiment in his letter of 29 March 1857, in which he recorded having no money left after the dissolution of the partnership (CL'ANA 0070).

2 Antonia misspelled the word "of". On 2 August 1856, Claire advised Antonia to tell Wilhelm and Pauline to monitor the color and quality of their stools as a way of prolonging their lives, explaining the portents of these indicators. She also recommended a daily dose of cod liver oil and an avoidance of "costiveness" (constipation). She advised beer and meat for Wilhelm (*CC* II: 574).

3 Antonia's concern was financial, as her letter to Claire confirmed (see CL'ANA 0347). Claire's gift of £50 to Pauline and Wilhelm made it possible for Pauline to book her passage home. By April 1857, Pauline was able to leave Australia for Europe, while Wilhelm used part of the money to make himself presentable for readmission into society (CL'ANA 0070).

81 • Antonia Clairmont to Claire Clairmont

241. Baden. 1 Nov. 1856.

My dearest Claire.

I can only write a line, today, being in all the turmoil of moving; I shall be glad and happy to be once again in a settled state of order and cleaness – I am also happy in having let my spare room, to a widow lady, a very nice person; the first quarter I shall have no profit, having had some furniture to buy, but afterwards it will pay half of my rent; and besides, I can now do without a servant, *[1] which will be the great saving in money as well as temper, for these young girls are pert useless, rude, and good for nothing and I shall thank God to have done with them: your last of 25th causes me great uneasiness;[2] to know your ailing and suffering is most painful – if you were here it would be much better; I wish I could comfort you; if Willy does not enter into details, it is because the dreadful distance hinders him, to take our advise, even if we could give any; he must act for himself, he cannot wait for our answers, think that 8th months must pass, and all is changed in so long a time; I think of the dear children every moment of the day – now they must have all the letters,[3] and have no doubt but they will do all they can to get away, at least Willy, and I think Pauline will come too, I don't think she will seperate from her brother; do not fret and sorrow so much, they are in His guidance! to his will let us resign ourselves! I have been Währing[4] to see the graves of the dear angels – I found a wreath of white roses on Sidi and Emmy's – dear little Hermine had taken it out;[5] it is here the fashion to ornament the graves in a most expensive and fanciful manner for All soul's day which is to morrow[6] – but I had only some flowers planted; but here is a poor deformed girl, and I got some clothing for her, and a poor sick boy and I do for him what I can and I hope the dear children in Heaven will be pleased with it – the rum and ising glass[7] I got and made it, but ½ an ounce me gives 10 glasses full it does me good but thanks for your kind offer; I hope you go on satisfied with your doctor: good bye ever yours affect:

A.C.

Address: Miss Clairmont/ ~~South Street, Epsom/ Surrey~~. England
Mrs Bartlett/ West by [illeg.]/ Brighton/ Surrey.
Front postmark: BADEN/ 2/11/4. [illeg.]
Rear postmark: [illeg.] ON THAMES/NO 7/1856; FF/5 NO 5/1856

Unpublished. Text: M.S., Pf. Coll., CL'ANA 0346

1 Antonia drew a star in the letter and then added the following words next to an X at the top of the page: "for before I was alone in the whole of the first floor".

2 The letter has been lost.

3 Informing them of Emily's and Charley's deaths.

4 See CL'ANA 0042.

5 Mrs. Drathshmid's niece. See CL'ANA 0364.

6 See CL'ANA 0347.

7 Antonia meant to write "isinglass". Isinglass was a form of gelatin and was a made from the bladders of certain fish (The Editors of Encyclopaedia Britannica. "Sturgeon". *Encyclopaedia Britannica Online*. Encyclopaedia Britannica Inc., n.d. Web. 24 October 2015. http://www.britannica.com/animal/sturgeon-fish). It was used in the production of beer and also to treat consumptive patients.

82 • Antonia Clairmont to Claire Clairmont

241. Baden 8th Nov. 1856.

My dearest Claire.

How shall I thank your sending off 50 pds – to the dear children; God be thanked, they are not without kind and loving friends! what relief it will be to them to find themselves enabled to undertake the journey directly, for I am sure Willy will be, for setting off directly, also Pauline, if she ~~g~~ can leave the Suttors so suddenly; if once I had proofs in hands, that they know all, I cannot tell you how I tremble to hear how they bore it; I am glad your health is improving, to be sure an attendant must be a great comfort to you, especially one of the better sort; a mere menial is disagreeable to have always about one. I have now parted with the servant girl I had, since I have let my room, I am not so entirely alone – my cough is rather worse and sore throat added owing to the bustle of moving – but now I will nurse myself carefully; the isingglass[1] I have taken regularly; but you cannot think how the rum affects me; for two hours I have violent beating of the heart, and such a pulsation – but when it is over I sleep very quietly – Yesterday I had to go to town; I missed a chest of books, it had been left behind but was found – I then went from the Landstrasse[2] to Mrs. Strimasko[3] it is a great way off, I had a thick shawl on, and so I caught the sore throat; I am sorry to say Tetty does not look well, but no wonder seeing me affects them all, they are so good and affectionate; just the day before they had been to the churchyard, to take whreaths to the beloved tombs.[4] but I scolded Mrs. Strimasko for it; the poor young girls suffer too much – thank you dear Claire for your repeated invitation; your society would surely do me good, we would have such chats but, selfdenial and resignation is all our lot – besides I could not be a burthen upon you, and income in England, would be as nothing – here I live extremely cheap – fuel is very cheap and so is rent; especially now my room is let – my dinner comes to about 10 p. I have it from an eating house; a cup of coffee for breakfast and some tea for supper is all I want; my wash I contrive cheaply; but in England I could make no contrivances, all would fall upon you – I shall write to Knox some of these days may I tell him of your remittance? I am just preparing my isingglass – for I take it in the evening – as I mostly cough in the night – Good bye dearest Claire warmest thanks and blessings: all letters have come regular –

ever yours most gratefully
A.C.

Address: No envelope.

Unpublished. Text: M.S., Pf. Coll., CL'ANA 0347

1 See CL'ANA 0346.
2 The third municipal district of Vienna, spelled Landstraße.
3 Tetty's mother.
4 Sidi, Charley, and Emily were buried in Währing cemetary. See CL'ANA 0042 and CL'ANA 0346.

83 • Antonia Clairmont to Claire Clairmont

241. Baden 15–11–56.

My dearest Claire.

Your last of the 8th reached me very soon on the 11th, and I would have answered it directly for I was much affected with the idea of your sufferings, but I have been obliged to keep my bed for a couple of days with fever and cold, but I am quite well now, and my cough is thank God disappeared; I really think it is owing to the isinglass[1] which I have taken regularly till now, for in general my coughs last a long time and are very painful and tedious; the last I had three years ago, I had to keep my bed 4 or 5 weeks, then I had sweet dear Sidi to nurse me – Oh my dear Claire you suffered with me, these holydays; I did not know you were aware of our customs – how grateful I am to ~~the~~ my dear friends sympathy. I wish indeed the winter were over – but be sure that I attend to your advice to take care of myself – I have got acquainted with another family, and we meet sometimes, and they are all very kind, and attentive, so is Mrs. A.[2] my lodger; she has a son established in London, as musicmaster, and has herself been there, and speaks English – all this makes her a very agreeable companion to me; and do not think of sending me any money; thank God I have enough my wants are but few. but how happy I am to think the dear children have now the means in hands to pursue their journey, may their love and affection repay you, for I cannot thank you enough – have you no news of the new road? when is it to be opened? I see nothing of it in our papers.

I trust to hear your health is better and then your spirits will rise with your strength – we have both had to suffer and must look to a better world beyond – I feel quite resigned to His will, and so are you; – I must conclude now with my best blessings and love to you. ever yours

A.C.

I have not yet written to K.[3] you will tell me –

Address: Miss Clairmont/ Mrs Bartlett's/ West by Thames/
Kingston, Surrey,/ England.
Front postmark: BADEN/ [illeg.]/11/1. E.
Rear postmark: [illeg.]/[illeg.]/1856

Unpublished. Text: M.S., Pf. Coll., CL'ANA 0348

---

1 See CL'ANA 0347.

2 Mrs. Artaria. See CL'ANA 035. Rupert Ridgewell notes that the Artaria firm was established in Vienna in 1768 by Carlo and Francesco Artaria and that, by 1776, they had begun to trade in printed sheet music. Later, they published music under their own name. See *Music Publishing in Europe: 1600–1900* (Berlin: Berliner Wissenschafts-Verlag, 2005), p. 93. *A Handbook for Travellers in Southern Germany* recommends Artaria's Bookstore: "At Artaria's 1151, Kohlmarkt, engravings, guide-books, and excellent maps may be purchased" (*A Handbook for Travellers in Southern Germany* [London: John Murray, 1857], p. 193).

3 Knox.

84 • Wilhelm Gaulis Clairmont to Claire Clairmont

[28 November 1856]

My dearest aunt.

I recd yours of the 1st April but was so immersed in business that I could not find time to answer it when a second letter of yours come by the May mail makes it an imperative duty to me to write to you at once.[1] I will try and wake up for my silence by a good long letter, although I have in fact neither much nor good news to communicate to you. What with the sad, sad news from home[2] and the failures of my plans here this year[3] has been one of uncommon hardship and trials to me, indeed were it not for my spirit of opposition I think I should have sunk under the pressure of melancholy and disastrous news pouring in from all quarters; but depressed as I am I cannot but feel a hatred towards a fate which continues its hottest persecutions on me and I shall therefore exert my utmmost energies to carry my point in defiance of my fate. I cannot tell you what has been my grief about my poor dear sisters; healthy and blooming as I had them still before my eyes from the time we parted I cannot persuade myself to believe that they are now no more. So often I indulged in the sweetest dreams of how happy we should all be when I returned again, and how they would look and what alterations would have taken place in them and now, if ever I do return instead of all this nothing awaits me but the melancholy satisfaction of visiting their graves; and this is not all, for I can never dispell from my mind the gloomy thought that poor dear Charley too is perhaps consigned to his eternal resting place while I am writing these lines. I dont know whether to advise Mama to come out here with him or not. I take it for granted that on the score of his health this would be advisable but there comes the question whether now that my affairs have taken so unfavorable a turn I should be able to maintain them here; and supposing they did come and friends then failed us what would be the result? this reminds me of the glorious news you give me in your last letter that you were about sending £100 to my mother; it is the only good news I have heard for these years. I cannot say how thankful I am to you for this dearest aunt; it is a relief to me and has made my heart quite light despite sorrows and disappointment for whatever difficulties may befal me I care not, I shall always be able to fight my way through them. but it is not so with her, she is now on the decline of life; she has not the impetus not the elasticity of youth to carry her through; I am sure if you had given me a thousand pounds it would not have given me half the pleasure & satisfaction as the hundred to my mother just at this moment.

I am afraid you would think my letter very imperfect if I did not say something on business too; but as I now forget how much I have told you already in my last I hardly know where to begin. Our plan now, as we find that we cannot carry on much longer is to shear in spring as early as we can and then sell off it will [~~illeg.~~] greatly depend on the prices ranging at the time we have to sell whether we make a good job of it. the speculation in itself is perfectly sound and would prove very remunerative if we only had a little more capital. Our net income from the station that is after the working expenses have been deducted would amount (provided the debts were all paid off) to about £1500 or £500 each which is equal to 16 per-cent on the capital employed so that we could afford to borrow capital at 8 percent and then still have a profit of 8 percent on it. but the difficulty is to borrow as we cannot give security; the previous owner holding a mortgage on stock & station. As things stand with us at present our stumbling block consists in a heavy bill of £2500 due in August 1858;[4] we could by dint of a deal of [illeg.] and pushing carry on till then, but we {tear}could not meet that bill out of our current revenue and as there is in the absence of any {tear} no reasonable probability of our being able to effect {tear}a loan for that purpose it is not very enticing to go on with the [~~illeg.~~] sacrifice of time and labour at a risk of failing after all in two years time. I hope dearest aunt you are in better health now and pray do not deny to yourself those comforts so essential to your wellbeing; it would be very well if you could get rid in a decent manner of your operabox, for not to mention the pecuniary loss you are put to by the uncertainty of its returns I think the worry and anxiety has a very prejudicial effect on your health. Now goodbye dearest aunt pray write very soon & give my best compts. to Col. & Mrs. Pringle and Violet and believe me dear aunt

your affectionate nephew W.G. Clairmont

Address: Aerogramme. Miss Clairmont/ care of Messrs Haggard & Hale[5]/ 2 Angelcourt Throgmorton street./ City/ London.
Front postmark: PAID/GZ/28NO28/1856

Unpublished. Text: M.S. Pf. Coll., CL'ANA 0069

1 While Wilhelm's letter was undated, the postmark on this aerogramme reads "28NO28" (28 November). In this letter, Wilhelm mentioned the deaths of his sisters and the hope that Charley was still alive. Sidonia died on 29 January 1856 while Emily died on 2 March 1856. Charley would die on 7 May 1856. Wilhelm had no knowledge of his sisters' deaths when he wrote to Claire on 24 May 1856. His letter of 3 September 1856 suggested the possibility of returning to Vienna in case Charley should "meet his doom" (CL'ANA 0073).

2 The deaths of his sisters.

3 The failure of Kangaroo Hills.

4 As per their agreement with William Dangar, Wilhelm and Duboc were paying off the purchase price in installments.

5 The London broker firm of Messrs. Haggard, Hale, and Pixley.

85 • Wilhelm Gaulis Clairmont to Claire Clairmont

[1 December 1856]

My dearest aunt.

I have rec^{d} two letters from you one dated July & the other the ~~middle of~~ 1$^{st.}$ August.[1] I wrote to you my last note on Octob. 4th – I cannot tell you dearest aunt how grateful I am to you for writing to me so often for though all the tidings you give us from Europe are so melancholy still the desire to hear from the few we have left ~~still~~ increases in proportion

You must not be angry with me for writing such short letters but I am literaly drowned in business for we are shearing just now; besides I have a sore finger which although a mere ~~fl~~ trifle is still enough being just on the tip of the finger to prevent me from writing more than the most urgent correspondences.

I wrote to Mama last week explaining to her my present position that I have partly sold my share in the station,[2] but that I have reason to suppose that the party whom I was trating with will try to back out of the bargain on account of my now refusing to comply with a condition made (& to which I formerly acceded) viz my taking the management of other stations at Port Philip,[3] ~~but~~ which of course would involve my further stay in the colony which I now wish to leave at once. I have recd £100 on account already which I devoted to paying off my debt so that I am at any rate free of that – The remainder still due to me would just suffice to cover my expenses to Europe, whither I intend starting as soon as I have finished here which I trust may be about the beginning of February; should I not be able to get the remaining sum I shall make use of Mama's bill of exchange to raise sufficient money to carry me home. I think I shall arrive somewhere about June. Pauline says she will go with me; but the distance is so great ~~there is now a~~ the letters take 8 weeks there & back there is no possibility of arriving at any settled plan; we shall therefore have to leave that till we meet at Sydney. when we shall be in a better position to judge as to the most eligible mode of going home. I can hardly tell you dear aunt how I rejoice to see you & Mama again but the time seems to me still very long.

Give yourself no concern about my health. I assure you my life here is so regular and simple that it is next to impossible to take ill. my health is perfect & I am constantly taking ~~a~~ great care of it. so pray dont fret on my account, but rather take care of yourself & raise your spirits as high as you can. I was glad to hear that Her Majesty's opera has opened again but I see from the papers that Covent Garden[4] is going to be rebuilt therefore I think it would be best to get rid of so obnoxious an investment before the renewed opposition becomes formidable. Goodbye now dearest aunt I cannot tell you how anxious I am to see again the cliffs of Old England. it will be a blessed day. I live now already in my thoughts at least more in the old world than in the new. believe me ever your affectionate nephew

W.G.C.

Kangaroo Hills
~~Nov~~ December 1st 1856.
Miss Clairmont,

Address: No envelope.

Unpublished. Text: M.S. Pf. Coll., CL'ANA 0068

---

1 These letters have been lost.

2 There is no record of a partial sale made of Wilhelm's share in the station.

3 The bay was named for Governor Arthur Phillip (1738–1814), the first governor of New South Wales (Fletcher, B.H. "Phillip, Arthur (1738–1814)", *Australian Dictionary of Biography*. National Centre of Biography, Australian National University. Web. 1967. 20 May 2015. http://adb.anu.edu.au/biography/phillip-arthur-2549/text3471).

4 See CL'ANA 0404 and CL'ANA 0373.

86 • Antonia Clairmont to Claire Clairmont

241. Baden 21-12-56.

My dearest Claire.

your letters always give me consolation, may God Almighty prove your predictions true and we have the happiness of seeing the dear children as you say! I should have answered you directly, but for the circumstance of my last containing already the answer to the chief question of yours. believe me my writing to him would have no effect; I do intend to write again, but it will be of no use – I did not mean to say that Willy in commencing his present undertaking did in any way rely on Knox, but having formerly made a voluntary proposition of placing such monies in Willy's hands, he might have thought it likely in case of need to obtain assistance – in spite of all you say, and with all due attention to your view of Bankrupty – it makes me unhappy and I fear for the dear boy's health and spirits. Tetty I have not seen the whole winter – my position is pecularly delicate – my advances might encourage her – and Willy then have nothing to say to her[1] – only think that Knox has also sent a bust of poor dear Clary's to Australia, I heard so from a friend of Pauline's to whom she wrote it; she says it is a painful sensation to look at it, for though it is like yet the smile of death is upon it – he sent also one to Sidi I can never think with patience of it – dear Charley and Emmy dying what a sight for them – and poor Sidi – the shock to her affectionate mind – to see the features of a beloved sister, the necessitude of hiding it before the two others – but I did not allow the box to be opened – however in the evening of the same day she was taken ill, and died before the night was over – there was Emmy in the bed near her and Charley in the next room. Goodbye my dear Claire. I cannot say anything more – yours ever

gratefully A. C.

Address: Miss Clairmont/ West by Thames, Kingston/ Surrey,/ England.
Front postmark: BADEN/ $^{22}/_{12}$/ 4. E.
Rear postmark: FW/2[illeg.]DE 2 [illeg.]/1856

Unpublished. Text: M.S., Pf. Coll., CL'ANA 0349

1 See CL'ANA 0390.

87 • Antonia Clairmont to Claire Clairmont

241. Baden 26-12-56.

My dearest Claire.

It is really wonderful what sympathy there is between our thoughts – your questions about dear Tetty I partly answered in my last – I do not often see her, not knowing how Willy might be inclined, I must avoid raising hopes which might prove vain, so I am by no means sure that the marriage will take place, I cannot say it for certain – Willy may have fixed his affections on another, which is however not at all likely – her fortune is quite in order; £1500 she gets at her marriage and the same sum at her mother's death – Mrs S. has a fine large dwelling house in the Alservorstadt,[1] the rent of which is as sure as an English rentroll;[2] the girls being wards of Chancery their fortune is deposited at that office – there is not the least doubt or difficulty on that head; her health is good – I have just had a letter from her – and I thank you many times for entering so fully into my wishes on that point – but who knows what will happen! Mr Maier's illness is incurable and a very painful one – a cancer in the tongue dreadful – I can but offer my prayers to the Almighty to strengthen him in the sufferings that are before him! another reason of grief and nearer still I had, poor general Drathshmid has been very ill of the typhus fever – I don't know whether I told you that they lost their eldest son suddenly – it is just a year, he was shot by accident – it was a dreadful blow, and then the loss of poor Emmy whom they both loved as a daughter, and which affected them doubly, for herself and for Frederic's sake for he loved her so dearly, it will take years ere he recovers her loss, and so the poor parents had to mourn the death of one son and the happiness of the other.[3] he is now declared out of danger but so weak and reduced, that I hardly consider him so. – I don't think Willy ever gives a thought to politics, and now less than ever and being happily, a catholic, he would have nothing to fear from the immediate causes, of all these new institutions; and my fears and scruples do not go so far as to prevent his return or wish to go there myself – as you say the great point is to get him home – as to his affairs I spoke to nobody about them; ~~to~~ those few, to whom I told of his engagement for five years – find it quite natural that I should now desire him to return the only one likely to hear the truth is at Maier's, for there being a young man from Sydney at the counting house – I will write to Knox – but I can not laud him, for I never have; to own the truth, I am not well[4] inclined towards him, as dear Cläry's husband, I tried to think as well of him as I could for her sake, but now the less I hear of him, the better I like it;[5] but I shall write to him, though I do not hope he will do anything, that he did not propose himself – a party of pleasure were more to his taste; last year he wrote to Sidi, to come to Munich and join him in a tour through Switzerland – but never asked my consent – and begged her not to scruple but allow him as a brother to defray the expenses of the journey – of course I refused, and he was furious – he did nothing but work up the children against my authority and once or twice I remonstrated so you see I cannot praise him now, for he has done nothing to deserve it – let us turn from him and rather fasten upon the certainty that in future we shall have a more speedy exchange of letters than hitherto that thought is happiness indeed. Frederic D.[6] is still in Scottland, at Glasgow on business, and has not yet been to London – We have a sloppy wet winter one day it snows and freezes and the next it thaws – that is very disagreeable but the scenery is even in winter beautiful – Mrs Artaria, my lodger turns out terribly bad tempered – thanks for your letters they are a great consolation to me –

ever yours affect.

A. C.

Address: Miss Clairmont/ West by Thames, Kingston/ Surrey,/ England
Front postmark: BADEN/ $^{28}/_{12}$/4. E.
Rear postmark: FB/31 DEC 31/1856

Unpublished. Text: M.S., Pf. Coll., CL'ANA 0350

1 Mrs. Strimasko, Tetty's mother. Alservorstadt was a municipality of Vienna but was incorporated into the 8th and 9th districts after 1850.

2 Income from rentals.

3 On 12 May 1856, Claire expressed sadness over "poor young Mr. Drathsmid," whom Stocking incorrectly records as unidentified (*CC* II: 549). Emily was engaged to Frederic Drathshmid before her death. See CL'ANA 0233.

4 Antonia numbered the page here with the numeral "2".

5 Claire echoed similar sentiments on 26 July 1856 when she called Knox "a rash harebrained person" and his thoughts on the Australian enterprise "erroneous" (*CC* II: 572).

6 Frederic Drathshmid, Emily's fiancé.

88 • Wilhelm Gaulis Clairmont to Claire Clairmont

[29 March 1857]

My dearest aunt.

I duly recd your last letter dated Decbr. 1st[1] but being absent from Sydney longer than I expected I missed the last mail; you have however no doubt heard from P. what arrangements we propose to make. When I wrote my last to you from Kangaroo Hills I was under the impression that I should have no difficulty in making the £150 I was promised on the dissolution of our partnership concern On my arrival ~~here~~ in Sydney I found that it was quite hopeless to expect anything for the present at least, and the consequence was that I was without a penny so that I was compelled although most reluctantly to encroach on your cheque of £50 which you sent to P. in order to purchase the where with alls to present my self once more in civilized society which after a 2 years bush campaign I needed very badly.[2] The absence of funds of course put a categorical stop to my intended return to Europe; but in addition to that this latter would have been tantamount to a sacrifice of my £150 whereas by stopping here I have still every reasonable chance of recovering the sum in a year or two; moreover I had the offer of a situation from a large company[3] on most favourable conditions so that considering the loss of time, money etz I made up my mind to take a certainty here in preference to an uncertainty at home. My salary is £300 a year and besides a servant, a full supply of flour, meat, tea & sugar and a nice cottage with 6 rooms stables and outhouses etz:[4] this latter I attach most importance to as it enables me to offer you all a suitable home should you like to accept it. I confess that I do not feel quite as sanguine with regard to your acquiescence to my plan as that of Mama and considering your weak health and your long habituation to all the ease and comforts of a townlife I question whether you would feel comfortable in the Bush at any rate this consideration is enough to deter me from pressing you to urgently to come but I can say in favour of my proposal that my future home is in one of the most civilized districts of N.S.W. that it is within 24 hours sail from Sydney pr. steamer & that my cottage is only 18 miles from the landing place with a very passable road all the way; there is a doctor too only 15 miles off.[5] I will not however say any more on the subject as P. knows all the particulars & you will be able to talk it over all with her: I am now on my way to the Murumbidgee where I have some business for the C°. but in 6 or 8 mos. at furthest I shall be back to Twofold Bay[6] where my permanent quarters will be. I hope you will be satisfied with the arrangements we made for P's passage I believe the Waterloo[7] to be the safest vessel now in harbour & the captain is a very nice person & very highly connected. Goodbye dearest aunt I shall be very anxious to hear from you & Mama write soon & direct to the care of Messrs. Smith Croft & Co Sydney.[8]

Believe me dearest aunt

your affectionate nephew

WGC.

Liverpool[9]
March 29th 1857.

Address: No envelope.

Unpublished. Text: M.S. Pf. Coll., CL'ANA 0070

---

1 This letter has been lost.

2 See CL'ANA 0345.

3 The Twofold Bay Pastoral Association. See introduction to The Australian Sojourn, and CL'ANA 0075.

4 Wilhelm's new living space clearly contrasted with the small hut in which he resided on his arrival in Australia. See Gerald Walsh, *Pioneering Days* and CL'ANA 0209.

5 Dr. Richard Bligh. See CL'ANA 0077.

6 See CL'ANA 0072.

7 The *Sydney Morning Herald* of 15 May 1857 announced the departure of the Waterloo for London on 19 April (National Library of Australia, http://nla.gov.au/nla.news-page1495978, p. 12). The newspaper reported that Captain Young was at the helm and that passengers included "Miss Claramont . . . and 21 invalid soldiers". Pauline's last name was incorrectly spelled. See also CL'ANA 0072.

8 Smith, Croft and Company was originally started by Thomas Smith and his brother, Henry Gilbert Smith as "Smith Brothers, merchants, agents, and importers". Thomas Whistler Smith, son of Thomas Smith, assumed control of the business after the death of his father. He partnered with John Croft to form Smith, Croft and Company (V. Parsons. "Smith, Thomas Whistler (1824–1859)", *Australian Dictionary of Biography*. 1967. Web. 20 November 2014. http://adb.anu.edu.au/biography/smith-thomas-whistler-2673/text3729). *Lawson's Merchants' Magazine* lists Smith, Croft and Co as having shipped 17,430 ounces of gold in between January and August 1852 (B. Strousberg, (ed.) [London: T.A.A. Day, 1853], p. 371).

9 Liverpool is about 40 kilometers south-west of Sydney. Wilhelm would have traveled via Liverpool on his way to the Cuba station. Cuba was located some 631 kilometers south-west of Sydney on the Murrumbidgee River. Before going deeper into New South Wales, Wilhelm would have mailed his letter from Liverpool to Sydney and then to Europe. Liverpool did not feature very positively in new immigrant Sarah Davenport's account of her stay there. In her account of her move to Australia in the 1840s, Davenport explained that she was almost raped while lodging near a public house in Liverpool: "they was a lot of ruffians . . . they was a great deal of bad language used among them and fighting one among another and they was for pulling poor me from under the dray for their own brutal purpose we never spoke to them but we armed our selves my husband with a small axe and me with a carving knife i felt determined to defend myself" (Davenport's spelling. *No Place for a Nervous Lady*, p. 204).

89 • Wilhelm Gaulis Clairmont to Claire Clairmont

Cuba[1] July 2nd 1857

My dearest aunt.

I have to acknowledge (since the dispatch of my last to you about two mos. ago) the receipt of two letters from you 5th Janry. & 21st Febry. – I cannot tell you how thankful I am to you for writing so regularly, even Mama is not as punctual as you are in this respect, but more of her letters are lost than of yours as the postal communication between here & England is more direct than to Austria. You have by this time learnt all about our plans for the future, perhaps even ~~out of~~ (by the time you read this out of Pauline's own mouth.[2] I write to her by this post & ~~enclos~~ forward the letter to the care of your agents. O pray do make her write or write to me yourself the moment she arrives, for I shall feel uneasy till I receive news from her. the dangers & particularly for a single young lady are so many – at any rate we have as far as the judicious choice of a vessel goes, done all we could – the Waterloo[3] (she sailed on the 19th April) is not exactly one of the fastest but she is one of the safest staunchest vessels in the trade. Capt. Young is a very gentlemanly patron and has been captain for more than 20 years.

the vessel is one of Green's[4] with fine large cabins and well found in every respect what I chiefly regret is that the capt. delayed his departure so long that they will have to face the Horn[5] in the middle of winter. I shall be in great suspense till I hear which way Mama decides; still I would not like her to come out if she did it as a sacrifice & against her inclinations for if she felt unhappy hear we should all be miserable It is strange now Pauline can feel herself so much fascinated by Australia. if I thought it right to consult my inclinations I should have been back to old Europe long ago; the only thought that deters me from doing so even now is the unpleasant necessity of beginning a new career over again and the great loss of time consequent. For fear ~~your~~ my last letter may not have reached you I may repeat here that I only received the £50 you sent Pauline for me. as I just then returned from Kangaroo Hills to Sydney pennyless and was hard up for funds to defray my town expenses, recruite my wardrobe etz. this sum came most apropriately and I trust that although it was not spent in the manner you intended viz on my return you will not disapprove of the way in which it was laid out.[6] the second £50 which you talk of sending in March you need now of course not send – You know that I have now a salary of £300 a year.[7] this, house & all other necessaries of life (excepting clothing) being found besides \ goes a good way – living by myself I could save with economy from £200 to £240 a year. if Mama and P. join me our expenses will be a little more, but the pleasure of being together would far outway that. I am at present on the Murumbidgee[8] but my permanent quarters will be in Twofold Bay[9] a most delightful district within 24 hours sale[10] from Sydney the steamer gives {tear} I hope dear aunt you give {tear} concern on my account I mean in {tear}; you must remember I have a much {tear} situation now & need therefore do no hard work no more than I like to do, besides health is to me not only the only comfort I have, but it is also everything to me in point of business;

for although people may continue going to their counting houses in indifferent health nobody with a broken health could perform {tear} therefore I shall treasure health as the most viable capital I possess. I hope to hear in your next that you are quite recovered! I think the climate would suit you well out here, but not so the scarcity of doctors & drugshops. I wonder whether this latter circumstance has anything to do with the reputed healthiness of this country!?[11] I enclose a note to dear Mama pray be kind enough to forward it by the first opportunity & do be sure to let me know directly dear Pauline arrives. Believe me my dearest aunt

Your affectionate nephew
WGC.

The Pringles appear to have become quite French you always write they are either at Havre, Boulogne or Paris – Violet must be very beautiful; I hope dear girl she will marry well I do not mean in point of worldly connections, but of true love & happiness the latter is so often sacrificed to the first with people of the Pringles' position in life –

Please direct WGC. Kamaruka, Bombala[12]
Sydney. N.S.W.

Address: Aerogramme. Miss Clairmont/ Mess[rs] Haggard & Hale/
2 Angelcourt Throgmorton street/ City London.
Front postmark: PAID/ [illeg.]/ 1857; GUNDAGAI[13]/JY10/1857/N.S.W

Unpublished. Text: M.S. Pf. Coll., CL'ANA 0072

1 After the sale of Kangaroo Hills, Wilhelm worked on the Cuba run, 631 kilometers south-west of Sydney. John Peter, the licensee of Cuba, owned "15 runs in three districts" by 1859. According to the *Australian Dictionary of Biography*, Peter was considered "one of the most progressive pastoralists in the Murrumbidgee Area" ("Peter, John (1812–1878)," *Australian Dictionary of Biography*, National Centre of Biography, Australian National University. 1974. Web. 31 October 2014. http://adb.anu.edu.au/biography/peter-john-4392/text7157).

2 Pauline returned to England on 19 April 1857. See CL'ANA 0070.

3 See CL'ANA 0070.

4 George Green (1767–1849) founded the shipbuilding company Green's of Blackwell. See "The Green Blackwall Collection". Royal Museums Greenwich. Web. 5 May 2016. http://collections.rmg.co.uk/collections/objects/14199.html

5 Cape Horn, located at the southernmost part of Chile in South America. Known as the "graveyard of ships . . . more than one thousand ships and fifteen thousand lives" were lost over a period of 400 years. The completion of the Panama Canal in 1914 reduced the need for ships to navigate Cape Horn's waters ("Cape Horn". Web. 14 January 2015. http://libweb5.princeton.edu/visual_materials/maps/websites/pacific/magellan-strait/cape-horn.html).

6 See CL'ANA 0070.

7 See CL'ANA 0070.

8 At the Cuba run.

9 Patricia Clarke explains that Twofold Bay, located some 57 kilometers from Kameruka, started as a whaling station around 1828. She records that the town of Eden (located 2 kilometers from Twofold Bay) was surveyed and architecturally planned by 1842 and that, on 9 March 1843, land was first put up for sale. Scottish pastoralists and brothers – Peter, George, and Alexander Imlay – had arrived in the area in the 1830s and they soon acquired land for cattle and sheep stations stretching thousands of kilometers across the area. Kameruka was one of these stations. However, by 1844, due to financial losses resulting from drought, bush fires, and depreciation in the markets, the brothers were forced to sell their holdings to William Walker and Company (pp. 140–1). Vicky Small notes that when James and William Walker took over the Imlays' holdings, Kameruka comprised some eighteen thousand six hundred acres (*Kameruka*, p. 13). Small records that, at Pambula, the Walkers grew crops, built the Governor Fitzroy Hotel, the first National School, and "a splendid home, 'Oaklands'" (p. 14). Angela George explains that Pambula became the "seventh public school" in New South Wales, after the passing of the National Education Act of 1848. The school was opened in July 1849 in a "hut" provided by James Walker. Construction of a building with two rooms and two classrooms began in November 1849 (Angela George. "Pambula". *Monaro Pioneers*. Web. 7 December 2014. http://www.monaropioneers.com/towns/Pambula.htm). Yet, in spite of what looked like a financial success, the brothers were forced ultimately to sell their holdings in 1852 to the Twofold Bay Pastoral Association.

10 Wilhelm meant to write "sail".

11 See CL'ANA 0384 in which Claire derided the absence of qualified doctors in Hungary.

12 Bombala is a town in New South Wales in the Monaro region and is located about 483 kilometers south of Sydney and 60.5 kilometers from Kameruka. Tayor and Roach note that the Monaro plain extends from the coastal range to the Snowy Mountains in the southeastern area of New South Wales and that many rivers, such as the Snowy and the Murrumbidgee, cross the plain (G. Taylor and I. Roach, "Monaro Region, New South Wales". CRC Leme. 2003. Web. 7 December 2014. http://crcleme.org.au/RegLandEvol/Monaro.pdf). Major towns in the region include Bombala and Cooma. The word Monaro comes from the Indigenous Australian word, "Maneroo," which means "plains" (Pattrick Mould, "Aboriginals on the Monaro". Monaro Pioneers. From Felix Mitchell, "Back to Cooma". 1926. Web. 7 December 2014. http://www.monaropioneers.com/aboriginals.htm).

13 Town in New South Wales, along the Murrumbidgee River.

90 • Wilhelm Gaulis Clairmont to Claire Clairmont

[12 October 1857]

My dearest aunt. I have rec^d yours of the 6th July. you must excuse this little scrap of a letter the fact is I am in a great hurry to catch the mail and I thought a few lines better than nothing I wrote you a long letter by the September mail. I see dearest aunt that you have set an engine to work in my immediate vicinity to belabour me about health. I admire the intense energy which you display in prosecuting your object & still now thank you for the care & solicitude you thereby evince for my welfare but I wish for your own sake that you would not worry yourself so much I assure you I am as careful as a gouty old gentleman. I wrote to you in my last all about the excellent partie you intend for me but there is one point which struck me as suspicious; you say "of your own age" this maybe possibly a few years older in which case she would be just 10 years too old for me which I think would be an insurmountable difficulty.[1] the Waterloo was especially chosen on account of its being so safe & comfortable a vessel we rejected the Aberdeen[2] clippers because a friend of ours who had been a sailor told us that they were wretchedly off for "grub".[3] If it is ever my bright lot to sail I shall chance this latter difficulty. I am intensely anxious to hear about P.'s arrival & the decision Mama will arrive at. Goodbye dearest aunt I am of course perfectly well pray forward the enclosed to Mama & believe me dear aunt

your affectionate nephew
WGC.

Cuba Octob 12th[4] [1857]
Direct.
Mess. – Smith Croft & Co
Sydney N.S.W.

Address: No envelope.

Unpublished. Text: M.S. Pf. Coll., CL'ANA 0074

1 See CL'ANA 0351.

2 Clippers were ships with three masts, built primarily for speed and used from the mid-nineteenth century for the transportation of goods. Some of these "fast long-distance carriers" were constructed in Aberdeen, Scotland, and were known as Aberdeen clippers (W.H. Fraser [ed.], *Aberdeen, 1800–2000* [Scotland: Tuckwell Press, 2000], p. 76).

3 Colloquial term for food.

4 Wilhelm referenced Pauline's return to Europe, thereby dating this letter to 1857.

91 • Wilhelm Gaulis Clairmont to Claire Clairmont

[9 November 1857]

My dearest Aunt. I can hardly tell you how much I feel obliged & indebted to you for losing not a day in communicating to me our dear P.'s safe arrival. I was some distance from home when the English mails of August reached the blessed Murrumbidgee but I managed to fall in with a newspaper containing the last English intelligence from which to my great joy I gleaned the Waterloo's safe arrival; but considering the unpropitious season & ~~the~~ P's weak state of health (of which I only heard some 6 or 8 weeks after P's departure through dear Mrs Suttor) I still felt much uneasiness on her account; I therefore hurried home as fast as horses could go & there to my great joy I found your dear letter giving me as far as P.'s health & spirits are concerned even a better account than I dared to hope for. the same mail brought me a letter from my dear mother entreating me before she decided on so important a step to acquaint her with the precise state of my own wishes on the subject. I therefore write her the enclosed in reply assuring her that my own personal wishes tended to take me back to Europe as vigorously as ever. but that I consented to P's proposal[1] to stop here first because I had a home ready at once to offer to her & Mama & secondly because P. seemed to wish so fervently to stop here & Mama appeared at least indifferent as to whether she was here or there & if they were only happy & contented I for my part should soon become reconciled to the drawbacks of this country. If therefore by the time this letter arrives they have decided on and prepared for their departure let them not be affected by the contents of this on my account, for eternal vacillation is worse than even a step in the wrong direction; but if P. should after all find Europe not quite as insupportable as she expected & if she thinks herself bound to return here only for consistency's sake and the promise given me, let her be undeceived at once for I shall be anything but ~~under~~ disappointed if she do not return. As regards my 3 years' engagement I dare say I shall be able to get an abatement of the time ~~if~~ but of course I shall take no measures towards the attainment of that and until I receive positive intelligence as to Mamas steps. You must not think that my letters to Mama are written in German because they contain anything I should wish you not to know; it is because it comes more natural and unaffected to me to write to her in German than in English. but if P. be with you pray make her translate the letter to you I should like it as I have said some things more fully in it which I have no time to repeat here I must send Mama's letter through you for although she ~~may have~~ gives me her direction still I am afraid she may have left by this time. You are under a misapprehension with regard to my Murumbidgee sojourn I am not travelling I am resident the Company[2] have a branchestablishment here of which I am in temporary charge, it is true that it is on the very outskirts of civilisation and with a nasty hot climate but I shall be transferred to Kamaruka by Christmas where I shall have a nicer place. – Pray why do you give me instructions as to the selection of a wife? they are thrown away ~~at present~~ on me at present for I have dreamt 3 nights running of the beauty described by you with the £4000 how could I throw away such a chance![3] I am hitherto in excellent health; the approaching heat of the summer makes me feel languid, but that is because I past the two last summers in the delightful cool climate of New England[4] I daresay I shall get used to it again by & by. Pray write immediately I have written lately by nearly every mail your affectionate nephew

WGC

Cuba November 9th 1857.

Address: No envelope.

Unpublished. Text: M.S. Pf. Coll., CL'ANA 0075

---

1 "Proposal" was underlined three times.

2 The Twofold Bay Pastoral Association was formed in 1852 by pastoralists John Edye Manning, James A. L. Manning, William Montagu Manning, Robert Tooth, Edwin Tooth, Thomas Sutcliffe Mort, and John Croft. The Association purchased some 400,000 acres in the Monaro and Bega districts (Clarke, p. 249) and James Manning was selected as manager of the Association's holdings. Wilhelm and James Manning shared an alma mater at Hohenheim, Germany, although Wilhelm attended the college some ten years after Manning did (see CL'ANA 0355 for more information about Manning). German settlers were employed to make cheese at Kameruka in 1855 and James Manning was responsible for bringing German immigrants to the area (V. Small, *Kameruka*, p. 15). Mary Braidwood Mowle recorded the arrival of these immigrants in her diary entry of 10 March 1855: "The 'Caesar' with German emigrants arrived today – there being sickness on board she has been placed in Quarantine" (p. 258). According to Small, this first group of German immigrants arrived at Twofold Bay and walked to Kameruka to commence working there. James Manning's interest in employing Wilhelm probably stemmed from the fact that the two men had attended the same agricultural school in Hohenheim.

3 On 6 September 1856, Claire told Antonia of a young woman she hoped Wilhelm would marry. The twenty-four year old woman apparently was to receive £4,000 on her mother's death. Claire described the young lady as "a perfect pattern of womanhood" (*CC* II: 584).

4 William Gardner recorded the sale of Kangaroo Hills to Duboc and Wilhelm in 1855. If, as Wilhelm noted, he only spent two summers in New England, then the loss of Kangaroo Hills occurred some time before the summer of 1857. Wilhelm planned on participating in the January 1857 sheep clipping (CL'ANA 0073), which meant that Duboc and Wilhelm sold Kangaroo Hills some time between February 1857 and August 1857.

92 • Wilhelm Gaulis Clairmont to Claire Clairmont

[3 December 1857]

My dearest aunt.

I rec^{d} your kind note of the 8th Septbr. together with two from my dear mother & 2 from Pauline. But the latter at the date of her last had not yet joined Mama being engaged as it appears on an escapade all over the Continent and so I know nothing definite as yet as to Mama's intentions[1] – I wish however she may decide to stop, for I can plainly see that she dislikes the idea of coming out & to have her here after all the fatigues & risks of the journey to find herself then unhappy would indeed be the climax of wretchedness If Mama decides on remaining in Austria I shall of course join her there; I only hope we may come to some definite conclusion at last or we shall spend all our lives in the present state of vacillation I gather from the tone of your last letter although not from any direct expression in it that you found Pauline rather obstinately bent on her purpose and difficult to deal with. I have written to Mama on this subject at full length advising her provided she have made up her mind to stop and she find Pauline still persisting in her wild and extravagant practices not to put anything in the way of her return to Australia for I know she can be happy here and although I personally am similarly attached to her & would consider her many social accomplishments as the greatest acquisition to a dull country circle still I think it is better to live apart as friends than together like cats & dogs. As regards my health dearest aunt give yourself no concern for the present at least – I am well; I take great care too of my health avoiding everything that might be injurious – the Murumbidgee you know is perhaps the driest climate in the world and in sofar agrees with me – it amounts not simply to an exclusion of rain but actually of every~~thing~~ particle of humidity from the atmosphere during the summer months. in proof thereof I can relate you the following incident which occurred to me during [~~illeg.~~] my last sojourn on this river. – I one day went before the sheepwashing commenced to see what repairs might be required at that establishment to put everything in working order – While examining the rafters to see which were trustworthy & which would have to be rejected the one I was standing on gave way and I suddenly found myself in the deep pool below; having previously intended to have a swim afterwards I did not regret this my only inconvenience being that my clothes were wetted I accordingly stripped and laid them out in the sun keeping sentinel myself under the shade of a huge [~~illeg.~~] gumtree much in the costume in which man is generally born. – now for fear your fertile brain may at this juncture of affairs suggest the fearful the imminent peril I ran of being taken up by some policeman for "indecent exposure" I must by way of parenthesis inform you that I should be as likely to encounter on any part of our run a policeman or indeed any other [~~illeg.~~] man as you are likely to see lions & tigers mingle peacably among the crowds in Hydepark & Oxfordstreet[2] – But to return to my tale; would you believe it that in less than 20 minutes all my clothes including boots and a stout pair of fustian trousers were perfectly dry! Heat alone could have never effected it so rapidly; if evaporation

were not accelerated by the extreme aridity of the atmosphere which {tear} course increases its capacity of receiving he{tear}[3] from the objects it surrounds. – I also study {tear}comfort– I never go out during the heat of the day unless it is unavoidable; but the truth is that the busy season is over now. the Company were obliged to request me to stop on here a little longer as they could not find anybody suitable to succeed me – It was first put off till Christmas. But as travelling on horseback then in the very height of summer would be unpleasant I readily consented to stop here till end of February. but you will understand I am not travelling all that while I am stationary managing the Co's establishment here –
Now goodbye dearest aunt write soon again & I shall do the same

your affectionate nephew
WGC

– Cuba Decbr. 3rd 1857
I kept a memorandum of the letters I sent you within the last 6 mos. Here it is
July 2nd with enclosure to Mama
Septbr 18th dto – Pauline
Octob. 12 dto – Mama
Novb. 9 dto to Mama and Pauline –
the only month I did not write was August which being the shearing
I was fearfully busy –[4]

Address: Aerogramme. Miss Clairmont/care of Messrs Haggard, Hale &Pixley/ 8 Copthal Court/ City London.
Postmark: WAGGA-WAGGA/[illeg.]/N. S. W.

Unpublished. Text: M.S. Pf. Coll., CL'ANA 0076

1 On 16 June 1856, Claire admonished Antonia for considering a move to Australia. Reiterating what she had written to Wilhelm about the proposed trip, and saying that the four month sea voyage would likely "kill" Antonia, Claire refused to support Antonia's plan (*CC* II: 555).

2 Theo Barker and Andrew Jones tell a similar tale: In 1827, Ralph Entwistle came to New South Wales to serve a sentence of life imprisonment for theft in England. By 1829, he was working as a servant for John Liscombe on a station some twelve miles from Bathurst. While transporting wool to Sydney, Entwistle and a companion decided to take a naked swim at Bathurst when the governor, Sir Ralph Darling, arrived on an official visit. While the governor did not see the men, a second group of soldiers saw them and they were later brought before the Police Magistrate on a charge of "causing an affront to the Governor" (Jones, A., "Entwistle Family History Association". Web. 16 November 2014. www.entwistlefamily.org.uk/entwistle-stories/19th-c-rapid-change/the-ribbon-gang/). Publicly flogged and no longer able to receive his ticket of leave as a result of his activities, Entwistle then became the leader of the Ribbon Gang (Barker, T., *A History of Bathurst*, p. 80). While Wilhelm was unlikely to see a policeman, naked swimming would certainly have led to a charge of "indecent exposure".

3 The page is torn. Wilhelm perhaps meant to write "heat".

4 See CL'ANA 0073.

93 • Antonia Clairmont to Claire Clairmont

17 [illeg.]: 2 J[illeg.] Baden 1858[1]

My dearest Claire.

The boxes are arrived, actually here and unpacked, but all wet half of the linen with large brown spots, whether they will come out in washing we must see – Pauline is in town – I would not let her stay at home the holidays – so full of sad recollections – she is to go to Landshütz[2] in about a fortnight – My dear Claire your letter is full of kindness and generosity, I shall be most happy to see you and hope nothing will interfere with your coming; your young friend will find it very dull as Pauline is not at home; on the other hand if P. were able to profit by examples she might do so every day, for we have all to suffer and bear and forbear but those that submit patiently to their lot, she calls tame and dowdy and perhaps to herself, adds meanspirited for she sees nothing in its true light; my wishes and endeavour is, to put ourselves on such a footing, so as to live without wanting your assistance for I do not wish always to be a burden on you, and I wanted to buy a little farm in a cheap neighborhood and live there quietly till Willy's return on my proposing this to her, she said very cheerfully,'oh yes Mama, I shall like it of all things, I shall have a saddle horse, my piano and plenty of books –' a saddle horse? what an idea? who should take care of it, we shall have male servant said I – Ah I shall take care of it, why I've saddled my horse a hundred – the conclusion of it was that without a horse she does not like to live in the country – and on the whole she prefers to live in a high family – it was after that I wrote my last letter to you, and regret very much that it gave you so much uneasiness, but I think the more I let her free to go, the less she feels inclined to do so – the little farm I had in view is wonderful cheap 45 acres of ground and ~~cash~~ valued at £200; and not very far from Vienna about a days journey now, but it lies on the line of the new railway and then it will be an advantageous concern – and the most beautiful part of Austria, healthy and fertile – shall we ever see our W. settled here? Thanks my dearest Claire for your feelings to Tetty – if the poor girl knew but how will you think of her; but her mother repeatedly begged we should not tell her; and indeed, in prudence, she cannot act otherwise. I hardly think W. would come by Egypt – it is too expensive for him[3] – it is so long we have had no letter from him, but as you say his being up the country is the reason – so did I not guess right? A. is not the chosen one?[4] very odd all things seemed to agree in pointing her out to me – for the boxes I had to pay35 flz or £3–10s. steamboat included but the Newsealand arms were not sent, nor the ruggs which I meant to appropriate, nor the chair which P. said should be sent – so all these articles go to the sale – and ought nearly came up to the sum; the chair cost 2 ½ pds P. told me – about the 100 pds do so as you said – all is right so – May the year 58 bring home our jewel then we shall be happy in him and accept my warmest thanks for all your kindness in the past year – yours ever gratefully

A.C.

Address: Miss Clairmont/ Garbrand Hall,/ Ewell, Surrey./ England.
Front postmark: BADEN/ $^{2}/_{1}$ / 4. EXP.; EPSOM/JA/[illeg.]
Rear postmark: WIEN/ $^{2}/_{1}$ / 6. A.; LONDON/ BI/JA 5/ 58

Unpublished. Text: M.S., Pf. Coll., CL'ANA 0351

---

1 Contextually, this letter appears to be from January 1858. The month is illegible.

2 Known as Landschütz in German and as Cseklész in Hungarian, the town of Bernolákovo is situated today in Slovakia in the region of Bratislava. Bernolákovo is located some 96 kilometers east of Vienna. See CL'ANA 0354.

3 Ironically, in spite of Antonia's conviction that Wilhelm would not be able to afford a homecoming via Egypt, he set sail on 22 January 1861 bound for Alexandria, Egypt (See introduction to The Australian Sojourn). As noted, his route took him to Suez, via train to Cairo, and then to Alexandria.

4 Claire and Antonia were still adamant about finding a suitable wife for Wilhelm. Wilhelm's rejection of Ada Ramsbottom (CL'ANA 0074) provoked Antonia's question. On 12 October 1857, Wilhelm referenced the age of the woman Claire had chosen for him, noting that "the excellent partie you intend for me" was probably ten years too old for him. Ada Ramsbottom was apparently older than Wilhelm, a difference he made clear in his letter of 12 October 1857 he considered "insurmountable".

94 • Antonia Clairmont to Claire Clairmont

17 Baden. 3rd Jan. 1858.

My dearest Claire.

I have just received yours with the half of the Bankbill for P's 100 pds and hasten to tell you of it – P. is still in town and I expect her home next Tuesday or she would add her thanks to mine for all your kindness – I wrote to you yesterday in answer to yours of the 26th – I can well believe that the sight of family feasts and happiness makes you sad for me, only the most complete solitude will do – if it were not for the hope of seeing you here next summer I should leave this place before the beginning of the season – like the hermit who "had lost all his family and wanted to go and live all by himself in a cave" so do I feel now – solitude is my friend – your society will be happiness to me, we have the best feelings of our hearts in common and so we shall meet and agree in our love for the dear children – but oh my dearest Claire do not think it unkind of W that he staid[1] – you know he did so more from duty than inclination – ah shall we ever have the comfort of exchanging all our thanks about this and a 100 others occurences in our family – how often have we said in our letters if you knew all. and if ~~you~~ I could tell you – well what nice chatty hours we shall ~~we~~ have together – I am slow in having my hopes excited of seeing you here, but if ame alive, I shall feel it extremely if disappointed – our papers tell of the mild winter in England – ours is so too – but much illness – I am always well, no cough as yet; I hope soon to hear of your getting better – do not suffer your anxiety to grow so much upon you – let us think it is His will that he left us and submit – our next hope must be for letters from the dear boy but decisive they [illeg.] hardly be – before he got ours of 10th of sept: last – his last to P. has no doubt of her coming out – he tells her of some books to bring him et et and expresses great anxiety as to my determination, but no trace of his intending to return – now are you not teased with this long scrawl – yours

thankfully A.C.

Address: Miss Clairmont/ Garbrand Hall/ Ewell, Surrey/ England.
Front postmark: BADEN/ $^{4}/_{1}$ / 3. EXP.; EPSOM/ [illeg.]
Rear postmark: WIEN/ $^{4}/_{1}$ / 4A.

Unpublished. Text: M.S., Pf. Coll., CL'ANA 0352

1 In his letter of 2 July 1857, Wilhelm told Claire that he was going to continue staying in Australia. He explained that the "unpleasant necessity of beginning a new career over again" deterred him from returning to Europe (CL'ANA 0072). He vacillated over returning to Europe and planned to base his final decision on whether Antonia's proposal to join him in Australia would materialize.

95 • Antonia Clairmont to Claire Clairmont

[18 January 1858]

Cuba 12th oct. 57[1]

Meine theuerste Mutter.

I habe deinen Brief von 7th July erhalten aber leider zu spät, um ihn noch mit umgehender post zu beantworten. Ich war natürlich darauf gefaßt dass meine abermals nicht erfolgte Abreise dein Mißfallen erregen müße. Pauline hat dir aber ehedem alle die Verhältniße auseinander gesezt. Ich verstehe deine gegenwärtige Hoffnungslosigheit und Ungeneigtheit auf neue Unternehmungen einzugehen. Ich habe auch lebhaft nachgedacht über die Verantwortlichkeit, welche ich auf mich nehme indem ich dich zur Umsiedlung zu bewegen suche; und ich will es dir nicht verhehlen, dass mir der Gedanke viel Sorge und Aengstlichkeit gemacht. So wie ich dich von früher her kenne, war dein Ideal immer daß wir zusammen irgendwo auf dem Lande leben; wäre dieser wunsh einmal erfüllt, und wir [hät][2]ten die Mittel anständig und ohne Entbehrungen zu leben, so dachte ich würdest du dich nicht viel um die übrige Welt kümmern. Weil sich nun unter den jeztigen Verhältnißen dieser Plan weit shneller hier, als durch meine Rückkehr nach Europa realisiren ließe, so rieth ich zu deinem Herauskommen. Wenn du aber liebste Mutter deine Pläne oder Ansichten geändert, wenn du vielleicht seit den fürchterlichen Schlägen welche du erlitten, eine unverhoffte Neigung für einen Art oder Person gefaßt so bitte dich, breche solche Bande nicht mehr gewaltsam ab, unter keiner Bedingung thue irgend einen Schritt der dich Überwindung kostet, wenn dich die Seereise abschreckt, so bleibe; du schreibst nie über deine Gesundheit; frage einen Arzt ob du die Strapatzen der Seereise ertragen kannst. Es wäre mir die größte Pein dich hier zu haben und nicht glücklich zu wißen. Was mich selbst betrifft so fühle ich daß ich mich allmählig mit den Mängeln Australien's, die mir sonst so peinlich waren aussöhne. Ich habe mir meine carriere hier gebrochen. Während meiner Lehrzeit habe ich mehr harte Arbeit gethan, mich mehr Strapatzen, Entbehrungen und Unannehmlichkeiten unterzogen als Leute in Europa während eines Lebensalters erfahren; ich fange nun eben an die Früchte davon zu genießen; Es wäre daher von dießem Gesichtspunct allein betrachtet unpolitish diese carriere gegen eine neue zu vertaushen in welcher ich wieder von vorn anfangen müßte. Zudem werde ich bis mein gegenwärtiges engagement aus ist 30 Jahre alt sein; das ist zu alt um als Adjunct mit 200 fl anzufangen; würde sich eine paßende Stelle finden? Ich könnte unmöglich daran denken von deinen oder der Aunt's Geschenken zu leben. Aber bitte dich liebe Mutter laß mich ganz aus der Frage; kommst du nicht, so kehre ich gewiß früher oder spatter zurük; allein es ist fruchtlos Pläne für so lange Zeit in Vorhinein zu machen. Deine Einwendungen wegen meiner möglichen Heirath, glaube ich sind nicht sehr bedeutend – für eine Liebesheirath habe ich hier wenig chance und eine Geldheirath würde ich nur machen wenn es wirklich der Mühe werth wäre, und das würde unsere Verhältniße natürlich ganz umgestalten; Ich brauche dir nicht zu sagen wie sehnsüchtig ich Nachrichten erwarte, von Paulinens Ankunft und dem Resultat eurer Berathungen. Ich bitte dich shreibe gleich adreßire in Trieste

dein dich liebender
Sohn W. C.

This my dearest Claire is the Copy of dear W's letter – you will see by it he does not think of coming for the present so you may make your plans for next summer without fear of hindrance I shall write with the next mail which goes from Triest[3] on the 26th and shall no more press him to return – for I cannot disagree with what he says, that he now begins to reap the fruit of his previous labour; the other letters for P. are also arrived, and I am going to post them alltogether – My dearest Claire we must submit, it is destiny. Pauline will have written already from Landshütz[4] – she is satisfied and comfortable – I have been unwell with cold and cough like every body else – Grippe[5] Grippe every where – you will have received my last acknowledging the 2d half bank bill – Good by my dearest Claire; I never ~~at~~ indulged in the hope of seeing him next summer, and yet I feel so dreary – ever yours affect

A.C.

18th Jan: 1858

English Translation (German transcription and English translation provided by Ann Sherwin):

My dearest Mother,

I received your letter of July 7th, but unfortunately too late to reply to it by return mail. I was naturally anticipating that my failure again to depart would arouse your displeasure. But Pauline has already explained all the circumstances to you. I understand your present desperation and your reluctance to consent to new ventures. I have also given serious thought to the responsibility I am shouldering as I try to persuade you to move; and I will be frank to admit that the thought has caused me much worry and anxiety. Knowing you as I do from yore, your ideal was always that we should live together in some rural setting; it this wish were fulfilled some day and we had the means to live respectably and without deprivation, so I thought, you would not worry much about the rest of the world. And because under the present circumstances this plan can now be realized much faster here than by my returning to Europe, I advised that you come out here. But if you have changed your plans or views, dearest Mother, if perhaps since the terrible blows you have suffered you have developed an unexpected affinity toward a way of life or a person, do not forcibly break such ties; do not, under any circumstances, take a step that requires an effort of will. If the sea voyage scares you, then stay. You never write about your health; ask a doctor whether you can tolerate the strains of a sea voyage. It would pain me no end to have you here and know that you are not happy. As for me, I feel that I am gradually becoming reconciled with the shortcomings of Australia that once distressed me so. I launched my career here. During my apprenticeship I did more hard work and underwent more strains, privations and vexations than people in Europe experience in a lifetime; I am just now starting to enjoy the fruits of this. Therefore, from this point of view alone, it would be impolitic for me to trade this career in for a new one in which I would have to start all over. Besides, by the time my current commitment is finished, I will be 30 years old; that is too old to start as an assistant with 200 gulden; would a suitable position? I couldn't possibly think of living off your or Aunt's gifts. But I beg you, dear Mother, leave me entirely out of the question; if you do not come, I will surely come back sooner or later; but to make plans this far ahead of time is fruitless. I don't think your objections regarding my possible marriage are of any significance. I have little chance of marrying for love here, and I would marry for money only if it were really worth the trouble. Naturally that would totally change our circumstances. I need to tell you how eagerly I await news of Pauline's arrival and the result of your deliberations. Please write at once and address it to Trieste.

Your loving son, W. C.

Address: Miss Clairmont/ 5 Surbitten Terrace/ Surbitten[6] – Surrey/ England
Front postmark: BADEN/ $^{18}/_{1}$ / 5. EXP.
Rear postmark: LONDON/ [illeg.]/JA 21/ 58; LONDON/10/JA 21/58

Unpublished. Text: M.S., Pf. Coll., CL'ANA 0353

1 The date, 1857, has been added in pencil.
2 The word is covered by an inkblot, but is still legible.
3 German for Trieste, a port in the north-east of Italy. During the nineteenth century, Trieste was part of the Austro-Hungarian Empire.
4 See CL'ANA 0351.
5 German for "influenza".
6 Antonia meant to write Surbiton.

96 • Antonia Clairmont to Claire Clairmont

17 Baden 30th Jan. 1858.

My dearest Claire.

I received yours of the 25th with W's inclosed, and I am extremely sorry your health is again attacked by the cold, and you are so lonely! if I could but nurse you – but the fates have decided otherwise, we must each go our solitary way, and only think of those we love instead of enjoying their society! You exhort me not to consent to his stay – that I do not, but I submit to the will of God – if every hair of our head is counted[1] – if Good and evil we receive from Him – so this separation all painful as it is, was wrote down in my destiny; what use to struggle – my strength is broken, yesterday was the anniversary of my poor dear Sidi's death she was an angel on earth blooming in loveliness of youth and innocence – and she was taken from me suddenly – and poor E. and Ch. followed – and I should struggle and resist! – I have shown poor dear Willy the deep grief his stay causes me but said I would submit for the present but he must not hope of my coming; in that I remain firm; oh do not my dear Claire be displeased with the dear boy he is but doing what he thinks his duty – I hope also his young friend, Mr Zöpf's letter will have some influenze.[2] Pauline is well satisfied of her situation but complains much of the cold – she has had a swelled face but it is gone off now – I dare say she caught cold, in crossing the passages not sufficiently covered they are coming to town in Febru so I shall see her – I am glad she is not with me now – for the cold is immense and our lodging not very well served against it – and then also these sad anniversari~~y~~es – my Baden friends are very kind and attentive to me, and whenever I feel inclined to go out a rubber at whist is at my service, and though I formerly used to despise cards, now I often feel the benefit of ~~it a~~ game[3] – it takes off my thoughts from sad things and turns them another way If only our climate were better so that you could come here and we live together – I think we should do well and suit each other – but I cannot come to England, my means are too limited to live in a dear country – besides I have all my furniture and house hold goods, which you have not – therefore you could easier make a trial – Pauline also complains of our separation, she says we are only four, and so dispersed in all the quarters of the world! shall we ever be united? Write soon again to tell me you are well – my cough is almost gone I have now kept at home 3 days for the cold is immense. ever

yours affect. A. C.

Pauline's direction
Miss P. Clair____
Landschütz par[4] Pressburg
Hungary

Address: No envelope

Unpublished. Text: M.S., Pf. Coll., CL'ANA 0354

---

1 "But the very hairs of your head are all numbered" Matthew 10:30 (King James Bible); "But even the very hairs of your head are all numbered" Luke 12:7 (King James Bible).

2 Franz Zoepf was a school friend of Wilhelm while at Altenburg. Hitschmann's listing notes that he was born on 13 February 1831 in Vienna and that he entered the school in 1850–1. His whereabouts after leaving the college are unknown (p. 84). In his letter of 23 April 1866 from Ofseniţa to Ottilia in Vienna, Wilhelm recorded: "Only think Zoepf is married" (CL'ANA 0421, Box 1, bundle a, number 23, unpublished letter, Pforzheimer Collection).

3 The game of whist was originally known as "trump" and was an early form of bridge, although no bidding was involved. Partnership whist (four players divided into partnerships of two) is still played today. The word "rubber" refers to playing a series of games. The winning partnership usually won two out of three rounds. See Parlett, David. "Whist". *Encyclopaedia Britannica Online*. Encyclopaedia Britannica Inc. n.d. Web. 7 May 2016. http://www.britannica.com/topic/whist

4 "Par" is the German word for "via". Formerly known as Pressburg in German, the city of Bratislava is located today in Slovakia. After the defeat of the Hapsburgs in 1918, Pressburg was renamed Bratislava and it became the capital city of Slovakia, one of the provinces in the newly created country of Czechoslovakia. In 1993, after the dissolution of Czechoslovakia, Slovakia became an independent country with Bratislava as its capital city. Landschütz is the German name for the city of Bernolákovo which is located in Slovakia, about 22 kilometers east of Bratislava (Teich, M., et al. (eds.), *Slovakia in History* [Cambridge University Press: Cambridge, 2011], pp. 1–5). See also CL'ANA 0351.

97 • Antonia Clairmont to Claire Clairmont

17. Baden 12th febr: 1858.

My dearest Claire.

How happy your last made me I cannot express, I first read yours, I was afraid what I might find in his, but oh, my dearest sister you have felt with me and more than sympathised in my grief, you only can share my joy, for he says, he will come, if he knows for sure that I do not intend to go out; and as I know, I have never in my letters shown the least hesitation or uncertainty on that head, but always said plainly and firmly I would not go, so there will be nothing to make him waver in his blessed resolution to return, on the contrary he will have been confirmed in it by every subsequent letter he must have received; for I have written 6 times since dear P. is here; the one I received yesterday was written in answer to one of mine of the 7th of July ere Pauline arrived, and I said in it what my wishes were that he might know my feelings ere influenzed by P's representations and presence; Oh the dear boy! I shall write to him with the 26th that is the 2d Alexandrian postday,[1] the first thereof I missed by a day – he says also he thinks Mr Man:[2] will let him off before his years are out – but now to Pauline – she has not written to Mrs Drysedale[3], for ~~she is~~ they are just moving up to town and entering new apartments she has a great deal to do, also she was much vexed, after having just settled down in a little like order at Landshütz to have to break up again and unsettle all the children too, never having had a regular governess before have to be broke into a proper train and it was just time lost and trouble – she might have entered now; if I had known all this, if she had not written to you, I dare say ~~I~~ it was her wish to give you a better account of the state of things than she could give just then, that made her defer writing – about Mrs Ddale I know she is much vexed because she misses so many of her things – she says every day brings to her recollections of losses – I have now received your second letter with W's included; Pauline's letters arrived all right – also mine from W. I sent to her, so I cannot copy it out for her till I get it back. it does not contain anything materially differing from yours only something about Tetty - but it gives the certainty that he is happy to return – his speech about the 200fl means nothing at all – it was a joke – I understood Miss A[4] cannot touch her fortune till after her mother's death? Now pray for Goodness sake don't hurry the dear boy at his arrival or entangle him ere he well knows what he is about. else his happiness may be wrecked even more. Pauline sends her best love, is glad she is in town, complains of the dreadful cold – believe me ever yours gratefully A.C.

Address: No envelope.

Unpublished. Text: M.S. Pf. Coll., CL'ANA 0355

---

1 By the nineteenth century, Alexandria (in Egypt) was an important port for shipping. Mail was routed through Alexandria to various overseas locations. K.S. Ingliss records that mail was sent

via steamship to Alexandria, "overland to the Red Sea, and by steamship to Australia". He notes that, from 1852, the Peninsular and Oriental Steam Navigation Company took just over two months to deliver mail from England to Australia via Alexandria (see "The Imperial Connection: Telegraphic Communication between England and Australia, 1872–1902" in A.F. Madden and W.H. Morris-Jones (eds.), *Australia and Britain: Studies in a Changing Relationship* [London: Frank Cass and Company, 1980], pp. 21–2).

2 James Alexander Louis Manning (1814–1887) was born in Exeter, England, and attended Hohenheim Agricultural College (Koeniglich Württembergischen Land- und Forstwirthschaftlichen Academie Hohenheim) in Stuttgart, Germany, from 1831 until 1833. As noted previously, the college is the forerunner of today's Universität Hohenheim. Archival records from the institution show that "J.A.S. Manning" from London was admitted to the academy in the winter semester of 1831–32. Unfortunately, the detailed record for those years has been lost (Dr. Ulrich Fellmeth, Universität Hohenheim, Stuttgart, Germany, personal communication: 15 September 2014). Manning immigrated to Australia in 1834 and became a pastoralist. Manning, together with his brothers John Edye and William Manning, as well as Thomas Mort, John Croft, and another set of brothers, Edwin and Robert Tooth, formed the Twofold Bay Pastoral Association in 1853. In 1854, Manning assumed management of Kameruka and introduced cheese making operations to the station. By 1864, Manning was farming near Bega in New South Wales (S. Edgar. "Manning, James Alexander Louis (1814–1887)", *Australian Dictionary of Biography*, National Centre of Biography, Australian National University. Web. 6 May 2016. http://adb.anu.edu.au/biography/manning-james-alexander-louis-4149). Bega is located nineteen kilometers from Kameruka and is situated in the Bega Valley Shire. The shire includes the towns of Bega, Merimbula, Pambula, and Eden. See CL'ANA 0043.

3 *The Sydney Morning Herald* of 15 May 1857 reported the list of passengers who departed for England on April 19 on the Waterloo. There were 17 passengers on the ship and an additional 21 "invalid soldiers". Mr. and Mrs. Drysdale and their two children were listed amongst the passengers (National Library of Australia, http://nla.gov.au/nla.news-page1495978, p. 12). In her journal, Pauline recorded that she arrived in England on 7 August 1857: "Arrived again in old England – the coast looked beautiful & the land smell was delightful – all day long I was mournful . . . Mrs. Drysdale was there and we talked about meeting in London" (CL'ANA 0176, p. 267, unpublished manuscript, Pforzheimer Collection).

4 The young lady Claire hoped Wilhelm would marry.

98 • Antonia Clairmont to Claire Clairmont

Baden. 23[illeg.] Marh[1] 1858

My dearest Claire.

Business of all sorts have kept me from answering you, then came dear Willy's letter, which made me quite happy; and yesterday dear Pauline came to spend the day with me; and she took W's letter away with her, and promised she would copy it for you, as she is going to write to you; I had not seen her for 3 months; she looks well and cheerful; I think she is all the happier for having regulated occupation and she is conscientious in doing her duty, and valued and liked and well received by every body; if only Willy is once here so that she has a cheerful home with us and ~~such~~ society such as suits her, then she will not think of going away; we must have patience with her; it would appear from dear W's letter that we must not be too sanguine expecting him home so soon; I resign myself to two years more; we should only work our own disappointment by hoping him sooner! I have just written to him, to tell him of our happiness in knowing him determined to come back et et I am glad the cold is over for this year or else your admonitions would have frightened me but the dry cold always agrees with me, it is only the damp I cannot bear that makes me ill – we have now charming wheather a little windy, but such a deep blue skye lovely – however Pauline found it much colder here in Baden than in town – she shivered when I told her, you thought Baden was not sufficiently ventilated whereas we suffer terribly from the violence of wind and storm. I must now conclude for it is late and I must go to the post myself with W's letter, I begin already to arrange things a little for moving, I am sorry not to have P. but my new friends at Baden will all kindly assist me, so I hope to get through the trouble in time. ever yours

gratefully A.C.

Address: Miss Clairmont/ 5 Surbitten Terrace/ Surbitten Hill,/ Surrey/ England.
Front postmark: BADEN/ $^{28}/_{3}$/ 1. EXP.
Rear postmark: LONDON/FY/MR 27/ 58

Unpublished. Text: M.S., Pf. Coll., CL'ANA 0356

---

1 Either Marh (incorrect spelling for "March") or Marz ("März," German for "March").

99 • Wilhelm Gaulis Clairmont to Claire Clairmont

[27 March 1858]

My dearest aunt.

I rec^d your letter of the 10th Janry.[1] and trust that you too have had no reason to complain of my silence ~~the~~ having written to you direct or sent you a note through Mama by every mail but the last. the chief topic which you urge in your letter viz my immediate return under any circumstances and at all hazards I am afraid it is impossible to realize. Such a breach of contract as you propose would by our colonial laws make me liable to 3 mos. imprisonment. Do you think that after enforcing this law so often against refractory men I would now like to put myself on a par with them and set the example at running away? But doubtless you have abandoned this idea after hearing through my mother the answer I rcd from Mr Manning to my request to have the contract cancelled.[2] I was at the time on the road travelling from Cuba to this place and had not time to write more than the one letter; but in case this letter (which I dispatched by March mail) should not have reached ~~you~~ Mama I had better repeat the substance of it here: My contract as you are perhaps aware dates from March 27th 1857 for 3 years – one year is expired today leaving 2 years to carry out. of these Mr Manning has consented to remit me setting me thus at liberty on March 27th, 1859 just this day twelve month.[3] I thought Mr Manning's decision very reasonable for with the stupendous amount of business to be gone through it would be impossible to dismiss the head of the most important department all at a moment's notice. You will be glad to hear that I am now quite in civilized society. Mrs Manning[4] keeps her house in the style of a well kept Engl. country gentleman's house and I live with them. I have still my choice to go to Caudilo[5] the place [~~illeg.~~] two miles off (where I was to live with Mama & Pauline) but in their absence I should be dependent on a common hutkeeper for all the cooking & the chances are that I should be reduced again to the never varying salt beef & damper system which I have by this time enjoyed sufficiently long ~~to~~ thoroughly to abominate. I shall therefore prefer the minor nuissances attending my living with the M's such as having to dress in the evening after perhaps a long ride or other fatigue; the inconvenient time of their meal hours for my business, lots of prayers at all hours out of the 24 etz. I can tell you for your consolation that we have an excellent medical man at Panbula[6] which is only 20 miles from here. I have Mrs Mannings authority for saying so. one of her children[7] has a standing complaint (my belief is that it is scrophular)[8] the cure of which would very well admit of being directed by a doctor from Sydney as all changes work so slowly in such deep rooted complaints but M^rs. M. assured me she would as soon have Dr. Bligh[9] as any Sydney physician. the poor little girl reminds me very much of our Sidy and I am sure she has the same complaint. The unnatural protrusion of the chest is just the same, and her little pale face with contracted shoulders and stunted figure even her character is the same; quiet, sedate and extremely reflective as if the [~~illeg.~~] reduced physical energies caused a proportionate increase of the mental ones. But I quite forget that you never knew our dear Sidi & cannot therefore take great interest in this.

Now I hope dearest aunt for the remaining year that I have to stop here you will not go one[10] giving yourself useless concerns about nothing. I am here just as well off as at Tattenwill in Kent[11] or perhaps even better as the exercise on horse-back suits me better than on foot; indeed any exercise that does not draw on the breath I can bear very well – In this country I think all people are good horsemen. Mr Mannings niece[12] a young lady who got married some mos. back rode with Mr Manning 55 miles in one day & 35 miles the next. – and that without being knocked up after it. My work {tear} does not by any means consist in hard labour it is {tear} constant than intense. – I shall follow your request{tear} about directing letters via Marseilles. I had no idea that you watched the arrival of the mails so keenly as to make a difference between the two.

Goodbye dearest aunt believe me ever

your affectionate nephew
WGC.

direct W.G. C.–
Kamaruka, Bombala
Sydney.
March 27th 1858.

Address: Aerogramme. via Marseilles. Miss Clairmont/ Messrs Haggard, Hale & Pixley/ 8 Copthall Court City/ London.

Unpublished. Text: M.S. Pf. Coll., CL'ANA 0077

1 This letter has been lost.

2 Wilhelm was intent on returning to Europe and requested from James Manning that his contract be shortened. Wilhelm's reluctance to break his contract and the terms thereof are recorded in his letter.

3 In fact, as William noted, Manning did agree to reduce the length of the contract.

4 James Manning became manager at Kameruka (an Indigenous Australian word which means "wait until I return") and Wilhelm resided with Manning and his wife, Mary Firebrace Manning (see CL'ANA 0078). Manning managed the company's leases in the Bega Valley as well as in the Twofold Bay district. When the Twofold Bay Pastoral Association was dissolved in 1860 and the company's holdings were distributed amongst the shareholders, James Manning assumed control of Kameruka. The estate finally became the property of Frederick Tooth in 1861 and then his nephew, Robert Lucas Tooth, in 1864. See V. Small, *Kameruka*. In 1964, Bruce Ryan recorded that Kameruka was the largest privately owned estate in the Bega Valley and that it stretched for nine miles along the bank of the Bega River and consisted of 14, 592 acres/5, 905 hectares and fifteen dairy farms ("Kameruka Estate," p. 103). The squatters who began working in the valley in the late 1820s found a "savanna-woodland formation thriving on shallow but fertile soils" (p. 104) that was "capable" of sustaining sheep farming enterprises. Kameruka remained a part of the Tooth family holdings until Giles Pritchard-Gordon purchased it in 2007. Kameruka was again offered for sale in November 2014.

5 Wilhelm misspelled Candelo, a town in New South Wales in the Bega Valley Shire. Candelo is located 24 kilometers from Merimbula and about 2 kilometers from Kameruka.

6 Dr. Richard Bligh was stationed at Pambula, a mere 36 kilometers south of Kameruka. Arthur Manning, commissioner of Crown Lands for the Monaro and younger brother of James Manning, lived at Pambula with his family. Pambula is also referred to as Panbula. See CL'ANA 0072.

7 The Mannings had three sons and three daughters.

8 Scrofula was a form of tuberculosis that affected the lymph nodes. Charles Clairmont told Mary Shelley in November 1845 that Sidi (whom he referred to as "Sidy") was "healthy and pretty" until the age of about three and a half years. He explained that she was then "seized by a scrophulous complaint" which resulted in "sores" on her body and particularly in her joints. The disease was first treated as a "rash" but soon, he noted, Sidi was unable to look from side to side without turning her body completely, as her eyes had become "fixed" in her body. In fact, she had been barely able to move due to her physical weakness. Charles affirmed that, while Sidi had overcome the scrofula, her spine "has taken a wrong direction". She practiced daily gymnastic exercises to correct her spine on the advice of a homeopathic physician (*CC* II: 464).

9 Mary Braidwood Mowle revealed many consultations and meetings with Dr. Bligh in her diary. Born in England, Mowle came to Australia with her surgeon father in 1836 and her diary covered the years 1850–1851 and 1854–1855. On 23 August 1854, she recorded the arrival of Bligh in Pambula, noting that Bligh is "an elderly man" and "by no means the courtly mannered gentleman Mr James Manning described, he did several things in fact I thought abominably illmannered" (p. 225). According to Mowle, Dr. Bligh talked of fleas at the dinner table and he did not stand up when she said good night to him. She later amended her opinion of him, calling Bligh a "kind intelligent man" (p. 226) with a "free and easy manner," "very kind & attentive in his medical capacity" (p. 232) and his wife a "ladylike woman" (p. 231). On 11 December 1854, Mowle suffered an eye injury as a result of being hit with a stick and Dr. Bligh provided her with a lotion for her eye as well as a bandage (pp. 236–7). In 1855, she recorded that he vaccinated the children (p. 246) and that he took care of both her infants during their illnesses (p. 252). She also noted that Bligh was required to "prescribe" for her on a few occasions after she had taken ill (p. 235 and p. 238). In 1855, when the first German immigrants to the area were placed under quarantine due to illness on board the ship the *Caesar*, Mowle recorded that Dr. Bligh attended to some of the immigrants (p. 258).

10 Wilhelm meant to write "on".

11 Wilhelm perhaps intended to write "Tattersalls". Established in 1766 by Richard Tattersall (1724–1795), Tattersalls (the firm's name has no apostrophe) sells thoroughbred race horses ("Tattersalls". Web. 10 May 2016. http://www.tattersalls.com/). Wilhelm might also have meant Tunbridge Wells, a town in Kent, England. Wilhelm wrote to Claire from Malling, Kent, in 1849 (CL'ANA 0041). East Malling is located 17 kilometers from Tunbridge Wells and West Malling is about 19 kilometers from Tunbridge Wells.

12 James Manning was one of eight children and uncle to many nieces and nephews.

100 • Wilhelm Gaulis Clairmont to Claire Clairmont

[27 April 1858]

My dearest aunt.

Although I have nothing of importance to write to you I scratch off a few lines merely to let you know that I am going on as usually & in perfect health. – I have no letter to acknowledge from you; the steamer due here on the 10th of this month bringing the Engl. Felonary mails[1] had not yet arrived in Sydney at the date of our last mail from that place; it was feared that she had met with an accident – If you or Mama have written me by it I shall loose the chance of answering by the next home mail (May) as our next weeks mail to Sydney would be too late to catch the Engl. mail starting on the 11th May. – Hitherto I like Kamaruka very well. the climate is very pleasant indeed; it is also agreable to have a nice well kept house to live in – after the eternal saltjunk[2] & damper without even cabbage or potatoes to vary your diet I enjoy Mrs Manning's well appointed though simple ~~diet~~ table.[3] We have a meat breakfast in the morning dinner at two consisting of one or two sorts of meat & [~~illeg.~~] a pudding or fruit tart then tea at 7. Mrs Manning is a very nice person only terribly religious on Sundays I find it necessary to abscond in the bush as there are prayers all through the day. the children are all quite dear little things and I am getting quite fond of them; the oldest girl is nine years old & her brother who is seven have two nice ponies on which they ride out with me whenever they get permission. And now dearest aunt I have a piece of news to tell you of which I am truly proud: it is no less than this that I have actually and for the first time since my arrival in N.S.W. swallowed an entire bottle of medicin minus the glass of course and two pills which from their size and suspicious appearance (by themselves in a little red box) together with the baneful effects they had upon me (undesirable sensations of squeamishness mixed up with unearthly sounds proceeding from the nether regions) I have now no doubt were the dreaded "blue Pill".[4] Now pray tell me candidly did you find out Dr Bligh & prime him regarding [~~illeg.~~] my special medicinal wants or is it fate that persecutes me everywhere in the shape of Blue Pills? The circumstances of the case were these: I was a few days from home when one of the sudden changes of temperature so peculiar to this climate finding me not prepared gave me a sore throat. the doctor living only 20 miles from here I made up my mind, enticed by the novelty of the idea, to apply to him for some medicine; it is true that by the time I found leisure to go my throat was all or nearly well but that I thought was ~~only~~ the best excuse for my going to the doctor, being a sort of pledge for his success, moreover I had been told that he had a very pretty daughter and that the little newly formed township in which he lived was very picturesque and worth seeing. so I went in spite of difficulties and misgivings and this was the end of my enterprise: the daughter was from home; the [illeg.] township a dirty hovel from which I bolted with all speed still the same day and the medicine, those nefarious pills (I suspect your agency in the matter from the cunning clandestine manner in which the innocent looking doctor introduced them to me) put me to untold mental and bodily agonies relieved only by the consoling idea what a triumphant figure I should cut in the report I should give you of this unparalelled instance of [~~illeg.~~] voluntary selfinfliction of (more than suspected) blue pills.–

I shall write to Mama & Pauline by this same post and again by next. Goodbye for the present from your affectionate nephew.

WGC.

direct:
Kamaruka
Bombala Sydney
April 27$^{\underline{th}}$ 1858.

Address: Aerogramme. via <u>Marseilles</u>./ Miss Clairmont/Mess$^{\underline{rs}}$ Haggard Hale and Pixley/ 8 Copthall Court/ City London.
Postmark: SYDNEY/ AP29/1858/A./N.S.W.

Unpublished. Text: M.S. Pf. Coll., CL'ANA 0078

1 Wilhelm meant "felonry" mail. The last convict ships left for Australia in 1867, after which the transportation of convicts to Australia ceased.

2 Nautical slang for salted beef or pork.

3 James Manning died in 1887 at his home in Vectis, Double Bay. He was survived by his wife, the daughter of Major Firebrace, and three sons and three daughters (*The Sydney Morning Herald*. 27 October 1887. National Library of Australia, http://nla.gov.au/nla.news-article13679630, p. 9).
The Squatters Act of 1846–47 enabled pastoralists to purchase land for a period of fourteen years. By mid-1860, the Mannings had left Kameruka to farm in Bega.

4 The "blue pill" or "blue mass" was regularly prescribed during the nineteenth century for a variety of ailments. According to Hirschhorn, Feldman, and Greaves, the primary ingredient in the pill was elemental mercury. The toxicity of mercury is well-known today and Hirschhorn et al. observe that chronic mercury poisoning can lead to nerve damage and feelings of hypochondria and depression. Together with a laxative known as the black draught, the "blue pill" was also used to treat constipation, a fact Wilhelm confirmed when he informed Claire of the "unearthly sounds proceeding from the nether regions". When Hirschhorn et al. recreated a typical nineteenth-century "blue pill," they found it contained over 9,000 times the daily permitted amount of mercury ("Abraham Lincoln's Blue Pills" in *Perspectives in Biology and Medicine*, 44 [Summer 2001], p. 323).

101 • Antonia Clairmont to Claire Clairmont

490 Baden 1[~~illeg.~~]$^{\underline{t}}$ Mai 1858.

My dearest Claire.

I have just received a short letter from dear W. dated 1$^{\underline{s}}$ May Wa[~~illeg.~~]ga=Wa~~rr~~ga[1]– with Mr Manning's answer to him – stating that he cannot release him directly but he must remain another year – so dear W. will be free by this time next year – I am going to send M^{r} M's[2] letter to Pauline and she will then send it to you – but I would not make you wait so long – M^{r} M's letter is very obliging and does justice to W's merits – who also says they could hardly hope to find a competent person sooner – he is just on his road to Kameruka and says he will write to you as soon as he is arrived – but pray my dear Claire, you must return this letter of M^{r} M's to Willy as it contains his promise to release W from his contract in another year – Willy might want it – I cannot say I am much disappointed in this delay – for I did not hope he would come sooner, and the certainty is always preferable to doubt – it would have been too much happiness to have him here this summer – you can at least make your arrangement without hesitation I am not very well just now – that is the baths affect me in the beginning and then the 7$^{\underline{th}}$ Mai also the idea of Paulines departure for Hungary[3] – I hope you have got my last through dear P. I have found since your direction – pray write soon and tell me what you intend to do – and how your health is – it seems so long since I heard from you – believe me ever yours

gratefully A.C.

4 letters for her with this mail ship Emen.[4] We can now say to know for certain when our dear traveller will return – Pauline can arrange so as to be free and at home by next spring; I shall think of nothing but saving and scraping a little sum together, first to buy a good instrument for her, and then to have a little cash ready against the dear boys arrival – and thinking always of it will make the year seem very short – P. has a most affectionate heart I hope she will be happy in the end – one point I have still to touch – my poorness does not allow me, to say, come and welcome, so I must accept of your help but shall do what I can – Tetty I have not seen the whole winter and now they are gone to the country without coming to see me – I find it against my conscience to keep up hopes in the poor girl and her family which may prove nought after all don't you also think? Good bye dearest Claire, hasn't P. sent my letter? I'll scold her. ever yours

A.C.

Address: No envelope.

Unpublished. Text: M.S. Pf. Coll., CL'ANA 0358

---

1 Wagga Wagga is located 460 kilometers south-east of Sydney, on the Murrumbidgee River. The name means "crow" in the Wiradjuri language. The repetition of the word "wagga" indicates a

plural form in the Wiradjuri language. Hence the name Wagga Wagga means "the place of many crows" ("Wagga Wagga". Web. 19 November 2014. http://www.waggawaggaaustralia.com.au/visitor-information/about-wagga-wagga/the-name/).

2 Mr. Manning.

3 Pauline would become a governess in Rakičan, Hungary, some 228 kilometers south of Vienna. Rakičan is located today in Slovenia. A few years later, Pauline would leave her daughter, Georgina Hanghegyi, born out of wedlock, with Countess Károlyi in Rakičan until she finally brought Georgina to live with Claire in Florence in 1871. Maribor (known as Marburg in German), where Wilhelm would later farm, is about 58 kilometers west of Rakičan. 7 May was also the anniversary of Charley's death.

4 Royal Mail Ships (RMS) were ships assigned to carry mail on behalf of the British Royal Mail. Antonia has written the name "Emen" (possibly an incorrect spelling).

102 • Antonia Clairmont to Claire Clairmont

490 Baden 13th Mai 1858.

My dearest Claire.

I was just going to take my letter to the post when yours arrived and I add these lines that not a day may be lost ere you get our dear boy's news. you have a striking talent for guessing everything, you were quite right as to his being on the journey, and not in time to write regularly and a real wonder it seems to me that Mr M's[1] letter met him on his road – he says he is quite well, and travelling in easy stages at the rate of 30 miles pr. day; and says I should next direct to Kamaruka, Bombala, Sydney.[2] but now to your affairs – I shall do my best in answering your questions. but they are rather imperfect – you dont say whether you mean to go straight to Vienna or Karlsbad and Schwalbach first – Karlsbad would but make little difference – the cheapest route I should think is by rail, from Ostende through Belgium, Minden Hannover, Berlin Leipzig Dresden – from there you can either proceed to Prague and Vienna or go sideways to Karlsbad[3] – you could also go by the Rhine to Frankfurt and then down the Danube but that is longer and dearer; my children always went the above road, and the cost always came to about £10 – but of course young people travel cheaply, and quickly, they now and then take a stage 3d class, and live cheaply, what you cannot do, you must take time and rest, and that increases the expense – now about the lodging; you don't say whether you come alone or bring one or two persons with you; if you are alone you can lodge with me; I have a very comfortable cheerful and healthy apartment; consisting of two rooms, a kitchen a little anteroom, and a very small closet without a window; where I keep boxes of all sorts of odd things – now if you only bring a servant, and find the little place good enough for her to sleep in, I would have the things removed and a bed placed for her and try to make you as comfortable as possible, but if you bring your friend, you must take private lodgings, there are plenty to be had at all prices – first rate rooms are at about one pound pr week. and lower down - you will want about 2 rooms and a servant's if also a sittingroom it will make 4 – however you must tell me all more clearly and then I shall make inquiries and report again. do you object to a ground floor? I bitterly regret that poor dear P. is not at home when you come she would make us cheerful – for I am sad and dull – Mrs Schauer will be in Baden again this summer and quite near me – my brother is in Neustadt[4] as usual, but I see very little of him. There is no question now of Pressburgh[5] – the [illeg]'s[6] are going to another estate during the summer, and P. said in her last she hopes that both you and I ~~should~~ will be able to come and spend a few weeks near her – it would be too sad for her to miss you entirely – there have been[7]

Address: No envelope.

Unpublished. Text: M.S. Pf. Coll., CL'ANA 0357

1 Mr. Manning.

2 See CL'ANA 0072.
3 See CL'ANA 0191, CL'ANA 401 and CL'ANA 0403. Minden is located 499 kilometers north-east of Ostend (Belgium). Schwalbach is in Germany, 735 kilometers north-west of Vienna, while Karlsbad is in the Czech Republic, about 460 kilometers north-west of Vienna. Karlsbad is known as Karlovy Vary in Czech.
4 Georg Ghilain von Hembyze. See CL'ANA 0380.
5 See CL'ANA 0354.
6 Antonia wrote a single letter here. It looks either like a B, R, or N.
7 The letter ends here and is incomplete.

103 • Antonia Clairmont to Claire Clairmont

17 of Mai[1] Baden 490.
1858.

You will have got mine of the 12th

My dearest Claire.

This moment I received yours of the 12th and sit down directly to answer it – Pauline has taken a copy of Mr Mannings letter and you will receive it through her, and the original I shall return to the dear boy when I next write which will be on the 26th one of our Alexandrian postdays we have but two a month – I feel sure, you will now put of[2] your journey till next year, for what use would it be to come when both W. and P. are absent, and moreover poor P. quite unhappy about the whole affair of his returning it would be time and money thrown away – you would hardly be inclined to repeat the journey next year, when your presence will be necessary to our happiness and family union, and when it will be more in our power to make your stay pleasant and agreeable; by that time P will be at home and help me to bear the delight of expectation – you will receive the dear traveller in England and then come with him, you can go by the Rhine to Frankfurt from there by rail to Ratiobome[3] and then on the Danube down to Vienna – I dont say a word more on your journey as I don't expect it will take place – it wants but prove a source of regret to us all to poor Pauline, who engaged in her arduous duties, could not even come to see you, to me and to you for good reasons, so I do hope and entreat you to put it off till next year, and now I will copy dear W's letter.

Wagga Wagga.[4]
1st March 1858

Ich habe eben auf der durchreise durch diese höchst sehenswerthe Stadt am Murrumbidgee Mr Manning's Antwort auf mein Gesuch mich sogleich zu entlaßen erhalten, ich übersende dir seinen Brief, der dir am besten zeigen wird wie die sachen stehen. obwohl ich es als eine große täushung empfinde nicht gleich gehen zu könen so muß man doch billig sein und gestehen daß seine Handlungsweise gerecht ist; den er selbst ist ja nicht unabhängig sondern auch den directoren verantwortlich und er würde sich gerechten tadel aussetzen wen er einen so wichtigen posten plötzlich unbesezt ließe ehe er für einen fähigen Nachfolger gesorgt hat; ich würde auch in dem Verkauf meinen Pferde verloren haben die ich in der Voraussetzung hier zu bleiben gekauft hatte; ich bin jezt auf der Reise fon Cuba nach Twofold bay begriffen; ich habe 3 Pferde 2 für mich und das 3te reitet ein deutscher Junge den ich noch von Kangaroo Hills mit mir habe; die ganze Entfernung ist 400 Meilen. Ich mache mir aber bequem, und mache nicht mehr als 30 miles per day; glücklicherweise sind nur 4 inns auf der ganzen Strecke sonst wärs expensive aber wir übernachten in stations und auf dem Gebirge müßen wir campieren, im Sommer ist das aber nicht unangenehm, let P. explain it to you. Ich habe nicht Zeit an Aunt Cl. zu shreiben aber sobald ich in Kamaruka domesticirt bin werde ich ihr and Pauline shreiben. Indeßen lebe wohl liebste Mutter et et

---

that is the whole letter; whether he will have reached home so soon as to have written to you by the expected mail I cannot tell nor guess but at all events we have Mr M's word – – –" [I must therefore solicit your willingness to assist me for one year more, of the two unexpired years of your contract, after which time I will, if you still desire it at that time, consent to a cancelment of your compact with us".][5] these lines are clear and decisive, you will see all he says when you get the copy of the letter, but I shall warn W. of those words, I underlined to declare himself clearly and decisively too – thanks for Mrs Suttors lines, and if you write give my best remembrances – I wrote to her once, but I think my letter must have been lost as she never mentioned it – Pauline at first would not believe that the Australian letters must be franked – in the course of time 3 of hers to Mrs S – were returned and found their way back to Baden from England so the one where mine was inclosed may have been lost too; Poor P. she is quite vexed with W. for his wont ambition and God knows what and she is really unjust in her displeasure. Now God bless you my dear Claire write soon and tell me what you intend to do – if you are not sure that you have both spirits and money to come next year again so put it off till then, when our beloved children are here, for this year we should be sad and solitary to the great disappointment of your young Lady. ever yours. A. C.

Translation (German transcription and English translation provided by Ann Sherwin):

Wagga Wagga.

1st March 1858

Just now, on my way through this very lovely city on the Murrumbidgee, I received Mr. Manning's response to my request to be released at once. I am sending you his letter, which will best show you how things stand. Although I am very disappointed not to be able to go right away, one must be fair and concede that he acted correctly; for he himself is not independent but accountable to the directors, and he would be exposing himself to legitimate criticism if he suddenly left such an important post vacant before he had found a competent successor; I would also have lost my horses in the sale, which I had bought on the assumption that I would be staying here. I am now on my way from Cuba to Twofold Bay. I have three horses: two for me, and the third is being ridden by a German boy[6] that I still have with me from Kangaroo Hills; the entire distance is 400 miles. But I am taking it easy and not doing more than 30 miles. Fortunately there are only 4 inns along the entire stretch. Otherwise it would be expensive, but we are spending nights in stations and on the mountains we have to camp in summer but that is not unpleasant, let P. explain it to you. I don't have time to write to Aunt Cl. but as soon as I am settled in Kamaruka, I will write to her and Pauline. Meanwhile, farewell, dearest Mother etc. etc.

Address: No envelope.

Unpublished. Text: M.S. Pf. Coll., CL'ANA 0359

1 German for "May".
2 Antonia meant to say "off".
3 Antonia intended to write "Ratisbon," the German name for the city of Regensburg. Regensburg is located in Bavaria, Germany, on the Danube River.
4 See CL'ANA 0358.
5 Wihelm included these square brackets in his letter.
6 Probably one of the German immigrants brought to Australia by Kirchner (see CL'ANA 0071).

104 • Wilhelm Gaulis Clairmont to Claire Clairmont

[3 June 1858]

My dearest aunt.

I have to acknowledge the receipt of two letters from you one by the February the other by the March mail – I am afraid you will be displeased to find that there is now again a doubt thrown on my intended return indeed but for my promise to Mama I ~~w~~should decide on stopping here for I hear such dismal accounts of Austria & on the other hand I like my present position at Twofold Bay so much better than I anticipated that I cannot make up my mind to throw it up so easily and begin a new carreer over again – My prospects are now very good; ~~an~~ in Austria I should at best have to work for 10 years till I attained the same position as I hold here; before I had been in personal communication with Mr Manning I could not judge of the probable permanency of my situation here as had he turned out a disagreeable man no considerations should have enduced me to stop; as it is I think my present prospects very favorable. As for marriage I think it is quite right to try (if it can be done without any other sacrifice) to make money by it, but to look to it as an only resource and give up other certainties for it I think would be folly. I could not help laughing at your idea of my being romantic; I have not been often found fault with on that score; I was of course only joking when I told you that I dreamt about your young lady – as you tell me that I have seen her I cannot think that it is anyone else but Ada Ramsbottom.[1] But I do not think that she would be suited for me; she is older than I am and consequently 12 years or so too old to be my wife; nor would it be very gratifying to my vanity to be accepted by one who spent all her youth in looking for some better match.[2] If you were to introduce me to the Pringles again I should be far more likely ~~for~~ to fall in love with Violet than Ada – I am now in Sydney on business I am going home again tomorrow. I found a letter here from Pauline to Mama which had been all the way to Austria (as I can see by the postage stamps) and sent back again because not claimed at the postoffice this is very little encouragement for me to write to her to Baden direct for what is the use of so doing if she does not get the letters; if I have only time I should like to enclose a note to her in this. If I wait till I get home {tear} shall be too late for this mail.

My health is very good but my throat is still visibly inclined to be delicate; this is one great point in favour of my stopping here it is very possible the Austrian cold may disagree with me and if once in Europe how could I help myself I hope dearest aunt if you cannot make up {tear} mind yourself to come you will not set your {tear} against P.' & Mama's coming. I am sure M. would like this country provided I can offer her a suitable home which I am now in position to do. I shall write to you again by next mail, I have done so by each of the last three.

Believe me dearest aunt
yours most affectionately
W.G.C.

Sydney
June 3rd 1858.
Direct. Kamaruka
Bombala. N.S.W.

Address: Aerogramme. via Marseilles./ Miss Clairmont/Messrs Haggard, Hale & Pixley/ 8 Copthall Court City/Throgmorton street London.
Postmark: [illeg.]/JU 4/ 1858/ [illeg.]W SOUTH WALES

Unpublished. Text: M.S. Pf. Coll., CL'ANA 0079

---

1 See CL'ANA 0191.

2 Wilhelm would later marry Ottilia von Pichler, who was twelve years his junior (CL'ANA 0273). This letter and Antonia's to Claire of 25 June 1858 provide further proof of Claire's preoccupation with finding an appropriate match for Wilhelm. The conversation about securing a spouse for Wilhelm, and in particular this young lady, seems to have begun as early as 1856 (*CC* II: 584).

105 • Antonia Clairmont to Claire Clairmont (and Claire Clairmont to Antonia Clairmont)

25th June 1858. [illeg.]
49$^{0.}$

My dearest Claire!

I have received both your letters and thank you for communicating dear Willy's; I have none this time, but thank God he is well and comparatively well settled – but my dear Claire let me turn at once to the chief point of your letter; for God'sake what can make you so desirous of getting poor W.'s promise of marriage to a person he does not know, not even by name, and will not see for a year to come at least – and considering the circumstances, his coming home after such a long absence unsettled and looking about him without an income or fixed destination, the first thing he is to do is to marry – is your nephew then such a pitiful fellow, that he must rely upon a place his wife's connexions might procure him? for you did not say relations – high connexions you mentioned – why don't you tell me her name and family? you err greatly in thinking to promote W's happiness in giving him a wife used to a higher sphere of life than he moves in; it is generally the poor man's ruin to indulge his wife in these habits she has been used to – and can he have a happy moment when he must fear for ever she is comparing past and presence – and where are the great advantages that make you propose such an extraordinary step to a young man, to sign away his life and happiness to an unknown? and then you complain Willy does not take your advice – what young man would? I have written to him and begged most strenuously not to give this promise, for I can see no earthly use for it – but unhappiness and trouble would be the consequence; I have just here the same case, in a friend of mine, whose son made a match of that sort; they are now married four years and he is unhappy and ruined – his mother giving up all her own to him is fallen into melancholy – and her relations use and abuse him! now God forbid my dear Willy should have such a fate – so pray my dear Claire drop all thought for the present, and let Willy spend his remaining time in pleasant expectation of home – and think also if you entangle the poor boy into this marriage, you will bestow new unhappiness upon us all for I shall never go to settle in England, and W will not be happy in a new separation – and how you would reproach yourself then ! if the advantages you see in this match have no surer basis than the one you mentioned of letters given to our ministers by Earl so and so they are weak indeed – and can you think W. in need of such paltry recommendations here in his own country? you do not overrate his merits and character – but I must conclude else I shall get warm – excuse my plain speaking, but the mother in me is easily affected, and I wish W. to be happy in marriage, a treasure his love will be, ~~and~~ but it must be given with reflection, and not signed away like Esau's birthright for a dish of lentilles.[1] Pray write soon again and tell me you are not displeased with your affectionate

A.C.

My Answer 15 July 1858.[2]

My dear Tonie

I am not displeased at your not liking the marriage I proposed for Willy. We english are accustomed to allow every Individual the use of their judgment. But I certainly am much hurt at the tone in which you express your disapproval. I cannot think that if you had confidence in my understanding, or confidence in my affection for my relations, you could have written me the letter you have written. [illeg.] Therefore, of course, it wounds me to be distrusted, feeling as I do, that I do not merit distrust. Alas you have misconceived in one point, my intentions. I never wished to obtain from Willy a promise of marriage for a young lady he does not know. What I wished to obtain from him was that [~~illeg.~~] if he returned to England heart and fancy free he would make the acquaintance of the young lady and if they were mutually satisfied with each other, that they should marry. The next thing you ask me is, "whether I think Willy such a pitiful person that he must rely upon a place procured by his Wife's connexions". What can you think I must be made of, not to be wounded by such an implication? You ought, had you a just idea of me, to feel well assured that not only I never entertained any thing but respect and affection for your Son: so much so, that if I had not had a remarkable affection and esteem for him, I should never have been cruel and unjust enough to endeavour to marry to a "pitiful fellow," a young lady whom I admire and esteem so much as I do the one in question. Another passage of your letter is as follows: "if the advantages you see in this match have no surer Basis than the one you mentioned of letters given to our Ministers by Earl So and So, they are weak indeed; and can you think Willy in need of such paltry recommendations in his own country? You do not overrate his merits and character – but I must conclude else I shall get warm the Mother in me is so easily affected". Allow me in answer to these passages to recall to your Memory what it seems strange you should so entirely have overlooked; that long before I mentioned the young lady's connexions, I mentioned her virtues. It was the rare and peculiar excellence of her understanding, of her Soul and Heart that first drew me to her; I described to you her admirable qualities, her love of Order, of frugality, her Industry, never idle, but always employed in needlework or some household duty making with her own hands, her dresses her Bonnets and all her apparel; her love of domestic life and domestic occupations – her patience under disagreeable circumstances, and in a life of the utmost dullness, without one affection or Joy, without even one amusement except what she gathers from her music and flowers.[3] I told you these qualities sprang unbiassed from her own nature, as she has no one to direct or guide or incite or force her to the performance of any one duty whatever. Her sense of right is such, that of herself she keeps constant to the good path, and would suffer the extremity of pain rather than act wrongly in the smallest particular. Knowing how few of such characters are to be found, for the sake of these moral perfections I ardently hoped she might one day be united to Willy because it struck me their dispositions were so similar, their qualities so alike, they would be happy with each other. This was the great and principal advantage in my view of the question – afterwards I mentioned her connexions as a mere adjunct – a happy adjunct I will say, which would augment, not their happiness – but their worldly prosperity: for I do not think with you that connexions are paltry things. Far from it. So much so that in this scene of toil and struggle, one can never have too many good connexions, since however meritorious a person may be, it is difficult to get on without good connexions. In conclusion I beg therefore to state most decidedly that her virtues were my first inducement in wishing the union; her connexions were a corollary in my mind, not a primal cause.[4] I think I may further add that had you had that confidence in my Judgment and my affection for my relations which you ought to have, these reflections would naturally have presented themselves to your mind, and would have saved you the trouble of writing me a letter which appears [~~illeg.~~] to be scornful in its tone towards me, and also you would have saved me the pain of deeming myself totally misconceived, totally unappreciated, and entirely distrusted by you. Such is the impression your letter has made and under the circumstances I think it best for you and myself that I should decline taking any further interest in my dear nephew's marriage. I am never desirous of taking responsibility upon myself – only the idea that I should be acting a treacherous part towards you all, if I did not endeavour (when this excellent union presented itself,) to secure the prize for him, and to the young lady the prize of such a Husband as she would have had in Willy, this idea caused me to exert myself – But now having done my duty and entirely failed in my good intentions towards all parties, I am very content to withdraw.

Address: Miss Clairmont/ Handcross, Croyden[5]/ Surrey./ England.
Front postmark: Baden/ $^{26}/_{6}$ / 5. EXP.
Rear postmark: London/ [illeg.]/JU 30/ 58

Unpublished. Text: M.S., Pf. Coll., CL'ANA 0361

---

1 "Then Jacob gave Esau bread and pottage of lentiles; and he did eat and drink, and rose up, and went his way: thus Esau despised his birthright," Genesis, 25:34 (King James Bible).

2 Claire's response.

3 On 6 September 1856, Claire described the young lady in question, noting in particular her excellent domestic skills, her compassionate nature, and her conscientious attitude towards her work (*CC* II: 584).

4 In her letter to Antonia of 16 August 1856, Claire begged Antonia not to allow her penniless friend, Miss Falcon, to stay with her for fear that it would "expose him [Wilhelm] to her seductions" (*CC* II: 579). Claire felt that Wilhelm needed to marry someone "that may raise him in life" (p. 579). On 6 September 1856, while she mentioned the fortune of the young lady she intended for Wilhelm, she was concerned primarily with the lady's physical health, her family members' healthy constitutions, and the intended's domestic virtues. Antonia misrepresented Claire's intentions in her response and Claire was quick to correct her, as this second letter shows.

5 Claire was living with Mr. and Mrs. Giles Long in Handcroft Road, Croydon, Surrey. Antonia frequently wrote the address as Handcross Road. She also spelled Croydon incorrectly.

106 • Antonia Clairmont to Claire Clairmont

I add P's direction[1] 490 Baden 2nd July 1858

My dearest Claire.

After having given up all hope of having a letter from Willy, I got one dated 26th March – it does not contain anything new, but what he told you about his stay at Mr M's and the certainty of his coming home next year – to come home directly is quite impossible, for there is three months imprisonment in case a person leaves his trust and engagement in such a manner[2] so my dear Claire let us be satisfied in the hope of seeing him next year and rejoice that three months of the second year are already gone, for he tells me his contract was signed the 27th of March and we are now in July – I hope my dear Claire you are not displeased with me for not agreeing with you in the object you have so much at heart[3] – let us wait patiently till W. is here – and settled – then it will be time for him to think of marrying; and may be make himself and us happy by his choice. you say you concluded the match with Tetty was broken off – it was never on – it is by mere prudence that I kept back, so as not to entangle the poor fellow, or give hopes to her which may not be fulfilled, and then be highly unpleasant to both the parties so do you take my example, and let things take their course, and see what God will send us – I had a letter from Pauline, but she had none from you, perhaps it was lost, as you had not the right direction; she is well and in spirits, but so occupied she says she never had less time to think and feel than she has now; she sent me the whole of her half year's salary to buy in stock for her, of which I am very glad, as it proves her desire to do right – some fine presents she received in bonnets and dresses from both the Countesses and her skill in dress making enabled her to save the whole £40 – and here allow me to remark – you had the kindness to offer Pauline £60 pr ann. if she would stay at home, but she preferred exerting her own talents to living upon your bounty; but don't you think a small part of that sum would be well applied now as a reward of her industry and economie? if you were to add ten pds to her 40, it would encourage her to persevere, and as a proof of your approbation be doubly pleasant and agreable I could then with a little help from my side fill up the 2d share 1000 fl X of Mettalliques which would give her a sure interest of £10 per ann

X[4] the 1st and part of the 2d. I bought with the £100 –

which is in our money 100f [illeg.][5] and would be a nice pocketmoney for her if once W. is here and she at home with us – I shall be extremely happy to bring that to bear – she has always been a support to me, during her absence in England and Australia she has sent me at different times £200 – to help me on through all my troubles; as soon as W. is here and I can look to him in case of need, I shall make over the interest of that sum to her – I much regret your not coming, for we should have had so much to talk over – however under present circumstances it is better to leave it for next year – I am now so displeased with Baden, it is such a dear place, and in Winter I am so far from P. – I have now consulted another physician he forbids the warm baths – I must take cold ones – Vöslau[6] – but I must have washes backwards and forwards, so I am out of patience a little only – ever yours affect A.C.

Address: Miss Clairmont/Handcross, Croyden/Surrey, England.
Front postmark: K· K·FAHRENDES/OST MT N: 9[7]
Rear postmark: LONDON/JY 6/ 5[illeg.]; [illeg.]

Unpublished. Text: M.S. Pf. Coll., CL'ANA 0362

---

1 The word "direction" indicates an address.
2 See CL'ANA 0077.
3 See the correspondence between 1856 and 1858 on the subject of Wilhelm's marriage.
4 Antonia wrote the words, "the 1st and part of the 2d I bought with the £100 –" upside down at the bottom of the page. They were meant to be inserted at the first X.
5 See note 2, CL'ANA 0404.
6 Bad Vöslau was a spa town, some 35 kilometers from Vienna.
7 Probably "Postamt," (German for "post office").

107 • Wilhelm Gaulis Clairmont to Claire Clairmont

[4 July 1858]

My dearest aunt.

I duly rec^{d} yours of the 9th April. I am afraid as your last letter still shows you so eagerly bent on my return that the news communicated in my last must have been displeasing to you.[1] It is very harassing that this difference of opinion should exist; but what am I to do for myself on my return to Austria; to trust simply to marriage for a competency would in my opinion be madness; and I am getting too old now to submit to all the drudgery of beginning a new career over again. I am also very doubtful of the climate; Twofold Bay is ~~for~~ although very mild still colder than the Murrumbidgee being more exposed to the cold southerly winds coming across the Antarctica sea & I sometimes think that if it were much colder as cold as Pauline describes Austria I should not be able to bear it. You talk about my settling in Italy or Tyrol[2] – the first I should not like (otherwise than for a change) the second is very cold in winter but either would be unfeasible because I could not exercise a choice but should have to take employment wherever I could get it. I do not urge you to come out here because I do not think you would when once here arrived like this country. But with Mama it is different – she has not so many wants, she cares nothing about society, she is not as nervous & timid as you are; in fact I think from her past and present mode of life that she would not only bear up with but actually like the dullness and monotony of bush life which to your more lively disposition would prove insupportable I am however contented to let the matter rest in abeyance for a bit longer. I have as yet only seen the pleasant part of Kamaruka the busy season sets in on the 1st August and continues till Janry 1st perhaps it is better before we finally decide to wait and see how I can fight my way through the disagreeable part of the year. I might possibly find that it is too much fatigue for me – or the increased work cause some {tear} or other unpleasant state of things not so apparent during the easy time of the year and in such case I may be yet glad to relinquish my situation here.

I have nothing new or interesting to tell you I am out of sorts just now because my best horse died. he was only 4 years old I bought him last year for £40 as an unbroken colt and had him broken in under my immediate surveillance. he turned out so well and his temper and paces were so excellent that he was now worth £60. When I bought him it was still under the impression that I was to return [~~illeg.~~] with Mama & I intended him as a present to her. [~~illeg.~~] Another of my horses has a fistula that is a very bad wound on the {tear} rendering him for the present quite useless. so you see I have plenty of troubles Goodbye dearest aunt pray forward the enclosed to P. & believe me my dearest aunt

yours most affect.
WGC.

Kamaruka
July 4th 1858.

Address: No envelope.

Unpublished. Text: M.S. Pf. Coll., CL'ANA 0080

1 See CL'ANA 0079.

2 Tyrol is a state (Bundesland) in western Austria and includes cities such as Innsbruck and Kufstein. Known as Tirol in German, Innsbruck is its capital city. North Tyrol was originally part of the Habsburg's empire. However, after the First World War, North Tyrol became part of Austria while South Tyrol became part of Italy ("Tirol Unser Land". Web. 5 May 2016. https://www.tirol.gv.at/).

108 • Antonia Clairmont to Claire Clairmont

[29 July 1858]
490 Baden 29th 1858.

My dearest Claire.

I just received yours, and sit down directly to tell you what you wish to know – You are the only person I have spoken to about those anxieties that disturb me for some months already; to Paula I would not say anything, not to give rise to hopes and wishes, and to Willy it will cause painful uncertainty, what is he to do,? if I only give him hints or suggestions he cannot act upon them – and yet I cannot let matters go on as it is – I have been to town already, to see some friends – that is – some men of note, and wellwishers to our dear boy, such as can give advice upon more solid grounds than mere opinion – ~~I shall have~~ but they were out of town, I shall go again to morrow – their advice will be something then to guide me, in this most difficult matter – to state my doubts and fears will throw the poor fellow into perplexity and uneasiness and I am afraid injure his health for what is he to do? how is he to judge with certainty upon the steps he is to take? if I tell him stay it follows quite naturally – Paula and I shall come out[1] – and that is again wormwood and bitterness to me – You speak of going to the Tirol[2] - but who shall buy the farm? I have not money enough for such a purpose, and you may perhaps inwardly intend of doing so yourself, but you ~~may~~ would not do it in the end, for Tyrol is more strange to you than Australia – and you would not like to go and settle there I am sure – you would find yourself more at home in Austr: however I shall do nothing without informing you of it my dear Claire you said once – you had not been asked about the children's going to Austr and yet it was your opinion which chiefly got me to consent so easily – for you said once soon after my husband's death – "you robb your children of their birth right by keeping them in Austria" these words lay heavy upon my mind and guided me the more as I fully recognized the truth and the importance of their meaning – the persons I want to see in town are – one great lawyer – one statesman and one great merchant – and if they are all of opinion he is better there than here – what then ? your picture of the Lady is admirable, if she has all those virtues you mention she will make a husband happy indeed once more I aspire you my great objection was to his giving his promise without knowing her – could you manage to let her and P. go out if we decide upon his staying? we have now very bad wheather every day rain and wind – I have left off the warm baths, but not begun the cold ones – 30th just received your 2nd letter and am deeply touched with all you say – my first lines will ease your mind in so far as nobody knows as yet of my fears – for I am like you afraid of alarming the dear boy ~~and~~ which must not be done lightly – I have also often considered that point in Willy's character that he is not likely to mix or take great interest in politics – he used often to say – a farmer must be a conservative, because he wants quiet – for the moment I must conclude as I want this to get off – and shall write more fully on my return from town – and thanks my dear Claire for your love to my children ever

yours affect –
A.C.[3]

we have rain every day and this prevented me from going to town today as I intended to do – tomorrow is Saturday, and that is a bad day for finding people at leisure they hasten their business to go out of town – so don't wonder if you have to wait a couple of days for my next – good bye my dear Claire be sure I wish nothing more than to have him here, but am afraid of not doing my duty if I consider my wishes more than his good –

Address: Miss Clairmont/ Handcross, Croyden/ Surrey./ England.
Front postmark: BADEN/ $^{31}/_{7}$ / 5. EXP.
Rear postmark: [illeg.]oeln./2 8 III /Verviers.; LONDON/ AU 4/ 58

Unpublished. Text: M.S., Pf. Coll., CL'ANA 0363

1 The plan was for Antonia and Pauline to follow Wilhelm to Australia.
2 Tirol is the German spelling for Tyrol.
3 Antonia included a small insert with the following paragraph written on it.

109 • Antonia Clairmont to Claire Clairmont

[4 August 1858]
4th of August 858
15. Weikersdorf Baden.

My dearest Claire.

I have just received yours with the check for 7 p. 10 s. inclosed; accept my best thanks for it and for all your kindness; if I am called away, my children will have a friend and a mother in you, that thought consoles me! I am astonished such a small place as Epsom[1] has a Bank we have none here nor at any of the other towns, not even such as Prague or Lemberg[2] – I shall go to town with it, to Mr. Maier's he will cashe it for me – your approval of my thoughts for Willy makes me quite happy; I won't say plans because, he may be differently inclined your remarks about fortune et et are very just, and I should surely have looked to it, but there are no difficulties whatever; Mrs Sch.[3] the mother is a widow, and has only two daughters the oldest, is 20 and also engaged to an amiable young man – the second my darling Tetty is 18. they live in kindness and harmony; if God is propitious to my wishes we shall all be happy – towards Willy, I shall have to proceed with the utmost caution and delicacy on his account as on her's; I cannot let him know her preference – and therefore, it is ~~good~~ better I should reside at Baden at his arrival; I can then give her the advantage of a first impression, ere he gets to town and is invited out as I know he will be by all our friends; Mrs Drathshmid has two daughters and two nieces the former are rather too old for him - but the nieces are young and lovely and though I love them dearly, yet I should prefer Tetty for a daughter in law; and for Willy's wife; but I would not have you think the worse, of the others; sweet Hermine the youngest of the nieces I always looked upon as Charley's future[4] – oh you would love them all if you were here – Fritz[5] is now in England, he will also come to London; I did not dare to offer him an introduction to you; you were just then going into the country, I did not know how you would have liked, so I told Mrs D. the truth and gave him Knox's direction; he saw him at our house in Weidling, when the Knoxes were here.[6] however Knox does not mention him in his last – but my dear Claire, how can you divide a mother and children's interests? If I beg for my children or for myself, is that not the same? and I told you, I had proofs that K. does not mind his own promises: when poor Emmy went to England to nurse poor Clary, I think he ought to have paid her the journey. he ~~also~~ gave her some of Clary's linen and clothes, and said he would pay the carriage for these and also her journey, if she arrived home, she must write and tell him what it all comes to, and then he said, further he would give to Charley £40 pr. an: till he was 21. and the first remittance would come at such and such a time – the luggage cost a great deal, so the journey X[7]

Address: No envelope

Unpublished. Text: M.S., Pf. Coll., CL'ANA 0364

---

1 From July 1856, Claire was living in Epsom, Surrey. In her letter of 5 July, she asked Antonia to address her letters care of Mrs. Innerarity, Epsom, and she described Epsom as being "about 17 miles from London". Claire explained that the air in Epsom was satisfactory and that there was a railroad to London (*CC* II: 564). Her letters from 1858 were written from Croydon, Surrey, 16 kilometers from Epsom. By then, she was staying at the home of Mr. and Mrs. Giles Long.

2 Lemburg was the German name for the town of Lviv, located some 794 kilometers from Vienna. Lviv is part of Ukraine today. Prague is the capital today of the Czech Republic. The defeat of the Austro-Hungarian Empire in 1918 resulted in the creation of Czechoslovakia and Prague was chosen as the capital city. After the dissolution of Czechoslovakia in 1993, Prague became the capital city of the newly independent Czech Republic.

3 Antonia previously wrote Tetty's last name as Strimasko. See CL'ANA 0347.

4 Antonia may have misinterpreted Charley's affections. After Wilhelm's return from Australia in 1861, he went on a tour of various estates to look at possible farms for purchase, an account of which he recorded in his Sands and Kenny's Diary of 1861. In this unpublished diary, he writes on 20 April of visiting a friend of Charley's, Sophie Gratichy: "I took more than usual interest in her presence she was very much attached to Charlie; she & her parents spoke very much of him as did all the people there and at Hostitz" (CL'ANA 0177, unpublished journal, Pforzheimer Collection).

5 See CL'ANA 0393.

6 Pauline referred to Clara and Knox's visit in her letter to Emily of 8 July 1855. See CL'ANA 0233.

7 The letter is incomplete and ends here. Antonia certainly included additional pages (as the X indicates), but they are missing.

110 • Antonia Clairmont to Claire Clairmont

490. Baden 8th August 1858.

My dearest Claire.

We have such horrid rains that I have been prevented day after day from going to town, yesterday however, a half favorable wheather I went but alas, not a soul I found, it was all in vain – and I must write now to Willy I have already let two post days pass, so may God guide my pen that I may say neither too much nor too little – God knows wether it would not be for the best, to let him there to enjoy the fruits of his labours, and let poor Paula join him, what has the poor girl here? she must be a governess –. – and she greatly prefers Australia – your idea of going to live in the southern Tyrol is quite castles in the air – it is not a productive country for farming undertaking and though we could manage to live but do you think Willy would like such a position to be for ever dependent on his aunt and mother ? to take a farm such as would be worth Willy's time and exertions one must have capital – £1000 would be the least – I have so much, but I could not give it him – it being my sole maintenance for my and dear Paula's old age – besides if I made a sacrifice, it ought rather to be for Paula's settlement think how your mother[1] judged in that case – she said also my daughter shall have my all – and your brother did not think her wrong – Hungary is country for the farmer and there is also the danger for the future – I must tell poor W. of these things, also of our finances – you say I should sell out and buy a house or ~~grounds~~ land – the house I cannot buy for it would fix me to the spot, and if W. were to return or I should like to go to him I should have to sell again – as to land – but do not think me wavering and inconsequent. I am sitting here sad and solitary pondering over and considering things, looking at them from all sides – I should like to buy a piece of land, it sells cheaply too, in consequence of the bad state of finances that every body is involved – estates large and small are sequestered and sold by auction, and money being scarce there are not many bidders – but that would just be the means of bringing dear Willy back – and I have not resolved what is best for him? I am going to write now to him – to Pauline I have not said anything, she is well, but so much occupied she has hardly time to give me a line, poor girl she would be happy to return – I shall be most careful in what I say to him only hints – in a month or so Mr K.[2] Willis great friend will be back. he is in franzensbad[3] – then I shall know better – farewell my dear Claire I am most unhappy about all this uncertainty – ever yours

most gratefully A.C.

Address: Miss Clairmont,/ Handcross, Croyden,/ Surrey - England.
Front postmark: BADEN/ 8/8 / 1. EXP.
Rear postmark: WIEN/ 8/8 / 5[illeg.]

Unpublished. Text: M.S., Pf. Coll., CL'ANA 0365

1 Mrs. Godwin.

2 Karl von Kleyle (1812–1859). According to *Österreichisches Biographisches Lexikon*, Von Kleyle studied law and politics at the University of Vienna. In 1834, he worked for Archduke Karl and then, from 1847 onwards, for Archduke Albrecht in Silesia. In 1849, von Kleyle was in charge of farming, agriculture, and forestry in Teschen, Silesia. Later, Archduke Albrecht assigned von Kleyle to Galicia. From 1853 onwards, he was the head of the Forestry and Mining Department in Vienna. He designed a plow (Kleyle's Pflug) which was named for him ("Kleyle, Karl von". *Österreichisches Biographisches Lexikon.* 1815–1950, Bd. 3 (Lfg. 15, 1965), p. 400. Web. 20 April 2015. http://www.biographien.ac.at/oebl/oebl_K/Kleyle_Karl_1812_1859.xml). See also CL'ANA 0338.

3 Franzensbad is the German name for Františkovy Lázně, a spa town in the Czech Republic today. It is located some 552 kilometers from Vienna.

111 • Antonia Clairmont to Claire Clairmont

490. Baden 10th Aug: 1858.

My dearest Claire.

You must have got now mine where I told you of my failure in finding the friends I went to see – I sincerely regret giving you such uneasiness, you say how it comes I did not see things before – but these don't come at once to be seen; our newspapers we can have no confidence in, for they never may speak the truth being all under strict observance; it is now nearly a year since I wrote those letters – at Pauline's arrival – which made the dear boy determine to come home – and since then things have taken such an unfortunate turn. the concord at then newborn, is developing the financial crisis too,[1] and many other things we could not foresee then, and if I have been silent till now, it was the fear of giving uneasiness to all the parties – I have now written to Willy, and tried to speak lightly of it, I put in my letter some newspaper extract, a table of calculation of our new money, and two clerical edicts he will see by these how things are, and pause and consider – I did not seem to think my news of such weight as likely to prevent his return, do not you I beg you say anything about it in your letter, perhaps you had better not to write at all for this post, for your letter will only impart all the uneasiness you fell yourself – let what I told him, undisturbed by your fears and suggestions – work on his mind – and let us have the result of his own thoughts- and do not for Goodness sake talk about marriage to him it will disgust him I assure you nor can I say that the readiness of the relations to let the girl go out, throws a good light upon the whole affair or pleases me – however it is time to speak about that when W. has once declared his determination to stay where he is – I cannot believe of her knowing nothing of your plans, she must know of it by this time or she is no woman – now tell me candidly, have you not made an [~~illeg.~~] agreement with her family what to settle upon Willy in case he mar~~r~~ries her? I do not think I asked you whether you would [~~illeg. illeg.~~]buy a farm in Tyrol,[2] because I never thought you would – I also said Tyrol was not at all the country for agricultural undertakings – but I must break off wanting very much to get this off in times, in order to regulate your letter to dear Willy, pray believe me dear Claire, it is better on your part to say nothing to him about our difficulties – about foreigners buying landed property in Austria, I think you had satisfactory answers ten years ago when poor Charles made all those inquiries for you as you proposed then to buy an estate or house in town – for my part I shall not take any step till I have seen Dr B. and Mr Kl.[3] who will be back by the end of this month and can advise me; now try to keep quiet and let us leave all things to Gods management – when I feel I have done my duty I am always so, come what may – next time I'll answer fully your other questions.

yours most affect
A.C.

I have no letter from Willy, though the mail must have arrived for there were two for Paula

Address: No envelope

Unpublished. Text: M.S., Pf. Coll., CL'ANA 0366

---

1 From 1854 until 1857, Austrian forces occupied the principalities of Walachia and Moldavia. In 1857, the Austrian army withdrew its forces, leaving the principalities united under the title the "United Principalities of Wallachia and Moldavia". Each principality, however, had a separate government, ruler, and military. In 1859, the two principalities officially united after they each elected Prince Alexandru Ioan Cuza to lead them. By 1859, Austria was at war with France and Sardinia. See K. Hitchins, *A Concise History of Romania* (New York: Cambridge University Press, 2014).

2 See CL'ANA 0365.

3 Dr. Budinsky and Mr. Kleyle. See CL'ANA 0322 and CL'ANA 0365.

112 • Antonia Clairmont to Claire Clairmont

490. Baden. 16th Aug 1858.

My dearest Claire.

I received yours and Willy's letter yesterday, like you I am deeply grieved but not angry, I do not abuse and reproach – God does every thing for the best – and so I must also think now – if it is for his and poor P's best – I should submit – you think I had~~e~~ written to him long ago on all the anxieties I had – when I had repeatedly said that you are the only person I spoke to about I am sorry you have no better opinion of me; I have no plans how should I, the only thing I wish is to let Pauline depart as soon as possible. I have and announced to her the new turn of affairs, she will be astonished – if she can get off her place, I should let her sett out instantly so as to have all the sacrifice over – it is no use to struggle against destiny – but pray for Heaven's sake refrain from abusing the poor children in your letters to me, it grieves me deeply and they do not deserve it[1] – I cannot say any more and shall seek strength by Him who gives it. Who would have thought when I laid poor Charleys head to rest that my tri~~y~~als were far from being ended – ever yours

affect. A.C.

Can you give me some news about sailing, if P. can manage to be in England by the beginning of Nov. whether that is still a good time for sailing? and do not think it is she wishes to go – but I wish brother and sister to be together I am an old root and better not unhoused –

Address: Miss Clairmont/ Handcross, Croyden/ Surrey England.
Front postmark: K·K·FAHRENDES/POSTAMT [illeg.]
Rear postmark: Coeln./ 18[illeg.]/Verviers; LONDON/AU 19/58

Unpublished. Text: M.S., Pf. Coll., CL'ANA 0368

---

1 These letters are missing. For the year 1858, Stocking only includes two letters from Claire in *The Clairmont Correspondence*, one to Antonia dated July 1858 and another to Antonia dated August 1858. A letter from Claire to Dina Williams Hunt in December 1862 follows them. The next letters date from 1869.

113 • Antonia Clairmont to Claire Clairmont

490 Baden 28th Aug. 1858.

My dearest Claire.

Thank god your letter tells me you are not really ill, I was in great anxiety about you! and feel the truth of all you say, but what ~~I~~ can I do? after what Willy said, I cannot urge him to return, to give up the hard earned position he has got into to toil here and make a fresh beginning, it is however but natural that I wish Pauline to be with him – I cannot bear the thought of separating the two young beings – let them remain and grow old near each other and in the country they are to live in otherwise they will grow estranged to each other – I cannot be so selfish as to require P. to remain here for my sake and W. left alone – do not think Pauline will leave me lightly but she will do so at my request and God will give me strength to get through it <u>if required</u> – and P. knowing she does not leave me from any selfish motives, but at my express will, so as I [~~illeg.~~] think best for my children, will not I hope lose any of the esteem her friends formerly thought her worthy of – oh my dear Claire think of the visit poor Charles paid you at Paris, when you had not met before for so long, should not you have been happier to have spent the intervening time near him in the protection of his brotherly love and friendship than being thrown amongst strangers?[1] I shall then go and live in some cave in the mountains, my capital I will deposit somewhere that it will be sure to the children after my death, and so await my master's call – to be sure the children will not be happy, but who is? it is clear by Willy's letter that he wishes to marry – he says "in Austria I could not think of marrying till I had a home, and how long that might be is very doubtful but here I have already what I might there have years to wait for – can I ask him to give up all, and come home to ~~make~~ begin again? in the state our affairs are at present? so I can do nothing but submit and suffer – you might do more you might smooth all, bring Willy back, get the match to take place, and bring us all together to live in love and friend ship, but will you do so? I have already told you that now is the moment for buying landed property – many causes combine, one of them is government having made over to the national bank extensive crown lands in payment of certain debts – these are now selling by auction in smaller and larger ~~parcels~~ lots – I send you here an advertisement of a small but exquisite lot at the price of £2600;[2] you understand German read it how immensely cheap and advantageous a bargain it is – situated on the frontiers of Styria[3] near Rohitsh – a Gesundbrunnen[4] of a known healthy situation – fertile in the extreme, melons and figs growing in the open air, the near neighbourhood of Italy – then a dear friend of Willy's a Count Sermage,[5] who studied with him in Altenburg has his estates near – but that is an after consideration – buy this my dear Claire and you will make us all happy and surely you will not lose by it nor have to regret it – instead of going to Italy we should go there Pauline of course with us, I take the management of the concern in which Count Richard Sermage would be very useful to me – and then you living on your own estate in your own chateau you could invite your young friend over, and next may we should have to look forward for Willy's arrival and all would turn out as you wished – and do not think you would lose the interest of your money, in case you should not feel inclined to live there – Good God how pleasing a picture; in a commodious house of your own with coach at command and a loving and grateful family around you – oh my dear Claire do make up your mind to it. be the saviour of all the painful sufferings in store for us, if not awarded by your means – you said you are not disinclined to do such a thing so do it at once now the oportunity offers so temptingly – Willy will have nothing to say to M.M.[6] if he hears what expects him here and oh the happiness you will confer upon the poor boy, and upon us all – won't it be much better so, than to live all separated and sad and solitary – Now my dear Claire consider and tell me – if you say yes I shall [~~illeg.~~] take all the necessarry steps to do the thing right and tight – you might also write to Baron Eskeles[7] who is one of the bank directors – my great support Mr. Maier we have lost – but I know one or two other persons of note whom I shall try to interest, but only when you say yes decidedly for it would not do to trouble those people and take up their time merely to make inquiries – besides it costs a great deal of money coaches et to go to town and pay such visits – you see the sale takes place on the 22 Sept: so there is not much time to be lost – you would have to send me a power of Attorney – if you were very active you might come here at once but that would hurry you too much – better have the bargain concluded and I and P. go down set things in order a little and then you and your friend arrive, and we spend the winter together rejoicing dear W. with our narratives and hurrying him to come and join us – whether the buildings are out of repair I can not say, but should find it in the conditions of sale if I go to town – to be sure one ought to go and have a look at the premisses – but I have not the money to spare, and it would cost at least ten pds: there have been some great purchases made by foreign princes, German and also one French nobleman bought extensive landed property in Hungary – the nearness of the southern railroad is a great advantage to you, as you can go to Venice any day you like to spend the winter months there – now my heart is so easy, I think you will consent, if you do, send at once the power of Attorney; in which I think you must mention the sum I may go to in buying the estate in your name – then you are Madame la Chatelaine[8] – when I hold that inestimable paper in my hand I shall feel sure of seeing my dear Willy again – I expect dear P. to visit me – the Css.[9] gave her leave of absence for a few days so that we can talk over that most unexpected stroke- the poor girl is quite unhappy she says she can't think to be able to leave me. oh my dear Claire do relieve us all and be sure I would not propose it if there were the least danger for you as to loss of property – and knowing your kind and generous heart I think you will be happy with us.

ever yours affect – A.C.

Address: Miss Clairmont/ Handcross, Croyden./ Surrey, England.
Front postmark: BADEN/ $^{28}/_{8}$ / 5. EXP.
Rear postmark: WIEN/ $^{29}/_{8}$ /6 F

Unpublished. Text: M.S., Pf. Coll., CL'ANA 0367

---

1 In 1845, Charles Clairmont visited Claire, who was living in Paris and whom he had not seen for many years. In her letter to Mary Shelley of 1 August 1845, Claire described the visit, noting that she was delighted to see her brother. Evidently Claire gave Charles a letter from Mary Shelley at that time, because on 1–23 November 1845, Charles wrote to Mary Shelley to thank her for the letter, the monetary gift enclosed (which, he noted, he had used to buy presents for his children and wife), and for renewing their friendship. He observed that he felt the "long and icy silence" between himself and Mary Shelley had been occasioned by a loan she made him in 1829, even though he had paid her back, and thanked Mary Shelley for reestablishing contact with him (*CC* II: 462). Charles expressed the hope that they would be firm friends going forward.

2 Antonia included a newspaper cutting in this letter. What follows is a translation of the announcement:

Announcement

A corpus of land consisting of several parts of the domain of Miljana in Croatia, which is situated along the border of Styria, 3 hours from the Pöltschach railway station and 1½ hours from the Bath of Rohitsch, is offered for sale at auction.

Included with it are the castle and outbuildings and an official's residence in Miljana, then a grist mill on the Sutla River, also 6 joch 1475 square klafter of intravillan and garden lands, 75 joch 782 square klafter of fields, 88 joch 427 square klafter of meadow, 4 joch 1424 square klafter of vineyards, and 380 joch 1588 square klafter of woodlands, thus 556 joch 896 square klafter in a well-rounded complex; and finally the right to operate taverns in the towns of Miljana, Poljana, and Kosnica, as well as hunting and fishing rights.

This land will be offered for sale at public auction in Miljana on September 22, 1858, at 10 o'clock in the morning, subject to higher approval.

Anyone wishing to take part in the auction must pay one tenth of the bid price in cash, or in Austrian government securities, which are accepted at 2% below the Viennese exchange rate for the day to the Auction Committee.

Written offers are accepted until September 15, 1858, at the private Austrian National Bank in Vienna and then at the public proceedings until the conclusion of the oral auction.

These offers must be accompanied by the 10% vadium and, along with the specific amount, expressed in numbers and spelled out, a declaration that the offerer knows the purchase terms exactly and submits to them unconditionally.

The detailed terms of the auction can be viewed at the National Bank in Vienna, at the Imperial Royal Finance Land Administration in Zagreb, and at the Domains Office in Miljana; the National Bank Foreign Division will also provide it in writing upon request.

Those wishing to see the property must contact the Domains Office there.

Vienna, August 25, 1858.

(Translation provided by Ann Sherwin)

Joch = 1600 *Quadratklafter* (square *Klafter*). A Lower Austrian *Klafter* was 189.6484 cm

3 The Duchy of Styria (Steiermark in German) was an Austrian state located in the south-east of the country. After the First World War, parts of Styria, including the Styrian city of Marburg (Maribor), were given to Yugoslavia. Today, Styria is one of the nine states (Bundesländer) of Austria (The Editors of Encyclopaedia Britannica. "Steiermark". *Encyclopaedia Britannica Online*. Encyclopaedia Britannica., n.d. Web. 10 May 2016. http://www.britannica.com/place/Steiermark). Wilhelm would eventually farm in Maribor for some years.

4 German for "mineral spring".

5 Richard von Sermage (1831–1903) attended school with Wilhelm in Altenburg. Sermage married Princess Franziska Wurmbrand-Stuppach, and they had a daughter, Alexandrina Maria Luise Sermage who was born in Oroslavje in 1864. He later married Karoline Feldkirchen, with whom he had no children (S. Ream. "Bowie, Costello, Cox et al". Web. 14 December 2014. http://wc.rootsweb.ancestry.com/cgi-bin/igm.cgi?op=GET&db=suaream&id=I19427). The Sermage de Szomszédvár et Medvegrád family were originally of French origin from Besançon in eastern France. The family was conferred a noble title in 1749 and they were active in Hungarian and Austrian politics (*Magyar Nemzetségi Zsebkönyv* (Handbook of Hungarian Clans), József Szinnyei and László Fejérpataky (eds.) [Budapest: Magyar Heraldikai és Genealógiai Társaság, 1888–1905], vol. 1, pp, 212–14). Translation provided by Steven Tötösy de Zepetnek.

Hitschmann lists Oroslavje as Richard Sermage's birthplace and records that he was a "Gutsbesitzer" after graduation, the German word for "land owner" (pp. 68–9). See CL'ANA 0246.

6 Mr. Manning.

7 Denis, Baron von Eskeles (1803–1876). Denis von Eskeles was the son of Bernhard von Eskeles (1753–1839), an Austrian banker. Bernhard von Eskeles founded the Austrian National Bank in 1816. Earlier, in 1787, he founded the Bankhaus Arnstein und Eskeles with Nathan Arnstein. Eskeles's son, Denis, managed the bank after his father's death. Bernard's daughter married Count von Wimpffen (Isidore Singer and Gotthard Deutsch. "Eskeles, Bernhard, Freiherr von". *Jewish Encyclopedia*. 1906. Web. 24 October 2015. http://www.jewishencyclopedia.com/articles/5856-eskeles-bernhard-freiherr-von). See CL'ANA 0402.

8 French for "Mistress of the castle".

9 Countess.

114 • Antonia Clairmont to Claire Clairmont

490 Baden. 15th Sept. 1858.

My dear Claire.

I had just sent away my last when yours arrived, and I see by it that you will again give yourself up to the hope of W's return – but it will bring on a new disappointment – I shall hope no more to see him and only try to be consoled in the idea that he is well in health and prosperous – I have had a short letter from Pauline, she will come to see me on the 17th – [illeg.] things kept her the children are acting a play for the Grandmother's name's day Helen,[1] which is to day – so she could not get off before, besides they had the house full of visitors and they can't get on without her – what will the countess say to have to part with her ? as soon as we have talked over affairs and considered or fixed something I will write to you – perhaps the content of Willy's letter will guide us; I sent it off inclosed (spelling as is) with the others pr[2] Rezepisse,[3] so they are sure to get into her hands – and today there arrived another Sidney letter for her with Baden via Trieste – I can't conceive why W. should take it into his head that my letters are going to be lost, and trouble you with them however so much is sure that I have none this time – God knows but I have a sort of stoniness coming over me, submission I have, but not of the right kind I am rather stemmed by the repeated trials imposed on me – but let me not complain uselessly – about farming and all that we shall say nothing more for the present and let me beg you not to press W to return, at least do not mention me in the reasons you may urge to him; think how we should reproach ourselves, if he were to give up all and come here and fall ill – partly the climate and partly anxiety as to his success might have bad influence on his constitution I hope you are a little better now and do not listen to all those people that pester you for services and advice the latter I should chiefly distrust for having side purposes of their own, and I would look close whether my advice had really been taken – what a poor silly creature the Lady in pregnancy[4] must be – to make such fuss after the 9th child too, no doubt all her friends and husband to booth – wish her quietly in the tomb, and how can a woman of your sense believe such ridiculous nonsense – her I should also suspect of other designs upon me; your letter I have also sent to P. and as soon as I have got it back I'll return it. We have now beautiful whether,[5] I am taking long walks which is my only pleasure – Once more my dear Claire let us resign to our fate and believe me ever yours affecty

A.C.

Address: Miss Clairmont/ Handcross, Croyden/ Surrey, England.
Front postmark: [illeg.]/POSTAMT [illeg.]
Rear postmark: LONDON/F A/ SP 20/ 58; [illeg.]/ 17 9/BRESLAU

Unpublished. Text: M.S., Pf. Coll., CL'ANA 0339

1 The feast day of St. Helena is 18 August. Antonia mistook the date.

2 Abbreviation for "per".

3 German for "acknowledgment of receipt" (an outdated term).

4 Unidentified.

5 Antonia's spelling for "weather".

115 • Antonia Clairmont to Claire Clairmont

490 Baden. 5th Oct. 1858.

My dearest Claire.

Your letter with the half sovereign I received and thank you warmly for sending it and more so for the affectionate kindness that breathes in the whole letter; Pauline is indeed more cheerful than before; she is satisfied with her situation, being treated like a member of the family by all; she left me on the 30th ~~indeed~~ intending to stay a day on the road, with some acquaintances of ours who have a estate in Styria near Gratz, and yesterday I got a letter from her from at Georgen,[1] quite happy and charmed with the scenery and wanting me to rent a little cottage which old Baron Binder would let me have for a trifle – they should like to have us for neighbours, I should also like very well to go there, but for the hope of Willy's return, in which case it will be preferable to be here; [~~illeg.~~] I have 3 times begun to write to you and never to my satisfaction, I could say so much and writing is so insufficient you have several times expressed a wish I should join my capital to yours in buying a farm. which I refused thinking it more necessary to do something for Pauline's establishment than Willy's; however I do not think P. will be in a hurry to marry; she will never take a poor man, and if she should happen to find a rich one to suit her taste the 3 or 400 pds I could give her would be of little consequence on the other hand, her social position will be benefitted if W. is at home and we all united, living on our own property and will perhaps have a better chance of getting married than none. so I shall have no ~~consideration~~ objection to join if circumstances make it desirable and I shall write to W. to tell him of our intentions; however I cannot but again return to my doubts; you know the agreement he made with the society was, that if he staid 3 years he was to have £500 salary – well now, if they offer to give that salary directly, would it not be natural that he would like to stay a couple of years at least to reap the reward of his previous labours privations and hard ships and come home with a 1000 pds in his pocket ? if he does so I shall not find it in my heart to find fault with him – I do not say that it is so, but it may be – in his letter to Pauline he says – "except my promise to Mama, every thing is in favour of my present position" and he is expressing his fears of our climate speaking of a person they both knew that after having been for several years in Australia on his return to Germany ~~he~~ died the first winter in Germany of a violent attack on the lungs, adding, that might be my lot too – you can see my dear Claire how delicate an affair it is for me to press his return after having read this; I was unwilling to grieve you with all these doubts, but simple truth is the best – and you had better be prepared, or at least know the true state of my mind and views – I am thinking even now that the buying an estate would bring him back directly but there also numberless difficulties in that besides the question, should we force him back if he prefers to stay ? here every body advises me not to do so to let him stay till the present crisis be over – and it is this conflict of my mind that is so trying to one's spirits – his last letter to you I sent to P. and she forgot it at Rakitsăn,[2] but will send it to you – next Thursday I shall go to town make inquiries about Miljana and other lots I have seen put up for sale;[3] I wish you could come and try to spend one winter here to see whether you find them really so dreadful as P. says they are – and do not think my dear Claire for what I said, I give up all hope, I shall tell Willy of our present difficulties, but also how low the price of land, in consequence thereof and how advantageous to buy now, than two years hence – in fact I shall speak as if I knew nothing of his "exept my promise to Mama" there is no fear of a great and sudden crash in the finances, but all is undermined and hollow, the reassumption of the cash payments at the Bank in consequence of order from High and against the judgment of our financial men does not strengthen public confidence but is hoped to create a small rise in the papers and then I can sell out – the pain is as much concerning the rise of all necessaries of life which must result from our new coins and moneys as the fall of stock – we have no private banks in Austria – the national Bank is the only one in the whole Empire,[4] ~~I~~ if I were to put my money into Rothschilds[5] hands and the Valuta[6] sinks my money would sink just the same – I do not share the panic but for the rise in provisions and all other articles that will take place – the papers are low enough already, and may sell and now to great disadvantage fearing a diminuition of interest – but that I fear not – it would be impolitic an exposure of our poverty in foreign money markets – I shall not fail to point out to Willy the favourable conjunction for the agriculturist to get land low at a moment when provisions rise and whether that might not partly make up for ~~the~~ what he might give up in Australia – I am afraid you will despise me my dear Claire for wavering about so much, but as a mother I must feel for both sides – and if I admit the bad may also bring to account the good – fare well my dear Claire I pray with you may God prosper our endeavours to bring back the dear boy.ever yours affect

A.C.

Address: Miss Clairmont/ Handcross, Croydon./ <u>Surrey</u>, <u>England.</u>
Front postmark: BADEN/ $^{5}/_{10}$/ 5. EXP.
Written on rear: Gesa Poggenburg/ Gesina Georgina Poggenburg
Rear postmark: LONDON/ [illeg.]/OC 8/58; LONDON - E/[illeg.]/OC 8/58

Unpublished. Text: M.S., Pf. Coll., CL'ANA 0340

---

1 There are three towns named Sankt Georgen (St. George) in Styria: Sankt Georgen an der Stiefing (36 kilometers from Graz), Sankt Georgen ob Judenburg (98 kilometers from Graz), and Sankt Georgen ob Murau (137 kilometers from Graz). The family Binder von Krieglstein lived in Sankt Georgen an der Stiefing.

2 Stocking notes that Pauline was a governess in "Rakicsan," Hungary. *A Gazetteer of the World* from 1856 identifies "Rakicsan or Kakitsan" as "a town in Hungary, in the comitat of Eisenburg, 14 m. ESE of Radkersburg, and 29 m. NNW of Warasdin" (London: Fullarton and Company, 1856), p. 227. Apparently the town also enjoyed "an active trade in wine" (p. 227). Pauline's daughter, Georgina, born in 1864, would live there with Countess Károlyi, for whom Pauline

worked in 1858. In her letter, Antonia misspelled the town's name. The village is in Slovenia today and is known as Battyánfalva in Hungarian and Rakičan in Slovenian. Rakičan is 228 kilometers south of Vienna. The Károlyi family owned Castle Batthyány, which became a school after the Second World War. The castle was rebuilt in 1984 ("Castle Batthyány". *Zalaszentgrót Portál*. Web. 9 June 2015. http://en.zalaszentgrot.hu/).

3 See CL'ANA 0367. Miljana is in Croatia today. It is located about 315 kilometers south of Vienna.

4 The National Bank of Austria was approved on 15 July 1817. Charles Conant explains that "the bank was accorded for twenty-five years the exclusive privilege of note issues, was exempted from the stamp taxes, and was authorized to accept deposits and discount commercial paper . . . The charter of the bank expired in 1842, but the Emperor signed a patent renewing its privileges, with some modifications, until December 31, 1866" (*A History of Modern Banks of Issue* [London: Putnams and Sons, 1909], p. 225). Ivan Berend states that "aside from the Austrian National Bank (1816), private banks were founded, such as the Arnstein und Eskeles bank, and others by Salomon Rothschild, George Sina, and Samuel Wodianer" (*History Derailed* [Berkeley: University of California Press, 2003], p. 155). See also CL'ANA 0367.

5 Salomon Mayer von Rothschild (1774–1855) founded S.M. von Rothschild in 1820, the Austrian branch of the family's banking empire.

6 German for "foreign currency".

116 • Antonia Clairmont to Claire Clairmont

490 Baden 16th Oct. 1858.

My dearest Claire.

I hope you have got both my letters. I have written to dear Willy and I hardly know whether to wish my letter success or not – everything looks more and more dreary here; the confusion attending the new money affairs is incredible, as yet we are still trying to get into the new amounts on paper only; and those that can read detail to those that cannot – for it is just the poor people – lower classes that have most to do with the small coin; on the 1st of Nov. those Millions and millions of coins in the hands of 38 Millions of people are out of use – everyone tries to get rid of the coins; some must lose at last; every body cries shame at ~~those~~ such proceedings – it is if one may say so, a regular cheating.[1] I must repeat I hardly know whether to wish for Willys return. the new military law also contains matters of dou~~d~~bts – no young man may marry till his 22nd year be completed isn't that a renewal of the old feudal bondage – Miljana sold very high, for 60.000fl £.6000 – I suppose people were in despair of what is to become of our pounds which some consider like trash – I have not sold out – I am not clear it would have been effectually useful, and I hope in time things will settle again – at all events I should have lost now in selling – so at least I have my regular interest – it is well my letter to W. was sent off before that confusion set in – I should have little heard now – perhaps it will be best to make up our minds to let W. stay a couple of years more to see how things go on, and P. to remain here meanwhile – Austria appears like a falling house badly propping up – and yet the luxury and show you meet with every where! I have just had a letter from Mrs Bouseú[2] the Hungarian lady, she is most amiable, and yet so unhappy ! and how is your health and spirits my dear Claire, shall we ever talk over together our family affairs? or shall we go on living in that solitary way each of us 4 alone, looking for society and consolation to strangers? I wrote to W. two sheets Nr 1 Dark and desponding, I gave him my best blessing if he chose to remain and conjured him to assist me to get P. back to Austria Nr 2. I showed him what might be done at his return, what you were willing to do and what our joint means in his hands could accomplish – but God knows what will be for the best – I grieve to think my dear Claire that this letter is not calculated to cheer you but this is such a moment of general calamity that one cannot bear up against it – ever yours

affectionately

A.C.

there have been two Sydney letters for P. but none from W to me.

Address: No envelope

Unpublished. Text: M.S., Pf. Coll., CL' ANA 0341

1 A decree issued on 30 April 1858 stated that one third of all new bills issued from 1 November 1858 were to be "covered by coin or bullion and that the other two-thirds should be represented in the assets of the bank by securities or commercial paper" and, furthermore, "100, 000, 000 florins in small notes" were to be retired (Conant, p. 228).

2 Unidentified.

117 • Wilhelm Gaulis Clairmont to Claire Clairmont

[31 October 1858]

My dearest aunt.

I have only five minutes to write to you just to assure you that I am in perfect health. I rec^d^ your letters of June 30th & July 12th both together some days ago – In my circumstances here nothing new has transpired; I am anxiously awaiting Mama's decision I think she would like a life out here but I think you would think it too little variety.[1] As regards your plan for my marriage I do not see that we can settle on anything just now. Even had I gone home now it would have had to be put off for indefinite times for I could not without having a fortune myself marry at once without previously procuring the at least ostensible means of subsistence. I have not seen Dr Bligh lately and could not therefore consult him about my short breath; but I will do so next time I see him not that I expect any result from it but just to satisfy you; he will say its constitutional; thats a comfortable word; fits everywhere, sounds professionally and means nothing in particular – I am at the shearing just now & terribly busy I wish it were over it worries me so much – I hear this is the last mail steamer going we shall now be dependent on sailing vessels;[2] how miserable –
Now Goodbye dearest aunt I shall write soon again

yours affectionately
WGC

Kamaruka
Octob. 31st 1858.

Address: via Marseilles./ Miss Clairmont/Messrs Haggard Hale & Pixley/ 8 Throgmorton Court City/ London
Rear postmark: BOMBALA/ NO 3/ 1858/N.S.W; SYDNEY/ NO 10/ 1858/A/N.S.W.

Unpublished. Text: M.S. Pf. Coll., CL'ANA 0081

1 See CL'ANA 0363 for Antonia's view on Claire's proposed move to Australia.

2 Steamships that carried mail as well as passengers in the nineteenth century.

118 • Antonia Clairmont to Claire Clairmont

15th Nov 1858. Baden 490.

My dearest Claire.

yours of the 8th gave me great relief for I thought you seriously ill. I am very sorry the letter with the half sovereign is lost, pray do not send anymore. you are very kind and considerate, but it is a mere chance if it reaches me except you recommand the letters. however I do not think we shall buy anything before W's return, there are so many difficulties when you enter into details, that I despair of doing it to the satisfaction of us all – perhaps the best will be to lay all these harassing thoughts of looking about and choosing aside and wait quietly till W. returns – if he does return – I too have had a letter from him with nearly the same contents – that he is not inclined to think of marrying now in his present uncertainty is but natural – he says – if you insist I will come but arrange with Mr M.[1] to leave my place open – well this I don't like at all – I dont wish to insist – I shall not press him – but I am not without hope for a change of mind in him, produced by my last of the 10th Oct: in which I showed him what might be done by our joint capital, and gave a description of a most valuable property near Vienna combining immense advantages, which it was easy for me to make clear to him as he knows the place by sight, for we had to pass it on our road from town to Weidling. I know the proprietor personally he is a rich and generous man and as good as promised me to wait with the sale till Willy's return – the place is all we could wish for in every respect, and would make Willy a rich man in the course of 10 years or so – I shall, in my answer to him, once more lay before him the important advantages of that property, and add my determination of never going to Australia – and if he means to go back again, he should rather not come at all – and that I will write no more on this subject till I have an answer from him to this letter – and should he prefer to remain, I hope I shall have strength for my last task to get off P. to him so that the two poor children may be together; and also to you I will not say anything more till we have that answer – my letter to him will go of[2] by Trieste on the 26th of this month – he will get it full time enough to take his resolution before the 27th of March, so in about 5 months we may expect an answer from him containing a final settlement of the most painful hesitation and uncertainty of the last three years. Pauline is still at Rakicsán[3] they will remain till the end of Nov. on account of the snipe shooting which the Count won't miss – so if you write directly your letter will still find her there; the Venice direction I do not yet know: there must have been letters lost, certainly the one about the Shelly[4] papers for P. asked me what had become of the whole business, and I said of course A.Cl. has not mentioned it again – I can't guess where the disorder lies here or in Engl. I thank God dear P. is with such amiable people – you know they took a trip to Trieste and they[5] Count went over to Venise to take a house for the winter – going a shopping at Trieste P. was presented with a most beautiful brown English made cloak and two most beautiful dresses of which she sent me patterns in a letter; and she is so clever, she makes up all herself with the help of her own maid who must work for her, she economises a great deal – by these spendid[6] presents she was enabled to save almost her whole quarter, which has completed the 2^d share of Metallique[7] of which I spoke to you some time ago – I have neither lost in capital nor income as I did not sell out – but our loss can into in the rise of every thing – the confusion in the market concerns is dreadful; every thing is now to be rekoned in new money but as government is not ready with the new coins we must pay with the old ones[8] – people take advantage of this and often it happens from ignorance let us hope for better times and believe me ever yours gratefully

A.C.

Address: No envelope.

Unpublished. Text: M.S. Pf. Coll., CL'ANA 0342

---

1 Mr. Manning.

2 She meant to write "off".

3 See CL'ANA 0340 and CL'ANA 0358.

4 Antonia's spelling for "Shelley". Claire had in her possession papers connected to the Shelley family. These papers would later lure people like Edward Silsbee who courted both Claire and Pauline in an attempt to access the papers (see CL'ANA 0218). Silsbee was, however, unable to purchase the papers as Claire's price was too high. In her will, Claire left "a tin box containing letters directed by Shelley the poet partly to Godwin the philosopher, partly to me, and a hundred or more letters from Mrs. Shelley Shelley the poet's wife to me . . . two letters from Sir Percy the poet's son". She urged Cini, as executor, to sell all the Shelley papers to benefit Pauline and Georgina (*CC* II: 661). For an excellent account of the fate of the Shelley papers, see S. Hebron and E. Denlinger, *Shelley's Ghost* (Oxford: Bodlean Library, 2010).

5 Correct as stated.

6 Probably "splendid".

7 See CL'ANA 0054.

8 See CL'ANA 0341.

119 • Antonia Clairmont to Claire Clairmont

490 Baden 28th Nov. 1858.

My dearest Claire.

Pray tell me exactly when the dec. post goes to Australia and how I must direct my letter to W. so that it really goes by England – I have written to the dear boy on the 26th of this month by Trieste, but I should now like also to write again by your mail, so that if one should be lost he is sure to get the other, besides I have some new and important communications to make with regard to the coalmines he is to have, and if he does not come with such a prospect in view, I'll give up all hope of seeing him again and shall try to find consolation in the thought that he cherises his birthright as an English subject[1] so highly as to give up every advantage his motherland might offer – but I do think indeed not the gold pits in Austr:[2] bid a fairer chance of his making his fortune than those he has here – I have since learned from Mr N:[3] that he found amber as well as coal, ~~and I~~ of which he gave me some little specimens and I had an'other journey to town to ascertain the value of the former, I went to the Director of the Imp: Mineral Cabinet,[4] no less authority will do for W. but unfortunately did not find him – so I must go again and then I can tell him exactly how affairs are – I have also seen the deeds and papers, and as W. likely knows the site and situation of the property, he will understand – all very well – I am not of a sanguine or illusory character but this appears to me like a question: there is a million fl at your service if you choose to pick it up – I hardly know what I have told you already of the whole affair should not like to promise too much; in my last to W. I disapproved the idea of his coming here if he ~~and~~ intended to leave again – but I think I shall even recommend his coming over on those terms, if it will set his mind at ease – and look at my concern here – and everything agrees so well as to time – March his term is out, he gets off in April and can be here by Sept: we can't enter the farm before Nov: but Mr N. is so much my friend, he will make over the mortgage to me before that, so W. will have time to look about him, and be in his right to see about the mine – and most happy I am to tell you and to remind him, that we have some valuable friends in that line able and willing to give him advice or further his undertaking in any way – I am sure Willy will be charmed with his reception, he will take his place at once in society and rank with men of intellect sience and knowledge – and I should think will find some difference from the Australian farmers he is now associating with – cheer up my dearest Claire, we shall have him at last and be happy and proud in him – I have not ~~had~~ heard from P. since I wrote last, she is most happy to go to V.[5] the next time I shall have another new to tell you, an undertaking of mine which I hope will turn out prosperous to the family – I long to hear from you that you are well and in good spirits. I am well thank God, and full of pleasing hopes.

yours affect

A.C.

do not forget the direction –

Address: Miss Clairmont/ Handcross, Croyden./ Surrey,/ England.
Front postmark: K·K·FAHRENDES/ POSTAMT N·9

Unpublished. Text: M.S., Pf. Coll., CL'ANA 0360

---

1 Wilhelm continued to be a British subject throughout his life. In 1880, he obtained a letter from the British ambassador in Vienna that requested permission for the family to travel unhindered on the continent. The printed document stated as follows: "We . . . Request and require in the Name of her Majesty all those whom it may concern to allow Mr William Gaulis Clairmont, British subject, travelling on the continent, accompanied by his wife and his three children – Walter Claire – Alma – John Paul – to pass freely without let or hindrance and to afford him every assistance and protection of which he may stand in need" (CL'ANA 0408, unpublished manuscript, Pforzheimer Collection).

2 Wilhelm had no interest in digging for gold, as could be seen by the trajectory of his career.

3 Mr. Nowotny.

4 *The Illustrated Catalogue of the International Exhibition* of 1862 provided information about the various mineral resources found in the Austrian Empire. Under the heading "Mineral Products," the text listed the "most important of these mineral productions and their most abundant beds" (London: Her Majesty's Commissioners, Clay, Son & Taylor, 1862), vol. IV, p. xiv. Coal was one of these "important productions" and the author recorded that "the production of Fossil coals . . . has, within 30 years, increased to more than twelvetimes its former extent" (p. xvi). The catalogue also explained that "Fossil Coals are an article of very brisk trade" (p. xxi). It made no mention of amber, but "Hungarian Opals and the Bohemian Garnets, Agates and varieties of Jasper rank foremost" did appear (p. xv). The Austrian Imperial Mineral Cabinet was known as k.k. Hof Mineralien Kabinet.

5 Venice.

120 • Antonia Clairmont to Claire Clairmont

490 Baden. 31 dec. 1858.

This moment I rec. yours of the 28th dec.[1]

My dearest Claire.

I am really in despair about the irregularity of our post; though yours may be in fault too. I can't tell which, for there have been letters lost on both sides – first yours with the sovereign – and now too[2] of mine are missing - the last I received of yours is dated the 2nd dec. in answer to the one where I asked Willy's direction I answered it even before I wrote to Willy – and I find in my notebook. 6th dec: letter to Claire – building – Madeleine Court[3] – Mr N. – for my head being rather weak, in writing to W. or to you anything of importance I mark the heads of subjects. so I am quite sure as to this, besides I added part of a letter I had just got from P. with her direction and many details about her situation – I quieted yours as to my entering into any purchase of which there is no question, for the good reason that my capital is going to be employed in building and gave a full account of my acquaintance with Mr and Mrs Nowotny – by some service I did Mrs N. and how grateful they are both to me there was no question on his side of pressing the sale – no idea – many other particulars which I hoped would be consoling and soothing to you – I also said I would not tell W. about my building – it might startle him it was a double sheet – and I never got any answer to it – then on the 10th of dec: I wrote to Willy and after once more to you, to tell you what I had written to him and to send Pauline's direction at Venice – which I add again in Pauline's own writing – and I think I also told you that she had sent me a little chest of nice books so that I have stock for the whole winter which is very agreable to me – that letter must have been sent off about the 13th and I have been waiting with great anxiety for an answer to both these epistles – today I had a letter from dear P. she says she has written to you, I gave her your new direction Brunswick S.[4] perhaps you have got it by this time she has been in very good spirits for some time, to days letter is rather damped – it is always so when she gets or writes letters to Australia – and she had 2 Sydney letters with the Dec. mail but none from Willy – and you have been again ill and uneasy about us, and I not ill, but anxious for your health – I thought also perhaps you disapproved of my building, thinking I enter [illeg.] but you will see and rejoice with me in the success of my endeavour I have arranged all is well, my apartment consists of 6 pieces,[5] 2 rooms and kitchen for my use – and joined to it by a hidden door is a sleeping room for P. and then a fine large room and antichambre for yourself and maid so that we shall be really comfortable besides I shall have a fine large garret for Willy there will be room for all without disturbing the other lodgers and if you are not here I can let the rooms – I live in the sweet hope we shall see all this realised – next summer you should come without waiting for W – let him find you here – by the bye – the gentleman to whom I wrote about the farms saw it was quite impossible to give an answer without knowing the question – but farms there are of all sizes, prices and extent of time; the best thing is to come and see let your young man accompany you here next spring and then look about in Hungary – I told already about Mr Smallbones,[6] he can direct him – and you have the benefit of his society on the journey. good bye dearest Claire ever yours

affect. A.C.[7]

Palazzo Ferro
 Canal Grande
Venice[8]

to make our house more attractive than the salon Clary[9] which till now was the tip-top of the Viennese colony

Address: Miss Clairmont/ Mrs Giles Long's/ Handcroft
Road, Croyden/ Surrey/ England.
Front postmark: K·K·FAHRENDES/POSTAMT N 8
Rear postmark: [illeg.]/LONDON/ JA 3/ 59

Unpublished. Text: M.S., Pf. Coll., CL'ANA 0343

1 Antonia wrote this sentence above her salutation.

2 Antonia's spelling.

3 See CL'ANA 0335 and CL'ANA 0338. Madeleine Court is unidentified.

4 See CL'ANA 0403.

5 French for "rooms" ("pièces").

6 Mr. Smallbones was the estate manager of Prince Esterházy's estate. In his chapter "General Remarks upon Continental Farming" in *The Journal of the Royal Agricultural Society of England* (London: John Murray, 1856), v. 16, pp. 160–1, Peter Love recorded meeting Mr. Smallbones: "Mr. Haswell kindly introduced me to Mr. Smallbones, of Deutsch Kreutz, near Odenburg, in Hungary, consulting agent to Prince Esterhazy under whom he occupies an extensive farm, which is a model of what can be done by English ingenuity, industry, and perseverance. Mr. Smallbones is highly thought of in Hungary by both rich and poor" (p. 160). Smallbones managed the estate of Paul Anton III, Prince Esterházy (1786–1866) in Ödenburg, the German name for Sopron, Hungary.

The Esterházy family's weath was enormous. In *Picture of Vienna*, Prince Esterházy's palace on Wallnerstrasse is listed as one of the palaces in Vienna (p. 44). The section on "Remarkable buildings and gardens in the suburbs" provides information about Prince Esterházy's house: "The house of prince Esterhazy in the Alservorstadt, has 4 courts, with 150 lodgings" (p. 49). The library of Prince Esterházy had "36,000 volumes, chiefly splendid editions, natural history, voyages and travels, philology and classics" (p. 70). In *Hand-books for Travellers* from 1889, W. Pembroke Fetridge describes the imperial palace, as well as the palaces of Prince Esterházy, Liechtenstein, Metternich, Schwarzenberg, and Auersperg as "objects of interest . . . to the stranger" (New York: W. P. Fetridge, Fetridge & Co., 1889), v. II, p. 709. See "Esterházy-castle Fertőd". Web. 3 November 2015. http://www.esterhazy-palace.com/en/history/the_esterhazy_family.html

In September 1845, *The Morning Chronical* recorded that "Prince and Princess Nicholas Esterhazy and family are expected to arrive from Vienna early in the ensuing month, to visit the Earl and

Countess of Jersey" (*British Newspapers: 1600–1950*. Farmington Hills: Gale-Cengage Learning. Web. 2 April 2014), while *The Field* reported that the Prince "took great interest" in a tennis match played in Brighton on 28 October (49: 1, 262).

See also CL'ANA 0255 and CL'ANA 0421, Box 3, bundle g, number 185.

7 Antonia included a small insert in this letter. She wrote the address of the Palazzo Ferro on one side and the incomplete sentence on the other side. This insert is a fragment and appears to have been cut from a larger piece of writing.

8 The Palazzo Ferro Fini is located on the Grand Canal in Venice between the Accademia Bridge and St. Mark's Square. In 1860, the Palazzo Ferro Fini was created from two smaller buildings, the Palazzo Morosini Ferro and the Palazzo Flangini Fini. Pauline evidently stayed in the Palazzo Morosini Ferro. Today, the building is used by the Regional Council of Venice ("Consiglio Regionale Del Veneto". Web. 15 October 2015. http://www.consiglioveneto.it/crvportal/pageContainer.jsp?n=1&c=1&e=3&mdx_id=4).

9 The Palazzo Fiquelmont-Clary was the Venetian home of the Franco-Austrian Counts de Ficquelmont. Built in the seventeenth century, the building was purchased by the de Ficquelmont-Clary family and is still owned by members of the family today. The Palazzo gets its name from the combination of Count Karl Ludwig von Ficquelmont's name and that of his daughter, Princess Elisabeth Alexandra Clary und Aldringen. See James Chastain. "Karl Ludwig Count von Ficquelmont". *Encyclopedia of 1848 Revolutions*. 2005. Web. 5 July 2015. http://www.ohio.edu/chastain/dh/ficquel.htm and Allmayer-Beck, Johann Christoph, "Ficquelmont, Karl Ludwig Graf von". *New German Biography* 5 (1961), p.136 f [Online version]. Web. 5 July 2015. http://www.deutsche-biographie.de/ppn119022672.html

121 • Antonia Clairmont to Claire Clairmont

490 Baden 15th Febr: 1859.

My dearest Claire.

I have got yours of the 8th and hope you received mine of the 6 including one to dear W. and hope you got it off with this month's mail – I too had a letter from him, and like yours it is longer and in better spirits than usual. With regard to mine of the 10th August he says – "Was du über politi[illeg.] Trübe schreibst genirt mich weniger, es musste den so weit gehen dass es der indrustiellen Blüthe des Landes in den Weg träte; Eben weil ich in einem obwohl nicht seiner politichen doch seiner socialen Verfassung nach republikanishen Lande gelebt, kenne ich die Mängel und Wiederwärtigkeiten der democratie und werde mir gerne ~~einer~~ kleine Bürde anderer Art gefallen lassen um jenen zu entrinnen – so you see my letter has had no retarding influenze upon him, the whole letter is like yours – he speaks of his friend Zoepf[1] – you will recollect it was I that set Zoepf to give him all these details, for I said to him ~~yours~~ numbers and dates will have more weight Willy than my wishes and opinions; he does not mention Mr Manning – but dearest Claire if you were again to write to Mr. M. to implore him to let W go – you can write such powerful letters he could not withstand you, do write once more don't you think it would be well? if we have him but here, let him then undertake what he likes, I am sure he will always do well – but one heavy loss he has to bear again – he and Austria have reason to regret the loss of Mr. Kleyle – 46 years of age – a most distinguished man – and he was fond of Willy as of a younger brother[2] – his said one is inconsolable only one daughter – I got W's letter on the 11th so could not write with the first post, but shall do so on the 25th however I always think the letters of the 25th must wait at Alexandria till next month for the English post, for how should they proceed to N.S.W. ? and I always hear only of one English mail – I have taken every pains to ascertain the true state of this – but in vain we have two Alexandrien post days pr. m. 10th and 25th – the 10th might correspond with your 12th – but the other is a riddle to me – I have not had a letter from Pauline these 3 weeks but will tell her all you say – the fine wheather is setting in, and on the 1st of next month building will begin in good earnest – the masons and workpeople would not begin unless the proprietor of the ground gives the first stroke – so I had to perform this ceremonie[3] and then they were satisfied – I am really sorry you have so many things to vex you just at present but if only your health would be restored the other things are easier to be borne – but how will it go with your journey if you have so young a servant that you must watch over <u>her</u>? I am afraid this new hope of seeing dear W. will again retain you in England to receive him in Europe – your friends leaving your neighbourhood must be very painful to you, but with your railroads distances are nothing now a day. you ask what colours I wear, in dresses dark grey and brown not to appear particular. I am most tired of these disturbances one gets so used to them, and they end in nothing but the fear of the moment – our funds are shockingly low too, which is particularly unlucky for me just at present.– but thank God I have friends that will assist me to wait with selling out till things better a little – poor W. two of his friends and patrons lost, M[r] Maier and Kleyle my health is good a little weakness still remains in my right ancle, a few baths will set all right. I expect your answer about the lodging and Clairmont Court.[4] ever yours

affect. A.C.

Address: Miss Clairmont/ Mrs. Giles Long's Handcroft Road/
Croydon, Surrey/ England.
Front postmark: K·K· F[illeg.]HRENDES/ POSTAMT N [illeg.]
Rear postmark: WIEN/ $^{16}/_{2}$/ 7 A.; [illeg.]/ E 19/ LONDON/[illeg.]

Unpublished. Text: M.S., Pf. Coll., CL'ANA 0338

---

1 Antonia misspelled the word "geniert". The German translates as follows: "What you write about political [the last part of the word is illegible but the first six letters, "politi," appear clearly] dimness does not really bother me, it had to come that this gets in the way of the industrial boom of the country; I know about the deficiencies and tribulations of democracy precisely because I lived in a republican country according to its social not its political constitution, and I will acquiesce in little burdens of a different kind to escape from those" (translation provided by Anja Reiner). For information about Zoepf, see CL'ANA 0354.

2 See CL'ANA 0365.

3 Antonia's spelling for "ceremony".

4 Unidentified. Possibly another name for Madeleine Court. See CL'ANA 0343 and CL'ANA 0335.

122 • Antonia Clairmont to Claire Clairmont

[27 February 1859]
490 Baden 27th [illeg.]b 1859.[1]

My dearest Claire.

I answer yours of the 15th directly that our letters may not cross again as you must have meanwhile got mine of the 16th your account of the Panama post pleased me extremely and I hope it will soon be established,[2] what a comfort it will be, to exchange letters so speedily that they do not become stale by age – I include also here half a letter of dear P's – it is in answer to one in which I sent her Willy's letter of the 18th Oct: the short and melancholy one – and you see the influenze it had on her she has the kindest heart – her errors are all of the head – no doubt when the dear boy is once here we shall be happy in our union! she enjoys the carnival exceedingly, they go out, masked every day, and she reproaches herself with it as you will find in her letter[3] – I answered her directly to tell her the good news you gave of the Panama course to be opened and of the great propability of her crossing Willy on the road – just to keep her from taking a sudden resolution; and you my dear Claire will not I trust judge her too severely for the sake of her warm and affectionate love to her brother – with regard to your questions about my buildings as you say – you wish to know all or nothing – so I think I shall say nothing – it is very difficult to enter satisfactorily into details by letter I hardly know the proper technical terms – and things are managed so differently here – on the whole I can assure you of success – and the hope of seeing you here at the beginning of summer, where you will see every thing makes silence easier to me as it would have been otherwise; the ground is legally mine – the great difficulty for me is the fall of the funds but that we cannot help or rather as I told you already by the assistance of some friends I am enabled to hold out a little – retract I cannot now do I wish to do so – till now we have only preliminary works done – for though the winter is uncommonly mild, yet one must not venture begin too early for fear of a frost – but next week all will be in full activity –. how will your box affairs be this season? I have read several accounts in our papers of Her M's Opera I trust you are not a sufferer by the new arrangement and that you will not be prevented from coming over next summer[4] – Baden is an uncommonly dry place so little rain I never saw – Weidling was damp in comparison – we shall do very well together – at present I have an old charwoman, who comes in the morning does my rooms and cooks my little dinner and then she goes home again – and so if we like we can go out to dine – or have something prepared at home, as your little maid will know your taste – my Bauplatz[5] is at Baden, next door to the house I live. that makes it so convenient for Mr N.[6] to look after the business. Pray be under no uneasiness on my account – here people are in great fear of a French war [7]– as yet I hold out, I cannot believe it – it would be too dreadful – my foot is getting stronger every day – but I am quite out of practice of walking so do not go far – otherwise I am well I am teaching the little girl of

M[rs] N. English she is a sweet child – and I am persuading M[rs] N. to learn a little so that she can understand you a little at least – you owe me two letters now. ever yours affectionately.

A. C.

Venice 24. Feb.[8]

Dearest best Ma, I cannot describe to you the bad impression poor W.'s letter made on me & the self-reproaches which occupied my mind the whole evening how can I remain here seeking pleasure & my own advantages when that poor boy is not only working hard all day long – but has not a soul to comfort him in mind or body? Is it not selfish of me to a degree to have left him all alone when I feel so well that he had rather be in Europe upon his two-pence halfpenny as I call it than enjoy all the advantages of the new world – I would argue the subject – it may be a matter of opinion & even taste – but if he does not like why should he be forced to enjoy a thing he does not care for? Did not dear Clari in her romantic youthful ideas refuse that brilliant situation in Princess G's[9] house for some chimeric idea of independence & proper pride – W. is doing just the same thing he would be ready to give up positive gain for some utopian bright vision of his youthful days spent in Europe. I would argue upon either side of the question but as the principal object in this life is to choose such occupation as will enable one to lead a contented & useful life & as his ~~will~~ coming alone can enable him to find that or to convince him of his mistake I say – let him come – let him come as soon as possible & let us all be happy & contented. I am going to write him a most determined letter on this subject handling it in such a manner as will quickest find the way to his heart.

Address: Miss Clairmont/ M[rs] G. Long's Handcroft Road./
Croydon, Surrey./ England.
Front postmark: BADEN/ $^{2}/_{3}$/ 1. EXP.
Rear postmark: LONDON/ MR 5/ 59

Unpublished. Text: M.S., Pf. Coll., CL'ANA 0337

1 Probably February.

2 Graeme Milne records that Australia's "slow" population growth in the nineteenth century gave rise to serious discussions about whether or not the colony required a regular mail service. The British government preferred to incorporate an Australian service into its India service, a plan towards which the Peninsular and Oriental Steam Navigation Company (P&O) felt "unenthusiastic". In 1851, ideas were proposed to add a "direct service" via the Cape of Good Hope in Africa. However, as Milne states, "The colonists themselves favoured the route across the Atlantic and Pacific via Panama" (*Trade and Traders in Mid-Victorian Liverpool* [Liverpool: Liverpool University Press, 2000], p. 176).

3 The Venetian carnival is held annually and is famous for its festive parties and the colorful masks worn by participants. Over the years, the carnival was banned by the authorities, who forbad the wearing of masks and frowned upon the celebratory behaviour of the participants. Today's carnival starts two Fridays before its final day, Shrove Tuesday.

4 By 1858, Benjamin Lumley found himself unable to pay his debts. In particular, Lord Ward "demanded three quarters" of the rent due to him (L. Middleton, "Benjamin Lumley". See page 136 for citation information), which Lumley was unable to pay. By August, the theater had closed. See CL'ANA 0404.

5 German for "building site".

6 Nowotny.

7 See CL'ANA 0084.

8 This note from Pauline was written on blue paper and was included in Antonia's letter to Claire.

9 Clara had worked for the Princess Liechtenstein. See CL'ANA 0402. Princess G. is unidentified.

123 • Wilhelm Gaulis Clairmont to Claire Clairmont

[1 March 1859]

Direct for the future not Bombala or Twofold Bay but simply Kamaruka
Merimbula
Sydney.[1]

My dearest aunt.

I duly received your letter of the 13th Decbr. 58. I also saw one from you to Mrs Suttor and was especially with reference to this letter glad that I had taken steps to get my chest sounded as this seems to give you so much relief.[2] Enclosed you will find Dr Bligh's report which I send you in his own handwriting so that you may be quite easy on the subject of my health. Partly on the strength of Dr Bligh's opinion, partly allured by a higher salary, on the other hand deterred by the uncertainty of political stability and my personal success in Austria I have finally determined to renew my engagement with the Company. My salary will be as heretofore £300 fixed and a certain percentage on profits which I think will make an additional £200 or even more according as the season and the prices of wool may favour our years success so that I would have £500 a very fine income for me. If I return to Europe I have ~~only~~ my choice between only 3 alternatives to seek a situation and then I might wait 20 years till I got such an other – to live upon you or Mama doing nothing and that would be quite enough to make me wretched, or 3rdly to embark on some enterprize with the assistance of your or Ma's Capital. that too I dislike for since my Kangaroo Hills failure I have grown very cautious in matters of this description and if I were thus to squander the means [~~illeg.~~] which form your only support ~~through~~ for the rest of your lives I should be thoroughly miserable – It is a frightful risk to run and quite unjustifiable in our case where I am already in receipt of a handsome salary and can with a little perseverance save up a small capital in a few years. Then if you are still so inclined we can join with much greater security and more chance of success embarking all my money on the enterprize and living if need be for the first year or two when the return is likely to be small on the interest of your money.[3] If we succeed we shall have a handsome return; if not your money and position will at least not be affected. so I hope dearest aunt you will not be angry with my decision. I write to Mama by same mail to the same effect. Please dearest aunt take note that I am now wearing (not all of them at the same time) ½ doz. curious [~~illeg.~~] looking articles of some flimsey material resembling [illeg.] make a shift rather than a shirt cut through in the middle just there where an ideal line may be supposed to separate the body from the tail; these said curious habiliments Mrs Manning purchased for me herself in Sydney and insists on my wearing. Having got over certain sensations of heat and fleas observable on my first wearing them, they do not now affect my customs and [~~illeg.~~] habits otherwise, than by making the wearing of night shirts both undesirable and superfluous; the important consequences resulting therefrom are a saving of 4d effected in my weekly washing expenses and the solemn lying

in state (in my chest of drawers) of the 6 nightshirts my dear Mother gave me on my departure bidding fair to return to Europe whenever I may do so, in a most perfect state of preservation highly commendatory of their master's domestic habits. I have often thought what a serious difficulty would have arisen on that subject if your project of marriage had been carried out.
Goodbye dearest aunt I shall write more by next mail

yours truly WGC.

March 1st 1859.

Pambula[4]
Janry 16th /59

W.G. Claremont Esqre[5]

Sir,

I hereby certify that having made a stethescopic[6] examination of your lungs, I am satisfied that they are at present free from disease. But I am of opinion that the prevalence of Decline in your family, and the tendency you evince to laryngeal affectations, indicating thereby some predisposition to the same disease, would render it highly imprudent of you to expose yourself to less genial influences than you experience in this mild climate; more particularly as you are in the enjoyment of all requisite comforts, whilst pursuing an occupation which is not only agreeable to your taste but likewise highly conducive to your general health –
I am Sir

yours faithfully
Richard Bligh

Address: via Marseilles./Miss Clairmont/ Messrs Haggard Hale & Pixley/ 8 Throgmorton Court City/London.
Front postmark: LONDON/[illeg.]/59/PAID
Rear postmark: SYDNEY/MR 3/ 1859/A/N.S.W.

Unpublished. Text: M.S. Pf. Coll., CL'ANA 0082

1 Merimbula is a town in New South Wales, located seven kilometers north of Pambula and thirty-four kilometers southeast of Kameruka. Bombala is located 85 kilometers west of Merimbula. Wilhelm bracketed the words Kamaruka (his spelling), Merimbula, and Sydney with a curly bracket.

2 Doctors began using stethoscopes in 1819 for chest auscultation. Before 1819, the physician would listen to the patient's chest to monitor for signs of abnormality (The Editors of Encyclopaedia Britannica. "Auscultation". *Encyclopaedia Britannica Online*. Encyclopaedia Britannica Inc., n.d. Web. 20 November 2014. http://www.britannica.com/EBchecked/topic/43503/auscultation).

3 The enterprise eventually succeeded with the purchase of Nikolaihof in 1871. See CL'ANA 0296.

4 Dr. Bligh's letter began on a new page.

5 Dr. Bligh's spelling for Clairmont.

6 See note 2. In 1816, René Theophile Laënnec (1781–1826) invented the first stethoscope while working at l'hôpital Necker-Enfants malades in Paris. The American Diagnostic Corporation notes that the first stethoscope was monaural and was made of wood. By 1851, stethoscopes had become bi-aural ("History of the Stethoscope". American Diagnostic Corporation. Web 20 November 2014. http://adctoday.com/learning-center/about-stethoscopes/history-stethoscope. See also "Necker Enfants Malades". Web. 16 July 2015. http://hopital-necker.aphp.fr/

124 • Antonia Clairmont to Claire Clairmont

490 Baden. 21st March 1859.

My dearest Claire.

I received both your letters, that of the 7th and 18th of March – and can not express my grief and sorrow at this new stroke of fortune that has so suddenly fallen upon you, and causes you so much distress and trouble if we were but nearer and could live together it would be such a comfort – you ask my opinion of what you had best do – it is difficult for me to give an opinion at that distance – but the idea of your going to Ramsgate[1] separated from all your friends is extremely painful to me – if you are not afraid of an Austrian winter, and if your presence is not necessary early in spring in London next year – I think you should still come on to Baden as you intended to do – and take your servant with you, if your means ~~do~~ will not allow you to keep her, she will find plenty of places here, or I can easily find occupation for her a couple of hours per day, that will pay her wages and you will have her attendance for the rest of the time and I shall be your nurse, and most happy I shall be – and I am sure you would feel yourself well, your mind would be agreeably occupied with me in hopes and endeavors for the future – and then dear Pauline will come and pay us a visit – and how glad both the children will be to know you with me for both our sakes – now do my dear Claire consider whether that would not be the best plan – could not you put the affair of the box into some friend's hands, and come on here in May as you intended? I cannot think so ill of Mr Brookes[2] that he would neglect an old and valued friend for some indiscretion of her niece's sake – do make an attempt and you will find I am in the right – if you have put your business affairs in good hands, I shall be less afraid to urge your coming, for fear of our winter – for have you not also been unwell in England and suffering all the winter through? perhaps our dry freezing cold will be less hurtfull to you than you now think – and I have such cheerful apartments, so sunny and warm – and if you do come, I promise you to stay here another winter instead of moving into the new house – my income is £100 a year – and fully satisfied my wants and wishes which are very moderate however – if you add the same sum we shall be very comfortable – for the lodging will be the same – furniture and bedding for you I have – [iron bedstead as you mentioned I have none] and ~~if~~ the summer will fortify your health, you will take the baths, they will do you good – and if the bad season should bring on a return of your complaint, at least you will not have to sit alone and ponder and grieve but we shall sit together and chatt over a 1000 things or perhaps even P. or W may be with us – as we are expecting letters from them a few old ladies we have always at command for a rubber in the evening[3] – and would it not be better so, than be alone at Ramsgate in a cheap room? Oh do my dear sister consult with your friends whether that would not be the best, believe me we all shall suffer with you and in coming here you will relieve us all – if you can only compass the means of ~~the~~ making the journey, if once here all will be well. and do not mention 53 any more, it is too painful, poor dear Ch. and E – oh those dreadful family feuds![4] let all be forgotten but you know too well if there were angry sentiments they had nothing to do with money affairs. I think the chief question is, will your affairs allow you to leave England for a year or so – ? then coming here will be the best thing you can do; Pauline will not go to Vienna at all – they go to Rakicsán on leaving Venice – and then dear P. is promised leave of absence to pay me a visit – I have not been to town the whole winter, so you need not fear the state of health is much better now. thanks for your explanation about the past days – but I see now 26th is the better day – I have not written to Willy since his last – I wished first to hear from him – now about the buildings – when it is once fixed that you do not come, I will write every detail you can wish, but with the hope I entertain of seeing you I will only give you the assurance that it will turn out well and that I have every reason to hope to see my income doubled when all is arranged – true that the present fall of stock decreases my poor Capital dreadfully and creates difficulties, I could not foresee – I have no written contract for the price of the building if you order a dress at a mantua[5] maker's it will cost much dearer than if you buy the stuff and other materials yourself and take a work woman by the day – such is my case and I trust God will help me through; I own I have suffered much anxiety at first when the falling of the papers[6] began, and had many a sleepless night one night I suddenly found my room getting quite light, on going to the window, I saw a dreadful fire about 10 Engl. miles off far and in the plain – the storm was high and carried the flames hither and thither – in about 3 hours the whole village was in ashes – so many families houseless, poor and starving – thus God sends evils and we must bear them – these poor people had done nothing to provoke their fate, one may have been guilty of carelessness but the others not, yet they must all suffer – since then I am quiet and resigned – it is about the same thing as with your box– you acted according to your best judgment so did I – man can do no more – success or failure comes from above! Good bye dearest Claire I wish I could console you. I could if you were here – my health is well but my foot is not quite recovered the wheather is exquisite – too fine to last. oh do decide in favour of Austria, and think that I have one great claim on you before your other friends for our dearest interests are the same. ever yours affect. A.C.

Address: Miss Clairmont/ Mrs. G. Long's Handcroft Road./
Croydon, Surrey/ England.
Front postmark: BADEN/ $^{22}/_{3}$ / 5 EXP.
Rear postmark: WIEN/ $^{23}/_{3}$ / 5 F.; DA/ LONDON/MR 26/[illeg.]
London

Unpublished. Text: M.S., Pf. Coll., CL'ANA 0336

1 See CL'ANA 0374.

2 Betty Bennett identifies "Brooks, Son & Dixon" as Percy Shelley's bankers (*LMWS* I: 117). In *A Handbook of London Bankers*, Frederick George Hilton Price names William Brooks as the founder of the firm "Brooks and Company" (London: Leadenhall Press, 1891), p. 24. By 1802, the firm became known as "Brookes, Son, and Dixon" and by 1819, "Brooks and Dixon" (p. 54).

3 See CL'ANA 0354.

4 On 6 September 1853, Claire responded to Antonia in very strong terms, condemning Clara for her behavior (*CC* II: 547). Antonia's response of 21 November 1853 to this letter (see CL'ANA 0374) clearly stated her reaction to Claire's outburst: "I was much affected with it, you reproach me, you abuse my children and hurt me in many ways". By 1853, Charley had left for England and Emily was a governess and away from home.

5 The term "mantua" means a loose gown. Antonia probably used the term to indicate a dress-maker. The word comes from the French, "manteau" which means a coat.

6 The devaluation of Austrian currency.

125 • Antonia Clairmont to Claire Clairmont

490 Baden. 3rd April 1859

My dearest Claire.

I received yours of the 29th March with Willy's included. I too had a letter from him of the same date, containing about the same things as yours – only he adds – if he remains another three years, it is his dearest wish that P. should come out to stay with him if I can spare her – this shows that he had no attachment, and does not intend to stay away forever, he also says, that he keeps a Leipsic[1] newspaper by which he is aware of all the awful state of the Austrian finances – that our credit cannot recover soon and consequently land will be as cheap three years hence; than it is now – he also says, that he will wait for the letters of Nov. mail till he takes his decision – in that I wrote to him about the coalpits and M. Court[2] – what effect it may have produced I cannot tell – let us wait patiently till next mail – but do not defer your preparations for coming here – what a comfort it will be if we can talk over the whole affair if he decides for staying neither you nor I will ~~objects~~ to P's going out to be with him – then we two should remain together – I should have no objection to go with you to the south provided I can live as solitary as I wish you can see your friends and enjoy their society – and I shall take long walks and keep to my fireside – but two great affairs must first be got through, your box and my building. it will be a great blessing to have the sale taking place, though the difficulties seem insurmountable 40 boxholders – and 50 shops and Lord W.[3] and the Grand Landlord – I hope it won't interfere with your leaving England I have written to P. to tell her of W.'s letter but did not mention the wish he expressed of her going out – I thought it better to wait for the decisive letter of W. else I should create false hopes in her – I do not mean to write to W. just now, his resolution must be taken by this time – so what can one say till we know what it is – if he stays I shall strain every nerve to get P. off as soon as possible – for anything will be better than the state of suspense and useless struggle and uncertainty as disappointed hopes in which these last three years have been spent. you will wonder to see me so quiet but I am schooled in adversity – and then the present state of the country is so uncertain, should war break out it is the ruin of a agriculturist and how should I reproach myself for having caused him to give up a fine independence and find here troubles and confusion? I wish with you he were married, though we should have less chance of seeing him back again – Pauline and the family are already returned to their place in Hungary – there have been some scenes at Venice it was nothing but enough to disperse the foreign guests[4] many went also to Vienna to enjoy the Italian opera which had just begun – P. is in despair – Well my dear Claire Patience till next mail and then we shall know what we have to hope for. – perhaps by that time something may be nearer decision in your affairs mine will have advanced too – to give up building is quite impossible impossible[5] having gone too far – and all will go well I am sure – If our dear boy will stay and P. must go – at least let me not lose the hope of having you this summer

ever yours affect: A.C.

Address: Miss Clairmont/ Handcroft Road. Croydon/ Surrey/ England.
Front postmark: POST[illeg.]
Rear postmark: [illeg.]5/Verviers.[6]; D7/LONDON/AP 6/59

Unpublished. Text: M.S., Pf. Coll., CL'ANA 0335

---

1 Leipzig is a city in Germany. The *Einkommenden Zeitungen*, the world's first daily newspaper, was published in Leipzig in 1650.

2 Perhaps Madeleine Court. See CL'ANA 0343 and CL'ANA 0343.

3 Abbreviation for Lord Ward. See CL'ANA 0337. William Ward, 1st Earl of Dudley (1817–1885). He was responsible for calling in Lumley's debts, causing him thereby to sever ties with Her Majesty's Theater.

4 Venice was a city in the Kingdom of Lombardy-Venetia, which was part of the Austrian Empire. After the Franco-Austrian War in 1859, Lombardy was annexed to Sardinia. However, the resulting call for Italian unification led to discontent amongst the people in Venetia who agitated for political reform. By 1866, Austria was at war with Prussia. During this conflict, Venetia became part of an almost-united Kingdom of Italy. See A. Blumberg, *A Carefully Planned Accident: The Italian War of 1859* (Selinsgrove, PA: Susquehanna University Press, 1990). See CL'ANA 0084.

5 Antonia repeated the word "impossible".

6 This letter went via Verviers, a city in Belgium.

126 • Pauline Clairmont to Claire Clairmont

Rakicsán Ap 11. [1859]

Dearest Aunt

You must have received my letter in answer to yours sent with the transfer by this time & consequently be satisfied that that document has duly reached me as you desire I will sign it have it witnessed as well as is possible in this blessed solitude & return it to you with the greatest dispatch – but as that might take some time I mean 2 or 3 days I write to answer your last kind letter – which if it be realized would fulfil one of the greatest wishes of my youth. – and to tell you the truth I do not at all see the necessity of boxing myself up 9 months of the year in a solitary country house ou je meurs d'ennuie,[1] work all day long for 80£ & not even have a horse! I am beginning to get tired of it – tho in other respects I value my situation. Most likely we will remain here all the summer, hoping for a stray visit or two to cheer up the monotony of this sandy plain neighbours we have only one family both vulgar & stupid – I look forward to my visit to dear Ma & the meeting with you with the greatest pleasure as you may imagine ~~&~~ but will wait till you come – trusting that this change of air will do you all the good in the world – the weather here is also beautiful – everything green, violets & primroses cherrytrees in blossom & peaches & the air soft & balmy – that is my only consolation for having left Venice the beautiful the charming –

Mama will not be persuaded to come I will be bound to say – has she not refused Willy & Australia for her dear Vienna, for lovely Austria that seat of envy that nest of worms that pile of wickedness – is it not enough to have such a ruin of sad memories in one's heart but one must also go & visit in reality the spot where battle death & tears are written on every stone – what attaches her to this place she could not say herself unless it is the inherent austrian love of antiquity which like every thing else has a bright & dark side.

I can not tell you dearest Aunt how very glad I shall be to see you again it seems to me to have been separated from you for many long years – the air of Europe is unhealthy all except that of Venice which did me all the good in the world. I will not neglect to answer all the questions of your other letter & take all the precautions about signing & witnessing & dispatch it as soon as possible. but if your Opera box cannot be sold all our fine plans will evaporate, & I am afraid taking me with you to Italy will be a great expense to you – but let us hope for the best

your most affl
Pauline

Address: Miss Clairmont./ Mrs. G. Long's Handcross Rd/
Croydon Surrey/England.

Front postmark: [illeg.]/$^{12}/_{4}$
Rear postmark: ODERBERG/BRESLAU; [illeg.]/LONDON/ AP 16/ 59

Unpublished. Text: M.S., Pf. Coll., CL'ANA 0207

1 French: "where I die of boredom".

127 • Antonia Clairmont to Claire Clairmont

490 Baden 15th Mai[1] 1859:

My dearest Claire.

I cannot imagine what causes your long silence – your last to me was dated 29th march and was answered by me on the 3rd of April. six full weeks – never there was such a long interruption to our correspondence since my residence at Baden – I had news from Pauline that she had got a letter from you, but she says it is not a cheerful one – from W. I have heard nothing since March – perhaps you will say why did you not write – but alas! I had such troubles and anxieties to go through to procure the means of going on with my buildings without ruining myself outright with selling out at such an unpropitious moment that I could not write for fear of making you partake of my cares – which I did not like to do. Now I have succeeded in getting a loan, and am comparatively easy – and convinced that all will be well in the end. this is hardly a time to look forward with hope and joyful expectation of any kind, but else I would say I rejoice to see the moment, when you and the dear children see the result of my endeavors and enjoy it too – P. tells me you intend coming in the autumn, to proceed then to Italy for the winter – God knows how affairs will turn out there – we cannot say from today to tomorrow what is to happen – what do you think of Willy's silence? I think it very likely he is intending to return it must at least have been uncertainty which prevented his writing, for if he had actually signed his new contract he would surely have written to tell us so – I saw the arrival of the April mail in our papers announced on the 22nd; so the mail of Mai must soon be expected, and will most probably bring no letters; dearest Claire write soon to me, and tell me how you are and what is the cause of your silence, perhaps it was like with me the uncertainty of your affairs that made you defer till something had been decided – or are you displeased at my saying I wish the two children together wherever it may be – it is no selfish wish that you will grant, even if you are not of my opinion – but I am only thinking of them and not of myself!

We are now surrounded by warlike preparations – day and night the railroad is occupied in transporting men and implements of war – and isn't it dreadful, the railway having been sold to a French company with the permission of course of employing Frenchmen[2] – we have the ennemy settled in the country, and the whole of the purchase money is used up in the costs of these military transports – Oh for a lesson of A. Smith[3] – Government has made a new loan from the Bank of 2/3ds of 200 millions and they are to issue 5fl <u>notes</u> for it so think what a state our finances are coming to – and let us not regret so much if dear W. remains where he is – also we may congratulate ourselves in spite of present loss upon having my capital vested in a wellbuilt substantial dwelling house which will bring in a good rent, instead of having it in the funds, which are sinking everyday, and the interest of which has been now reduced by government under the name of income tax at 5 from H[4] – the houses have also heavy taxes to pay but at least the property is not injured – the railroad being closed now for the public – P. cannot come to see me, which we both regret extremely – this arrangement is painful also to the Baden people for the Viennese cannot come out to take lodgings, so all is empty and melancholy. good bye dearest Claire, write soon and tell me when the next mail is expected, and believe me ever yours affection.

A. C.

Address: Miss Clairmont/ Handcroft Road/ Croyden. Surrey/ England.
Front postmark: BADEN/ $^{17}/_{5}$/ 1 EXP.
Rear postmark: [illeg.]/LONDON/ MY 20/ [illeg.]

Unpublished. Text: M.S., Pf. Coll., CL'ANA 0334

1 German spelling for "May".

2 Albert Schram explains that the Austrian government forced all French employees of the Upper Italy Railway Company to leave Lombardy and Venetia during the 1859 war (*Railways and the Formation of the Italian State in the Nineteenth Century* [Cambridge: Cambridge University Press, 1997], p. 19). In *Europe in the Nineteenth Century*, Harry Hearder suggests that, "if the state acquired a hold on railways in France, and retained a firm control in Belgium and Germany, in Austria it sold railways for revenue" (London: Routledge, 2013), p. 80.

3 Adam Smith (probably 1723–1790), Scottish philosopher and economist who wrote *An Inquiry into the Nature and Causes of the Wealth of Nations* (1776), an important treatise on political economy, and *The Theory of Moral Sentiments* (1759).

4 Antonia meant at 5 percent. The German term is "fünf vom Hundert" which means "five out of a hundred".

128 • Antonia Clairmont to Claire Clairmont

490 Baden 27th Mai 1859.

My dearest Claire.

When I had sent off my letter to you I got one from dear W. containing about the same statements as yours; says rather less about his health, only that he is well; about P. he says, he does not know what we shall decide upon – for though has definitively only signed for one year longer, but there is little danger of his expectations not being realized, and then he will remain longer, and should be most happy to have her with him – so we are not called upon to decide directly – and I should much rather she should be here during the war, for ~~you~~ who knows what may happen, so for the moment we shall not talk of her journey; she poor girl would be quite satisfied to have him here and have this tiresome question at rest – but in fact we must all thank God for his staying in a good situation, good climate with the consolation and comfort of success instead of having him here, deprived of all he had earned by his own great exertions, about to encounter all the difficulties Austria presents now and will do so for a long time; It is a cruel fate that we 4 must be forever divided but we must bear with it – thanks my dear Claire for Dr Blighs letter,[1] it is a great comfort to know he is well – it would surely be better if the dear boy were married! May God make him happy in his choice! is my prayer I shall not be allowed to contribute to his happiness, for as he does not return now, he will not return at all, that you will see – and yet he is right; he says he would not for the world, endanger either your capital or mine, and what misery should I fail! poor dear boy! P. has not yet been to see me, for the railroad is now always closed for the Public latter when the family go to Landshütz[2] she hopes to get a week or ten days to spend with ~~with~~ me my health is pretty well; I have begun the baths again they always agree with me in respect of my reuhmatic[3] complaint, but they drive the blood to my head so I may only go twice a week; this is the 3d summer where we hope and wish to meet and always in vain! my building is going on well and prosperous, of course I have only begun two of the projected 4 but yet it will be splendid, if I can but keep them both; oh how I cherished the idea when you and P. should see them for the first time, but this sad war destroys all my hopes, in fact it has injured me before any others by the great fall of the papers – Good bye dearest Claire and do not remain so long without writing. we have beautiful wheather[4] now our air would do you good I am sure

ever yours affect A.C.

Address: Miss Clairmont/ Mrs. G. Long's Handcroft Road/
Croyden Surrey/ England.
Front postmark: BADEN/ 29/5 / 2. EXP.
Rear postmark: [illeg.]/LONDON/[illeg.]/59

Unpublished. Text: M.S. Pf. Coll., CL'ANA 0333

1 See CL'ANA 0082, Dr. Bligh's note of 16 January 1859.

2 See CL'ANA 0354.

3 Antonia's spelling for "rheumatic". The word is spelled "rheumatisch" in German.

4 Antonia's spelling for "weather".

129 • Antonia Clairmont to Claire Clairmont

490 Baden 22 June 1859.

My dearest Claire.

Yesterday I got yours with Willy's included, and if an angel had walked into the room to visit me it could hardly have given me more pleasure than its contents, for I had just been returned from town, cold wet and weary and quite disheartened by a negative answer from the saving bank, owing to the critical state of our finances they do not give money to private persons, in order to be prepared if government should call upon them for supplies – so you see, the capital amassed in the Saving B. though all coming from the poorer part of the population, yet in times of need they are denied the benefit of their own savings; to me it is particularly painful just now as my houses are half ready and I cannot go on without help – to let them stand open will be absolute ruin – for they cannot sell nor bring in any interest, and how am I to live? if on the other hand I can finish them, all will go well, I can then sell one, pay off the debts and so clear the other – if that unfortunate war had not began, all would have been well, that alone is the cause of my present difficulties – for not only did I lose about between 3 or 400 pds in selling out, but I cannot find help from my friends, for they also have their money in government shares, and if I were to ~~take~~ receive say – one 500 pd share – I should get but 258 pds for it on selling yet I should have to pay 5% interest upon the full 500 – and if in about a year or so when I should have to pay it back, the shares have risen it would be utter ruin for me – ready money is so scarce people ask 30% for it and more; Oh dearest Claire! help me save me, lend me £500, for Willy's sake do it. and believe you will not lose your money I will pay you 5% interest upon it and shall pay it back as soon as I have sold one of the houses I can also give you security, for till now the property is quite free and all my own – I have not begun building with borrowed money; but must finish so – and if that unfortunate war had not broke out it would have been quite a simple affair, I should have had about £600 debts upon the two houses; which I could have paid off in time and leave my children a fine property – I want now about £1000 to finish – but having arranged with the ~~work~~ trades people that only half the amount of their bills[1] is to be paid immediately, and the other half ~~in~~ 3 months after all is finished which ~~so that~~ will just be the time when dear W's money can arrive, I shall go on with 500 meanwhile and write to him directly, to beg him to send it without fail or loss of time, for I am lost without it – it was that hope of his sending his poor dear savings which refreshed me so much, for I could not have asked you to lend me the whole sum I want; but £500 I hope and trust from your kindness to receive, ~~and~~ to save me from my present great distress; and the exchange is so much in my favour now I shall have 6000fl instead of 5~~0~~; when dear Paula was I talked the whole matter over with her but then I had the hopes of the saving bank, and never thought they would deny me – but now this hope is lost – I declare I see no other way than going to Australia – though God knows bitter is the thought to me in my old age!

dear Claire save me from that fate – if you could have come and seen the houses I think you would have taken pleasure in them and willingly lent the money – as there is no loss to be feared – the loss for me being only in my inability of finishing – I commissioned P. to write to W. to prepare him for the sad possibility of our coming out to join him – but I am going to write now to him myself to explain more fully how badly every thing turned to my disadvantage – how impossible for my friends here to assist me for they are in moderate circumstances like myself having their capitals in government shares, which to take would be certain ruin to me. God knows how sorry I am to trouble you with this sad affair, happily you are in town which makes it easier to transact business, I should have liked to have your answer before writing to Willy but I cannot delay it, but must write to day, the 26th being our 2nd postday – if I must go to Austr. I should prefer going this very autumn instead of lingering the winter without any income for my capital is all in the building – here you have a sketch of the concern[2] – I could send you a list of the tradespeople's bills of what they have to furnish – estimates – I think you say in English – but 10,000fl I shall want, and if you kindly lend 500 pd and W. 4 – so with the profit in the exchange it will make 10000. once more forgive the cruel shock, but this would have been the same, if I had been obliged to tell you I am quite ruined – must go to Willy for support – dear P. was so sorry for your sake she said: do not tell Aunt C. she will be so uneasy – and that was[3] before I had the answer from the saving bank, this hope having failed, and at the same time also that of a speedy termination of that unhappy war I was obliged to tell – the value of the property when finished will be

492 – £2000
493 – 1600[4]
Baüplatz 200

the houses being new will be [~~illeg.~~] exempt from government taxes 15 years to come – only those of the community are to be paid – oh dearest Claire if you would buy one of the houses what happiness! that brings me to your question – foreigners may and can buy and possess land in Austr., Hungary or Bohemia – [I have been to see Dr Budinsky][5] but as to percentage he could not give a lengthy answer – these great lawyers have always people waiting, their time being money he said – all depends upon the purchase have the money ready, and if a good thing offers clutch it – do nothing without advice; sometimes you think to buy cheap and it proves dear – another gentleman whom I asked with regard to my own affairs said – why if you can only finish your houses they will sell rather better than other wise, stocks being almost worthless now, People will be glad to have real property; with trembling anxiety I shall expect your answer, let it be propitious for the dear children sake; assist me dear Claire in this great distress, I shall be your debtor in gratitude forever.

A.C.

I have now also written to Willy to the same effect – but as the Alexandrian post may be interrupted, would you mention the chief points again in your next to him?

and do tell him whether you can comply with my request or not? it will be such a comfort to the poor boy to know I am saved![6]

Address: Miss Clairmont/ 55 Cambridge Street, Hyde Park./ London./ England.
Front postmark: BADEN/ $^{23}/_{6}$ / 3 EXP.
Rear postmark: [illeg.]/BRESLAU; LONDON/JU 27/ 59

Unpublished. Text: M.S., Pf. Coll., CL'ANA 0332

---

1 Antonia commenced a new set of four pages by writing the number 2 at the left top of the page.
2 Antonia included a small sketch of her house.
3 The number 3 was inserted at upper left.
4 Antonia's two lodgings were numbered 492 and 493. The three items and their corresponding values are bracketed off by a set of two square lines forming an L shape.
5 See CL'ANA 0322.
6 This last section was written on a small insert.

130 • Antonia Clairmont to Claire Clairmont

[30 June 1859]
490 [illeg.] 30th Juny[1] 1859

My dearest Claire.

My letter to W. could not go off owing to the Alexandrien poste being interrupted by the war; So pray do you in your letter of July tell ~~him~~ and explain all to him – I shall also write with the English poste, but yours will go surer – Oh my dear Claire what will have been your feelings on receiving my former letter! and I do not know what will be my fate if you must refuse my request – and I wish only you were here to convince yourself of there being no danger for you to loose your money for I can give full security for ~~the~~ it and can pay it back as soon as I have sold one of the houses which will soon be done, for they have great advantages in point of situation, air, and each has a pump with particularly good water, which is rare at Baden, the water being generally tainted with sulphur; Oh I tremble what will be your answer ! this week the roofing is putting up, and I shall have to pay about the 15th of July the first half of the carpenter's and tiler's bill amounting to about £140 is being the heaviest part of all – if you wish it I shall send you the list of the different bills or rather Contos[2] that are to come in between now and 2 months the half of which is payable 3 m-ths after finishing. Is there no hope of your coming here in the course of the summer? I am sure you must and would approve of what I have done and wish to assist me in preserving such fine property to the dear children; or is there none of your acquaintances here or in town to whom I might prove the state of my affairs, to attest that I only want a little timely help to get all in order again and to show how only that unfortunate war caused all my present difficulties, and that I did not enter giddily in an undertaking too great for my powers, for in ordinary cases there would have been no difficulty to my getting any sum I might have wanted from the saving bank, which is always given for twenty years, and paid back by installments; that I am denied that benefit is my misfortune of course I shall pay you 5% interest – for the children's sake, assist me dear Claire – by lending me £500 you will save them a 1000 – for if must sell the houses unfinished my all will be lost – ever yours affectionately.

A.C.

Address: Miss Clairmont/ 55 Cambridge Street/ Hyde Park/ London./ England.
Front postmark: BADEN/ $^{30}/_{6}$ / 3 EXP
Rear postmark: [illeg.]/LONDON/ JY 4/ 59

Unpublished. Text: M.S., Pf. Coll., CL'ANA 0331

1 Antonia misspelled "Juni," German for "June".
2 Antonia meant to write "Kontos," which is the German for "accounts".

131 • Wilhelm Gaulis Clairmont to Claire Clairmont

[4 July 1859]

My dearest aunt.

I rec^d yours of the 8th April I wrote you a long letter by last mail – this time being in a great hurry I shall only write a few lines just to assure you that I am going on as well as you could desire. I am sorry to find that you still complain about illhealth. I hope however that the spring & summer will have done you good – I should much like to know whether you carried out your intention of going to Vienna and if so how you liked it? I am afraid you are too English to like any part of the continent as a permanent residence and that is part of the reasons why I did not place much faith in your [~~illeg.~~] plans of settling near Trieste – If Pauline comes out now it would spoil our plans; but I have no doubt before you all agree on her starting you will wait to receive my answer to Mamma's last projects which is adverse to her coming out, for I wrote to Mamma that if she continued to send me favourable reports concerning her plan of partnership between Mr Nowotni & myself – I should certainly return to Europe as soon as the expiration of my engagements here would permit me which would be in April next at latest. But of course I should not do so if it turned out in the mean time that Mr Nowotni had altered his mind or that any other insurmountable difficulties were in the way. I am happy to think that you must have received long ago the document from Dr Bligh on which you seem to lay such stress.[1] I should not have thought it worth much myself as it appeared to me worded very much in the fashion of the famous Oracles of Delphi mouldable into anything.[2] but if you are contented I shall be delighted to use what I wrote to you last about my increased weight is infinitely more conclusive
Goodbye now dearest aunt

Believe me yours most affectionately
WG Clairmont

Kamaruka
Merimbula
July 4th 1859
Please forward enclosed to Mamma[3]

Address: via Marseilles/ Miss Clairmont/ Messrs Haggard Hale & Pixley/ 8 Copthall Court City/London.
Rear postmark: SYDNEY/ [illeg.]/1859/[illeg.]/N. S. W.

Unpublished. Text: M.S. Pf. Coll., CL'ANA 0083

1 See CL'ANA 0082 and CL'ANA 0084.

2 The Temple of Apollo in Delphi attracted visitors who believed that the Pythia, the priestess of Apollo and known as the Oracle, could predict the future and might change it if they paid her.

3 The enclosure has been lost.

132 • Antonia Clairmont to Claire Clairmont

490 Baden 10th July
1859

My dear Claire.

I am sorry my letters made you ill – if I had known your capital was ~~in~~ taken out of the funds I should not have asked you to assist me in my present difficulties – you shall hear no more of it – but why will you persist in thinking that building ruined me? when it is merely the war that caused my misfortune! To Willy I have written already – so do not exert yourself to write on my account, I only asked you as you said you were going to write to him; I directed via Southampton and hope it was right[1] – you say I should procure a delay – you little know how things are managed here, those little tired people cannot wait for their money, you must even pay something beforehand to enable them to begin the work – but let us say no more of it – you are at least prepared for the close of the whole affair, that I could not have saved you; your kind offer of going to the Isle of Jersey[2] with you, I cannot accept but thank you most warmly for it – if I must be a burthen to someone, my son is the proper person to whom I should look to for support. that Austria ~~is~~ for many years to come has but dreary prospects for a young man in Willy's situation, is but too true, so perhaps all will turn out for the best and God's will be done! let me soon hear that your health is recovering and your affairs going on well, it will be some consolation to me.

Yours most affectionately,
A.C.

Address: Miss Clairmont/ 55 Cambridge Street/ Hyde Park/London/ England.
Front postmark: BADEN/$^{12}/_{7}$; 3. EXP.
Rear postmark: DC/LONDON/ JY 16/ 59

Unpublished. Text: M.S., Pf. Coll., CL'ANA 0330

1 See Wilhelm's letter of 29 July 1859 in which he informed Claire that he had sent a second letter via Southampton due to the war (CL'ANA 0084).

2 The Bailiwick of Jersey is one of the Channel Islands situated some 30 kilometers from the coast of Normandy.

133 • Antonia Clairmont to Claire Clairmont

490 Baden 25t July 1859

My dearest Claire.

I received yours of 18th July and am very glad to hear you are in better health, and leaving London, for in the extreme heat we suffer from, the L. atmosphere must be dreadful; I write only as you desire me to do so, for I have little or nothing good to communicate, not having been able to raise the sum I want, I am in great trouble and the danger of being forced to go to Australia is by no means removed but it will hardly be possible to have all over before next spring; so you might come and spend the winter here God knows how happy I should be to see you, but sorry not to be able to receive you as I should wish to do; for several reasons I am going to leave my fine lodging to take a cheaper one. all depends on my being able to go on with my building – next spring cannot help me – now is the pressing moment – I have ~~the~~ a promise ~~of~~ from the court of chancery to get the necessarry sum by the month of December and even with this promise which is no empty word, I cannot find means to procure it for the space of the intervening 4 or 5 months and yet I have good security to give, so scarce is ready money; Excuse my shortness to day my dear Claire but I can say no more but assure you of my best wishes that you at least will prosper in your affairs I shall write again as soon as I have any thing good to communicate: can you imagine that moneylenders ask 30–40 and even more percentage? shocking today we have blessed rain after the most dreadful heat; thank God my houses are under roof now, and don't suffer by the wet; I didn't tell poor Pauline the extent of my troubles; nor to dear Willy either – I won't make the dear children unhappy – as they cant change anything and only suffer from it –

Goodbye dear Claire, I cannot think you will have war; people's mind have been so long occupied with thinking of it, they can't change suddenly but tell me all about it you think. ever yours affect

A. C.

I have no Metalliques[1] left, having sold out all – as yet I have no debts except the carpenter who took my bills for £2.40, but the other bills and accounts are coming in every week and I ought to pay them, and except the joiner none can give credit for they are poor and needy and no lawyer could make things otherwise than they are – in England credit is given so freely, that you cannot imagine how it is here – things being so different here, I cannot give an opinion on the annuity you mention –

Once more I bid you goodbye
let us hope for better times –[2]

Address: Miss Clairmont/ Mrs Long's Handcroft/ Road.
Croydon/ London/ England.

Front postmark: BADEN/ $^{26}/_{7}$/1. EXP.
Rear postmark: DM/LONDON/ JY 29/ 59

Unpublished. Text: M.S., Pf. Coll., CL'ANA 0329

---

1 See CL'ANA 0046 and CL'ANA 0054. Carl-Ludwig Holtfrerich notes that the Métallique was instituted as a "new type of bond" because the value of Austrian money had declined due to inflation: "What distinguished 'Métalliques' was that interest on them was paid in 'Konvention' – standard coin" (*Frankfurt as a Financial Center* [München: Oscar Beck, 1999], p. 145). See also CL'ANA 0404 for information about the value of money in nineteenth-century Austria.

2 Antonia wrote this section on a separate sheet of blue paper.

134 • Wilhelm Gaulis Clairmont to Claire Clairmont

[29 July 1859]

My dearest aunt.

I duly received your note of the 14th May that mail for a wonder having come punctually; I was sorry however to find there was no letter from Mamma, especially as this is the second mail running she has kept me without news from her. and as for Pauline I do not understand her at all; she used to be so good a correspondent but since her return to Europe I believe she has only written me once. You may imagine how astonished I was to read the news in the May mail of war having been declared between Austria & France[1] I was disagreeably surprised at the news as I fear it may mar my prospects on my return to Austria; this latter event I have lately been looking forward to with the more satisfaction as circumstances have occurred which render the continuation of my engagement here doubtful even though I had no thoughts of leaving the colony. the most important of those circumstances is the fact that the Company's leases of their runs expire in 1860 – there is a low, radical, popularity hunting party in power just now which will in all probability to gain favour with the mob curtail the company's runs and throw them open for sale; the consequence will be that the Company for want of room will have to considerably restrict their pastoral operations so that like on a small station a mere overseer at a low salary will suffice for the management in which case it would of course not pay me to stop.

I must say I thought you took the news of the war very coolly as if it were a mere vent of illtemper on one or both sides which must blow over before the summer is over. I hope it may be so, perhaps by the time this reaches you all is settled; the want of money on both sides is certainly a strong fact in favour of the probabilities of peace but I do not see that even if war were to continue for longer than this summer (as long as it does not revolutionize the whole of Hungary) that it would be a positive bar to my return; for if the turmoil were confined to the south western corner of the monarchy the chances are that the necessarily high prices of provender would make agriculture a profitable pursuit carried on of course in a secure corner. I am afraid my dear mother has become very lowspirited about this matter and afraid to betray her fears & anxieties has preferred not to write at all.

I shall send this via Marseilles agreably to your request; I shall however dispatch another epistle via Southhampton for fear the first mentioned route should be what in a colonial phrase is termed "knocked on the head".[2] the last news from Europe sounds so doubtful that I should be not in the least surprised if France & England were scratching each other's eyes out by this time. and then goodbye to Marseilles route –

I am vexed to find from your last that you had not yet received Dr Bligh's precious report.[3] I do not exactly remember when I sent it to you but I am pretty sure that if you did not receive it by this time you may give it up as lost. but there will not be much harm done as you would not be much wiser after its perusal than before. the main fact is that I am in excellent health. I wish I could hear a better report of your health. Goodbye dearest aunt give my love to Mam. & Paul.[4] and believe

me ever yours most

affectionately
WGC

Kamaruka
Merimbula
Sydney N.S.W.[5]
July 29th 1859.

Address: No envelope

Unpublished. Text: M.S., Pf. Coll., CL'ANA 0084

---

1 In April 1859, Austria declared war on France, following the creation by Napoléon III and Count Cavour of a military plan to rid Italy of Austria and to create a new confederation of Italian states in July 1858. The French defeated the Austrians in a series of battles that resulted in Austria relinquishing its control of Lombardy. Known as the Franco-Austrian War, the Second Italian War of Independence, or the Austro-Italian war, it ended with the call for Italian unification (J. Marino. "Italy". Encylopaedia Britannica. *Encyclopedia Britannica Online*. Encyclopaedia Britannica Inc., n.d. Web. 9 May 2016. http://www.britannica.com/place/Italy/Unification#ref318914).

2 Colloquial speech for the thwarting of a plan.

3 See CL'ANA 0082.

4 Mama and Pauline.

5 Wilhelm bracketed the address with a single curly bracket to the left of the address.

135 • Wilhelm Gaulis Clairmont to Claire Clairmont

[1 August 1859]

My dearest aunt.

Although I have written to you already via Marseilles I write this note via Southhampton partly for fear the first may not reach you and partly because it will offer me a good opportunity to enclose a few lines to my mother, the "via Trieste" route being now blockaded.[1] – Mamma has not written to me for the two last successive mails and I am very uneasy on her account – I hope nothing has gone wrong in her house speculation; if so it would be best to let me know at once so that I may if possible retrieve the losses by keeping if I can my present lucrative situation

I am glad you received the letter from Mrs Suttor which appears to have given you so much pleasure; she is a very nice person I get a letter from her occasionally. I regret very much that your valiant resolution to spend the summer at Vienna was upset by this horrid war; it would have been such a treat to Mamma to see you again after so long a separation; perhaps however you will defer your visit now & perhaps I may be back by next summer & thus we shall all be very happy together.

I see from your last that you are still uneasy on the score of my health; I assure you dearest aunt that you can with perfect ease dismiss all anxiety on that subject – I am in most perfect health I have not had a sore throat[2] for ever so long and am only troubled with an inconveniently active digestion which gives me an insatiable appetite.

I wrote you in my last via Marseilles that I was afraid the war in Austria may have the effect of materially impairing my prospects there on my return – there is no doubt that the scheme of partnership with Mr Nowotni would fall to the ground as people would not be apt to build much under the pressure of such a crisis but the pursuit of agriculture in a quiet out of the way corner maybe rather favoured than otherwise in as much as the increased consumption of the war is sure to cause a rising of the price of all provender. However it is no use speculating on such distant events now; pray [~~illeg.~~] forward the enclosed[3] to my dear mother and give Pauline a good scolding for being so lazy & never writing and believe me dearest aunt

your affectionate nephew
WGC

Kamaruka
Merimbula
Sydney N.S.W.
[~~illeg.~~] August 1st 1859.

Address: No envelope.

Unpublished. Text: M.S. Pf. Coll CL'ANA 0085

---

1 Because of the conflict with France.

2 See Claire's earlier concerns for Wilhelm's health when he lived in England. She frequently took him sea-bathing to treat his goiter.

3 The enclosure has been lost.

136 • Antonia Clairmont to Claire Clairmont

490 Baden 25th August 1859.

My dearest Claire.

I did not succeed in getting in a letter for Coblenz[1] as I hoped I would – no doubt you can get one in London; I am most impatient to know what you decide upon, and whether we shall meet this blessed summer. I hope we shall, and you will hear all my troubles, and see how all goes. since your last letter gave me the hope of succour; things were a better aspect; with the money I got I had to pay the carpenters £300 the joiner £200, brickmaker 200 – so very little remained for the remaining expenses – that ~~and so~~ I could not have engaged so many workpeople as to act expeditiously – however we have now 10 masons more and I promised each man 10 kreutzers a day extra pay, and the overseer one additional pound a week, on condition that in 5 weeks all should be ready and now all goes so brisk and fresh it is a pleasure to see them; it is impossible to describe my troubles and distress since I begun this undertaking – Mr. Nowotny promised so much and spoke so fair, I trusted and believed him, but he did not act honestly – he persuaded me to build two superior houses, instead of the two small ones such as would have suited my means – and ~~promised~~ offered to lend the necessary money, for my capital, was only about £1400 of which unfortunately I lost a good deal in selling out, and was soon used up, the unfortunate war made all money transactions more and more difficult – at last he procured me some Metalliques for which I had to pay enormous interest, but he gave me a bond that he resigned all right to have this sum secured upon my property, so when I wrote to you the houses were quite free from debts, meanwhile I had found out his dishonesty, and by the advice of some friends, I distrusted him entirely and demanded an account of him all along I had been gathering proofs against him, but declining a regular lawsuit, I merely stated my case to a public notary here, who arranged with him, that he was to pay me in compensation 200 pounds, which he was forced to do, but being irritated by this, he went and had my debt to him prenotirt[2] on both the houses; that means not a regular mortgage, but a prevention of a mortgage being made without paying his debt first. My difficulties were much increased by this step – if you or Mrs Schauer, or some friend could have helped me it would have been well for me – go on with my building I must at any price, or I am entirely ruined – for if not finished before Nov:[3] so that I can get regular mortgages from the saving Bank upon the property N: or chancery will seize and sell all for nothing; so I had to go to a moneylender – I got £400 at such awful interest! and cannot yet finish the affairs, for one must pay down ready money for everything as I told you at the beginning of my letter – again I begins to look about me in despair where to turn for help, when your letter came and gave me relief; do not fear anything; if you come you will see and judge yourself, and if you do not come, I will send the documents I mentioned from the Notary and signed by the Embassy. Do tell me whether you agree with [~~illeg.~~] this proposal – ever yours

affectionately
A.C.

No answer from Pauline[4]
There appeared an advertisement in the Austrian papers – of 654.000fl being lent in the Austrian monarchy on moderate terms from one to 20.000fl Apply to M Tom, Camber well 12 Albany Terrace, London. 5. I wrote on the 18 an English letter, stating my case – and asked a loan of one thousands pounds, have no answer as yet – could this be a hoax? I send the advertisement for you to see and judge[5] – Now God bless you dear Claire, and speed you! what I then said is still true, that your loan will save me, and help to arrange everything – I shall finish my houses, obtain the means of clearing of the debts and have regular mortgages at 5% upon the houses, and can pay of[6] or sell at leisure whereas these two debts are upon bills the one due on the 16th of Nov. and the other ~~at~~ on the 6th of Febr. 1860 and if not paid at the moment will subject me to the rigour of the law – our institutions will not lend money upon unfinished houses, and if I must once more ressort to insurers, I shall be ruined either way. I am afraid this is but a confused account.

I am already washing and cleaning a mattress for your use[7]

Address: Miss Clairmont/ Mrs G. Long's Handcroft Road/
Croyden, <u>Surrey</u> /England.
Front postmark: BADEN/ $^{26}/_{8}$/ 1. EXP.
Rear postmark: [illeg.]/LONDON/ AU 29/59; LEIPZIG/ 2781/[illeg.]

Unpublished. Text: M.S., Pf. Coll., CL'ANA 0328

1 Coblenz (Koblenz in German) is a city in Germany. Mail was interrupted as a result of the war and substitute routes were created. The Nordeutscher Lloyd shipping company was started in Germany in 1857 with the aim of providing an alternative route from England to the colonies. In 1857, the company began service between Bremen and England. The company's souvenir *Guide Through Germany, Austria-Hungary, Italy*, (Berlin: Reichmann & Cantor, 1896) explained that in 1857 service was "carried on but by three small steamers" and that it "consisted during the first year only of one line to England" (p. vii). Antonia's letter probably went from Vienna to Coblenz and then on to Bremen, thereby circumventing France.

2 Antonia probably meant "pre" (as in "before") "notiert," the German word for "to write down".

3 November.

4 Antonia wrote the following paragraph on a small blue insert which she included in the envelope.

5 The advertisement has been lost.

6 Off.

7 Antonia cross-wrote the final sentence.

137 • Antonia Clairmont to Claire Clairmont

490 Baden 29th Aug. 1859.

My dearest Claire.

Just received yours of the 27th and am inexpressibly sorry that all I say gives you so much uneasiness – and does not agree with your thoughts and wishes; I said all along it is difficult to explain by letters, one should confine oneself to yes or no – you know I did not tease you with complaints or further demands for assistance – your first refusal silenced me, and when you later spoke of borrowing money I begged you not to do so, but let me fight it out alone, for I well know I am in a difficult possition; but when you wrote again to say you had borrowed it, of course I thought you would send it if you could not come yourself, and that made write as I did, not that I wanted to urge you to send the money; and now that you have explained yourself to take only the first mortgage, and I have already 1000 pds as first m. there is nothing more to be said; I must find an other lender – and you dispose of your money otherwise – in my last I have tried to explain how matters stood, but insufficiently. I am sorry I wrote that letter it will only be disagreeable to you – consider it as not written and do not think any more of my troubles – what to advise about your coming I do not know – for me it is quite impossible to leave here – for I am the whole day on the Bau,[1] and as they are just finishing I must look to everything myself to have all done as I wish it; the houses will be perfection, in every respect; – I have already told you I did not succeed in getting any letter for Coblenz; yours that I received today I will send off to Pauline if she can go she will – but I greatly doubt, her time is not her own, she will then write to you, so that you get the news sooner – but where will you spend the winter? Genna[2] and Florence won't be safe and Venice very questionable; P. can tell you that the Venetians begin to be very rude to the Strangers as soon as these risings begun, so that all the strangers dispersed rapidly; also the Bath's[3] left suddenly – but you'll know all this by your own newspapers your letter about dear W's account of his weight I got, and if I did not mention ~~it~~ and thank you for it you must excuse me, but my head is sometimes quite turned and giddy. Let me once more beg you not to bring the money over on my account. I will not have it said, that I urged you on against all you said; besides it will cause great expenses to you, to go to a first rate lawyer, to have him send out here, have the houses valued, will cost a great deal; surely about £50; and then it will take so much time, that my houses must be finished before that ~~time,~~ and I shall have been obliged to take up money to get them done and if I have to go through my present difficulties unaided, it is much better than to take from the Saving bank – Well what will be the end of all these trials? God Knows! Cannot you find an English family going to Vienna? so many are going to Italy and passing Vienna?

ever yours affectionately
A.C.

Address: Miss Clairmont/ Henry Batson's Esqr Westmoreland/ Lodge, Inner Park Road/ Wimbledon/ near London.
Rear postmark: OT/ London/ P 2/ 59

Unpublished. Text: M.S., Pf. Coll., CL'ANA 0327

---

1 "Bau" is the informal use of either the German word "Baustelle" ("construction site") or "Bauplatz" ("building site").

2 Antonia no doubt meant Genoa (Genova in Italian), a port city on the Mediterranean Sea in northwestern Italy. By 1860, Genoa was part of the movement for Italian unification as Garibaldi began his "Expedition of the Thousand" from Genoa which led to the incorporation of Naples and Sicily into the Kingdom of Sardinia. See The Editors of the Encyclopaedia Britannica. "Expedition of the Thousand". *Encyclopaedia Britannica Online*. Encyclopaedia Britannica Inc. n.d. Web. 24 October 2015. http://www.britannica.com/event/Expedition-of-the-Thousand and Charles Killinger, *The History of Italy* (Westport, CT: Greenwood Press, 2002), pp. 115–6.

3 Possibly the Bathurst family. In 1844, Claire told Mary Shelley that she met Mrs. Bathurst whose daughter had drowned while Mary Shelley and Claire were in Rome (see *CC* II: 402). Claire was staying with Lady Sussex Lennox at the time she met Mrs. Bathurst.

Lady Mary Margaret Sussex Lennox married Lord Sussex Lennox in 1828 (See *CC* II: 350, 373). Claire told Mary Shelley in 1844 that the couple quarrelled frequently and that they had "driven" her "wild" with their arguments (p. 389). Emily Sunstein records that Lady Sussex Lennox had an affair with Carlo Guitera, Italian revolutionary, member of the Carbonari, and friend of Gatteschi (see CL'ANA 0378). Sunstein also notes that Lady Sussex Lennox and Gatteschi became lovers in early 1845 (p. 367).

138 • Antonia Clairmont to Claire Clairmont

490 Baden 4th Sept.1859.

My dear Claire.

You do drag me from hot water. into cold – one letter gives hopes the next reproach and repulse, you said so distinctly you would have none but the first mortgage why then will you make me hope again? what use is it to give you all the particulars you demand. as you cannot know to what amount the property may be safely mortgaged? I shall try to explain, but our customs and expressions are so different, I fear I shall make a poor thing of it: the houses are mortgaged twice – simultan[1] that is both together – the first is Mr. N.'s. and is only a prenotation:[2] he procured me 10.000fl mettalliques which I sold ~~out~~ under 58 and got 5700fl for them – these must be paid back by the 16 of Nov: – these shares are now at 75, ~~now~~, they may rise they may fall between this and november so the amount of the first mortgage is very uncertain, it is generally surmised or feared the papers will fall when the new loan is negotiated this would be well for me, but one cannot know; it will also depend upon my having command of the money to buy in the moment they fall – they may not fall at all, but rise and then my loss will be accordingly. the second mortgage was made when I first asked you for the 500pd then the property was quite free – no friendly hand being stretched to me, I had to go to a regular money lender, he gave me 400 pd and I had to give a bond for £600 payable on the 6th of Febr. Him I also said that he would have first mortg: but when my lawyer came to the office, we ~~had~~ found that N. had been secretly beforehand and had his debt prenotirt – a shabby trick for he has no right to come upon the mortgage but Mr V. the moneylender – who is not at all Shylock like but a most elegantlooking handsome Greek who drives a fine carriole[3] said he had no objection to take the 2nd post, he having seen the houses said he was fully satisfied; so that was so arranged – and I received on the whole about £950 for there were taxes and fees to be deducted, and [~~illeg.~~] have now 300 pds debts ~~upon~~ the houses which may be more or less as the papers may happen to rize or fall; when I last wrote I said I had about 200 pds left of this money since then I have disbursed about 50 pds more - I must now make a third mortgage of £500[4] which the property will bear very well – it is essential to the success to have all finished this autumn the garden must be laid out and the lodges built up so far as to be inhabitable and look nice by next spring; if I carry this through, I shall still make a good job of it – in spite of the dreadful losses I had – on my own capital I lost about £300 in selling out; on the two mortgages – 400 about makes 700[5] and if I must again go to a moneylender who will screw me down to some horrid sacrifice, I shall be overpowered and dead and gone – nobody will ever know the sufferings those buildings cost me; the[~~illeg.~~] day when that carpenter's bill was presented, which I had not the money for, I nearly fainted, which had only happened once before in my life, and that was when the physician told me there was no hope for dear Charley, and it always was my lot to bear all without any support whatever – You told me lately,

I take no notice of what you say, but keep on urging you to send the money – I can't tell you how that hurt me – I could in return say, that you take no notice of what I say, viz– that now is the difficult moment for me to procure money, when the houses are unfinished, late help is no help – when I have all accomplished by ruinos sacrifices you can do me no more good – I said in my former I had engaged 10 masons more, there are now 25 masons at work and as many labourers, there is a great deal of inside work, our houses are built so heavily and substantial – the walls were hastened up to have the roof up. I have not heard from dear Willy but am going to write to him now nor from Pauline though I sent her your last. the letters to her run longer than those to England Pray write directly and tell your intentions

ever yours A.C.[6]

I send you here a little sketch of the Bauplatz; the size ~~and~~ shape and situation is beautiful, and when ready will be fit for any noblemans residence the small corner buildings may be used as lodges or else sold separately – my original plan was to build on the north side as on the south – but it is better so, the houses have such a lovely view on the beautiful hills around, and more space for garden and offices et I think the laying out and distribution of the whole does me some credit – for you may turn either way, sell it whole or divided into two; or the small houses will sell well by themselves each – and each part has fine air and position in a good street. If our dear boy returns we could at time exchange this property for an estate in any of the provinces – there are underhand reports here current of disturbances in the Venitian territory: what will you do? Trieste will hardly do, and is shamefully dear.

Pray write directly – A.C.

Address: Miss Clairmont/ Westmoreland Lodge/ Inner Park Road/ Wimbledon./ Surrey./England.
Front postmark: BADEN/$^{5}/_{9}$ / 5.EXP.
Rear postmark: DZ/ LONDON/[illeg.] 9/59

Unpublished. Text: M.S., Pf. Coll., CL'ANA 0326

---

1 German for "simultaneous". Although she claimed she would "make a poor thing of it," Antonia explained her financial concerns quite capably.

2 There are two possible meanings for this word. "Notation" is the German noun meaning "recording, record or note". In this instance, Antonia may have referred to a pre-recording of the mortgage. Alternatively, the English word "notation" means "the act of noting down". See CL'ANA 0328 for Antonia's dealings with Nowotny.

3 A horse-drawn carriage, used for only one person.

4 It is not clear if Antonia meant to write £300 or £500.

5 Antonia summed the numbers 300 and 400 to yield a total of 700.

6 Antonia enclosed a note with a plan of the Bauplatz on the one side and the following short note on the other side. Her sketch indicated two houses side by side and numbered 491 (48 German feet) and 492 (72 German feet). Each house had its own water pump in the shared garden. Antonia indicated the following features: "space for garden," "courtyard planted with trees," "place for lodge or small house," "place for stables," "Lodge," and "gardeners house".

139 • Wilhelm Gaulis Clairmont to Claire Clairmont

[7 October 1859]

My dearest aunt.

I rec^{d} yours dated July 8th Cambridge St; but being in the midst of the shearing I have leisure only to write a very few words. –
the only news I can give you with reference to myself is one of some importance viz. that the Company for [~~illeg.~~] reasons too long to detail here have been obliged to ~~dis~~ determine on disposing of their sheepproperty and that therefore my engagement with them will terminate on the 1st April.[1] Pauline gives me such a doleful account of prospects in Austria in general and of Mama's affairs in particular that there is not much encouragement in looking to Europe – I shall wait till I receive your & M.'s & P.'s reply to the letters conveying the intelligence of the ceasing of my connection with the Twofold B Past C^{o} this I can have before the 1st April and then be guided by your advice. I thought of insisting on ~~getting~~ taking no lower salary than £500 – this I must confess would be a great temptation to me for I could lay by £400 a year but anything short of that I do not think would tempt me. I am sorry you have so much worry with your operabox it is a most unsatisfactory property, I could not help smiling at the idea of your regretting that I was not there to assist you. I am afraid my opinion would turn out not worth having. I have written to you although short letters still regularly every mail not missing one I believe for the last 12 mos. You have not acknowledged the letter enclosing Dr Bligh's opinion.[2] I am perfectly well & only wish you were as well

Believe me dearest aunt
yours truly
W.G. Clairmont

Kamaruka
Merimbula
Octob. 7th 1859.

Address: No envelope.

Unpublished. Text: M.S. Pf. Coll., CL'ANA 0086

1 According to Vicky Small, the *Illawarra Mercury* (New South Wales) reported in 1860 that the Twofold Bay Pastoral Association had dissolved its partnership. The runs were rented to Robert and Edwin Tooth, while James Manning held on to Kameruka and Wolumla (p. 17). Wolumla is some twenty kilometers south-east of Kameruka.

2 See CL'ANA 0082.

140 • Wilhelm Gaulis Clairmont to Claire Clairmont

[5 November 1859]

My dearest aunt.

I duly rec<u>d</u> your letter dated Croydon 13<u>th</u> August in which you announce to me your intention of starting almost immediately for austria. I hope your visit may have had a satisfactory result as far as Mamas affairs are concerned. I rec<u>d</u> at the same time a letter from Mamma in which she requests me to send immediately all the money I can spare, but she does not say anything about your anticipated arrival. but then Mamma's letter is a hole[1] ~~week~~ month behind time, for judging by its date it ought to have arrived by the last but one mail instead of the last and very likely they received intelligence of your proposed visit in the interval. Mamma wrote to me as I told you before to send her all the money I could spare, but I cannot possibly do so now as I cannot get away from home for a single day, and this business could not be accomplished without my presence to sign sundry documents etz. etz. and of course it is here in the country without legal assistance equally impossible to obtain a power of attorney. I do not know when I shall go, but if necessary I might manage in January when the shearing is over.
I am at present in an unpleasant uncertainty as to my own movements. I have no courage under the present aspects of affairs to return home to Europe; it is [~~illeg.~~] all but certain that Kamaruka will be given up and as to Cuba it is quite uncertain as to whether the Company will retain it or not, but I am inclined to think that the probability is they will <u>not</u> retain it. In that case I should have to look for another place, but the question is whether I may find another good one in a hurry. to return home <u>now</u> seems very risked perhaps I may find Mamma in difficulties and [~~illeg.~~] [~~illeg.~~] more likely to require my assistance than able to give me hers. As soon as anything is settled on that point I shall write to you, at any rate you may depend on getting a letter from me regularly (if only a short one) by every mail for I can appreciate the comfort it must give you from the satisfaction I myself derive out of your regularity in corresponding & somehow the postoffices appear to be more regularly conducted for not a single letter seems to miscarry. Goodbye dearest aunt believe me

yours most affectionately

I am perfectly, well WG Clairmont

Kamaruka
Merimbula
Novb. 5<u>th</u> 1859.

Address: No envelope.

Unpublished. Text: M.S. Pf. Coll., CL'ANA 0087

---

1 Wilhelm's spelling for "whole".

141 • Antonia Clairmont to Claire Clairmont

8th Jan. 1860.

My dear Claire.

I trust you have received mine of the 28th Dec. and rejoice with me in the favourable turn affairs have taken. the great danger is avoided and as you will see from Pauline's letter I have hope to be able to extricate myself from all the difficulties I am beset with – accept my best thanks for your kind feelings and intentions towards me; your plan of us three living together awaiting Willy's return would quite meet my wishes,[1] but not under such sad circumstances – of all this we shall speak later, for now I have to strain every nerve to get through my task I am sorry to hear you talk of your sick room, but now the severity of the season is broken into – and warm weather returned, you will feel better – and also Pauline's cough will easily be cured; that she wants repose and quiet I always said and I hope it will restore her fully – my wish of seeing her under her brother's protection is only for her sake. I cannot bear the idea of her being a dependent among strangers any longer – I should be happy to have her with me, if what I can offer her, will make her so – for the present we can't decide anything nor is it necessary we should – poor dear girl – [2]
I must conclude now being obliged to go out and wishing to take the letters with me – as soon as any thing takes place I shall be sure to tell you – once more my best thanks and believe me
ever yours most affectionately

A.C.

Address: No envelope

Unpublished. Text: M.S., Pf. Coll., CL'ANA 0323

---

1 Wilhelm would return from Australia in 1861. See CL'ANA 0245.

2 Pauline returned from Australia in 1857. After a stay in London with Claire, she became a governess in Hungary, as previous letters have recorded. By 1860, Pauline joined Claire in Florence, where Claire had resided since 1859. The letters show that Pauline spent time from 1860 through 1863 in Baden with Antonia as well as in various European locations. In 1863, she joined Wilhelm in Hungary. She would give birth to her daughter, Johanna Maria Georgina Hanghegyi, in 1864.

142 • Antonia Clairmont to Claire Clairmont

Baden 2 Febr: 1860.

My dear Claire.

I am quite at a loss what to think of your never having any letters from me – I wrote to you twice lately – in the first I thanked you for your kindness to dear Pauline[1] and was so glad the physician found all right – in the second I sent the direction of Dr Budinsky; I have of course not the least objection into his looking into my affairs, for I have no secrets, the debts I have upon the houses are a misfortune but no dishonour – I only thought and said also on a former occasion it would cost you much to consult him – but I sent you his direction – there is no possibility of postponing beyond the month of april, indeed it is the greatest favour done to me to have ~~it~~ the term stretched so far, but farther if cannot go – I have a very clever advocate – from W. Neustadt[2] and thanks to him and our Bezirks Vorstand [Judge of the circle][3] I was so kindly treated; I shall even gratefully remember the kindness of the latter, for without this interference my name would be in the gazette by this time for Now:[4] had already lodged his complaint against me – I hope to get 14000fl from the saving bank – and then with 400[illeg.] English money I shall be quit of the high interest for even to my brother and Mr S.[5] I must pay nearly 8 pct – owing to the bad state of the papers when I sold out – but if I could buy it back now when the papers are again very low. – I should have no new loss – oh dear Claire if you could see the houses how beautiful and substantial they are; every lady is charmed – in every respect they are praiseworthy – I ought now to begin laying out the garden, but I am so short of money – I can't do much – but it is a beautiful place – the frontside has a southern aspect, is so nice and warm that I sit in the morning without a fire, in spite of the frost out of doors – the best rooms have fine Swedish stoves to heat from within with doors of open work in iron which looks so pretty and thank God all the rooms heat well; it would be of immense advantage if I could furnish one lodging in the first floor,! if rich people that squander 1000fl for a whim or nothing at all knew the value of that sum to others! there is a countess just now leaving Baden to join her husband – she wants to sell off her furniture and has been to offer it to me – I was obliged to refuse – but I could make more of the lodgings if ~~I~~ furnished – in one thing I am better of than before; I have very good Hausmeisterleute[6] – he must look after the houses and she serves me, does my rooms fetches my dinner – so that I do not want servants, she is a steady woman and an honest one – and I am free from vexation in that quarter at least – have you not heard from Willy? I think he will come over this time, if he is is[7] once here it must be our endeavour to make him happy here, and not let him regret his wilderness – at least Pauline's and mine – and I know you will support us, if he should write to announce his return, should you not then try to come here so that he find us all together? but I must conclude, thanks for all your kindness to Pauline she is quite happy with you, and says she feels so much better! Pray write soon my dear Claire and believe me ever yours affectly,

A.C.

An
Herrn Dr. August Budinsky[8]
Hof und Gerichts Advokat
in
Hohenmarkt No 541. Wien.

Address: a/ Madame de Clairmont/ Casa Scarpa/Borgo ogni Santi[9]/II ºº Piano[10]/Firenze/Toscana
Front postmark: RECOM:
Rear postmark: FIRENZE/ 7/ FEB/ 1860; [illeg.]ILANO/ 5/FEB/60/[illeg.]

Unpublished. Text: M.S., Pf. Coll., CL'ANA 0322

---

1 Pauline was with Claire in Florence.

2 Wiener Neustadt is about 63 kilometers south of Vienna and 31 kilometers south of Baden.

3 Antonia translated this German term as "Judge of the circle". The official translation is "district board". She enclosed the words in square brackets.

4 Mr. Nowotny, with whom Antonia was engaged in a financial disagreement.

5 Antonia's brother Georg von Hembyze. Mr. S. is unidentified. The *Jahrbuch Der Kais. Kön. Heraldischen Gesellschaft "Adler"* of 1913 lists the death in 1836 of Karoline Ghilain von Hembyze, aged 31 years. Her survivors were Anna Ghilain v. Hembyze (mother) and her siblings Anna Hofinger, Antonia Clairmont, Marie Rismondo, and Georg Ghilain v. Hembyze (Wien: Carl Gerold's Sohn, 1913), p. 116.

6 German for "caretakers".

7 Correct in the original document.

8 Translation: To Mr. Dr. August Budinsky, Attorney (Royal and public attorney) in Number 541 Hohen Markt (the name of the street), Vienna.

9 Antonia's spelling for "Borgo Ognissanti," a road in Florence meaning "All Saints Village".

10 Italian for "floor".

143 • Antonia Clairmont to Claire Clairmont

492. Baden 2.3 Febr. 1860.[1]

My dear Claire.

I had two letters from you, one of the 7th of this month and ~~both~~ one a week earlier, both containing sundry advice, hopes, hints and insinuations – then I had a visit from dr Habeler[2] on the part Dr Budinsky – he knows English, so I showed him Willy's letters and yours, and told him, what I had asked of you, in short I spoke plain simple truth, which some people are incapable of doing; his answer will be according to the impressions your own letters to me, and Willy's letters made on him; your account of Pauline's health surprise me, I am not easily alarmed, but if there is a shadow of real danger she ought at once proceed to Australia, what an idea to send her to Elba[3] – no believe me it will be an imperative duty to send her there where kind and affectionate friends ~~and~~ will be glad to welcome her, and where she is happy with her brother in his society and protection[4] – I do not think Willy will return – we aught hardly to wish it, for a new blow has fallen upon poor Austria, and it will prove the death blow of her – die nun declarirte Besitzfähigkeit der Juden wird der Krim von Österreich sein bereits sind alle Pachtungen von Grundbesitz, und Gewerben eg. Wirth häuser Brauereien Brantwein und Essig erzeugung et et in Mähren Pohlen u Ungarn in ihren Händen der Adel der zwei lezteren KronLanden ihnen verschuldet – ist ganz in ihrer Macht – mehr oder weniger auch in den übrigen Provinzen – unsere strengen Wuchergesetze haben Veranlassung gegeben zu einer Umgehung derselben wie sich nach und nach in ein System gebildet hat, und für den Schuldner viel Verderben bringender ist als der Wucher in seiner nackten Gestalt – die mit voller pupillar Sicherheit größten Hypothekar Schulden werden nam lich auf Wechsel, diese durch die dritte Hand verkauft werden auf der Realität einverleibt und dann hat der Gläubiger vermöge der Wechselrechte die Macht in den Händen binnen 4 Wochen die grösten estates um einen Spottpreis loszuschlagen, während es auf gewöhn {section cut out of page} jetzt{line cut out of page} fehlen, in 3 Jahren wird Österreich ein Juden-reich sein! let your German friend translate and explain this – some time ago I asked Mr. Landesman whether the Jews really did expect another Messiah but now I am answered; I think they have found him! indeed I deeply grieve for Austria[5] – and tremble for dear Willy –

I must conclude; if one considers such a great national calamity one almost ceases to think of one's own difficulties; I also suffer from that very system I mentioned, but I shall bear what is decreed – only my children I do not wish to involve[6]

English Translation (German transcription and English translation provided by Ann Sherwin)

the now-declared ability of Jews to own property will be the Crimea of Austria.[7] Already all leases of property and businesses, such as inns, breweries, brandy and vinegar production, etc. etc., in Moravia, Poland, and Hungary are in their hands.

The aristocracy of the latter two crown lands is encumbered with debts to them – is totally under their power – more or less in the rest of the provinces as well – our strict usury laws have given rise to circumnavigation, which has gradually turned into a system and is much more ruinous for the debtor than usury in its stark form – in that the biggest mortgage debts, with full pupillary security, become bills of exchange, are sold by third parties, are incorporated into the real estate, and then the creditor, by dint of the exchange laws, has the power in his hands to release the largest estates within 4 weeks for a ridiculous price, whereas it {section cut cut of page} now {line cut out of page} miss,[8] in 3 years Austria will be a Jewish empire!

Address: Madame de Clairmont/Pensione Scarpa 4030 Borgo/
Ogni Santi/à/ Florence.
Rear postmarks: FIRENZE/ [illeg.]; MIL[illeg.]/ 26/FEB/60

Unpublished. Text: M.S., Pf. Coll., CL'ANA 0324

1 Antonia's notation for 23 February.

2 Franz Haberler was listed as one of the "Hof-und Gerichts-Advocaten" practicing in Vienna in the *Hof- und Staats-Handbuch des Kaiserthumes Österreich: 1868* (Wien: G.J. Manz Buchhandlung, 1868), p. 263. The book's title translates as "Court and State Manuel of the Austrian Empire" and provides names of advocates who were approved to practice law.

3 The island of Elba is the biggest of the islands in the Tuscan archipelago. It lies some 155 kilometers from Livorno. Maria Gisborne, friend of the Shelleys and Claire, lived in Livorno (known in English circles as Leghorn) and in 1819 Claire and the Shelleys moved into a home in Livorno. In 1814, Napoléon Bonaparte was exiled to Elba where he lived until he returned to Paris in 1815. See The Editors of the Encyclopaedia Britannica. "Elba". *Encyclopaedia Britannica Online*. Encyclopaedia Britannica Inc., n.d. Web. 10 August 2015. http://www.britannica.com/place/Elba-island-Italy

4 Although Antonia was not impressed by Australia, her fears for Pauline's health explain this remark. Stocking notes that Antonia "inexplicably" encouraged Pauline to return to Australia (*CC* II: 593). Evidently, Claire also encouraged her because of concern about her single surviving niece's health.

5 In 1781, the Edict of Toleration permitted Jews and other minorities to own property in certain parts of Bohemia, Silesia, and Moravia, but Jews were forbidden to own property in Austria. On 18 January 1860, the Jews of Lower Austria "were permitted to aquire real estate" (Joseph Jacobs and Meyer Kayserling. "Vienna". *Jewish Encyclopedia*. 1906. Web. 23 May 2015. http://www.jewishencyclopedia.com/articles/14699-vienna). On 18 February 1860, "legislation . . . gave to the Jews of most of the Austrian provinces full right to hold property" (Gotthard Deutsch. "Austria". Jewish Encyclopedia. 1906. Web. 23 May 2015. http://www.jewishencyclopedia.com/articles/2152-austriaee). The "messiah" to whom Antonia refers is Emperor Franz Joseph I, whose government finally gave Jews permission to purchase property.

6 The letter ends here and is incomplete.

7 In this section of the letter, someone has deliberately cut sections of the text, possibly to destroy them and perhaps to obscure Antonia's anti-Semitism. See CL'ANA 0404, CL'ANA 0326, and CL'ANA 0421, Box 3, bundle g, number 185. Antonia alluded to the Crimean War of 1853–6 and Russia's defeat by the combined forces of Britain, France, and Turkey. She saw the purchase of Austrian land by the Jews as a type of "Crimea" in which Austrians would lose their land to foreigners. Antonia's view that Jews were not true Austrians and that they had designs on taking over Austria ("Austria will be a Jewish empire") reflected typical anti-Semitic notions of the time.

8 The verb form is unclear without an appropriate context. It could also mean "be lacking".

144 • Wilhelm Gaulis Clairmont to Claire Clairmont

[28 February 1860]

My dearest aunt

I recd your two last letters one from Novb. & the other Decemb.. I am sorry that I missed last mail – I was absent from home calculating however to be back just in time to catch ~~the~~ our coasting steamer for the departure of the Sydney mail steamer.[1] I was however delayed by floods several days and in consequence too late to write to you by last mail –

As you wrote to me ~~for~~ in your last that you could not lend Mamma any money as your absence from home made it impossible to you to borrow – I made arrangements to send her my this years salary – I have not got the draft yet but I hope to get it in time to forward it by this mail – After deducting my expenses I think it will amount to £250 – this is all I can do for the present, the £450 I have in steamboat shares I cannot realise just now as for reasons which I have explained to Mama before these shares will not sell just now.

I hope this will suffice to give her a lift out of her difficulties. My only fear is, that if not enough to rescue her it will ~~go~~ be swallowed up with the rest and go to the benefit of her cheating creditors instead of herself. I have therefore remitted the amount through an English Bank where it will be out of the power of those villains to pounce upon it.

Under these circumstances, I have not much inclination to return to Europe – I think there is little doubt that something promising may turn up even though I should leave Twofold Bay. I am quite well. I recd a distressing letter from Pauline about her troubles and distaste of European life. she did not tell me though of the happy manner she has of seeking recreation from the fatigues of her duties by little "solo" excursions to Venice. I wish very much to write to her but I cannot as I do not know her address please will you tell me how I can direct – a letter to her. but not to go through Mamma's hands – If I stop in this country and Mamma & Pauline still continue to live apart so that Mamma can reap no possible benefit from P.'s society I do not see why the latter had not better come out again more especially if she really persists in prefering Australia to Europe. I think I shall be in a position to offer her a home (although with the most decided objections to such solo performances) and if I should not succeed just at first to get a proper situation for myself she is so much liked that she could get a temporary situation or a home as a friend about anywhere. Believe me dearest aunt your affectionate nephew

WGC

February 28th 1860

Address: No envelope.

Unpublished. Text: M.S. Pf. Coll., CL'ANA 0088

---

1 Coasting steamers were steam ships designed to carry cargo to and from certain ports. See Mancuniensis, *80th Thousand Facts and Figures in Favor of The Proposed Manchester Ship Canal* (London: John Heywood, 1882).

145 • Wilhelm Gaulis Clairmont to Claire Clairmont

[7 April 1860]

My dearest aunt.

The last letter I rec^d from you is dated Florence 13th Janry. I was very glad to ~~get~~ hear of the pains you had taken about Pauline's health – I have no doubt that the harassing, fatiguing life she had been leading in her former position[1] would have a tendency to wear her out and therefore a life of rest & ease in a delightful climate would of itself without the existence of the various ails put her to rights again, accept my sincerest thanks dearest aunt for the exercise of that vigilant forethought & kindness which has no doubt averted a great calamity from us in this instance. If the Doctors really are of opinion that Pauline cannot live in Austria I think she had better return to Australia – With Mamma's difficulties at home and my excellent position <u>here</u> contrasted with the doubtful career I should have to commence in Austria I do not think I shall return at least not for some years to come, but it is a subject on which I should not press her because I know your and Mamas wishes in that respect to run the contrary way. As regards my own movements I told you in my last months letter that there was nothing as yet decided – now however it is. the Twofold Bay P. Compy have dissolved themselves but I have reengaged with the principal shareholder Mr. Robert Tooth[2] (his father lives in a country place near Maidstone)[3] to undertake the management of ~~a~~ the sheepstations which he got from the Company.[4] In the winter I shall live at Cuba and in the summertime at Tantangara[5] which is on the Australian Alps at the head of the Murrumbidgee about 5000 feet over the level of the Sea and near to those new diggings called Kiandra of which you have no doubt heard.[6] I was up there just now – it is a delightful country in the Summer time – this you will however perceive is not a permanent arrangement so that if Cuba does not agree with my health I shall be at liberty to break off any time and on the other hand Mr Tooth will be at liberty to break off the engagement if the station did not pay as well as he expects or if he should loose the right of run through the diggings. but in any case I think I may look forward to permanent employment from him. as if he sold these stations he would go into{tear} other investment likely to afford me {tear} ning. My salary now is £500 pr. an {tear} a chance although a very uncertain one {tear}aking a trifle extra in the way of percentages on fut[7] stock sold. As regards poor Mammas affairs I am glad that you think of lending some money although I am afraid that Budinski's report will not be to the effect that you can under the circumstances lend the money quite without risk. I sent M- a draft in favour of Haggard H. & P. [8] (they being the only people I know of in London) for £252„14„8^d I shall try and send her a little more by next mail. – I cannot without a complete sacrifice get a sale for my steam navigation shares. Looking at it merely in a commercial point of view I consider it a great pity to send this money back to Europe for I could get 10 pr. cent on it here in any ordinary investment and 15 or 20 pr cent provided I could scrape together enough to go into some squatting operation whereas Mamma will barely realise 3 pr. cent but of course the question is now not how to invest this money to best advantage but how to help Mamma out of her difficulties – I enclose a letter for dear Pauline Goodbye dearest aunt

believe me yours truly

Kamaruka W.G. Clairmont

April 7th 1860

Direct Cuba, Wagga Wagga

Sydney[9]

Address: Aerogramme. via Trieste./Madame Clairmont/alle cure del Signor Cini[10]/ 496 bis via dei Giraldi/ Firence/Italy.

Rear postmark: SYDNEY/ AP11/1860/E/N.S.W.

Unpublished. Text: M.S. Pf. Coll., CL'ANA 0089

---

1 As a governess.

2 Robert Tooth (1821–1893) was one of the seven men who founded the Twofold Bay Pastoral Association. G. P. Walsh notes that, together with his brother Edwin (1822–1858), he acquired the Kent Brewery in 1844 and they formed the firm R. and E. Tooth. A third brother, Frederick (1827–1893), joined the company in 1860 under the name R. and F. Tooth and Company. After the dissolution of the Twofold Bay Pastoral Association in 1860, Robert acquired various runs, was a director of the Bank of New South Wales, and maintained businesses in both Australia and England (G. P. Walsh, "Tooth, Robert", Australian Dictionary of Biography. National Centre of Biography, Australian National University. 1976. Web. 7 May 2016. http://adb.anu.edu.au/biography/tooth-robert-4731).

3 The Tooth brothers' father, Robert Tooth, lived in Cranbrook, Kent, where Robert was born. Maidstone is located in Kent and is some 16 kilometers from Cranbrook. Kent is a county in south-east England.

4 According to Small, the earliest records of R. and F. Tooth and Company date from 1860–64. The Tooth family owned stations in Candelo, Bemboka, as well as eight dairy stations (p. 17).

5 Tantangara is located in New South Wales about 6 kilometers from Kiandra. The Kiandra Historical Society records that gold was discovered in 1859 and that, by March 1860, 10,000 diggers were looking for gold in the area. The rush, however, lasted a mere 18 months. As Wilhelm observed, the headwaters of the Murrumbidgee River are formed some twenty kilometers from Kiandra. (Kiandra Historical Society. Web. 19 November 2014. http://www.kiandrahistory.net/index.html).

6 In his narrative, banking agent George Preshaw records his 1860 visit to Kiandra, or Snowy River, as it was commonly known. He went by steamer from Melbourne to Eden, Twofold Bay, and then traveled overland the 150 miles from Eden to Kiandra. He found himself "cold and miserable" at the local hotel (p. 52). Preshaw observed that Sundays were very busy in Kiandra as diggers came to meet friends, shop, and frequent public houses which did a "roaring trade" (p. 54). In "*Back to Cooma*" *Celebrations*, Felix Mitchell observes that "settlement increased more rapidly" with the Kiandra gold discovery in 1859 and the rush in 1860. Mitchell also notes that telegraphic communication commenced between Sydney and Kiandra in October 1860 (Sydney: The Direct Publicity Company, 1926), pp. 7–8.

7 future.

8 The London broker firm of Messrs. Haggard, Hale, and Pixley.

9 As the postal address reflects, mail went from Sydney to Wagga Wagga and then to Cuba.

10 Italian for "care of Mr. Cini".

146 • Wilhelm Gaulis Clairmont to Claire Clairmont

May 4th 1860.
Sydney

My dearest Aunt.

I have only five minutes time to write this for I am in a great hurry. I write this from Sydney whither I came on business. I leave again for ~~Cuba~~ Kamaruka tomorrow morning but wish to write before I leave town lest the mail from the Country should be too late. I have sent Mama another £150 which I got in advance on my this years salary. I hope her prospects will soon brighten again I am very anxious to hear what sort of a report Budinsky will give. I shall write to you more by next mail – if our country mail is still in time for this vessel I shall write to Pauline from Kamaruka Tell her everyone here is very amiable and inquiring much after her. I wonder whether she will come out. again I dont know whether to send her boxes or not. I am perfectly well & wish you were the same

Believe me dearest aunt,
yours truly
W.G. Clairmont

Direct for the future.
WGC
care of Leopold Rawack Esqr.
Sydney N.S.W.[1]

Address: Aerogramme: Via Marseilles/ Madame Clairmont/ alle cure del Signor Cini/ 496bis via dei Giraldi/ Firence/ Italy.
Postmarks: 60/MY 4/B/ SYDNEY; AUSTRALIA/[illeg.]/60/[illeg.]/FIRENZE/ 10/LUG[2] 60/VII; DA ALESSANDRIA A BOLOGNA [illeg.][3] /9/LUG./60

Unpublished. Text: M.S. Pf. Coll., CL'ANA 0090

1 Graeme Skinner provides bibliographic information on Leopold Ravac (Rawack), a musician who moved to Australia in 1852 and who died in Darlinghurst in 1873 at the age of 54 years. Skinner identifies Rawack as a violinist and merchant. Rawack was apparently one of the organizing committee members of the Sydney University Musical Festival of 1859 and his wife, Amalie Mauthner Rawack, was a Viennese musician who immigrated with him to Australia. Skinner cites the journal of Dr. Karl Scherzer who wrote, "All the world congratulated the charming, highly educated, but impecunious Miss Mauthner when they heard that she was going to marry a rich merchant from the gold mining district of Australia". According to Skinner, Amalie Rawack divorced Leopold Rawack in 1861 and returned to Vienna (*A biographical register of Australian colonial musical personnel–R, Australharmony* Web. 26 April 2015. http://sydney.edu.au/paradisec/australharmony/register-R.php). *The Sydney Morning Herald* of 1 August 1856 included an article entitled "Insolvency of Rawack and Company" in which Leopold Rawack was described as "one of the

insolvents" (National Library of Australia, http://nla.gov.au/nla.news-article12985514, p. 4). On 19 February 1864, the newspaper listed him as one of the members of the Committee For General Purposes of the New South Wales Free Trade Association (National Library of Australia, http://nla.gov.au/nla.news-page1476549, p. 6).

2 Abbreviation for "luglio," the Italian word for "July".

3 Italian for "from Alexandria to Bologna".

147 • Wilhelm Gaulis Clairmont to Claire Clairmont

[25 May 1860]

My dearest aunt.

I received your letter of the 14th March just as I was on the point of leaving Kamaruka for Cuba – and regretted exceedingly that it came too late [~~illeg.~~] to make me return to Europe I having thus already definitely arranged with Mr Tooth to undertake the management of Cuba & Tantangara.[1] the tenor of my previous letters however no doubt prepared you for this decision as I believe I thus told you that I should remain in Australia if any acceptable offer should be made me. I am exceedingly sorry that my inability to return at once should difficulties in the way of your kind intention towards Mama but I think both you & Pauline greatly overrate my ability of assisting Mama – It is true I could have gone to England for you to save you the journey there, but by the time I could have got to you it would have been summer & then very likely you will enjoy the trip your self and as for assisting Mama in this difficulty I do not see what us I could have been for I do not understand that sort of business myself As for myself pray give your self no anxiety on my account the Murrumbidgee now is quite a different place to what it was 7 years ago when I first went to it civilization has progressed wonderfully, there are now numbers married gentlemen living with their families where formerly there was only a convict stockman. there is mail twice a week to Melbourne & once a week to Sydney it is quite a rising locality and the work for me now is not so severe as I have attained a superior position Looking at the mere prudential side of the question I think still that I have acted for the best in stopping here for Mamas income of £200 would barely suffice to cover the interest on her debts and my presence would only entail additional expense and the consciousness of it would render me miserable. I am now on my way to Cuba being determined by Floods at a place called Tumut.[2] I shall write to Pauline by this post – pray direct for the future: WGC care of L. Rawack Esqr – Sydney[3] who will forward my letters – Goodbye dearest aunt believe me

dearest aunt yours affectionately

WGC.

May 25th 1860

Address: No envelope.

Unpublished. Text: M.S. Pf. Coll., CL'ANA 0091

---

1 See CL'ANA 0089.

2 Tumut is located at the foot of the Snowy Mountains, some 410 kilometers south-west of Sydney and about 255 kilometers east of Cuba.

3 See CL'ANA 0090.

148 • Wilhelm Gaulis Clairmont to Claire Clairmont

[3 September 1860]

My dearest aunt.

Your last letter of the 7th June (dated from Borgo alla Collina)[1] was a great source of consolation to me. in as much as it was of a somewhat more cheerful strain than the letters received pr same mail from Mamma & Pauline. I recd the batch only today owing to loss of time occupied in overland transmission from Kamaruka to Cuba. but I hope this may reach Sydney in time to be dispatched by the September mail – It was a great consolation to me to find that you too have or are going to contribute towards helping Mamma. As you know by this time I sent £150 more which I borrowed last May and I hope that my friends in Sydney will succeed in selling my shares and send off the proceeds by this mail. if not by this mail they are sure to follow by next – the amount realised on them ought to be about £665 (less commission on sale of shares & transmission of money) the shares having in the mean time risen greatly in value and they would rise even much higher could I retain them – but as it is, it is not a bad investment I bought them 18 months ago at £450. – My reluctance to send money arose not from any wish to keep it to myself but from this reason: I have as you all know come out here with the avowed purpose to make some money for myself & family. this I cannot accomplish without some little capital to start with. Now if I had been left alone for another year and [illeg.] I should have accumulated nearly £2000 which would have been the certain foundation of a fortune not only to me but to us all. instead of this you cripple all my endeavours ~~by~~ in the very bud by taking the means from me to make a start and for what purpose? to build a wretched house ~~in a~~ with a frightful burden of debt & returning wretched £200 pr. ann. & that uncertain. & supposing the speculation fails after all Mamma has deprived herself of the chance of attaining the competency I am almost sure I might have realised for us all if left alone – Do not however imagine dearest aunt that I say this in an ill natured spirit – I simply propound my views as to the relative merits of the two schemes my sheepfarming and Mamma's house building plan. But here one member of a family has travelled 16.000 miles ~~to~~ expressly to reach a place reputed favourable to the making of money it looks like bad management that the means wanted for making a start should after all be sent back to the old country instead of being invested here. I would not like to mention this to Mamma as it might hurt her feelings & after all she meant it for the best but you are sufficiently impassionate to perceive that I am merely giving my opinion as to the financial merits of the case. As a contribution from me to my dear mother I send the money most cheerfully but looking upon it from a mere commercial point of view I look upon it as a most suicidal act in as much as it will throw me back if not prevent me altogether from ever gaining a competency for all of us. Of course I cannot until the house is paid off entertain the idea of going to Europe to get a salary of £20. or £30 there while I can get £500 here. but I wish among other things to impress you with the necessity of discontinuing your ungrounded fears of dangers brought by a residence on the Murrumbidgee or any other part of this colony. the Murrumbidgee

of now is not a bit more like the Murrumbidgee that was when I first came to it moreover I am 200 miles nearer to Sydney than I was at Mr Morris's station[2] – then the country had been just only taken from the Blacks; now they are nearly all dead there are houses, paddocks, etz. springing up in all directions.[3] I myself am getting a very nice cottage put up with 8. rooms.
I am glad to find that Florence agrees so well with you and that also in a pecuniary point of view it suits you I shall send Mama very likely £150 more by the mail starting Janry. 14th and half yearly instalments after that – If you wish it I can therefore guarantee you the interest on the money you may lend Mamma (as long as I have health and employment) to be ~~first~~ paid first of all out of the instalments forwarded to Mamma the rest to be disposed of by her as she may think fit. But you can settle that with M. as you please. Now Goodbye dearest aunt.

yours truly
WG Clairmont

Cuba, ~~August~~ Septemb. 3rd 1860.
Direct WGC – care of Leopold Rawack Esqr
Sydney.[4]

Lest this letter should give you an erroneous impression with reference to the sale of my shares I must add here that it is only of late that they were saleable, they were exceedingly low first but they are rising fast now owing to the contemplated arrival of a new steamer from London; once this is at work they will rise even much higher than they are now. Mr. E. Manning[5] a brother of the one who is at Kamaruka is Director & manager of the Company and let me into the secret of the matter or else I should not have had the courage to purchase – At first I could not have sold the shares at my price – and even now they are being sold at a sacrifice.

Address: No envelope

Unpublished. Text: M.S. Pf. Coll., CL'ANA 0092

1 Borgo alla Collina is about 51 kilometers west of Florence. The village is located in Arezzo province.

2 Pauline's letter of 8 July 1853 confirmed that Wilhelm was working 600 miles from Sydney on Augustus Morris's station (CL'ANA 0210). Darlington Point, where Cuba was located, is 392 miles from Sydney. Wilhelm was correct in stating that his location at the Cuba run was two hundred miles closer to Sydney than was Morris's run.

3 Wilhelm meant Indigenous Australians who lived in the country for over 45,000 years before the arrival of the English. Between massacre by conquering colonists and disease against which the Indigenous Australians had no resistance, many died.

4 Wilhelm cross-wrote the next paragraph on the first page of the letter.

5 Edye Manning (1807–1889) was James Manning's brother and one of the seven businessmen who founded the Twofold Bay Pastoral Assocation in 1852. His son, John Edye Manning (1831–1909), married Caroline Suttor. See CL'ANA 0075.

149 • Antonia Clairmont to Claire Clairmont

Baden 5th Sept. 1860.

My dear Claire.

I received yours of the 30th August with directions about £70 which you are so kind as to give to me. take my best warmest thanks I shall go to town tomorrow to write to England about it – my not answering your letter about P. was not neglect, but when there are so many difficulties one must weigh, and consider, P. should have liked to come, and I to let her go – but there were many and important reasons to demand her staying here[1] – I shall try to explain – the taxes on houses and landed property are dreadfully high in this country and in a town like Baden, where the income of house rent depends mostly on the influx of strangers it is difficult to fix what income you will have – it is therefore a usual practice here, for one member of the family to rent the whole house. if Willy had been here, he would have been the tenant, but so it was fixed on Pauline – in the month of July, I announced her as my tenant, it cost me much trouble to get her accepted, but it is now done and saves us a world of trouble and annoyance, and money too, but of course she must stay here at least the first winter, she has to sign papers and now and then to show herself, for another winter she ~~may~~ will be able to go away but for this it would be highly imprudent, as all the advantages gained by her being named my tenant would be lost, and I might be fined – there is another reason for her own sake – she has had an offer of marriage, but does not feel inclined to accept I should have liked to see her settled but would not persuade her, however if by having an oportunity of knowing the young man better by seeing him oftener she might decide for him,[2] I should be very glad, you will agree with me her staying here this winter is also advisable in this respect, besides the assistance she will give in furnishing half the repayments to the saving Bank, which I cannot possibly compass, besides it is her native air – and we consulted a physician and you shall have his opinion in writing – I am in great hurry to day and shall write more the next time – we had two good offers, and cho~~o~~se the situation in town which in every respect desirable; once more my best thanks, as soon as I have an answer from England I shall write again; and pray dear Claire send off her boxes directly – I cannot say how sorry I am you are to be worried with these things – I know what it is; she ought to have brought them with her.

ever yours gratefully
A. Clairmont

Dearest best Aunt – How can we sufficiently thank you for all your kindness! – the Lord & your own conscience will reward you – I am afraid you will not from what Ma has said quite understand the <u>tenant</u> business – as ma has said, the taxes ~~rents~~ are so awfully high – that it would be ruination to us & every landlord – we therefore walk round the law – I rent the houses & thereby engage to pay a certain sum every year, which certainly is more acceptable to government than having to calculate a percentage upon every 10£ that we receive – of course we have fixed the average of our income as low as possible – should we not let any lodgings I should have to pay the same sum – but if we let the lodgings as is presumable I am the gainer as you must know that the taxes are calculated according to the yearly rents received – I enclose a photographic view of the two houses.[3]

Ever your affte
Pauline

Address: No envelope

Unpublished. Text: M.S., Pf. Coll., CL'ANA 0325

---

1 By September 1860, Pauline had returned to Austria.

2 In her unpublished journal, Pauline expressed a distinct dislike of marriage, a theme to which she frequently returned in her musings. When Willie Suttor's romance with his future wife Adelaide Agnes Henrietta Bowler became evident, Pauline wrote in her journal, "I feel certain that AB will make him an excellent wife five hundred times better I could have done" (8 November 1856, CL'ANA 0176, pp. 166–7, unpublished manuscript, Pforzheimer Collection). The poignant sentiments she expressed in her journal clearly showed her love for Willie. In December 1856, she wrote: ". . . deeply did I long for you to love me & protect me though life" (p. 183). In thinking of her life back in Vienna, she acknowledged that, amidst the splendours of Europe, "I shall walk in the glittering ballroom in glittering dress in the crowded Operahouse surrounded by music perfume elegance with mirth & flattery all my senses charmed with magic art – & like a dream like a vision on the distant ocean shall I see Australia with her sad gumtrees her starlight her rocky solitudes her silent calm moonlight nights & remember the time when we loved each other" (13 December 1856, pp. 173–4). And before her departure for England, she wrote, "Had you loved me as I loved you, nothing would have separated us" (25 January 1857, p. 191). See also CL'ANA 0421, Box 3, bundle g, number 201 bis, for more information on Adelaide Bowler.

3 These photographs have been lost.

150 • Wilhelm Gaulis Clairmont to Claire Clairmont

[2 October 1860]

My dearest aunt.

Yours of the 12th July has given me great relief in as much as I conclude from it that Mammas affairs are brightening up a bit and that you have come forward very generously to help her. I got Mr John Manning[1] to sell my shares for me but he could find a purchaser only for 100 of them they sold at £5. the proceeds £492 he tells me he has forwarded to Pauline. I asked him to sell my remaining 33 shares as soon as possible and to forward proceeds in the same manner

You must excuse me for writing so hurriedly – the shearing is on just now and I am busy from morning to night but I shall write to you regularly – I always receive your letters punctually and I assure you they are great source of comfort to me. direct to care of L. Rawack Esqr Sydney.[2] as I shall not always be at Cuba during the summer and he will always know my direction.

I write to Pauline and Mamma by this mail

yours most affectionately
WGC

Octob 2nd 1860

Address: No envelope.

Unpublished. Text: M.S. Pf. Coll., CL'ANA 0093

---

1 Son of Edye Manning, and husband of Caroline Suttor. Edye and Caroline were married in 1859.

2 See CL'ANA 0090, CL'ANA 0092 and CL'ANA 0094.

151 • Wilhelm Gaulis Clairmont to Claire Clairmont

[30 October 1860]

My dearest aunt

I duly rec^{d}. yours of the 13th August sent to the care of Mr. Rawack. continue to direct your letters to him I shall always keep him au courrant of my movements so that I shall get any letters through him without delay. We are now in the midst of shearing and I in consequence very busy but as I have no news to tell you a few lines to assure you of my health etz. will suffice I rec^{d} a letter from Mamma pr. last mail which made me breath a little freer. I am so thankful that she is out of this difficulty. You will about~~h~~ this time receive a rather cross letter from me written under the sting of what I conceived a very great Injury. I still think that you were wrong in saying what you did say or rather wrote but as you have written me some good kind letters since I should be sorry that my cross letter coming some 5 or 6 months afterwards should appear like the raking up of an old difference please therefore never to mind what I may have said; and let us be friends it is more than probable that I may never see you or Mamma again. and to turn what scanty means of communication with you I have left me into messages of quarrel & discord would be highly repugnant both to my heart & head. If I therefore said anything in that letter calculated to cause a coolness between us I now retract it most cheerfully. the aspect of Europe is so threatening that I am in a pecuniary point of view glad I did not go home again.

Believe me dear aunt yours most affectionately
WGC.

Cuba
Octob 30th 1860.

Address: Via Trieste./ La signora Clairmont/ alle cure del
Signor Cini/ 496 ^{bis} Via dei Giraldi/ a Firenze
Front postmark: TARCUTTA/ NO 2/ 18[illeg.]/ N.S.W.
Rear postmark: [illeg.]DNEY/ NO 5/ 18[illeg.]

Unpublished. Text: M.S. Pf. Coll., CL'ANA 0094

152 • Wilhelm Gaulis Clairmont to Claire Clairmont

[10 December 1860]

My dearest aunt.

I received no letter from you by last mail (that leaving in September). I have nothing new to tell you and just write these few lines to keep you from fretting about me.

Believe me dearest aunt
yours most affectionately
WGC.

Cuba
(Tarcutta)[1]
Decemb 10th 1860.

Address: via Trieste./Mademoiselle Clairmont/alle Cure del Signor Cini/ via dei Giraldi / Firenze/Italy.
Front postmark: TARCUTTA/ DE 11/ 18[illeg.]/ N. S. W.
Rear postmark: FIRENZE

Unpublished. Text: M.S. Pf. Coll., CL'ANA 0095

1 Tarcutta is located 438 kilometers south-west of Sydney. Tarcutta is 48 kilometers west of Wagga Wagga and about 200 kilometers west of Cuba. Mail would have been routed overland from Sydney via Tarcutta or Wagga Wagga. Wilhelm's address confirms the mail route from Cuba to Sydney via Tarcutta. The postmark on the envelope reads "Tarcutta".